popgun

volume one

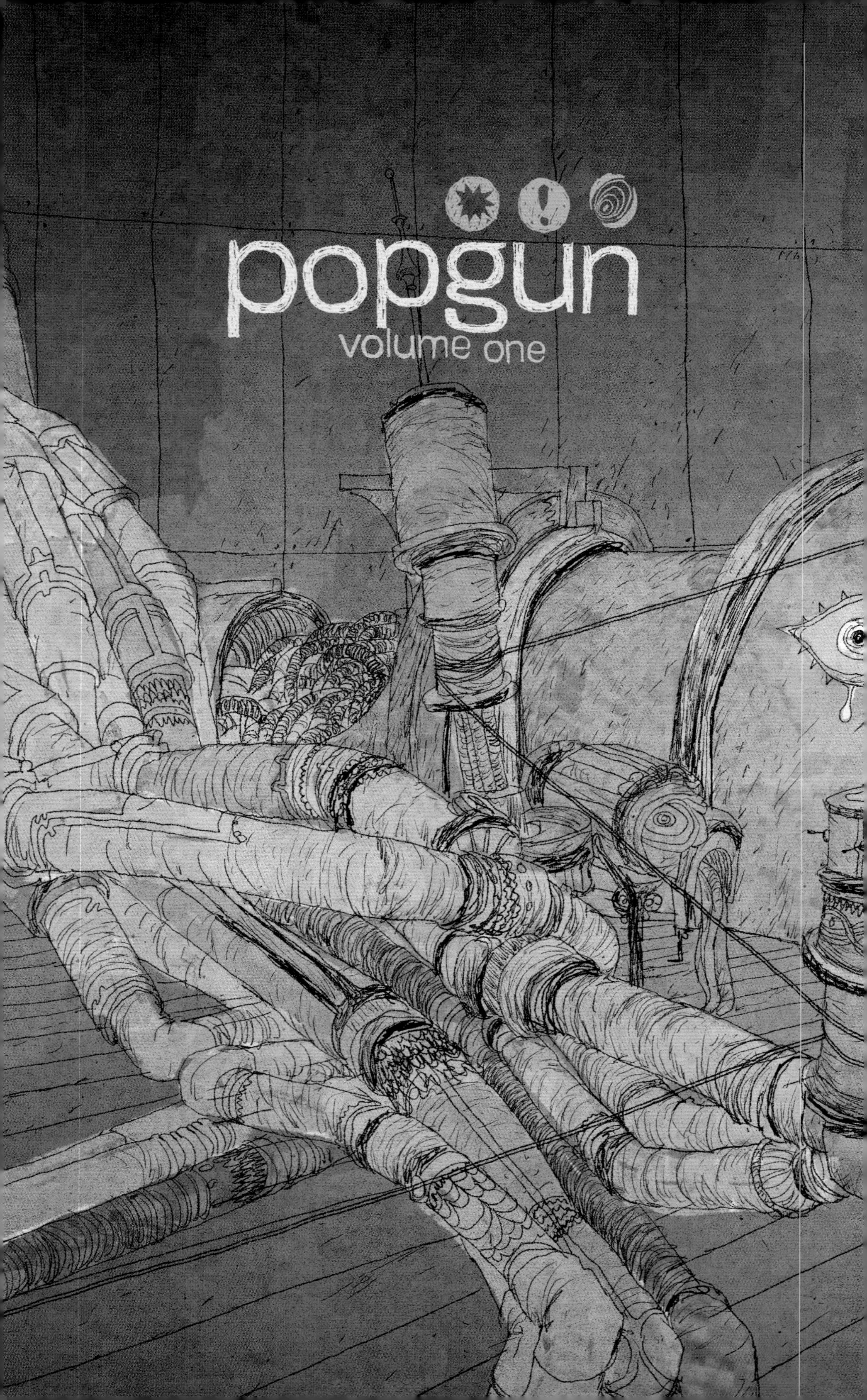
popgun
volume one

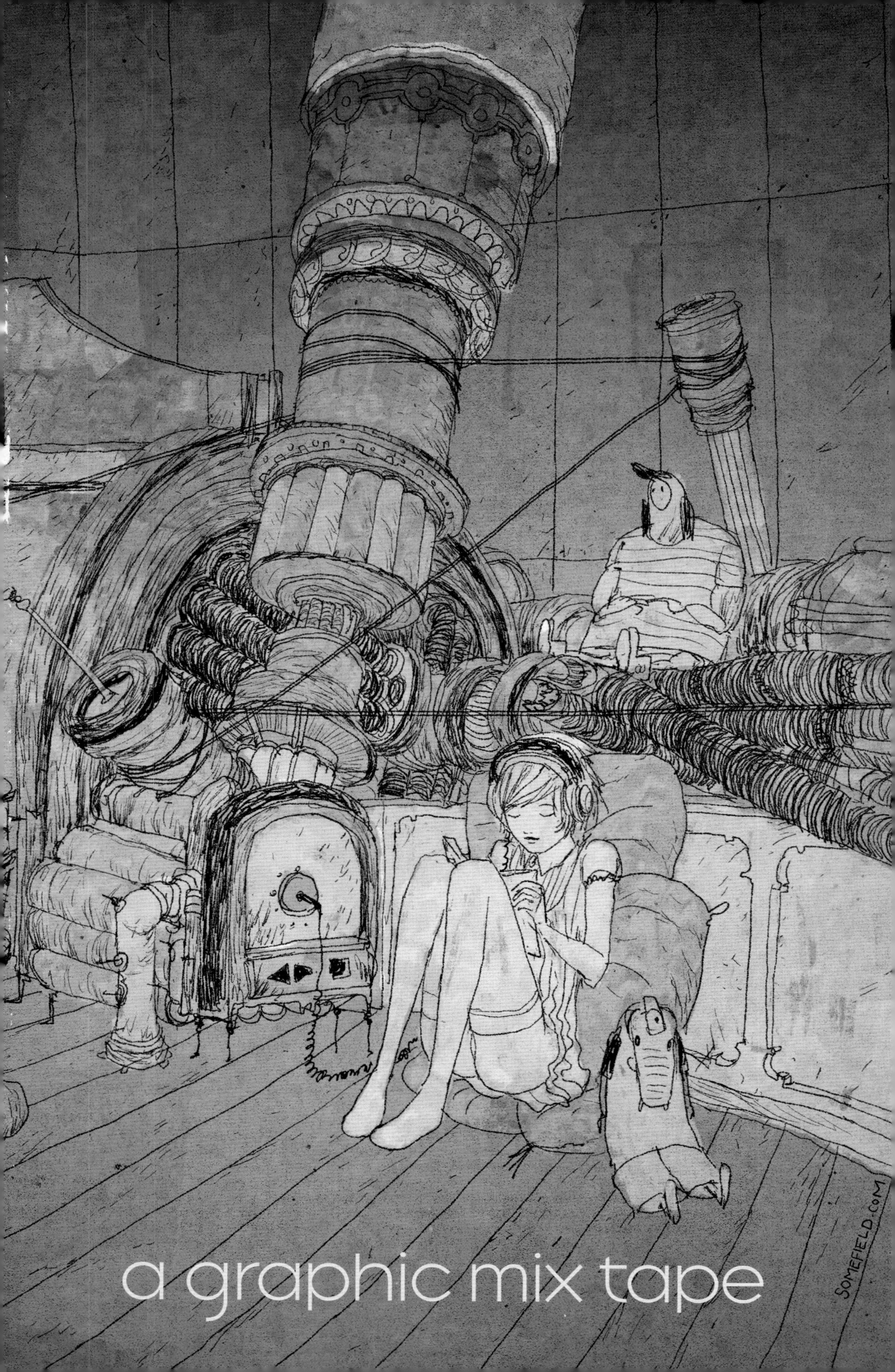
SOMEFIELD.COM
a graphic mix tape

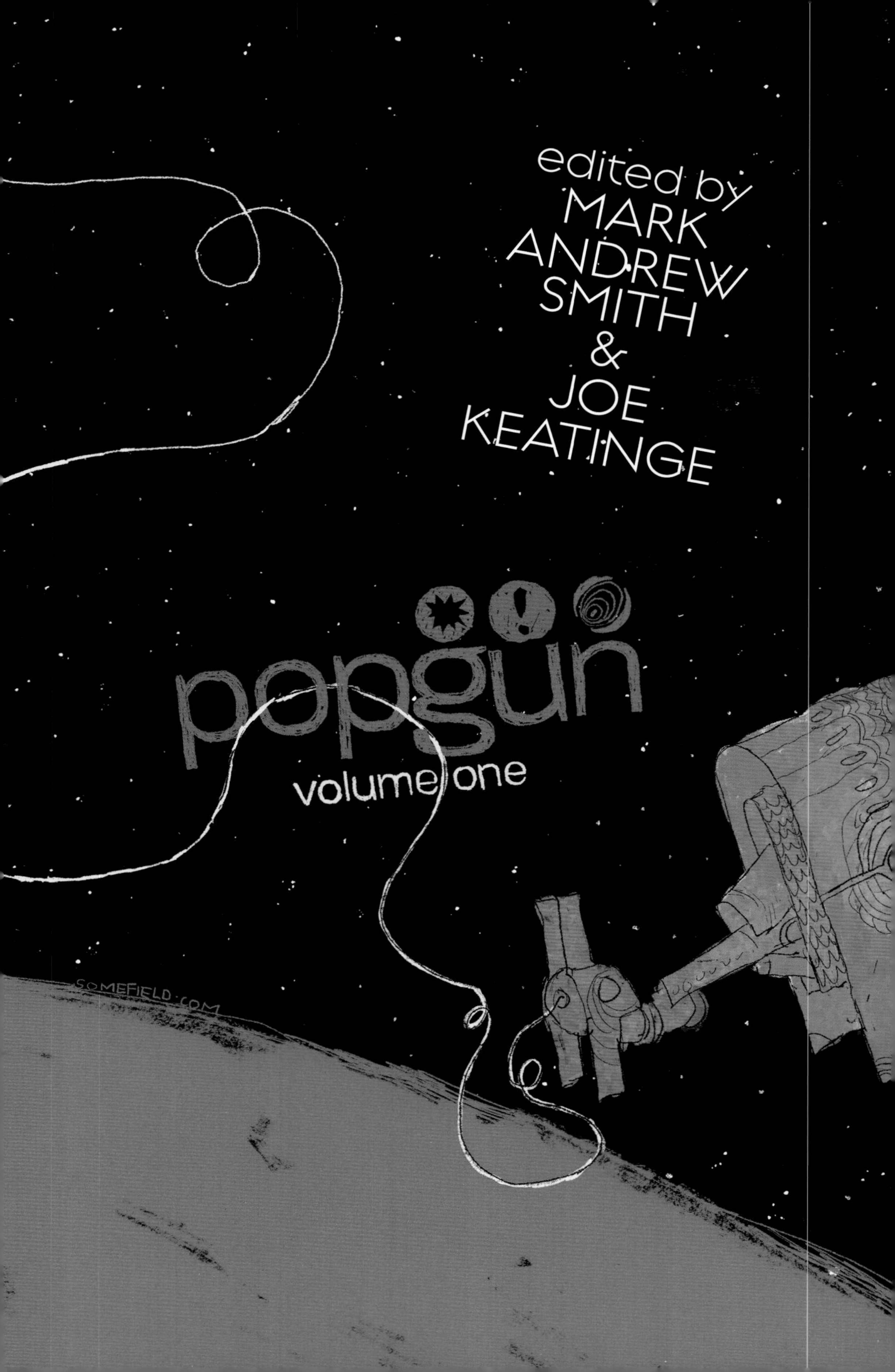
edited by
MARK ANDREW SMITH
&
JOE KEATINGE
popgun
volume one
SOMEFIELD.COM

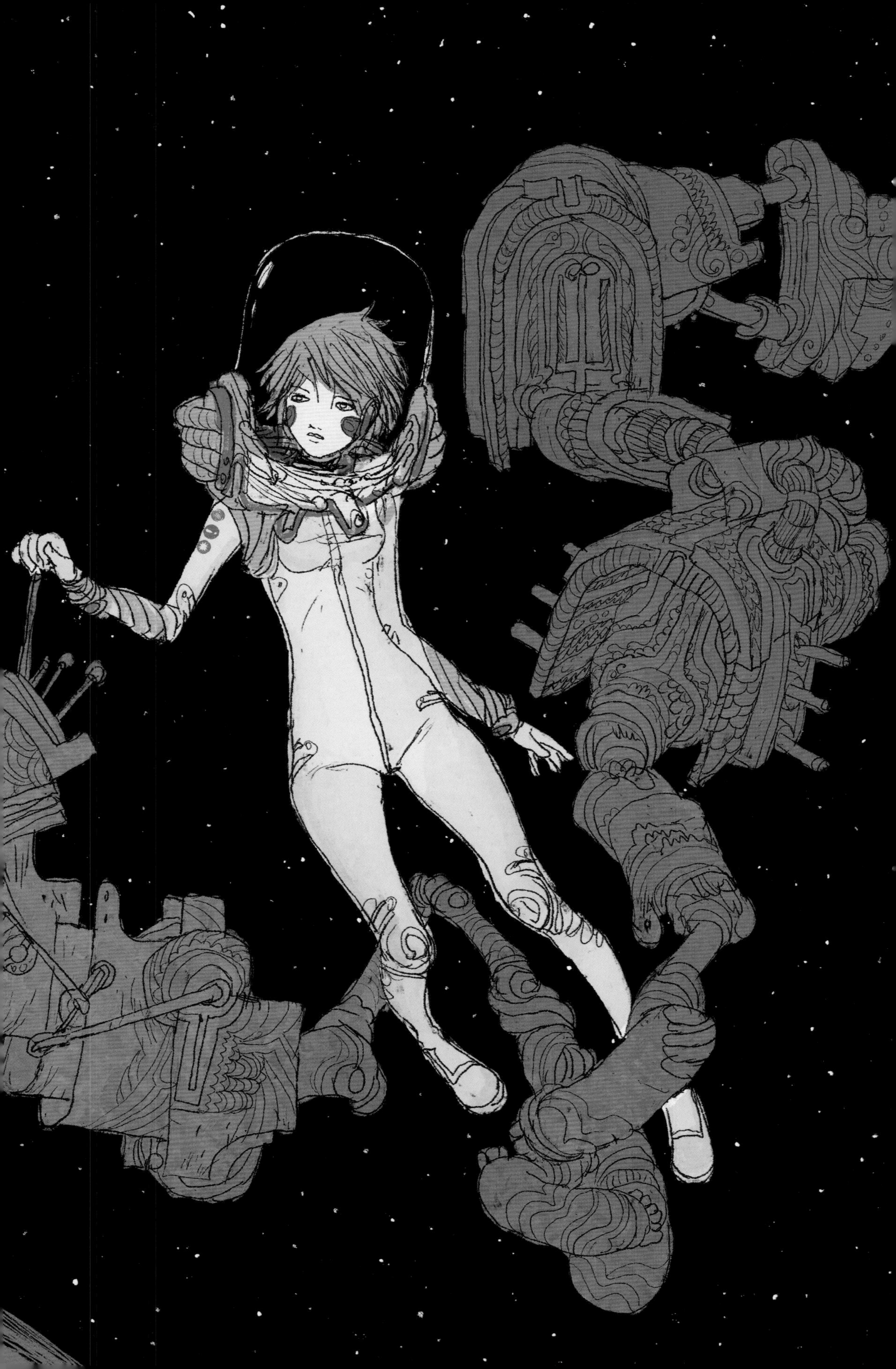

MARK ANDREW SMITH
JOE KEATINGE
editors

THOMAS MAUER
S. A. FINCH
production editors

D. J. KIRKBRIDE
assistant editor

MICHAEL ALLRED
LAURA ALLRED
cover art

FONOGRAFIKS
cover design

JOE FLOOD
inside front–page 1
page 448–inside back

BARNABY WARD
pages 2–3, 4–5, 10

JOSEPH MICHAEL LINSNER
pages 443, 444–445

YERAY GIL HERNANDEZ
pages 446–447

a very special thanks to
SATELLITESODA.COM

IMAGE COMICS, INC.

Robert Kirkman - chief operating officer
Erik Larsen - chief financial officer
Todd McFarlane - president
Marc Silvestri - chief executive officer
Jim Valentino - vice-president

ericstephenson - publisher
Joe Keatinge - pr & marketing coordinator
Branwyn Bigglestone - accounts manager
Tyler Shainline - administrative assistant
Traci Hui - traffic manager
Allen Hui - production manager
Drew Gill - production artist
Jonathan Chan - production artist
Monica Howard - production artist

www.imagecomics.com

POPGUN, VOL. 1. Second Printing. Published by Image Comics, Inc. Office of publication: 1942 University Avenue, Suite 305, Berkeley, California 94704.
PRINTED IN CHINA
ISBN: 978-1-58240-824-8
International Rights Representative: Christine Jensen (christine@gfloystudio.com)

Track Listing

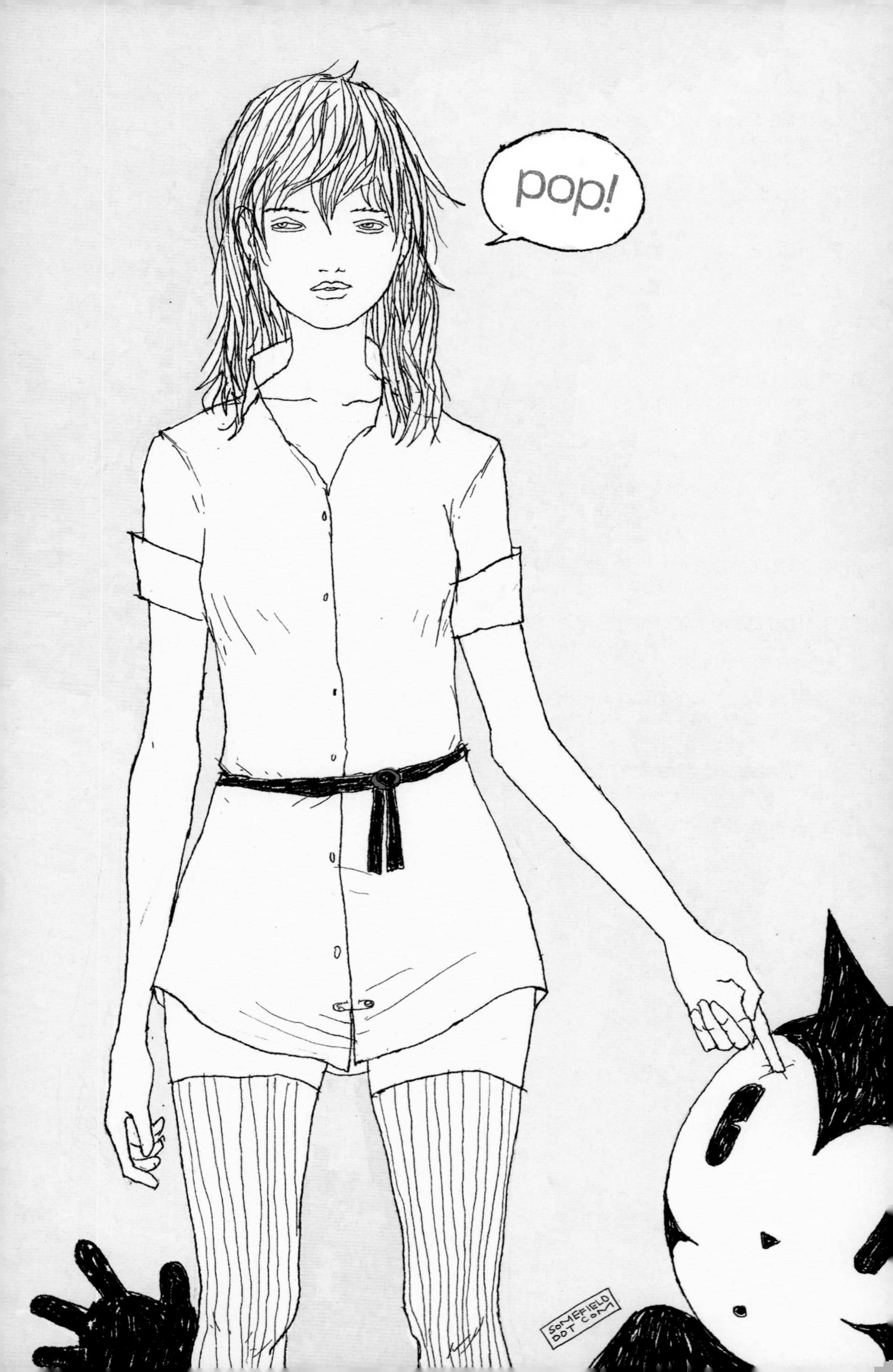
pop!
SOMEFIELD DOT COM

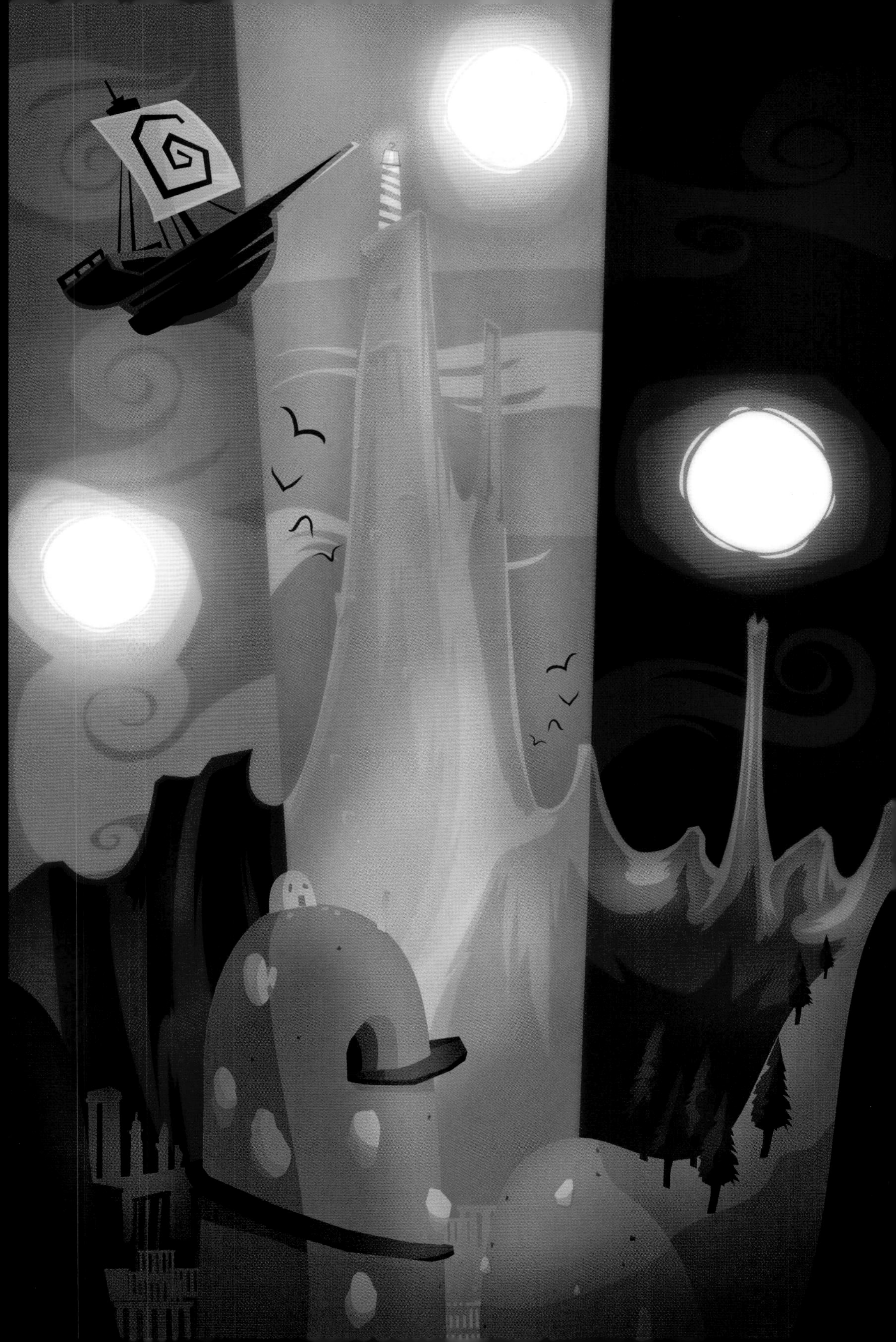

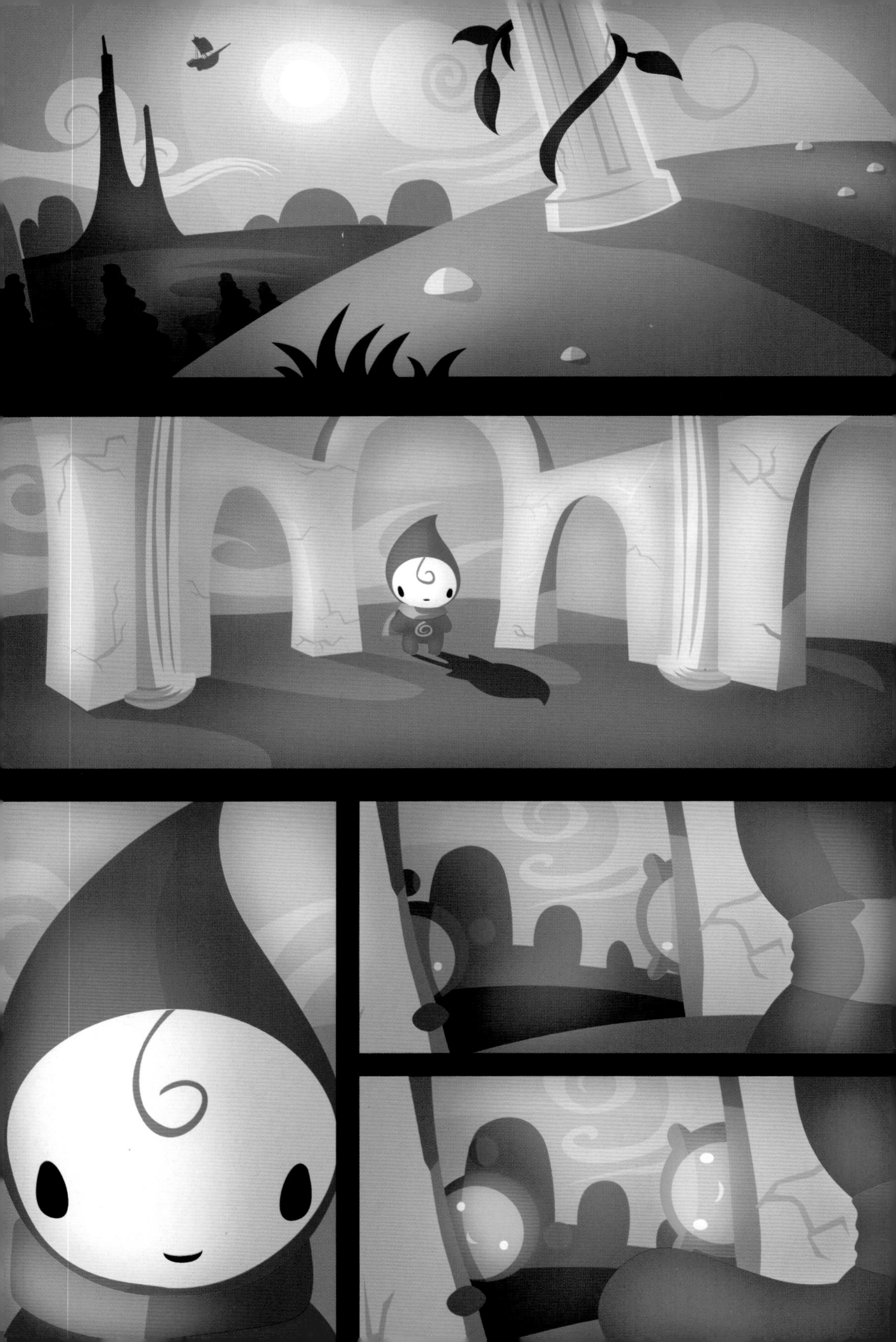

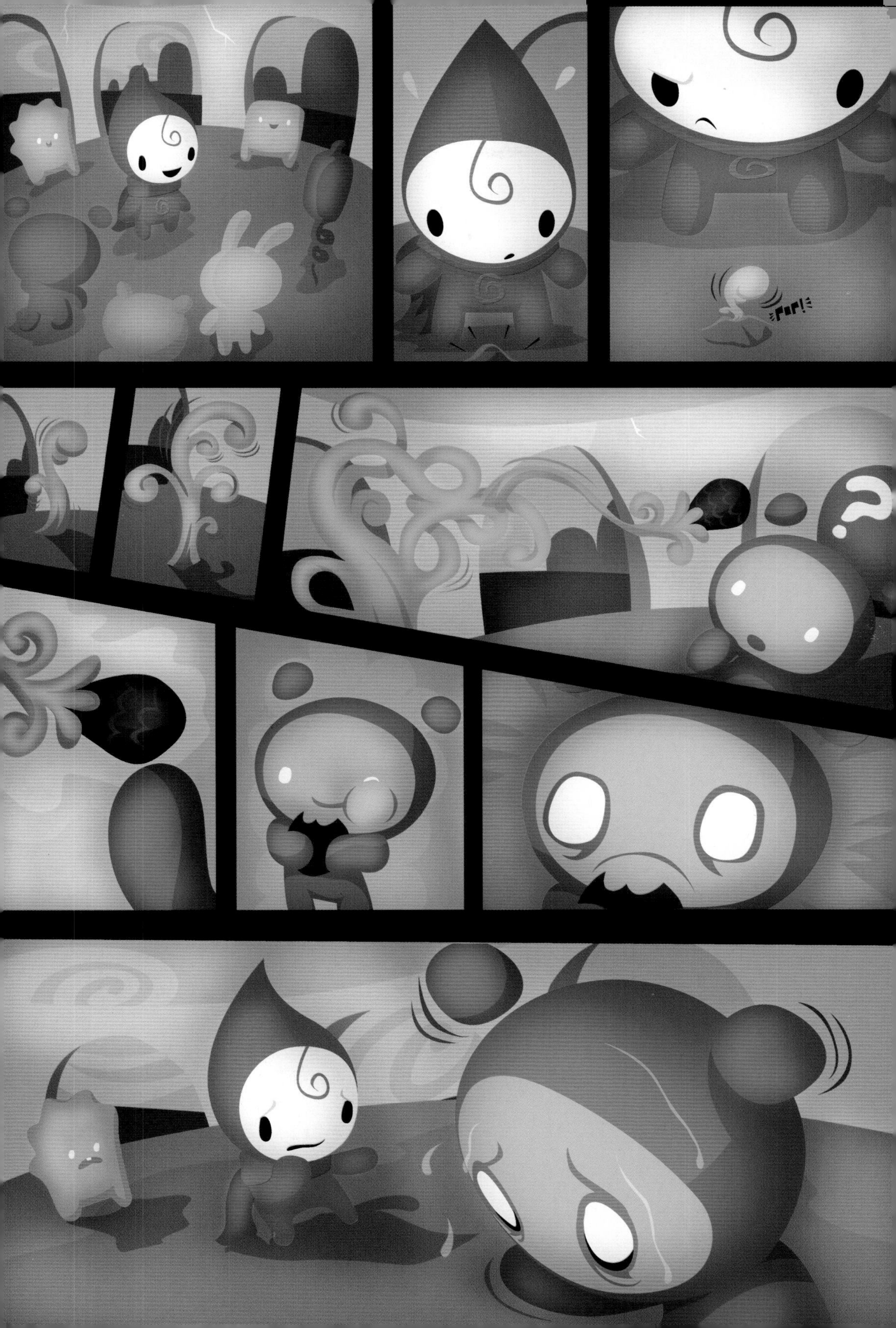
POP!
?

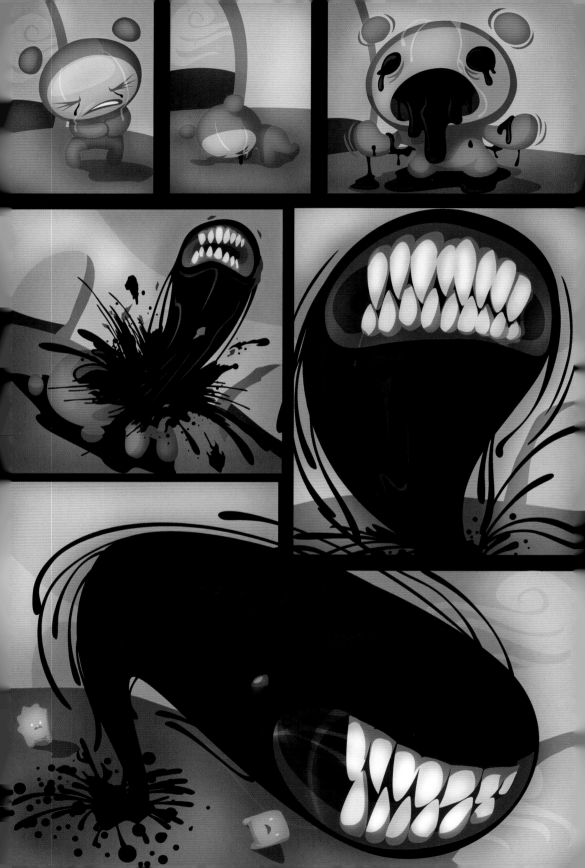

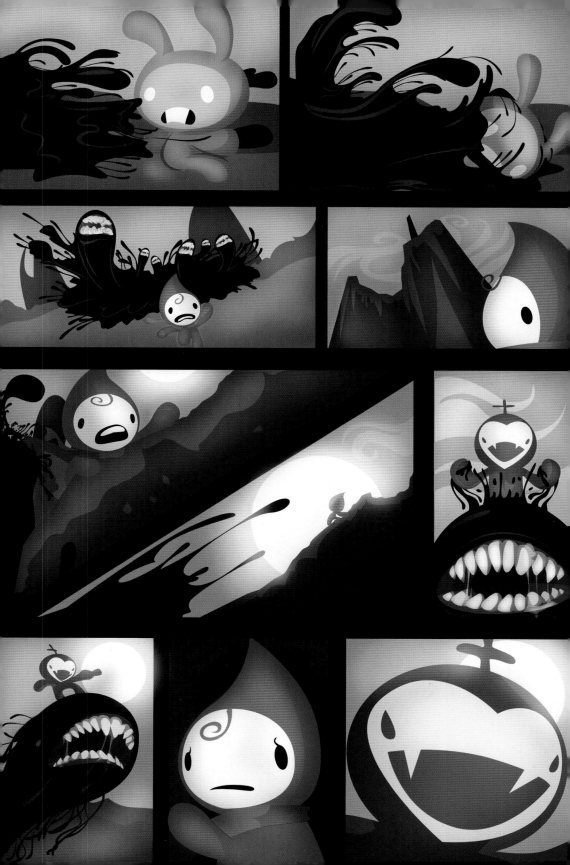

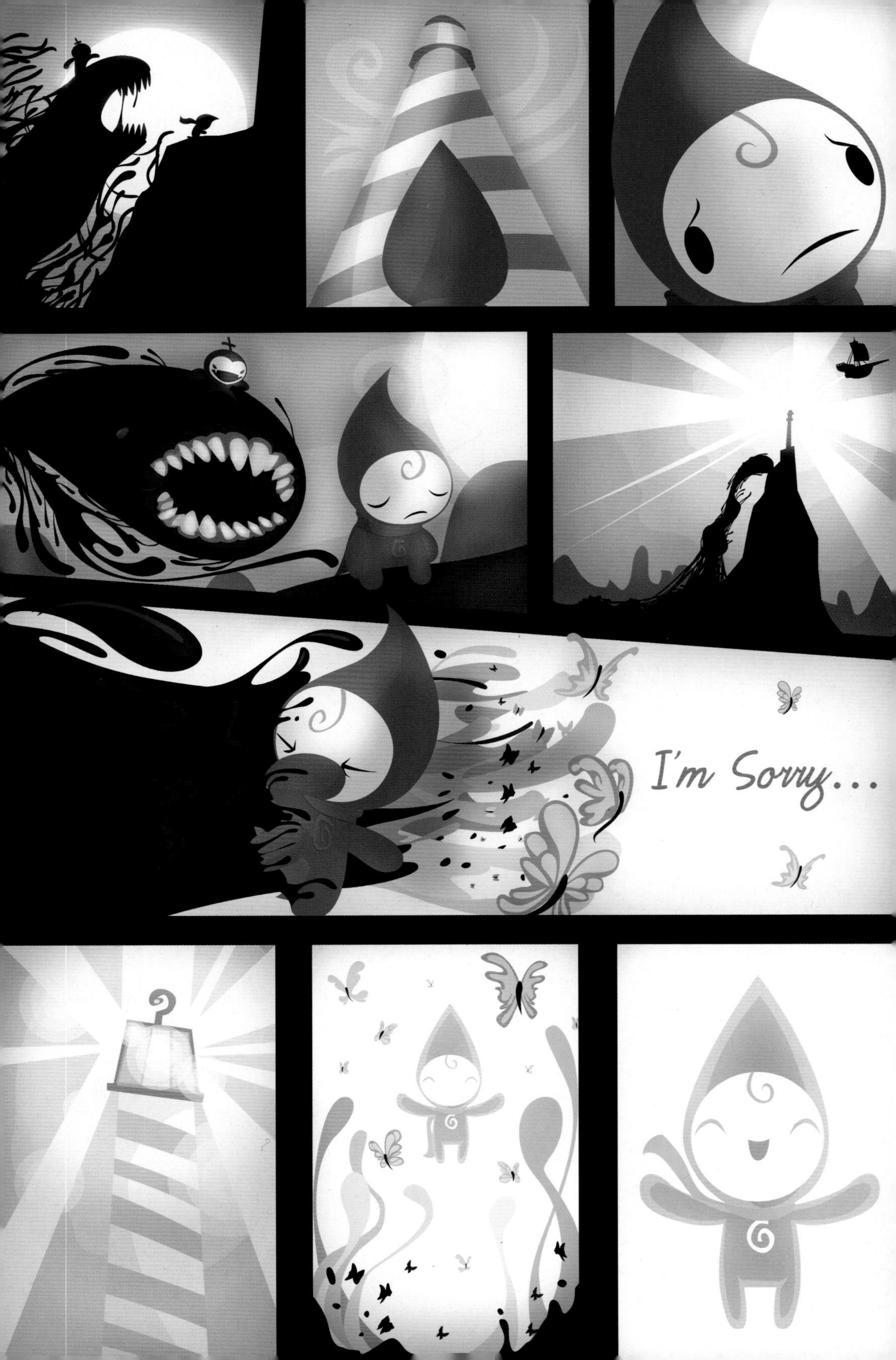
I'm Sorry...

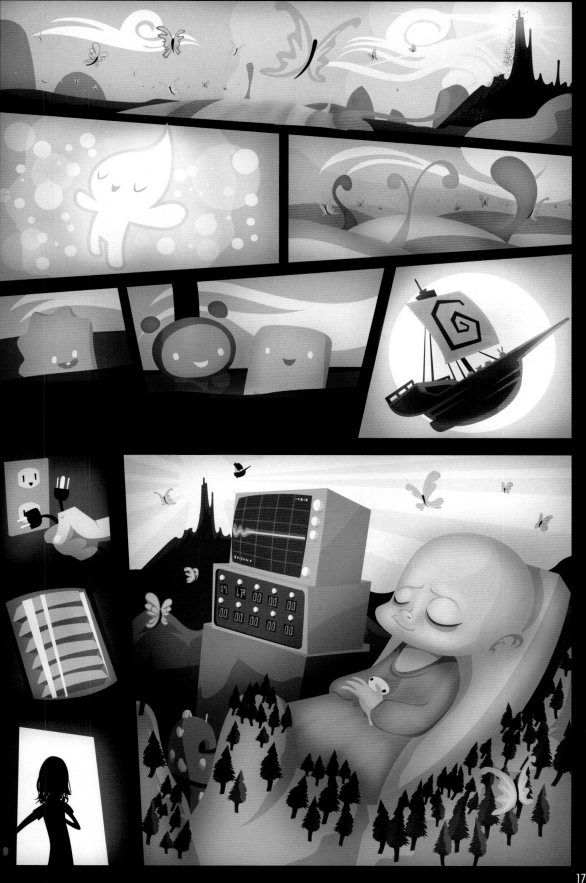

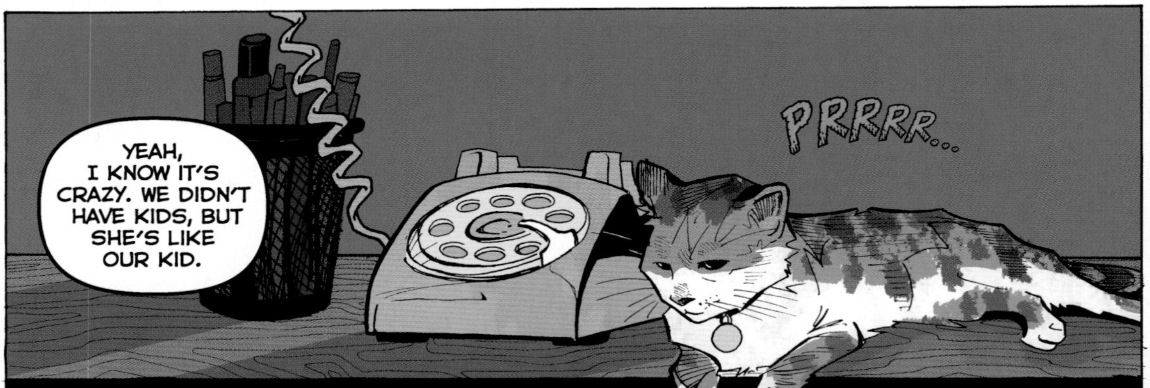
YEAH, I KNOW IT'S CRAZY. WE DIDN'T HAVE KIDS, BUT SHE'S LIKE OUR KID.
PRRRR...

"ME & THE CAT OWN THE LEASE ON THE FLAT"

by Jamie S. Rich & Joëlle Jones

Coloring and lettering by Keith Wood Special thanks to J-Lu.

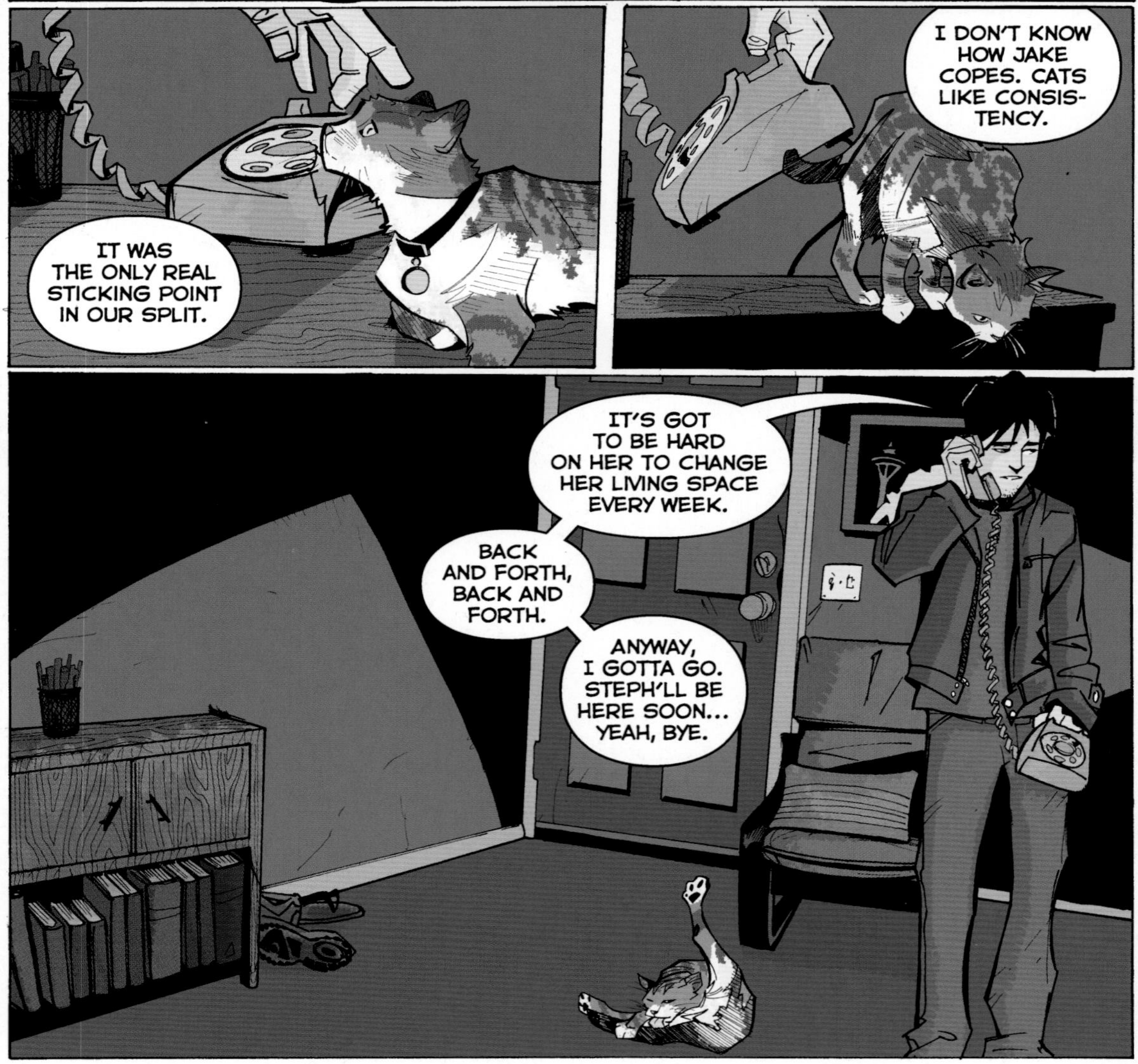
IT WAS THE ONLY REAL STICKING POINT IN OUR SPLIT.
I DON'T KNOW HOW JAKE COPES. CATS LIKE CONSIS-TENCY.
IT'S GOT TO BE HARD ON HER TO CHANGE HER LIVING SPACE EVERY WEEK.
BACK AND FORTH, BACK AND FORTH.
ANYWAY, I GOTTA GO. STEPH'LL BE HERE SOON... YEAH, BYE.

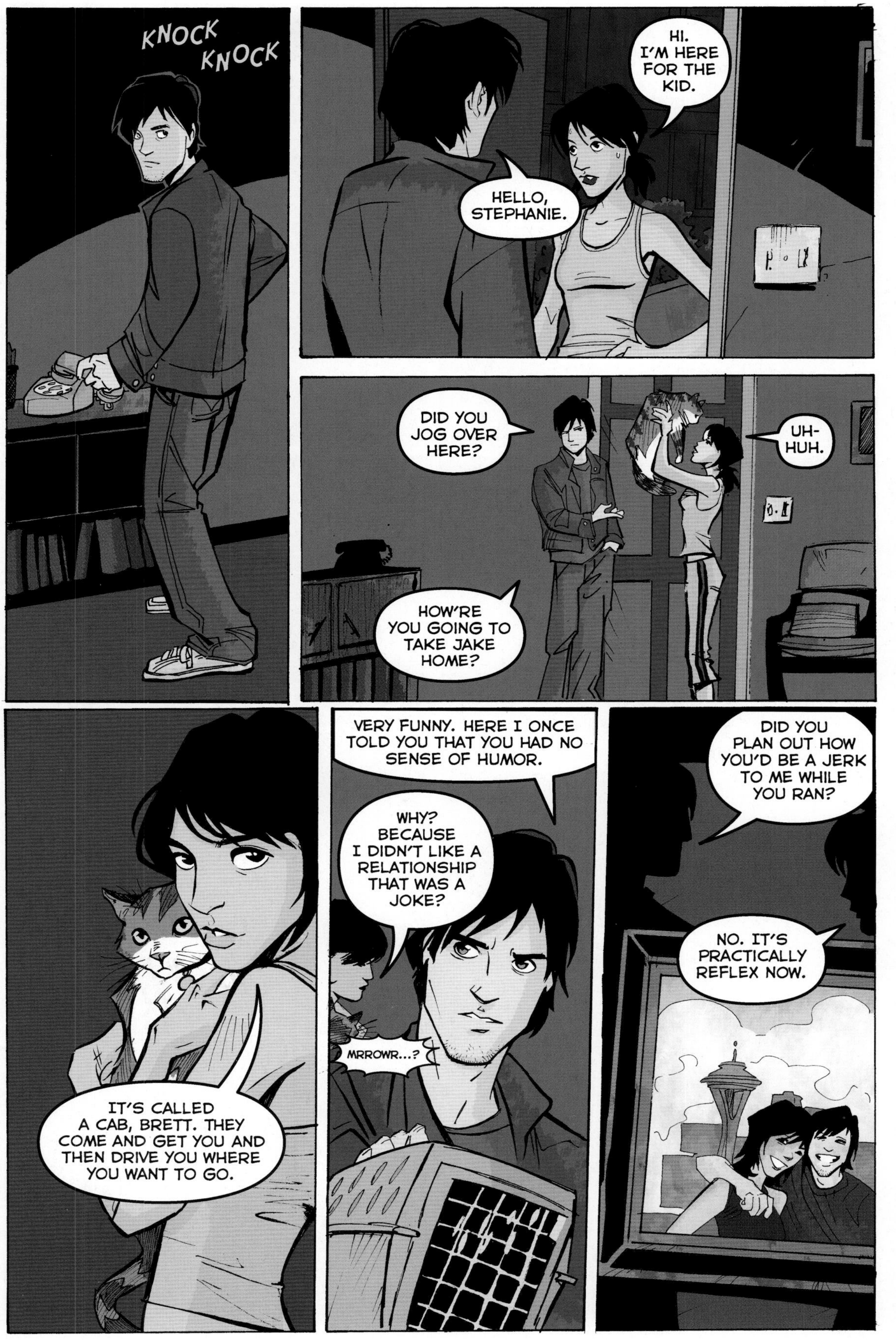

KNOCK KNOCK
HI. I'M HERE FOR THE KID.
HELLO, STEPHANIE.
DID YOU JOG OVER HERE?
UH-HUH.
HOW'RE YOU GOING TO TAKE JAKE HOME?
IT'S CALLED A CAB, BRETT. THEY COME AND GET YOU AND THEN DRIVE YOU WHERE YOU WANT TO GO.
VERY FUNNY. HERE I ONCE TOLD YOU THAT YOU HAD NO SENSE OF HUMOR.
WHY? BECAUSE I DIDN'T LIKE A RELATIONSHIP THAT WAS A JOKE?
MRROWR...?
DID YOU PLAN OUT HOW YOU'D BE A JERK TO ME WHILE YOU RAN?
NO. IT'S PRACTICALLY REFLEX NOW.

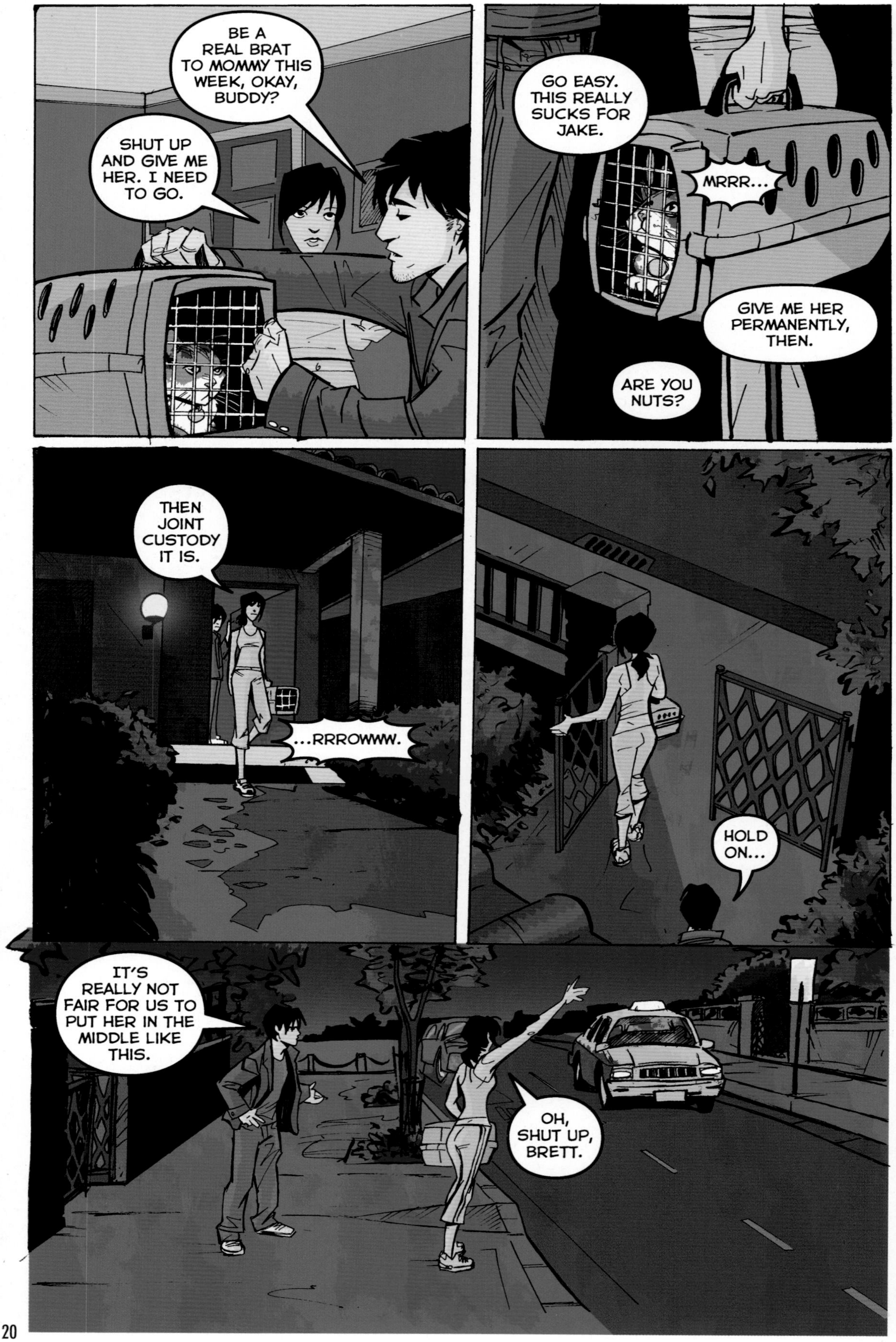

BE A REAL BRAT TO MOMMY THIS WEEK, OKAY, BUDDY?
SHUT UP AND GIVE ME HER. I NEED TO GO.
GO EASY. THIS REALLY SUCKS FOR JAKE.
MRRR...
GIVE ME HER PERMANENTLY, THEN.
ARE YOU NUTS?
THEN JOINT CUSTODY IT IS.
...RRROWWW.
HOLD ON...
IT'S REALLY NOT FAIR FOR US TO PUT HER IN THE MIDDLE LIKE THIS.
OH, SHUT UP, BRETT.

DAMNIT!

YOU DIDN'T EVEN WANT A CAT.

AND AS USUAL, WHAT I WANTED DIDN'T MATTER, YET I MADE THE BEST OF IT.

WHO TOOK CARE OF HER ALL THAT TIME YOU WERE TRAVELING ON BUSINESS?

ARE WE GOING TO HARP ON MY CAREER GOALS AGAIN? JUST BECAUSE YOU'RE FINE SERVING COFFEE ALL YOUR LIFE...

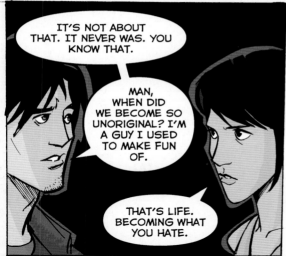

IT'S NOT ABOUT THAT. IT NEVER WAS. YOU KNOW THAT.

MAN, WHEN DID WE BECOME SO UNORIGINAL? I'M A GUY I USED TO MAKE FUN OF.

THAT'S LIFE. BECOMING WHAT YOU HATE.

I'M SORRY THEN. I WISH I COULD MAKE YOU SEE ME FOR THE GUY I MEANT TO BE.

YOU KNOW WHAT?

YOU DON'T NEED TO BRING JAKE BACK. YOU KEEP HER.

SHE'S ANOTHER LIVING BEING, AND IF I CARE ABOUT HER AS MUCH AS I CLAIM, THEN I CAN LET HER GO.

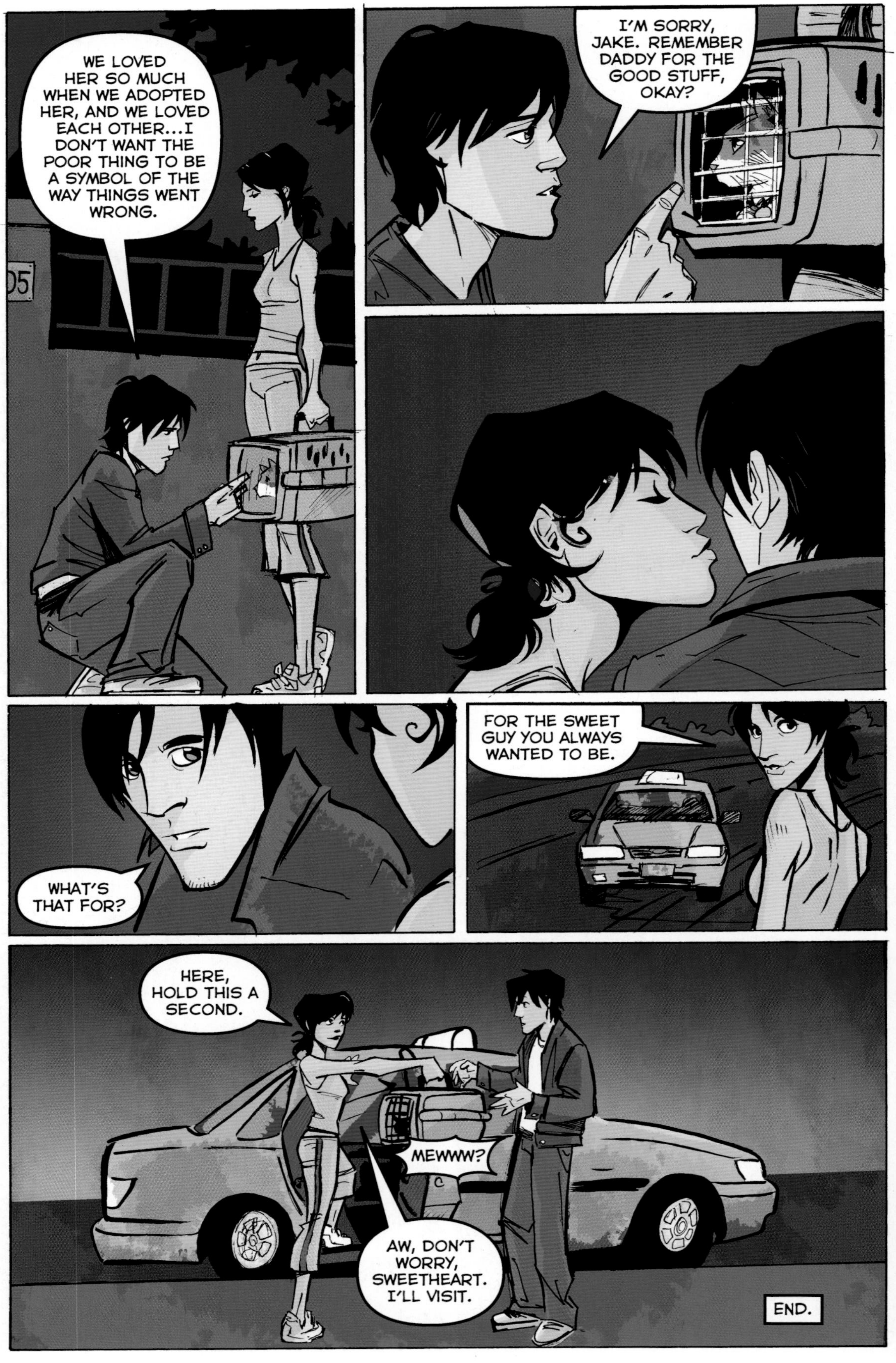

WE LOVED HER SO MUCH WHEN WE ADOPTED HER, AND WE LOVED EACH OTHER...I DON'T WANT THE POOR THING TO BE A SYMBOL OF THE WAY THINGS WENT WRONG.
05
I'M SORRY, JAKE. REMEMBER DADDY FOR THE GOOD STUFF, OKAY?
WHAT'S THAT FOR?
FOR THE SWEET GUY YOU ALWAYS WANTED TO BE.
HERE, HOLD THIS A SECOND.
MEWWW?
AW, DON'T WORRY, SWEETHEART. I'LL VISIT.
END.

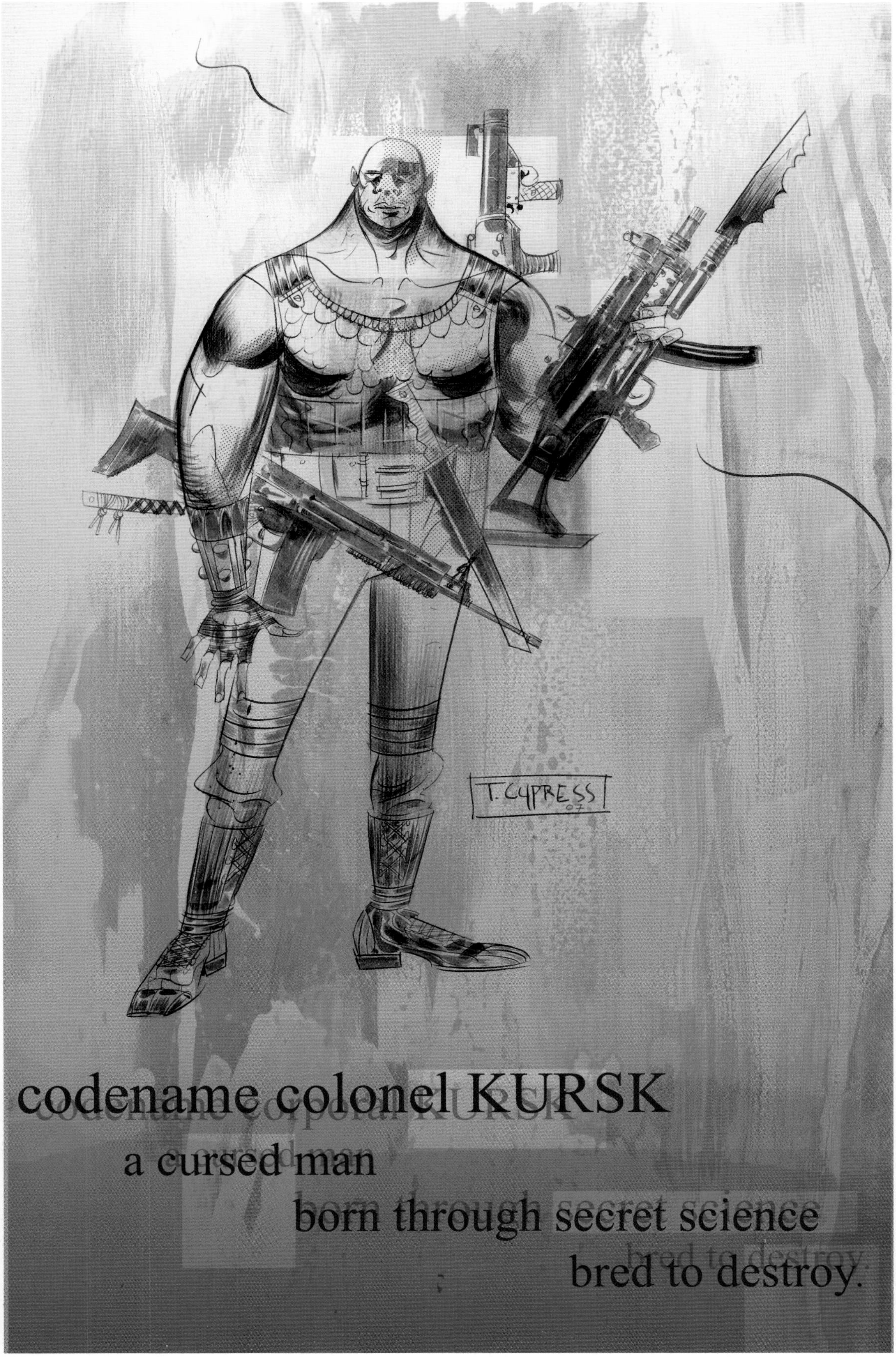
T. CYPRESS 07
codename colonel KURSK
a cursed man
born through secret science
bred to destroy.

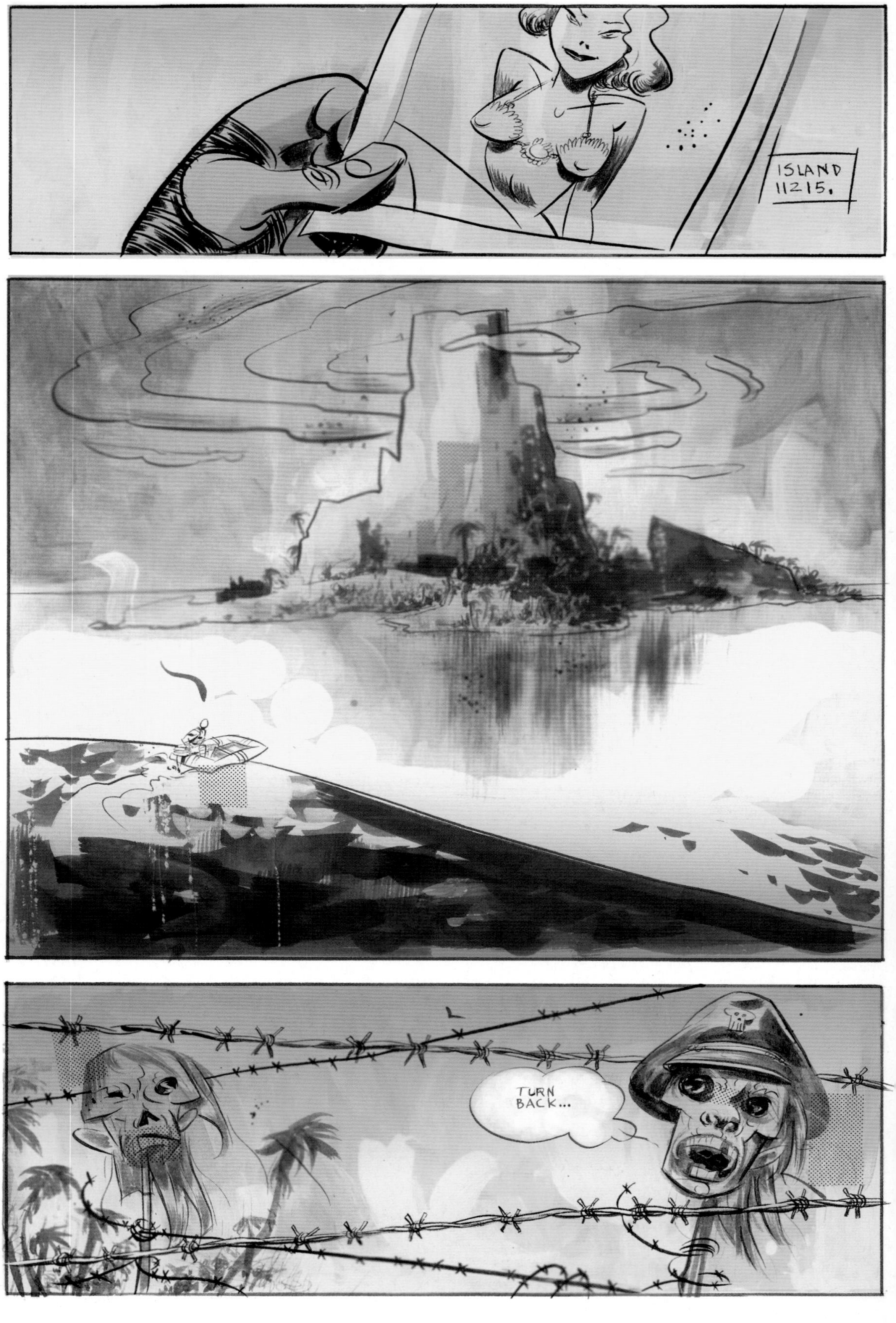
ISLAND
11215.
TURN BACK...

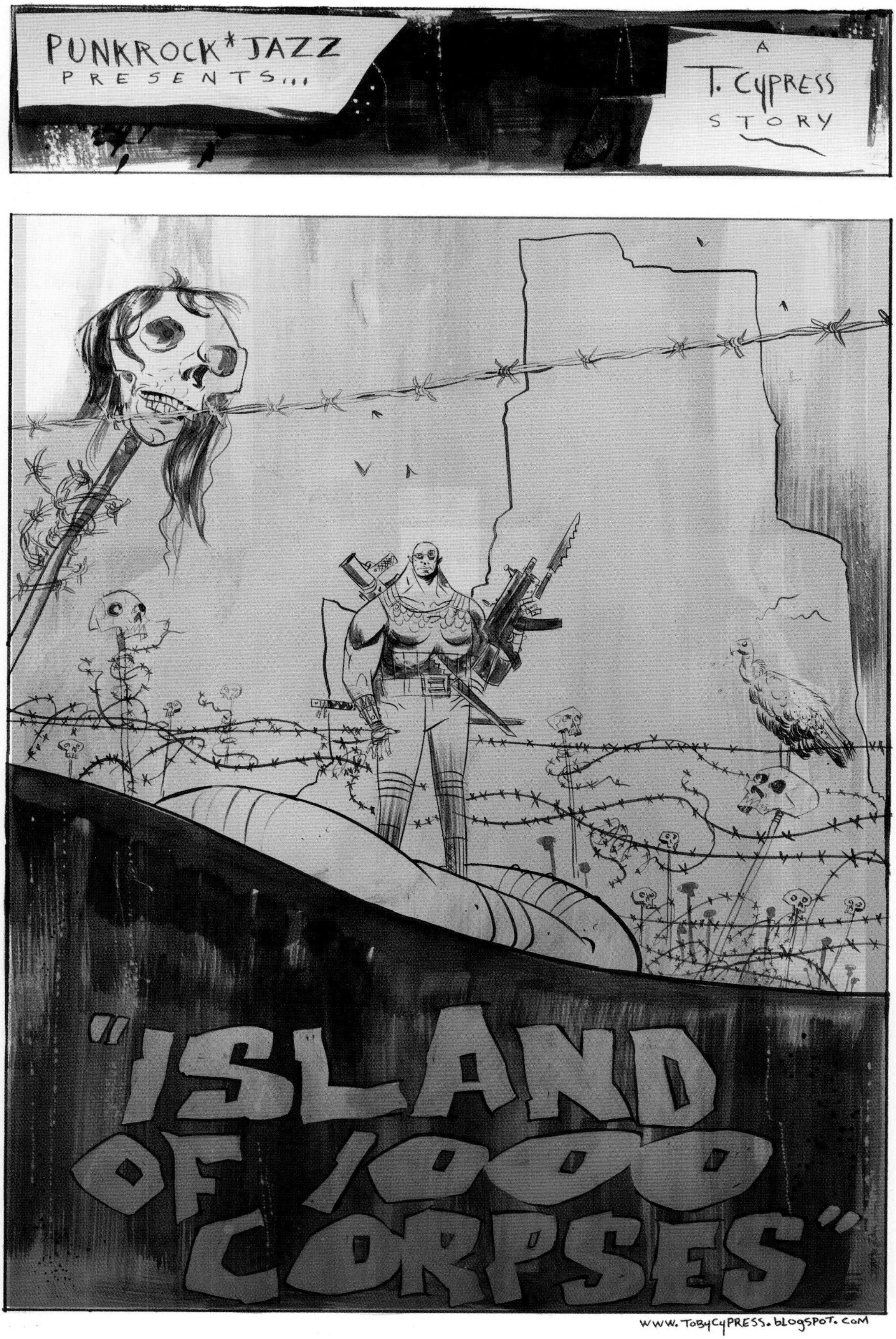
PUNKROCK*JAZZ PRESENTS...
A T. CYPRESS STORY
"ISLAND OF 1000 CORPSES"

WWW.TOBYCYPRESS.BLOGSPOT.COM

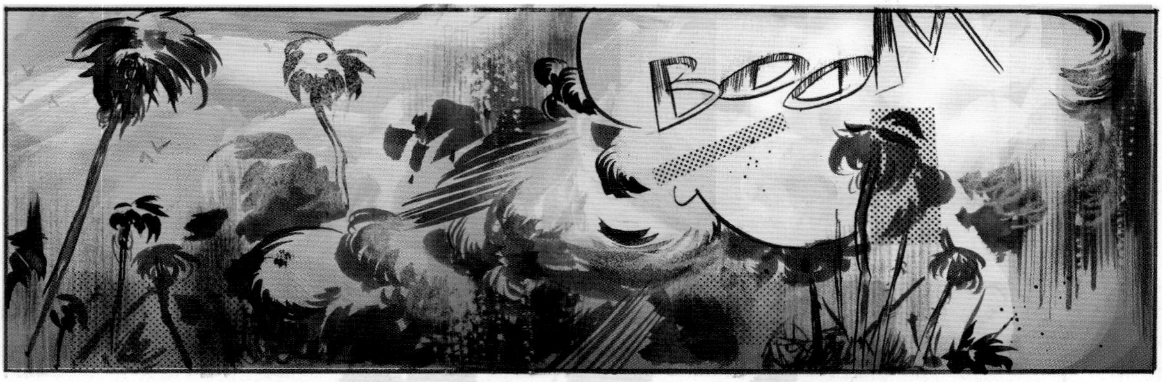
BOOM

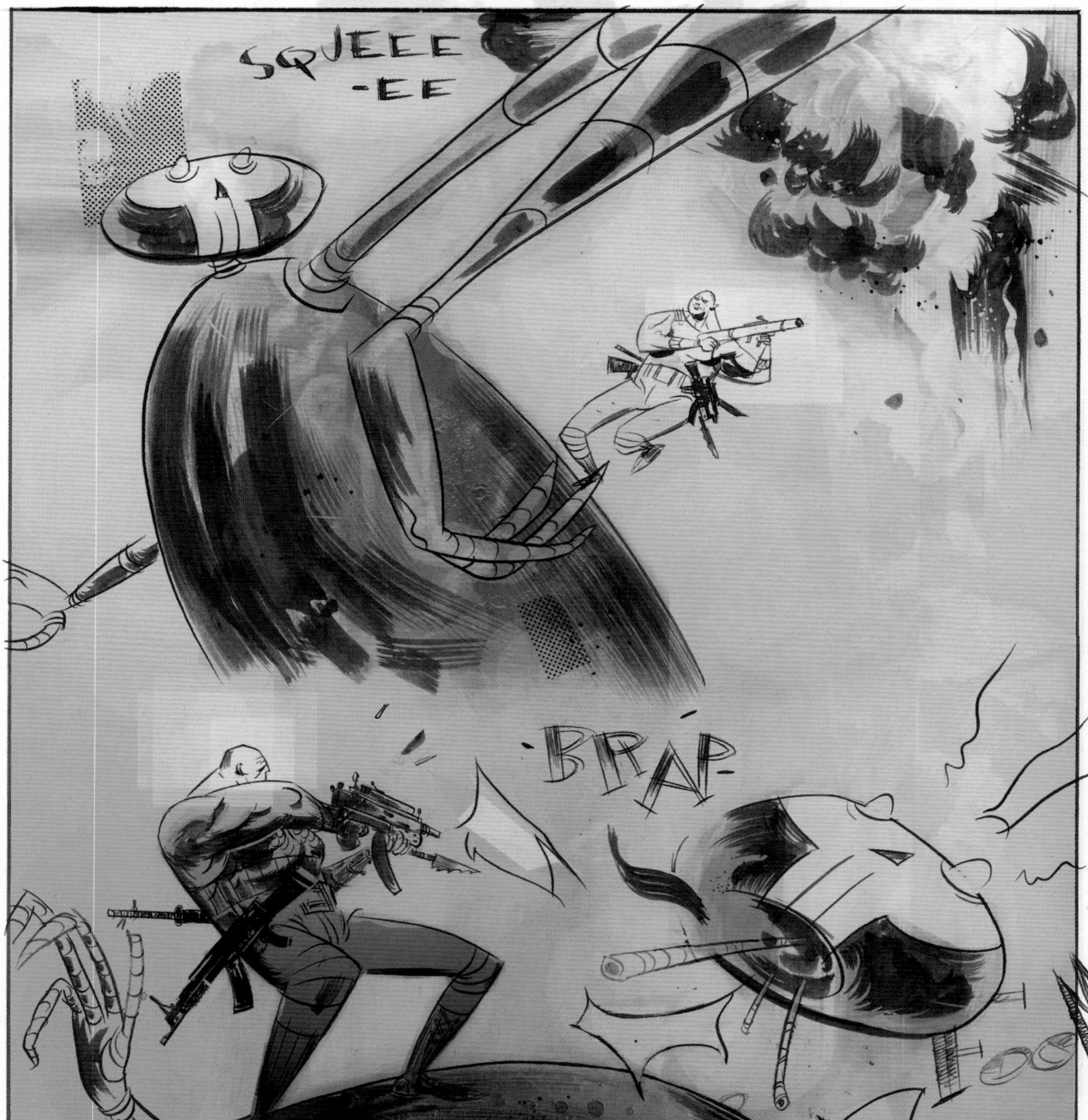
SQUEEE
-EE
BRAP
FOOM

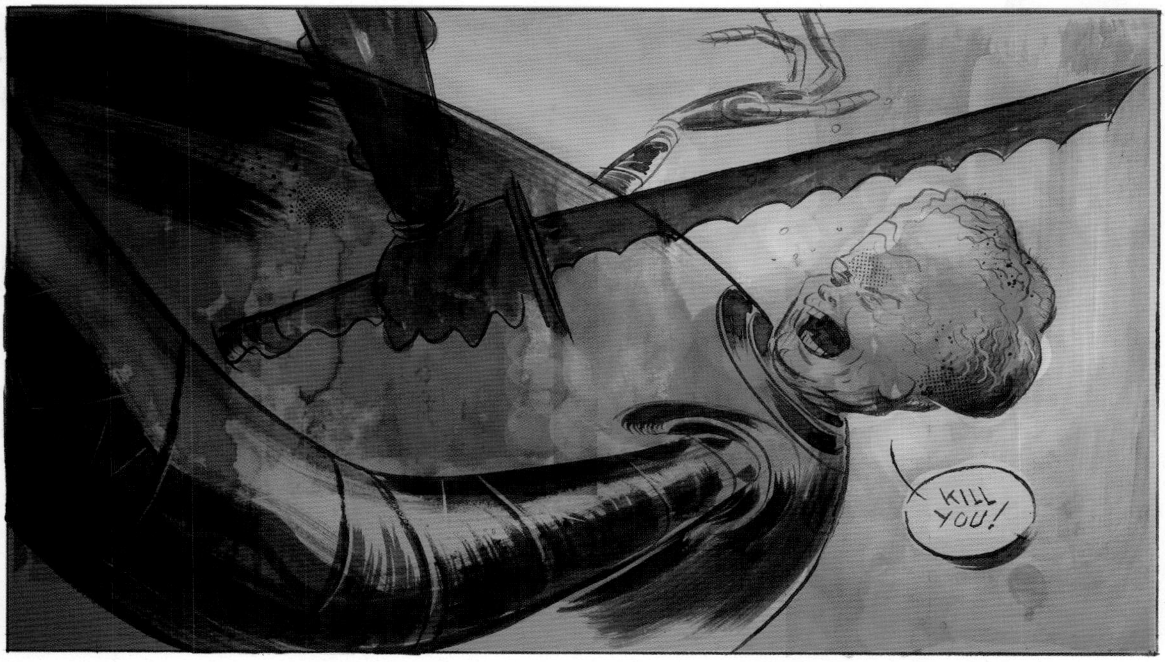
KILL YOU!

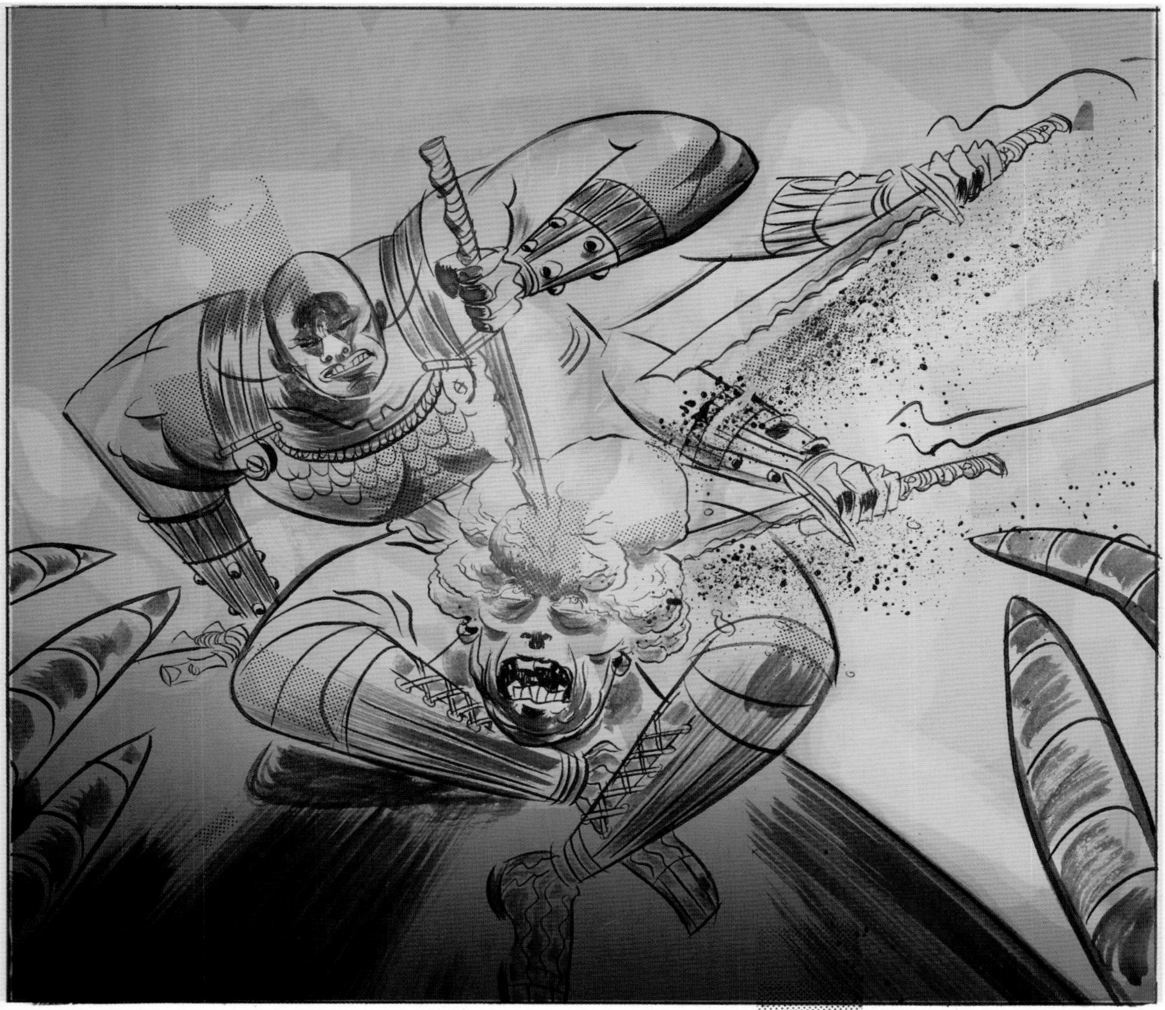

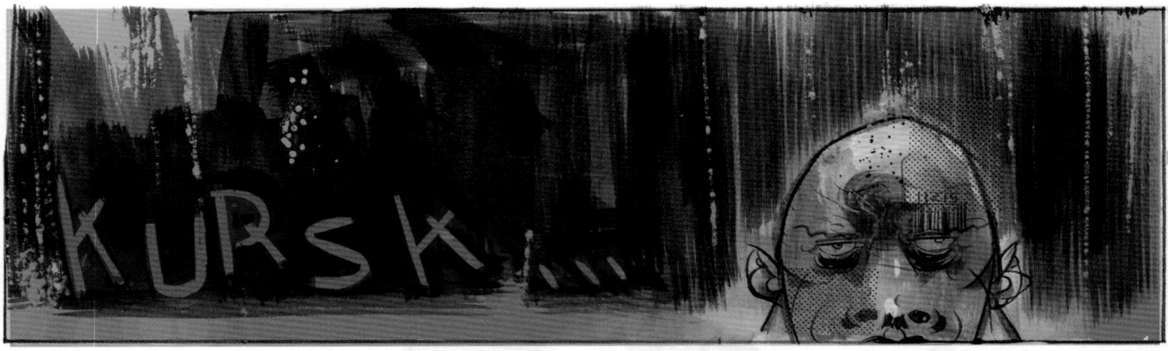
KURSK...

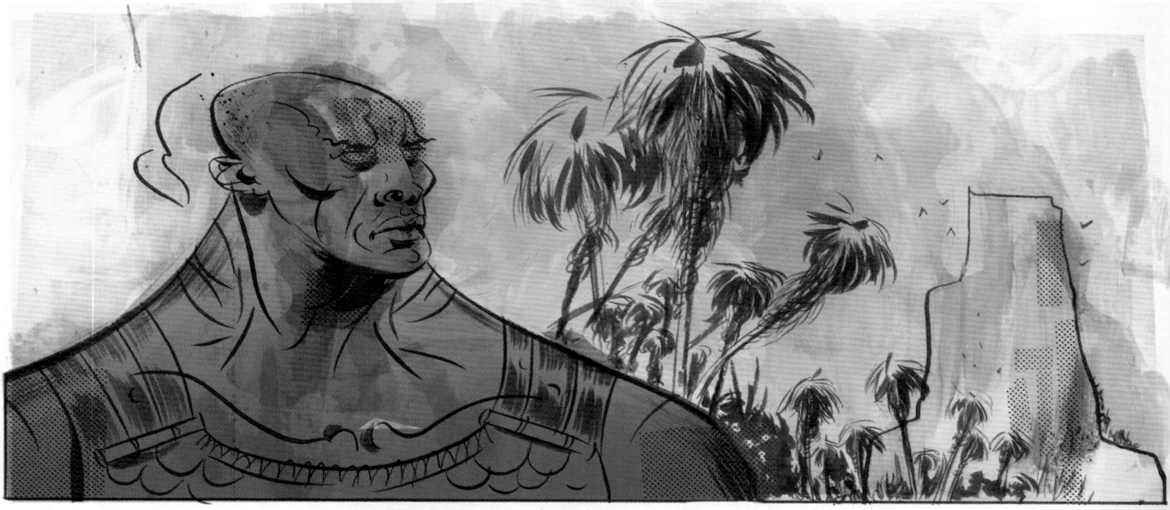

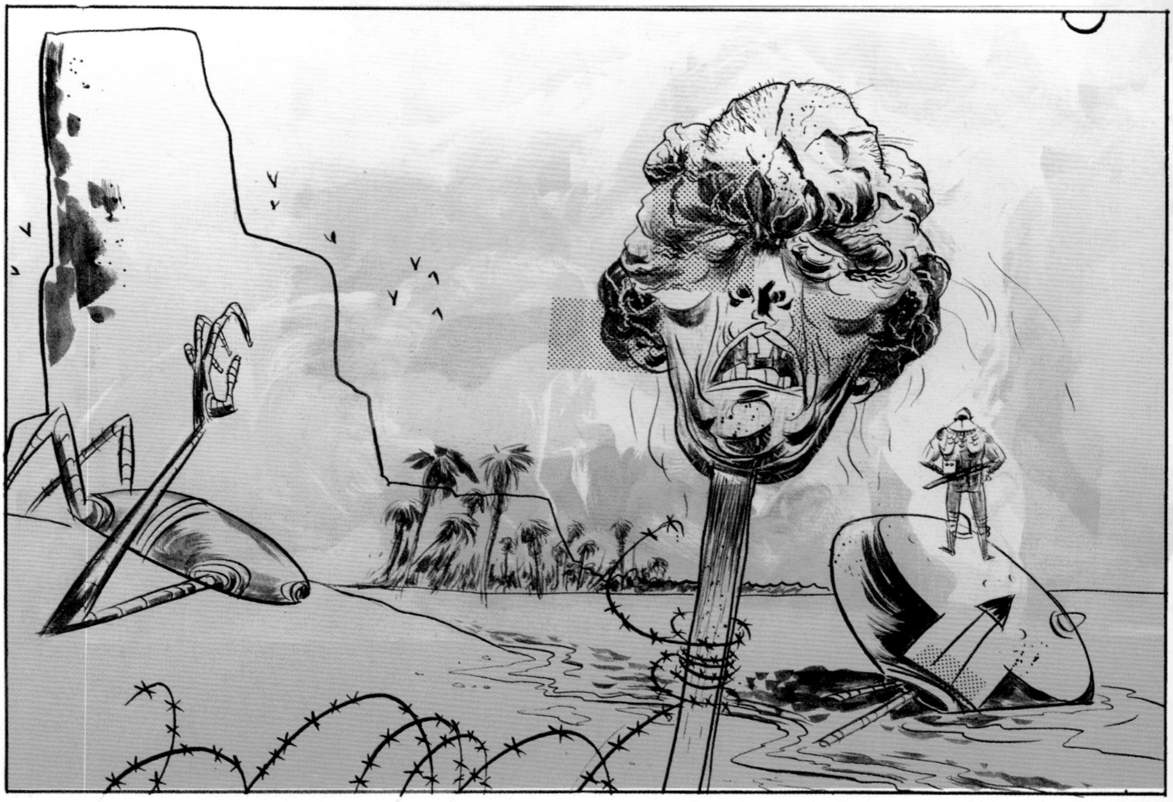

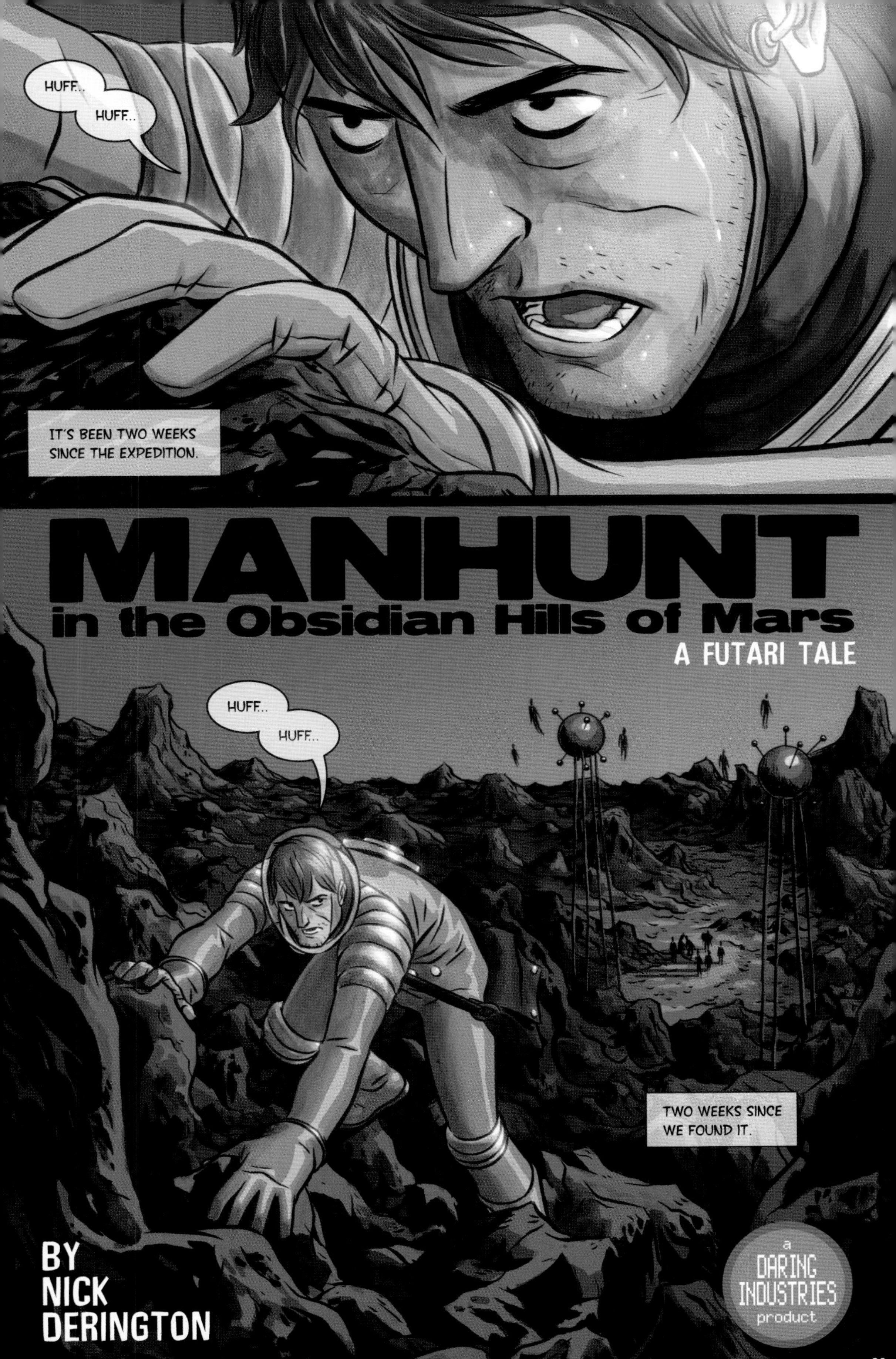
HUFF...
HUFF...
IT'S BEEN TWO WEEKS SINCE THE EXPEDITION.
MANHUNT
in the Obsidian Hills of Mars
A FUTARI TALE
HUFF...
HUFF...
TWO WEEKS SINCE WE FOUND IT.
BY NICK DERINGTON
a DARING INDUSTRIES product

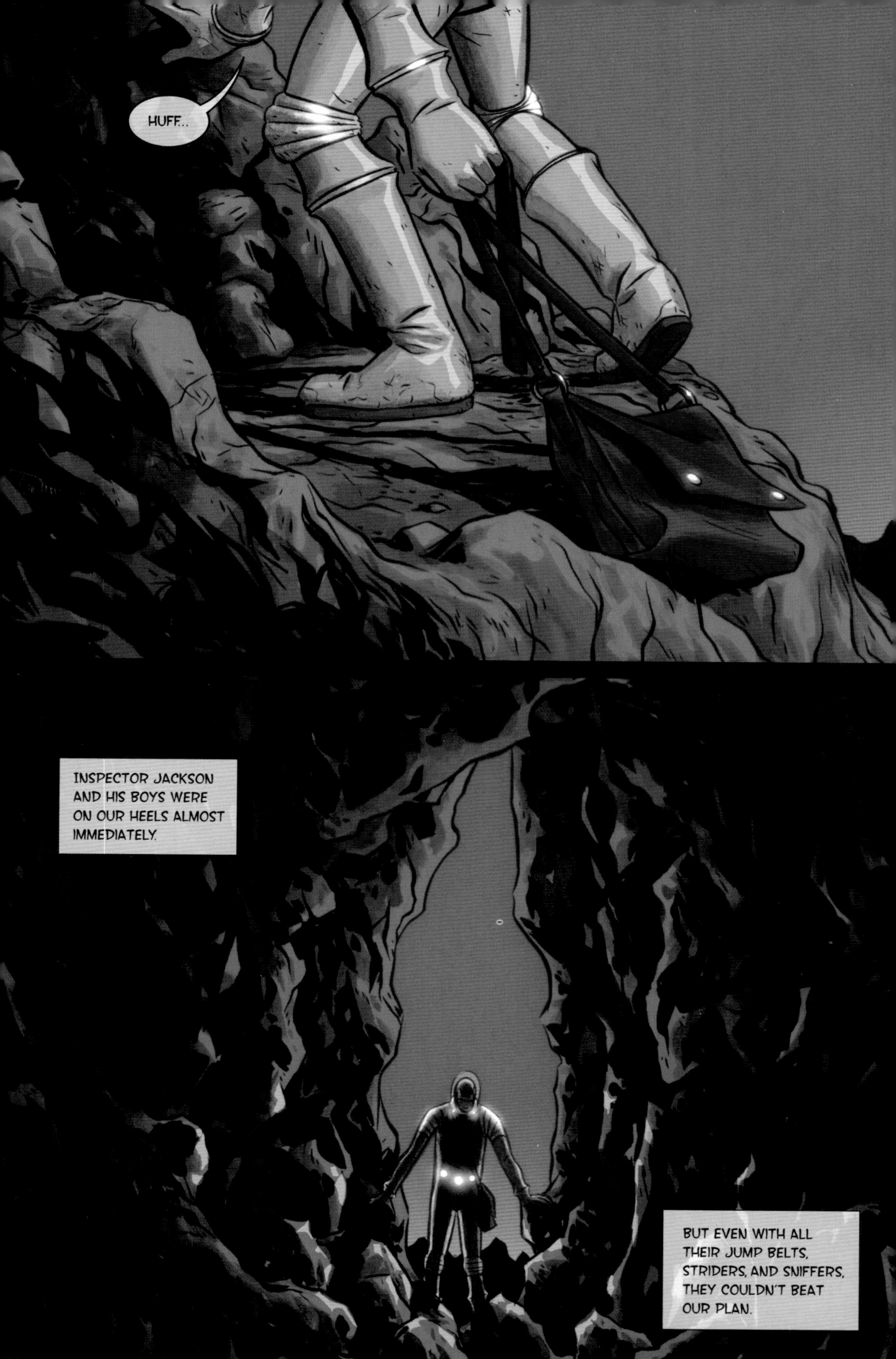
HUFF...
INSPECTOR JACKSON AND HIS BOYS WERE ON OUR HEELS ALMOST IMMEDIATELY.
BUT EVEN WITH ALL THEIR JUMP BELTS, STRIDERS, AND SNIFFERS, THEY COULDN'T BEAT OUR PLAN.

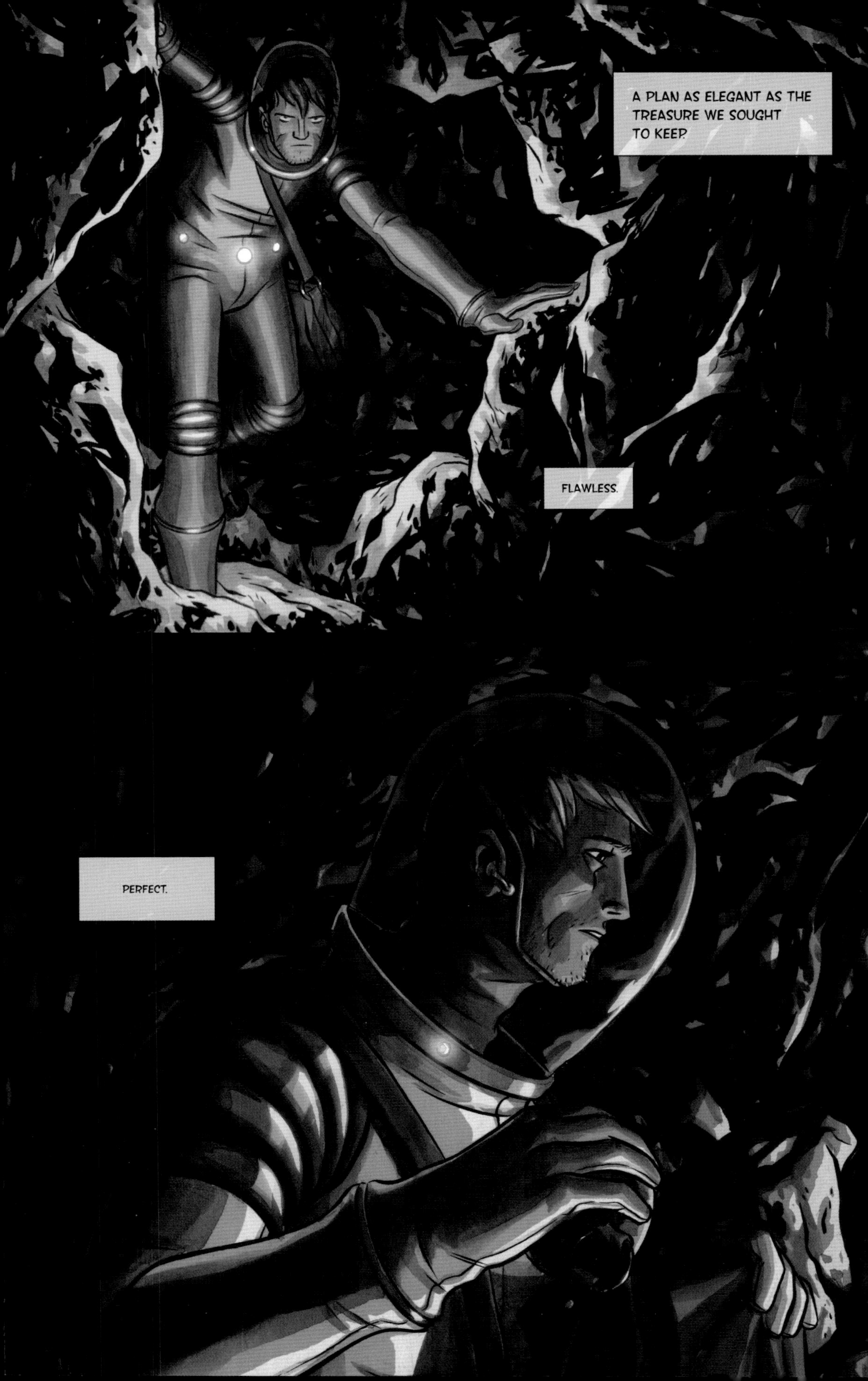
A PLAN AS ELEGANT AS THE TREASURE WE SOUGHT TO KEEP.
FLAWLESS.
PERFECT.

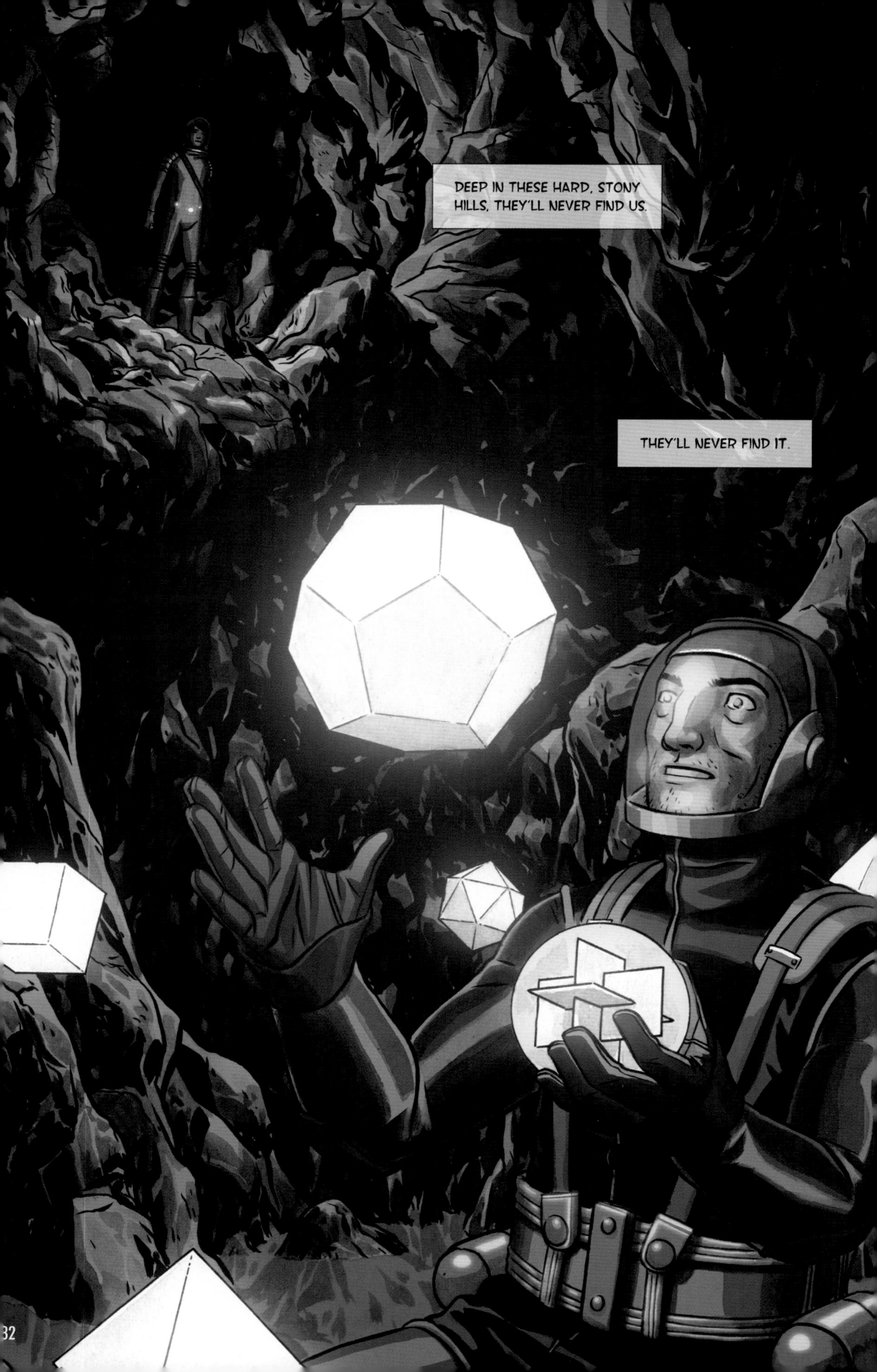
DEEP IN THESE HARD, STONY HILLS, THEY'LL NEVER FIND US.
THEY'LL NEVER FIND IT.

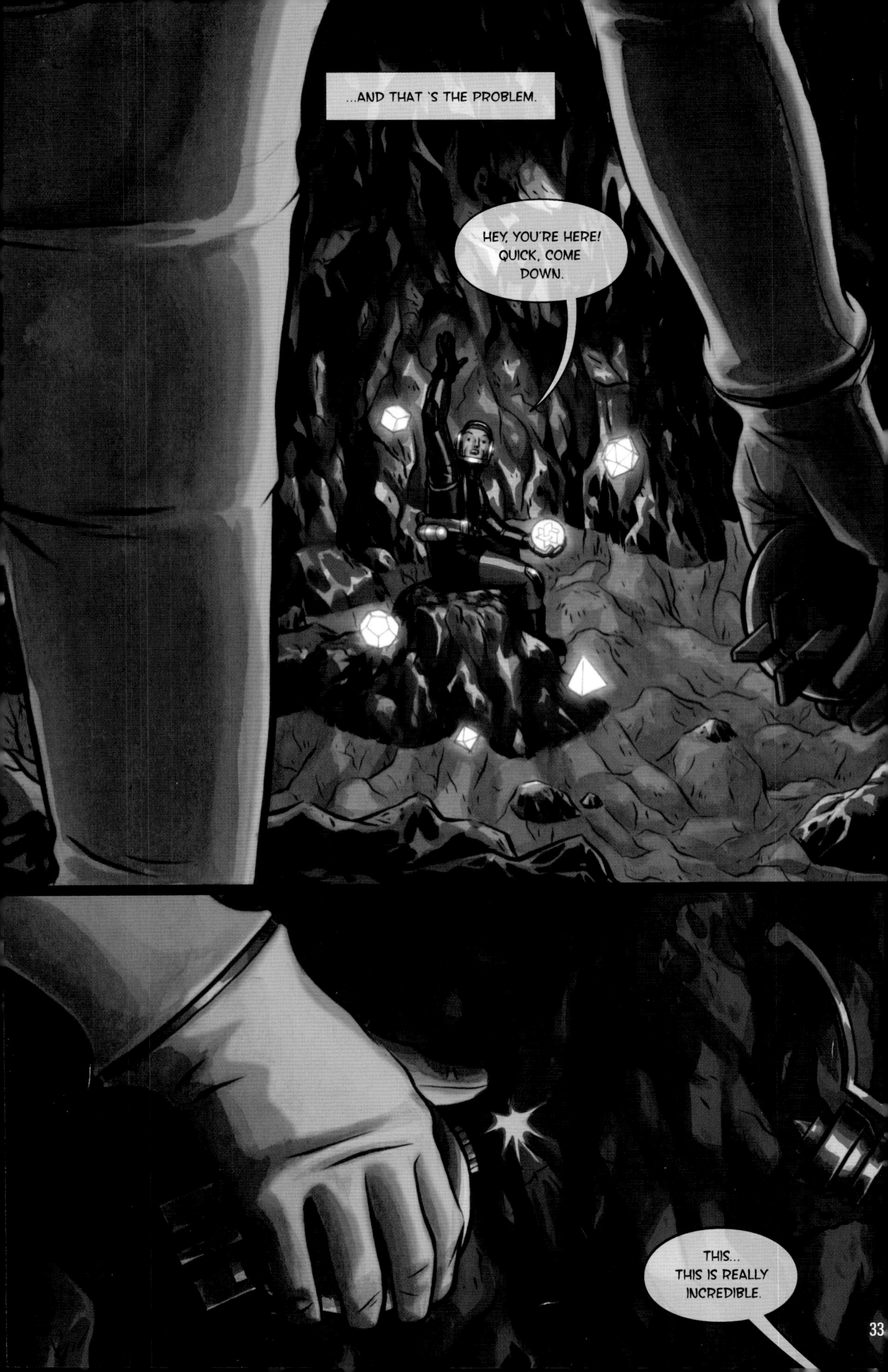

...AND THAT 'S THE PROBLEM.
HEY, YOU'RE HERE! QUICK, COME DOWN.
THIS... THIS IS REALLY INCREDIBLE.

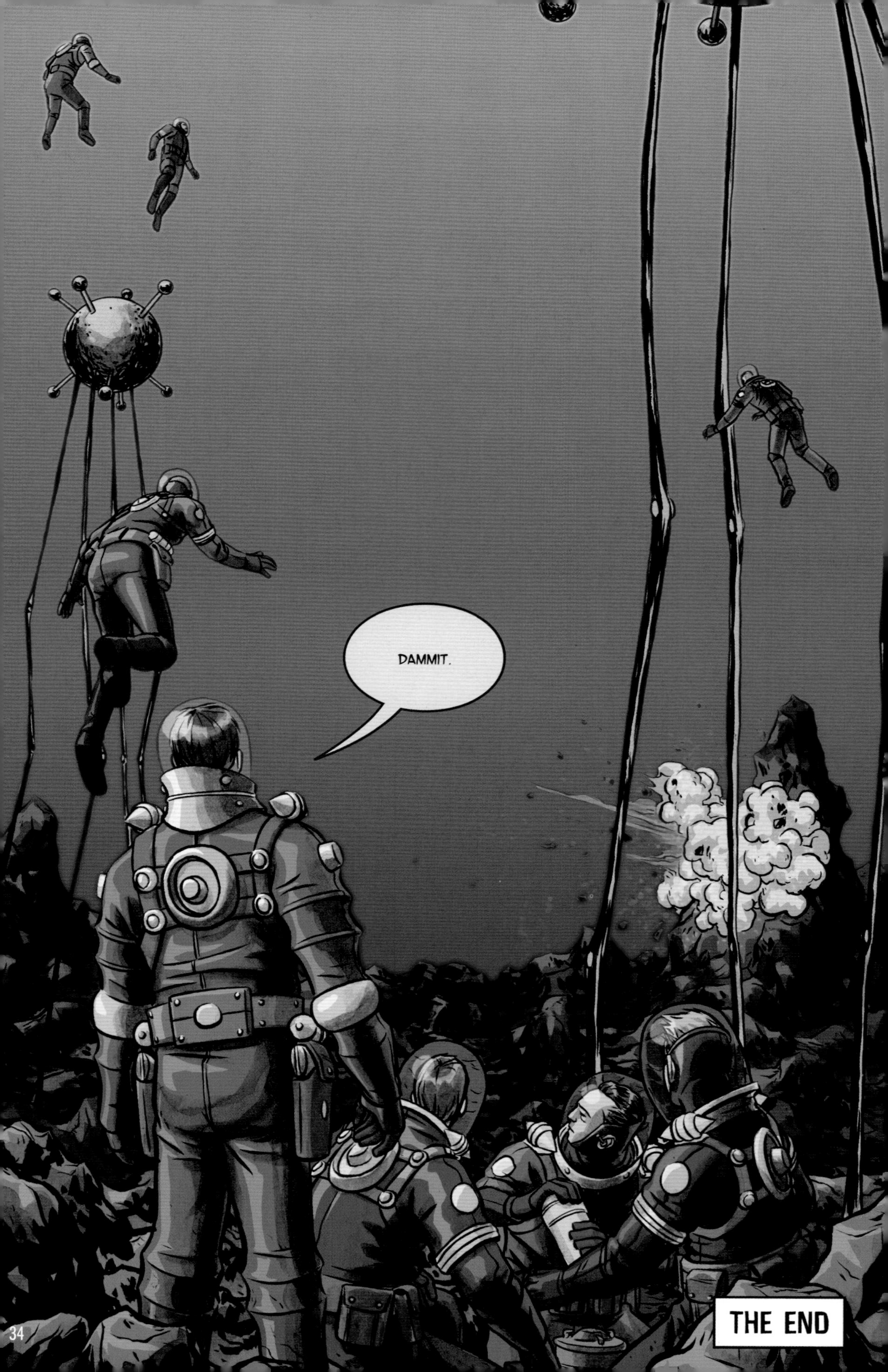
DAMMIT.
THE END

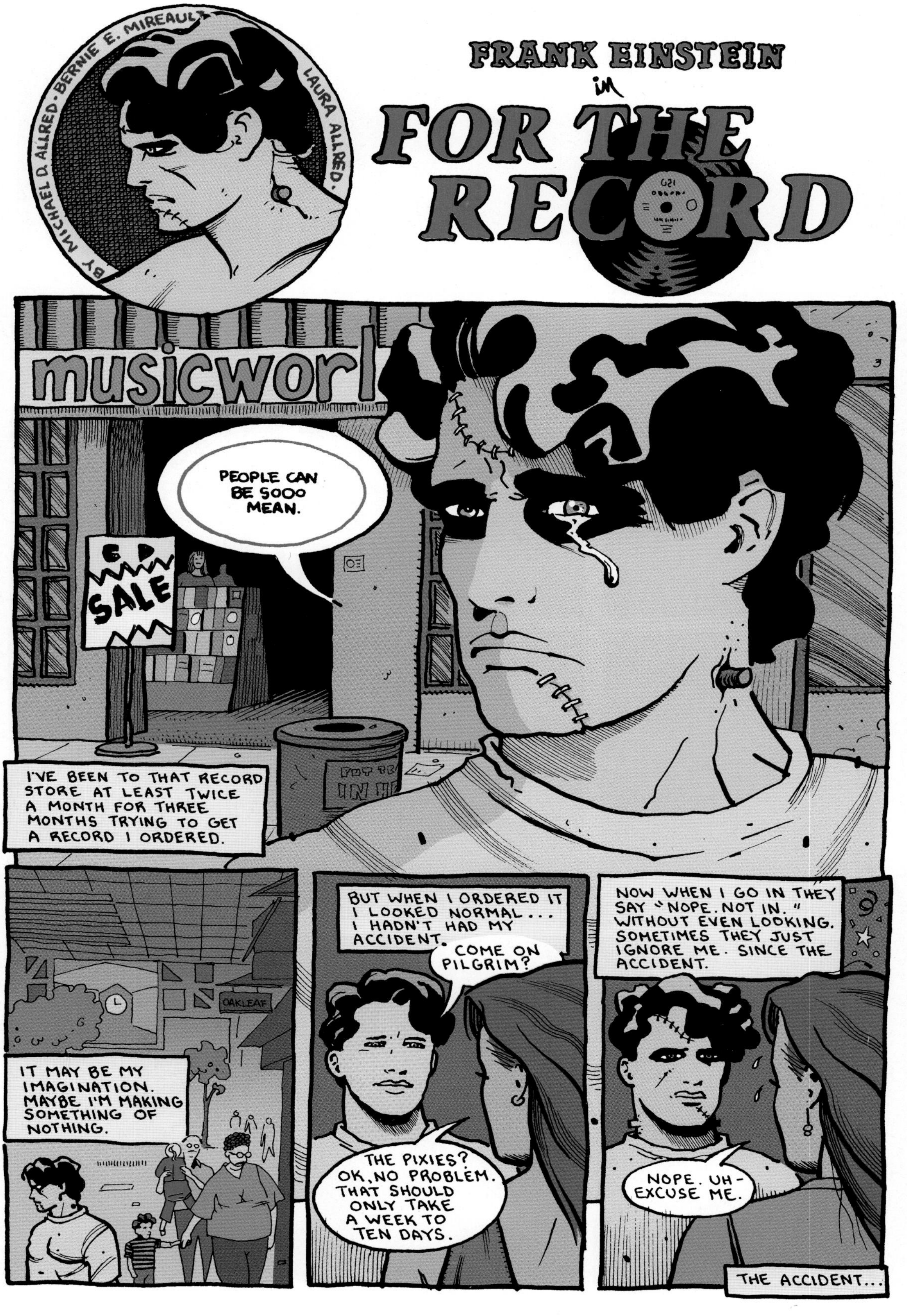
BY MICHAEL D. ALLRED · BERNIE E. MIREAULT · LAURA ALLRED.
FRANK EINSTEIN
in
FOR THE RECORD
musicworl
PEOPLE CAN BE SOOO MEAN.
SALE
I'VE BEEN TO THAT RECORD STORE AT LEAST TWICE A MONTH FOR THREE MONTHS TRYING TO GET A RECORD I ORDERED.
OAKLEAF
IT MAY BE MY IMAGINATION. MAYBE I'M MAKING SOMETHING OF NOTHING.
BUT WHEN I ORDERED IT I LOOKED NORMAL... I HADN'T HAD MY ACCIDENT.
COME ON PILGRIM?
THE PIXIES? OK, NO PROBLEM. THAT SHOULD ONLY TAKE A WEEK TO TEN DAYS.
NOW WHEN I GO IN THEY SAY "NOPE. NOT IN." WITHOUT EVEN LOOKING. SOMETIMES THEY JUST IGNORE ME. SINCE THE ACCIDENT.
NOPE. UH- EXCUSE ME.
THE ACCIDENT...

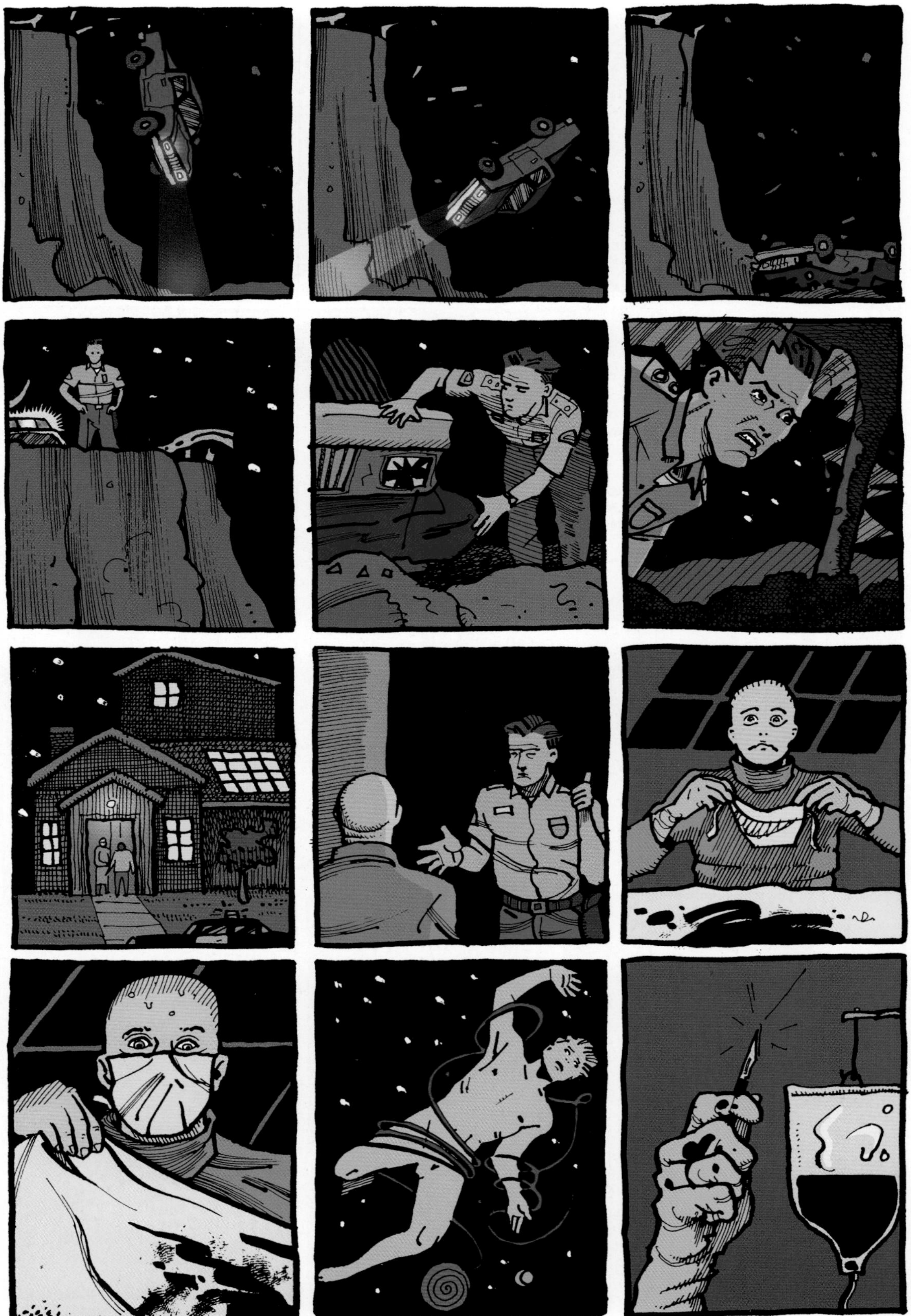

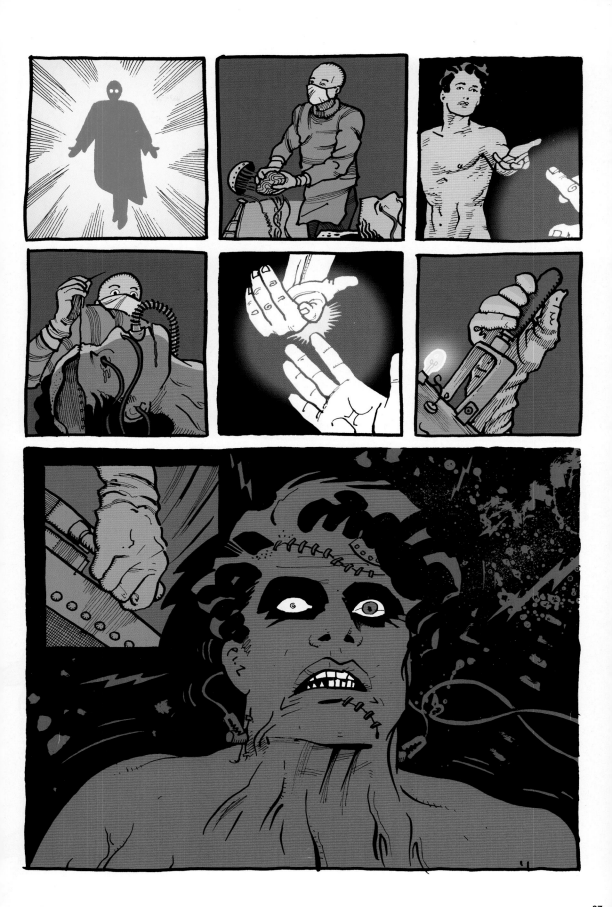

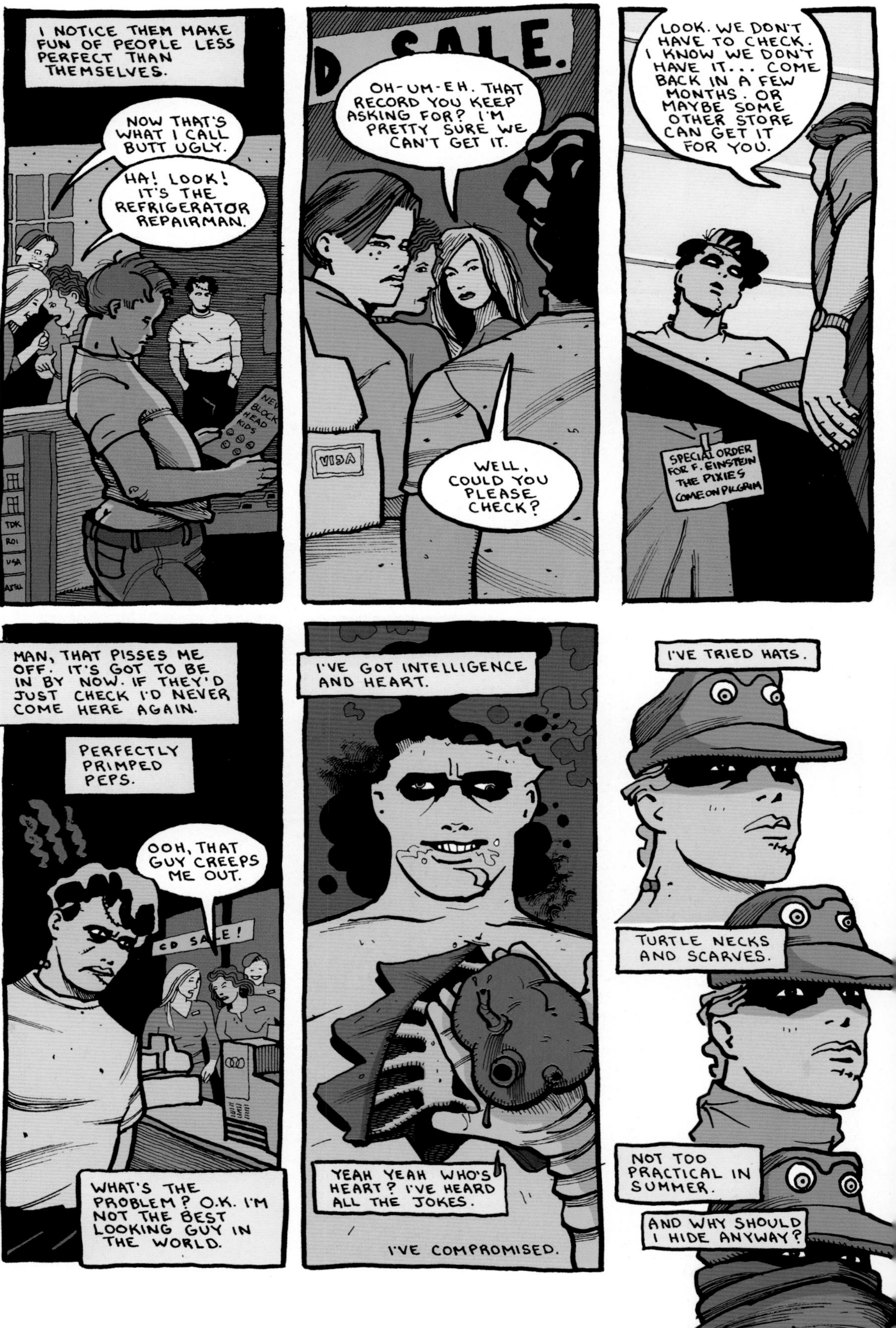

I NOTICE THEM MAKE FUN OF PEOPLE LESS PERFECT THAN THEMSELVES.
NOW THAT'S WHAT I CALL BUTT UGLY.
HA! LOOK! IT'S THE REFRIGERATOR REPAIRMAN.
NEW BLOCK HEAD KIDS
TDK
SALE.
OH-UM-EH. THAT RECORD YOU KEEP ASKING FOR? I'M PRETTY SURE WE CAN'T GET IT.
VISA
WELL, COULD YOU PLEASE CHECK?
LOOK. WE DON'T HAVE TO CHECK. I KNOW WE DON'T HAVE IT... COME BACK IN A FEW MONTHS. OR MAYBE SOME OTHER STORE CAN GET IT FOR YOU.
SPECIAL ORDER FOR F. EINSTEIN THE PIXIES COME ON PILGRIM
MAN, THAT PISSES ME OFF. IT'S GOT TO BE IN BY NOW. IF THEY'D JUST CHECK I'D NEVER COME HERE AGAIN.
PERFECTLY PRIMPED PEPS.
OOH, THAT GUY CREEPS ME OUT.
CD SALE!
WHAT'S THE PROBLEM? O.K. I'M NOT THE BEST LOOKING GUY IN THE WORLD.
I'VE GOT INTELLIGENCE AND HEART.
YEAH YEAH WHO'S HEART? I'VE HEARD ALL THE JOKES.
I'VE COMPROMISED.
I'VE TRIED HATS.
TURTLE NECKS AND SCARVES.
NOT TOO PRACTICAL IN SUMMER.
AND WHY SHOULD I HIDE ANYWAY?

YEAH, WHY SHOULD I HIDE?

PEOPLE WHO ARE DIFFERENT SHOULD BE CELEBRATED NOT OUTCAST.

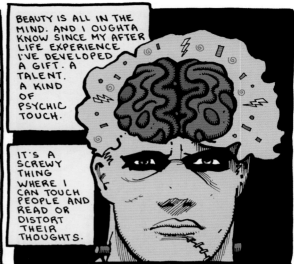

BEAUTY IS ALL IN THE MIND. AND I OUGHTA KNOW SINCE MY AFTER LIFE EXPERIENCE I'VE DEVELOPED A GIFT. A TALENT. A KIND OF PSYCHIC TOUCH.

IT'S A SCREWY THING WHERE I CAN TOUCH PEOPLE AND READ OR DISTORT THEIR THOUGHTS.

THE REAL ME.

BUT BODIES REALLY ARE JUST VESSELS TO SAIL THROUGH LIFE IN.

UNFORTUNATELY.

MORE OFTEN THAN NOT YOU'RE JUDGED ON YOUR VESSEL INSTEAD OF YOUR CREW.

1ST PLACE

I SHOULDN'T WHINE. I DON'T HAVE IT SO BAD. I SAW A MAN ONCE, HIS WHOLE NOSE WAS MISSING. HE DIDN'T TRY TO HIDE IT.

WHOAH!

SUN-LICKED ORANGES 40¢/lb.

AND MY OLD FRIEND, CHARLIE. THIS IS AN OLD EXAMPLE BUT VERY IMPORTANT. IF HE TOOK HIS FAMILY TO A RESTAURANT, IN SOME PARTS THEY WOULDN'T GET SERVED.

MISS?

NIGGERS.

SICK.

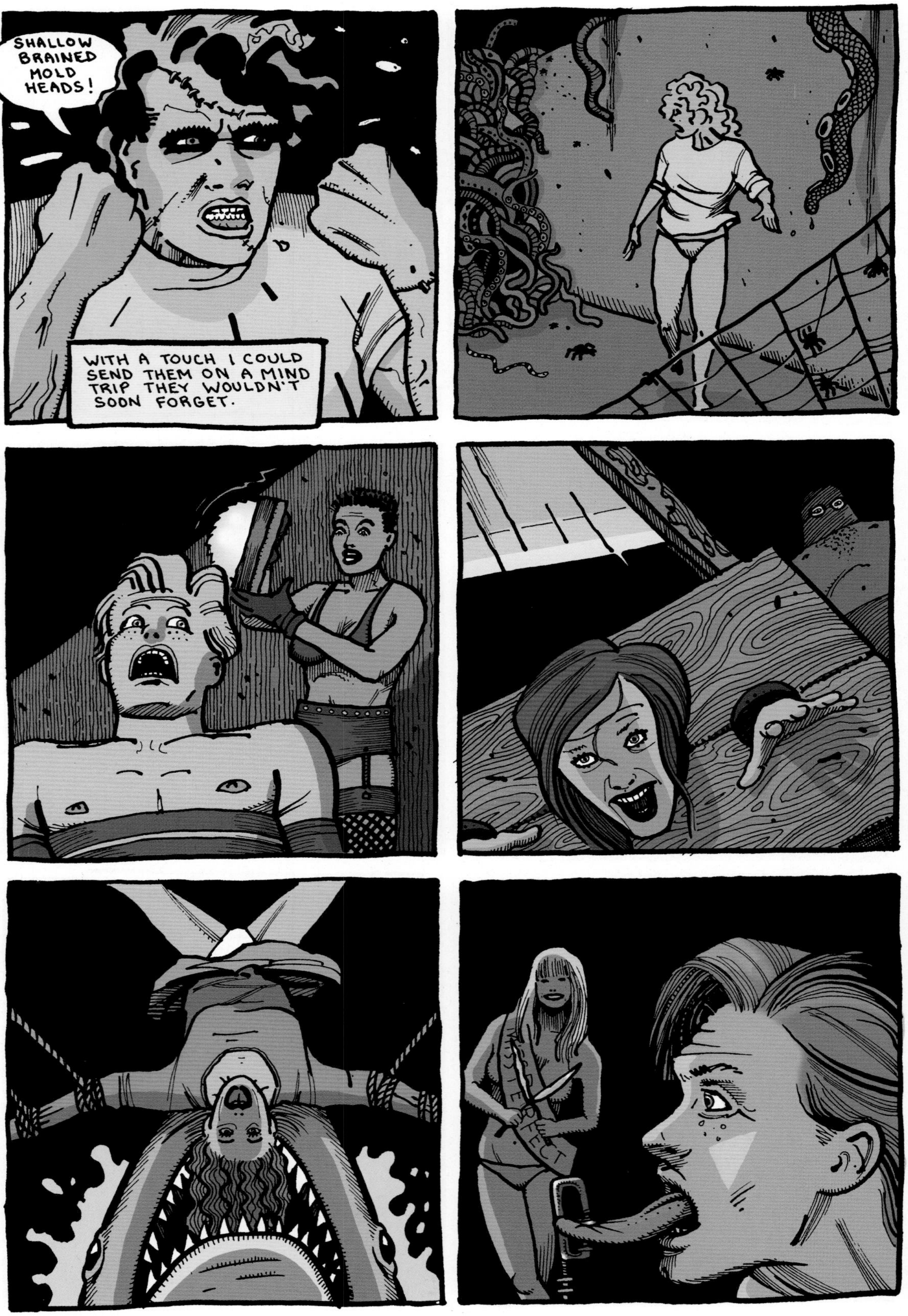
SHALLOW BRAINED MOLD HEADS!
WITH A TOUCH I COULD SEND THEM ON A MIND TRIP THEY WOULDN'T SOON FORGET.

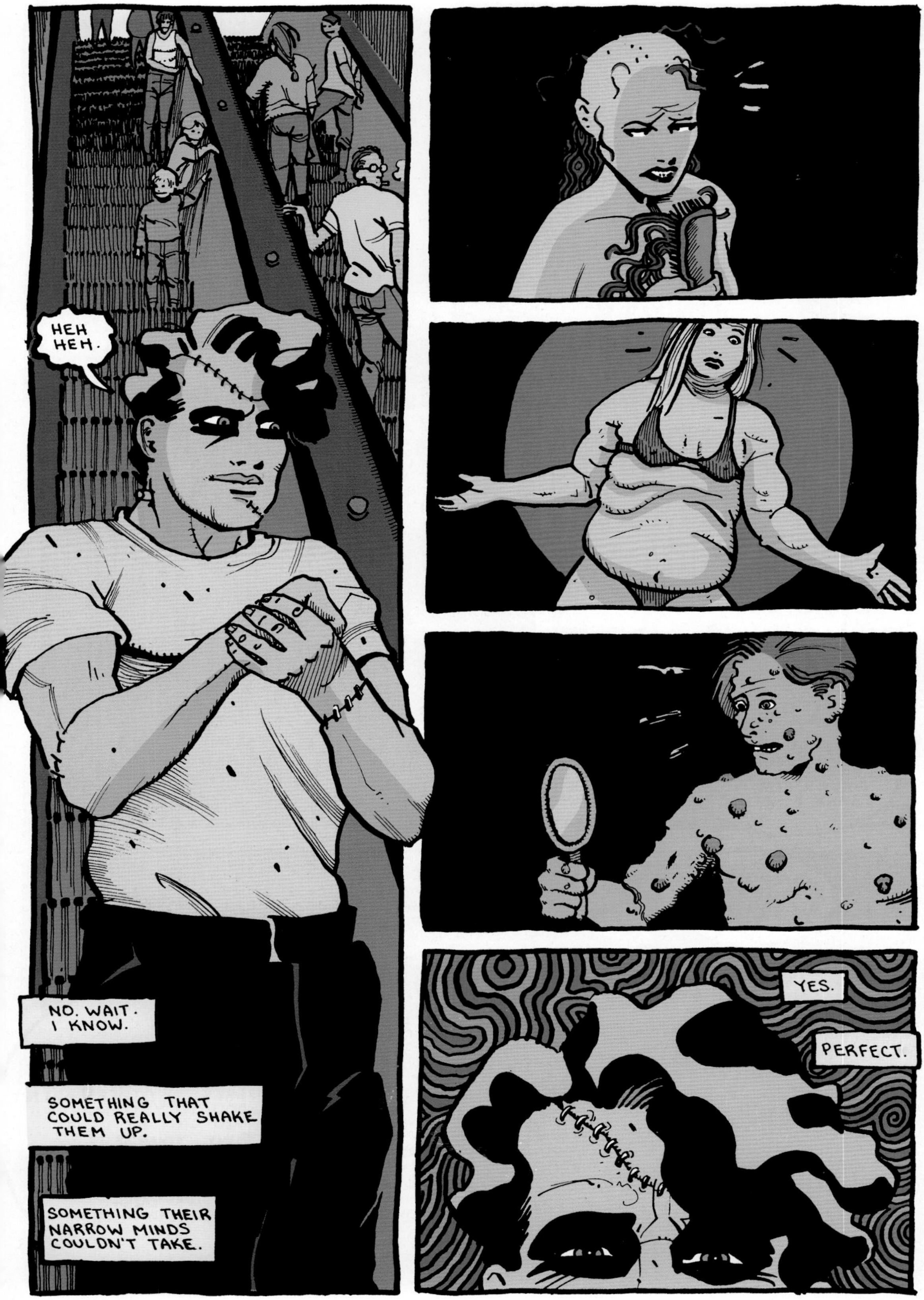
HEH HEH.
NO. WAIT. I KNOW.
SOMETHING THAT COULD REALLY SHAKE THEM UP.
SOMETHING THEIR NARROW MINDS COULDN'T TAKE.
YES.
PERFECT.

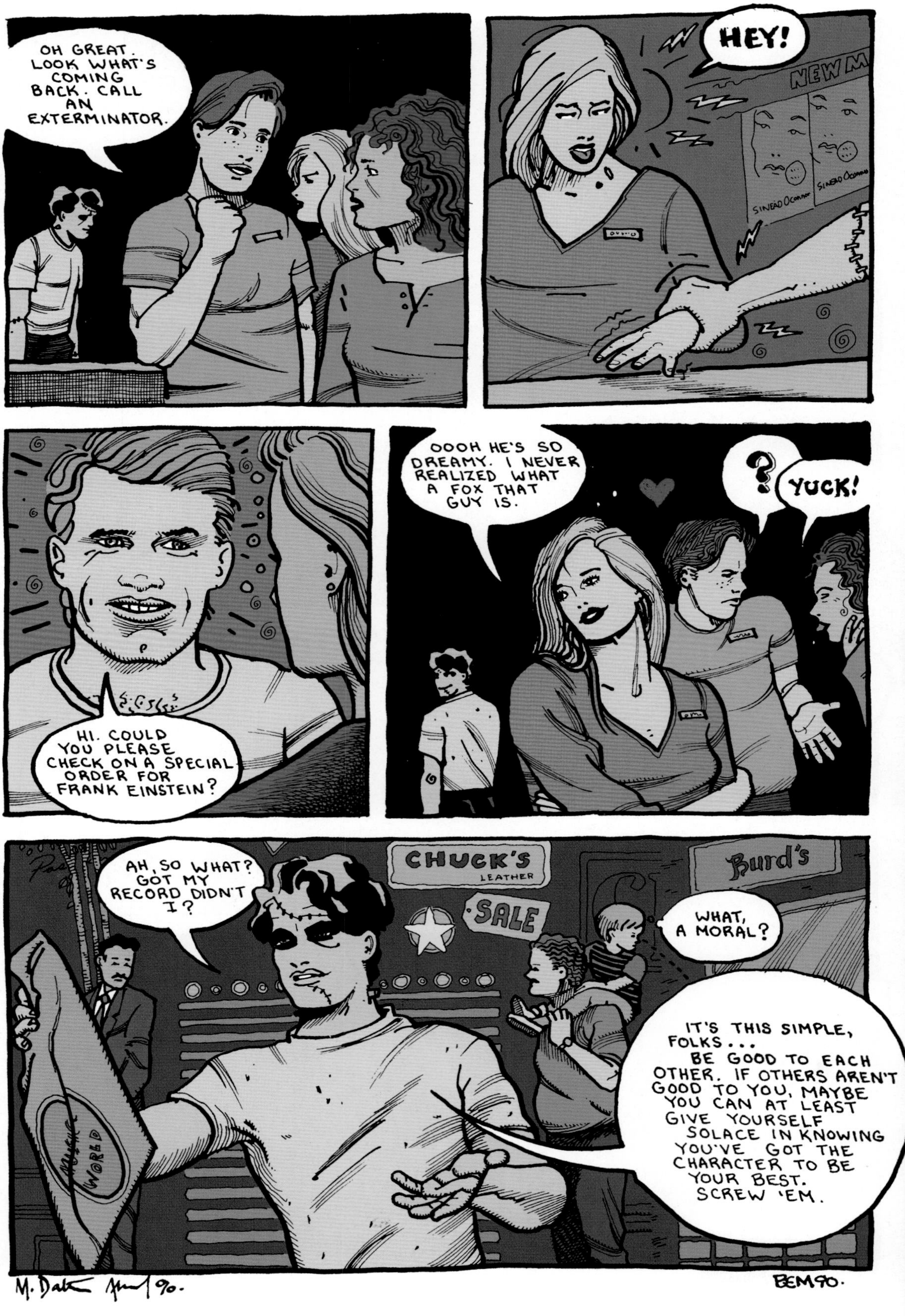

OH GREAT. LOOK WHAT'S COMING BACK. CALL AN EXTERMINATOR.
HEY!
NEW M
SINEAD OConnor
SINEAD OConnor
HI. COULD YOU PLEASE CHECK ON A SPECIAL ORDER FOR FRANK EINSTEIN?
OOOH HE'S SO DREAMY. I NEVER REALIZED WHAT A FOX THAT GUY IS.
?
YUCK!
CHUCK'S LEATHER
Burd's
SALE
AH, SO WHAT? GOT MY RECORD DIDN'T I?
WHAT, A MORAL?
IT'S THIS SIMPLE, FOLKS... BE GOOD TO EACH OTHER. IF OTHERS AREN'T GOOD TO YOU, MAYBE YOU CAN AT LEAST GIVE YOURSELF SOLACE IN KNOWING YOU'VE GOT THE CHARACTER TO BE YOUR BEST. SCREW 'EM.
MUSIC WORLD
M. Dalton April 90.
BEM90.

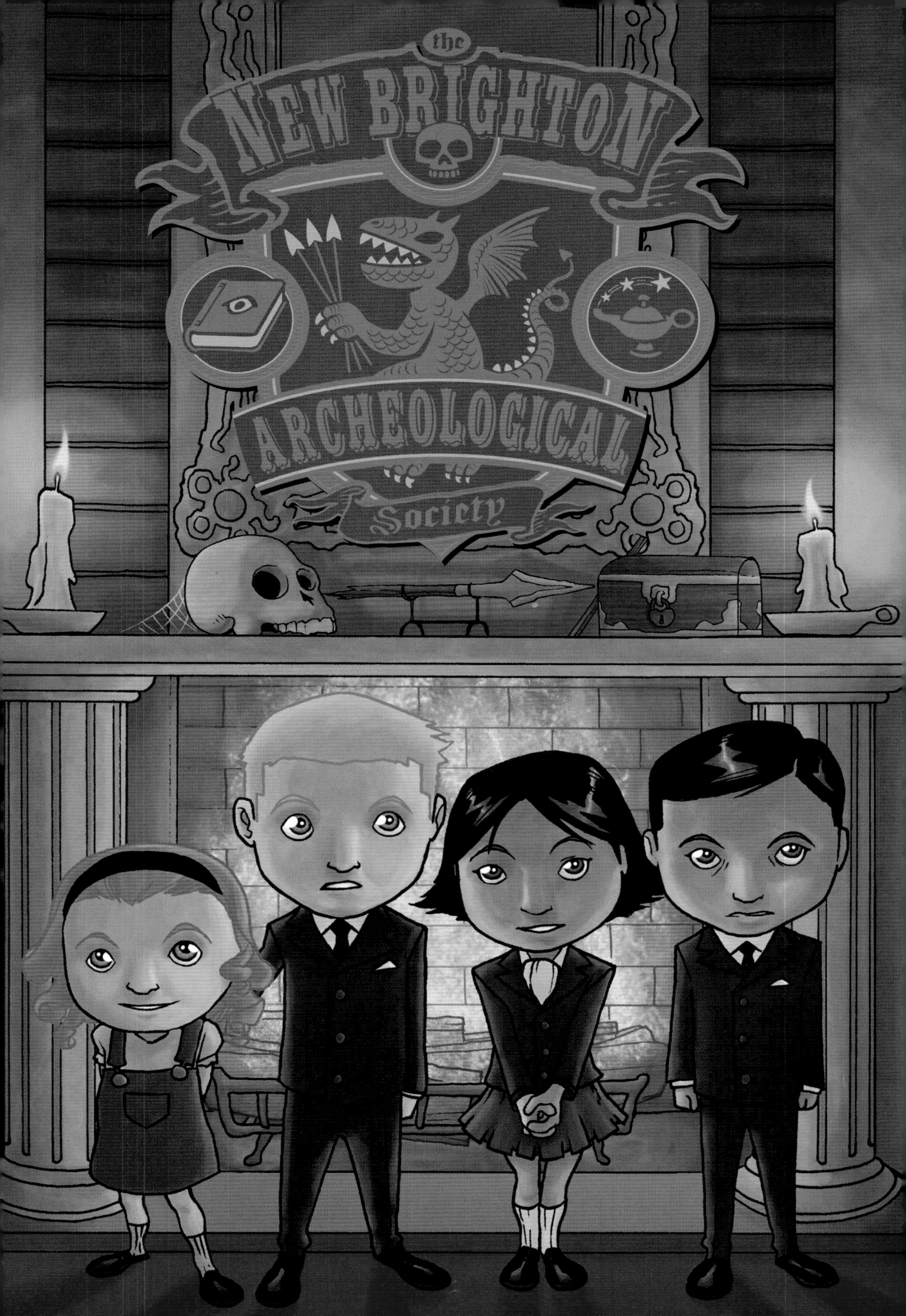

the
NEW BRIGHTON
ARCHEOLOGICAL
Society

MARK ANDREW SMITH · **MATTHEW WELDON** · **JACOB BAAKE** · **FONOGRAFIKS**
writer · artist · colorist · letters

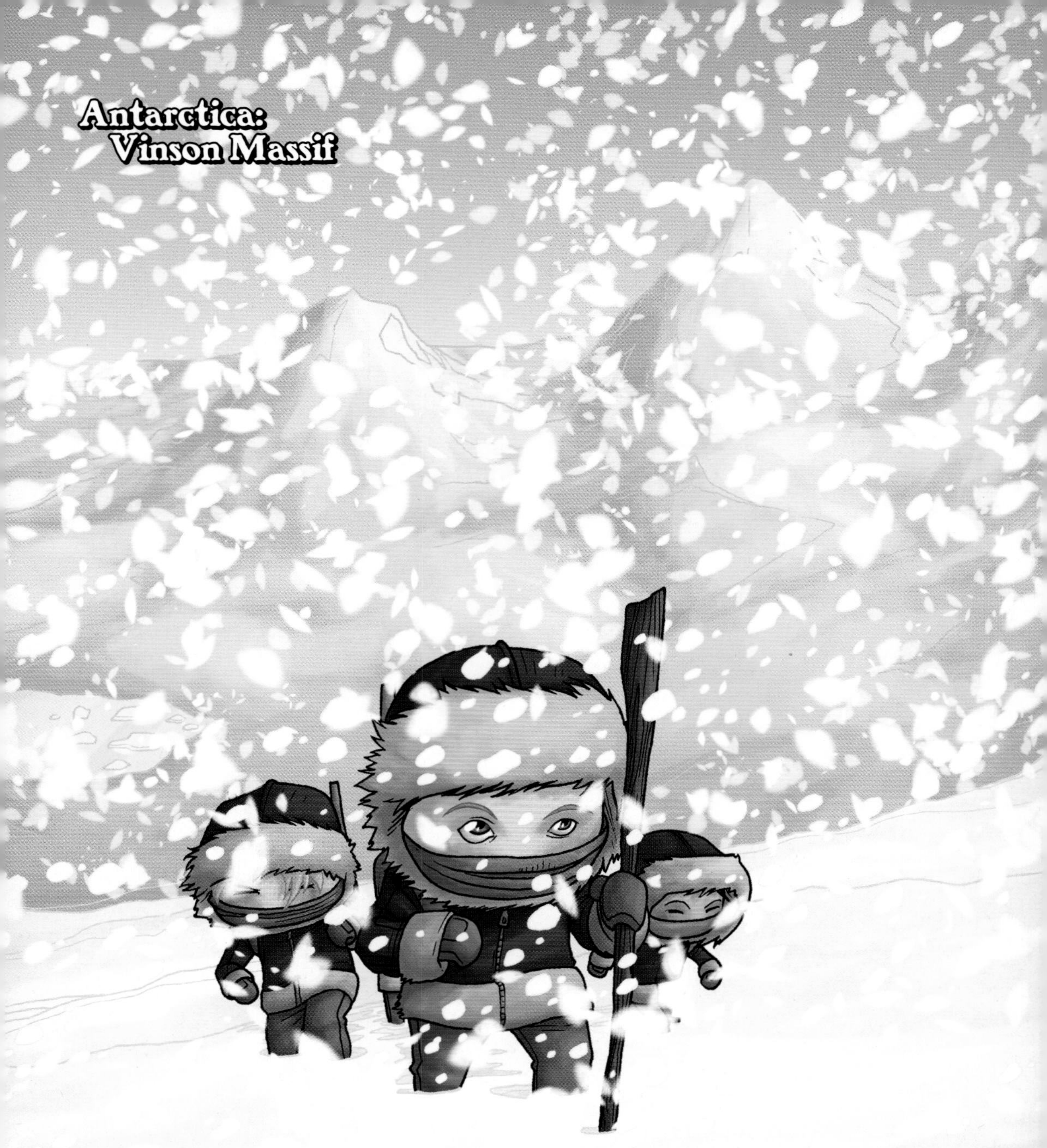
Antarctica:
Vinson Massif
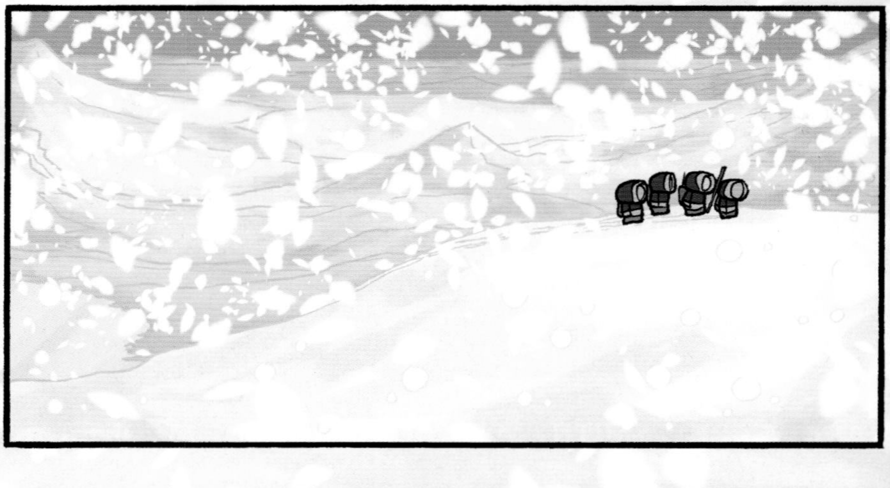

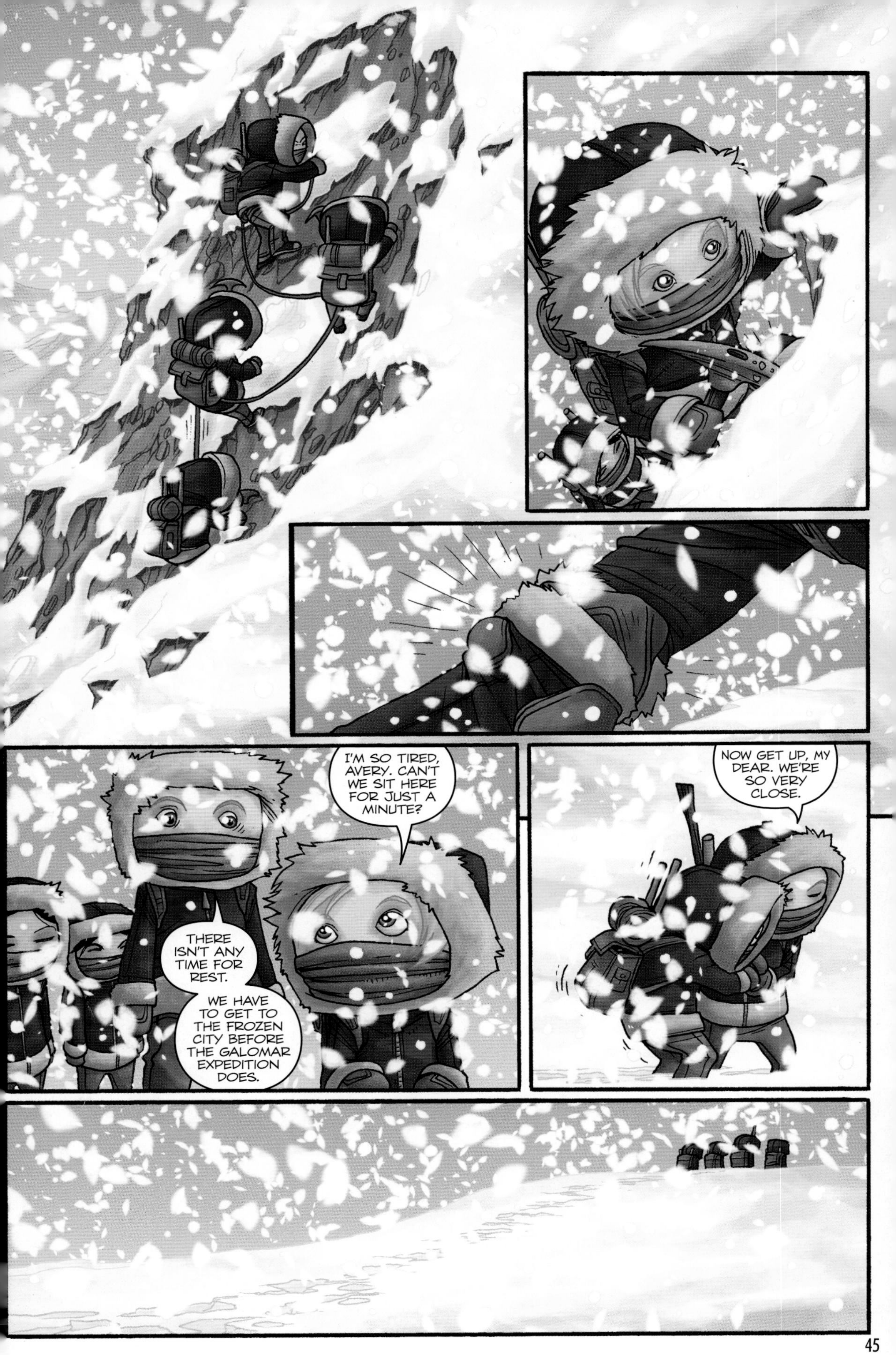
I'M SO TIRED, AVERY. CAN'T WE SIT HERE FOR JUST A MINUTE?
THERE ISN'T ANY TIME FOR REST.
WE HAVE TO GET TO THE FROZEN CITY BEFORE THE GALOMAR EXPEDITION DOES.
NOW GET UP, MY DEAR. WE'RE SO VERY CLOSE.

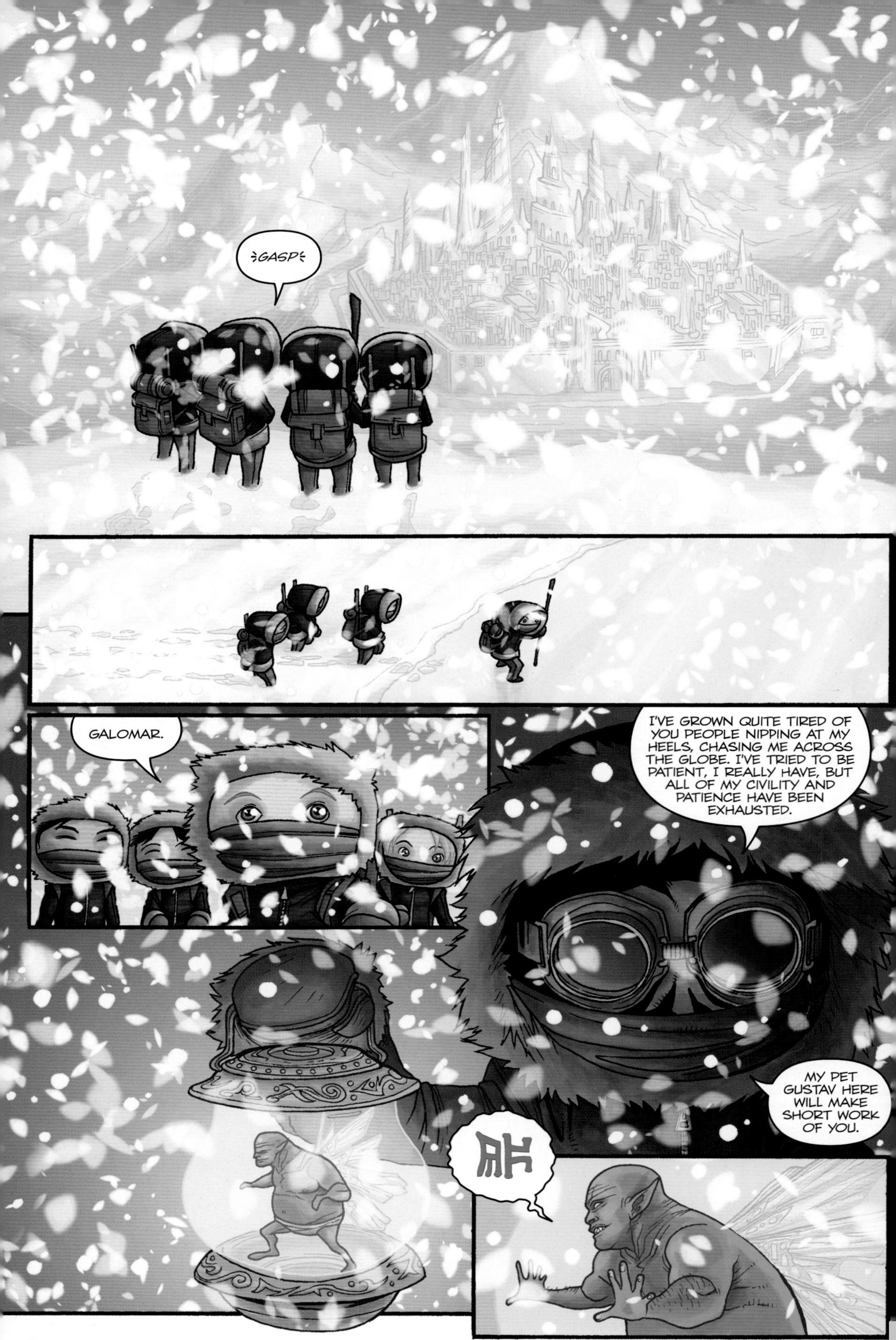
GASP
GALOMAR.
I'VE GROWN QUITE TIRED OF YOU PEOPLE NIPPING AT MY HEELS, CHASING ME ACROSS THE GLOBE. I'VE TRIED TO BE PATIENT, I REALLY HAVE, BUT ALL OF MY CIVILITY AND PATIENCE HAVE BEEN EXHAUSTED.
MY PET GUSTAV HERE WILL MAKE SHORT WORK OF YOU.

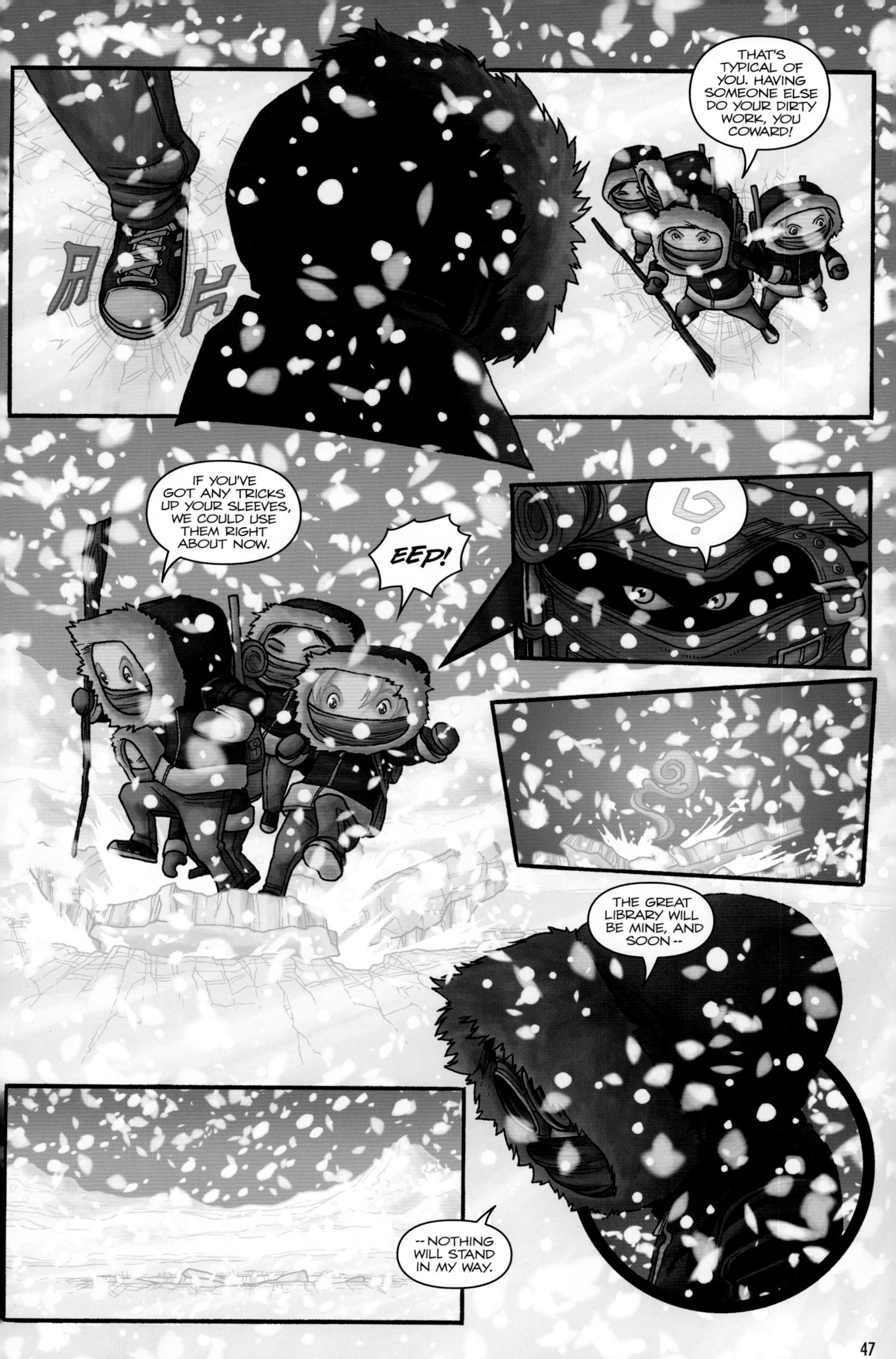
AH
THAT'S TYPICAL OF YOU. HAVING SOMEONE ELSE DO YOUR DIRTY WORK, YOU COWARD!
IF YOU'VE GOT ANY TRICKS UP YOUR SLEEVES, WE COULD USE THEM RIGHT ABOUT NOW.
EEP!
THE GREAT LIBRARY WILL BE MINE, AND SOON --
-- NOTHING WILL STAND IN MY WAY.

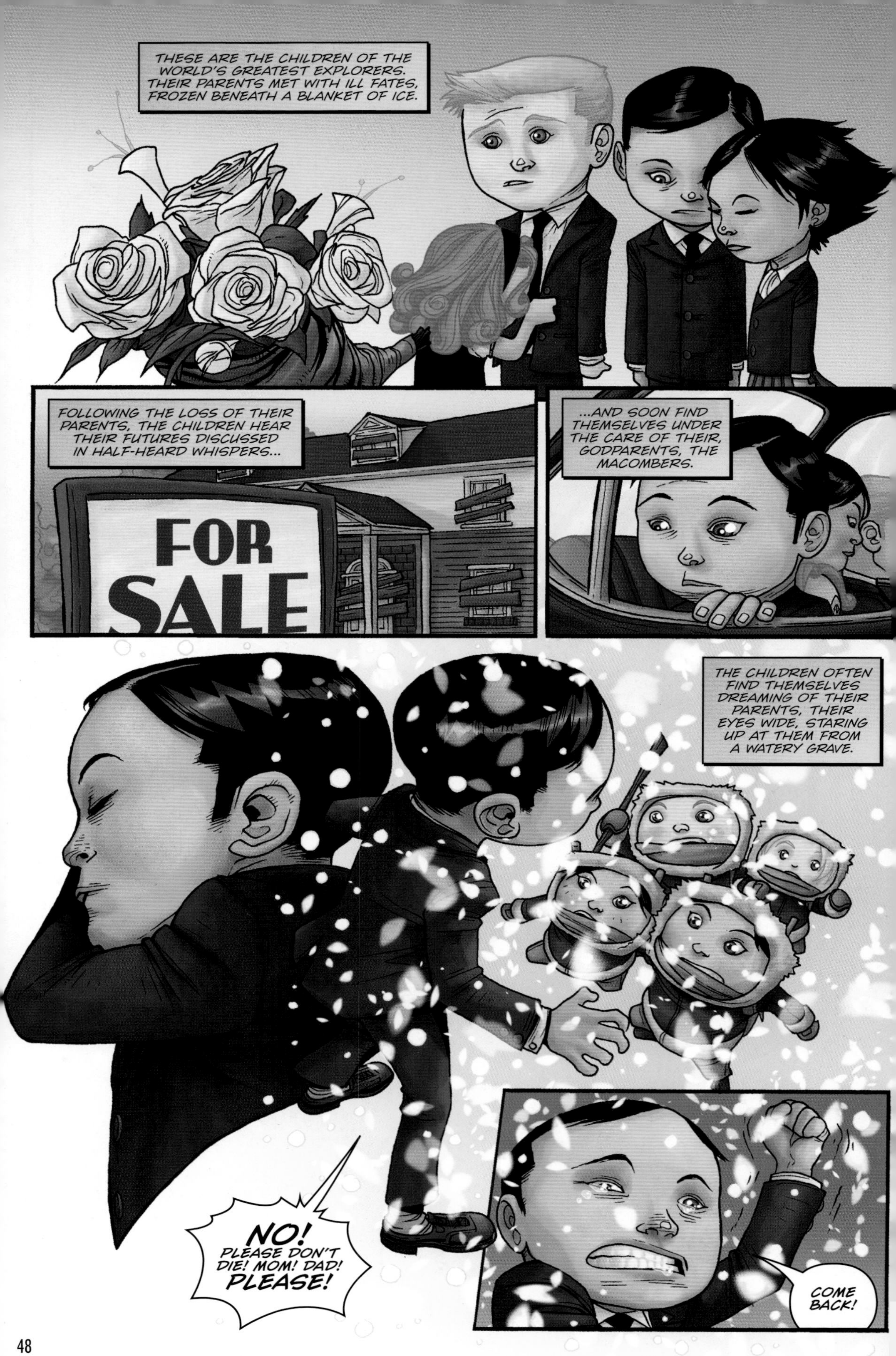
THESE ARE THE CHILDREN OF THE WORLD'S GREATEST EXPLORERS. THEIR PARENTS MET WITH ILL FATES, FROZEN BENEATH A BLANKET OF ICE.
FOLLOWING THE LOSS OF THEIR PARENTS, THE CHILDREN HEAR THEIR FUTURES DISCUSSED IN HALF-HEARD WHISPERS...
FOR SALE
...AND SOON FIND THEMSELVES UNDER THE CARE OF THEIR, GODPARENTS, THE MACOMBERS.
THE CHILDREN OFTEN FIND THEMSELVES DREAMING OF THEIR PARENTS, THEIR EYES WIDE, STARING UP AT THEM FROM A WATERY GRAVE.
NO! PLEASE DON'T DIE! MOM! DAD! PLEASE!
COME BACK!

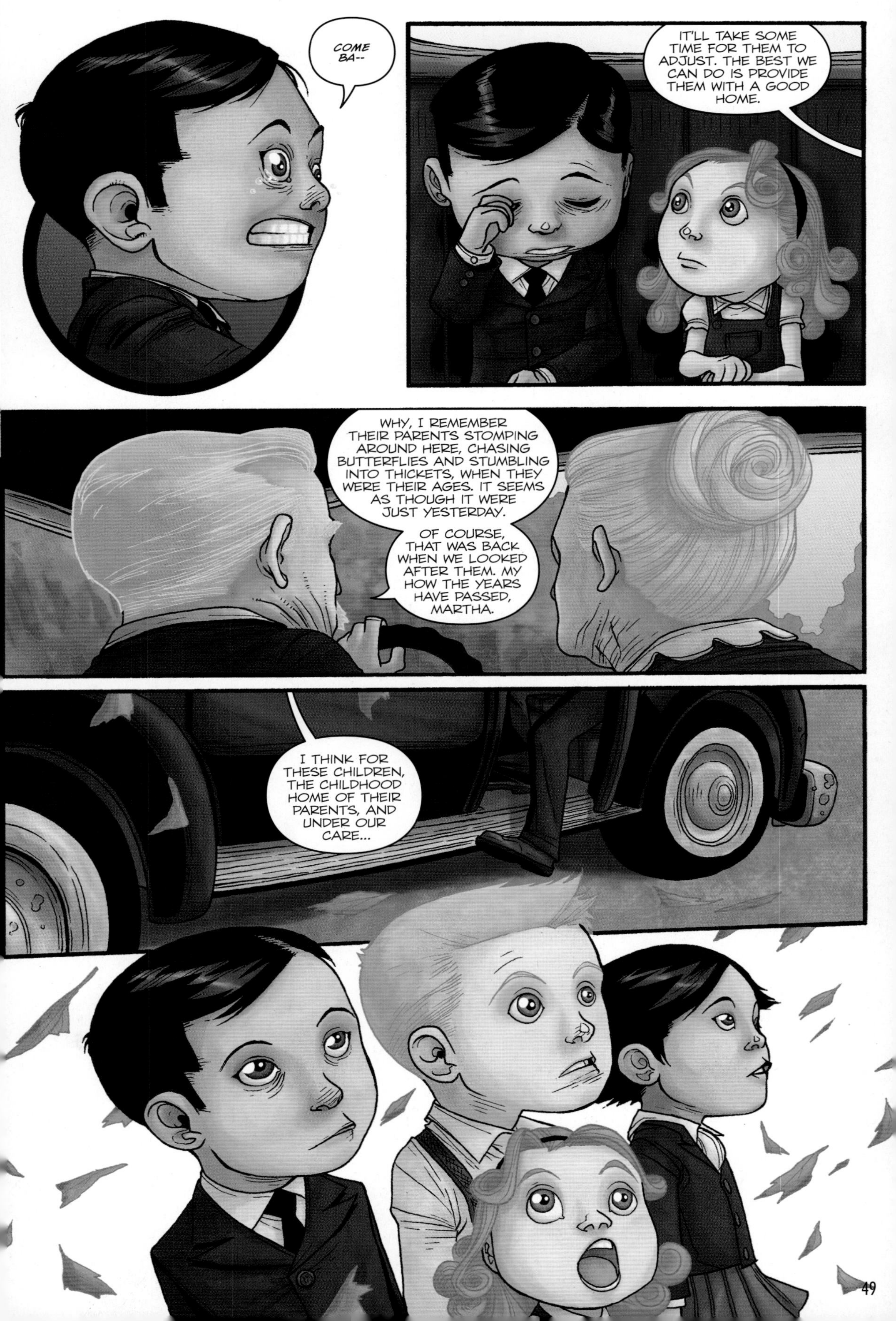
COME BA--
IT'LL TAKE SOME TIME FOR THEM TO ADJUST. THE BEST WE CAN DO IS PROVIDE THEM WITH A GOOD HOME.
WHY, I REMEMBER THEIR PARENTS STOMPING AROUND HERE, CHASING BUTTERFLIES AND STUMBLING INTO THICKETS, WHEN THEY WERE THEIR AGES. IT SEEMS AS THOUGH IT WERE JUST YESTERDAY.
OF COURSE, THAT WAS BACK WHEN WE LOOKED AFTER THEM. MY HOW THE YEARS HAVE PASSED, MARTHA.
I THINK FOR THESE CHILDREN, THE CHILDHOOD HOME OF THEIR PARENTS, AND UNDER OUR CARE...

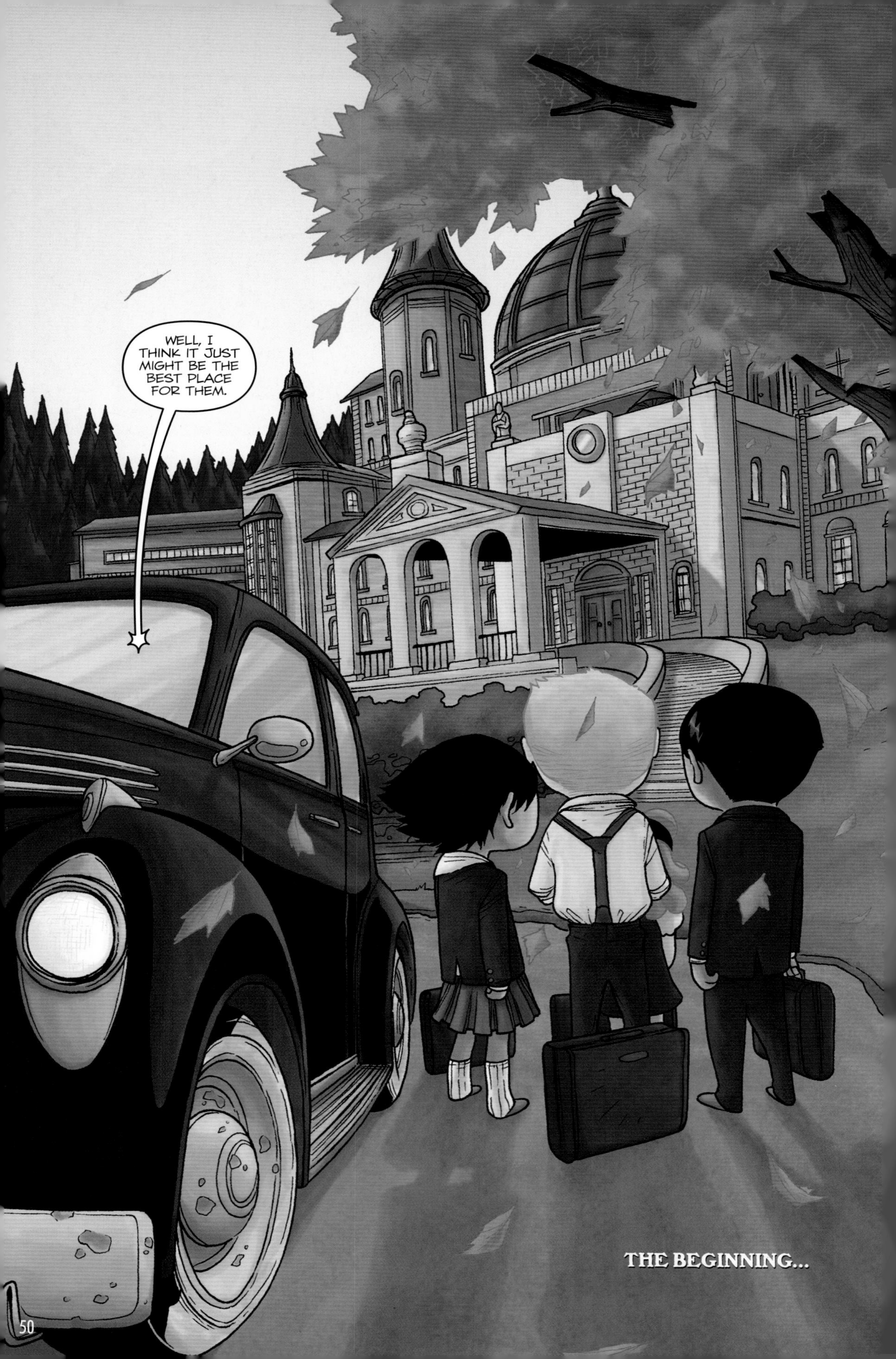
WELL, I THINK IT JUST MIGHT BE THE BEST PLACE FOR THEM.
THE BEGINNING...

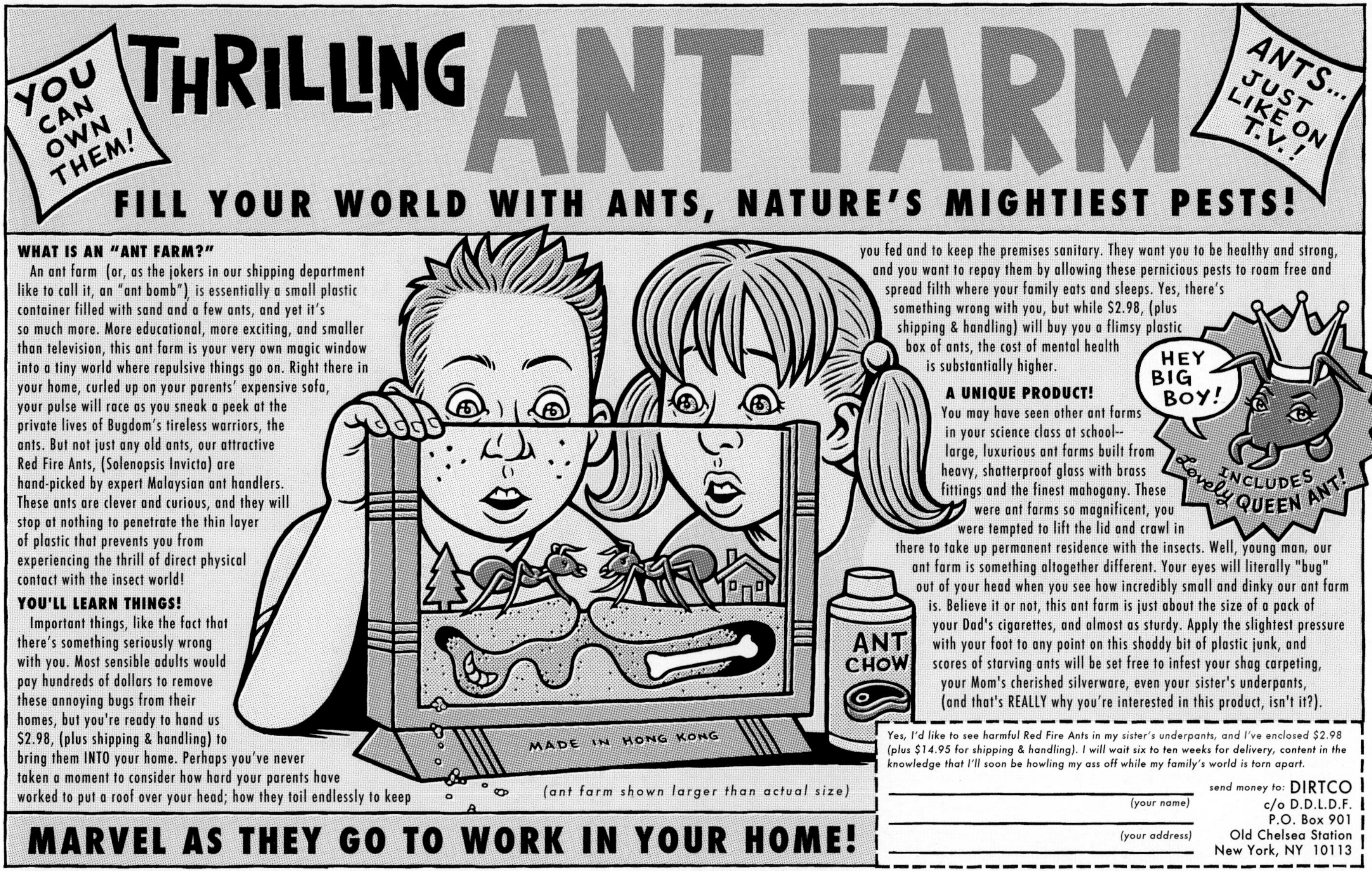
YOU CAN OWN THEM!
THRILLING ANT FARM
ANTS... JUST LIKE ON T.V.!
FILL YOUR WORLD WITH ANTS, NATURE'S MIGHTIEST PESTS!
WHAT IS AN "ANT FARM?"
An ant farm (or, as the jokers in our shipping department like to call it, an "ant bomb"), is essentially a small plastic container filled with sand and a few ants, and yet it's so much more. More educational, more exciting, and smaller than television, this ant farm is your very own magic window into a tiny world where repulsive things go on. Right there in your home, curled up on your parents' expensive sofa, your pulse will race as you sneak a peek at the private lives of Bugdom's tireless warriors, the ants. But not just any old ants, our attractive Red Fire Ants, (Solenopsis Invicta) are hand-picked by expert Malaysian ant handlers. These ants are clever and curious, and they will stop at nothing to penetrate the thin layer of plastic that prevents you from experiencing the thrill of direct physical contact with the insect world!
YOU'LL LEARN THINGS!
Important things, like the fact that there's something seriously wrong with you. Most sensible adults would pay hundreds of dollars to remove these annoying bugs from their homes, but you're ready to hand us $2.98, (plus shipping & handling) to bring them INTO your home. Perhaps you've never taken a moment to consider how hard your parents have worked to put a roof over your head; how they toil endlessly to keep you fed and to keep the premises sanitary. They want you to be healthy and strong, and you want to repay them by allowing these pernicious pests to roam free and spread filth where your family eats and sleeps. Yes, there's something wrong with you, but while $2.98, (plus shipping & handling) will buy you a flimsy plastic box of ants, the cost of mental health is substantially higher.
A UNIQUE PRODUCT!
You may have seen other ant farms in your science class at school--large, luxurious ant farms built from heavy, shatterproof glass with brass fittings and the finest mahogany. These were ant farms so magnificent, you were tempted to lift the lid and crawl in there to take up permanent residence with the insects. Well, young man, our ant farm is something altogether different. Your eyes will literally "bug" out of your head when you see how incredibly small and dinky our ant farm is. Believe it or not, this ant farm is just about the size of a pack of your Dad's cigarettes, and almost as sturdy. Apply the slightest pressure with your foot to any point on this shoddy bit of plastic junk, and scores of starving ants will be set free to infest your shag carpeting, your Mom's cherished silverware, even your sister's underpants, (and that's REALLY why you're interested in this product, isn't it?).
HEY BIG BOY!
INCLUDES Lovely QUEEN ANT!
MADE IN HONG KONG
ANT CHOW
(ant farm shown larger than actual size)
Yes, I'd like to see harmful Red Fire Ants in my sister's underpants, and I've enclosed $2.98 (plus $14.95 for shipping & handling). I will wait six to ten weeks for delivery, content in the knowledge that I'll soon be howling my ass off while my family's world is torn apart.
(your name)
(your address)
send money to: DIRTCO
c/o D.D.L.D.F.
P.O. Box 901
Old Chelsea Station
New York, NY 10113
MARVEL AS THEY GO TO WORK IN YOUR HOME!

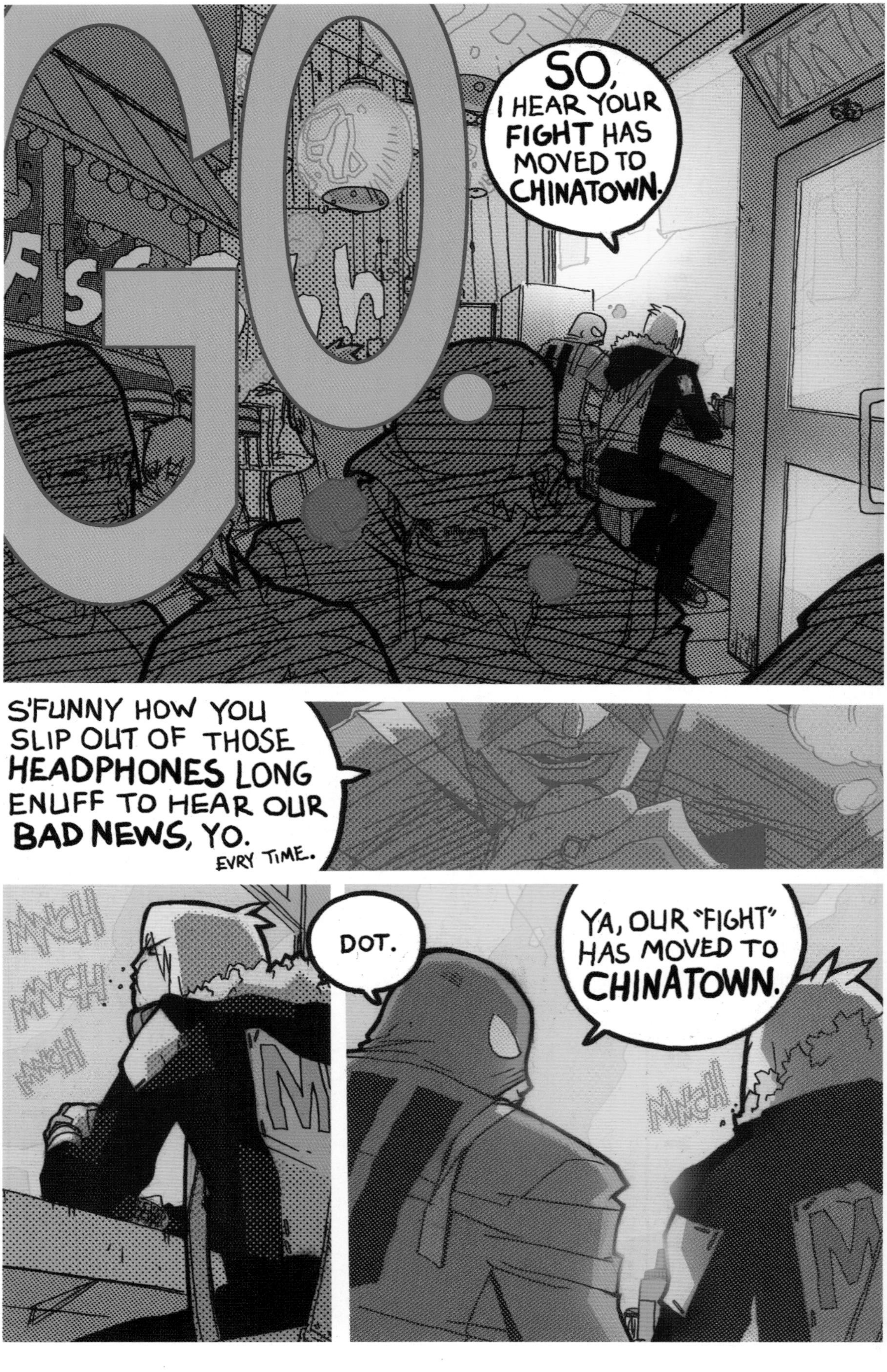
GO.
SO, I HEAR YOUR FIGHT HAS MOVED TO CHINATOWN.
S'FUNNY HOW YOU SLIP OUT OF THOSE HEADPHONES LONG ENUFF TO HEAR OUR BAD NEWS, YO. EVRY TIME.
MNCH MNCH MNCH
DOT.
YA, OUR "FIGHT" HAS MOVED TO CHINATOWN.
MNCH

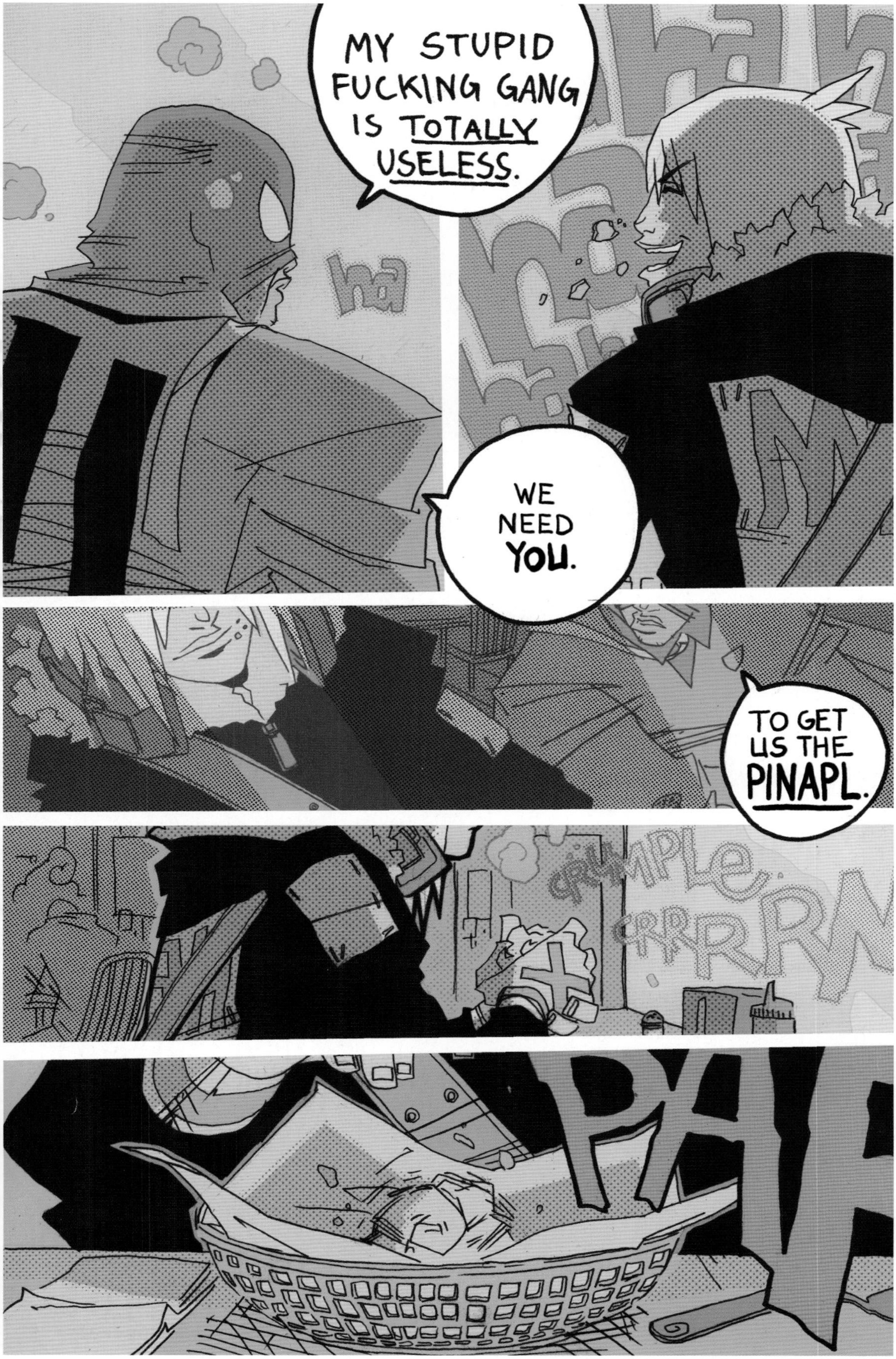
MY STUPID FUCKING GANG IS TOTALLY USELESS.
ha
WE NEED YOU.
TO GET US THE PINAPL.
CRUMPLE
CRRRRRW

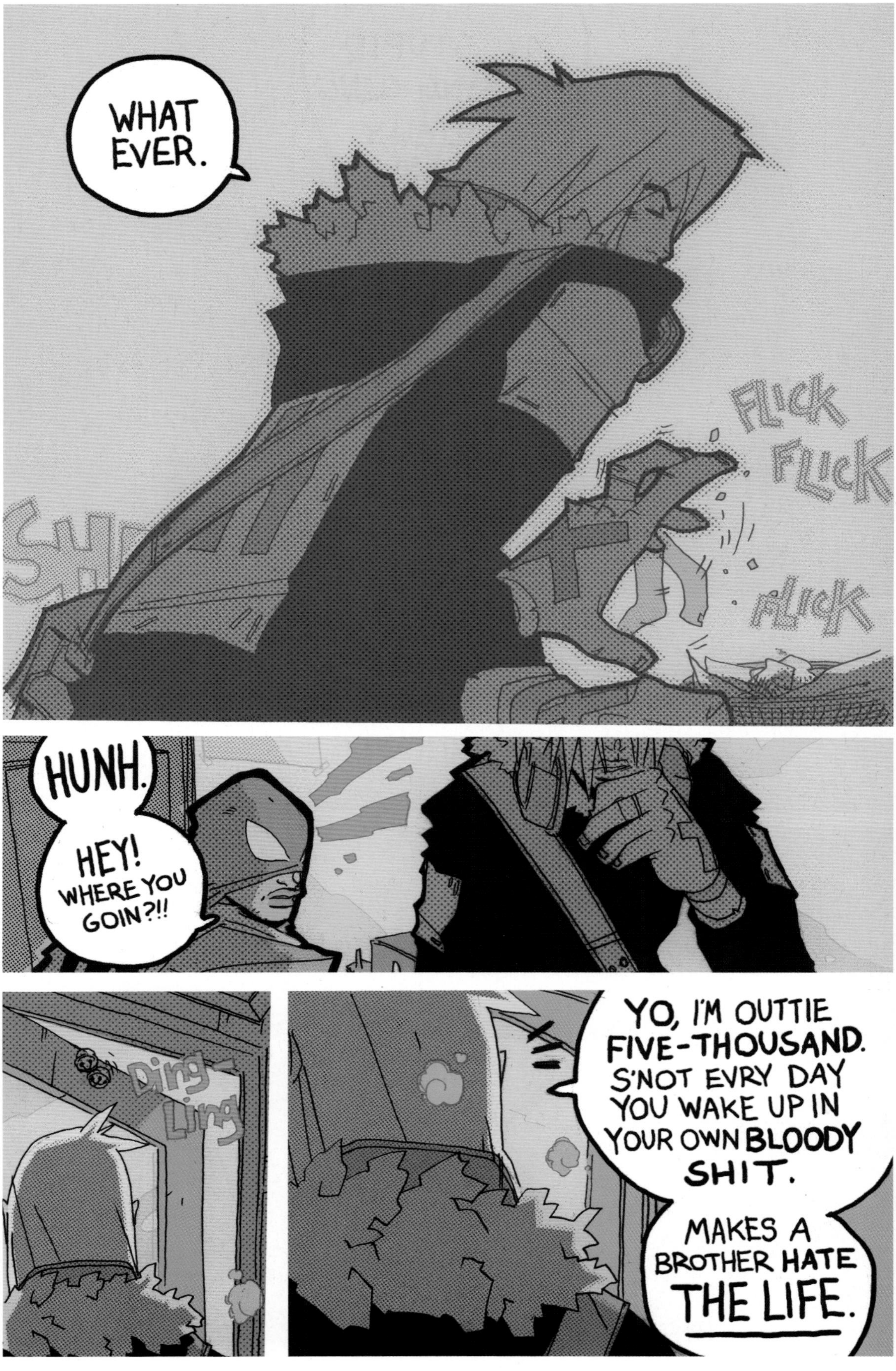
WHAT EVER.
SHH
FLICK
FLICK
FLICK
HUNH.
HEY! WHERE YOU GOIN?!!
Ding-Ling
YO, I'M OUTTIE FIVE-THOUSAND. S'NOT EVRY DAY YOU WAKE UP IN YOUR OWN BLOODY SHIT.
MAKES A BROTHER HATE THE LIFE.

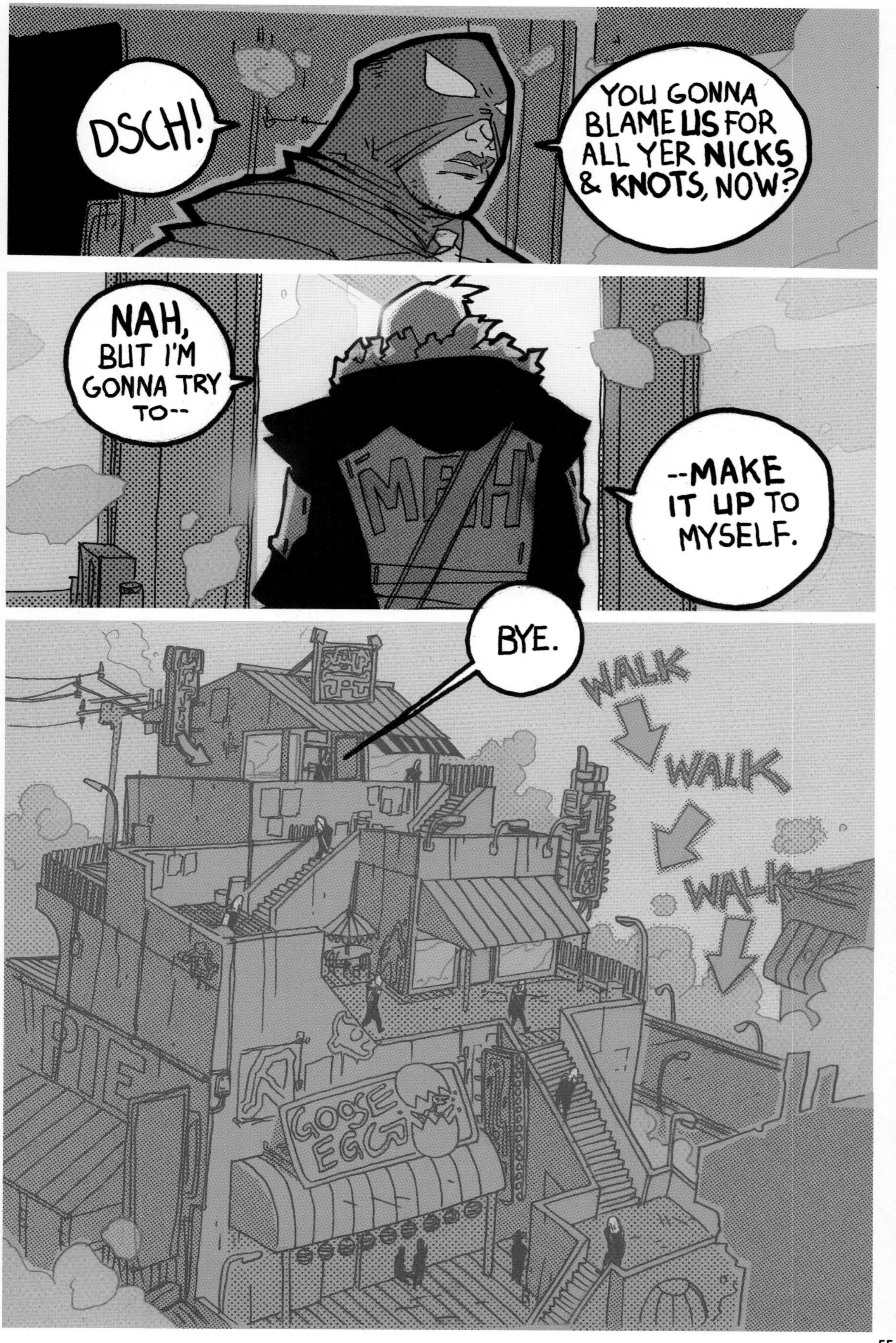

DSCH!
YOU GONNA BLAME US FOR ALL YER NICKS & KNOTS, NOW?
NAH, BUT I'M GONNA TRY TO--
--MAKE IT UP TO MYSELF.
BYE.
WALK
WALK
WALK
GOOSE EGG

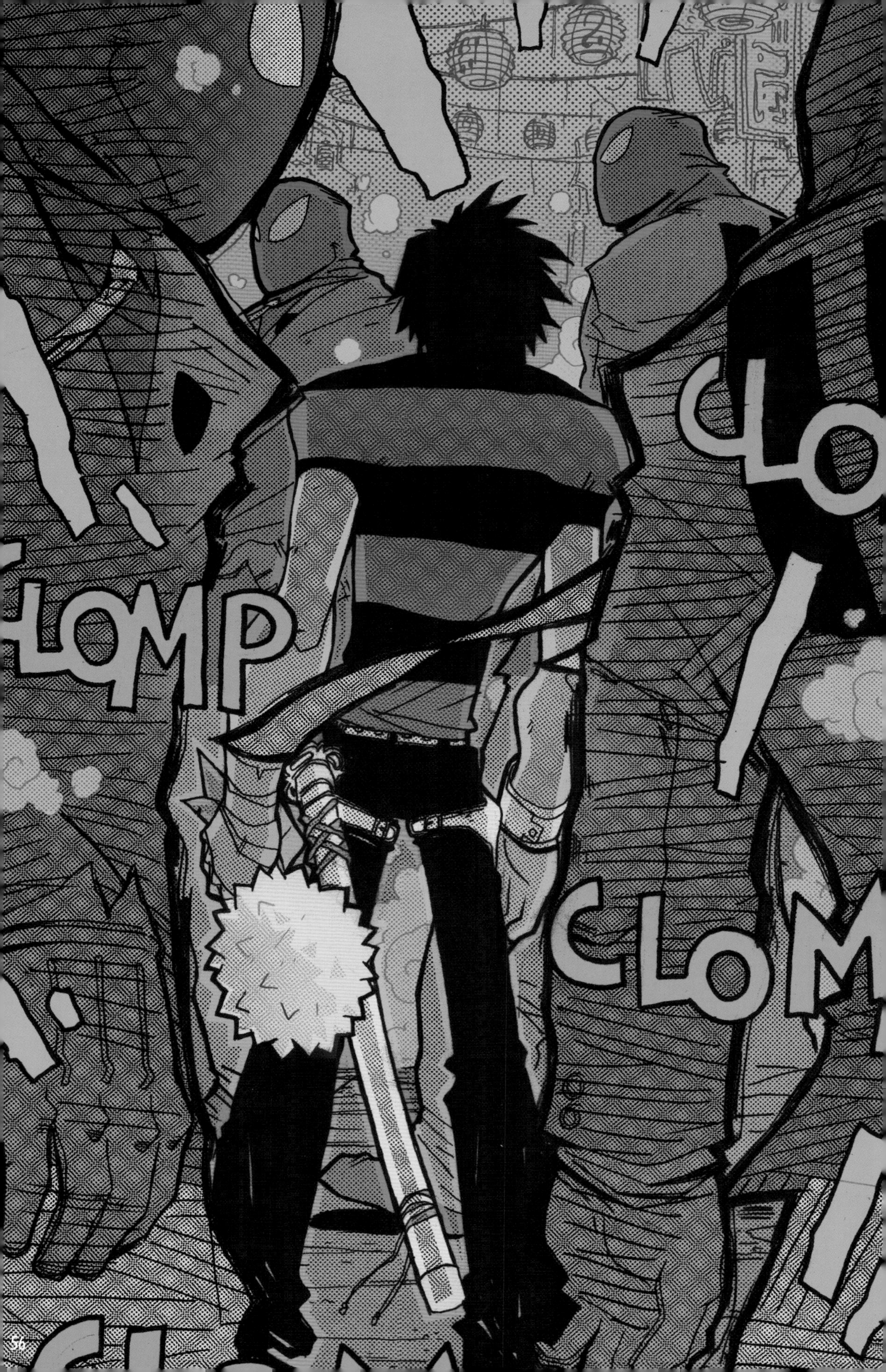
CLOMP
CLO
CLOM

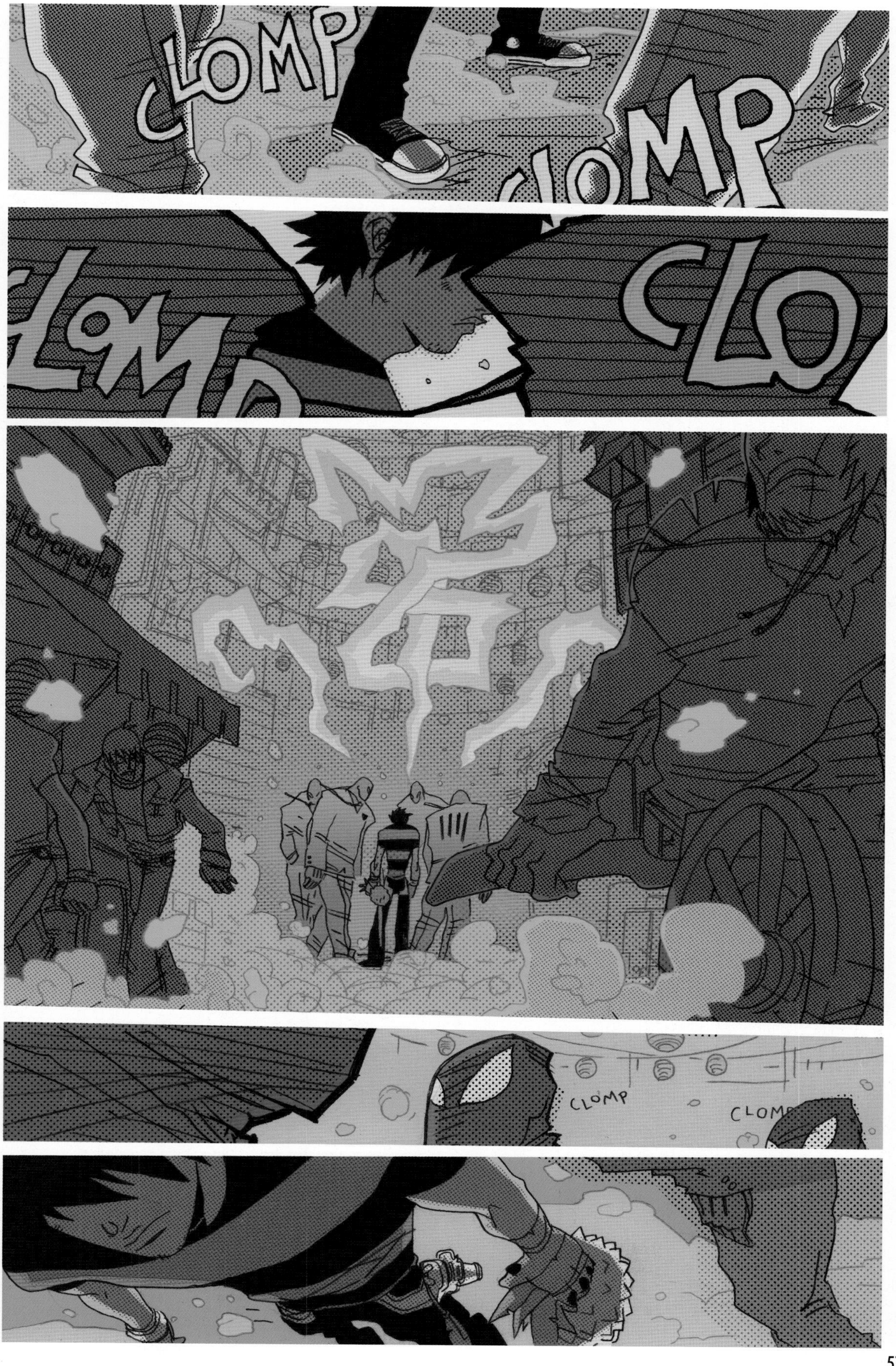
CLOMP
CLOMP
CLOMP
CLO
CLOMP
CLOMP

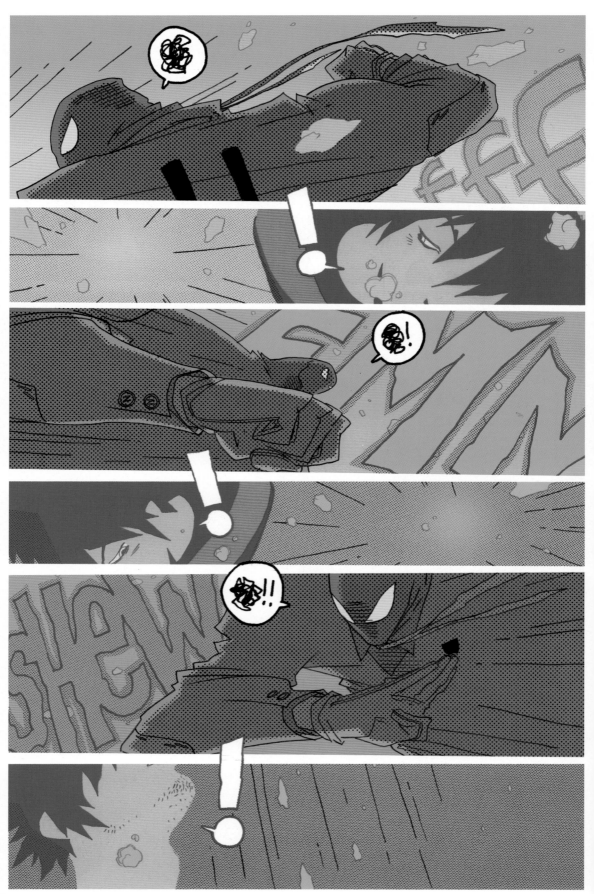

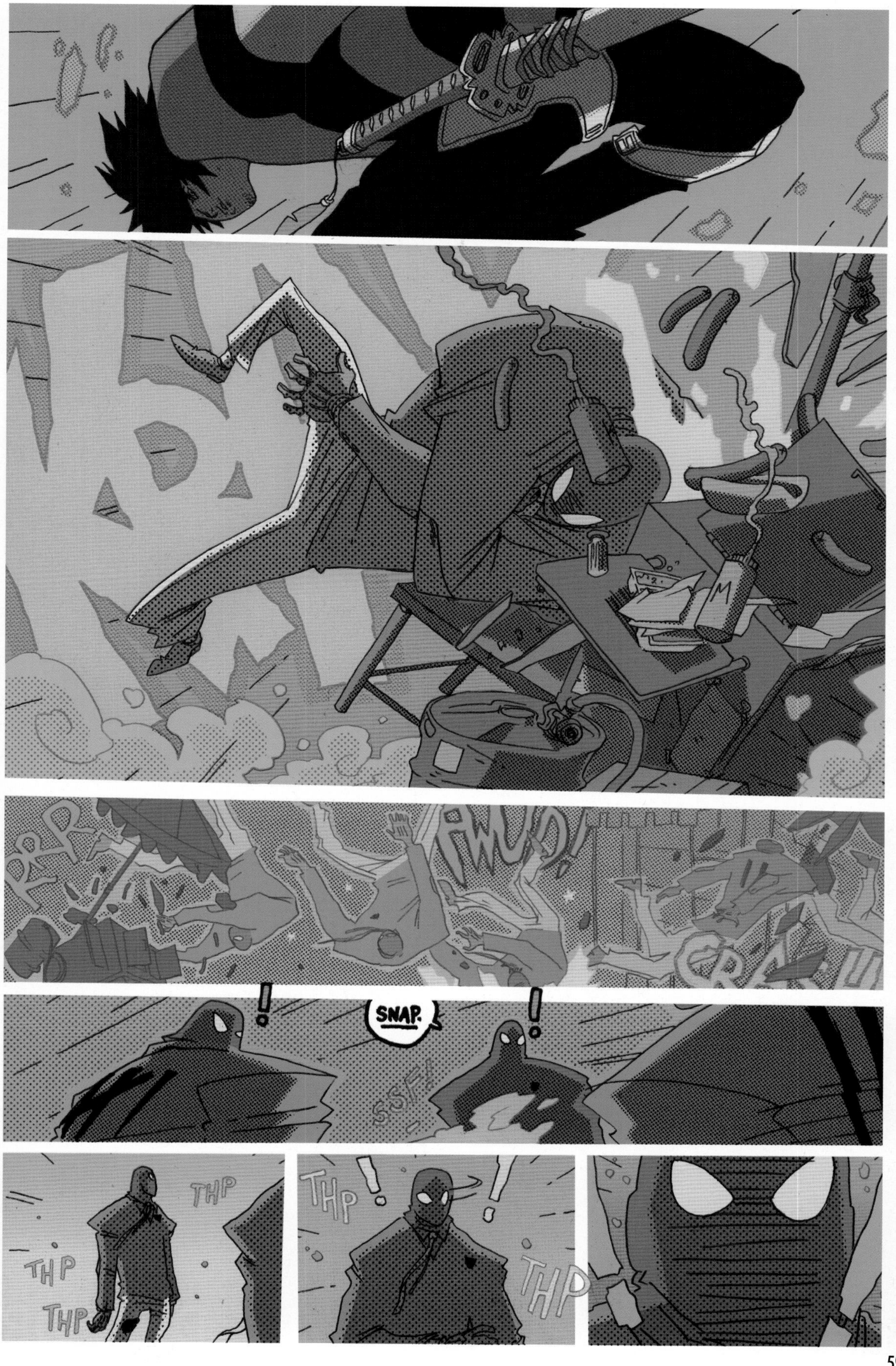
!
SNAP.
!
THP
THP
THP
THP
!
!
THP

ZAFRETTA DIVEBOMBER NO.6 DIES

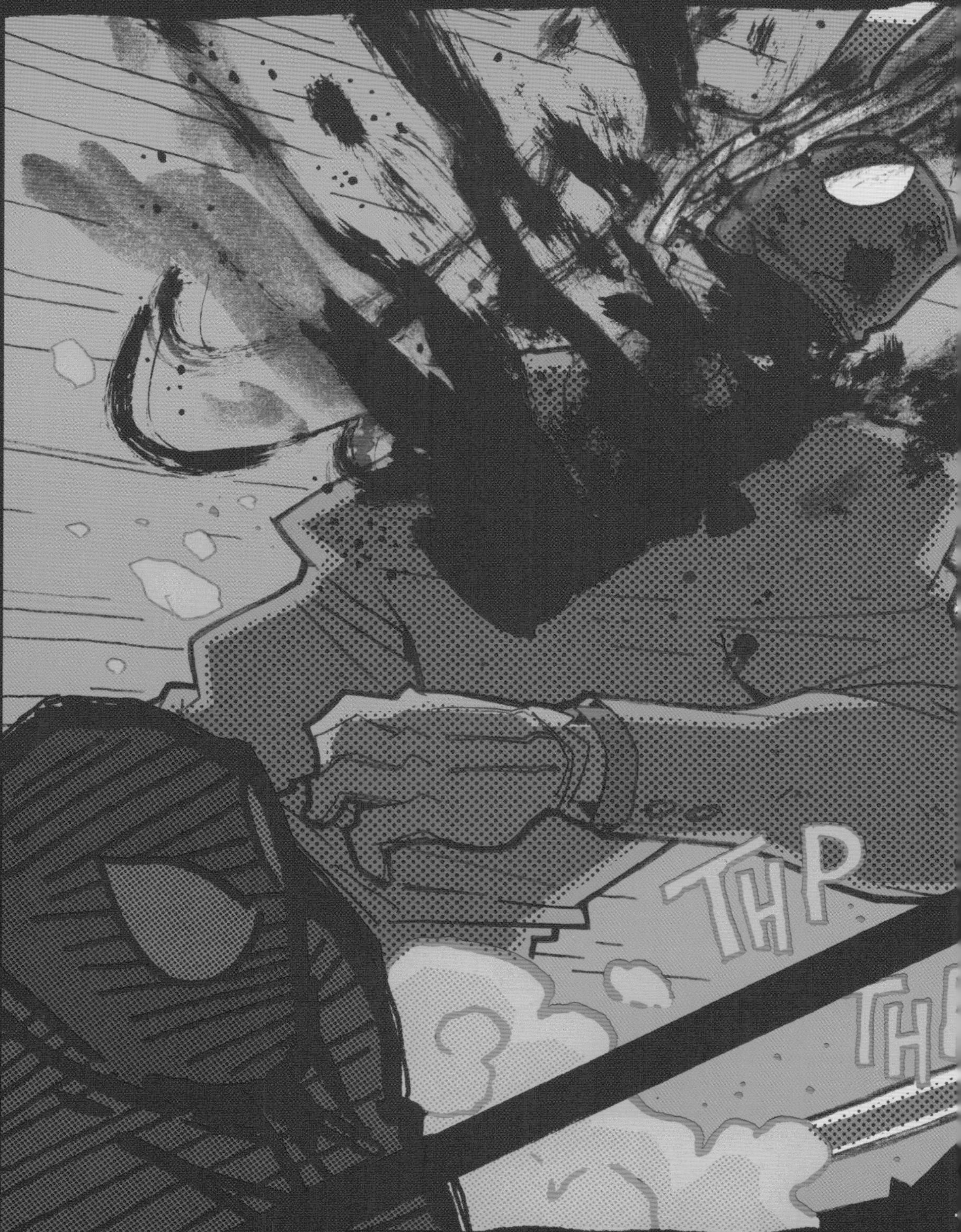
THP

NINE MORE PEOPLE WILL DIE FOR

INSTANTLY, HIS NAME WAS JOSH.

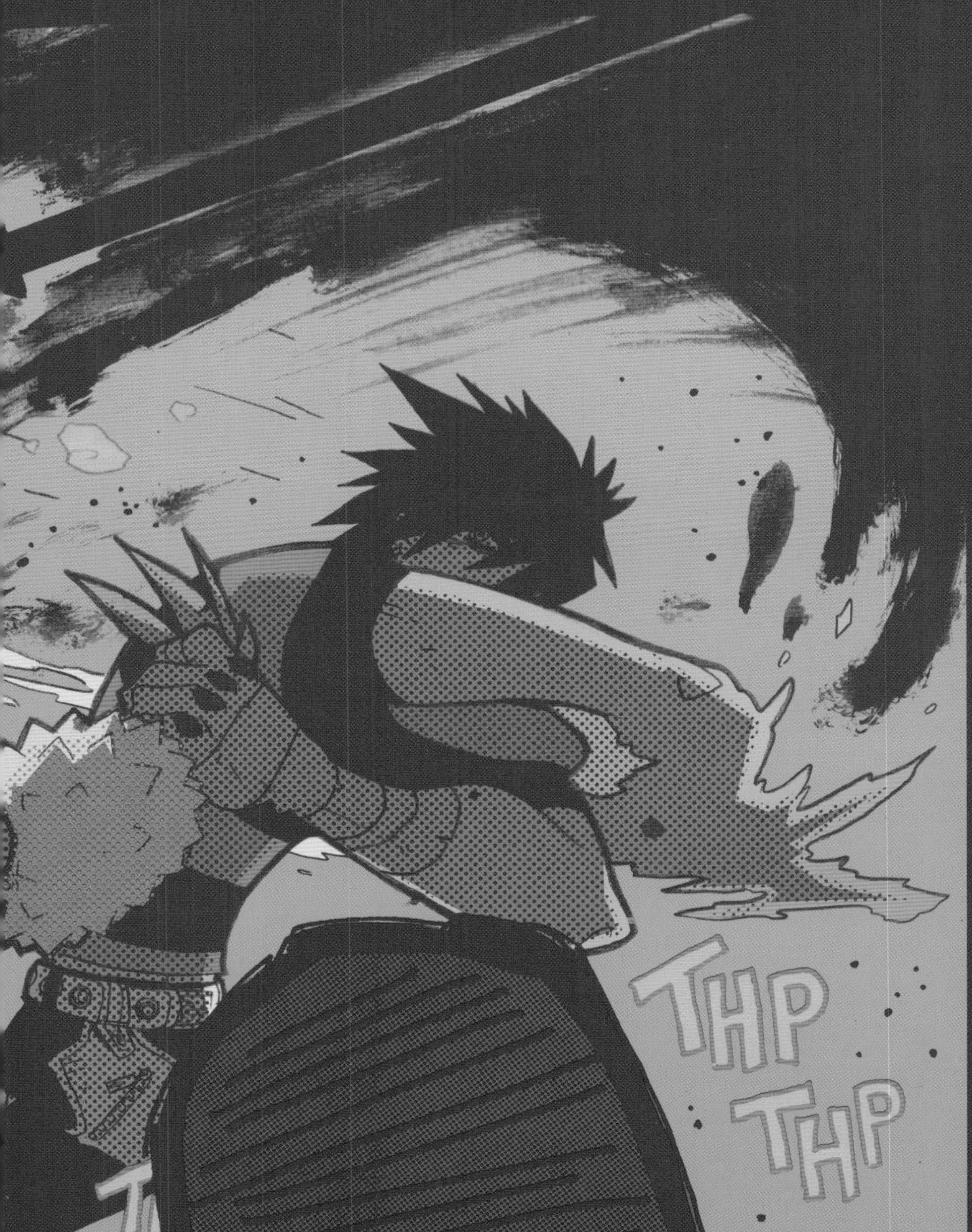
THP
THP

THE RIGHT TO POSSESS THIS.

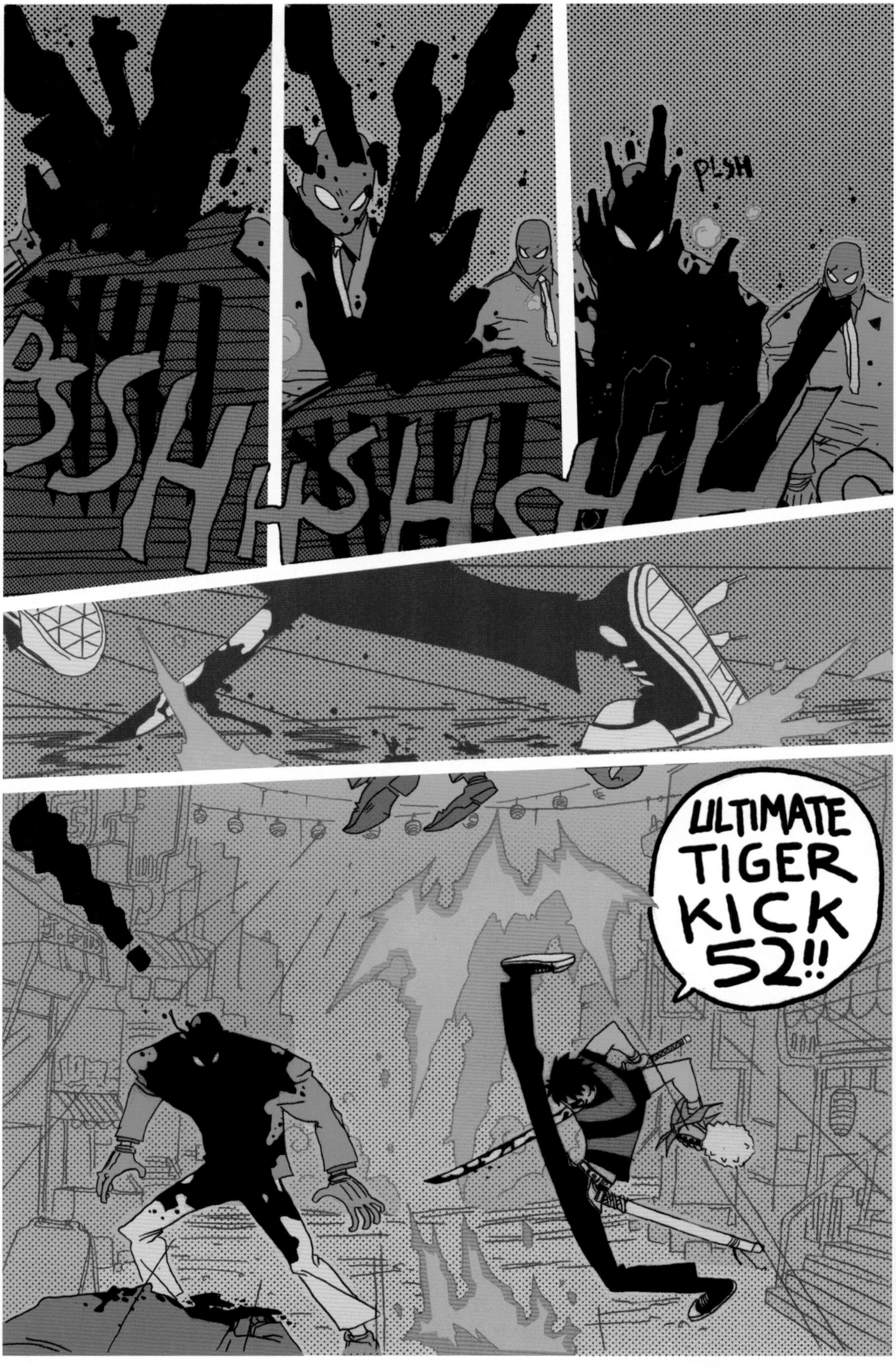
PLSH
ULTIMATE TIGER KICK 52!!

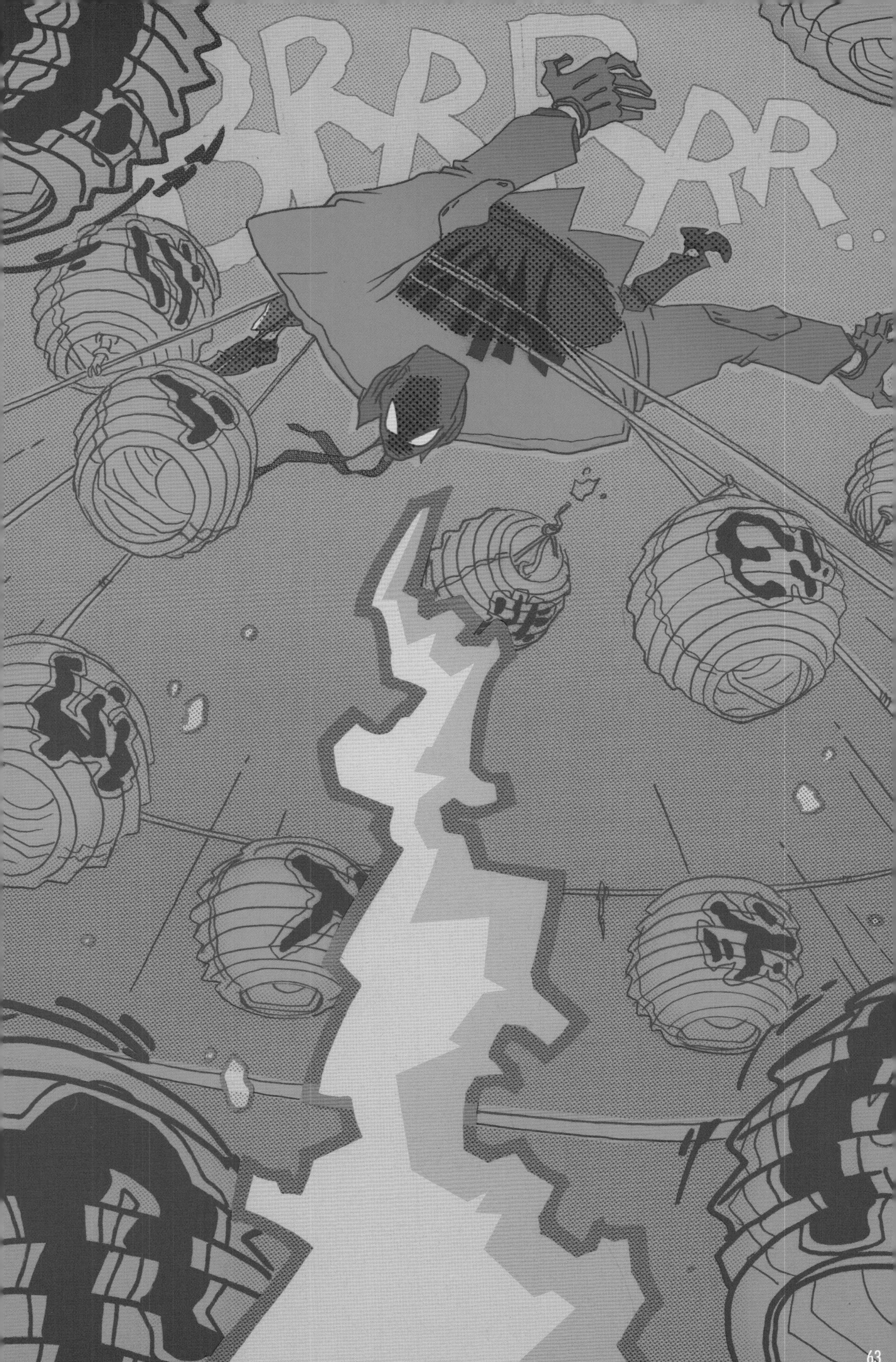
RRRRAR..

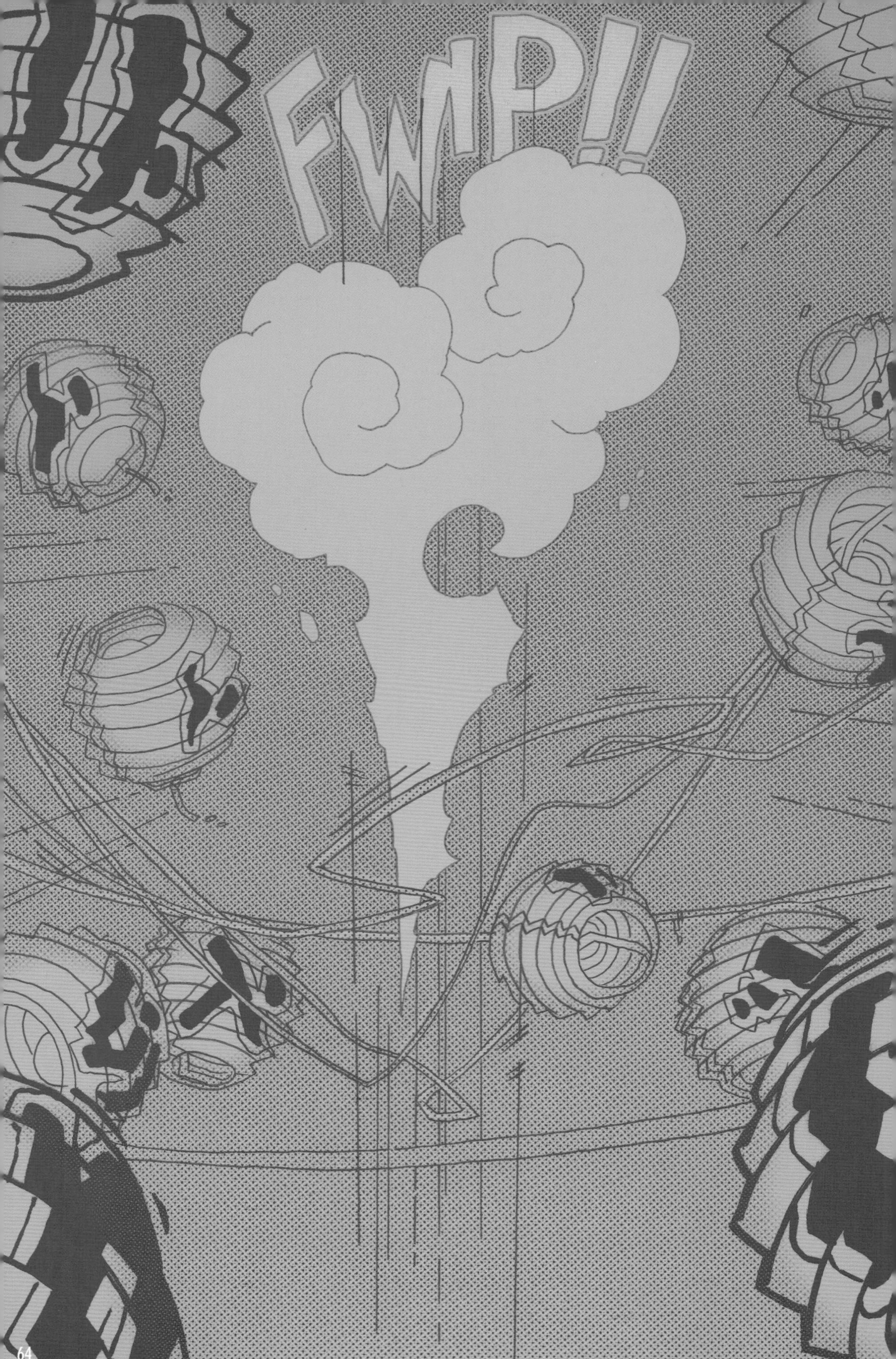
FWIP!!

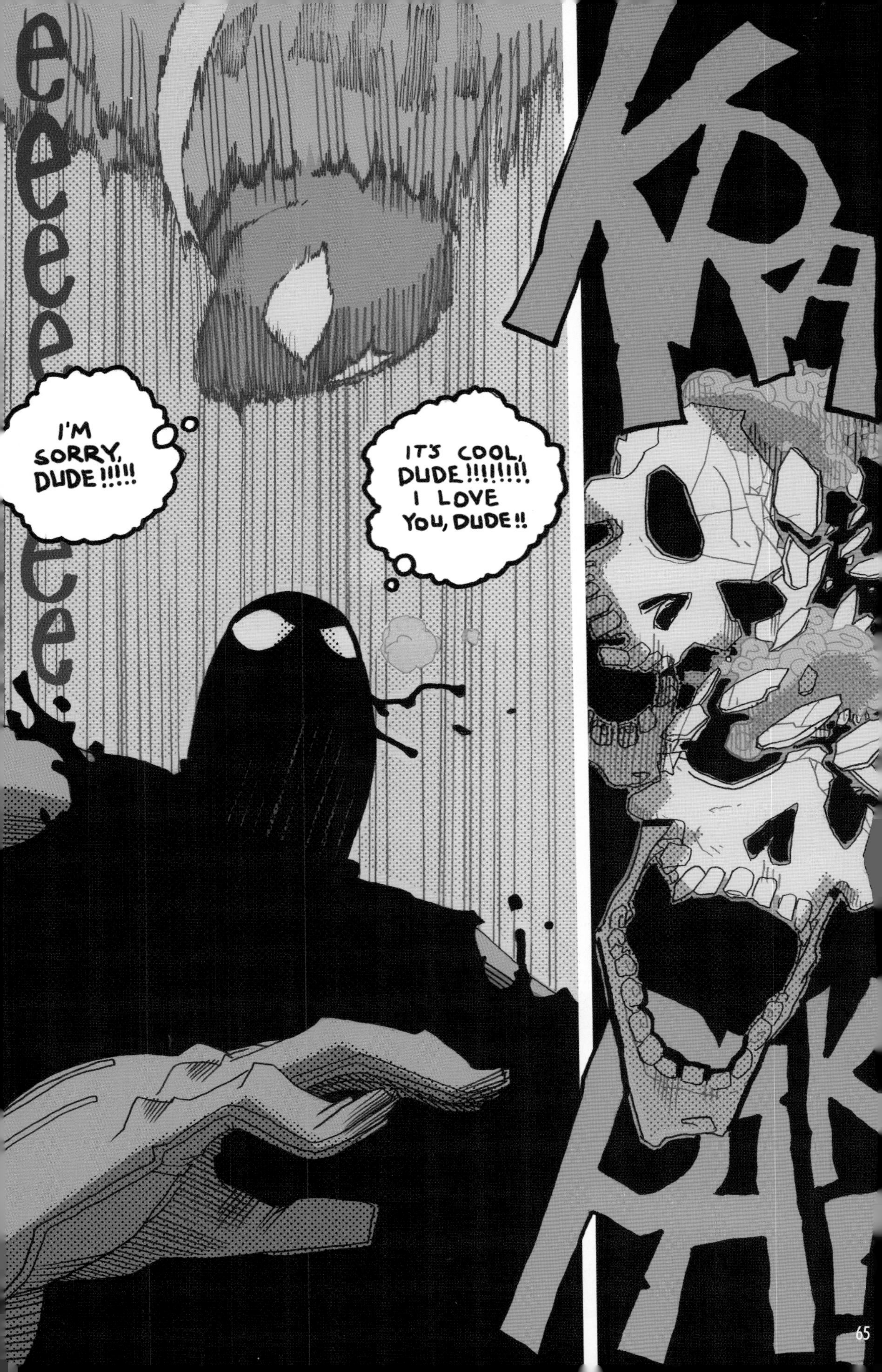
I'M SORRY, DUDE!!!!!
IT'S COOL, DUDE!!!!!!!!! I LOVE YOU, DUDE!!

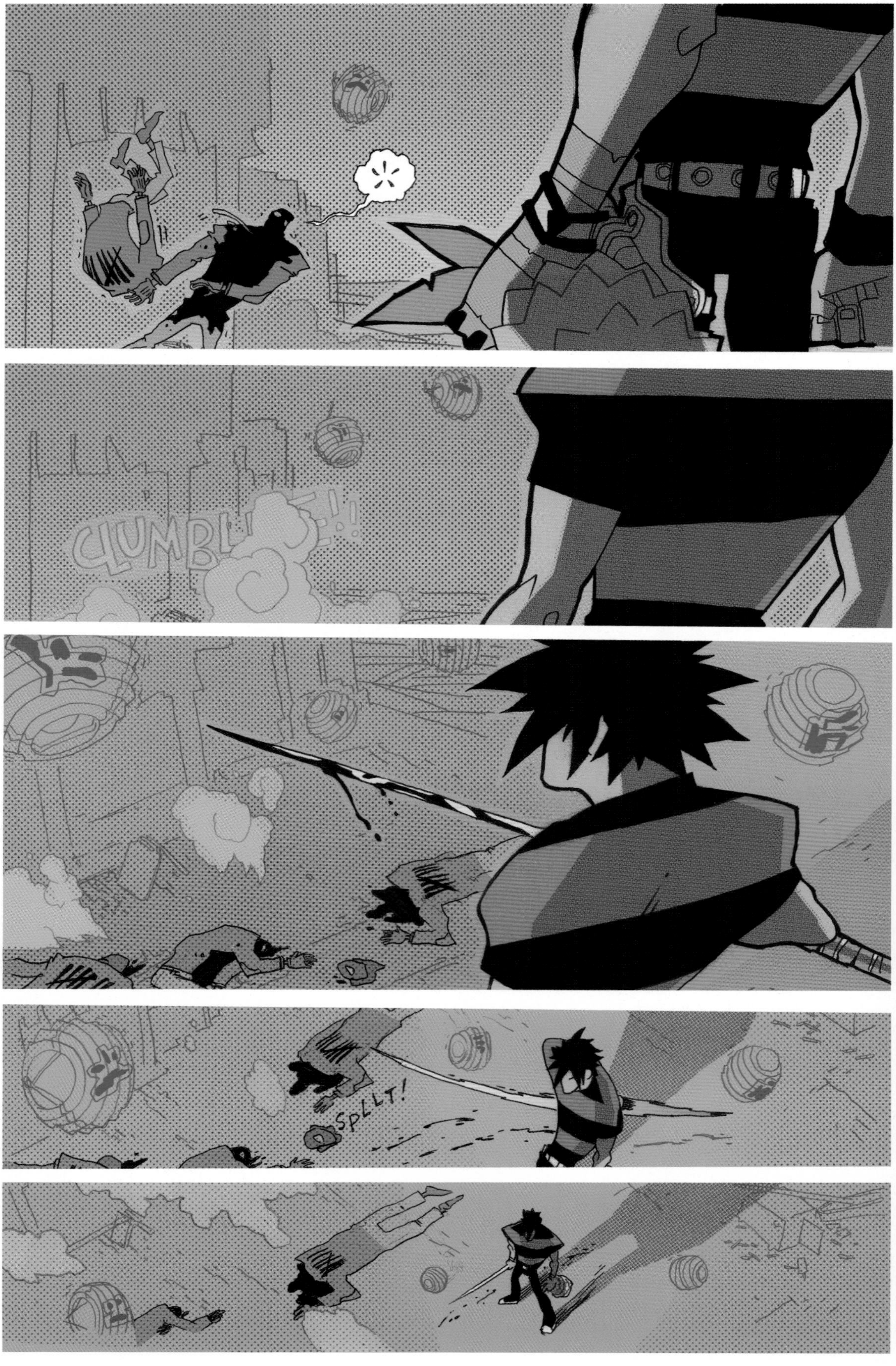
CLUMBLE!!
SPLLT!

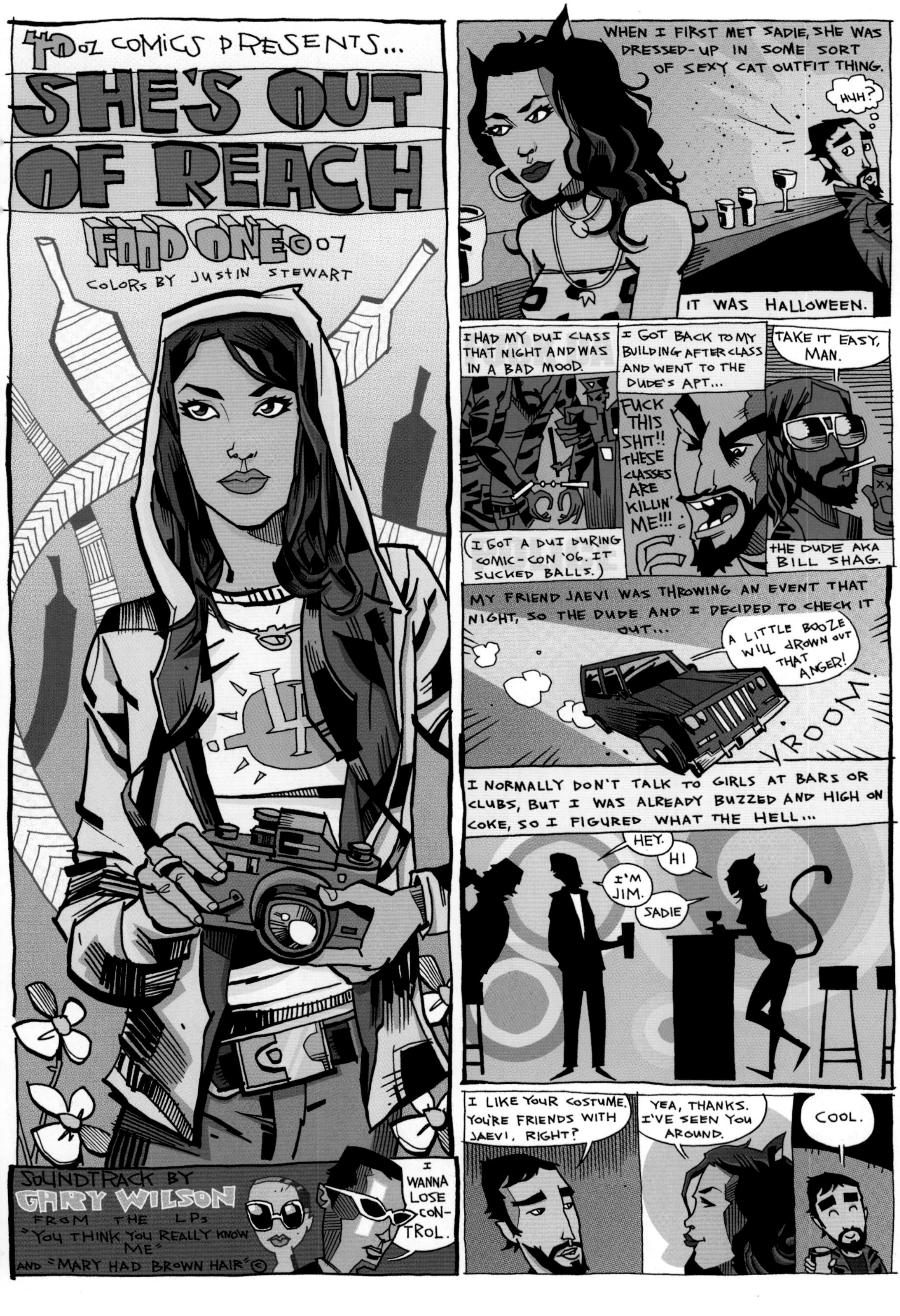
40 OZ COMICS PRESENTS...
SHE'S OUT OF REACH
FOOD ONE © 07
COLORS BY JUSTIN STEWART
SOUNDTRACK BY
GARY WILSON
FROM THE LPs
"YOU THINK YOU REALLY KNOW ME"
AND "MARY HAD BROWN HAIR" ©
I WANNA LOSE CONTROL.
WHEN I FIRST MET SADIE, SHE WAS DRESSED-UP IN SOME SORT OF SEXY CAT OUTFIT THING.
HUH?
IT WAS HALLOWEEN.
I HAD MY DUI CLASS THAT NIGHT AND WAS IN A BAD MOOD.
(I GOT A DUI DURING COMIC-CON '06. IT SUCKED BALLS.)
I GOT BACK TO MY BUILDING AFTER CLASS AND WENT TO THE DUDE'S APT...
FUCK THIS SHIT!! THESE CLASSES ARE KILLIN' ME!!!
TAKE IT EASY, MAN.
THE DUDE AKA BILL SHAG.
MY FRIEND JAEVI WAS THROWING AN EVENT THAT NIGHT, SO THE DUDE AND I DECIDED TO CHECK IT OUT...
A LITTLE BOOZE WILL DROWN OUT THAT ANGER!
VROOM!
I NORMALLY DON'T TALK TO GIRLS AT BARS OR CLUBS, BUT I WAS ALREADY BUZZED AND HIGH ON COKE, SO I FIGURED WHAT THE HELL...
HEY.
HI
I'M JIM.
SADIE
I LIKE YOUR COSTUME. YOU'RE FRIENDS WITH JAEVI, RIGHT?
YEA, THANKS. I'VE SEEN YOU AROUND.
COOL.

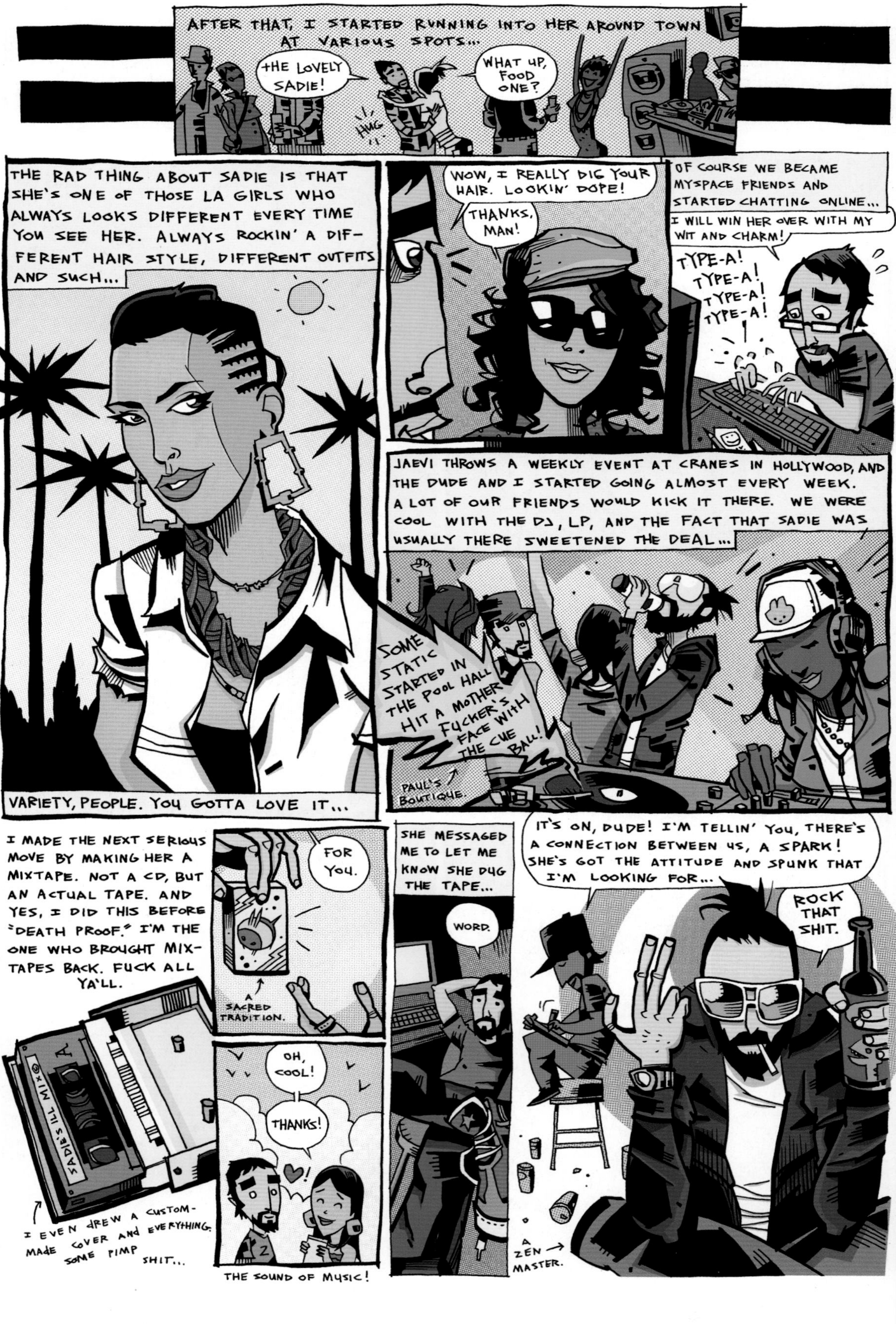
AFTER THAT, I STARTED RUNNING INTO HER AROUND TOWN AT VARIOUS SPOTS...
THE LOVELY SADIE!
HUG
WHAT UP, FOOD ONE?
THE RAD THING ABOUT SADIE IS THAT SHE'S ONE OF THOSE LA GIRLS WHO ALWAYS LOOKS DIFFERENT EVERY TIME YOU SEE HER. ALWAYS ROCKIN' A DIFFERENT HAIR STYLE, DIFFERENT OUTFITS AND SUCH...
VARIETY, PEOPLE. YOU GOTTA LOVE IT...
WOW, I REALLY DIG YOUR HAIR. LOOKIN' DOPE!
THANKS, MAN!
OF COURSE WE BECAME MYSPACE FRIENDS AND STARTED CHATTING ONLINE...
I WILL WIN HER OVER WITH MY WIT AND CHARM!
TYPE-A! TYPE-A! TYPE-A! TYPE-A!
JAEVI THROWS A WEEKLY EVENT AT CRANES IN HOLLYWOOD, AND THE DUDE AND I STARTED GOING ALMOST EVERY WEEK. A LOT OF OUR FRIENDS WOULD KICK IT THERE. WE WERE COOL WITH THE DJ, LP, AND THE FACT THAT SADIE WAS USUALLY THERE SWEETENED THE DEAL...
SOME STATIC STARTED IN THE POOL HALL HIT A MOTHER FUCKER'S FACE WITH THE CUE BALL!
PAUL'S BOUTIQUE.
I MADE THE NEXT SERIOUS MOVE BY MAKING HER A MIXTAPE. NOT A CD, BUT AN ACTUAL TAPE. AND YES, I DID THIS BEFORE "DEATH PROOF." I'M THE ONE WHO BROUGHT MIXTAPES BACK. FUCK ALL YA'LL.
A
SADIE'S ILL MIX
I EVEN DREW A CUSTOM-MADE COVER AND EVERYTHING. SOME PIMP SHIT...
FOR YOU.
A SACRED TRADITION.
OH, COOL!
THANKS!
THE SOUND OF MUSIC!
SHE MESSAGED ME TO LET ME KNOW SHE DUG THE TAPE...
WORD.
IT'S ON, DUDE! I'M TELLIN' YOU, THERE'S A CONNECTION BETWEEN US, A SPARK! SHE'S GOT THE ATTITUDE AND SPUNK THAT I'M LOOKING FOR...
ROCK THAT SHIT.
A ZEN MASTER.

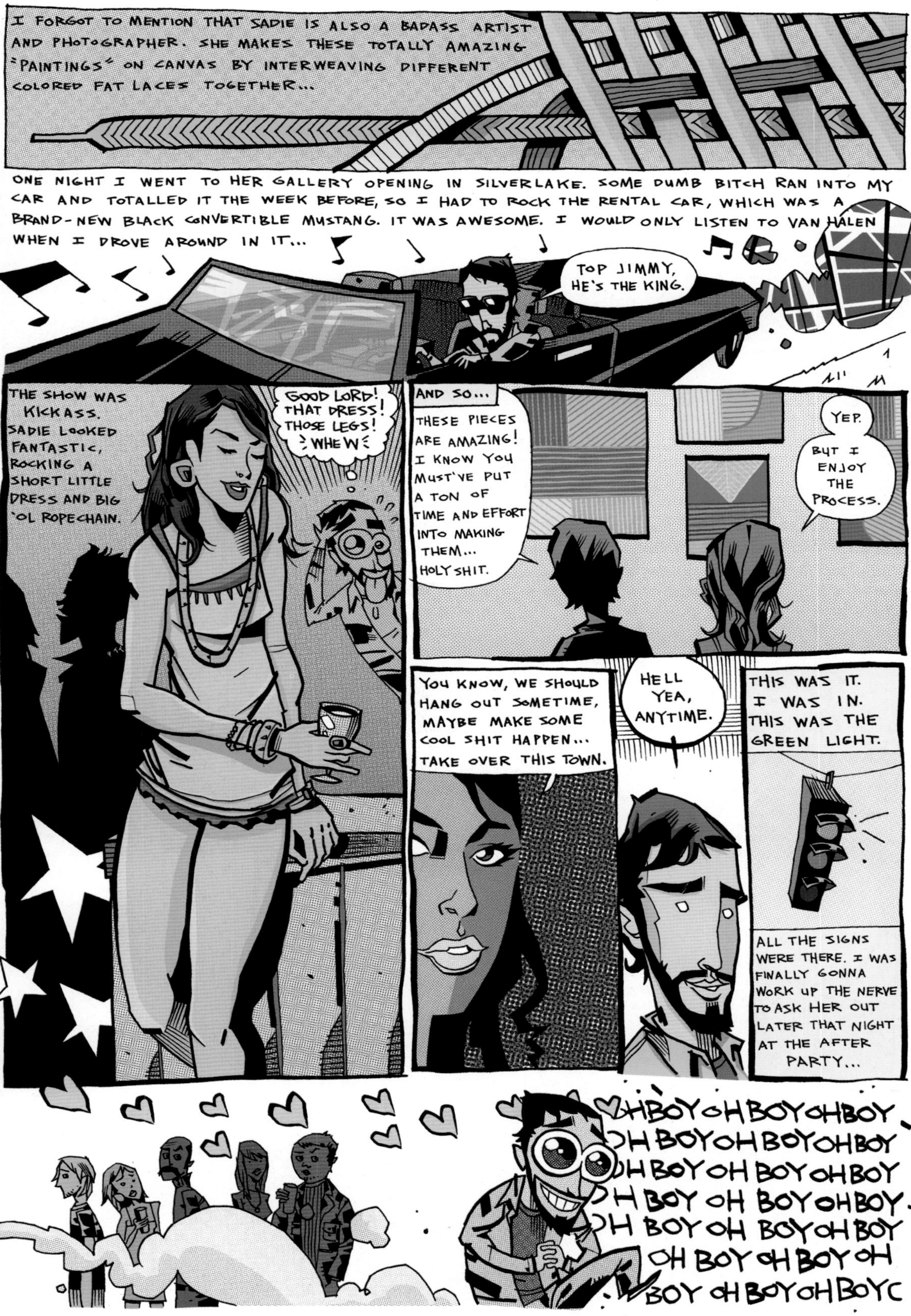
I FORGOT TO MENTION THAT SADIE IS ALSO A BADASS ARTIST AND PHOTOGRAPHER. SHE MAKES THESE TOTALLY AMAZING "PAINTINGS" ON CANVAS BY INTERWEAVING DIFFERENT COLORED FAT LACES TOGETHER...
ONE NIGHT I WENT TO HER GALLERY OPENING IN SILVERLAKE. SOME DUMB BITCH RAN INTO MY CAR AND TOTALLED IT THE WEEK BEFORE, SO I HAD TO ROCK THE RENTAL CAR, WHICH WAS A BRAND-NEW BLACK CONVERTIBLE MUSTANG. IT WAS AWESOME. I WOULD ONLY LISTEN TO VAN HALEN WHEN I DROVE AROUND IN IT...
TOP JIMMY, HE'S THE KING.
THE SHOW WAS KICKASS. SADIE LOOKED FANTASTIC, ROCKING A SHORT LITTLE DRESS AND BIG 'OL ROPECHAIN.
GOOD LORD! THAT DRESS! THOSE LEGS! WHEW!
AND SO...
THESE PIECES ARE AMAZING! I KNOW YOU MUST'VE PUT A TON OF TIME AND EFFORT INTO MAKING THEM... HOLY SHIT.
YEP.
BUT I ENJOY THE PROCESS.
YOU KNOW, WE SHOULD HANG OUT SOMETIME, MAYBE MAKE SOME COOL SHIT HAPPEN... TAKE OVER THIS TOWN.
HELL YEA, ANYTIME.
THIS WAS IT. I WAS IN. THIS WAS THE GREEN LIGHT.
ALL THE SIGNS WERE THERE. I WAS FINALLY GONNA WORK UP THE NERVE TO ASK HER OUT LATER THAT NIGHT AT THE AFTER PARTY...
OHBOY OH BOY

I DROPPED MY CAR OFF AT HOME AND WAITED FOR JAEVI AND PETER TO PICK ME UP SO I COULD DRINK...

WE POUNDED A BUNCH OF DRINKS ON THE RIDE THERE...

DOWN THE HATCH, FOOD!

CHEERS!

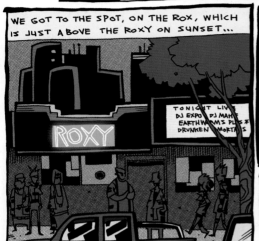
WE GOT TO THE SPOT, ON THE ROX, WHICH IS JUST ABOVE THE ROXY ON SUNSET...

ROXY

TONIGHT LIVE DJ EXPO, DJ MAH, EARTHWORMS PLUS DRUNKEN MORTALS

I SAW SADIE WHEN I WALKED IN...

SADIE DOOWAP! BUY YOU A DRINK?

SURE, THANKS!

IT'S OOOOOOOON!!!

THE BARTENDER THERE SORTA KNEW ME AND KEPT POURING ME THESE STRONGASS DRINKS...

A VERY LARGE AND AFFORDABLE GLENLIVET ON THE ROCKS.

I GOT DRUNK QUICK...

FUCK THIS. THE TIME IS NOW. TIME TO MAKE THE MOVE!

SPILL!

SO LISTEN, I WAS WANDERING... UM, I'D, I-I WOULD LIKE TO TAKE YOU OUT SOME-TIME. I'D LIKE TO HANG OUT WITH YOU, YA KNOW? WOULD YOU BE COOL WITH THAT?

OH.

WELL, UM... I'M WITH LP.

DID YOU KNOW THAT?

I'M... WITH HER.

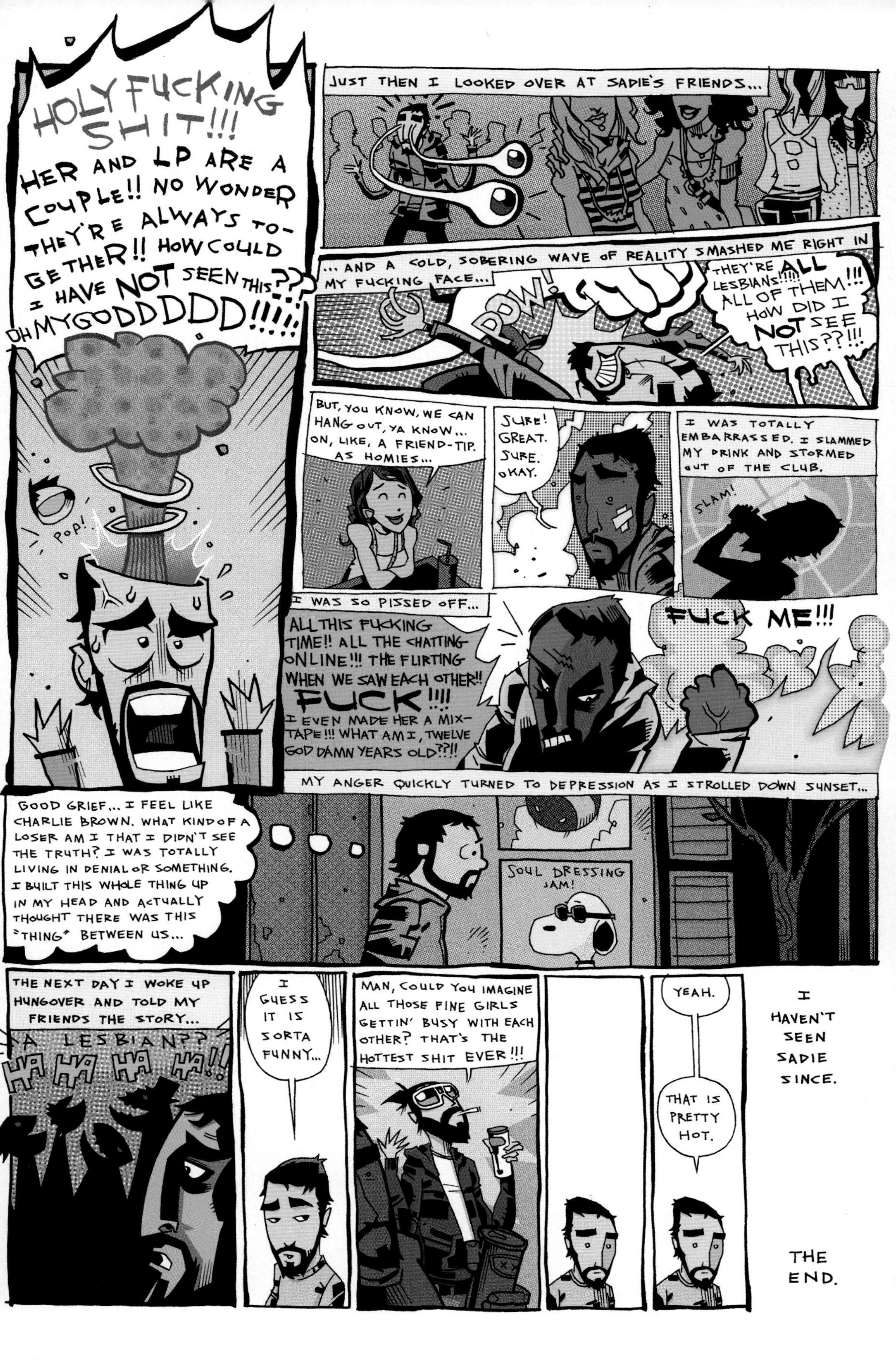

HOLY FUCKING SHIT!!! HER AND LP ARE A COUPLE!! NO WONDER THEY'RE ALWAYS TOGETHER!! HOW COULD I HAVE NOT SEEN THIS??? OHMYGODDDDDD!!!!!!
POP!
JUST THEN I LOOKED OVER AT SADIE'S FRIENDS...
...AND A COLD, SOBERING WAVE OF REALITY SMASHED ME RIGHT IN MY FUCKING FACE...
POW!
THEY'RE ALL LESBIANS!!!! ALL OF THEM!!! HOW DID I NOT SEE THIS??!!!
BUT, YOU KNOW, WE CAN HANG OUT, YA KNOW... ON, LIKE, A FRIEND-TIP. AS HOMIES...
SURE! GREAT. SURE. OKAY.
I WAS TOTALLY EMBARRASSED. I SLAMMED MY DRINK AND STORMED OUT OF THE CLUB.
SLAM!
I WAS SO PISSED OFF...
ALL THIS FUCKING TIME!! ALL THE CHATTING ONLINE!!! THE FLIRTING WHEN WE SAW EACH OTHER!! FUCK!!!! I EVEN MADE HER A MIX-TAPE!!! WHAT AM I, TWELVE GOD DAMN YEARS OLD??!!
FUCK ME!!!
MY ANGER QUICKLY TURNED TO DEPRESSION AS I STROLLED DOWN SUNSET...
GOOD GRIEF... I FEEL LIKE CHARLIE BROWN. WHAT KIND OF A LOSER AM I THAT I DIDN'T SEE THE TRUTH? I WAS TOTALLY LIVING IN DENIAL OR SOMETHING. I BUILT THIS WHOLE THING UP IN MY HEAD AND ACTUALLY THOUGHT THERE WAS THIS "THING" BETWEEN US...
SOUL DRESSING JAM!
THE NEXT DAY I WOKE UP HUNGOVER AND TOLD MY FRIENDS THE STORY...
A LESBIAN?? HA HA HA HA!!
I GUESS IT IS SORTA FUNNY...
MAN, COULD YOU IMAGINE ALL THOSE FINE GIRLS GETTIN' BUSY WITH EACH OTHER? THAT'S THE HOTTEST SHIT EVER!!!
YEAH.
THAT IS PRETTY HOT.
I HAVEN'T SEEN SADIE SINCE.
THE END.

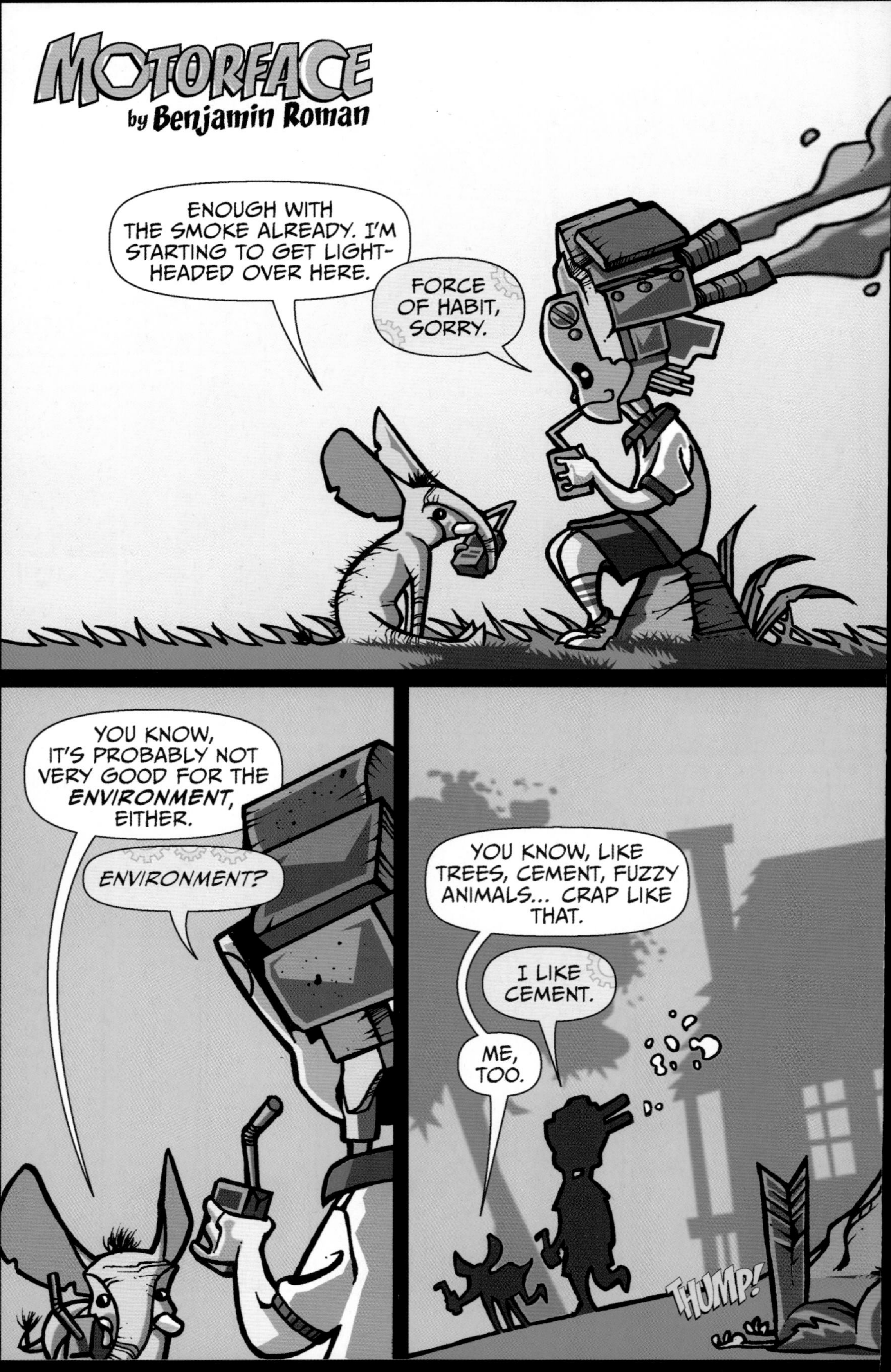
MOTORFACE
by Benjamin Roman
ENOUGH WITH THE SMOKE ALREADY. I'M STARTING TO GET LIGHT-HEADED OVER HERE.
FORCE OF HABIT, SORRY.
YOU KNOW, IT'S PROBABLY NOT VERY GOOD FOR THE *ENVIRONMENT*, EITHER.
ENVIRONMENT?
YOU KNOW, LIKE TREES, CEMENT, FUZZY ANIMALS... CRAP LIKE THAT.
I LIKE CEMENT.
ME, TOO.
THUMP!

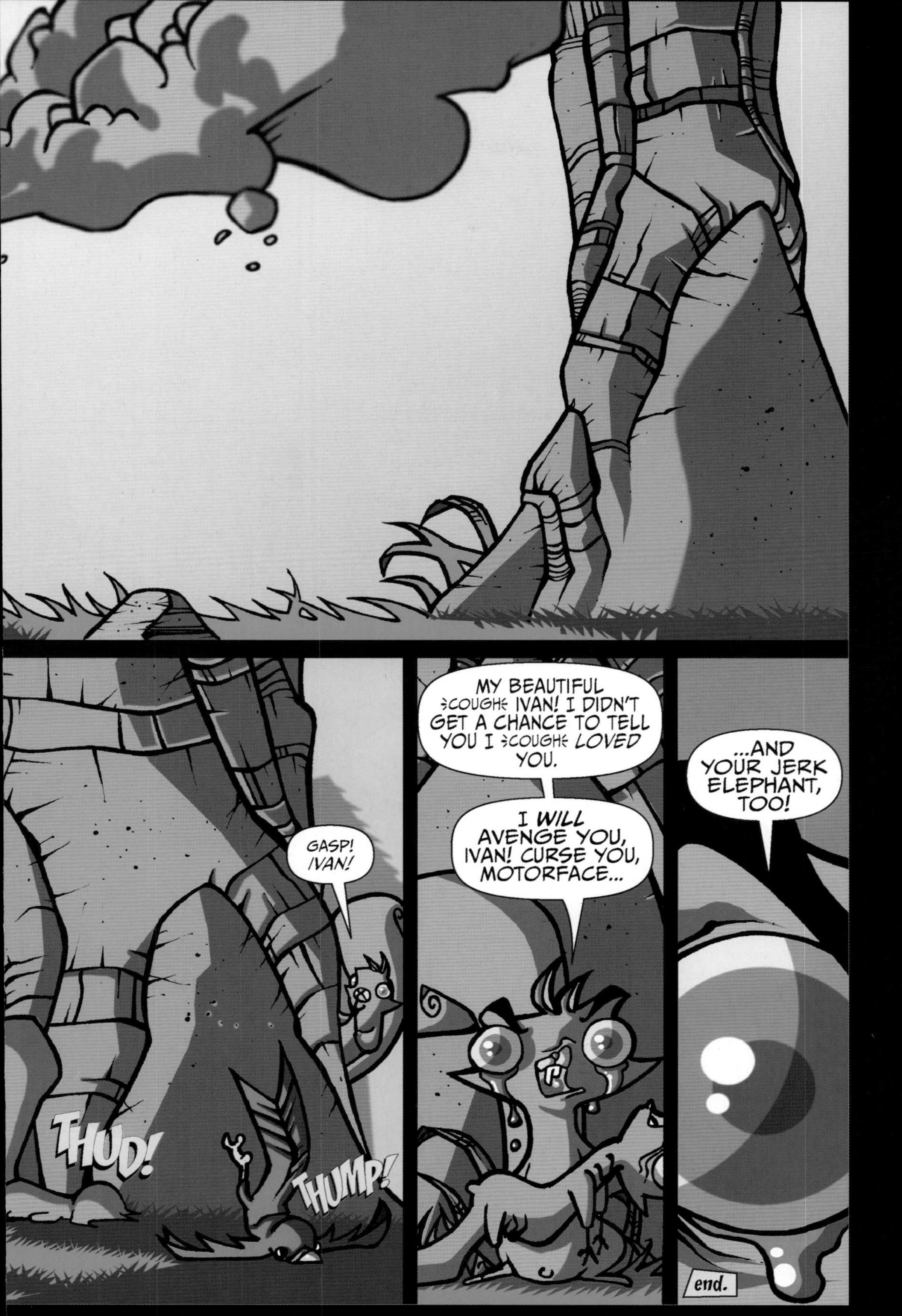

GASP! IVAN!
THUD!
THUMP!
MY BEAUTIFUL ≷COUGH≶ IVAN! I DIDN'T GET A CHANCE TO TELL YOU I ≷COUGH≶ LOVED YOU.
I WILL AVENGE YOU, IVAN! CURSE YOU, MOTORFACE...
...AND YOUR JERK ELEPHANT, TOO!
end.

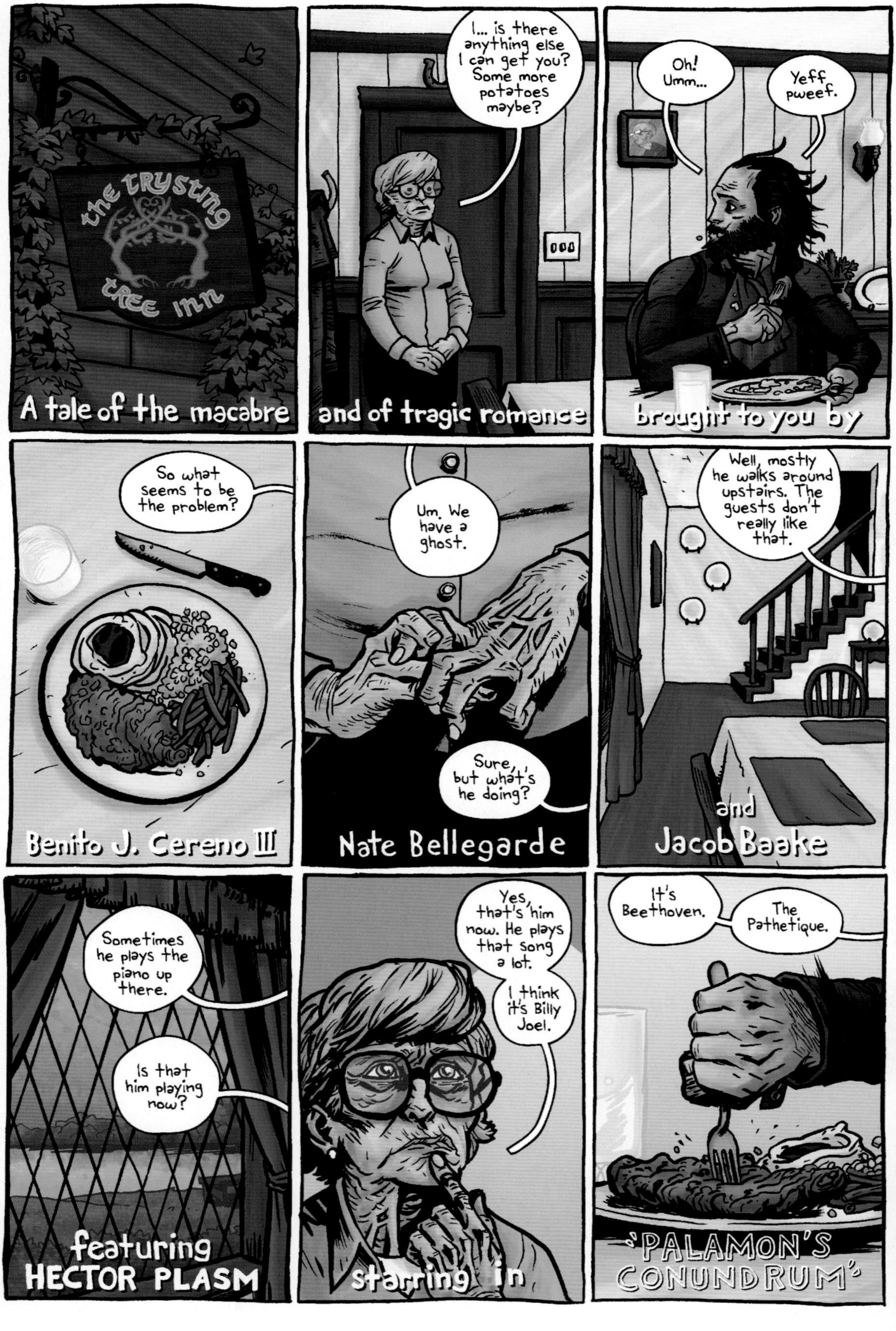
A tale of the macabre
the trysting tree inn
I... is there anything else I can get you? Some more potatoes maybe?
and of tragic romance
Oh! Umm...
Yeff pweef.
brought to you by
So what seems to be the problem?
Benito J. Cereno III
Um. We have a ghost.
Sure, but what's he doing?
Nate Bellegarde
Well, mostly he walks around upstairs. The guests don't really like that.
and
Jacob Baake
Sometimes he plays the piano up there.
Is that him playing now?
featuring
HECTOR PLASM
Yes, that's him now. He plays that song a lot.
I think it's Billy Joel.
starring in
It's Beethoven.
The Pathetique.
'PALAMON'S CONUNDRUM'

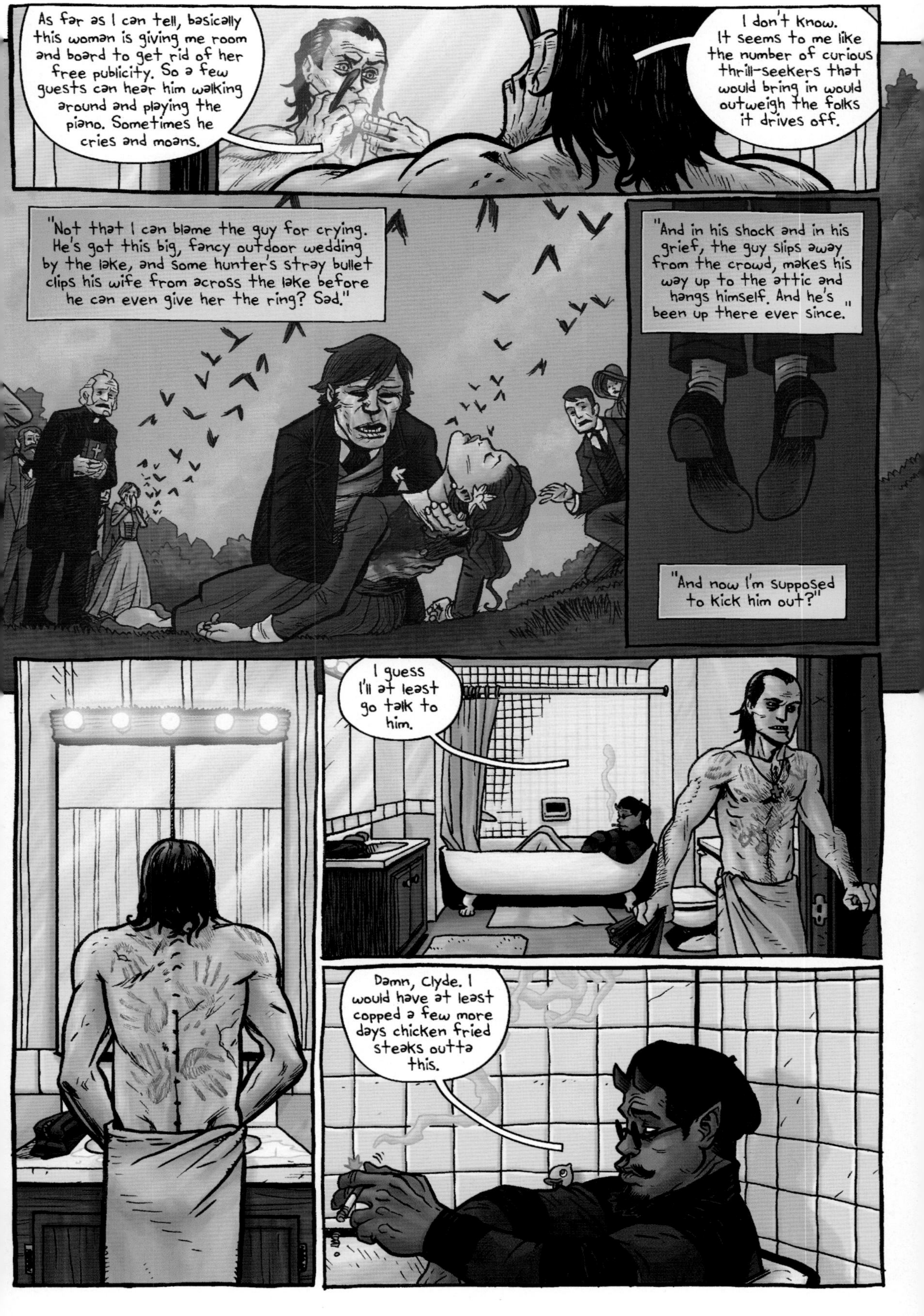

As far as I can tell, basically this woman is giving me room and board to get rid of her free publicity. So a few guests can hear him walking around and playing the piano. Sometimes he cries and moans.
I don't know. It seems to me like the number of curious thrill-seekers that would bring in would outweigh the folks it drives off.
"Not that I can blame the guy for crying. He's got this big, fancy outdoor wedding by the lake, and some hunter's stray bullet clips his wife from across the lake before he can even give her the ring? Sad."
"And in his shock and in his grief, the guy slips away from the crowd, makes his way up to the attic and hangs himself. And he's been up there ever since."
"And now I'm supposed to kick him out?"
I guess I'll at least go talk to him.
Damn, Clyde. I would have at least copped a few more days chicken fried steaks outta this.

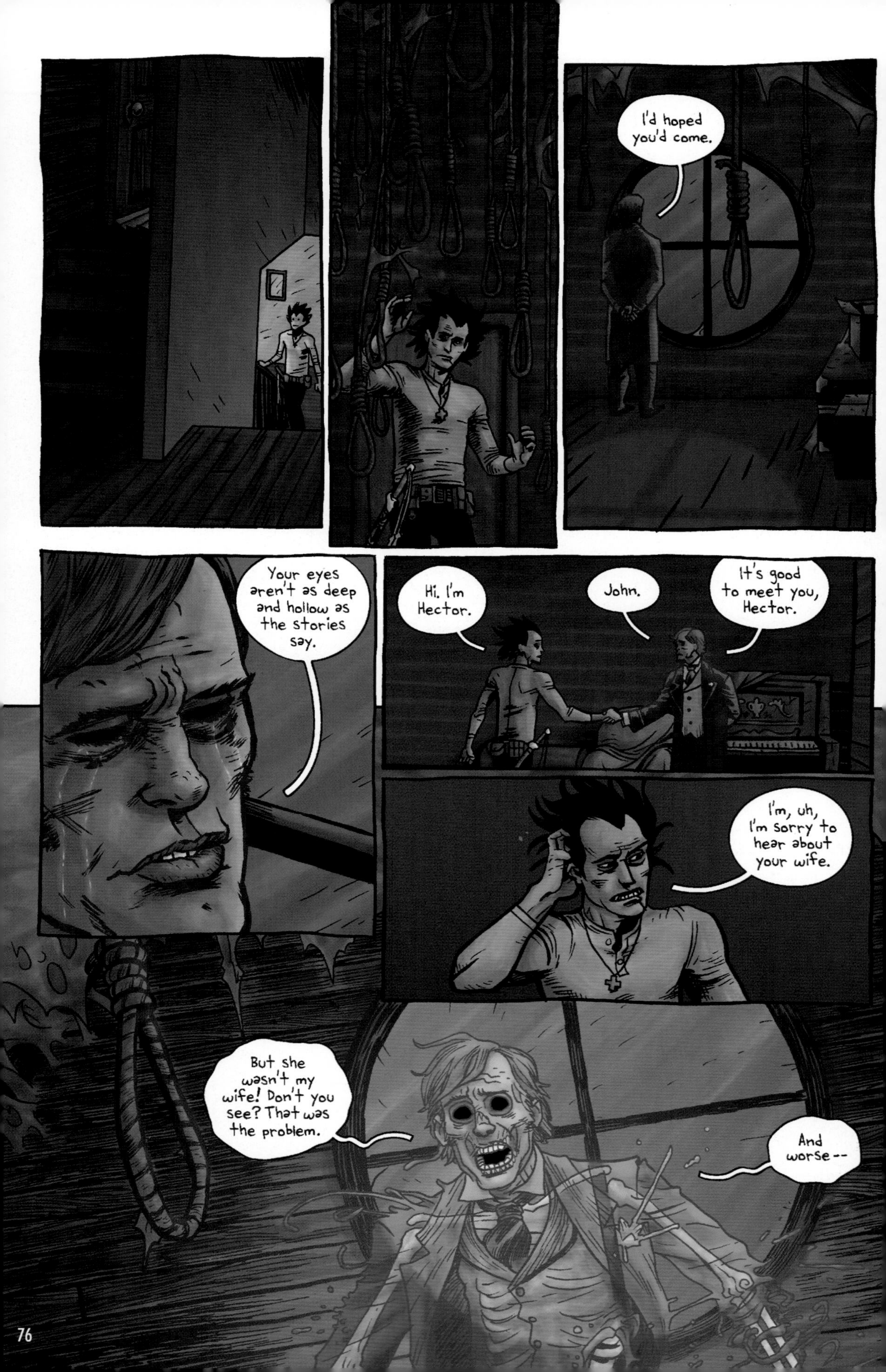
I'd hoped you'd come.
Your eyes aren't as deep and hollow as the stories say.
Hi. I'm Hector.
John.
It's good to meet you, Hector.
I'm, uh, I'm sorry to hear about your wife.
But she wasn't my wife! Don't you see? That was the problem.
And worse --

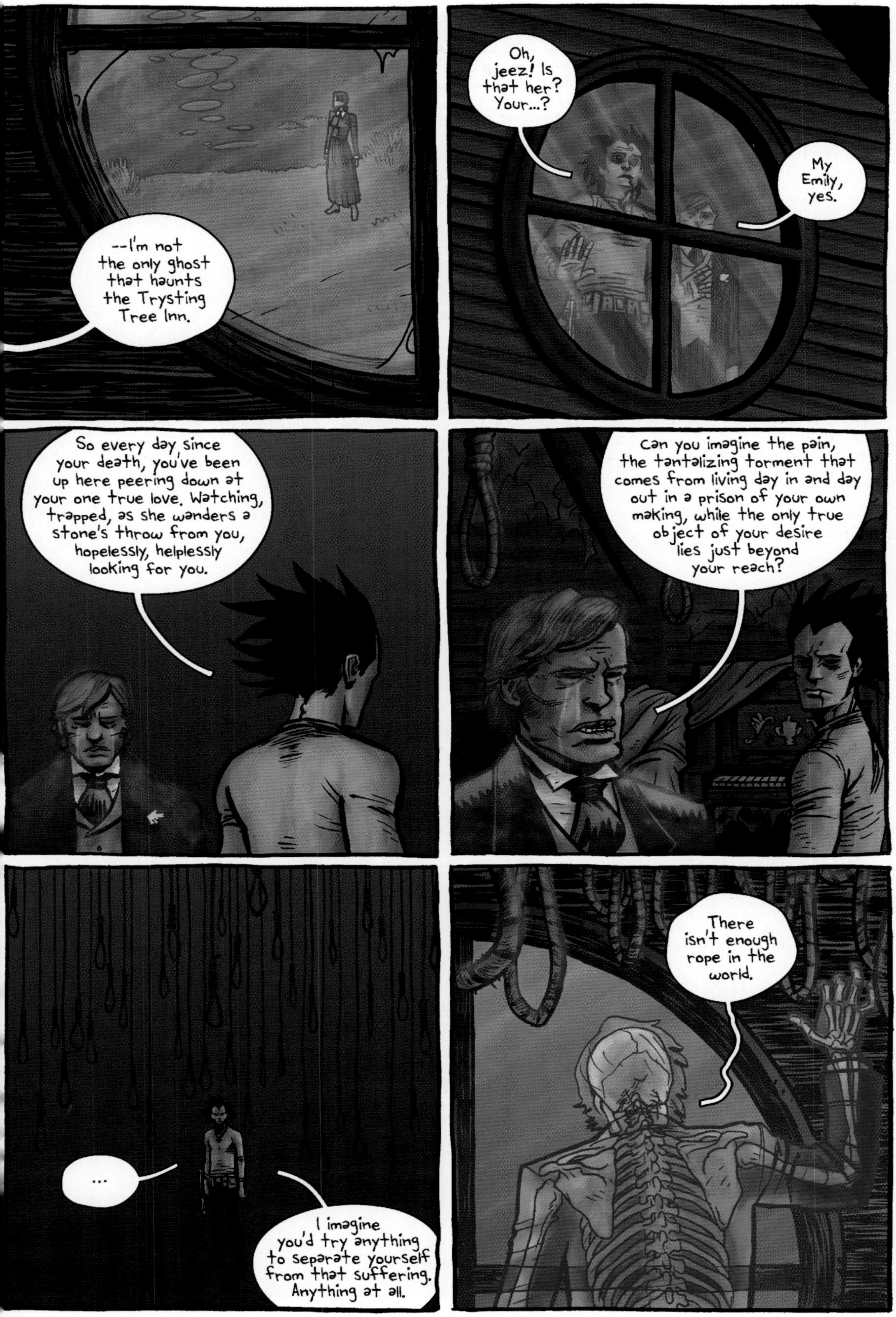
--I'm not the only ghost that haunts the Trysting Tree Inn.
Oh, jeez! Is that her? Your...?
My Emily, yes.
So every day since your death, you've been up here peering down at your one true love. Watching, trapped, as she wanders a stone's throw from you, hopelessly, helplessly looking for you.
Can you imagine the pain, the tantalizing torment that comes from living day in and day out in a prison of your own making, while the only true object of your desire lies just beyond your reach?
...
I imagine you'd try anything to separate yourself from that suffering. Anything at all.
There isn't enough rope in the world.

I... I came up here not expecting to do anything. I thought we might chat, maybe play a duet on the piano... I'm not really prepared. I didn't bring...

You brought your sword.

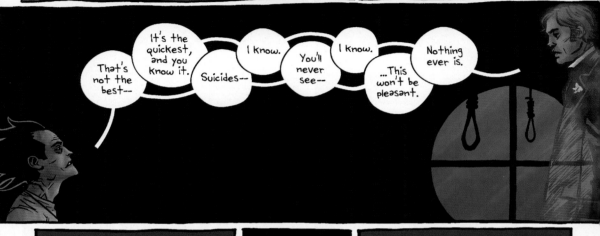

That's not the best--

It's the quickest, and you know it.

Suicides--

I know.

You'll never see--

I know.

...This won't be pleasant.

Nothing ever is.

tnk
tnk

78

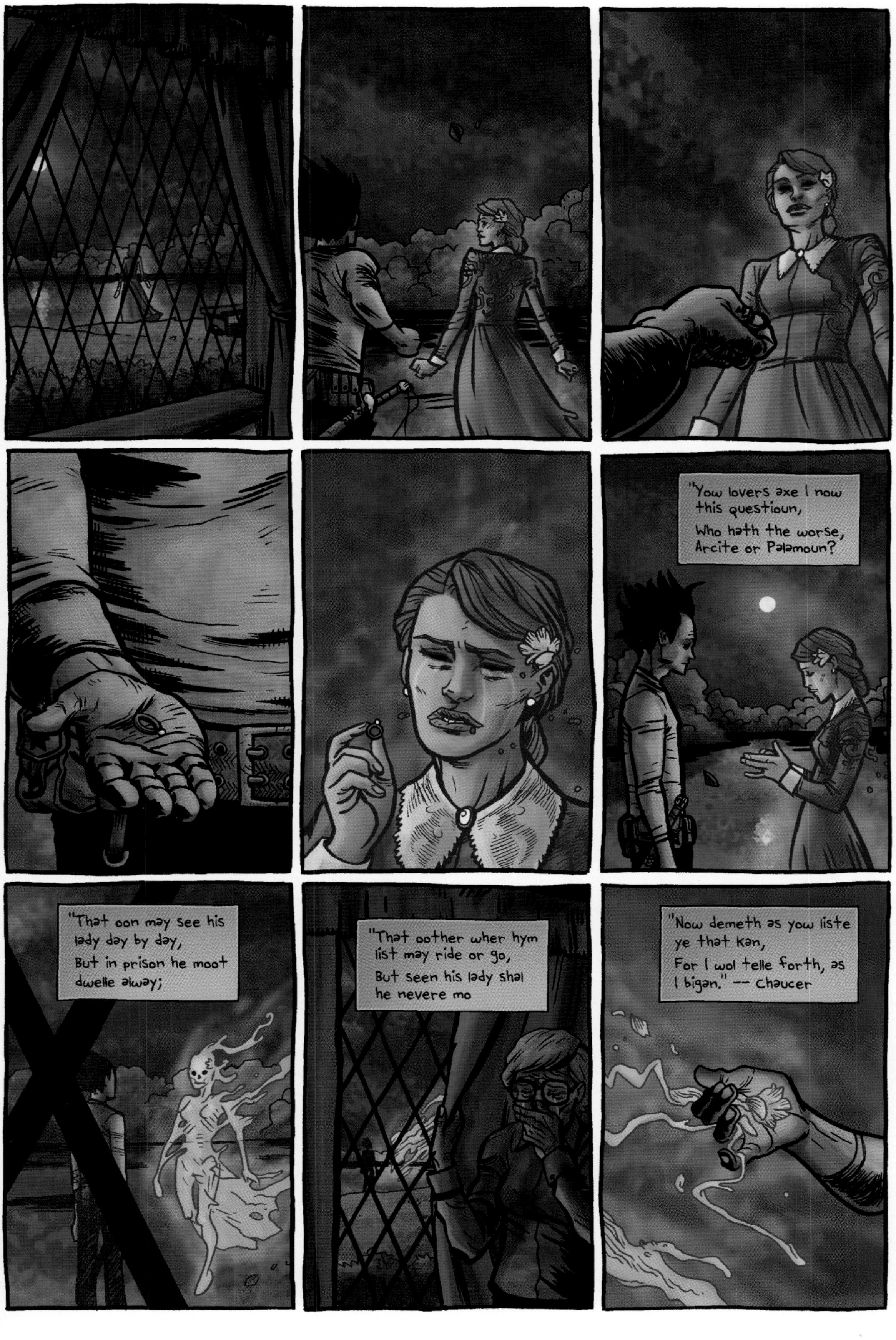
"Yow lovers axe I now this questioun,
Who hath the worse, Arcite or Palamoun?
"That oon may see his lady day by day,
But in prison he moot dwelle alway;
"That oother wher hym list may ride or go,
But seen his lady shal he nevere mo
"Now demeth as yow liste ye that kan,
For I wol telle forth, as I bigan." -- Chaucer

End.

Nate♡07

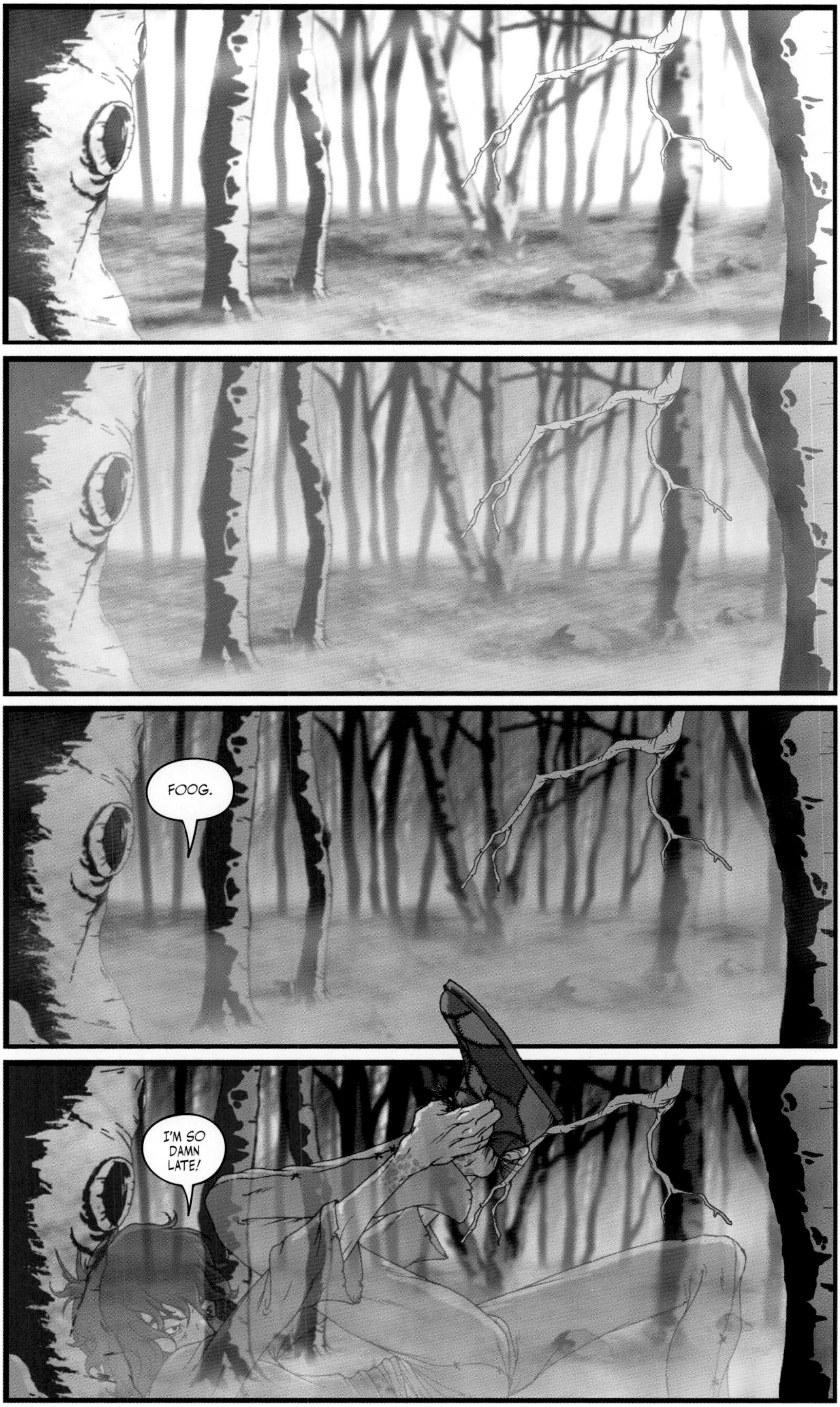
FOOG.
I'M SO DAMN LATE!

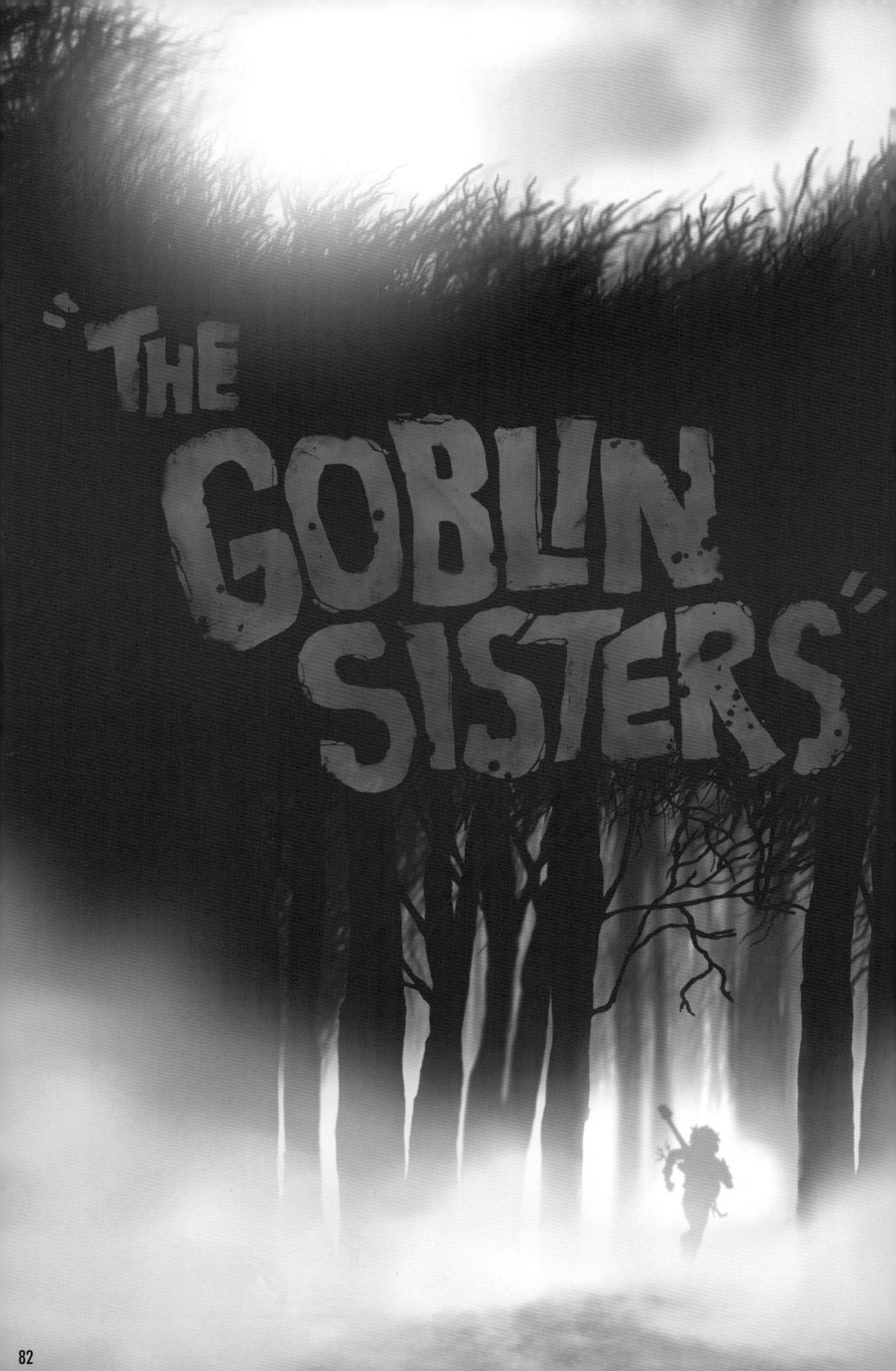
"THE GOBLIN SISTERS"

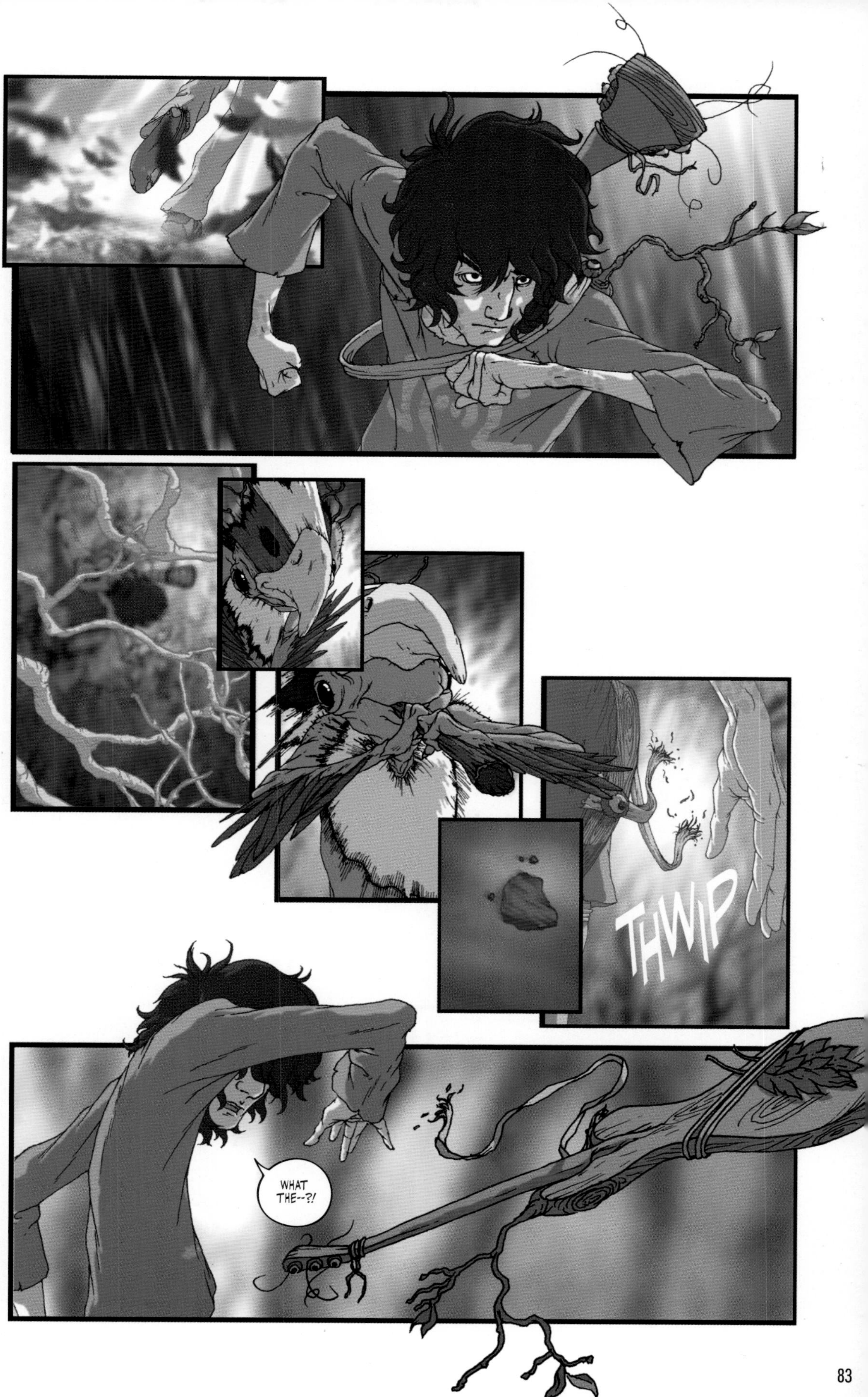
THWIP
WHAT THE--?!

WAKEY BREAKY!

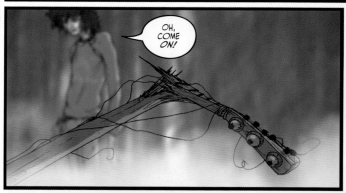

OH, COME ON!

I'M GONNA FEED YOU IMPS TO THE GOBLIN SIST--

ERR...

WHATEVER.

84

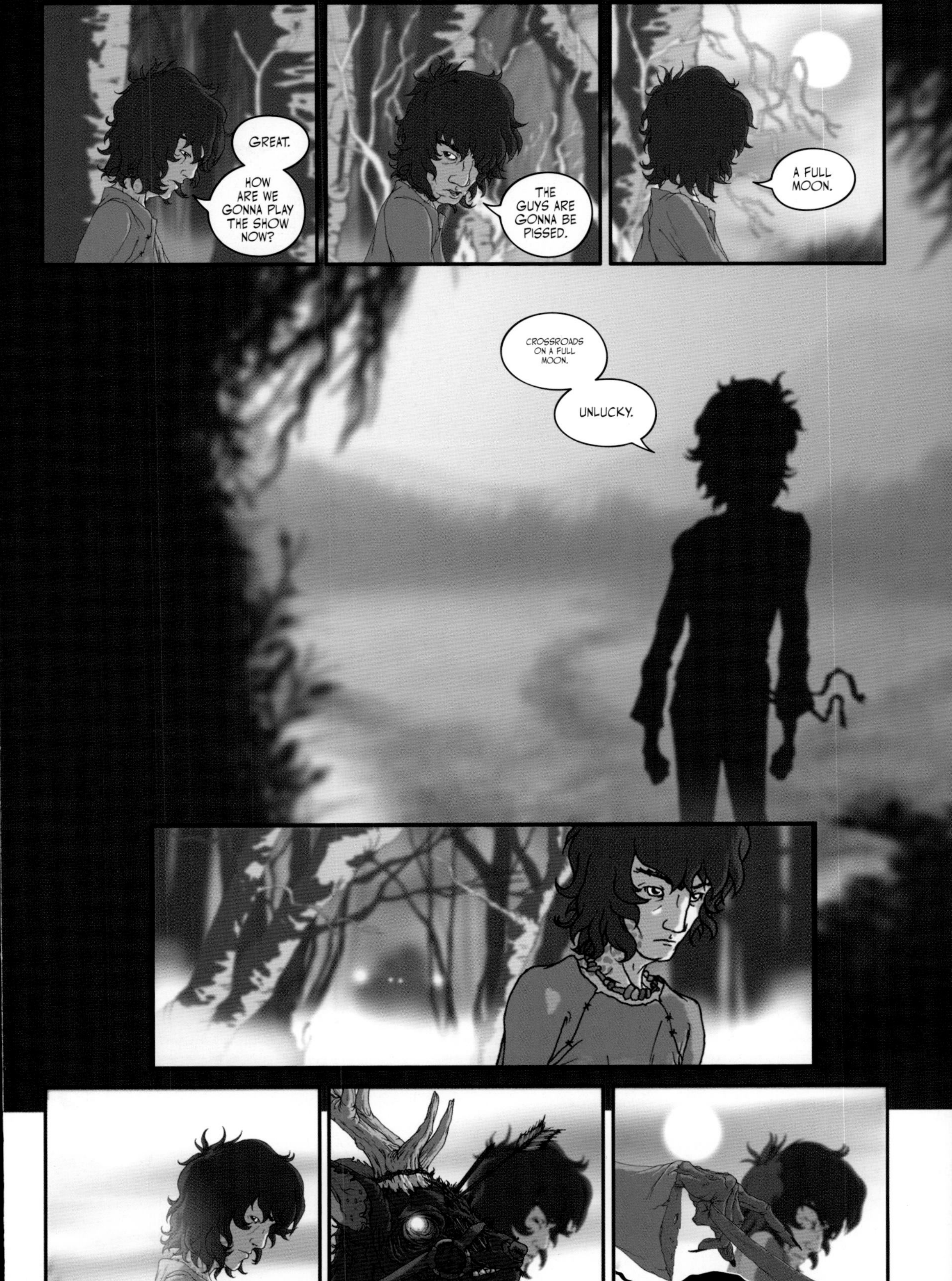
GREAT.
HOW ARE WE GONNA PLAY THE SHOW NOW?
THE GUYS ARE GONNA BE PISSED.
A FULL MOON.
CROSSROADS ON A FULL MOON.
UNLUCKY.
ME EARS IS BURNIN', CHILD...

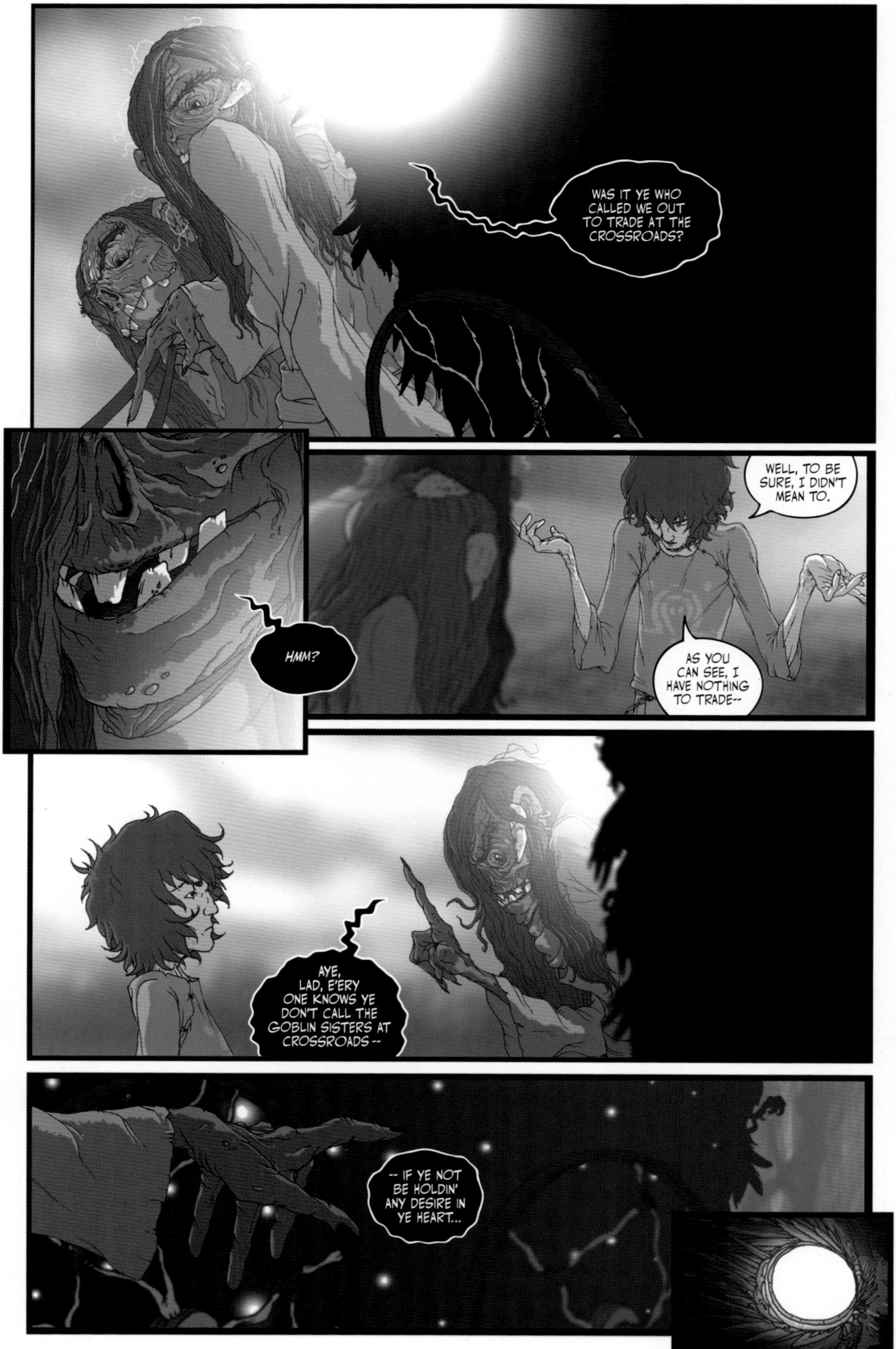
WAS IT YE WHO CALLED WE OUT TO TRADE AT THE CROSSROADS?
HMM?
WELL, TO BE SURE, I DIDN'T MEAN TO.
AS YOU CAN SEE, I HAVE NOTHING TO TRADE--
AYE, LAD, E'ERY ONE KNOWS YE DON'T CALL THE GOBLIN SISTERS AT CROSSROADS--
-- IF YE NOT BE HOLDIN' ANY DESIRE IN YE HEART...

THE 'ELL?

AND WHAT WOULD YE GIVE FOR THIS TRINKET?

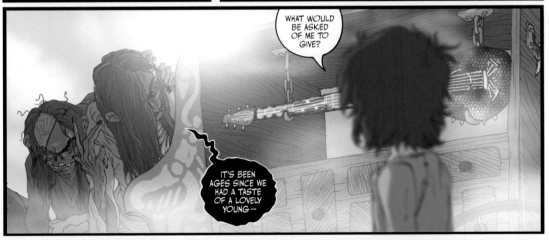

WHAT WOULD BE ASKED OF ME TO GIVE?

IT'S BEEN AGES SINCE WE HAD A TASTE OF A LOVELY YOUNG --

WE WANT THEM SHOES!

GIT! THE SHOES?! WE WANTS THE HEART!

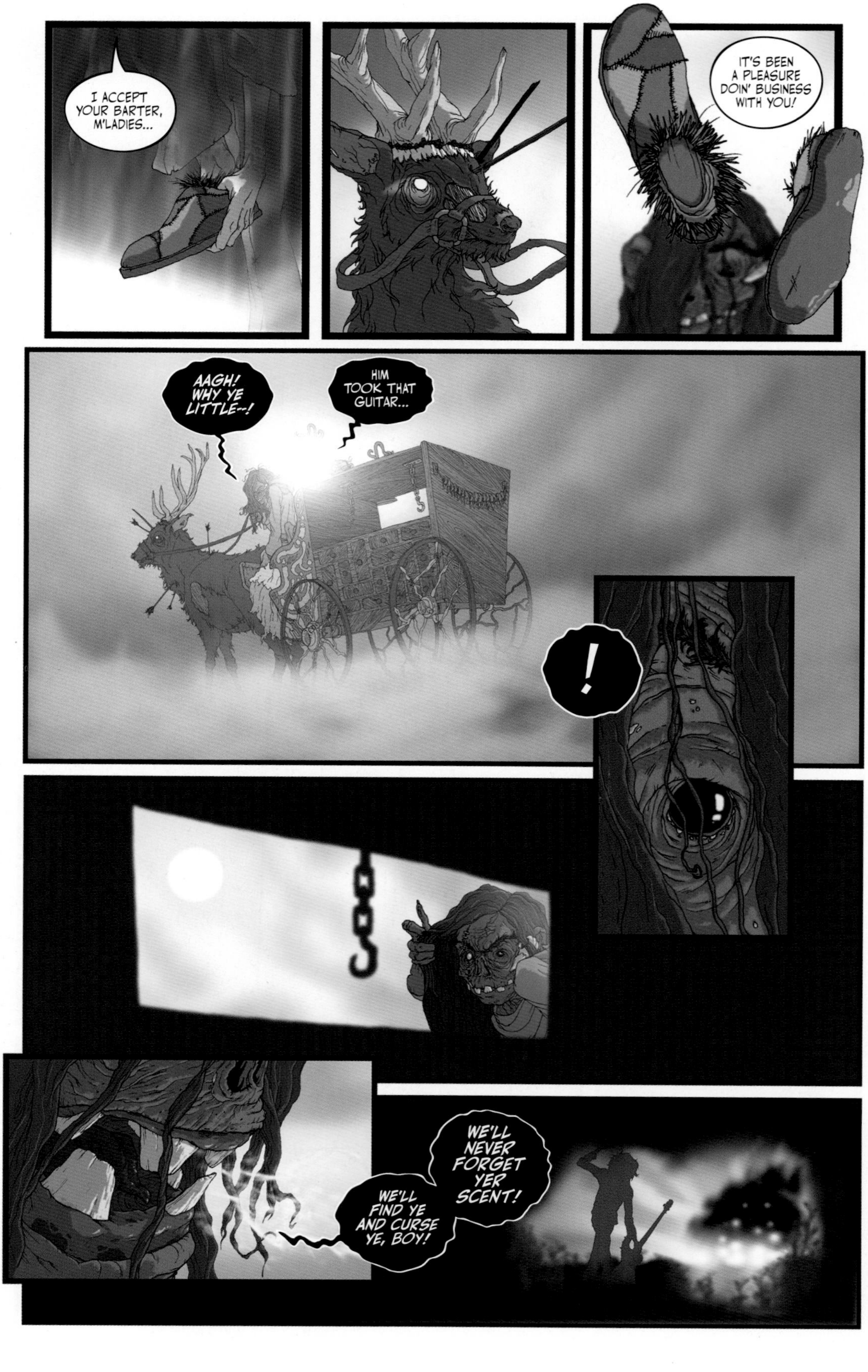
I ACCEPT YOUR BARTER, M'LADIES...
IT'S BEEN A PLEASURE DOIN' BUSINESS WITH YOU!
AAGH! WHY YE LITTLE--!
HIM TOOK THAT GUITAR...
!
WE'LL NEVER FORGET YER SCENT!
WE'LL FIND YE AND CURSE YE, BOY!

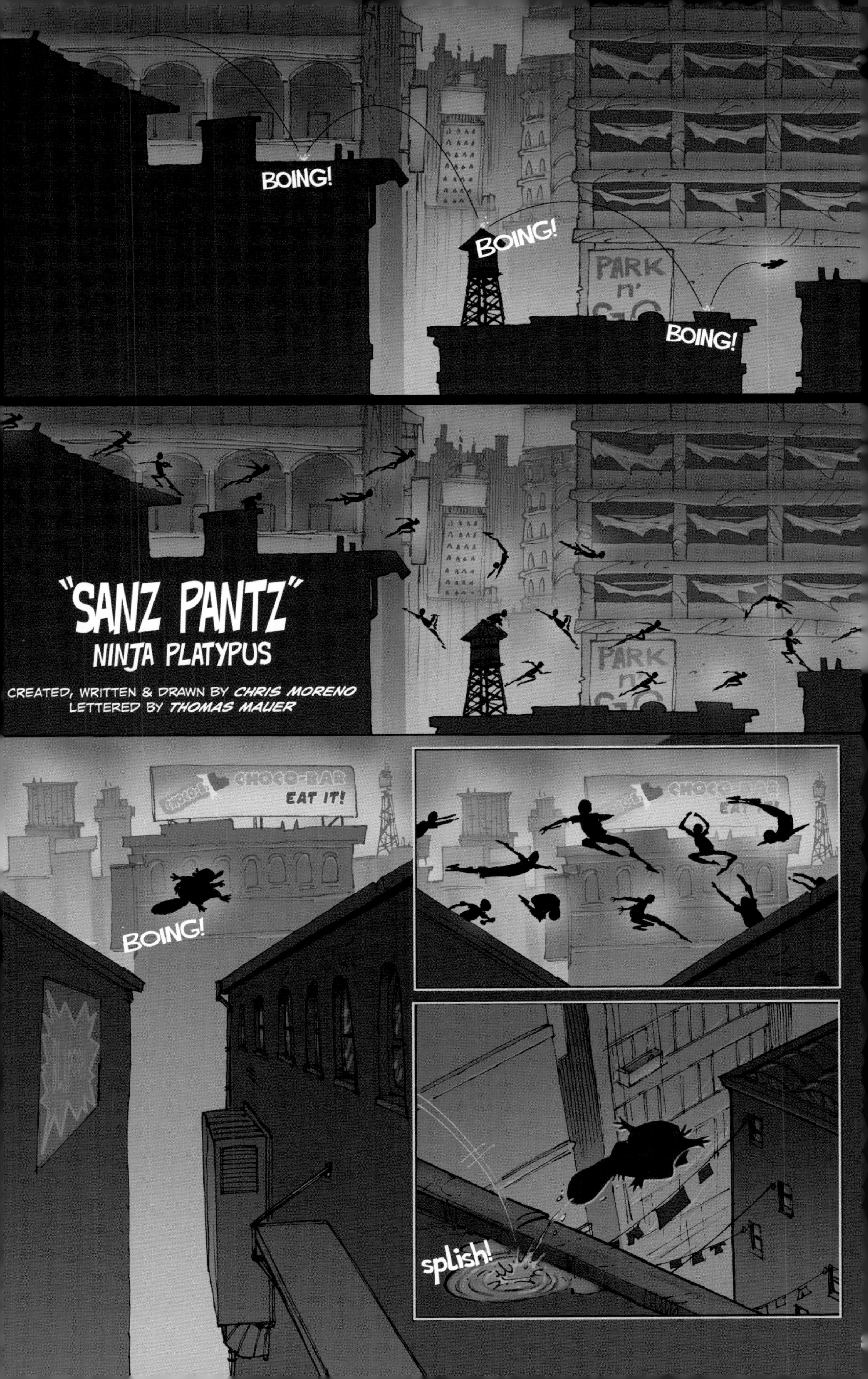
BOING!
BOING!
BOING!
"SANZ PANTZ"
NINJA PLATYPUS
CREATED, WRITTEN & DRAWN BY CHRIS MORENO
LETTERED BY THOMAS MAUER
CHOCO-BAR
EAT IT!
BOING!
splish!

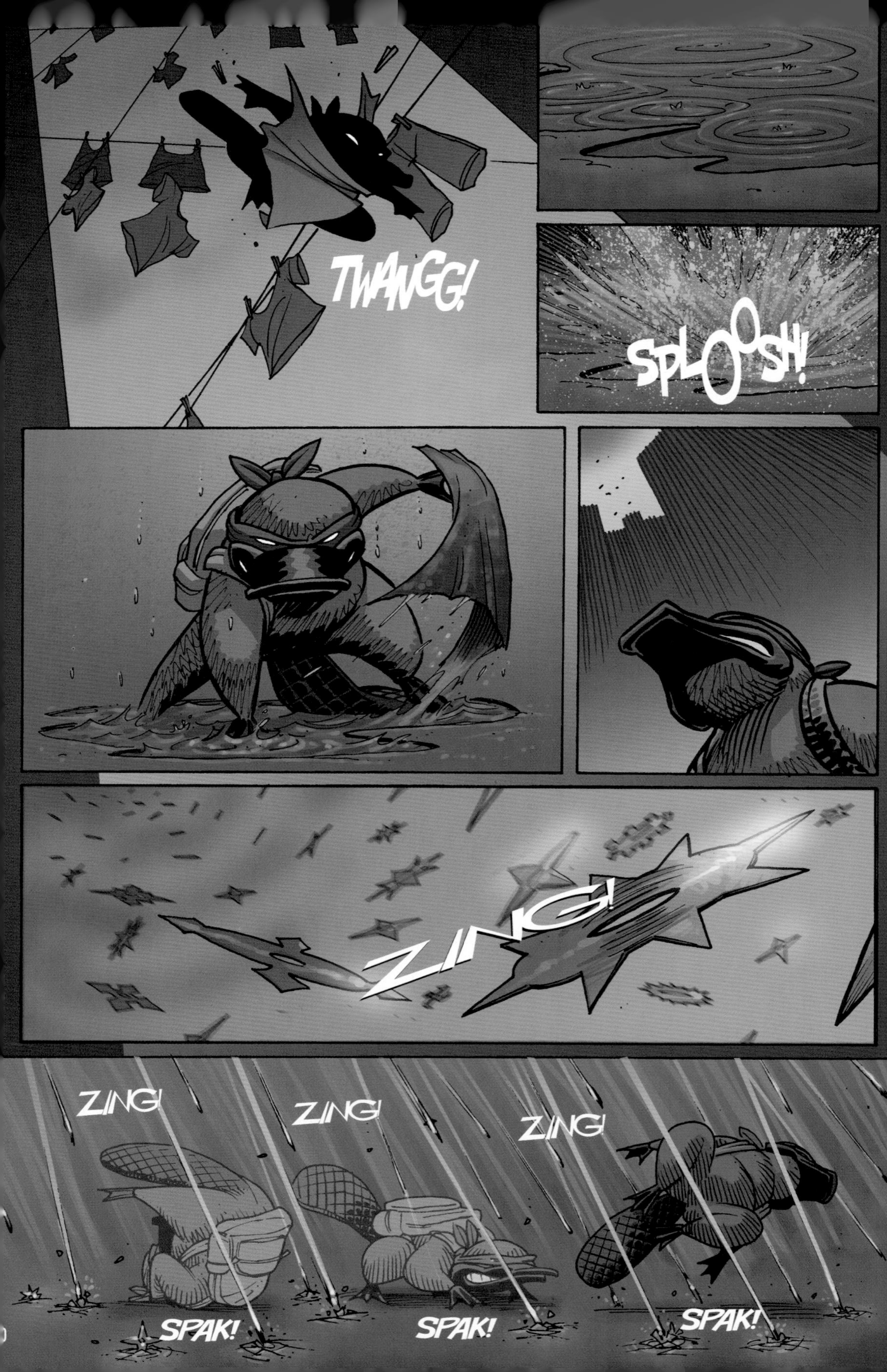
TWANGG!
SPLOOSH!
ZING!
ZING!
ZING!
ZING!
SPAK!
SPAK!
SPAK!

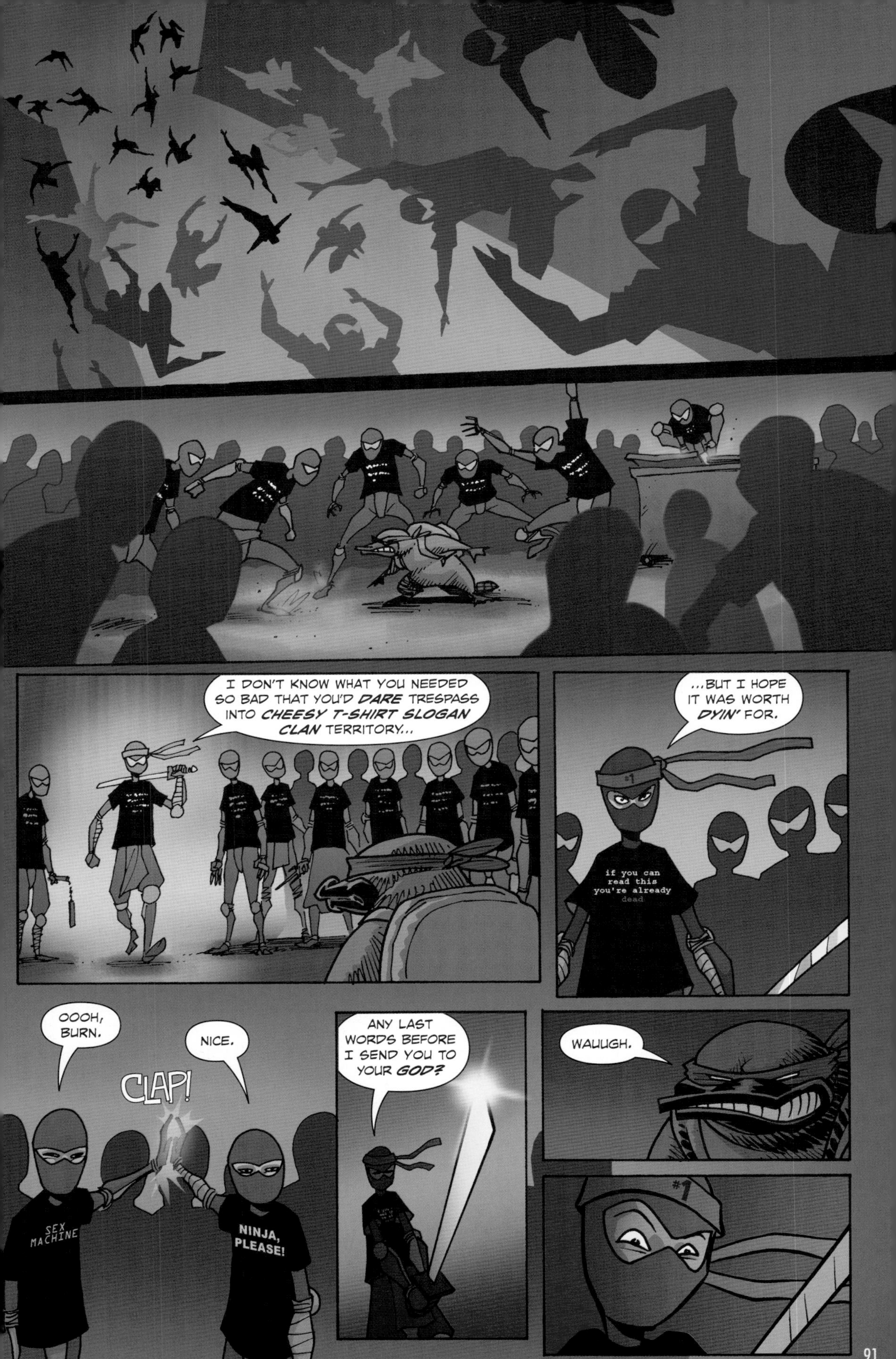
I DON'T KNOW WHAT YOU NEEDED SO BAD THAT YOU'D *DARE* TRESPASS INTO *CHEESY T-SHIRT SLOGAN CLAN* TERRITORY...
...BUT I HOPE IT WAS WORTH *DYIN'* FOR.
#1
if you can read this you're already dead
OOOH, BURN.
NICE.
CLAP!
SEX MACHINE
NINJA, PLEASE!
ANY LAST WORDS BEFORE I SEND YOU TO YOUR *GOD?*
WAUUGH.
#1

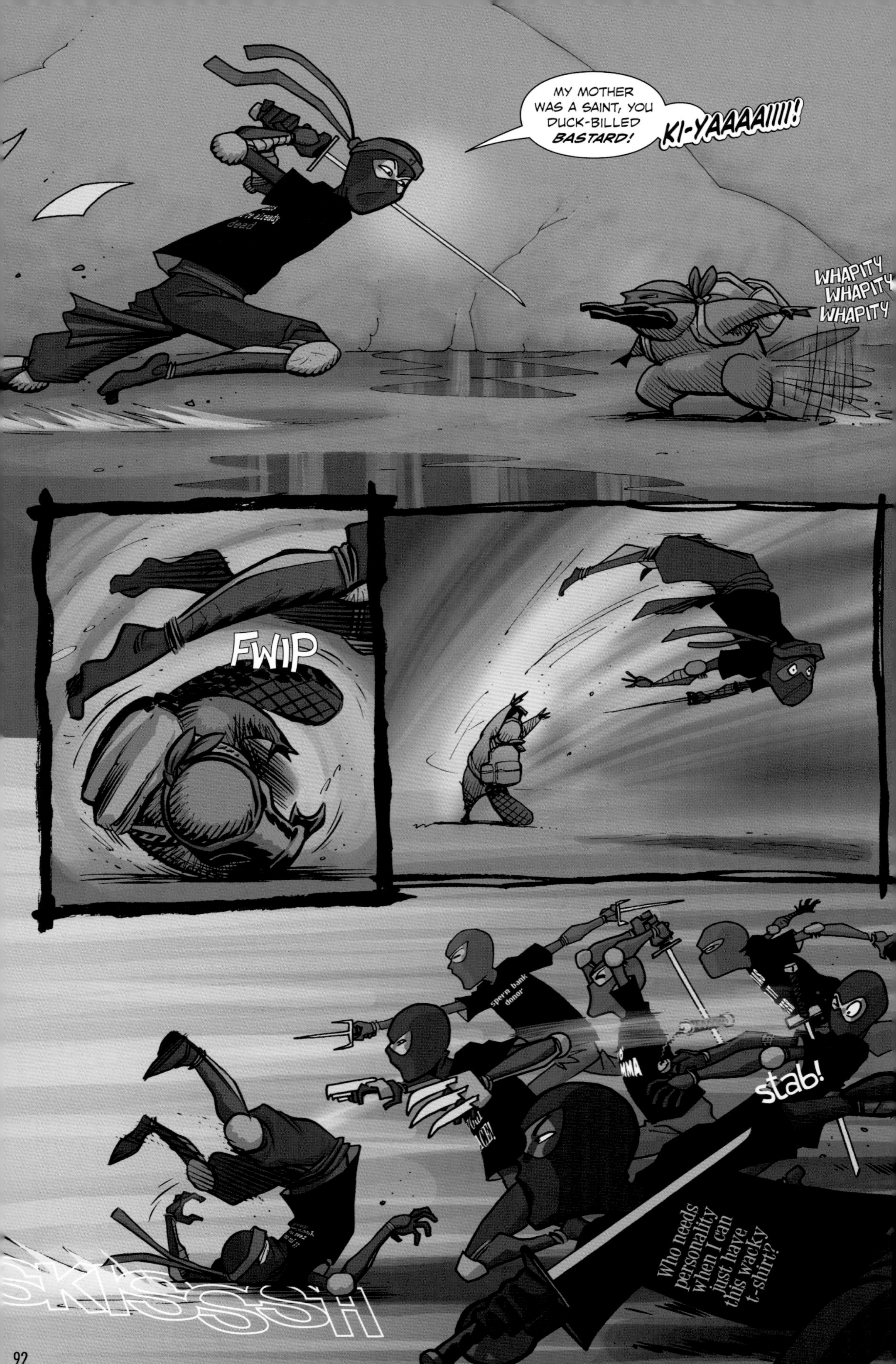
MY MOTHER WAS A SAINT, YOU DUCK-BILLED BASTARD!
KI-YAAAAIIIII!
WHAPITY WHAPITY WHAPITY
FWIP
sperm bank donor
stab!
Who needs personality when I can just have this wacky t-shirt?
SKISSSH

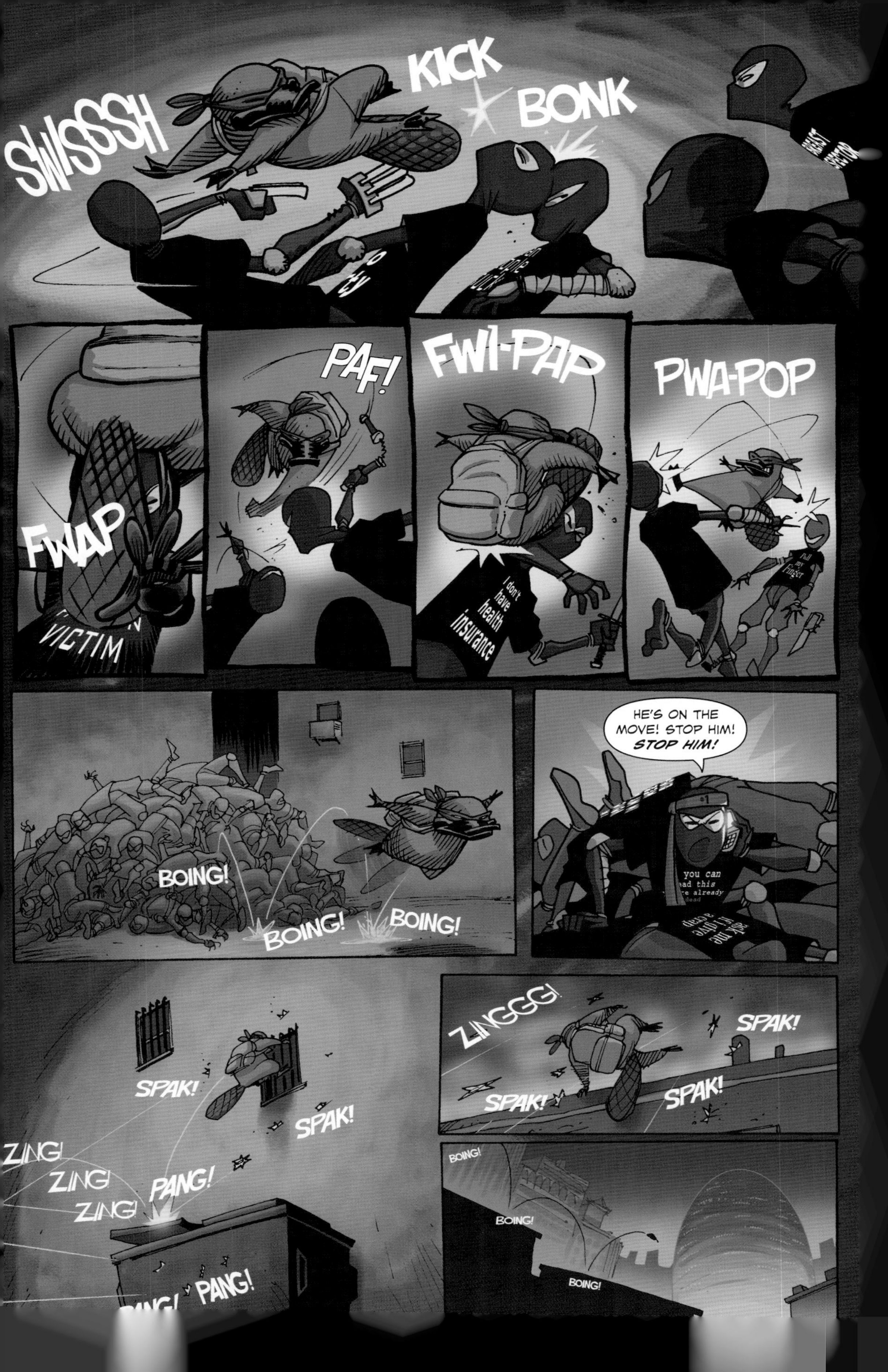
SWISSSH
KICK
BONK
FWAP
VICTIM
PAF!
FWI-PAP
I don't have health insurance
PWA-POP
BOING!
BOING!
BOING!
HE'S ON THE MOVE! STOP HIM! STOP HIM!
SPAK!
SPAK!
ZINGGG!
SPAK!
SPAK!
SPAK!
ZING!
ZING!
ZING!
PANG!
PANG!
BOING!
BOING!
BOING!

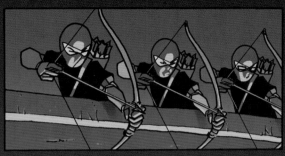

BEWN!

BEWN!
WHIF!
SPAK!
WHIF!
SPAK!
WHIF!
BEWN!
SPAK!

KSSSH

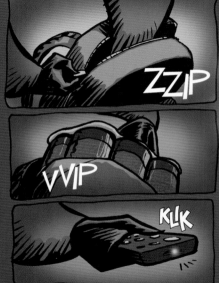
ZZIP
VVIP
KLIK

glug! glug!

WE'LL GET RIGHT BACK TO OUR *SHO KOSUGI NINJA MOVIE MARATHON* RIGHT AFTER THIS MESSAGE FROM *BANZAI BREW*--THE BEER WORTH *DYING* FOR!

BURRRRP!

END

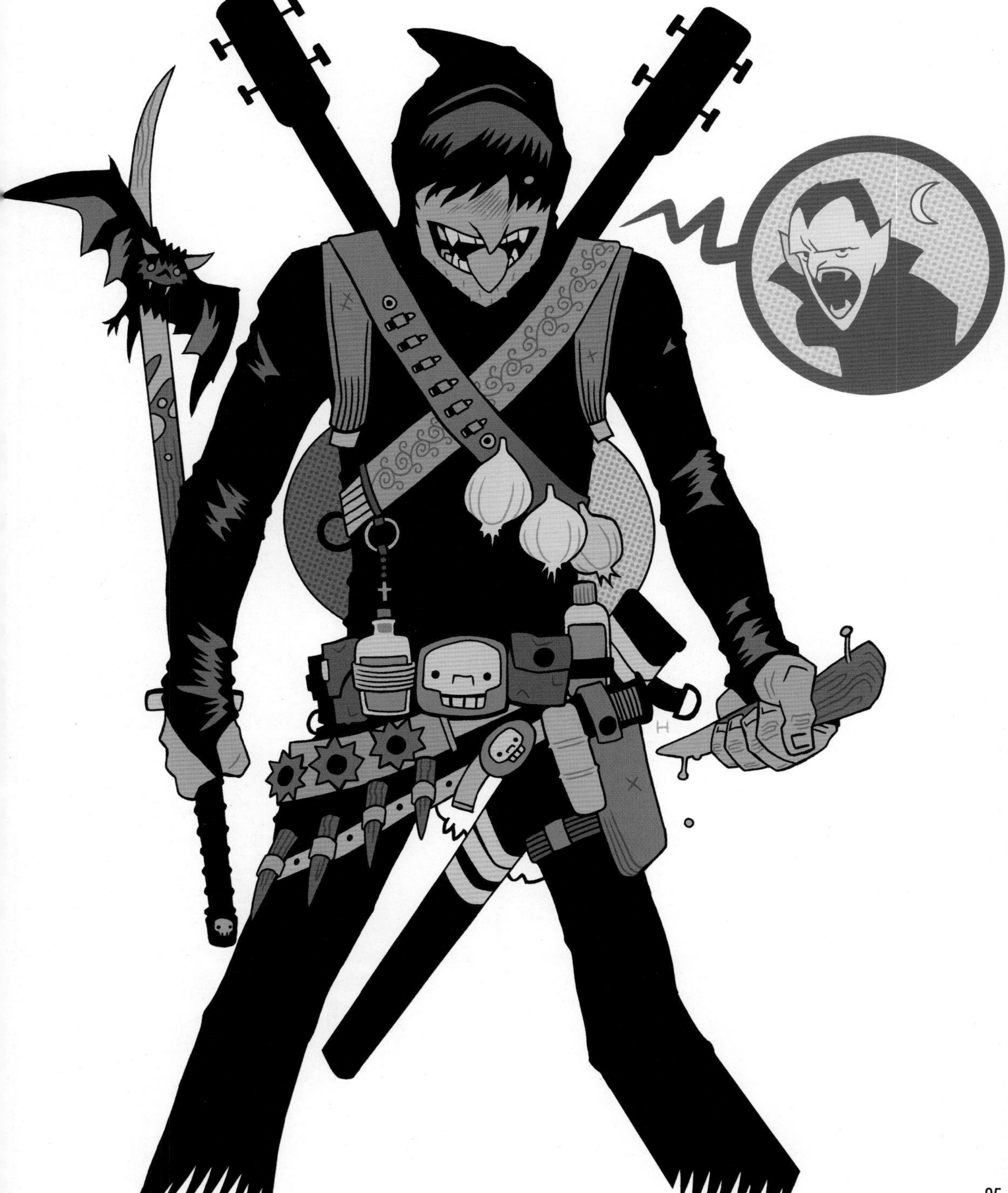

Smith & Hipp's THE AMAZING JOY BUZZARDS starring in THE FEARLESS VAMPIRE HUNTERS or (EXCUSE ME, BUT YOUR STAKE IS IN MY HEART).

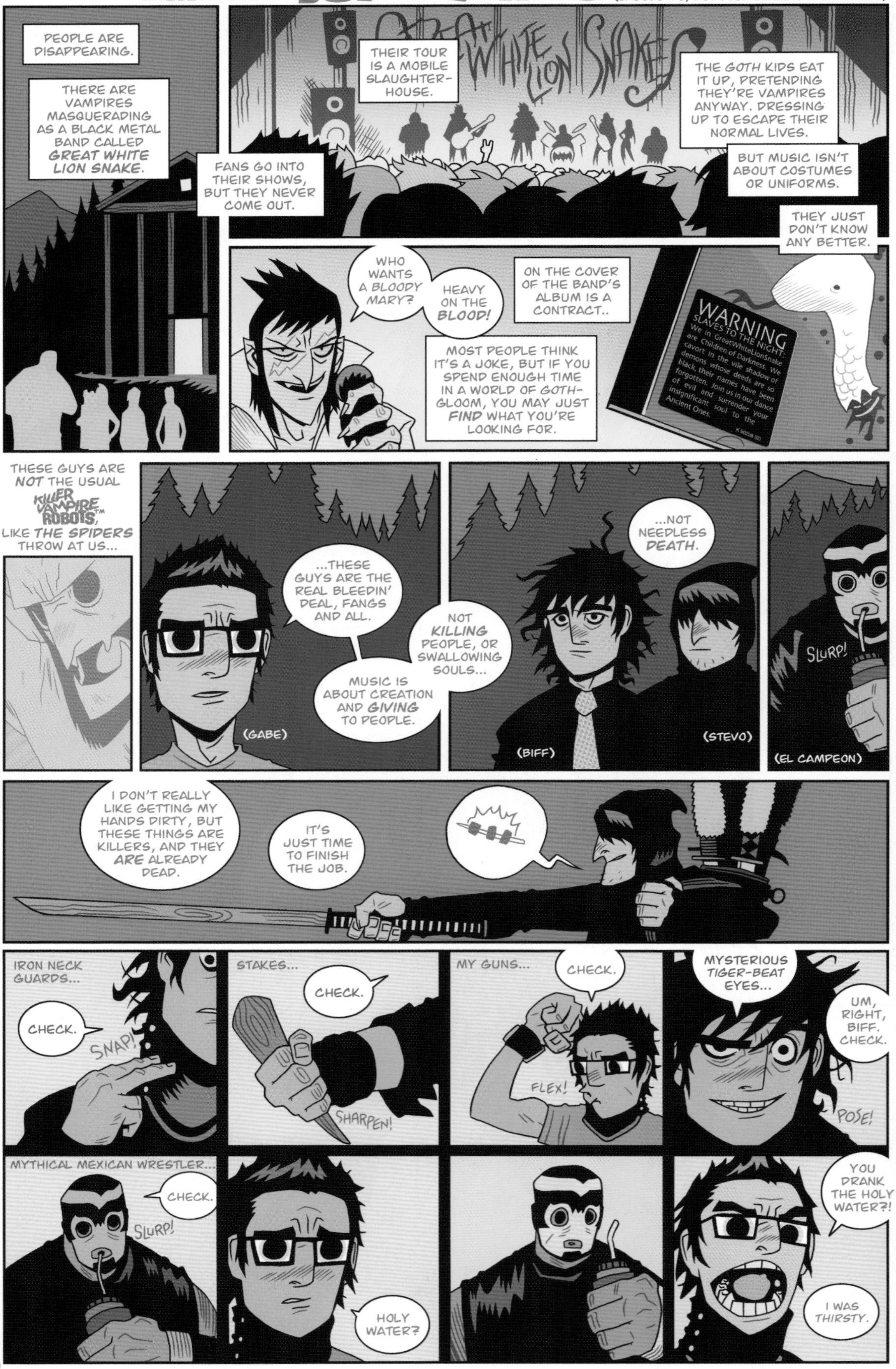

PEOPLE ARE DISAPPEARING.
THERE ARE VAMPIRES MASQUERADING AS A BLACK METAL BAND CALLED GREAT WHITE LION SNAKE.
FANS GO INTO THEIR SHOWS, BUT THEY NEVER COME OUT.
THEIR TOUR IS A MOBILE SLAUGHTER-HOUSE.
GREAT WHITE LION SNAKE
THE GOTH KIDS EAT IT UP, PRETENDING THEY'RE VAMPIRES ANYWAY. DRESSING UP TO ESCAPE THEIR NORMAL LIVES.
BUT MUSIC ISN'T ABOUT COSTUMES OR UNIFORMS.
THEY JUST DON'T KNOW ANY BETTER.
WHO WANTS A BLOODY MARY?
HEAVY ON THE BLOOD!
ON THE COVER OF THE BAND'S ALBUM IS A CONTRACT..
MOST PEOPLE THINK IT'S A JOKE, BUT IF YOU SPEND ENOUGH TIME IN A WORLD OF GOTH-GLOOM, YOU MAY JUST FIND WHAT YOU'RE LOOKING FOR.
WARNING
SLAVES TO THE NIGHT:
We in GreatWhiteLionSnake are Children of Darkness. We cavort in the vile shadow of demons whose deeds are so black, their names have been forgotten. Join us in our dance of evil and surrender your insignificant soul to the Ancient Ones.
THESE GUYS ARE NOT THE USUAL KILLER VAMPIRE ROBOTS™ LIKE THE SPIDERS THROW AT US...
...THESE GUYS ARE THE REAL BLEEDIN' DEAL, FANGS AND ALL.
MUSIC IS ABOUT CREATION AND GIVING TO PEOPLE.
(GABE)
NOT KILLING PEOPLE, OR SWALLOWING SOULS...
...NOT NEEDLESS DEATH.
(BIFF)
(STEVO)
SLURP!
(EL CAMPEON)
I DON'T REALLY LIKE GETTING MY HANDS DIRTY, BUT THESE THINGS ARE KILLERS, AND THEY ARE ALREADY DEAD.
IT'S JUST TIME TO FINISH THE JOB.
IRON NECK GUARDS...
CHECK.
SNAP!
STAKES...
CHECK.
SHARPEN!
MY GUNS...
CHECK.
FLEX!
MYSTERIOUS TIGER-BEAT EYES...
UM, RIGHT, BIFF. CHECK.
POSE!
MYTHICAL MEXICAN WRESTLER...
CHECK.
SLURP!
HOLY WATER?
YOU DRANK THE HOLY WATER?!
I WAS THIRSTY.

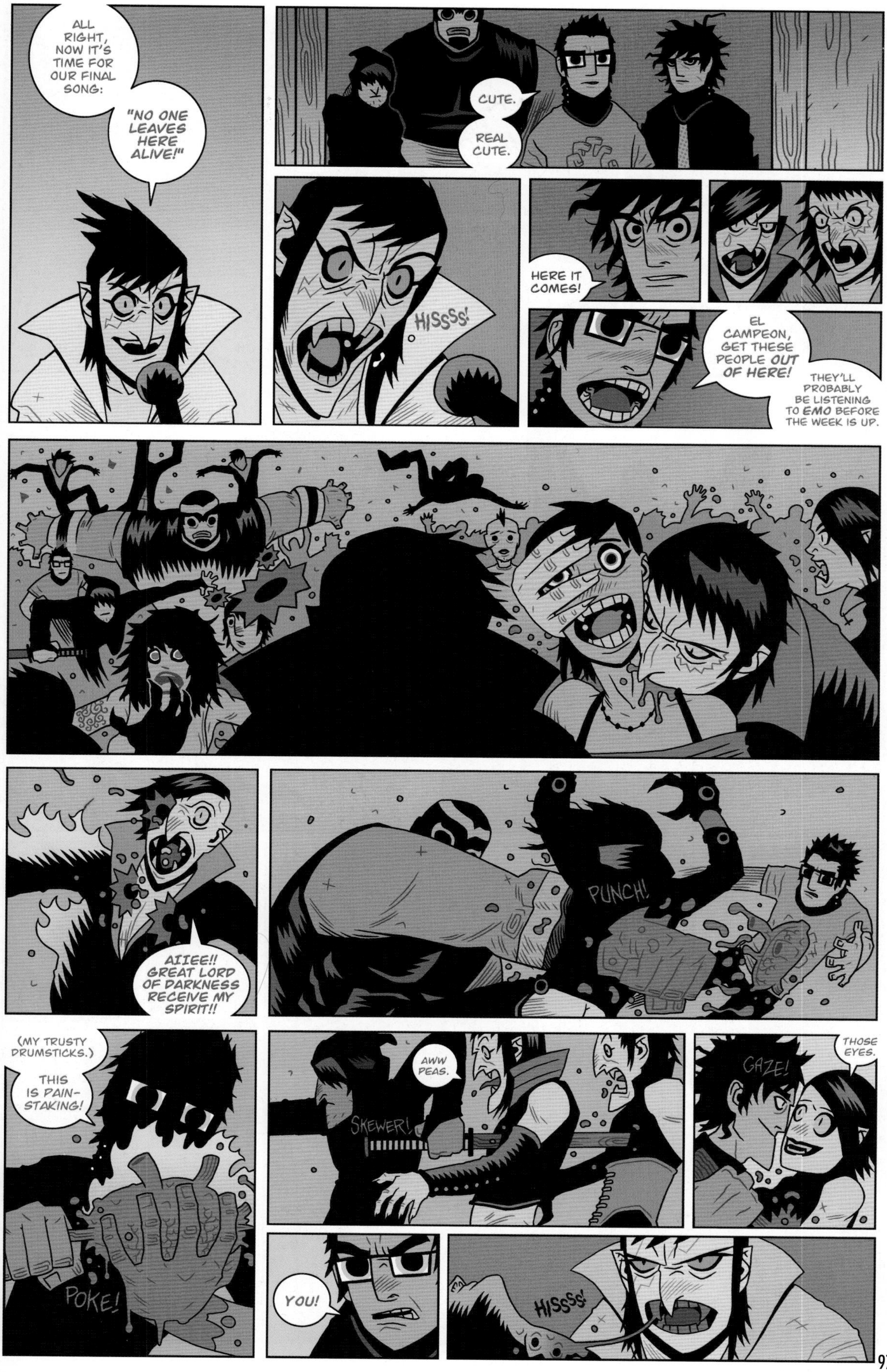
ALL RIGHT, NOW IT'S TIME FOR OUR FINAL SONG:
"NO ONE LEAVES HERE ALIVE!"
CUTE.
REAL CUTE.
HISSSS!
HERE IT COMES!
EL CAMPEON, GET THESE PEOPLE OUT OF HERE!
THEY'LL PROBABLY BE LISTENING TO EMO BEFORE THE WEEK IS UP.
AIIEE!! GREAT LORD OF DARKNESS RECEIVE MY SPIRIT!!
PUNCH!
(MY TRUSTY DRUMSTICKS.)
THIS IS PAIN-STAKING!
POKE!
AWW PEAS.
SKEWER!
THOSE EYES.
GAZE!
YOU!
HISSSS!

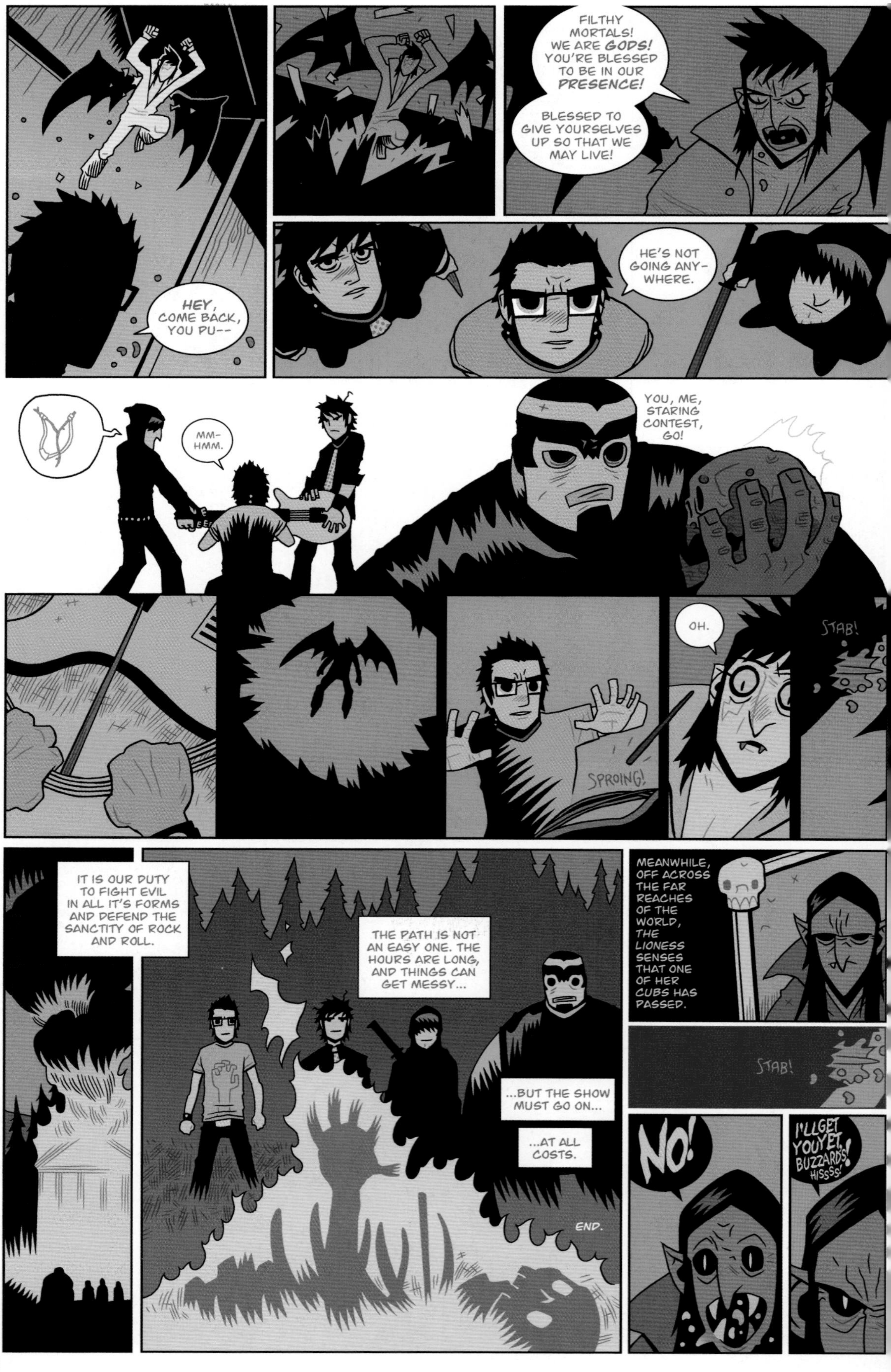

HEY, COME BACK, YOU PU--
FILTHY MORTALS! WE ARE GODS! YOU'RE BLESSED TO BE IN OUR PRESENCE!
BLESSED TO GIVE YOURSELVES UP SO THAT WE MAY LIVE!
HE'S NOT GOING ANYWHERE.
MM-HMM.
YOU, ME, STARING CONTEST, GO!
OH.
SPROING!
STAB!
IT IS OUR DUTY TO FIGHT EVIL IN ALL IT'S FORMS AND DEFEND THE SANCTITY OF ROCK AND ROLL.
THE PATH IS NOT AN EASY ONE. THE HOURS ARE LONG, AND THINGS CAN GET MESSY...
...BUT THE SHOW MUST GO ON...
...AT ALL COSTS.
END.
MEANWHILE, OFF ACROSS THE FAR REACHES OF THE WORLD, THE LIONESS SENSES THAT ONE OF HER CUBS HAS PASSED.
STAB!
NO!
I'LL GET YOU YET, BUZZARDS! HISSSS!

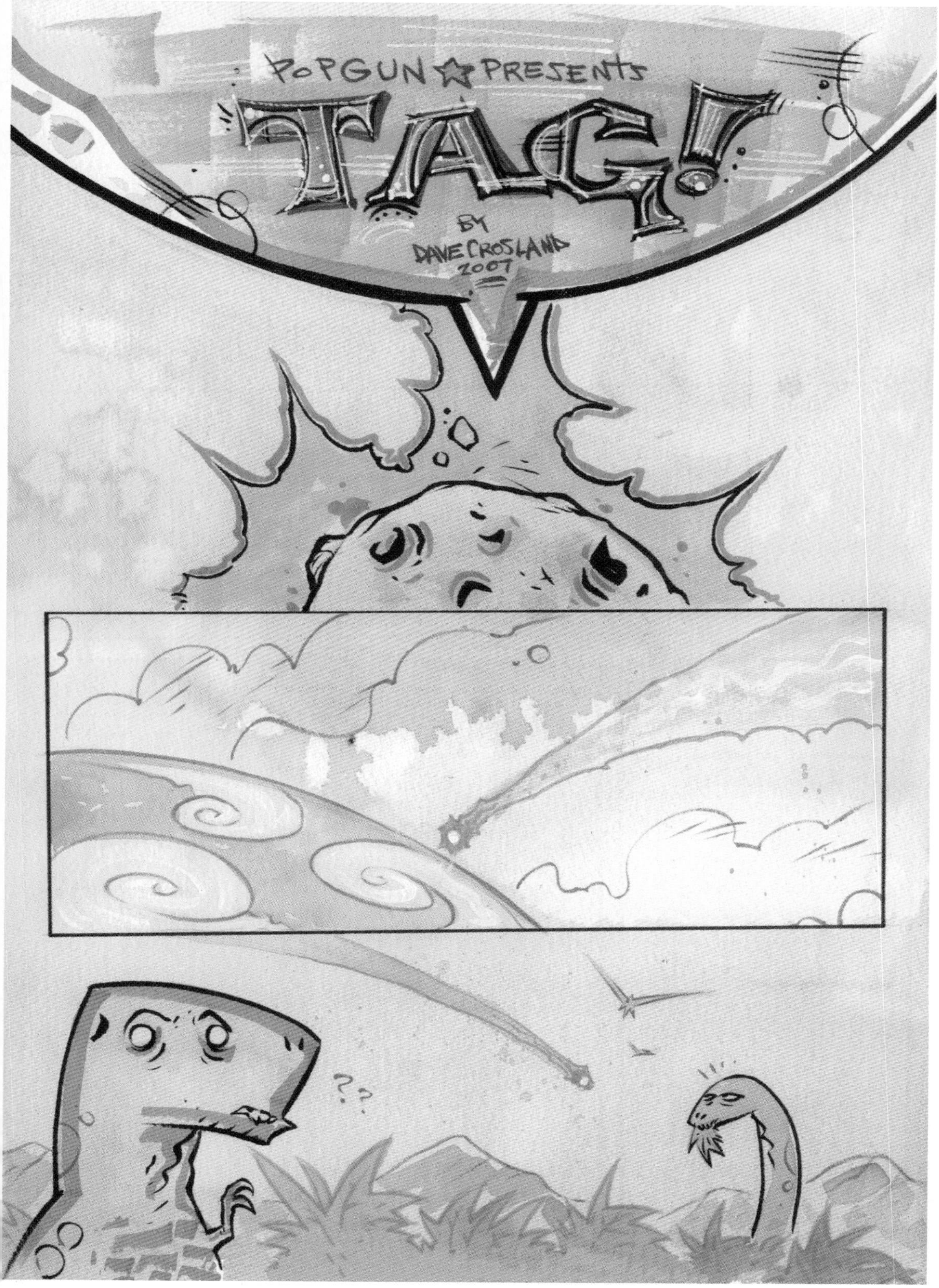
POPGUN PRESENTS
TAG!
BY
DAVE CROSLAND
2007
??

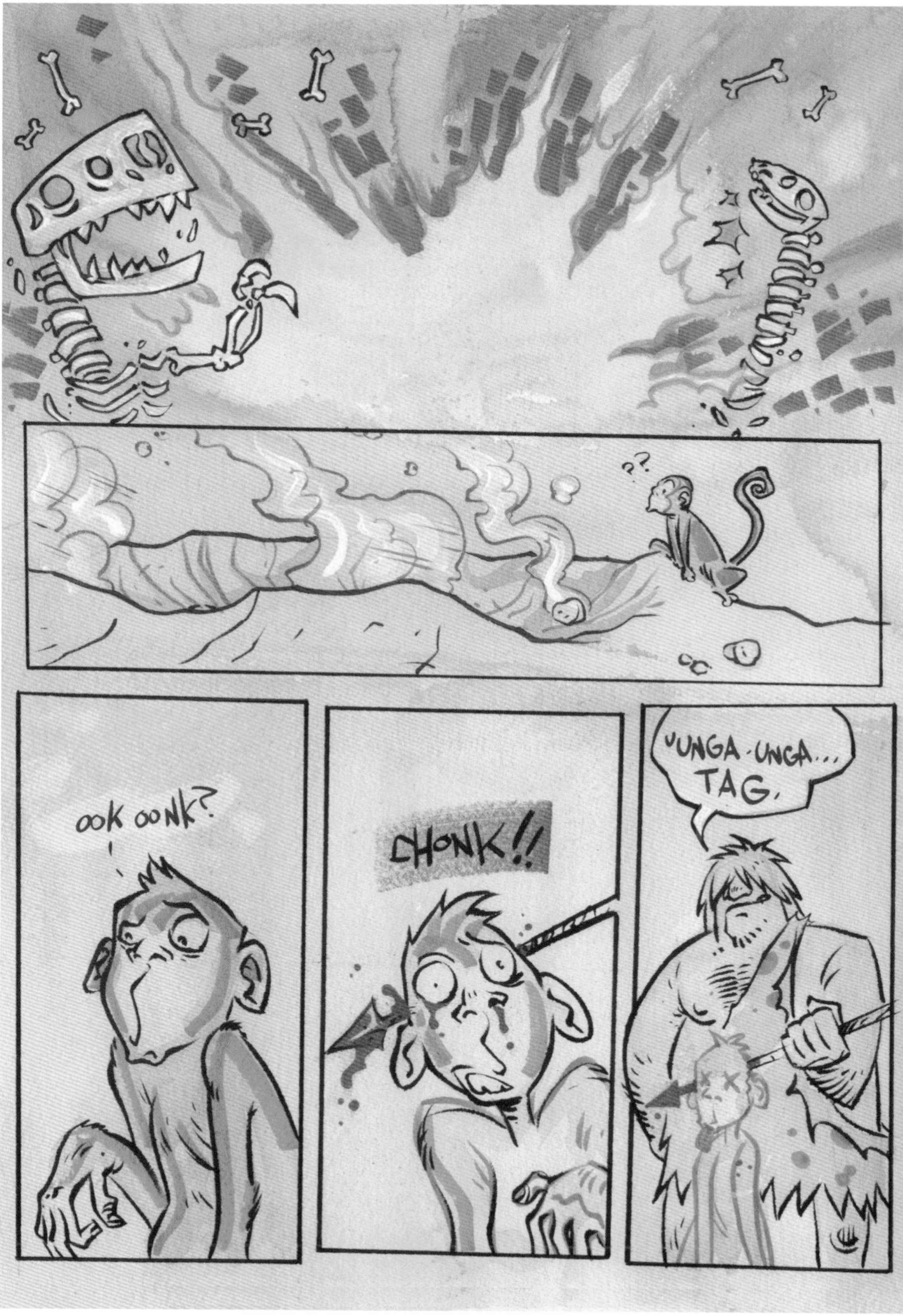
?
OOK OONK?
CHONK!!
UNGA-UNGA...
TAG.

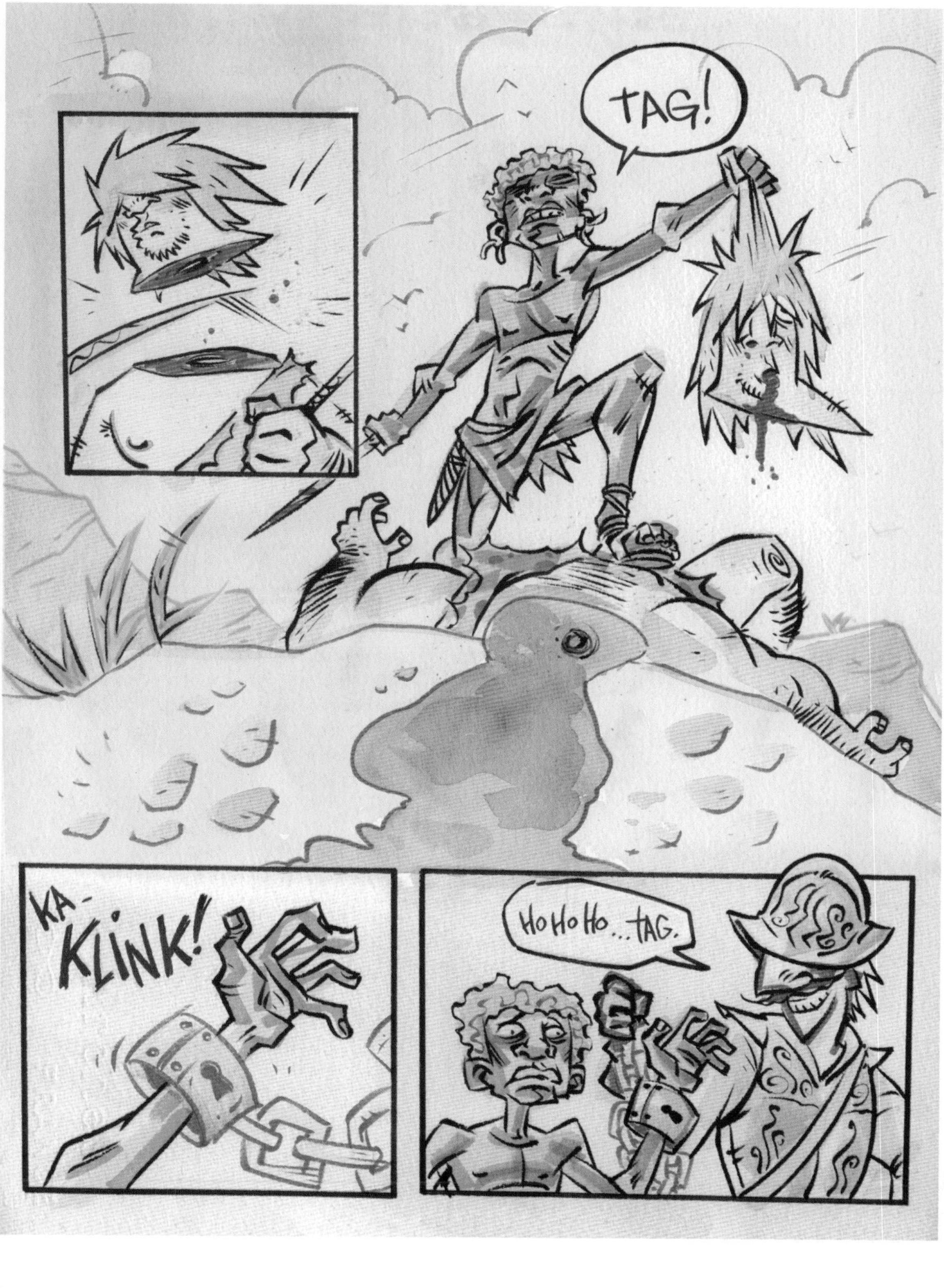
TAG!
KA-
KLINK!
HO HO HO... TAG.

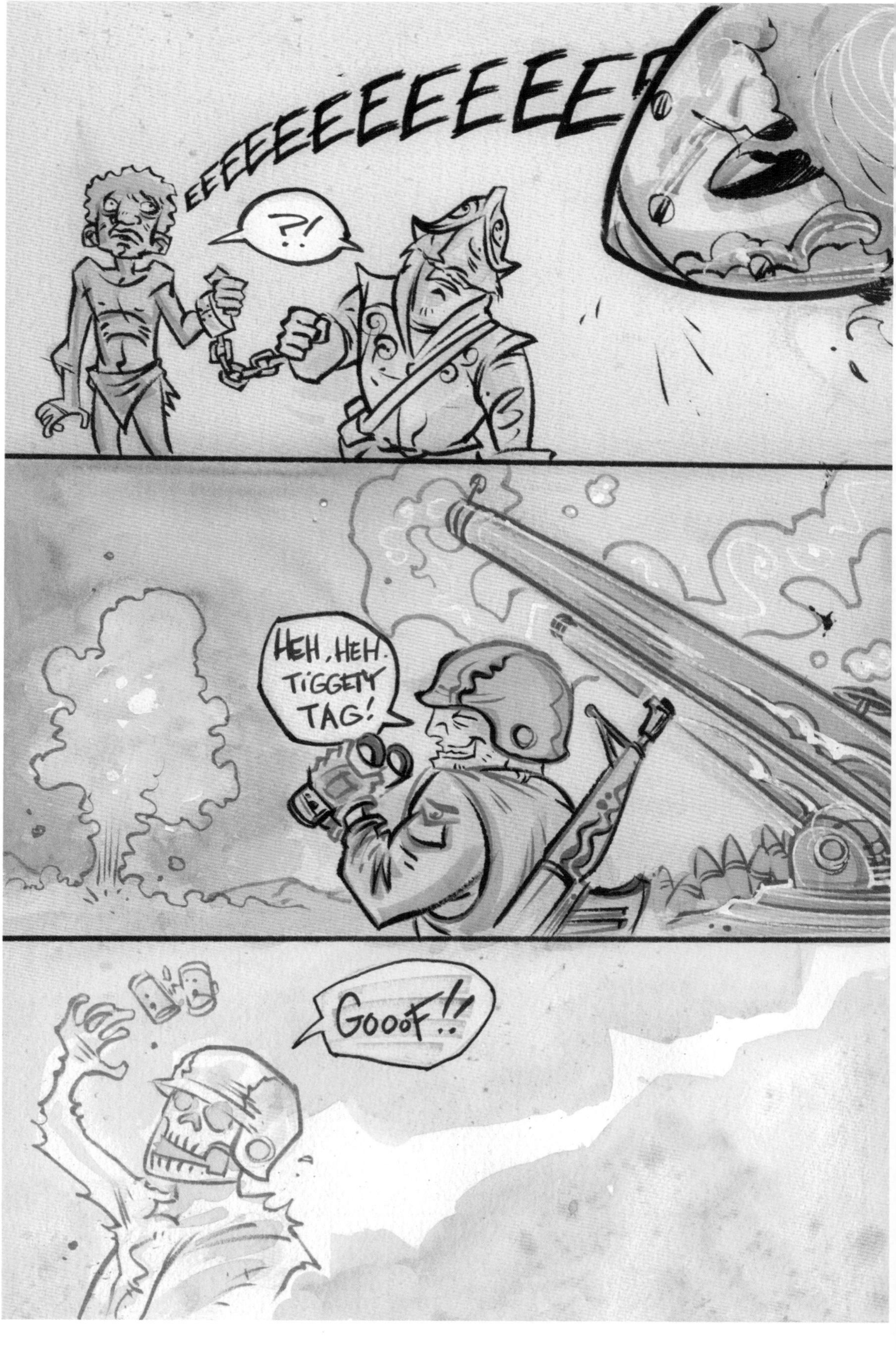
EEEEEEEEEEEEEEE
?!
HEH, HEH. TIGGETY TAG!
GOOOF!!

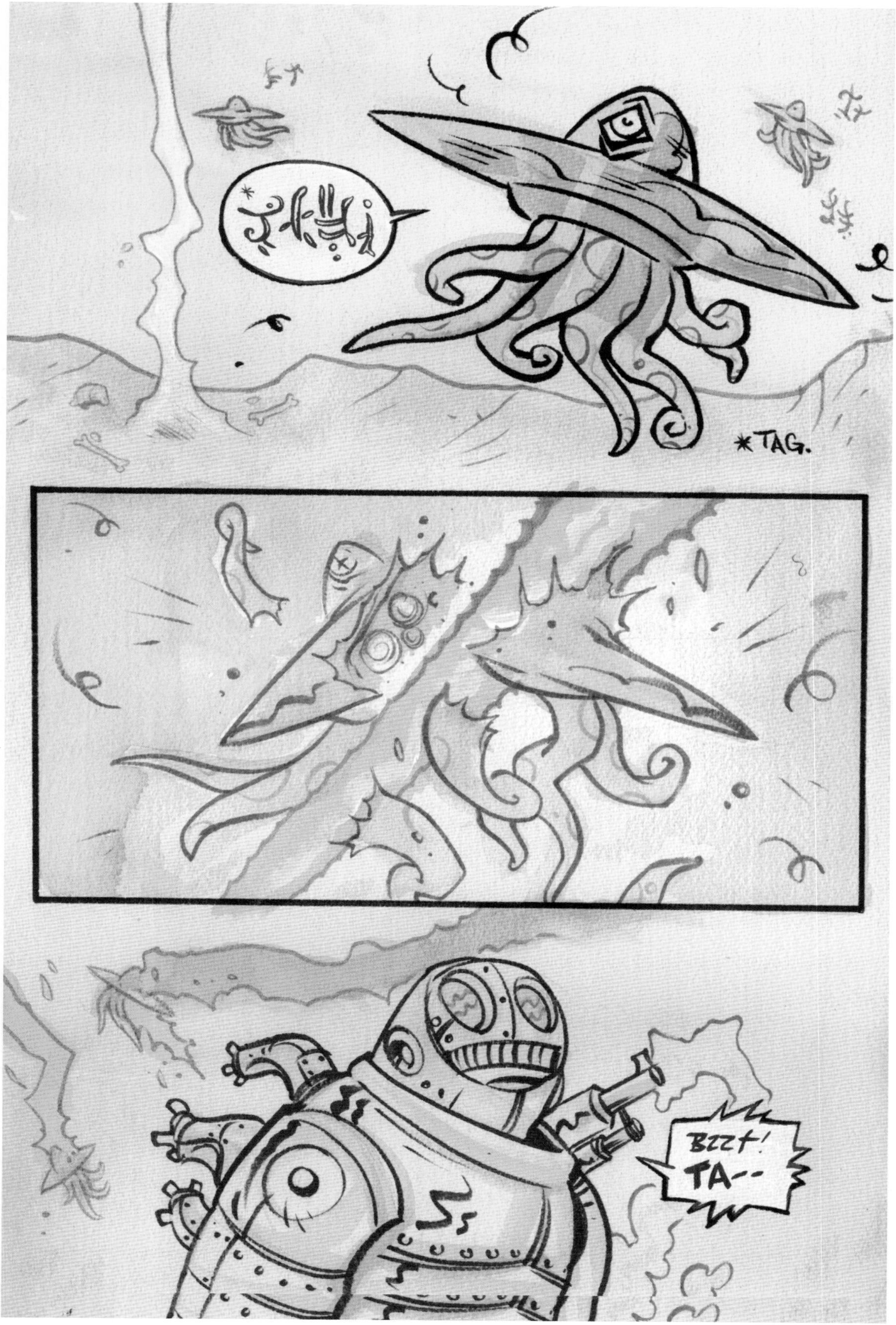
*TAG.
BZZT!
TA--

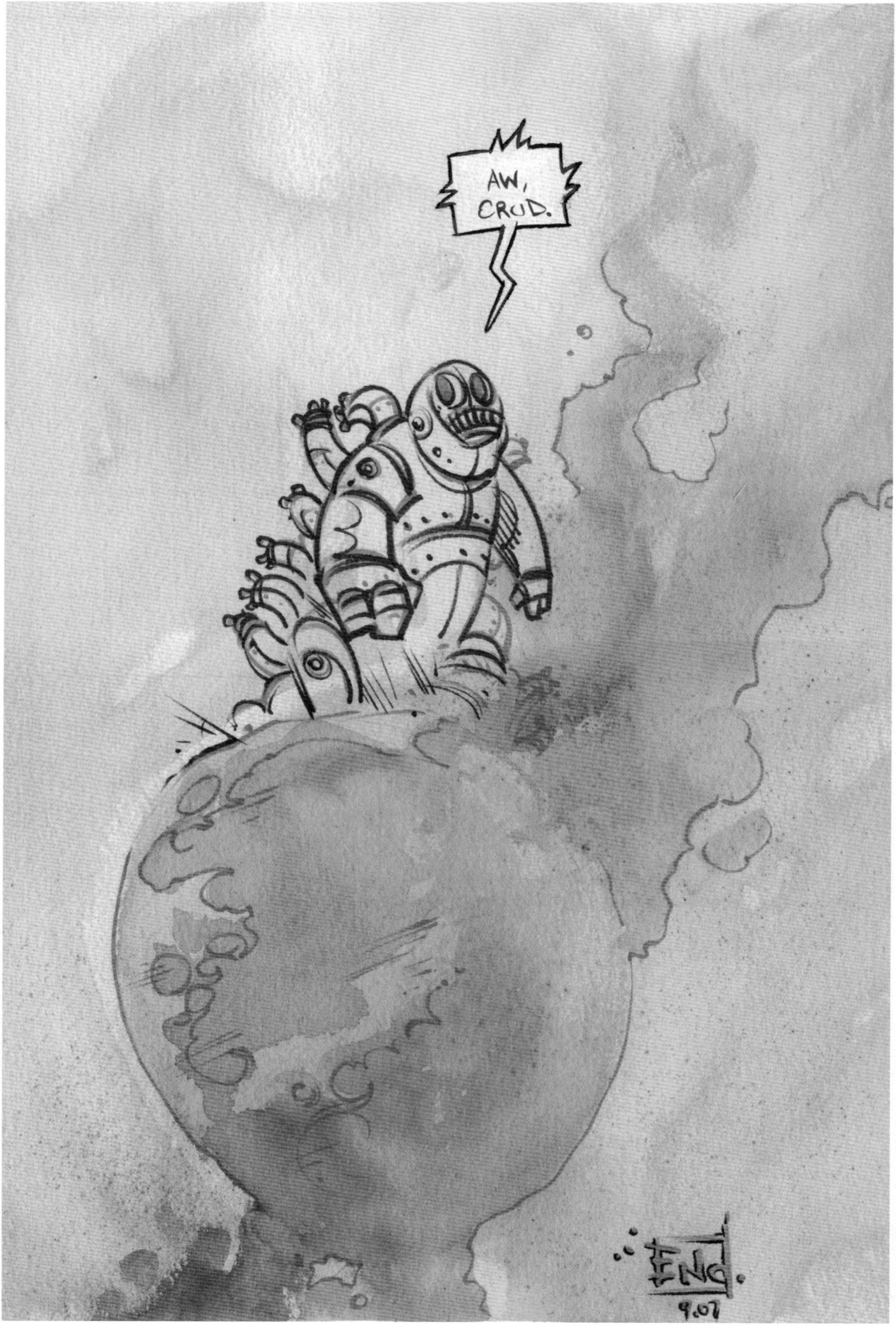
AW,
CRUD.

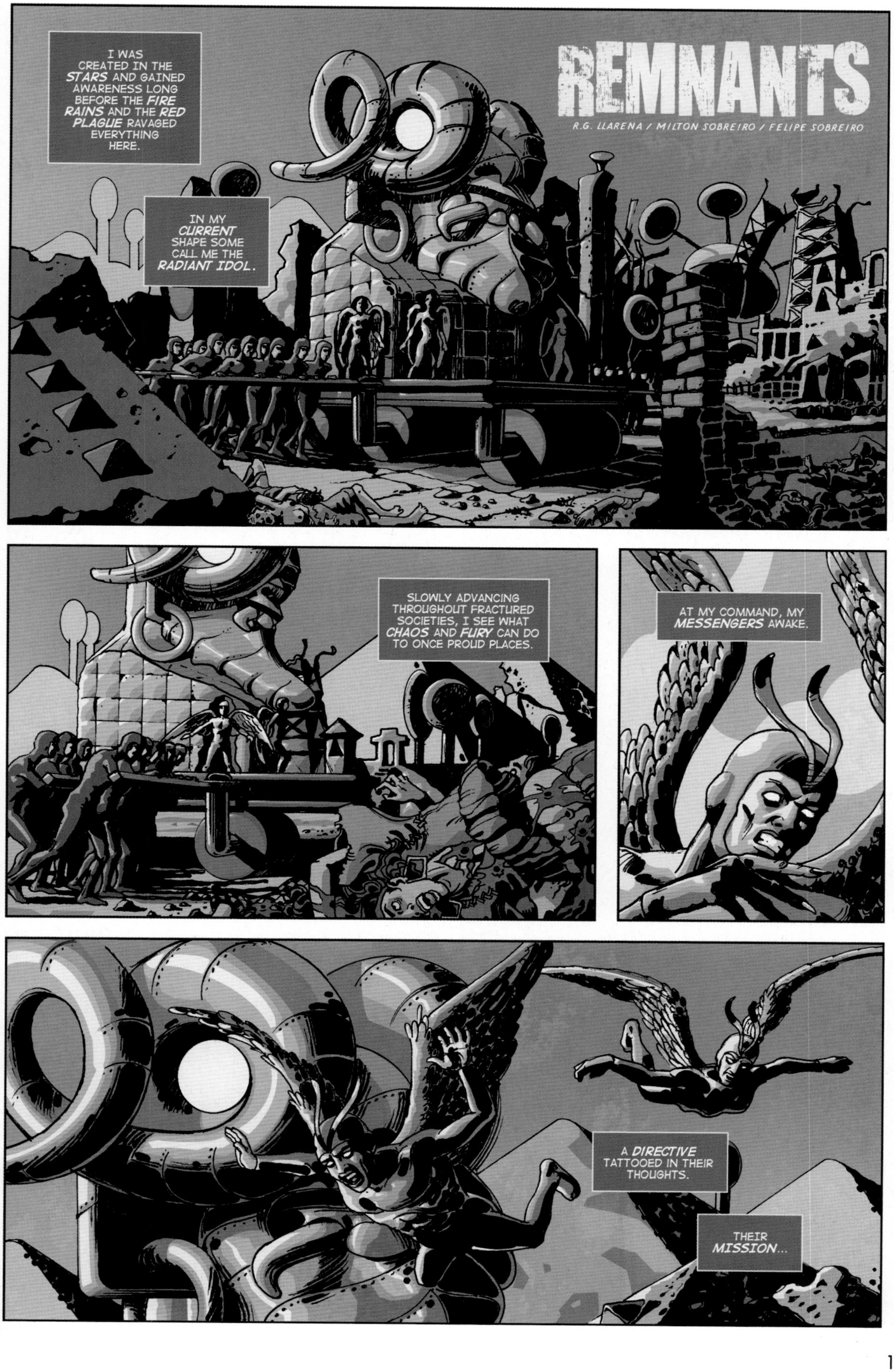
I WAS CREATED IN THE STARS AND GAINED AWARENESS LONG BEFORE THE FIRE RAINS AND THE RED PLAGUE RAVAGED EVERYTHING HERE.
REMNANTS
R.G. LLARENA / MILTON SOBREIRO / FELIPE SOBREIRO
IN MY CURRENT SHAPE SOME CALL ME THE RADIANT IDOL.
SLOWLY ADVANCING THROUGHOUT FRACTURED SOCIETIES, I SEE WHAT CHAOS AND FURY CAN DO TO ONCE PROUD PLACES.
AT MY COMMAND, MY MESSENGERS AWAKE.
A DIRECTIVE TATTOOED IN THEIR THOUGHTS.
THEIR MISSION...

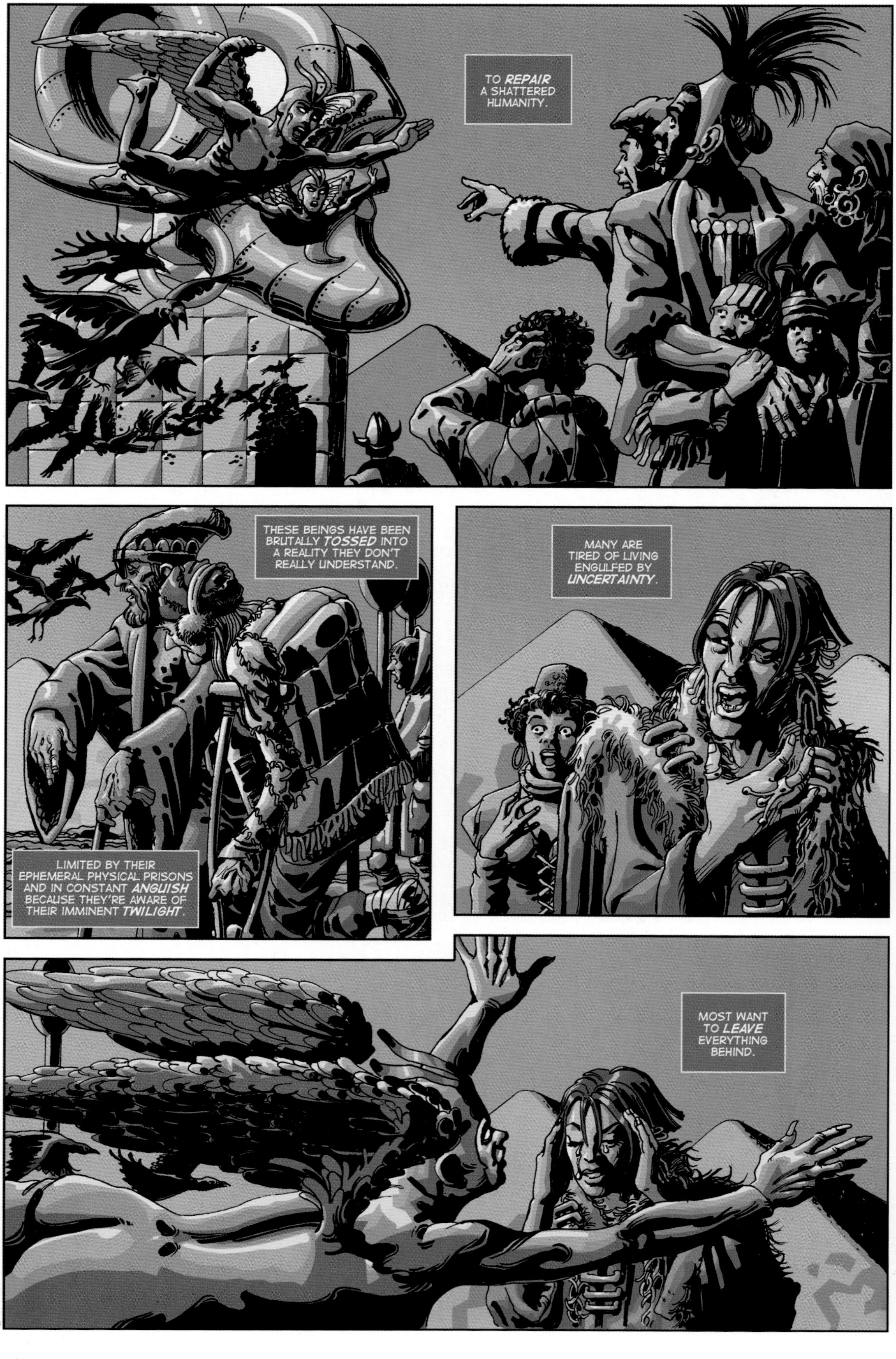
TO REPAIR A SHATTERED HUMANITY.
THESE BEINGS HAVE BEEN BRUTALLY TOSSED INTO A REALITY THEY DON'T REALLY UNDERSTAND.
LIMITED BY THEIR EPHEMERAL PHYSICAL PRISONS AND IN CONSTANT ANGUISH BECAUSE THEY'RE AWARE OF THEIR IMMINENT TWILIGHT.
MANY ARE TIRED OF LIVING ENGULFED BY UNCERTAINTY.
MOST WANT TO LEAVE EVERYTHING BEHIND.

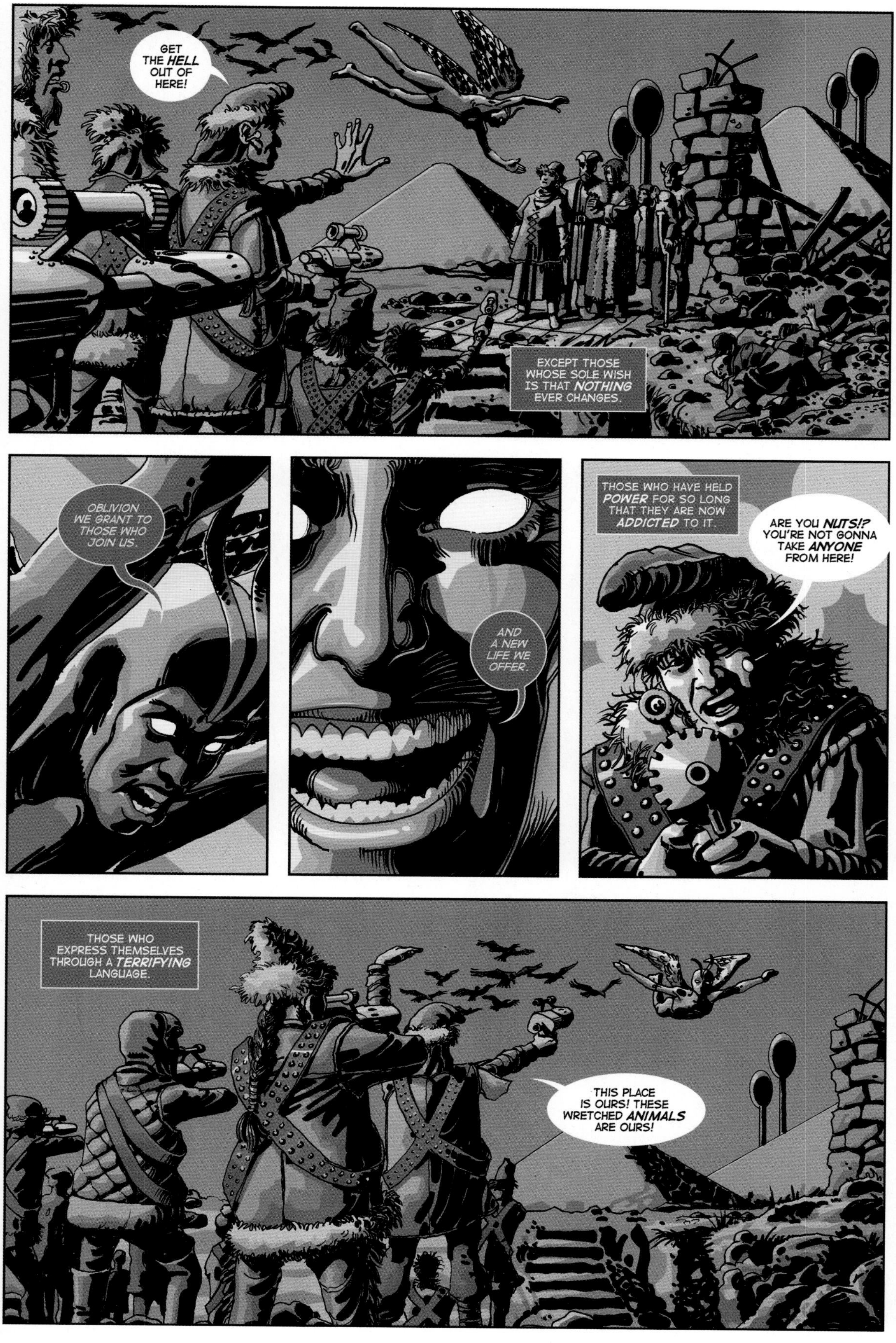
GET THE HELL OUT OF HERE!
EXCEPT THOSE WHOSE SOLE WISH IS THAT NOTHING EVER CHANGES.
OBLIVION WE GRANT TO THOSE WHO JOIN US.
AND A NEW LIFE WE OFFER.
THOSE WHO HAVE HELD POWER FOR SO LONG THAT THEY ARE NOW ADDICTED TO IT.
ARE YOU NUTS!? YOU'RE NOT GONNA TAKE ANYONE FROM HERE!
THOSE WHO EXPRESS THEMSELVES THROUGH A TERRIFYING LANGUAGE.
THIS PLACE IS OURS! THESE WRETCHED ANIMALS ARE OURS!

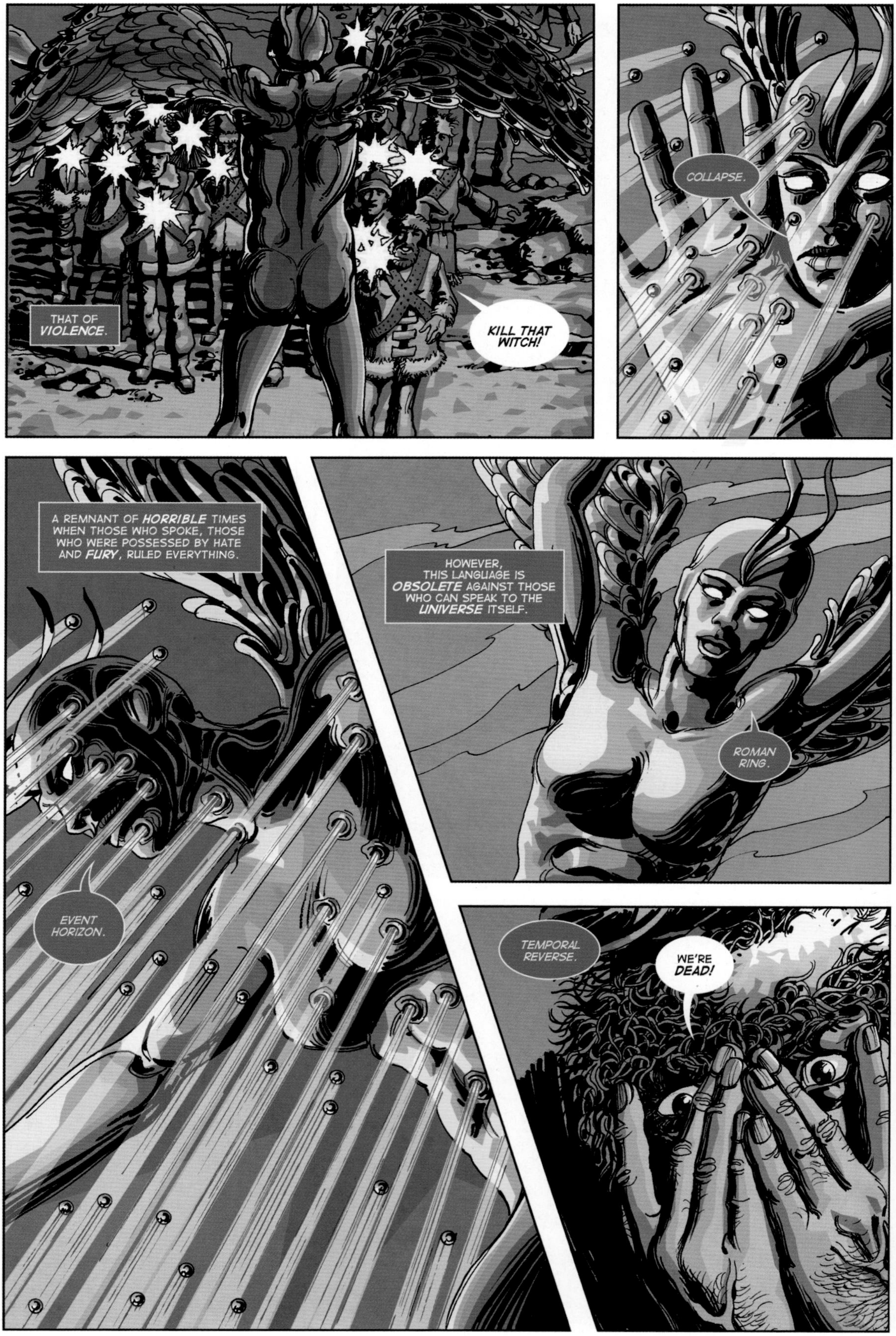
THAT OF VIOLENCE.
KILL THAT WITCH!
COLLAPSE.
A REMNANT OF HORRIBLE TIMES WHEN THOSE WHO SPOKE, THOSE WHO WERE POSSESSED BY HATE AND FURY, RULED EVERYTHING.
EVENT HORIZON.
HOWEVER, THIS LANGUAGE IS OBSOLETE AGAINST THOSE WHO CAN SPEAK TO THE UNIVERSE ITSELF.
ROMAN RING.
TEMPORAL REVERSE.
WE'RE DEAD!

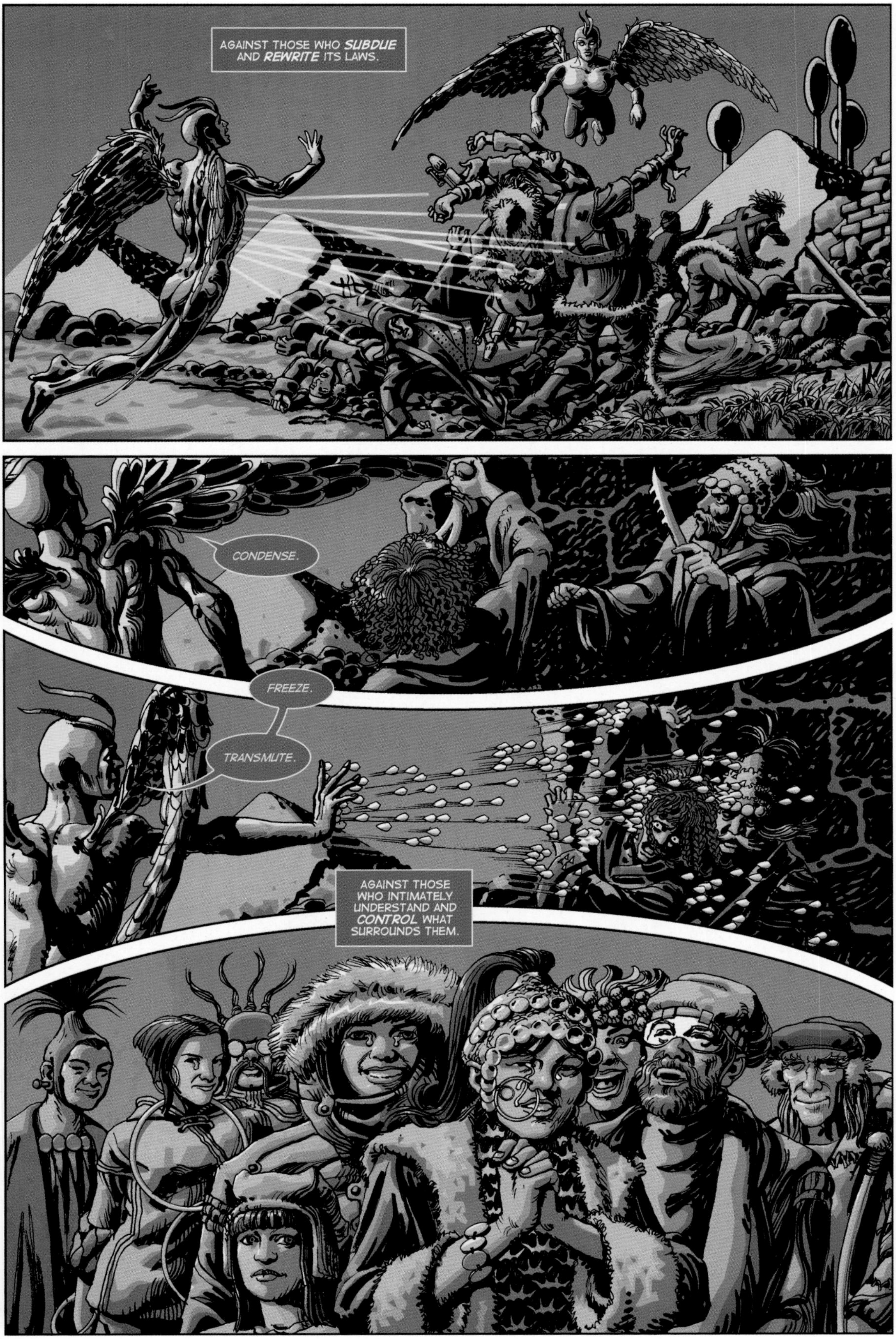
AGAINST THOSE WHO SUBDUE AND REWRITE ITS LAWS.
CONDENSE.
FREEZE.
TRANSMUTE.
AGAINST THOSE WHO INTIMATELY UNDERSTAND AND CONTROL WHAT SURROUNDS THEM.

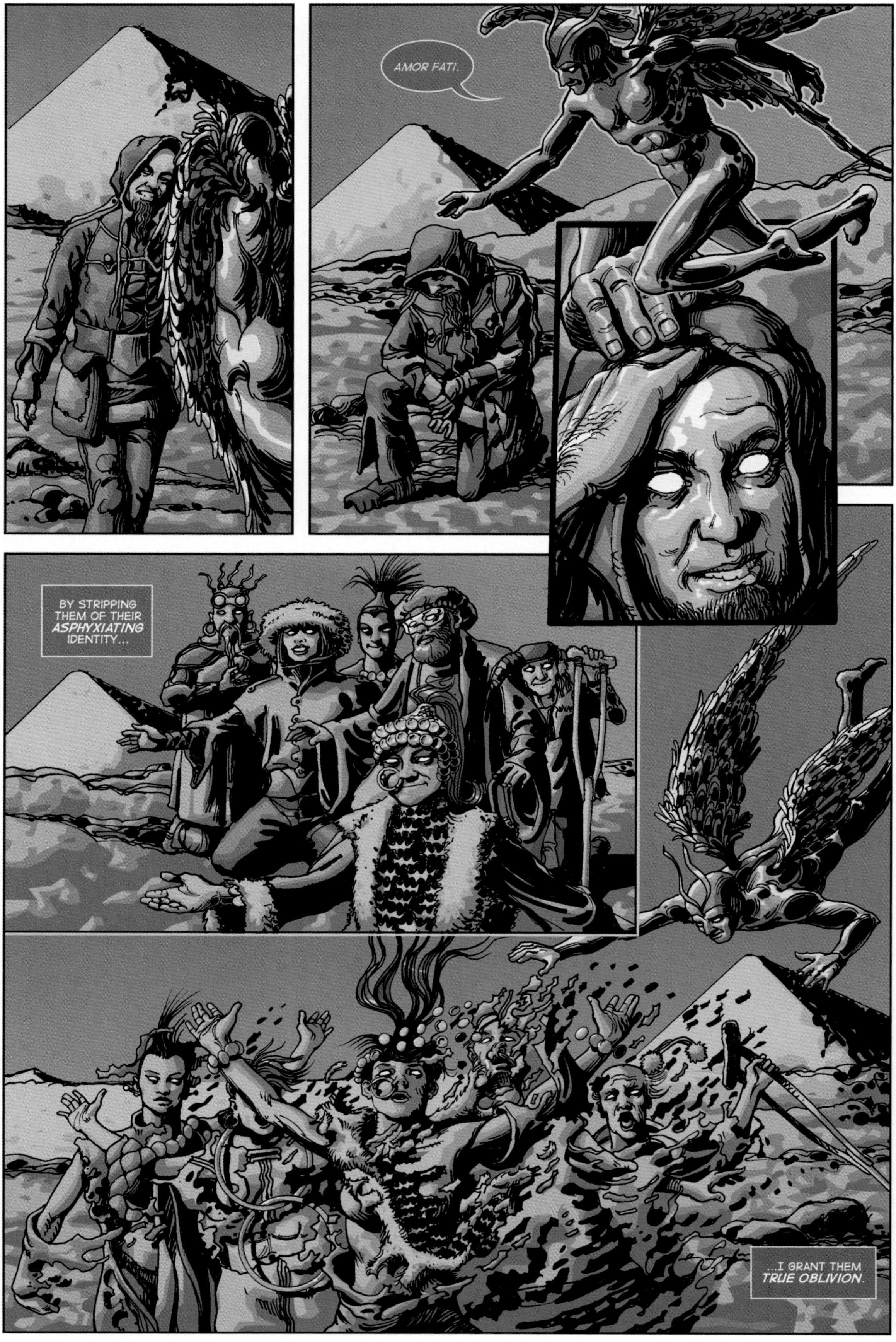
AMOR FATI.
BY STRIPPING THEM OF THEIR *ASPHYXIATING* IDENTITY...
...I GRANT THEM *TRUE OBLIVION*.

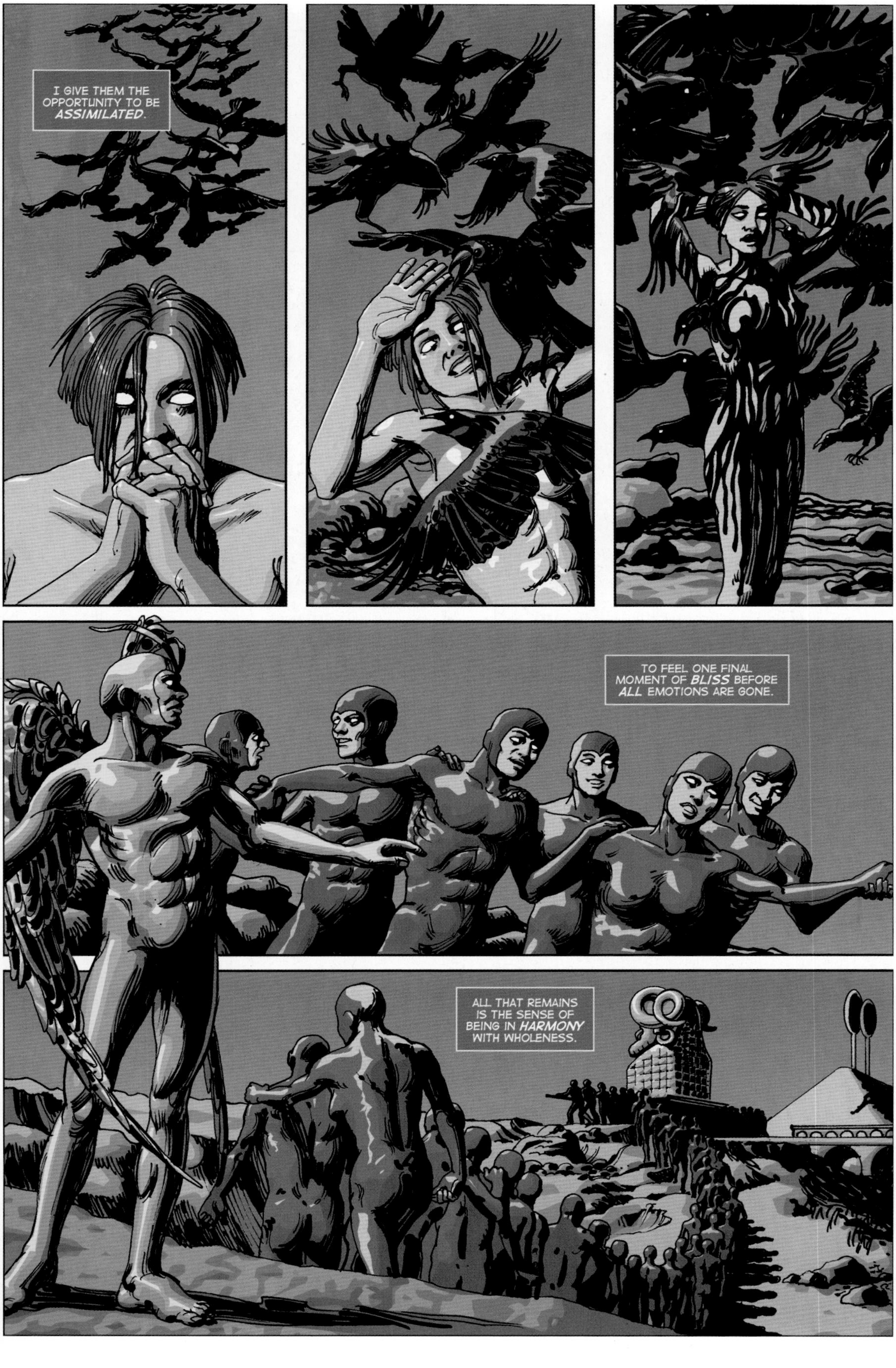
I GIVE THEM THE OPPORTUNITY TO BE *ASSIMILATED*.
TO FEEL ONE FINAL MOMENT OF *BLISS* BEFORE *ALL* EMOTIONS ARE GONE.
ALL THAT REMAINS IS THE SENSE OF BEING IN *HARMONY* WITH WHOLENESS.

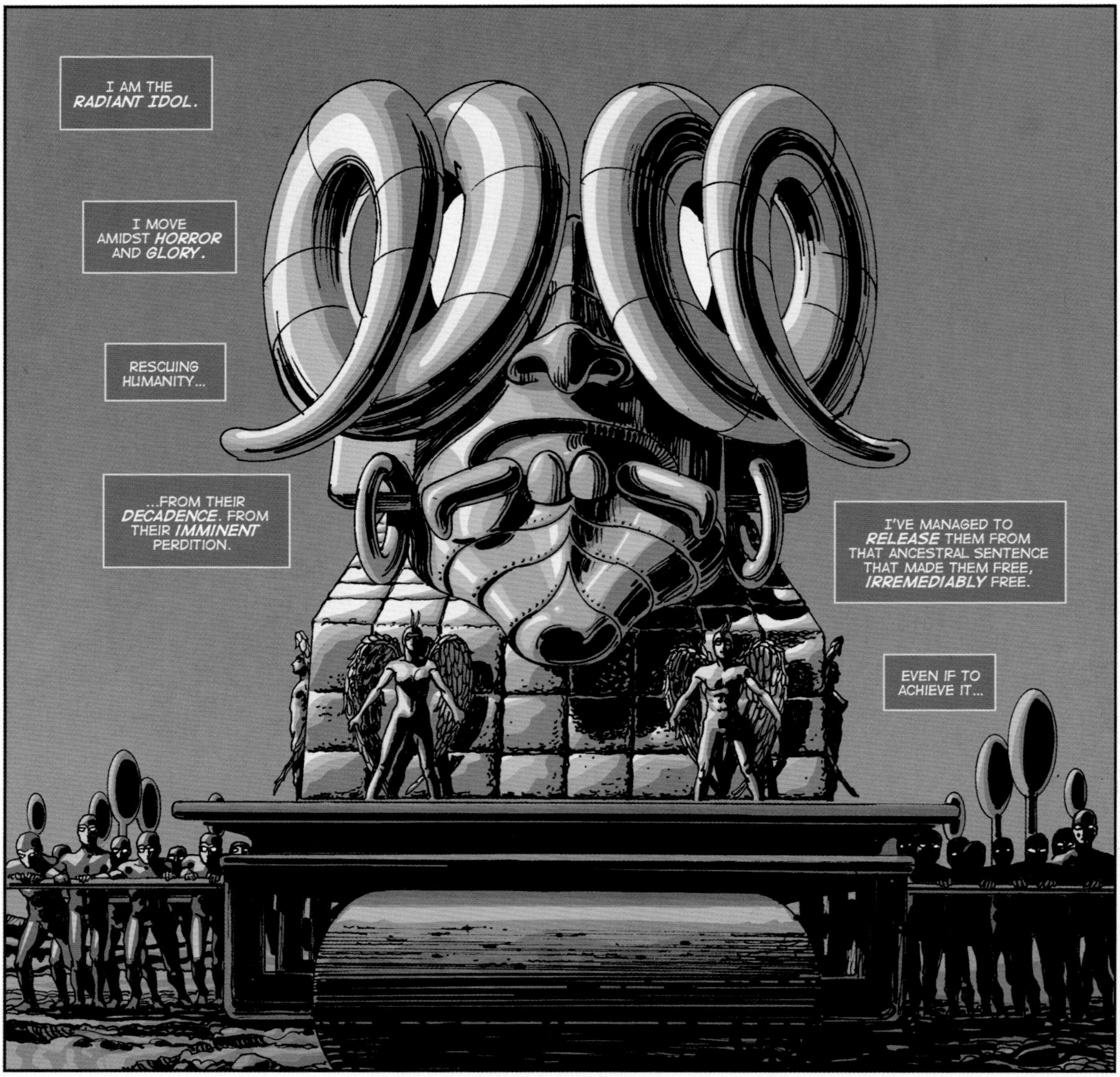
I AM THE RADIANT IDOL.
I MOVE AMIDST HORROR AND GLORY.
RESCUING HUMANITY...
...FROM THEIR DECADENCE. FROM THEIR IMMINENT PERDITION.
I'VE MANAGED TO RELEASE THEM FROM THAT ANCESTRAL SENTENCE THAT MADE THEM FREE, IRREMEDIABLY FREE.
EVEN IF TO ACHIEVE IT...

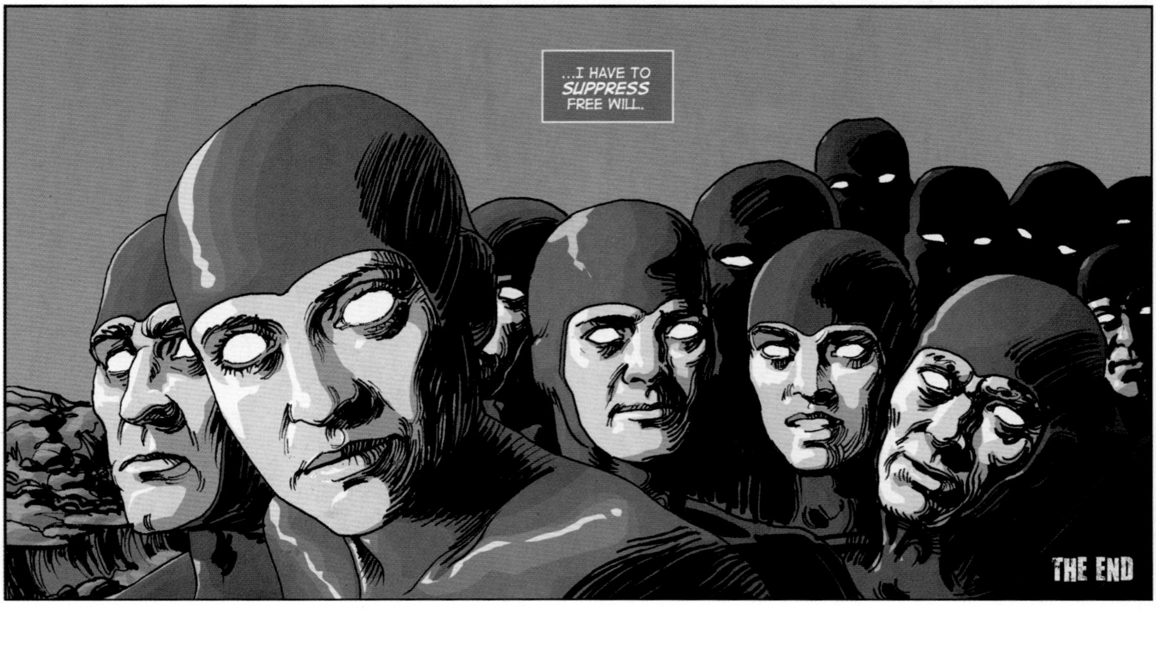
...I HAVE TO SUPPRESS FREE WILL.
THE END

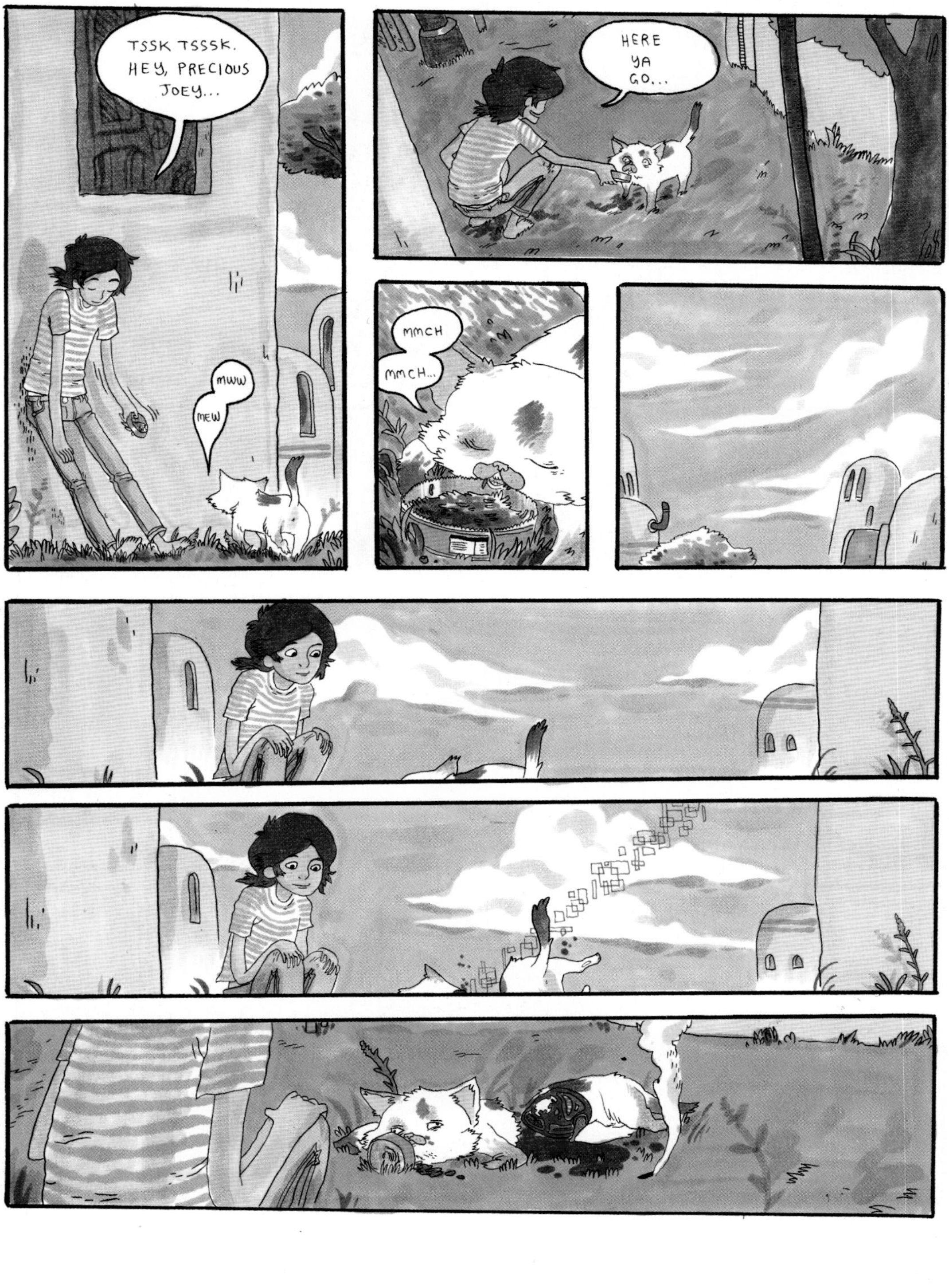
TSSK TSSSK. HEY, PRECIOUS JOEY...
MWW
MEW
HERE YA GO...
MMCH
MMCH...

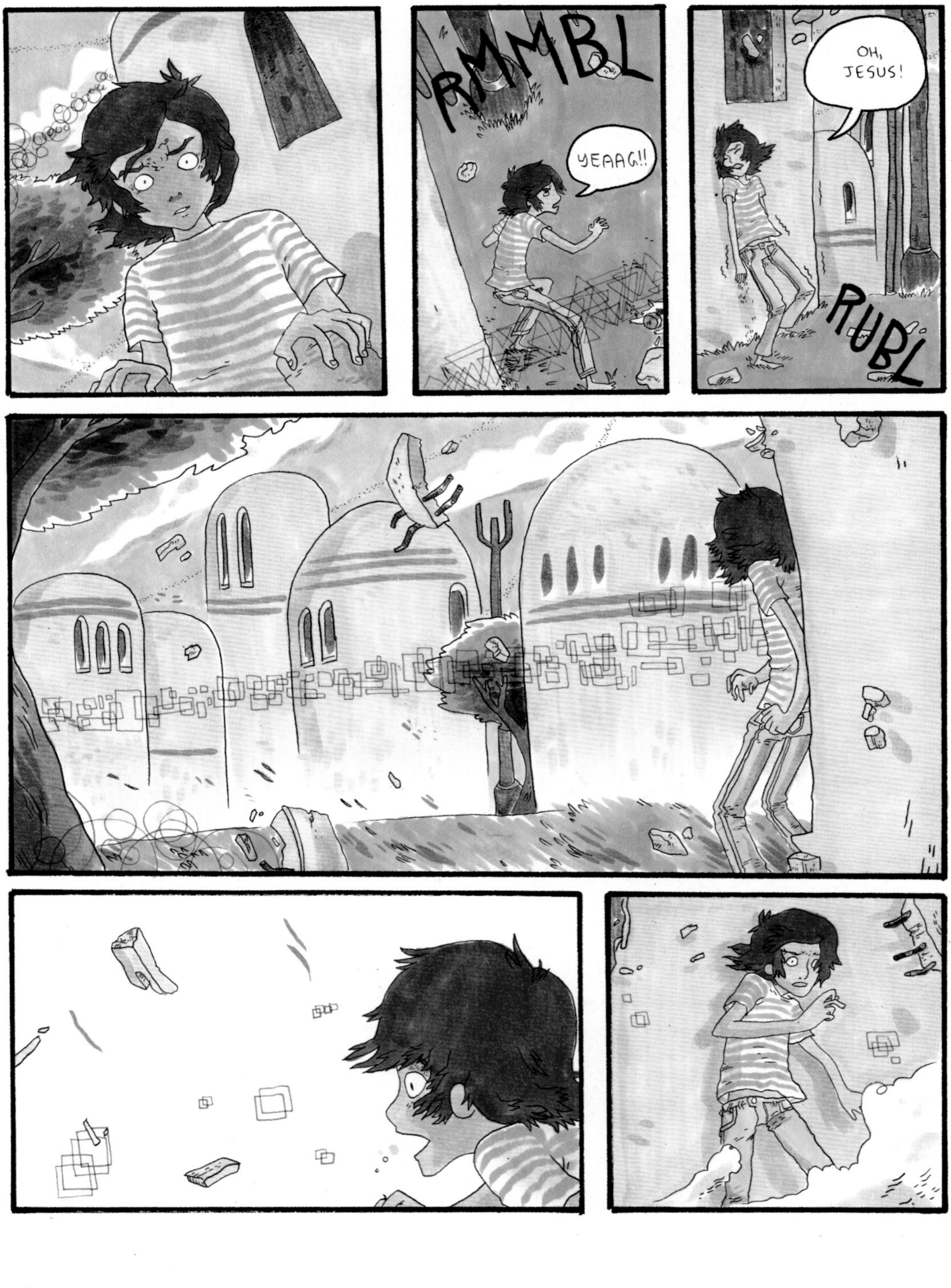
RMMBL
YEAAG!!
OH, JESUS!
RUBL

THE FALL
OF
GEOMETRY
by coleman engle

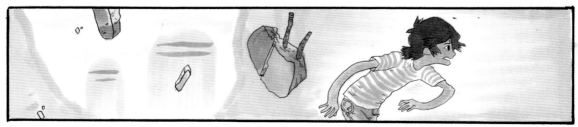

DOUGLAS!!!

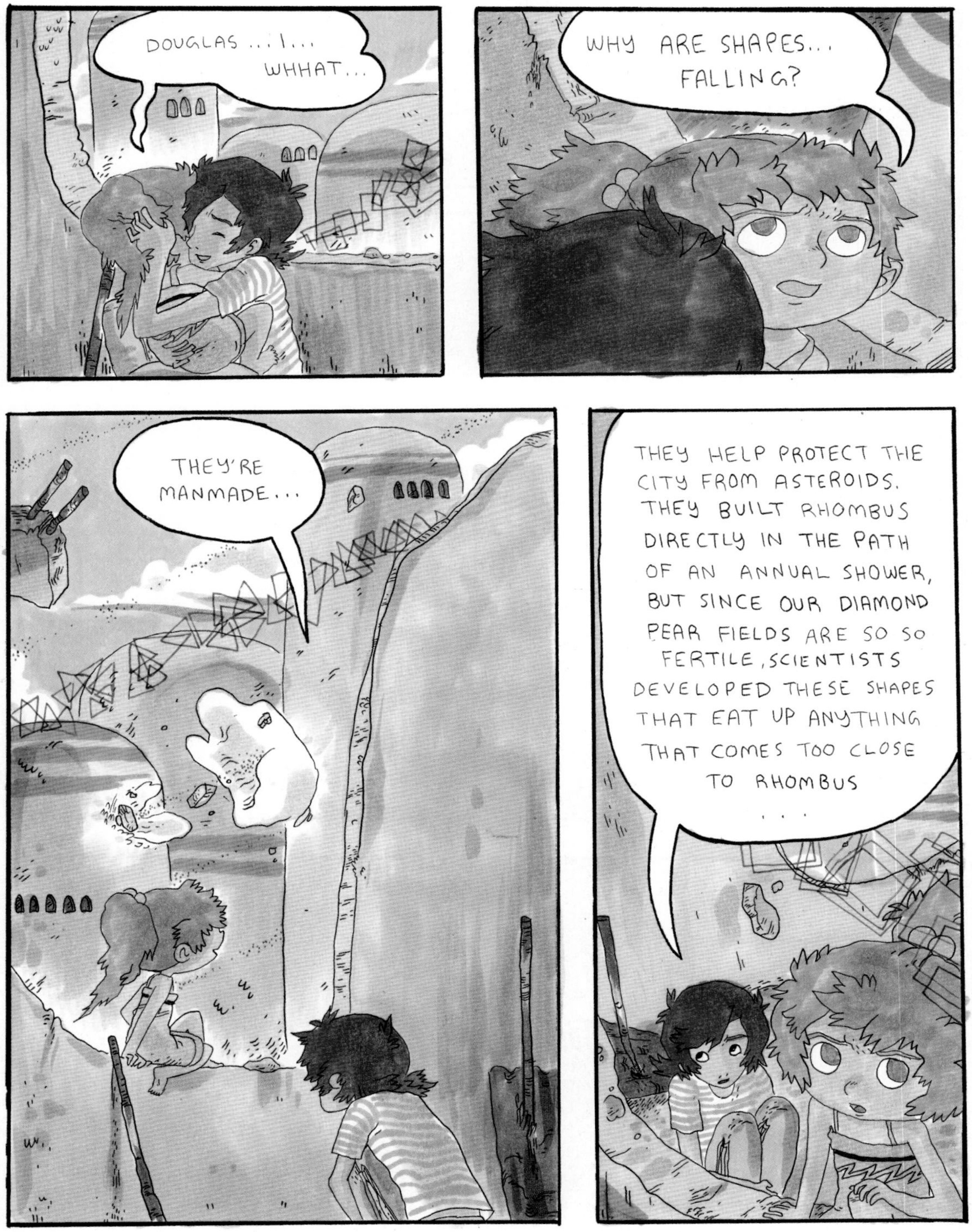
DOUGLAS ... I ... WHHAT ...
WHY ARE SHAPES... FALLING?
THEY'RE MANMADE ...
THEY HELP PROTECT THE CITY FROM ASTEROIDS. THEY BUILT RHOMBUS DIRECTLY IN THE PATH OF AN ANNUAL SHOWER, BUT SINCE OUR DIAMOND PEAR FIELDS ARE SO SO FERTILE, SCIENTISTS DEVELOPED THESE SHAPES THAT EAT UP ANYTHING THAT COMES TOO CLOSE TO RHOMBUS ...

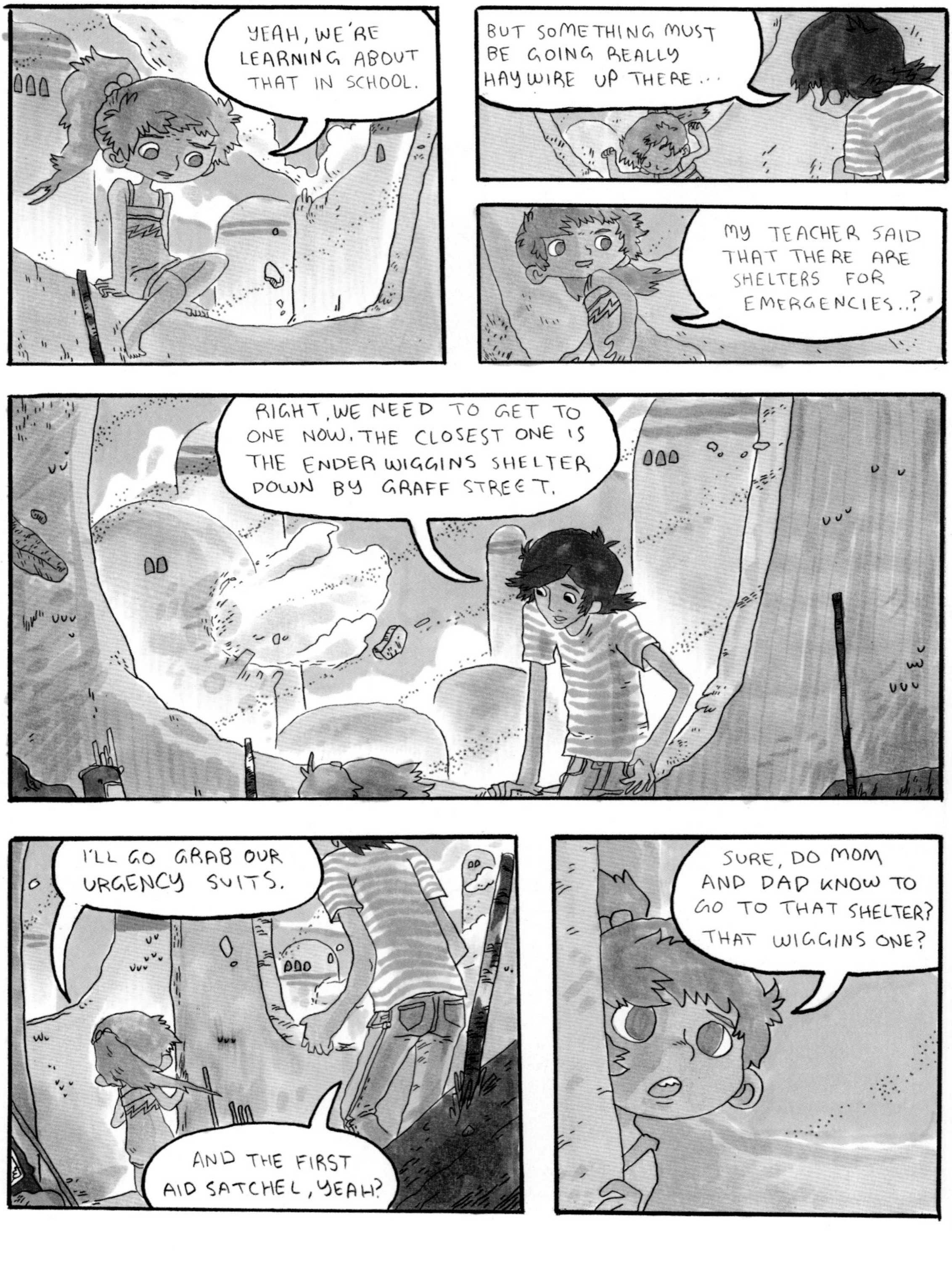
YEAH, WE'RE LEARNING ABOUT THAT IN SCHOOL.
BUT SOMETHING MUST BE GOING REALLY HAYWIRE UP THERE...
MY TEACHER SAID THAT THERE ARE SHELTERS FOR EMERGENCIES...?
RIGHT, WE NEED TO GET TO ONE NOW. THE CLOSEST ONE IS THE ENDER WIGGINS SHELTER DOWN BY GRAFF STREET.
I'LL GO GRAB OUR URGENCY SUITS.
AND THE FIRST AID SATCHEL, YEAH?
SURE, DO MOM AND DAD KNOW TO GO TO THAT SHELTER? THAT WIGGINS ONE?

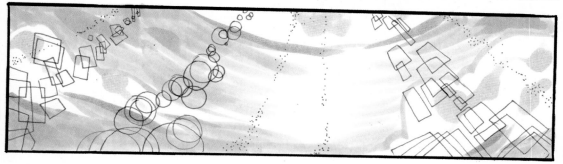

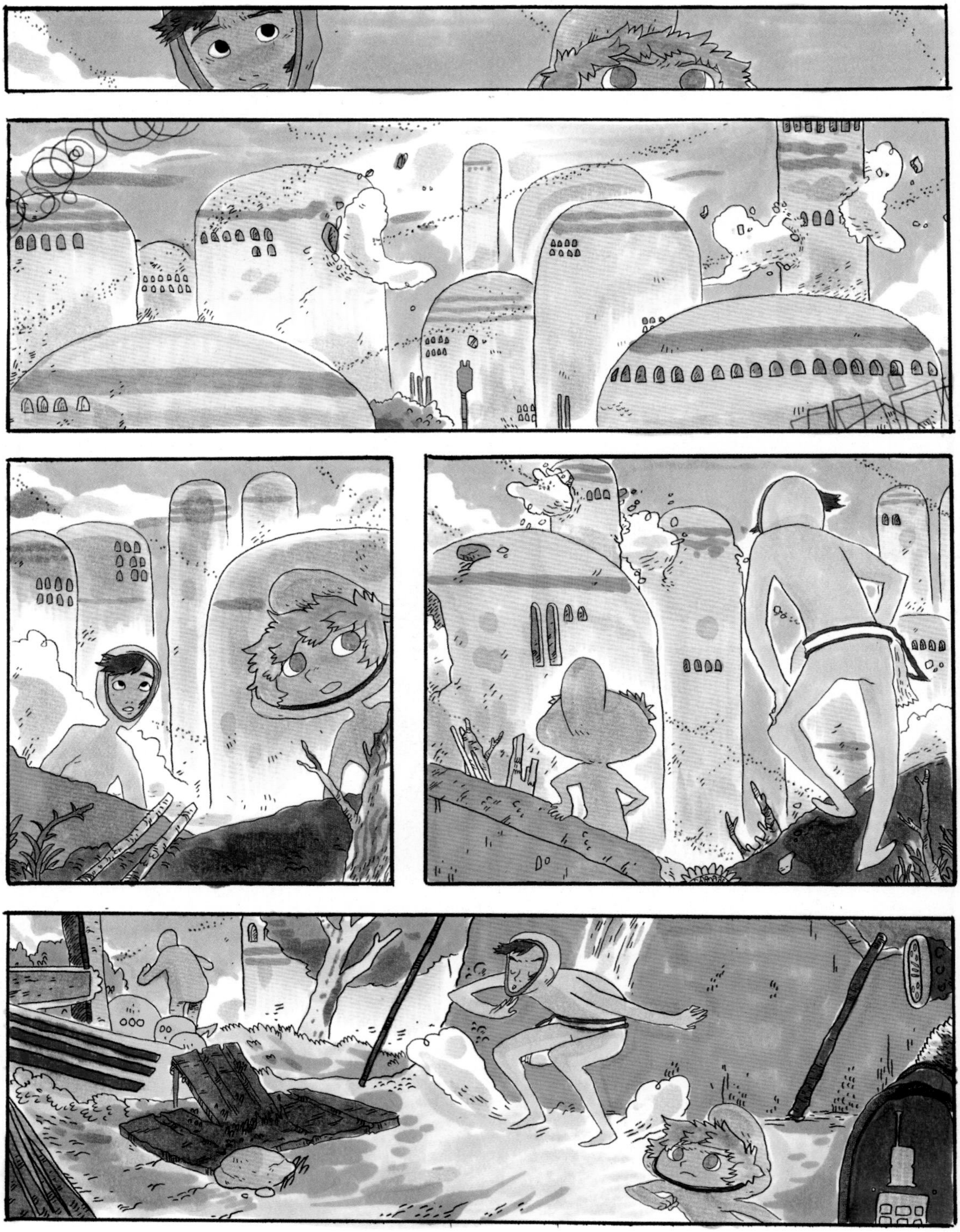

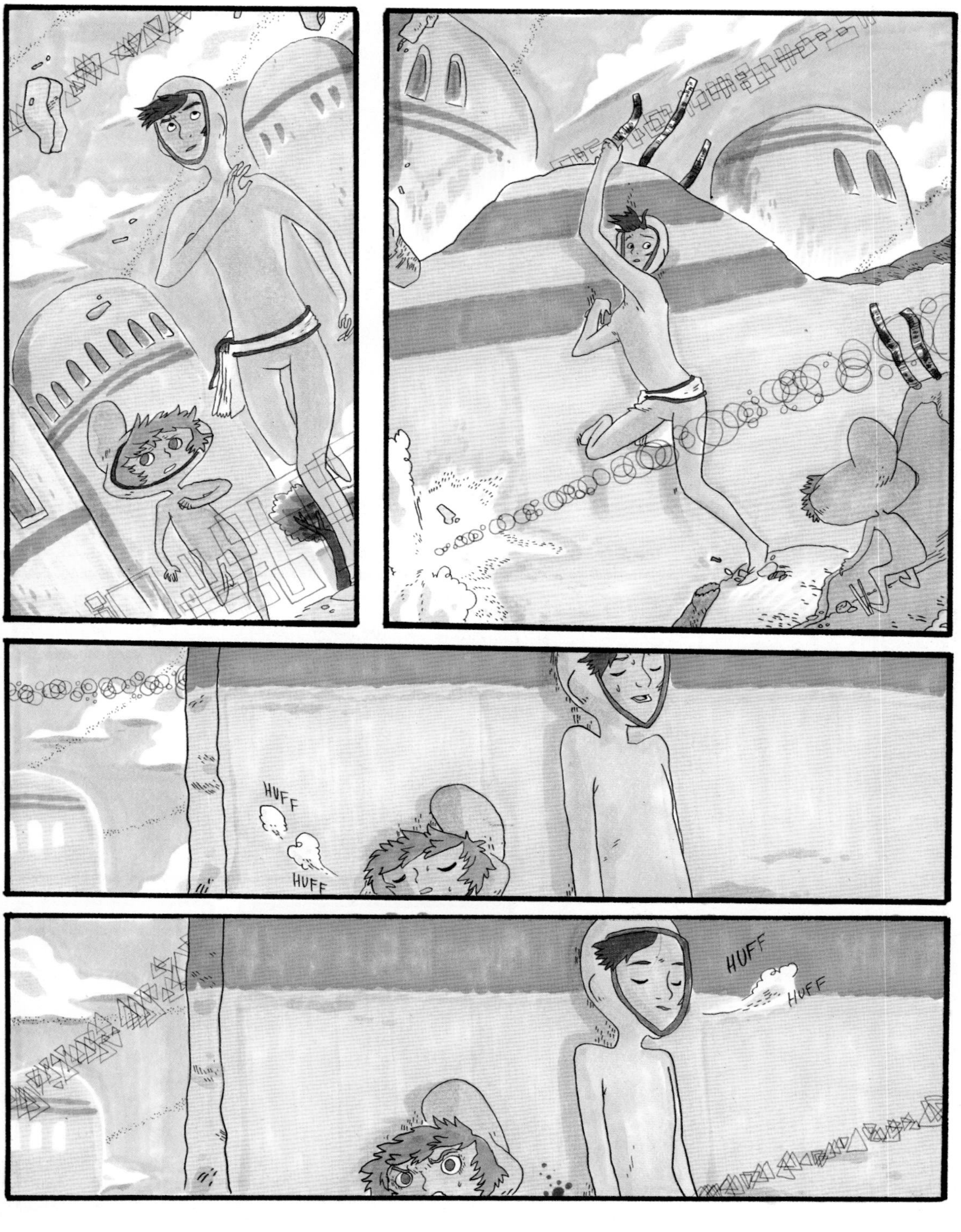
HUFF
HUFF
HUFF
HUFF

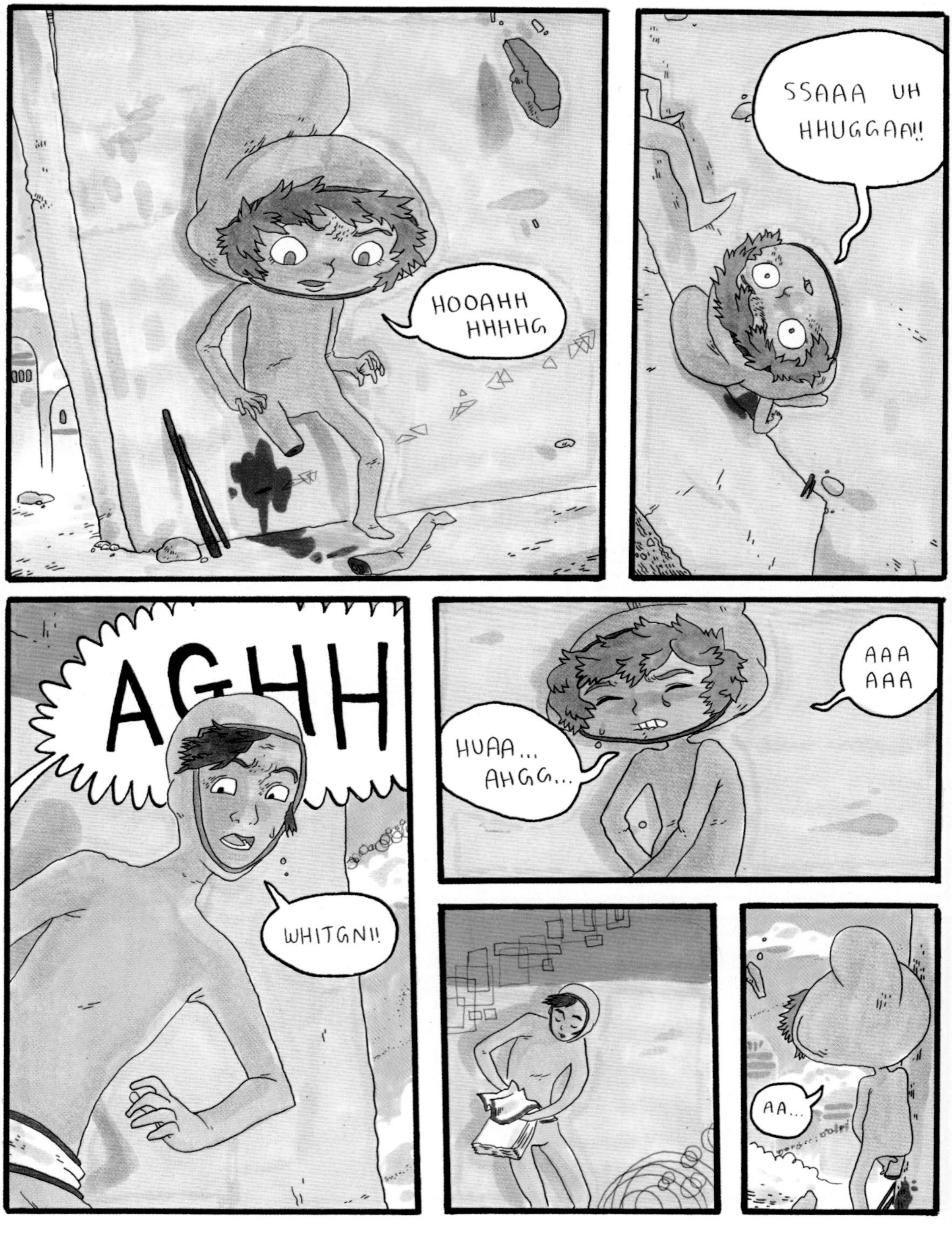
HOOAHH HHHHG
SSAAA UH HHUGGAA!!
AGHH
WHITGN!!
AAA AAA
HUAA... AHGG...
AA...

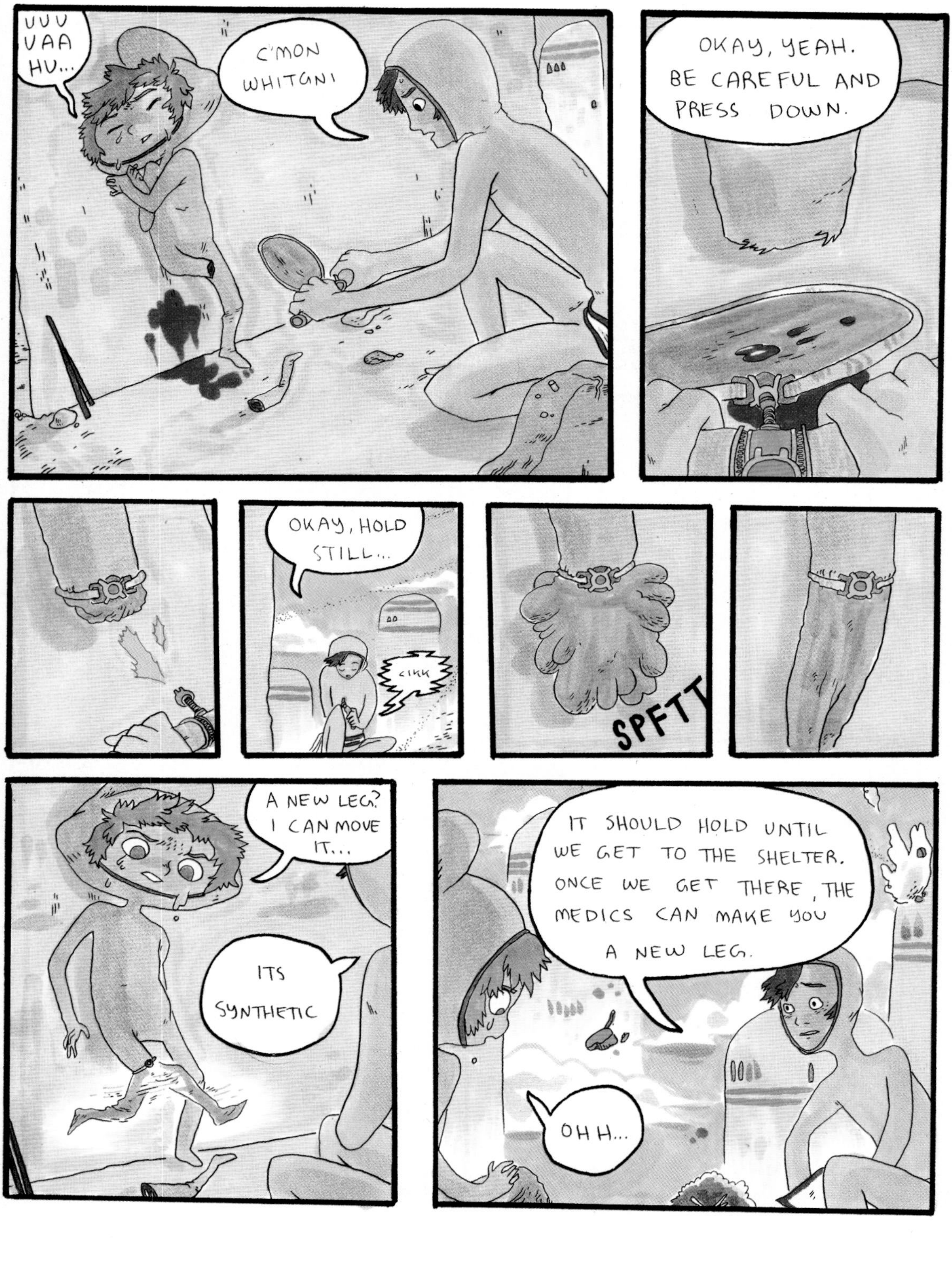
UUU VAA HU...
C'MON WHITGNI
OKAY, YEAH. BE CAREFUL AND PRESS DOWN.
OKAY, HOLD STILL...
CIKK
SPFTT
A NEW LEG? I CAN MOVE IT...
ITS SYNTHETIC
IT SHOULD HOLD UNTIL WE GET TO THE SHELTER. ONCE WE GET THERE, THE MEDICS CAN MAKE YOU A NEW LEG.
OHH...

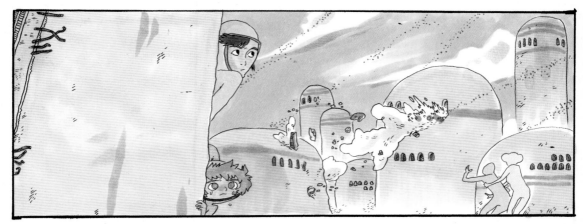

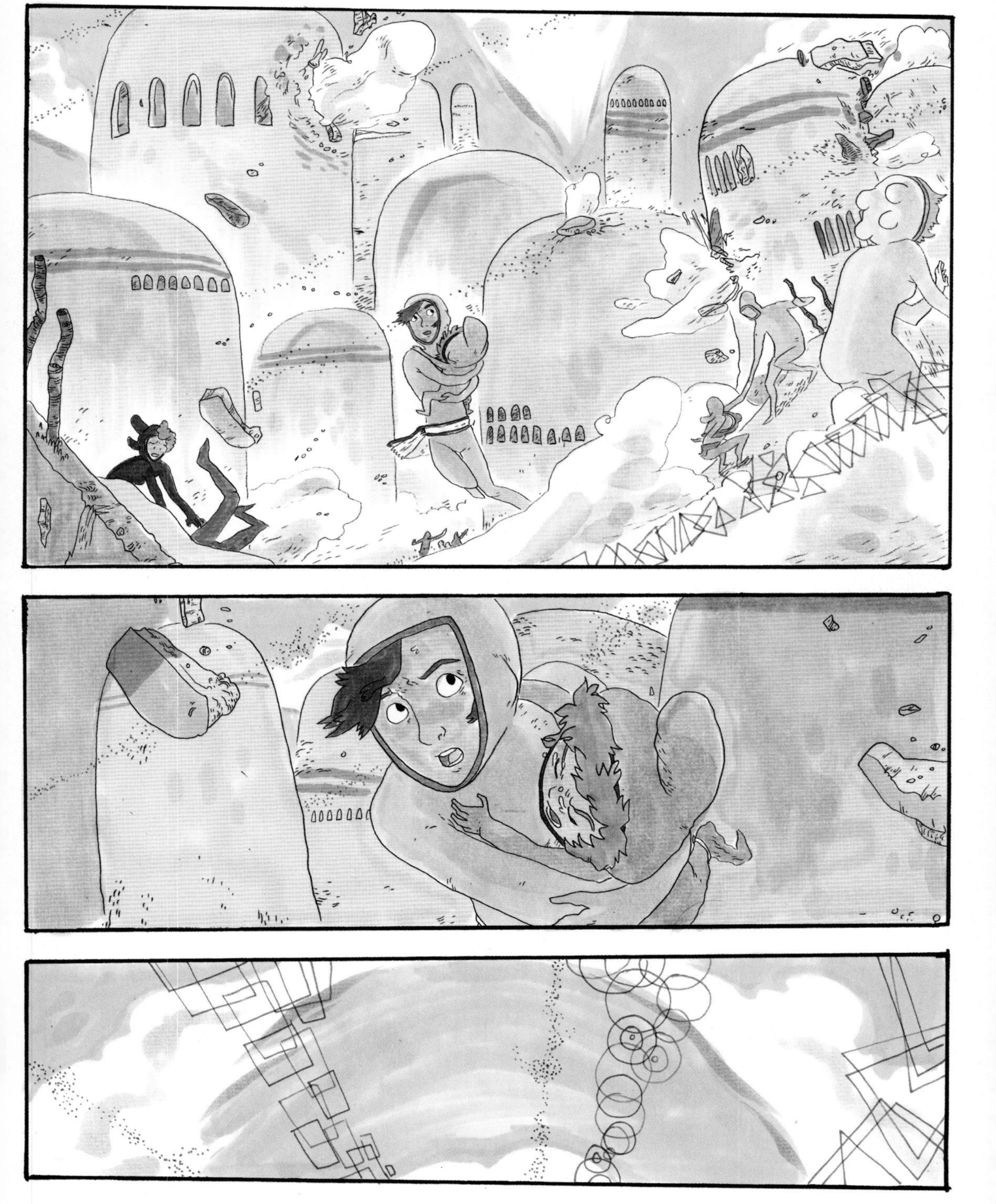

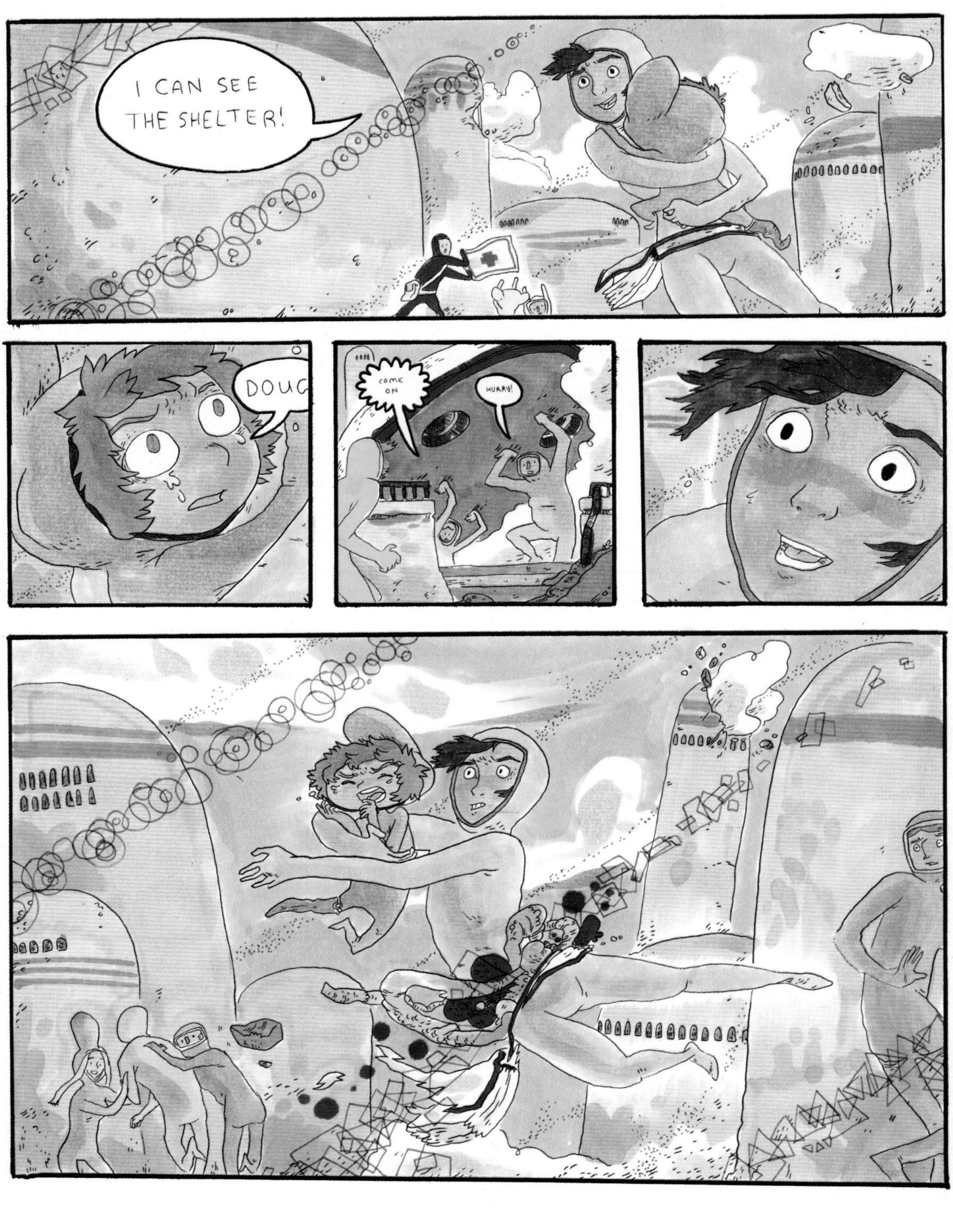
I CAN SEE THE SHELTER!
DOUG
COME ON
HURRY!

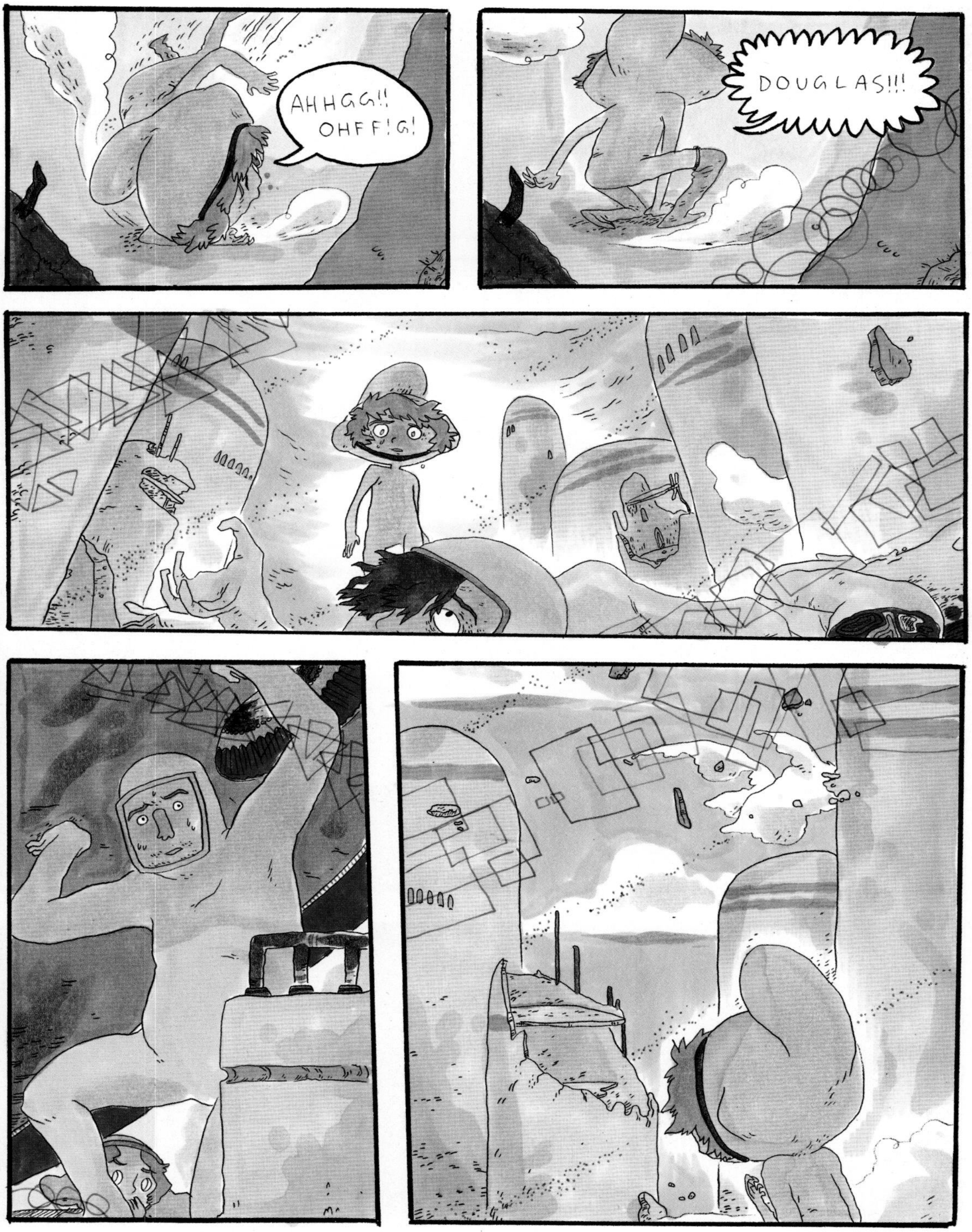
AHHGG!! OHFF!G!
DOUGLAS!!!

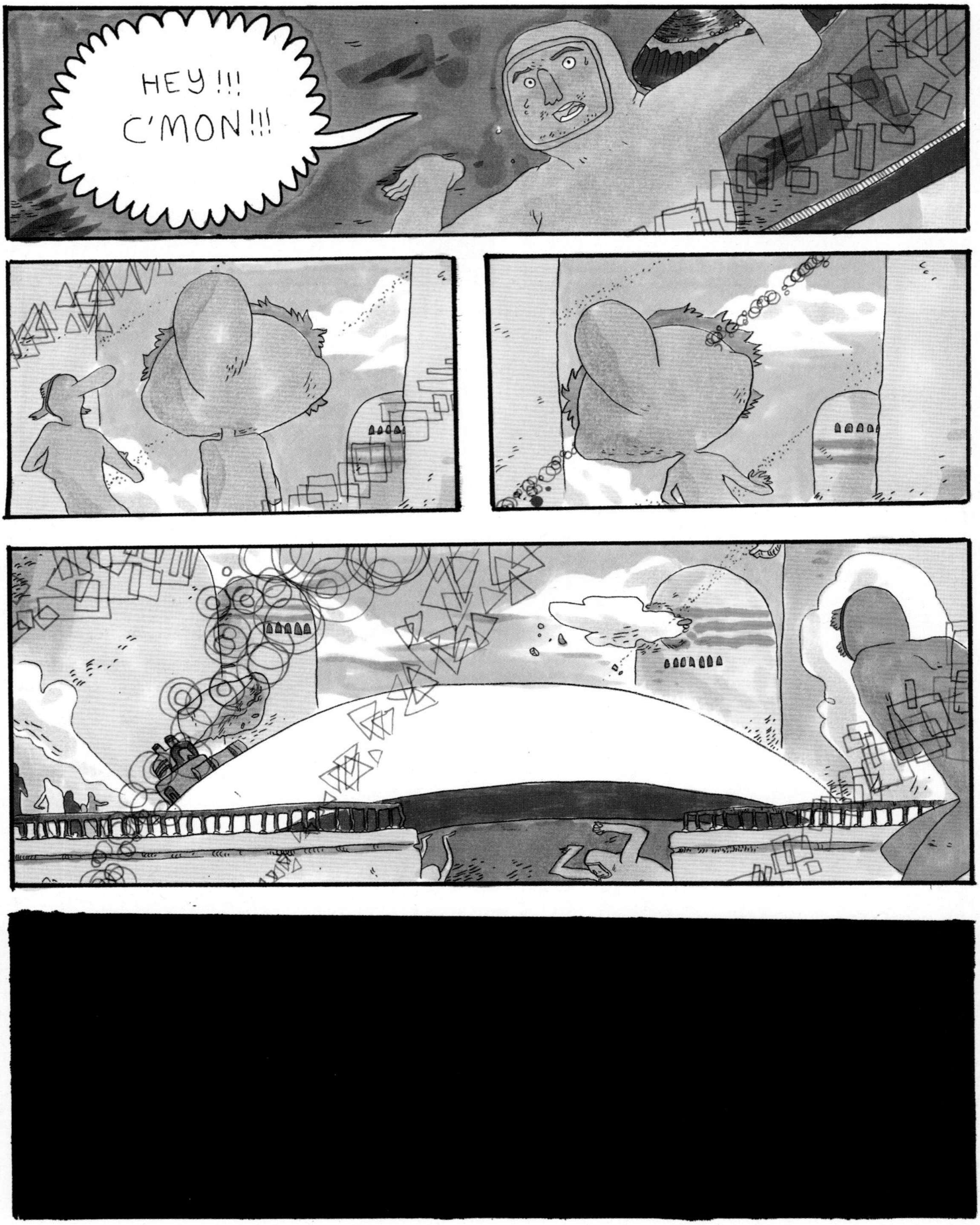
HEY!!! C'MON!!!

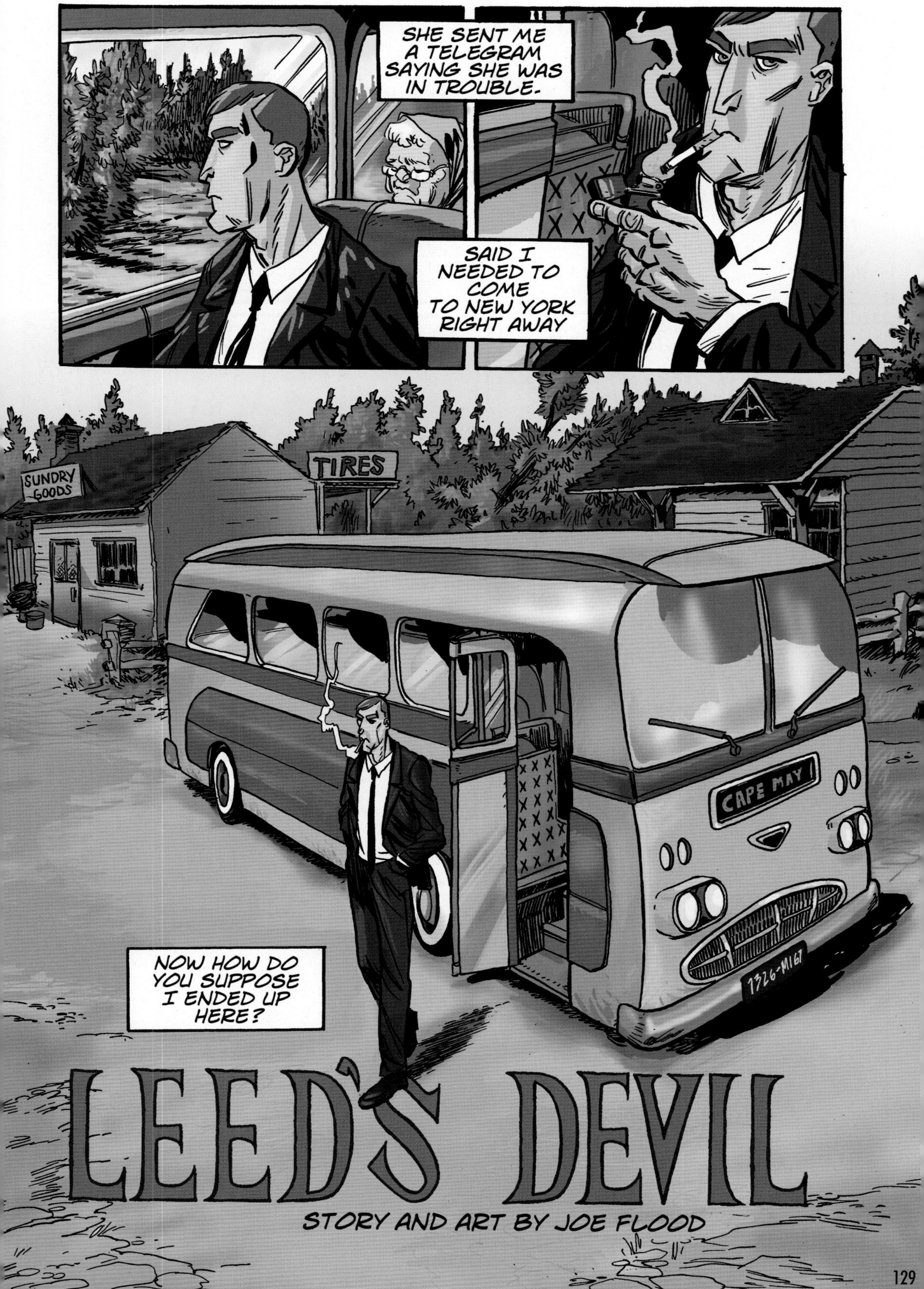
SHE SENT ME A TELEGRAM SAYING SHE WAS IN TROUBLE.
SAID I NEEDED TO COME TO NEW YORK RIGHT AWAY
SUNDRY GOODS
TIRES
CAPE MAY
1326-M167
NOW HOW DO YOU SUPPOSE I ENDED UP HERE?
LEED'S DEVIL
STORY AND ART BY JOE FLOOD

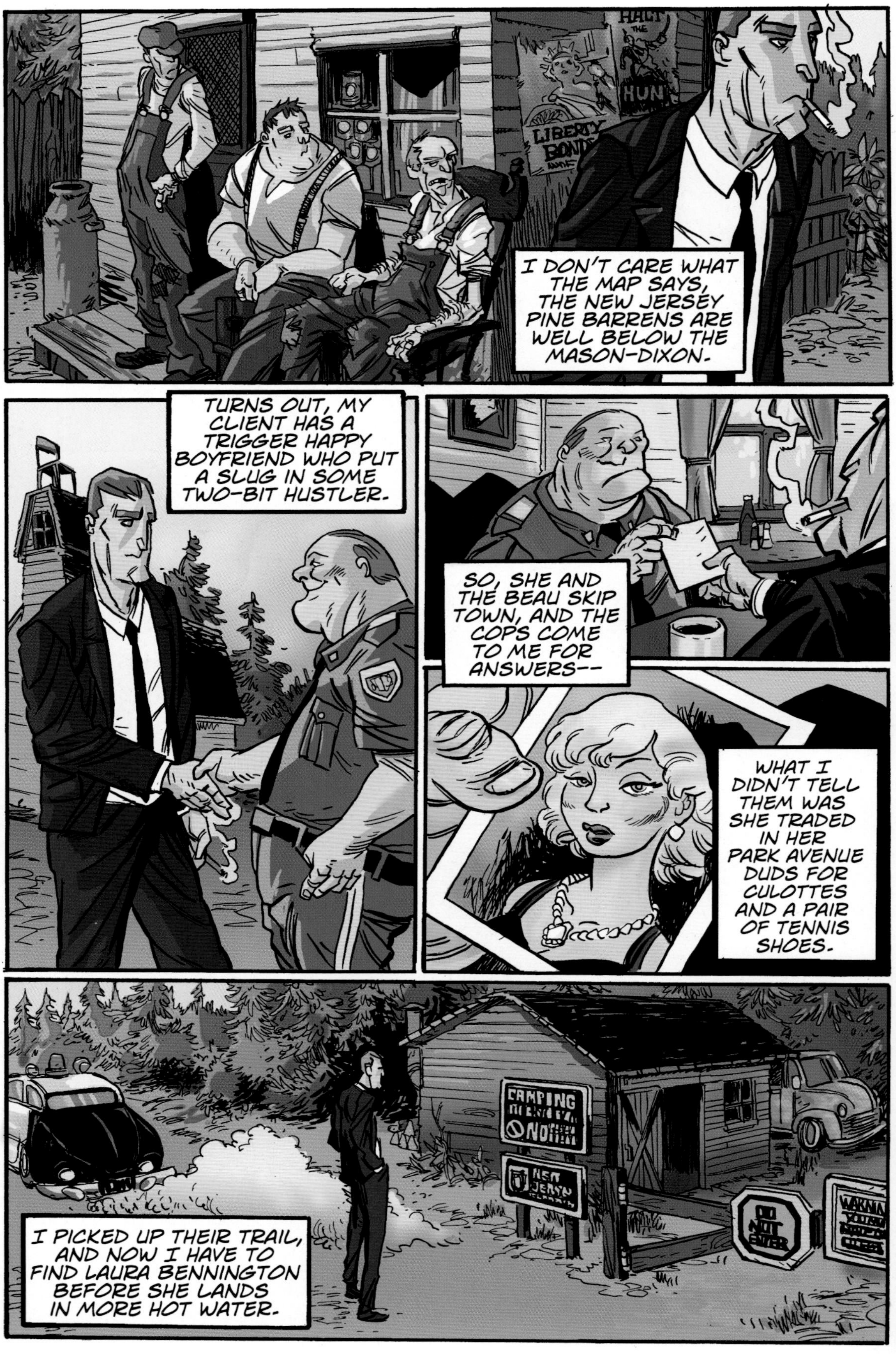
HALT THE HUN
LIBERTY BONDS
I DON'T CARE WHAT THE MAP SAYS, THE NEW JERSEY PINE BARRENS ARE WELL BELOW THE MASON-DIXON.
TURNS OUT, MY CLIENT HAS A TRIGGER HAPPY BOYFRIEND WHO PUT A SLUG IN SOME TWO-BIT HUSTLER.
SO, SHE AND THE BEAU SKIP TOWN, AND THE COPS COME TO ME FOR ANSWERS--
WHAT I DIDN'T TELL THEM WAS SHE TRADED IN HER PARK AVENUE DUDS FOR CULOTTES AND A PAIR OF TENNIS SHOES.
I PICKED UP THEIR TRAIL, AND NOW I HAVE TO FIND LAURA BENNINGTON BEFORE SHE LANDS IN MORE HOT WATER.
CAMPING
DO NOT ENTER

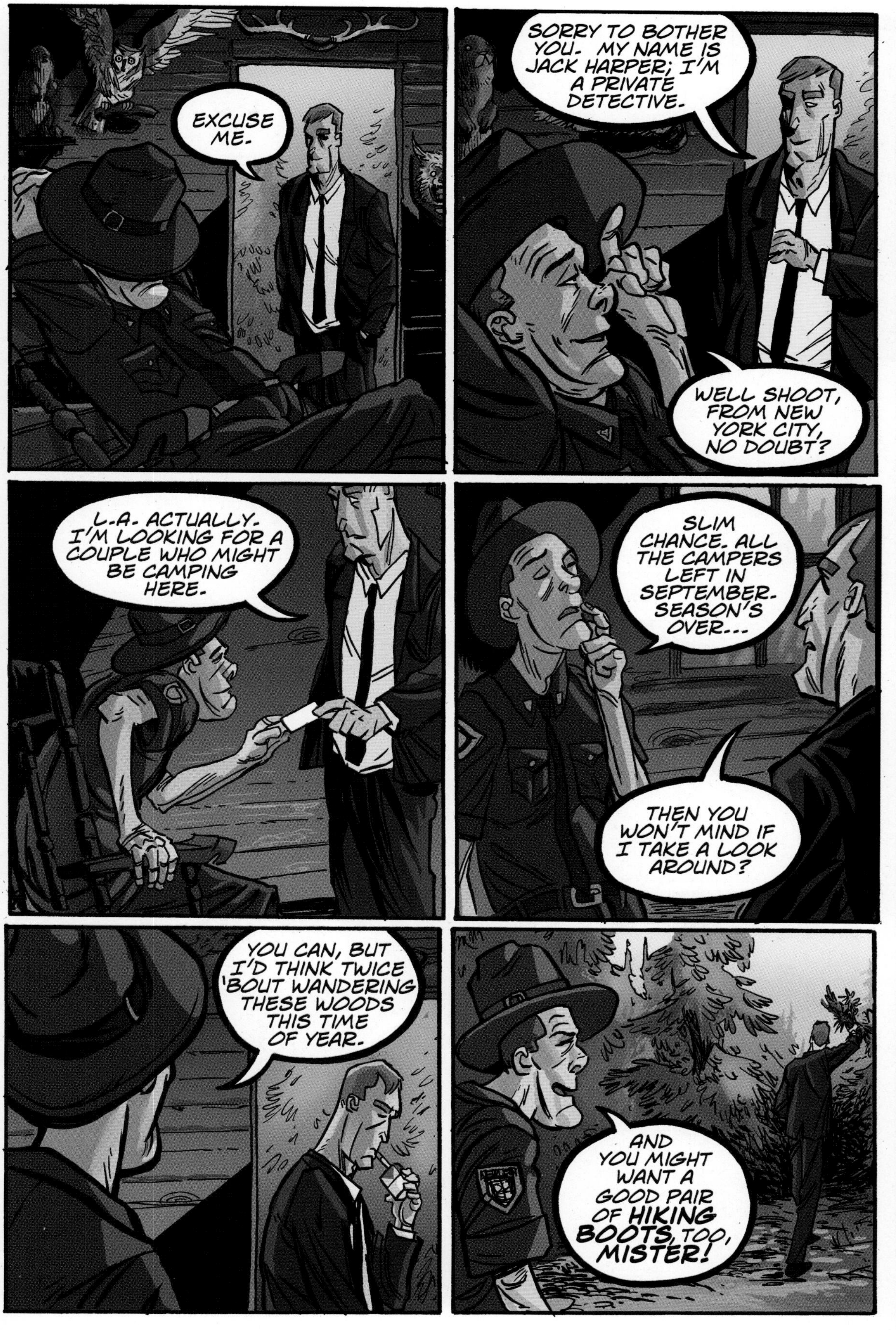
EXCUSE ME.
SORRY TO BOTHER YOU. MY NAME IS JACK HARPER; I'M A PRIVATE DETECTIVE.
WELL SHOOT, FROM NEW YORK CITY, NO DOUBT?
L.A. ACTUALLY. I'M LOOKING FOR A COUPLE WHO MIGHT BE CAMPING HERE.
SLIM CHANCE. ALL THE CAMPERS LEFT IN SEPTEMBER. SEASON'S OVER...
THEN YOU WON'T MIND IF I TAKE A LOOK AROUND?
YOU CAN, BUT I'D THINK TWICE 'BOUT WANDERING THESE WOODS THIS TIME OF YEAR.
AND YOU MIGHT WANT A GOOD PAIR OF **HIKING BOOTS**, TOO, **MISTER!**

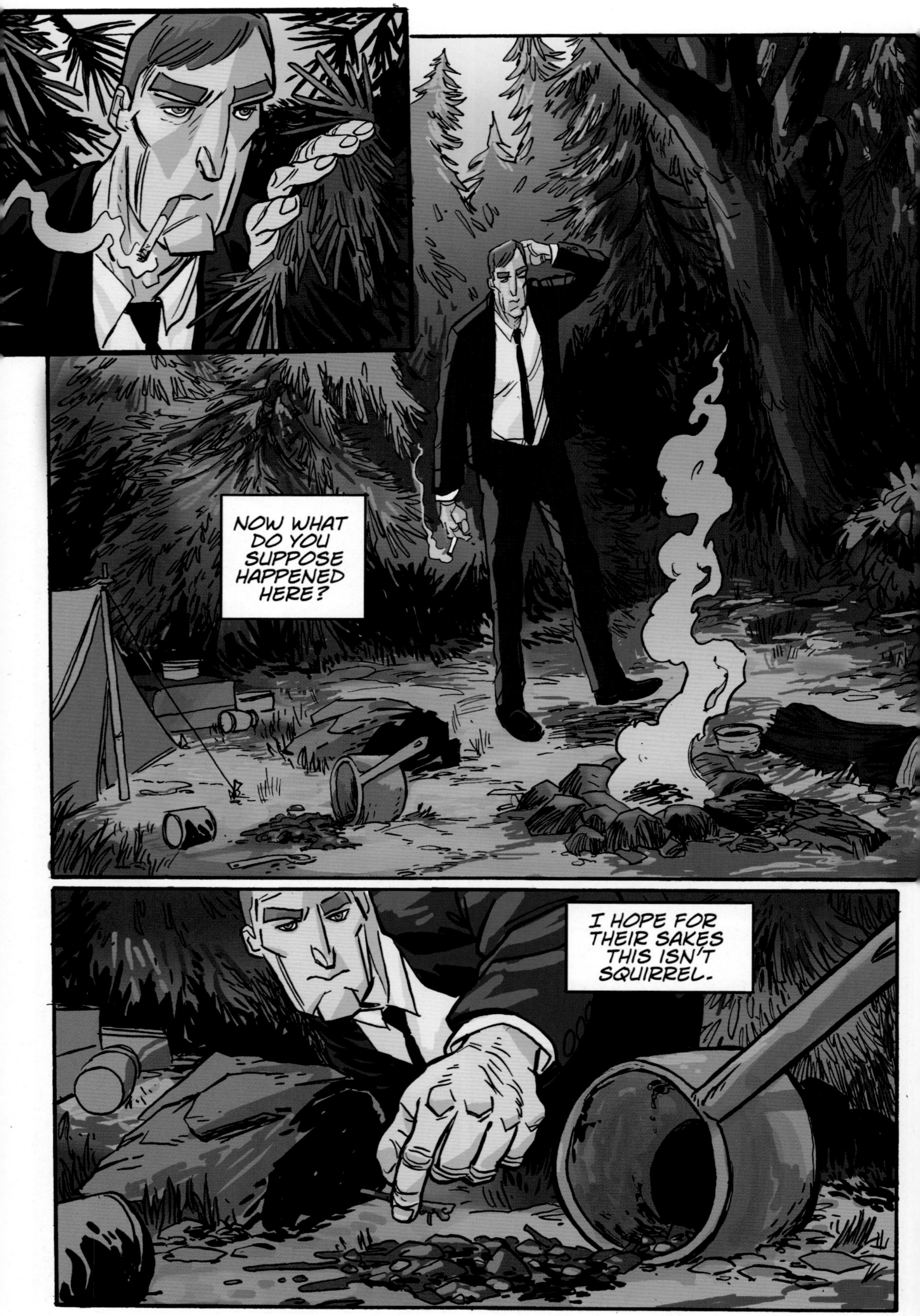
NOW WHAT DO YOU SUPPOSE HAPPENED HERE?
I HOPE FOR THEIR SAKES THIS ISN'T SQUIRREL.

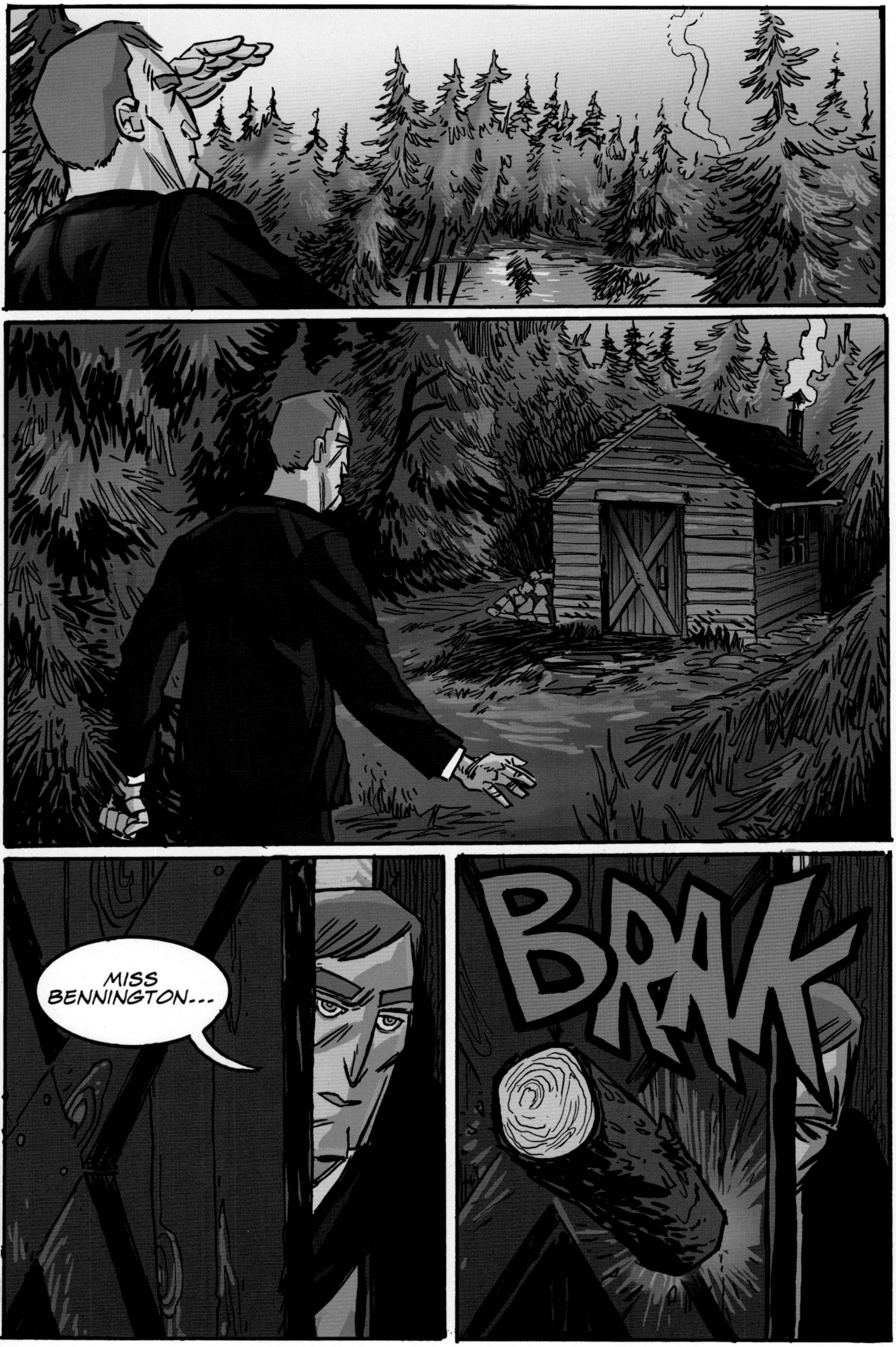
MISS BENNINGTON...
BRAK

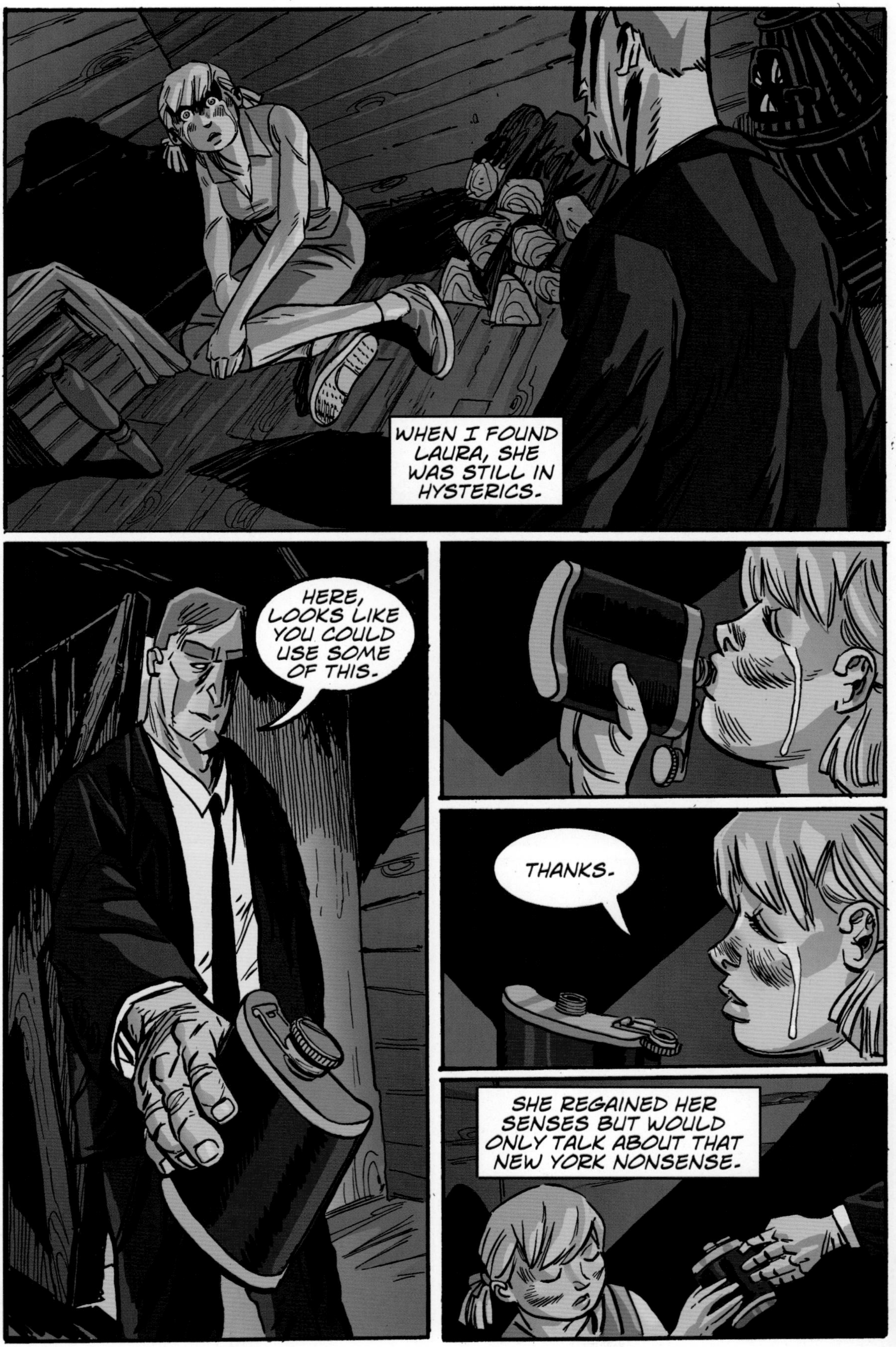
WHEN I FOUND LAURA, SHE WAS STILL IN HYSTERICS.
HERE, LOOKS LIKE YOU COULD USE SOME OF THIS.
THANKS.
SHE REGAINED HER SENSES BUT WOULD ONLY TALK ABOUT THAT NEW YORK NONSENSE.

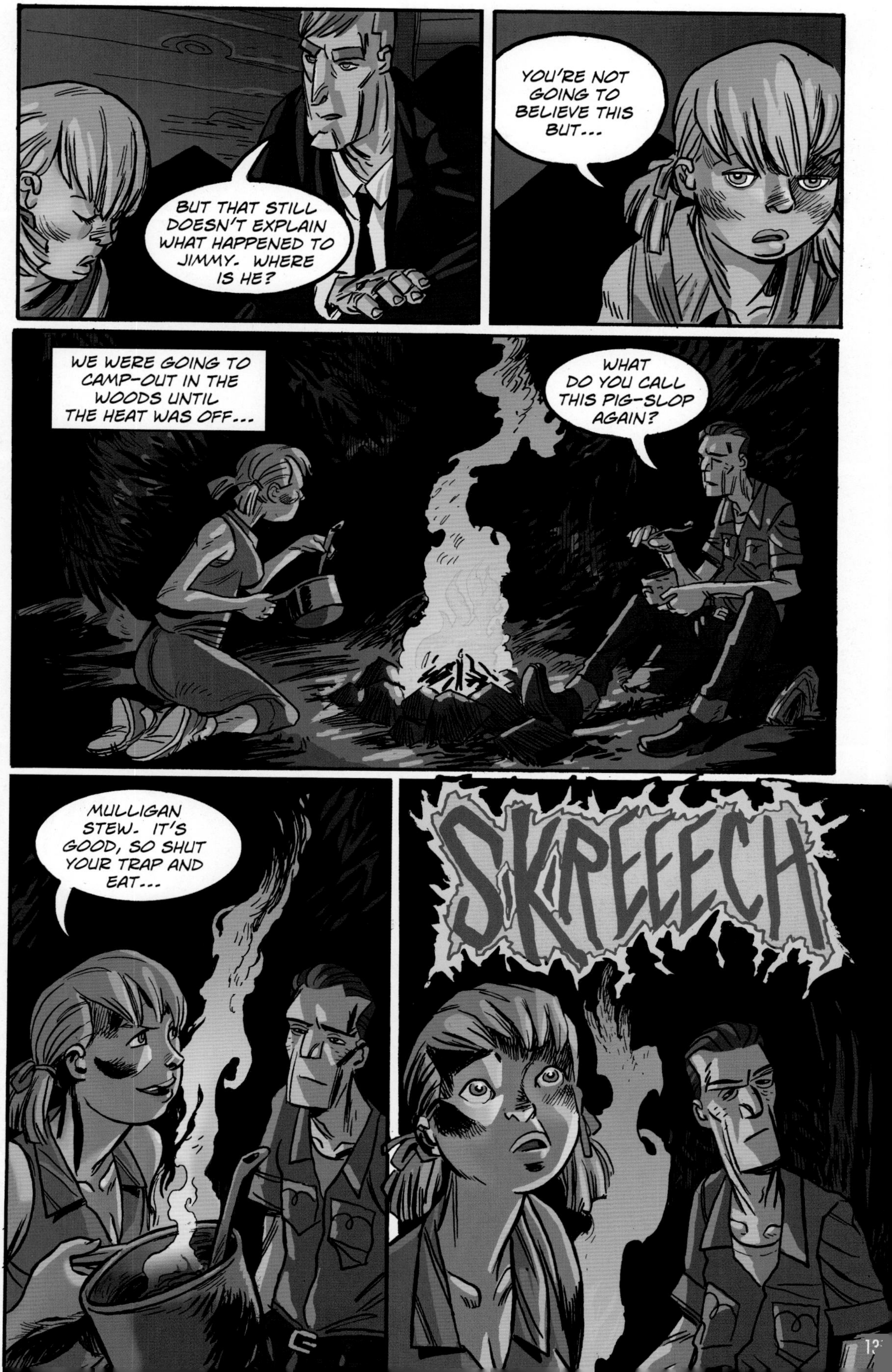
BUT THAT STILL DOESN'T EXPLAIN WHAT HAPPENED TO JIMMY. WHERE IS HE?
YOU'RE NOT GOING TO BELIEVE THIS BUT...
WE WERE GOING TO CAMP-OUT IN THE WOODS UNTIL THE HEAT WAS OFF...
WHAT DO YOU CALL THIS PIG-SLOP AGAIN?
MULLIGAN STEW. IT'S GOOD, SO SHUT YOUR TRAP AND EAT...
SKREEECH

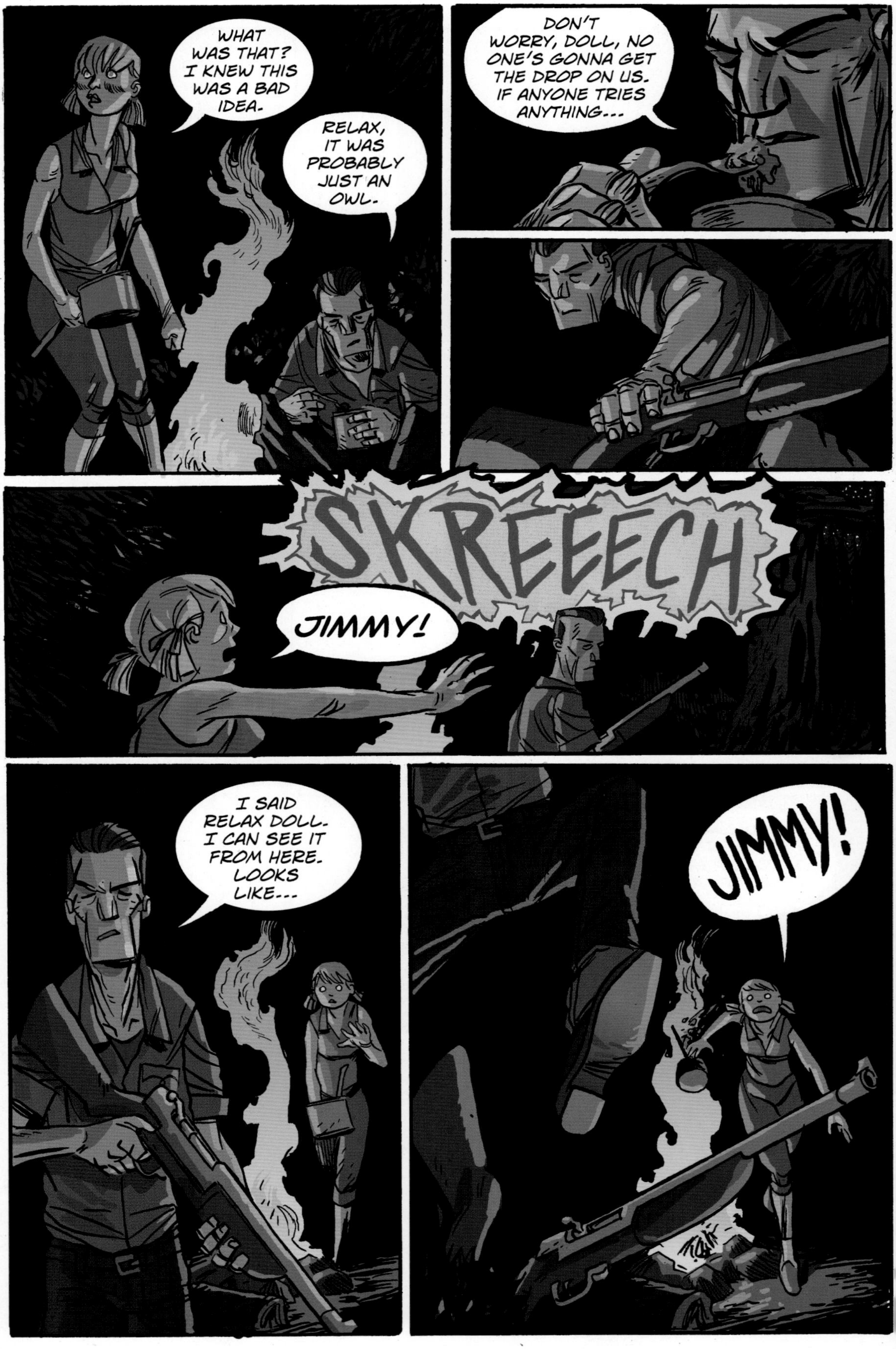
WHAT WAS THAT? I KNEW THIS WAS A BAD IDEA.
RELAX, IT WAS PROBABLY JUST AN OWL.
DON'T WORRY, DOLL, NO ONE'S GONNA GET THE DROP ON US. IF ANYONE TRIES ANYTHING...
SKREEECH
JIMMY!
I SAID RELAX DOLL. I CAN SEE IT FROM HERE. LOOKS LIKE...
JIMMY!

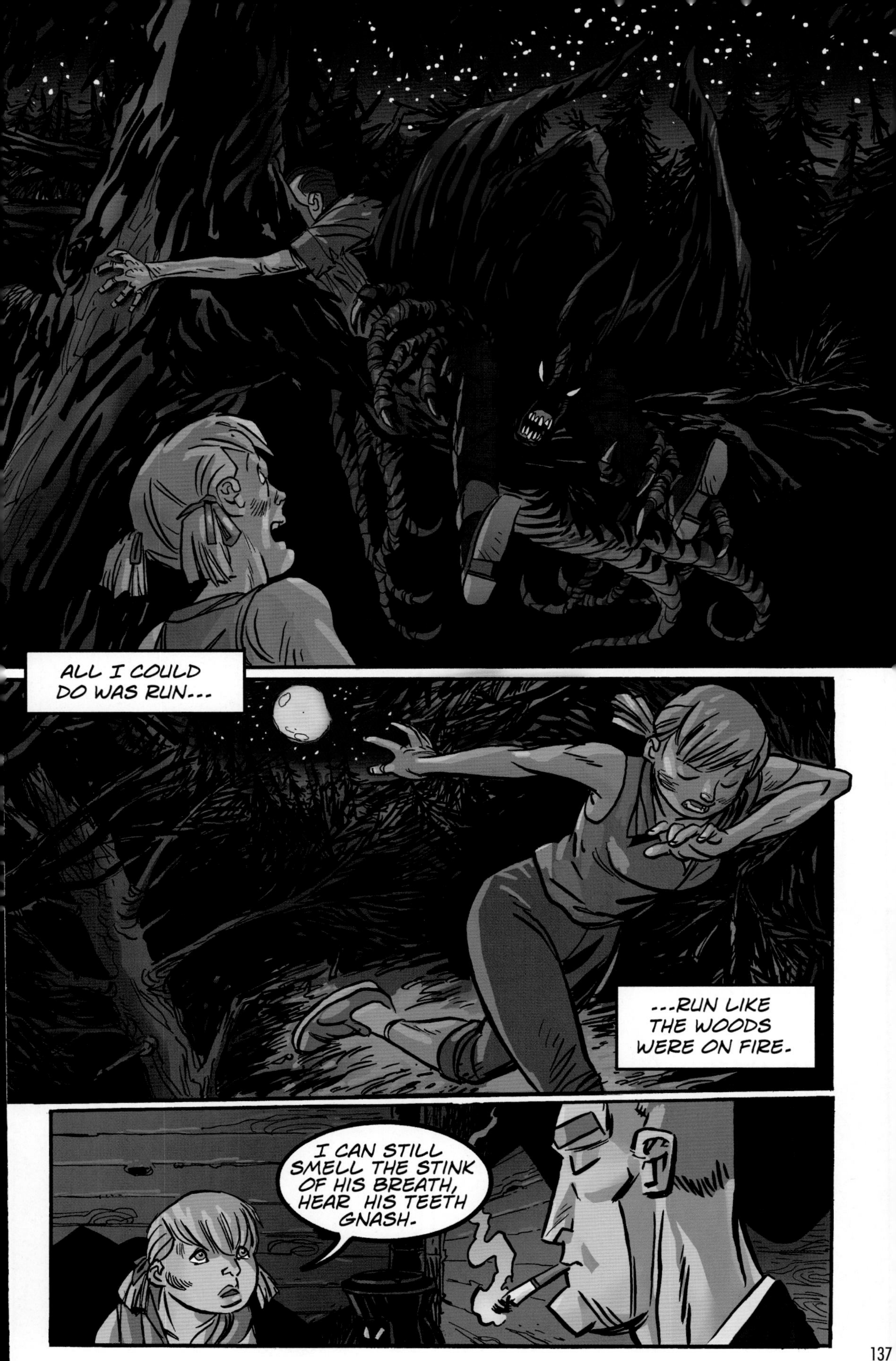
ALL I COULD DO WAS RUN...
...RUN LIKE THE WOODS WERE ON FIRE.
I CAN STILL SMELL THE STINK OF HIS BREATH, HEAR HIS TEETH GNASH.

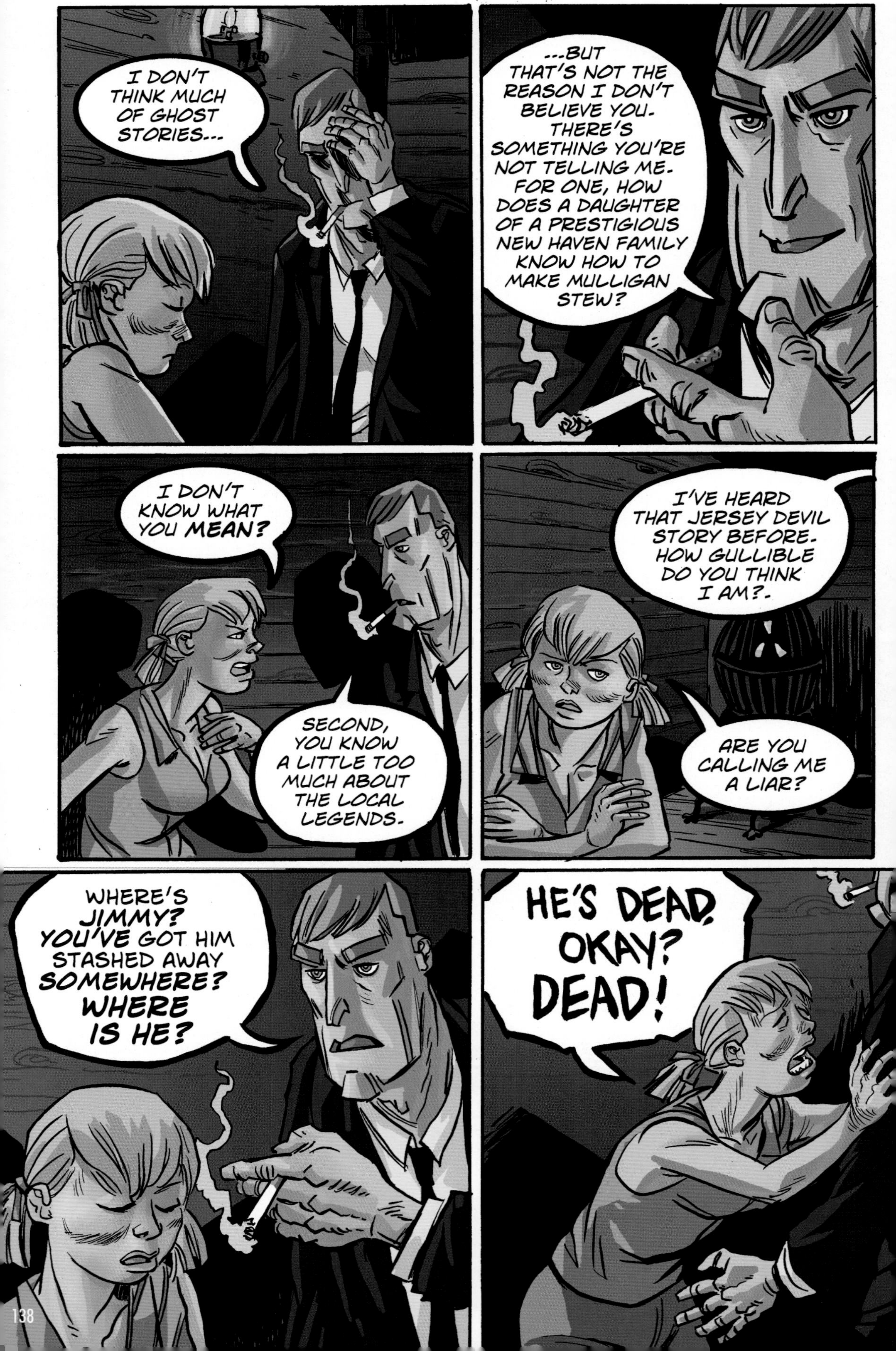
I DON'T THINK MUCH OF GHOST STORIES...
...BUT THAT'S NOT THE REASON I DON'T BELIEVE YOU. THERE'S SOMETHING YOU'RE NOT TELLING ME. FOR ONE, HOW DOES A DAUGHTER OF A PRESTIGIOUS NEW HAVEN FAMILY KNOW HOW TO MAKE MULLIGAN STEW?
I DON'T KNOW WHAT YOU MEAN?
SECOND, YOU KNOW A LITTLE TOO MUCH ABOUT THE LOCAL LEGENDS.
I'VE HEARD THAT JERSEY DEVIL STORY BEFORE. HOW GULLIBLE DO YOU THINK I AM?.
ARE YOU CALLING ME A LIAR?
WHERE'S JIMMY? YOU'VE GOT HIM STASHED AWAY SOMEWHERE? WHERE IS HE?
HE'S DEAD, OKAY? DEAD!

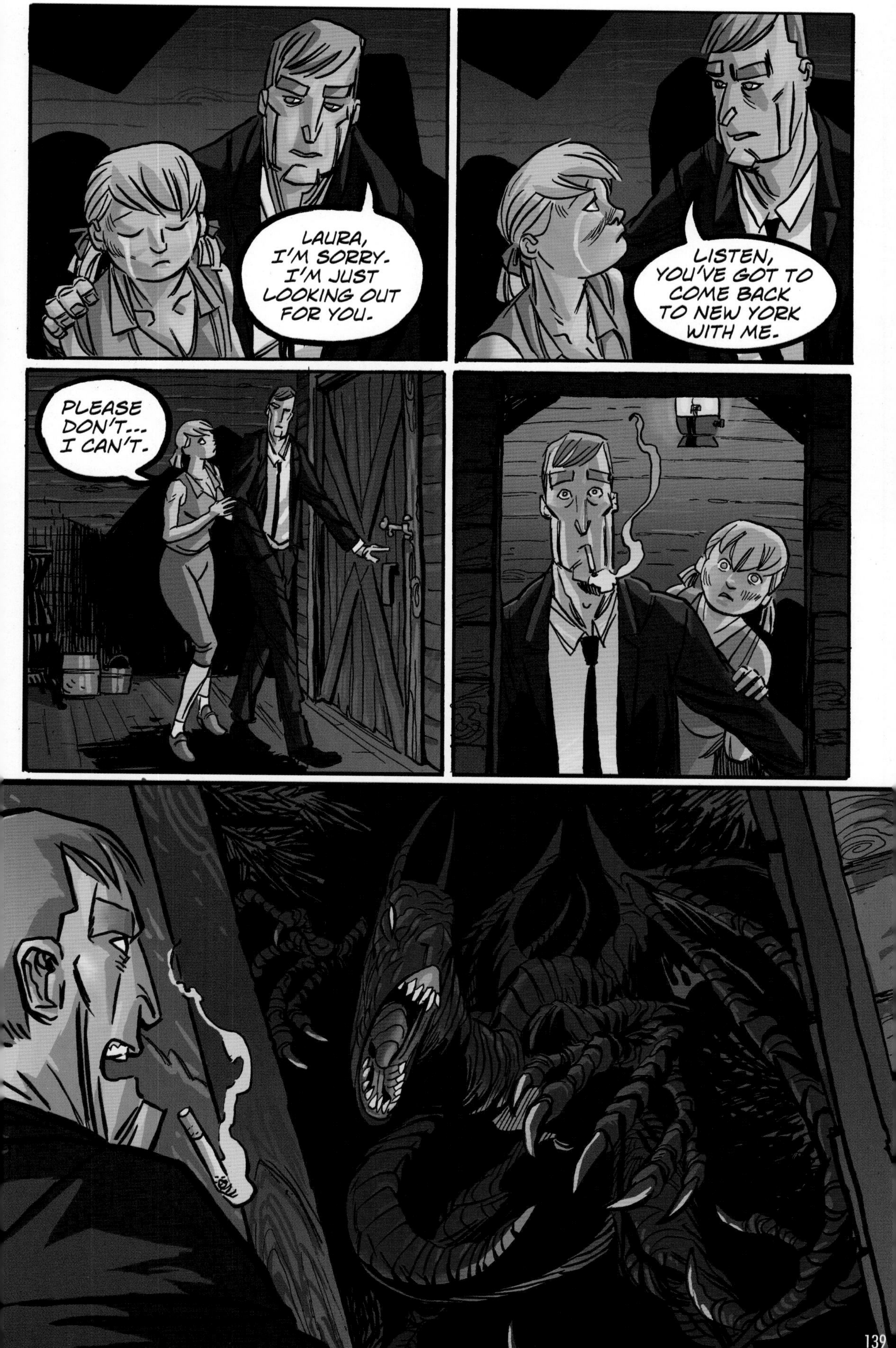
LAURA, I'M SORRY. I'M JUST LOOKING OUT FOR YOU.
LISTEN, YOU'VE GOT TO COME BACK TO NEW YORK WITH ME.
PLEASE DON'T... I CAN'T.

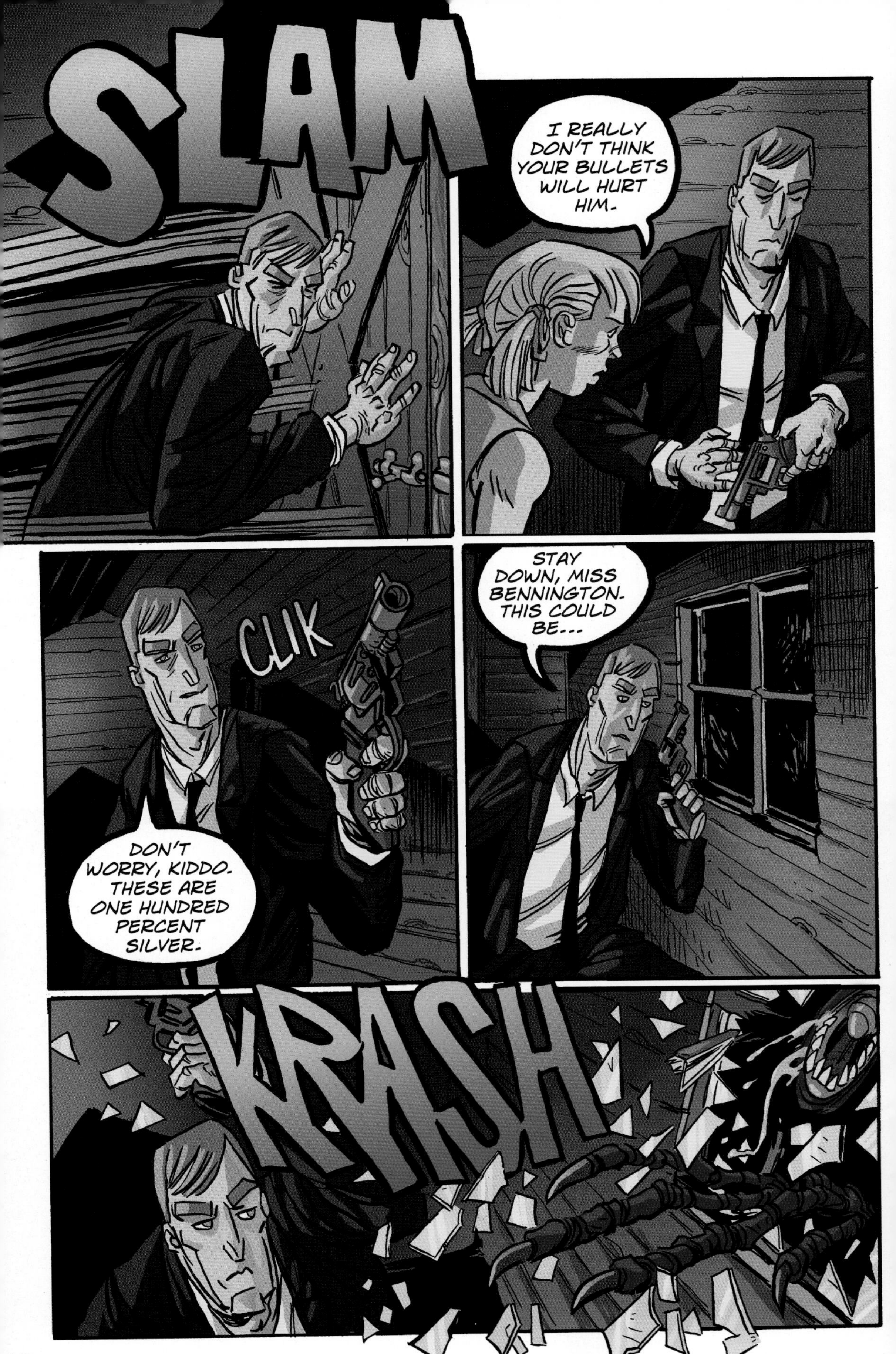
SLAM
I REALLY DON'T THINK YOUR BULLETS WILL HURT HIM.
CLIK
DON'T WORRY, KIDDO. THESE ARE ONE HUNDRED PERCENT SILVER.
STAY DOWN, MISS BENNINGTON. THIS COULD BE...
KRASH

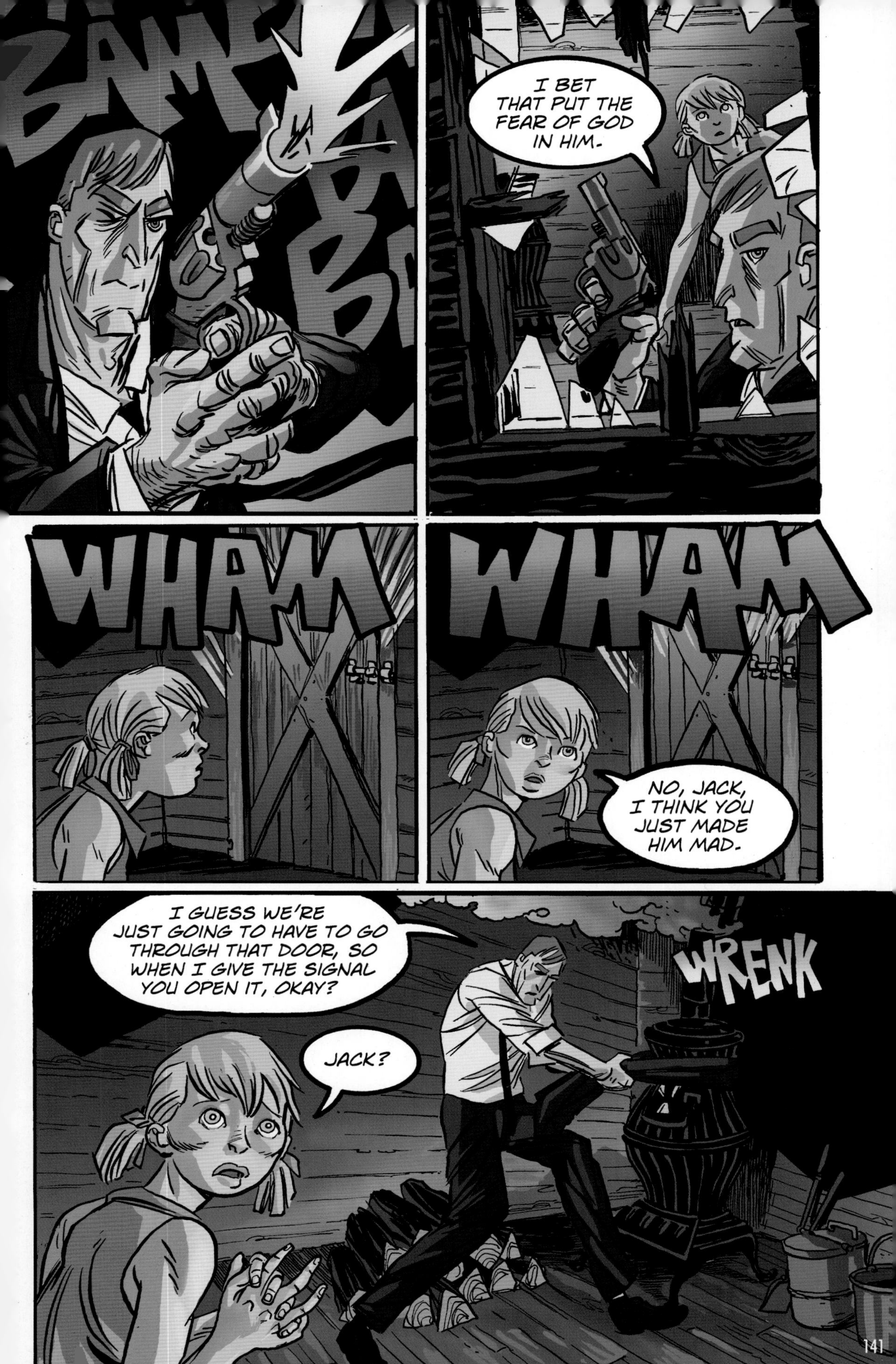
BAM! BA BA
I BET THAT PUT THE FEAR OF GOD IN HIM.
WHAM
WHAM
NO, JACK, I THINK YOU JUST MADE HIM MAD.
I GUESS WE'RE JUST GOING TO HAVE TO GO THROUGH THAT DOOR, SO WHEN I GIVE THE SIGNAL YOU OPEN IT, OKAY?
WRENK
JACK?

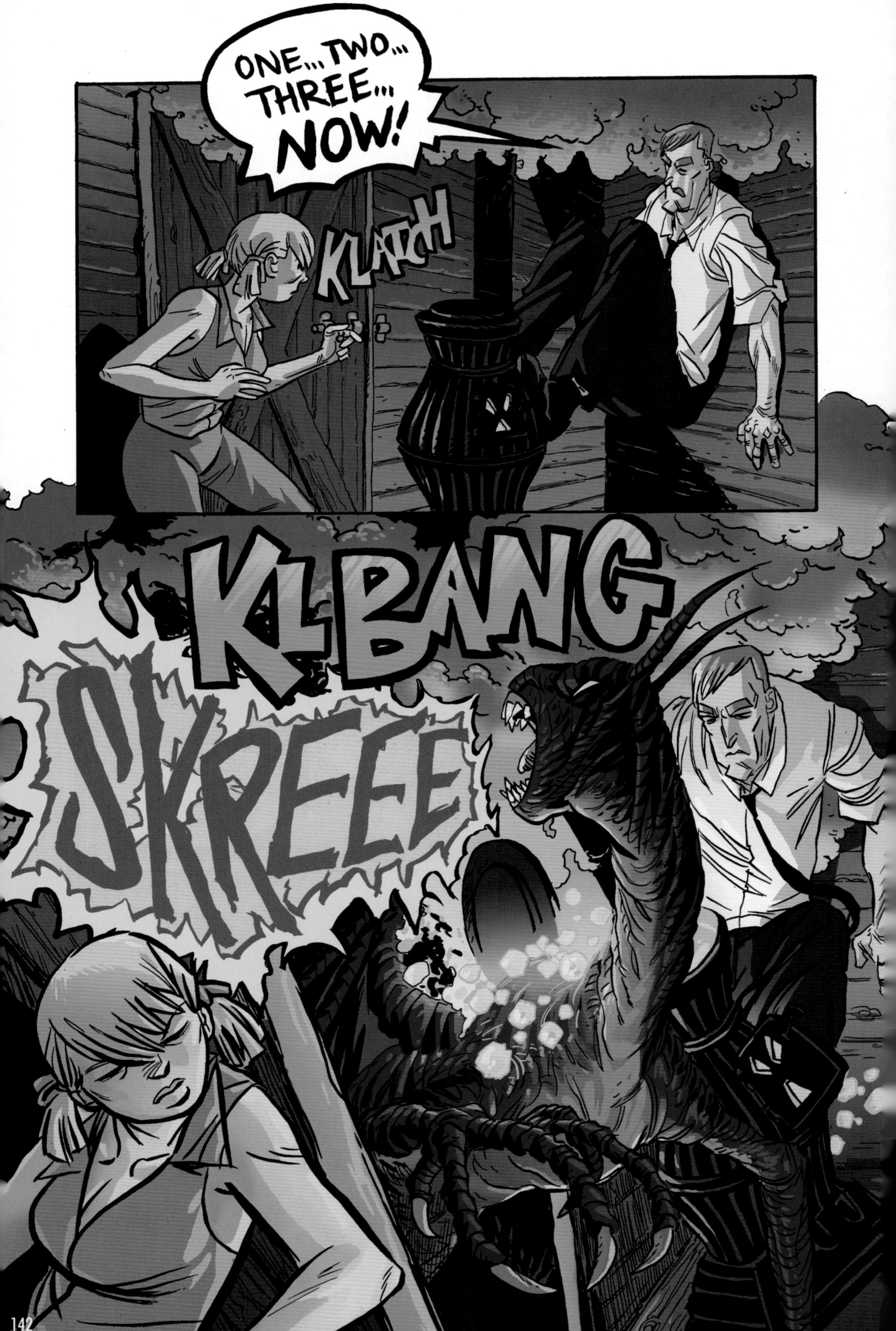
ONE... TWO... THREE... NOW!
KLATCH
KLBANG
SKREEE

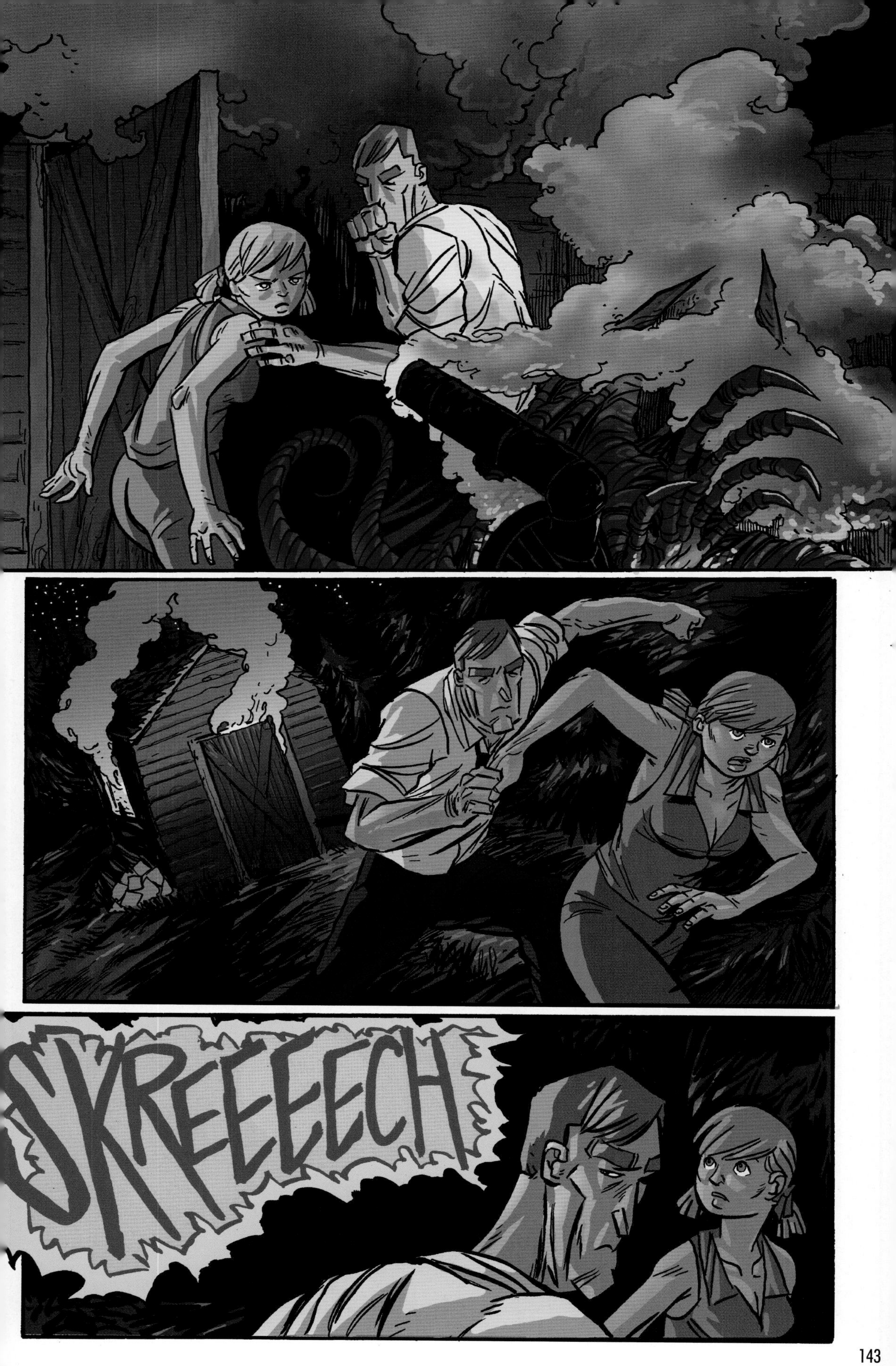
SKREEEECH

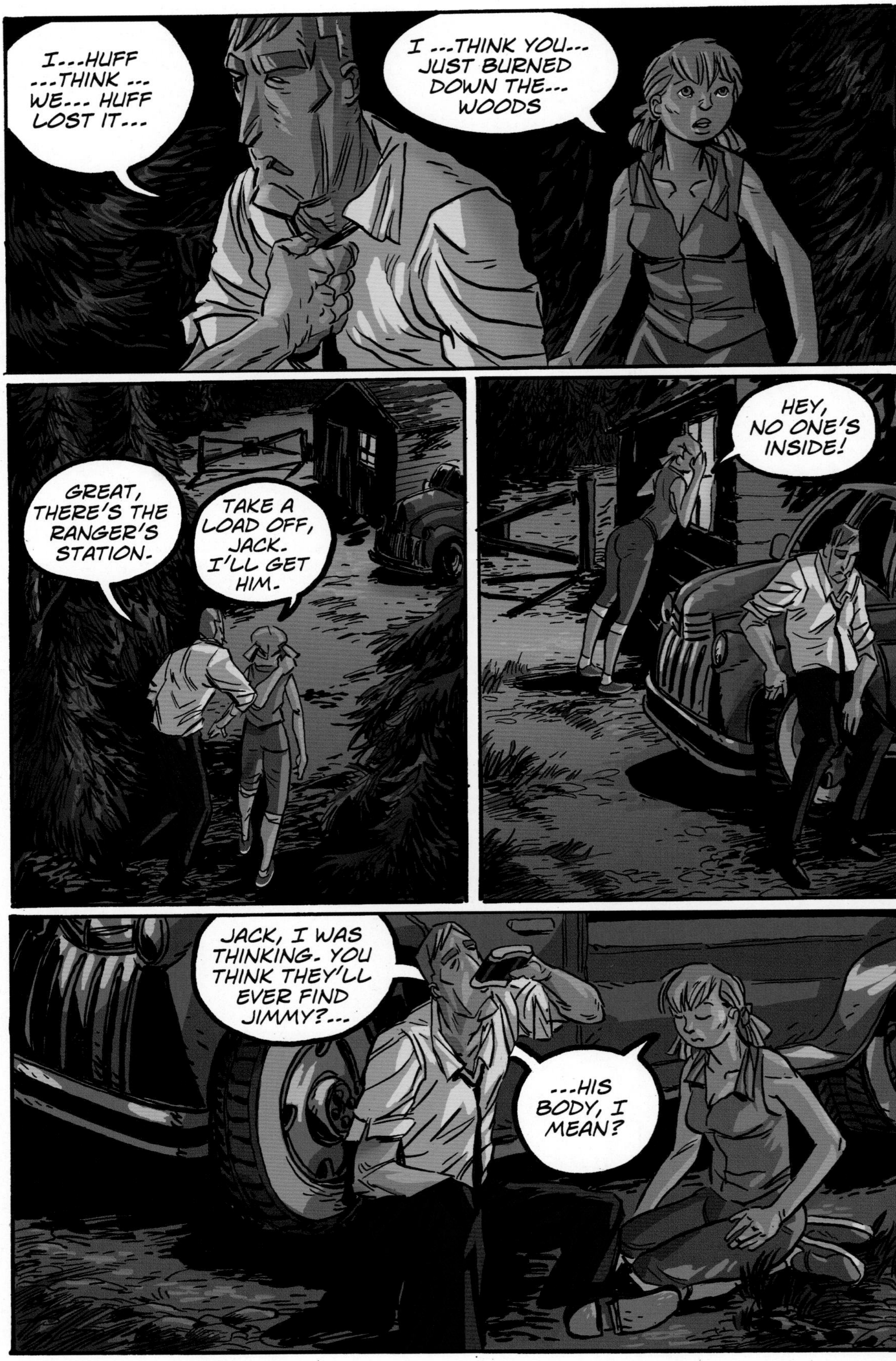
I---HUFF ---THINK --- WE--- HUFF LOST IT---
I ---THINK YOU--- JUST BURNED DOWN THE--- WOODS
GREAT, THERE'S THE RANGER'S STATION.
TAKE A LOAD OFF, JACK. I'LL GET HIM.
HEY, NO ONE'S INSIDE!
JACK, I WAS THINKING. YOU THINK THEY'LL EVER FIND JIMMY?...
---HIS BODY, I MEAN?

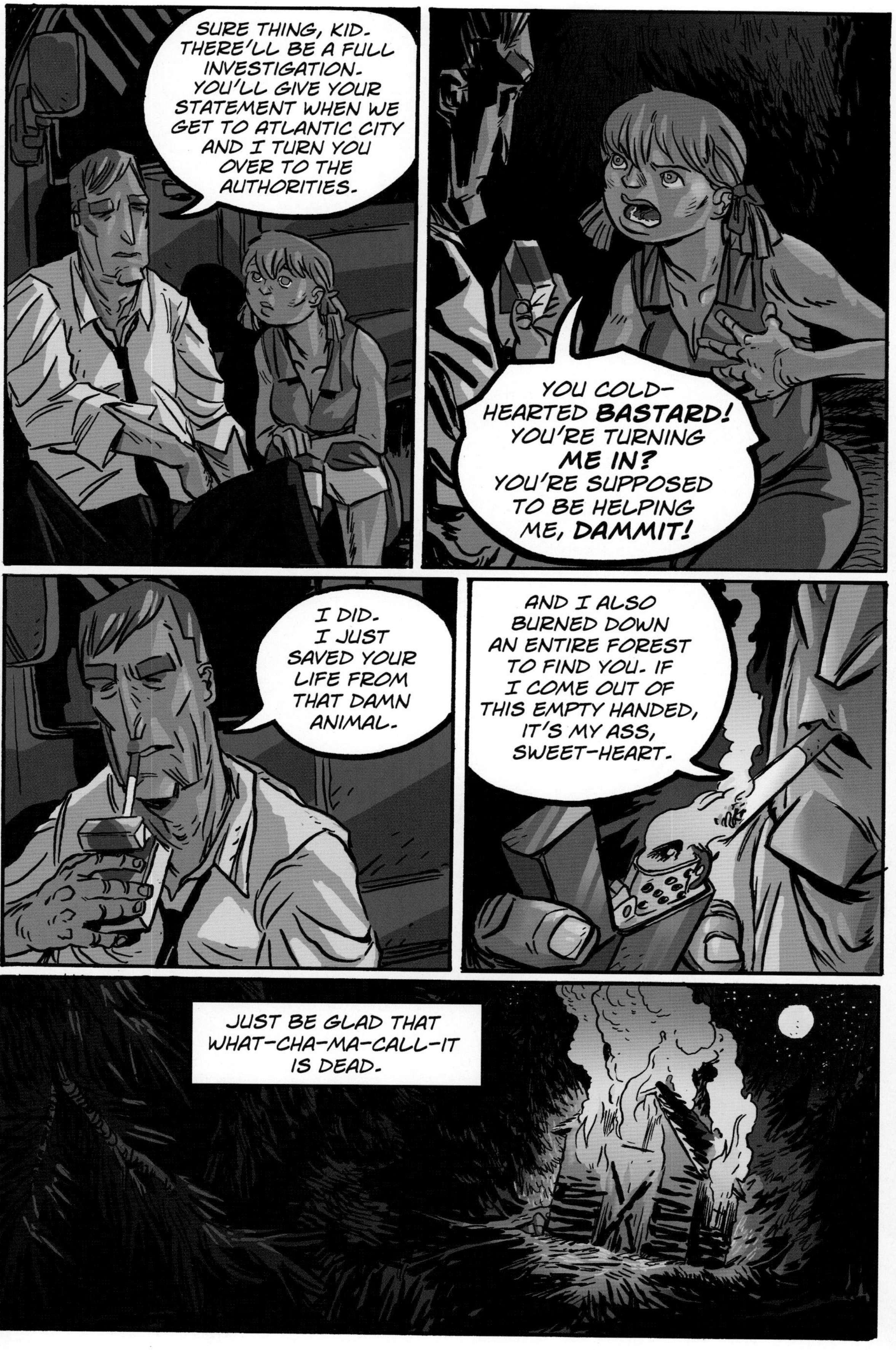
SURE THING, KID. THERE'LL BE A FULL INVESTIGATION. YOU'LL GIVE YOUR STATEMENT WHEN WE GET TO ATLANTIC CITY AND I TURN YOU OVER TO THE AUTHORITIES.
YOU COLD-HEARTED BASTARD! YOU'RE TURNING ME IN? YOU'RE SUPPOSED TO BE HELPING ME, DAMMIT!
I DID. I JUST SAVED YOUR LIFE FROM THAT DAMN ANIMAL.
AND I ALSO BURNED DOWN AN ENTIRE FOREST TO FIND YOU. IF I COME OUT OF THIS EMPTY HANDED, IT'S MY ASS, SWEET-HEART.
JUST BE GLAD THAT WHAT-CHA-MA-CALL-IT IS DEAD.

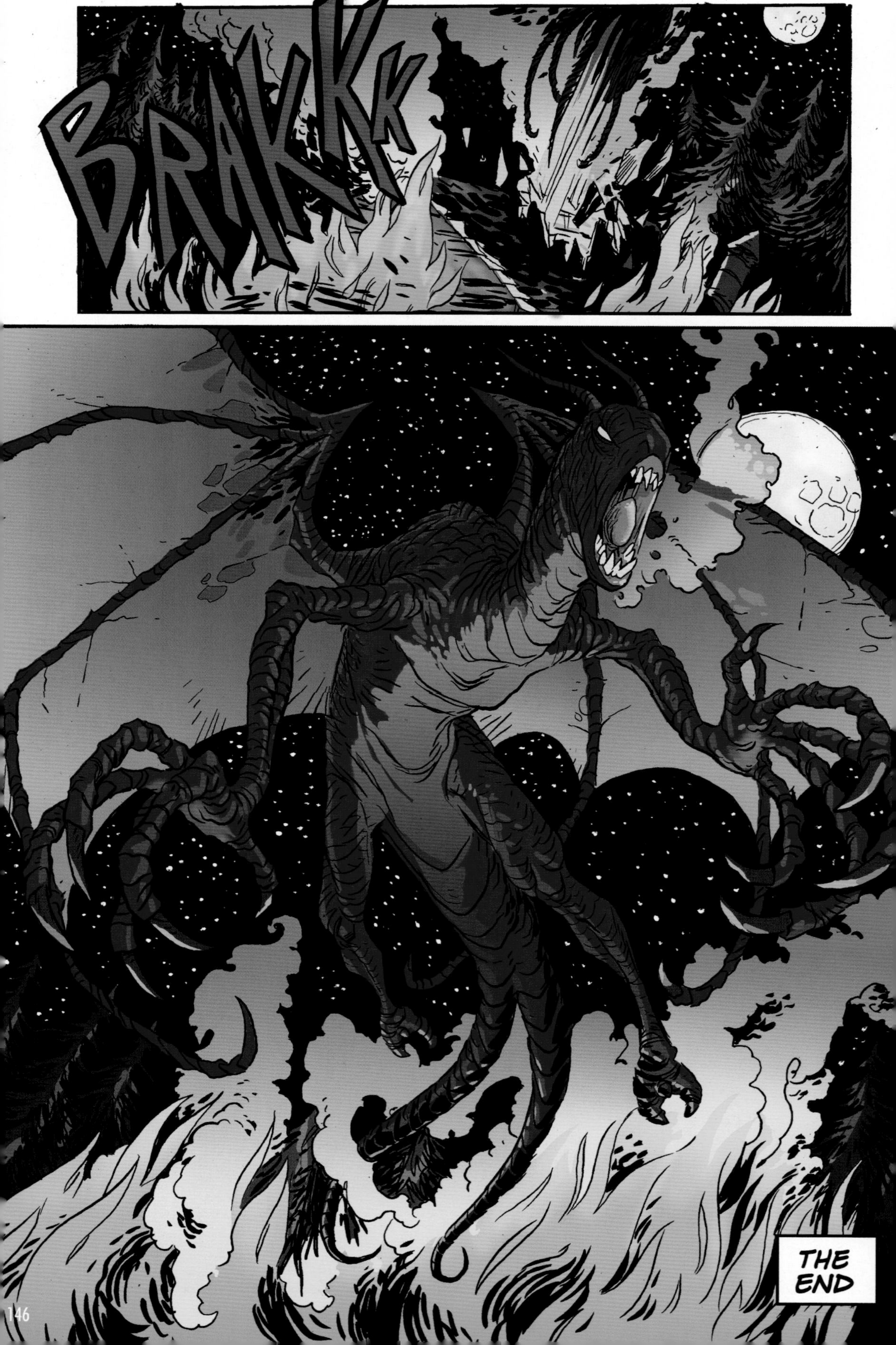
BRAKKK
THE END

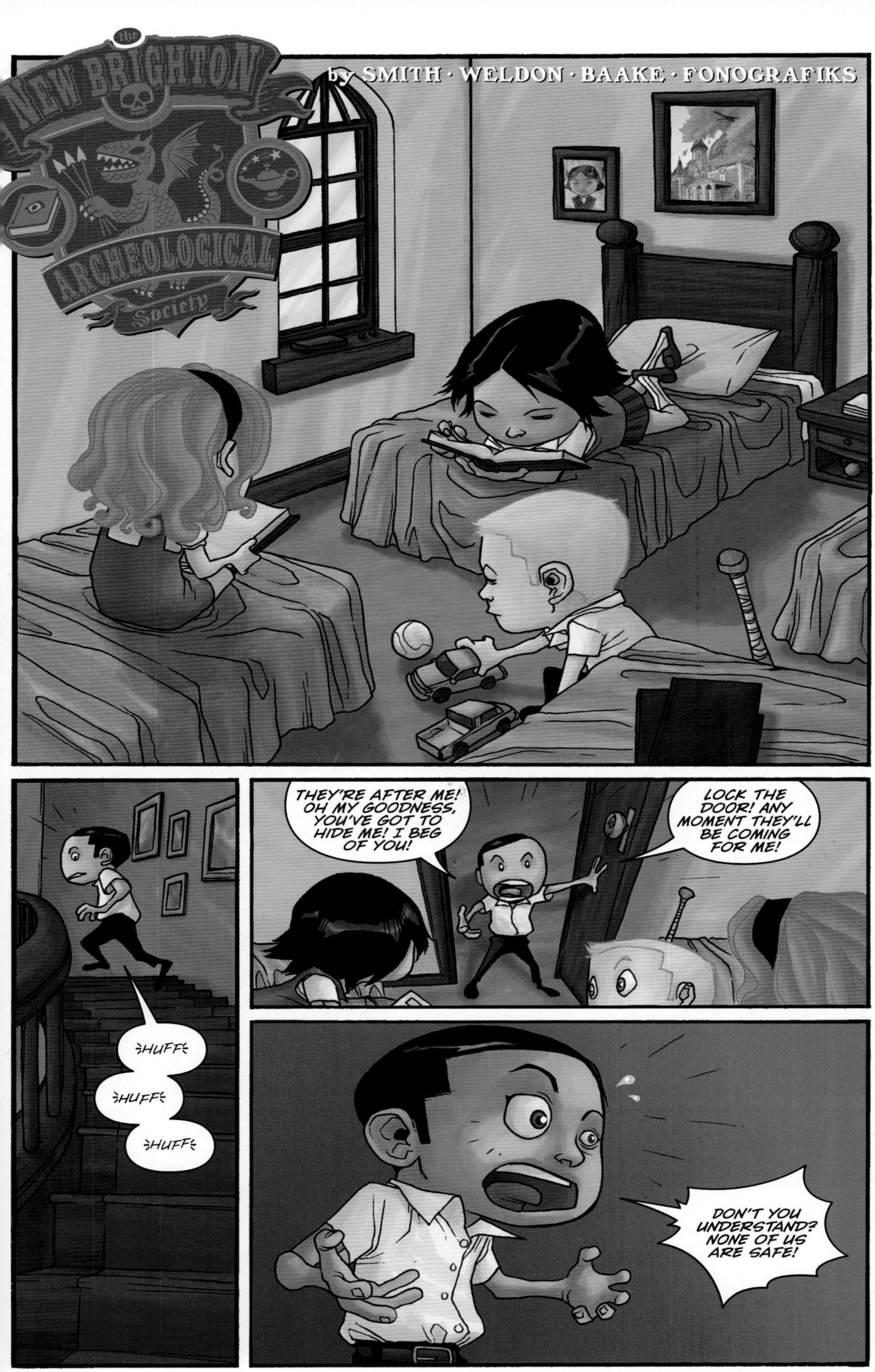

the NEW BRIGHTON ARCHEOLOGICAL Society
by SMITH · WELDON · BAAKE · FONOGRAFIKS
HUFF
HUFF
HUFF
THEY'RE AFTER ME! OH MY GOODNESS, YOU'VE GOT TO HIDE ME! I BEG OF YOU!
LOCK THE DOOR! ANY MOMENT THEY'LL BE COMING FOR ME!
DON'T YOU UNDERSTAND? NONE OF US ARE SAFE!

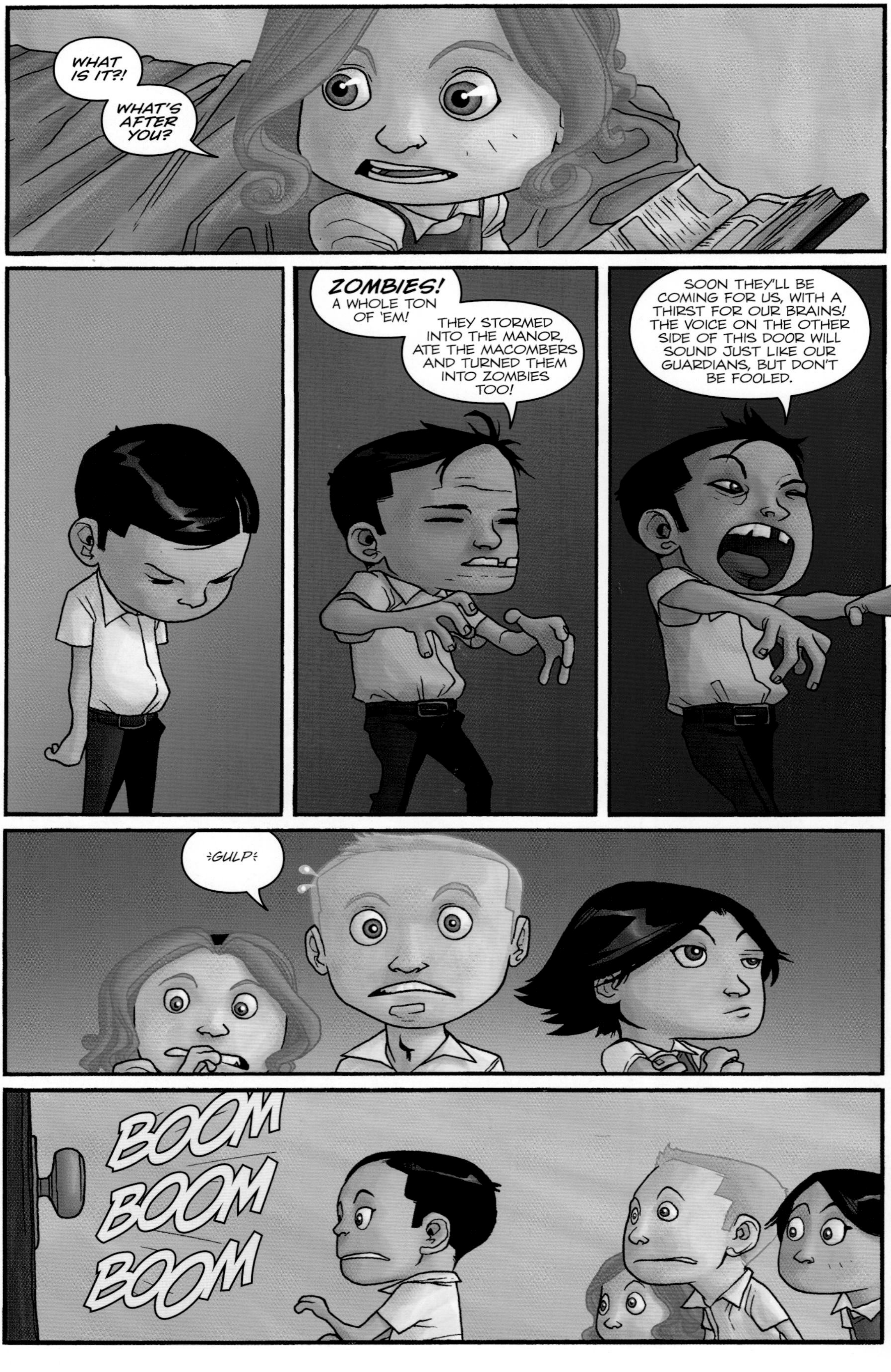
WHAT IS IT?!
WHAT'S AFTER YOU?
ZOMBIES! A WHOLE TON OF 'EM!
THEY STORMED INTO THE MANOR, ATE THE MACOMBERS AND TURNED THEM INTO ZOMBIES TOO!
SOON THEY'LL BE COMING FOR US, WITH A THIRST FOR OUR BRAINS! THE VOICE ON THE OTHER SIDE OF THIS DOOR WILL SOUND JUST LIKE OUR GUARDIANS, BUT DON'T BE FOOLED.
GULP
BOOM
BOOM
BOOM

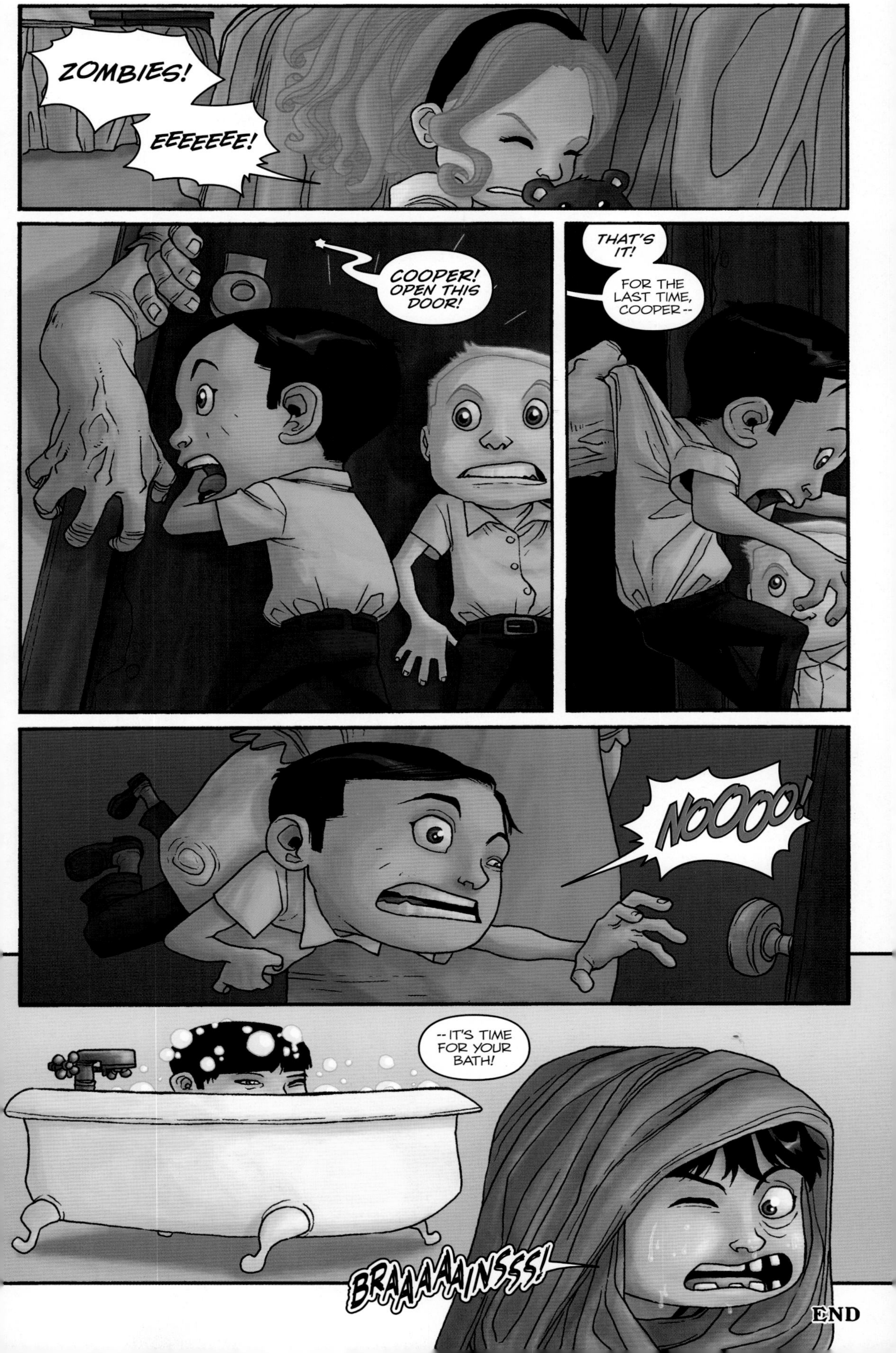
ZOMBIES!
EEEEEEE!
COOPER! OPEN THIS DOOR!
THAT'S IT!
FOR THE LAST TIME, COOPER--
NOOOO!
--IT'S TIME FOR YOUR BATH!
BRAAAAAINSSS!
END

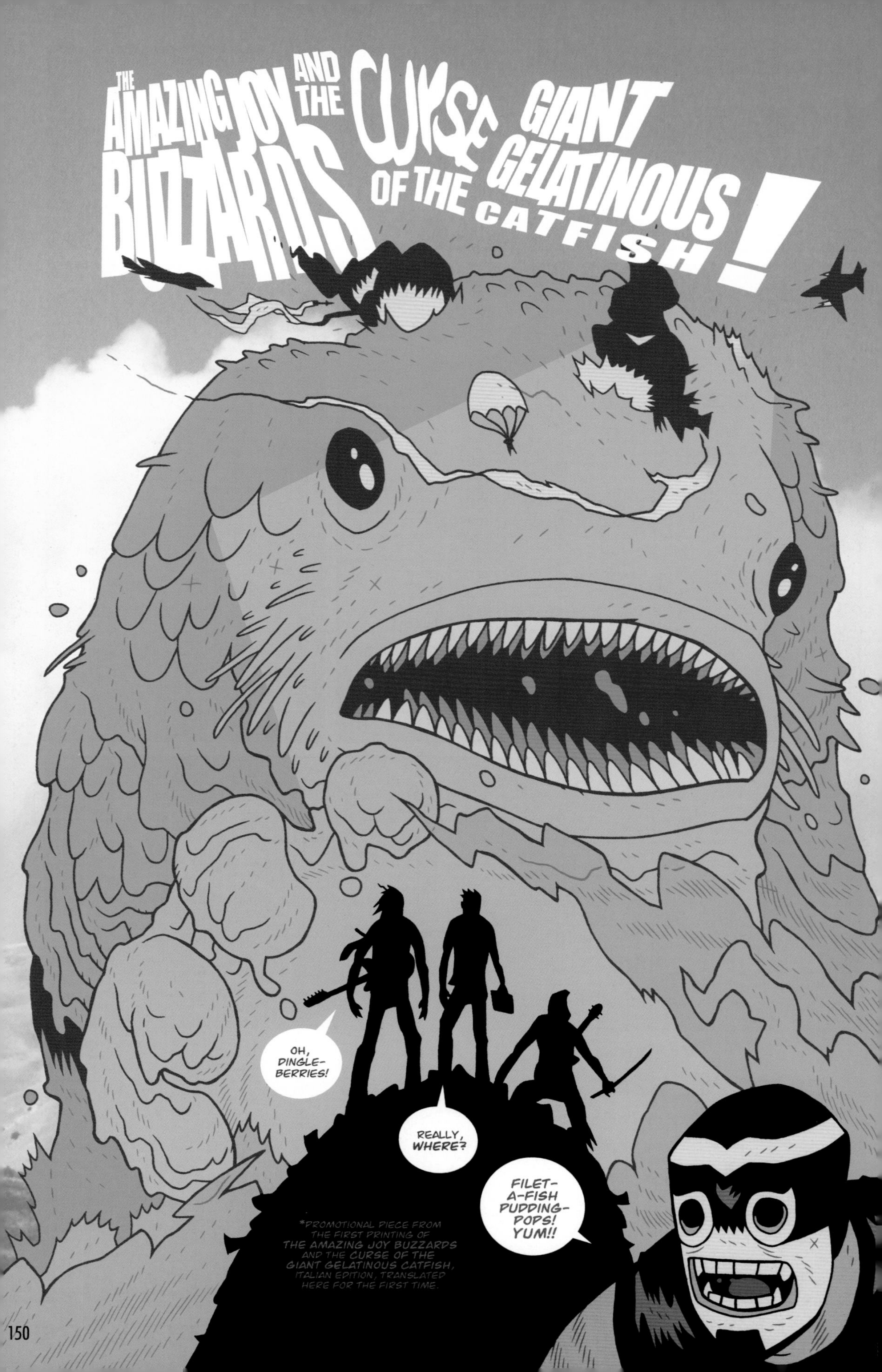
THE AMAZING JOY BUZZARDS AND THE CURSE OF THE GIANT GELATINOUS CATFISH!
OH, DINGLE-BERRIES!
REALLY, WHERE?
FILET-A-FISH PUDDING-POPS! YUM!!
*PROMOTIONAL PIECE FROM THE FIRST PRINTING OF THE AMAZING JOY BUZZARDS AND THE CURSE OF THE GIANT GELATINOUS CATFISH, ITALIAN EDITION, TRANSLATED HERE FOR THE FIRST TIME.

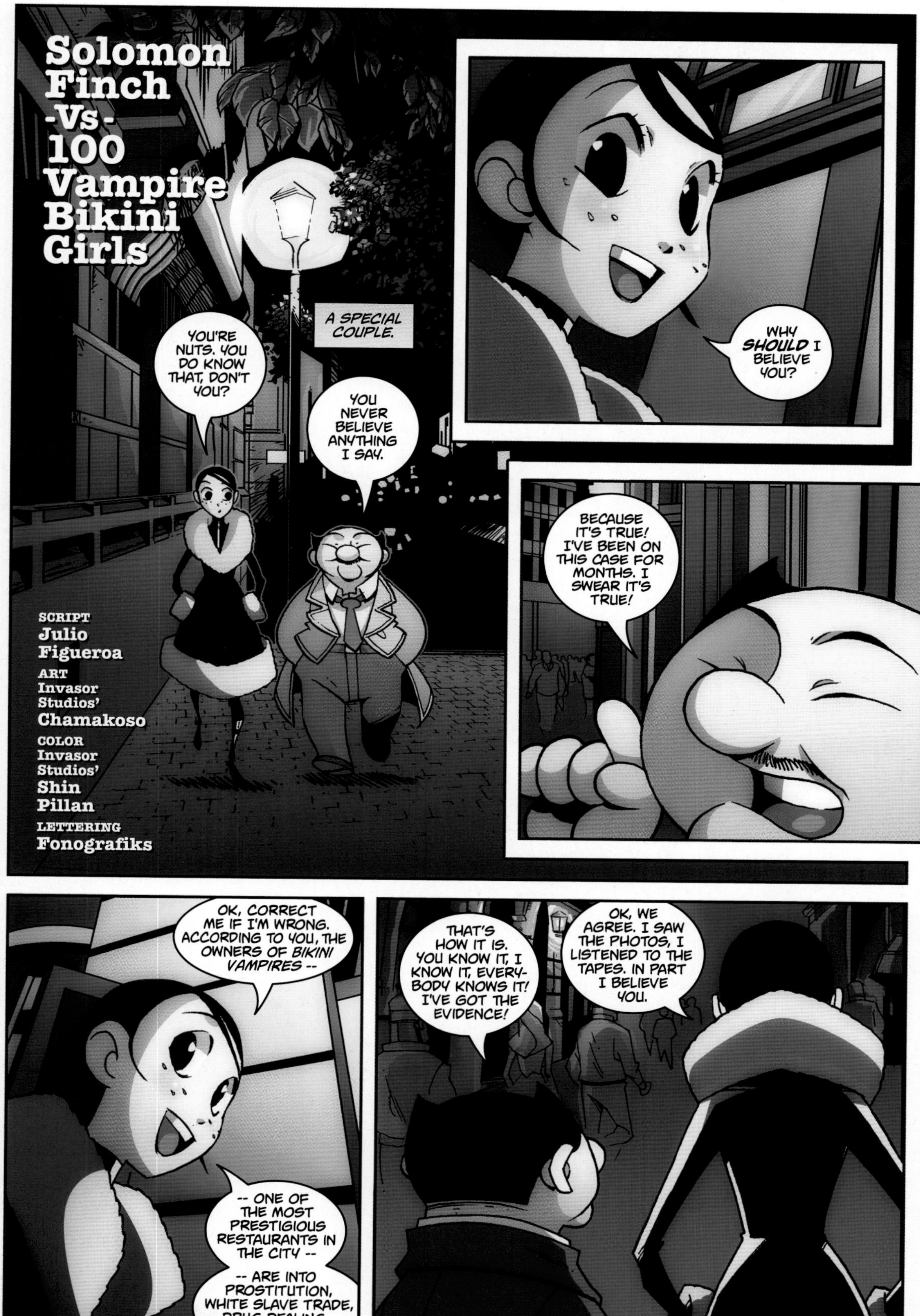
Solomon Finch -Vs- 100 Vampire Bikini Girls
A SPECIAL COUPLE.
YOU'RE NUTS. YOU DO KNOW THAT, DON'T YOU?
YOU NEVER BELIEVE ANYTHING I SAY.
SCRIPT Julio Figueroa
ART Invasor Studios' Chamakoso
COLOR Invasor Studios' Shin Pillan
LETTERING Fonografiks
WHY SHOULD I BELIEVE YOU?
BECAUSE IT'S TRUE! I'VE BEEN ON THIS CASE FOR MONTHS. I SWEAR IT'S TRUE!
OK, CORRECT ME IF I'M WRONG. ACCORDING TO YOU, THE OWNERS OF BIKINI VAMPIRES --
-- ONE OF THE MOST PRESTIGIOUS RESTAURANTS IN THE CITY --
-- ARE INTO PROSTITUTION, WHITE SLAVE TRADE, DRUG DEALING...
THAT'S HOW IT IS. YOU KNOW IT, I KNOW IT, EVERYBODY KNOWS IT! I'VE GOT THE EVIDENCE!
OK, WE AGREE. I SAW THE PHOTOS, I LISTENED TO THE TAPES. IN PART I BELIEVE YOU.

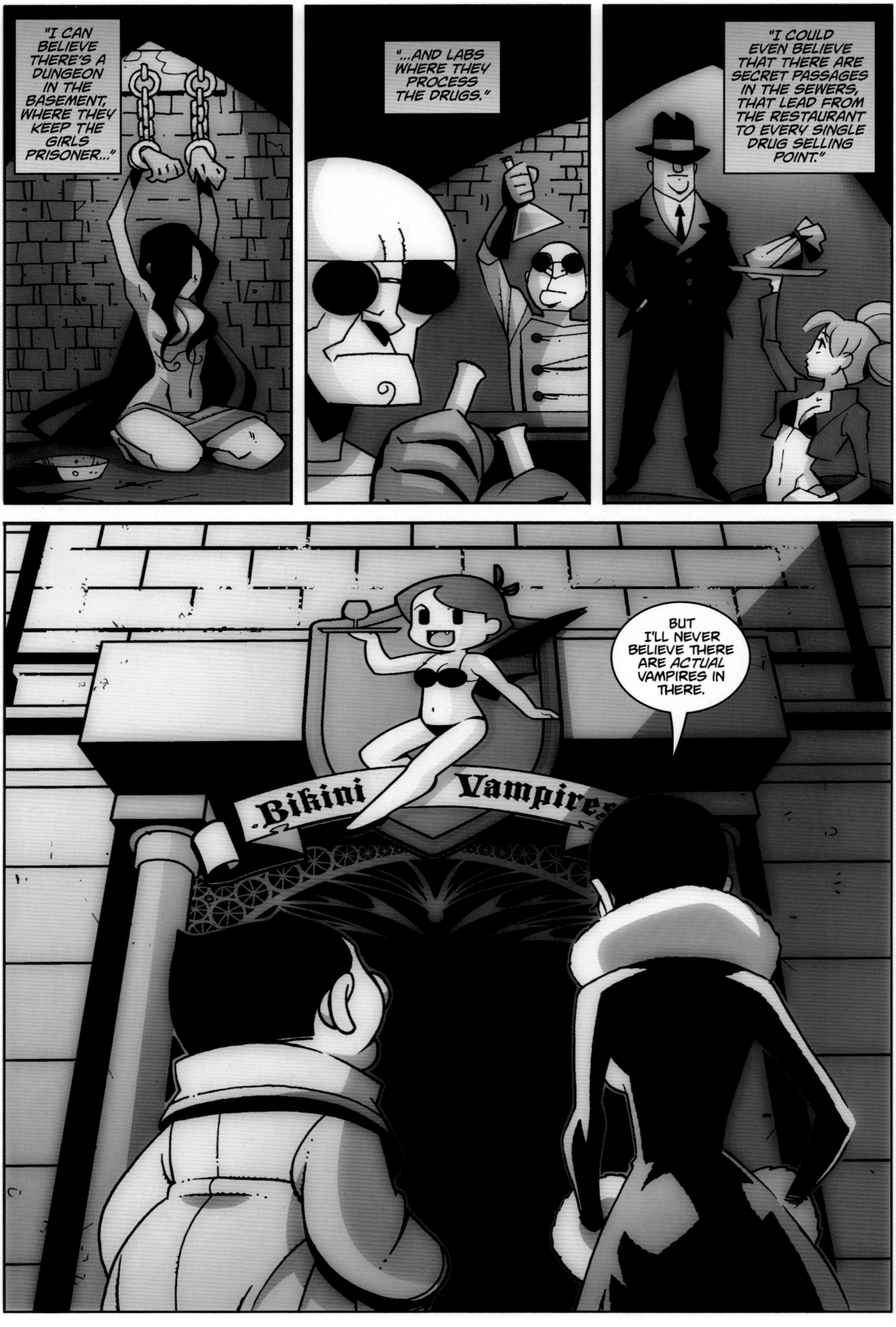
"I CAN BELIEVE THERE'S A DUNGEON IN THE BASEMENT, WHERE THEY KEEP THE GIRLS PRISONER..."
"...AND LABS WHERE THEY PROCESS THE DRUGS."
"I COULD EVEN BELIEVE THAT THERE ARE SECRET PASSAGES IN THE SEWERS, THAT LEAD FROM THE RESTAURANT TO EVERY SINGLE DRUG SELLING POINT."
BUT I'LL NEVER BELIEVE THERE ARE *ACTUAL* VAMPIRES IN THERE.
Bikini Vampires

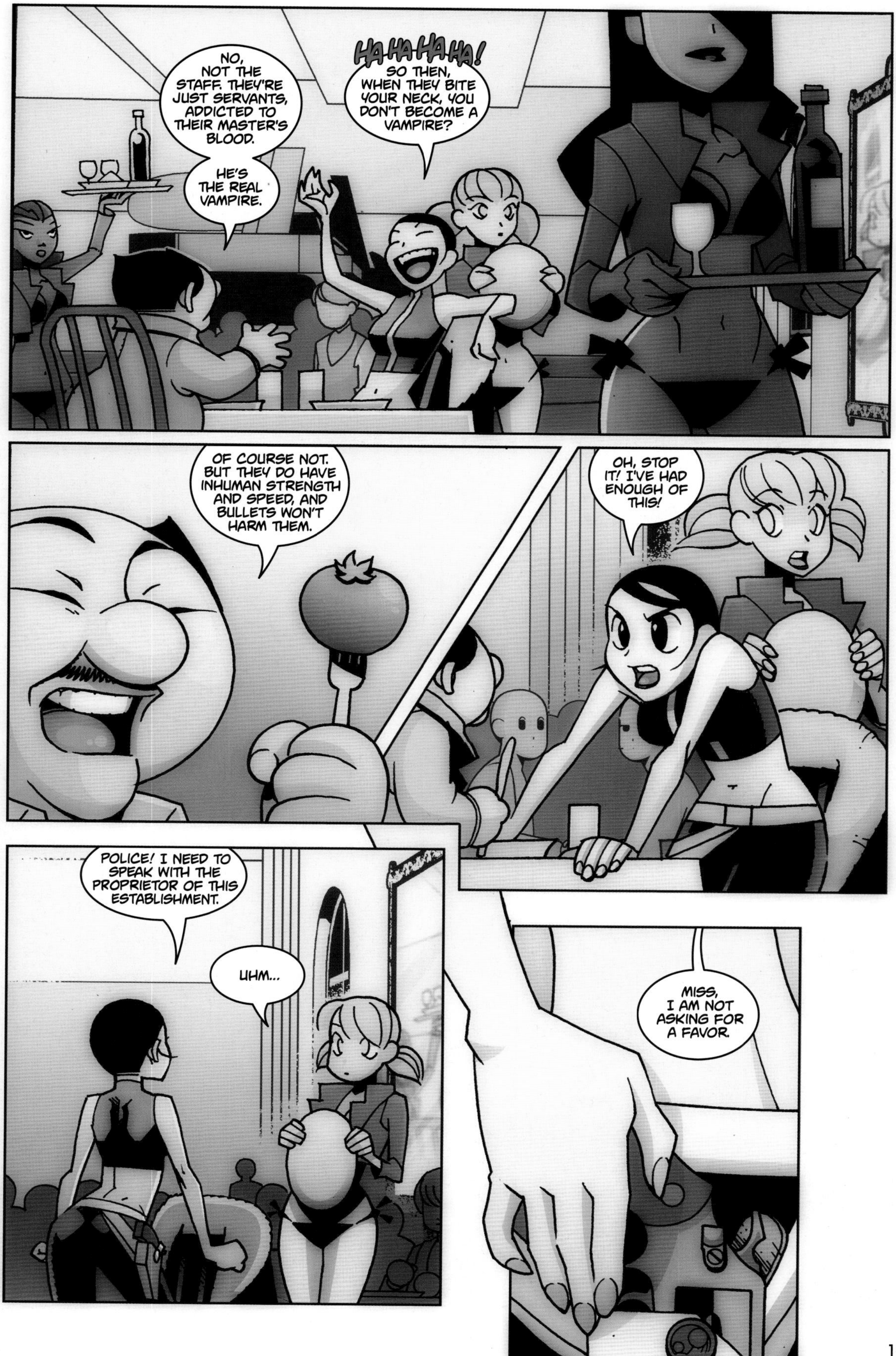
NO, NOT THE STAFF. THEY'RE JUST SERVANTS, ADDICTED TO THEIR MASTER'S BLOOD.
HE'S THE REAL VAMPIRE.
HA HA HA HA!
SO THEN, WHEN THEY BITE YOUR NECK, YOU DON'T BECOME A VAMPIRE?
OF COURSE NOT. BUT THEY DO HAVE INHUMAN STRENGTH AND SPEED, AND BULLETS WON'T HARM THEM.
OH, STOP IT! I'VE HAD ENOUGH OF THIS!
POLICE! I NEED TO SPEAK WITH THE PROPRIETOR OF THIS ESTABLISHMENT.
UHM...
MISS, I AM NOT ASKING FOR A FAVOR.

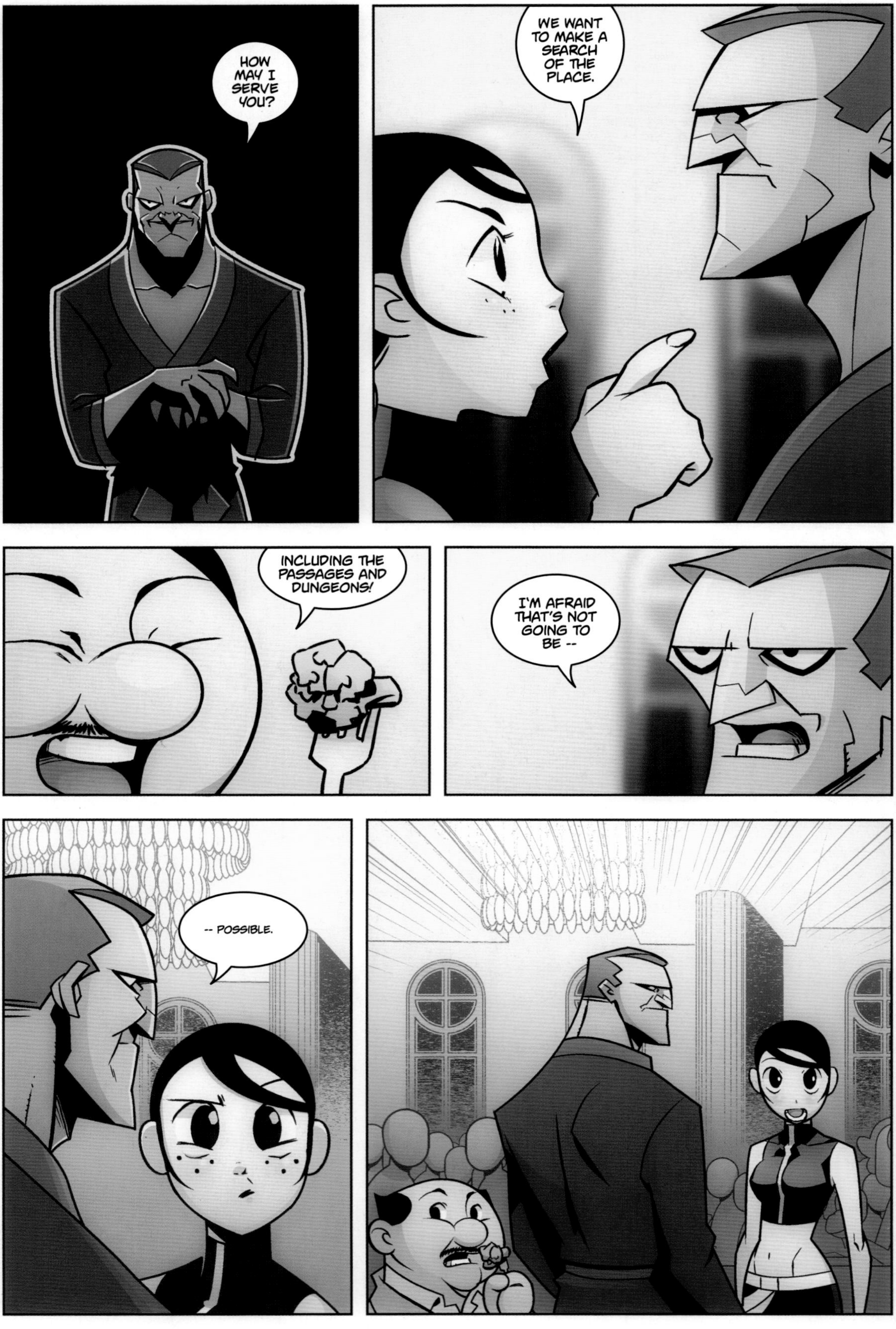
HOW MAY I SERVE YOU?
WE WANT TO MAKE A SEARCH OF THE PLACE.
INCLUDING THE PASSAGES AND DUNGEONS!
I'M AFRAID THAT'S NOT GOING TO BE --
-- POSSIBLE.

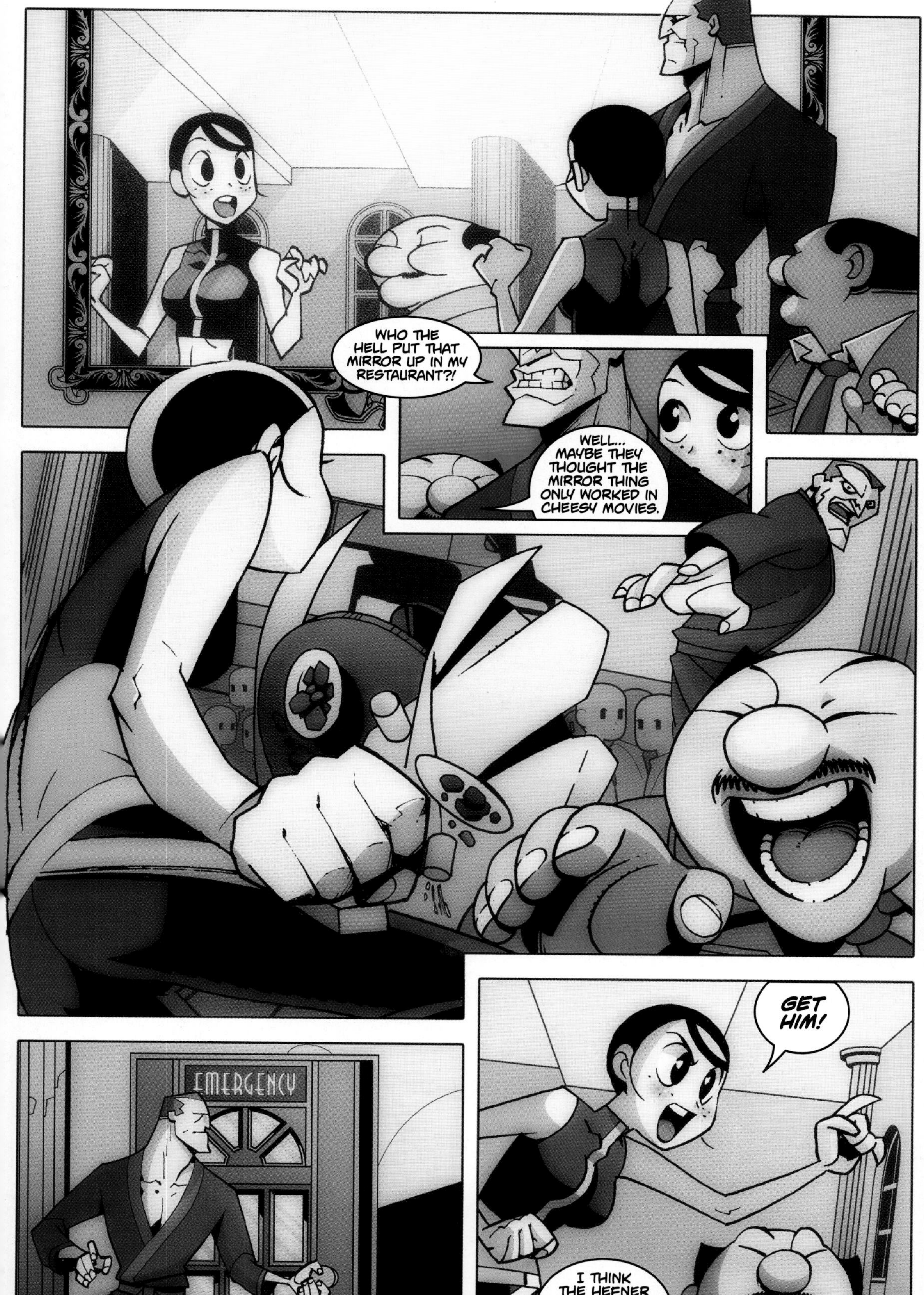

WHO THE HELL PUT THAT MIRROR UP IN MY RESTAURANT?!
WELL... MAYBE THEY THOUGHT THE MIRROR THING ONLY WORKED IN CHEESY MOVIES.
EMERGENCY
GET HIM!
I THINK THE HEFNER STYLED DRACULA CAN WAIT...

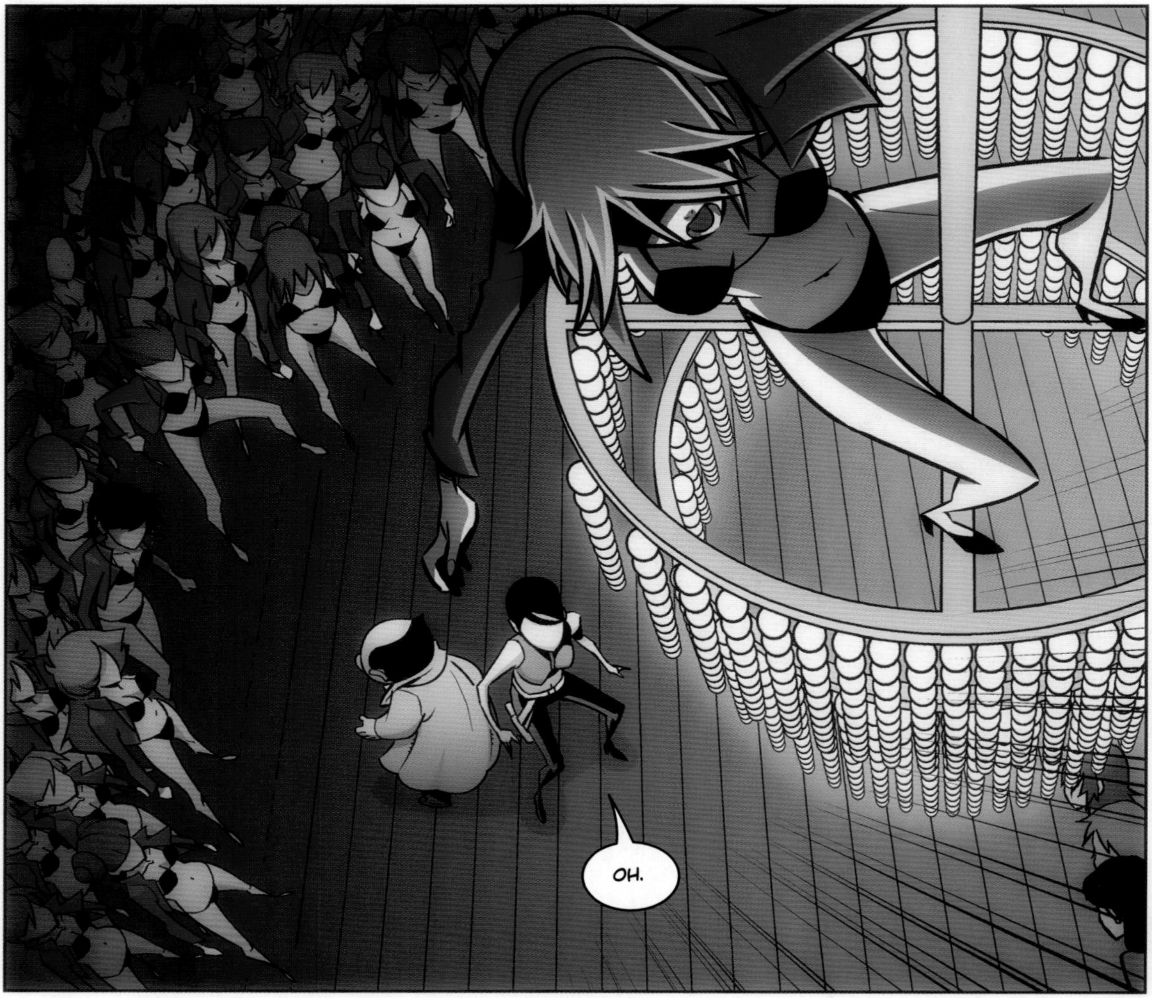
OH.

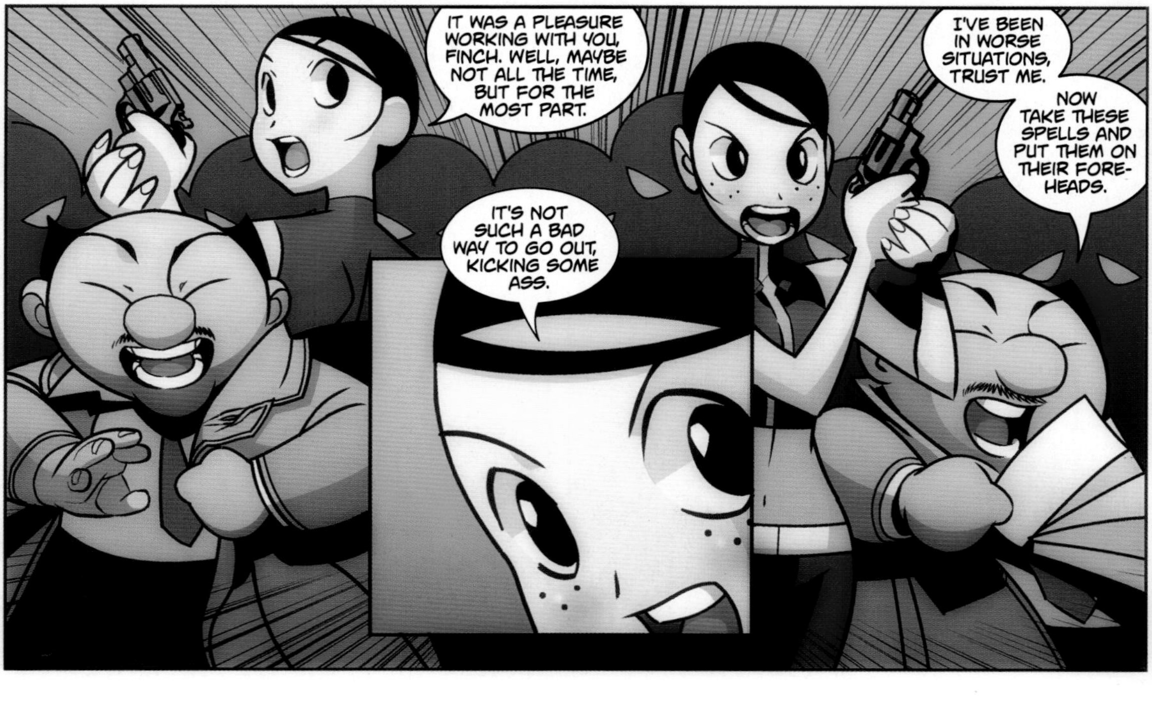
IT WAS A PLEASURE WORKING WITH YOU, FINCH. WELL, MAYBE NOT ALL THE TIME, BUT FOR THE MOST PART.
IT'S NOT SUCH A BAD WAY TO GO OUT, KICKING SOME ASS.
I'VE BEEN IN WORSE SITUATIONS, TRUST ME.
NOW TAKE THESE SPELLS AND PUT THEM ON THEIR FORE-HEADS.

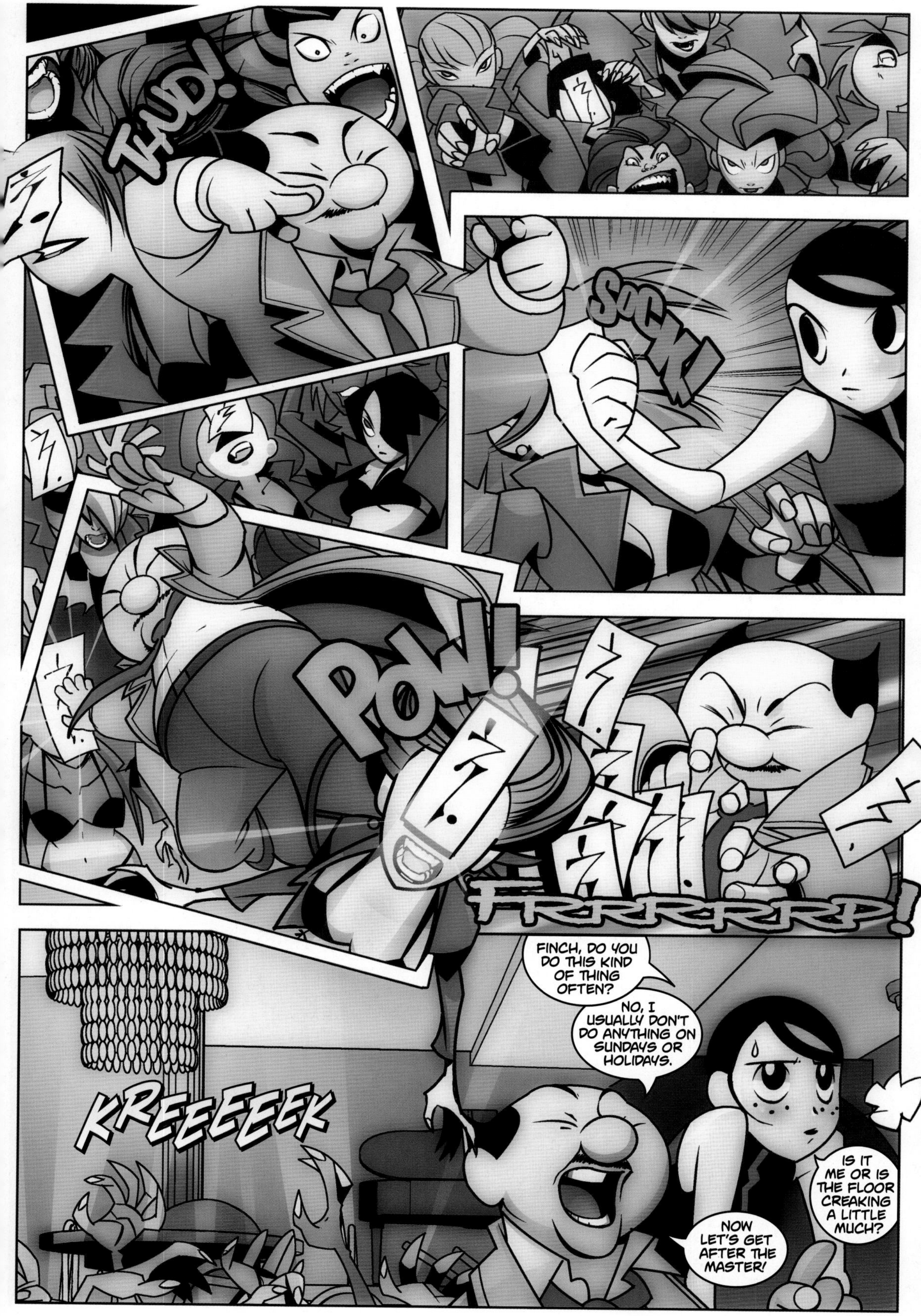
THUD!
SOCK!
POW!
FRRRRRRP!
FINCH, DO YOU DO THIS KIND OF THING OFTEN?
NO, I USUALLY DON'T DO ANYTHING ON SUNDAYS OR HOLIDAYS.
KREEEEEEK
IS IT ME OR IS THE FLOOR CREAKING A LITTLE MUCH?
NOW LET'S GET AFTER THE MASTER!

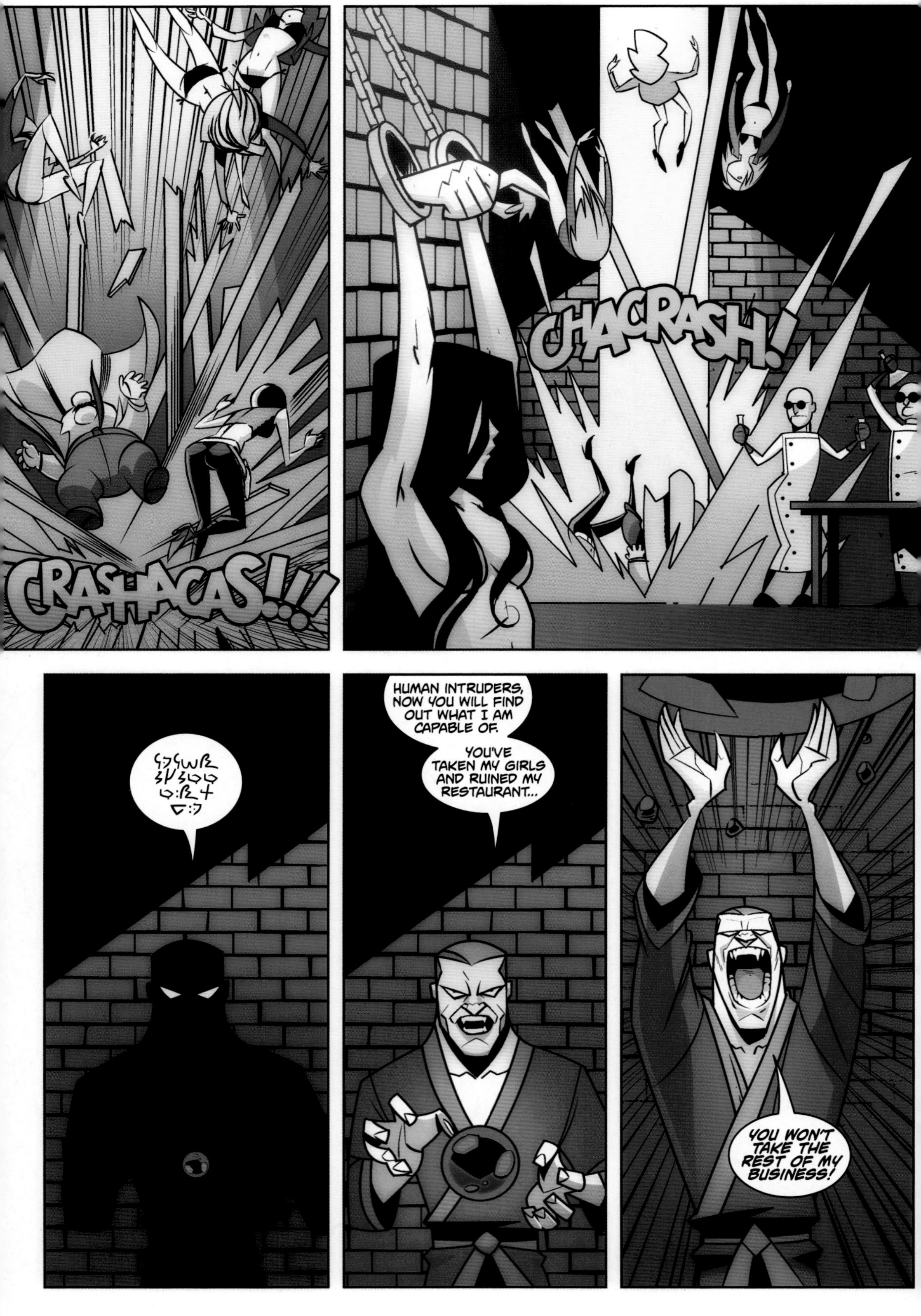
CRASHACAS!!!
CHACRASH!
HUMAN INTRUDERS, NOW YOU WILL FIND OUT WHAT I AM CAPABLE OF.
YOU'VE TAKEN MY GIRLS AND RUINED MY RESTAURANT...
YOU WON'T TAKE THE REST OF MY BUSINESS!

BLOOD OF THE ETERNAL NIGHT... CURSE THEM!

AAAH!

THAT WILL TEACH THEM. THAT'S WHAT YOU GET WHEN YOU MESS WITH A VAMPIRE OF MY LEVEL.

GROSS! I LOOK LIKE FREAKIN' CARRIE.

THAT WASN'T VERY NICE, VLAD. THIS IS MY FAVORITE COAT.

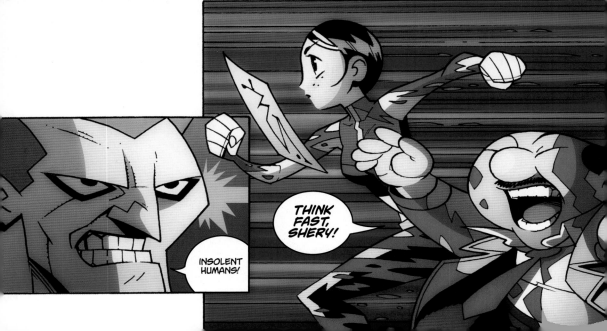

INSOLENT HUMANS!

THINK FAST, SHERY!

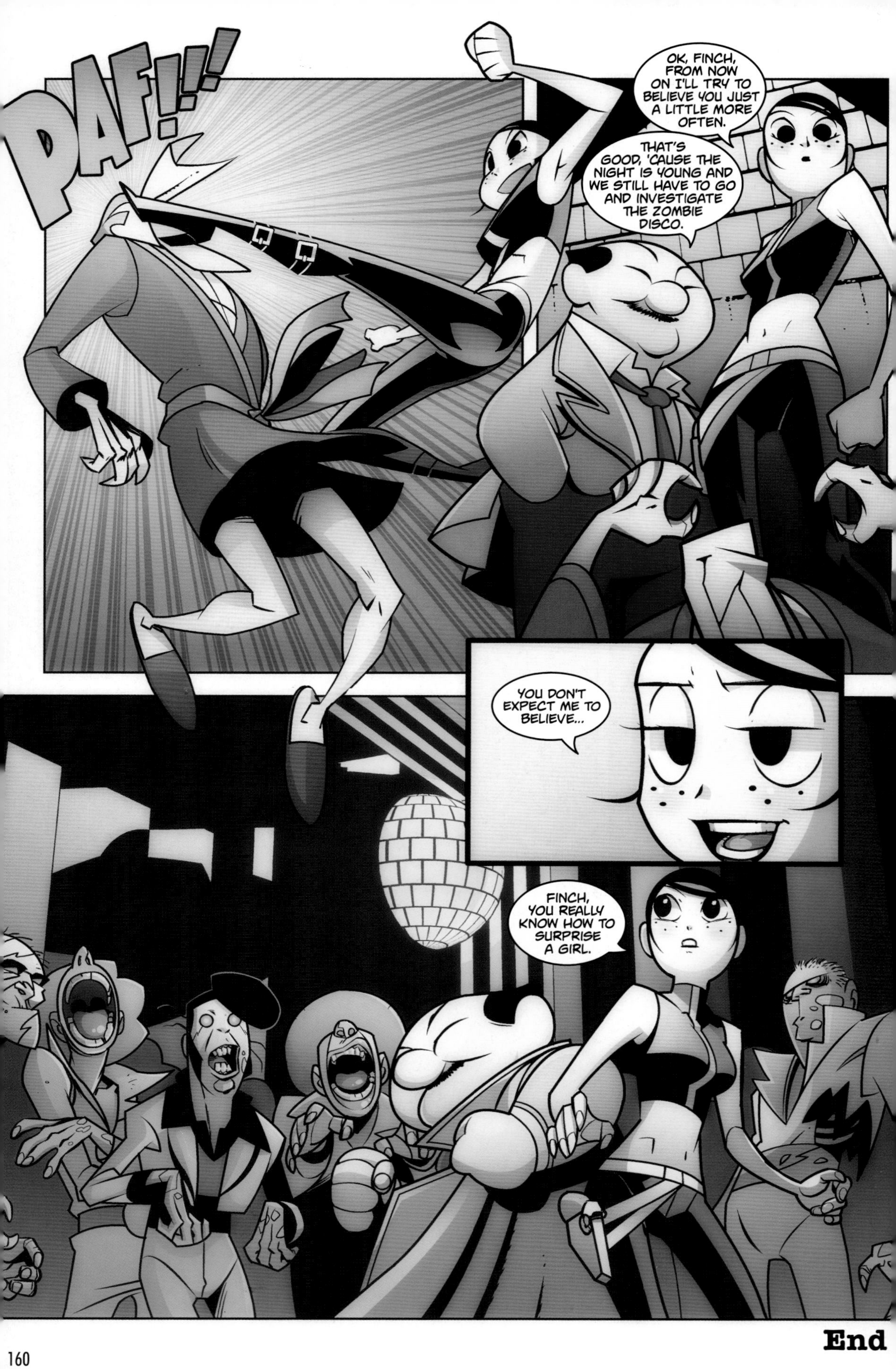
PAF!!!!
OK, FINCH, FROM NOW ON I'LL TRY TO BELIEVE YOU JUST A LITTLE MORE OFTEN.
THAT'S GOOD, 'CAUSE THE NIGHT IS YOUNG AND WE STILL HAVE TO GO AND INVESTIGATE THE ZOMBIE DISCO.
YOU DON'T EXPECT ME TO BELIEVE...
FINCH, YOU REALLY KNOW HOW TO SURPRISE A GIRL.

End

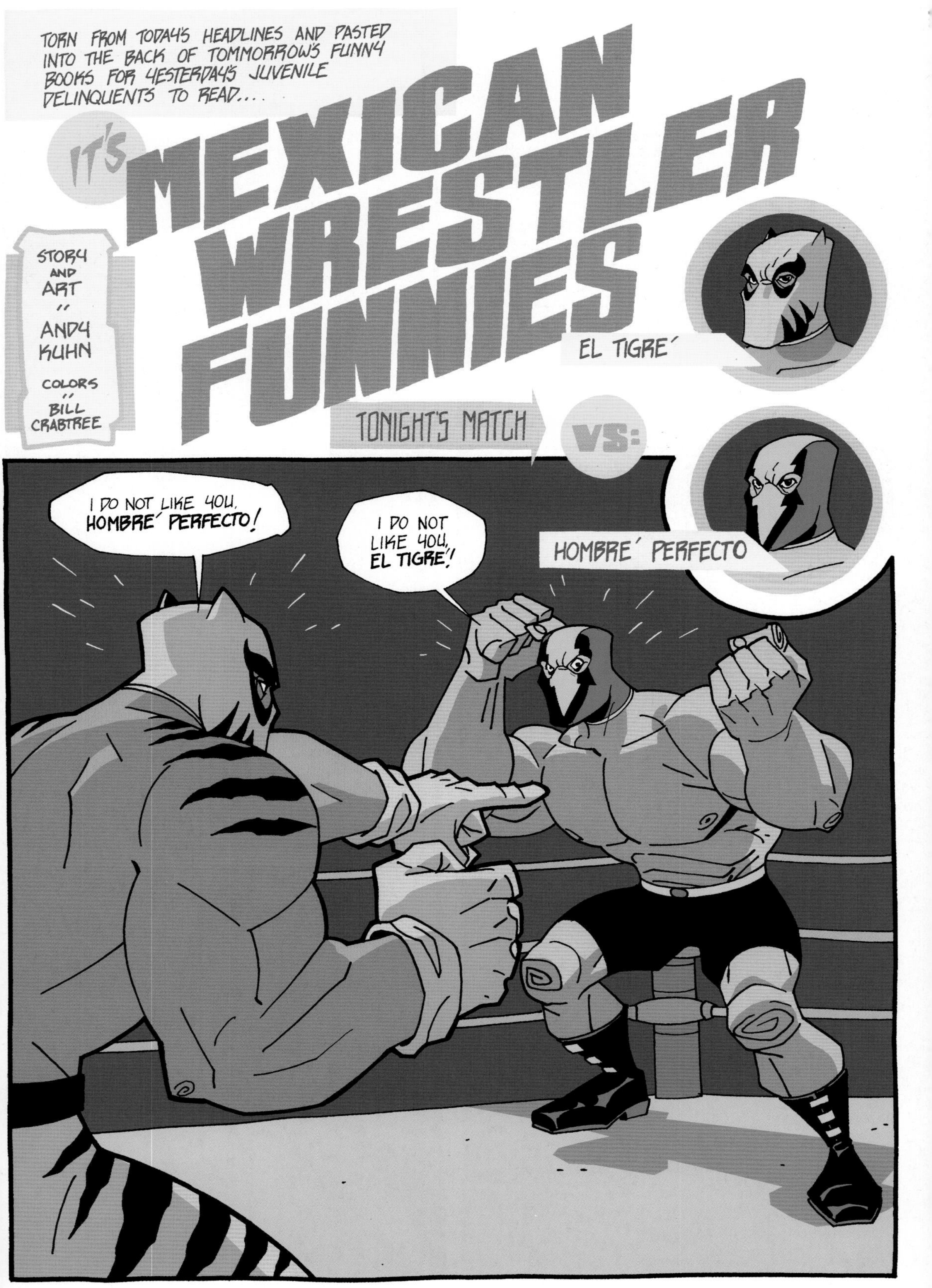
TORN FROM TODAY'S HEADLINES AND PASTED INTO THE BACK OF TOMMORROW'S FUNNY BOOKS FOR YESTERDAY'S JUVENILE DELINQUENTS TO READ....
IT'S
MEXICAN WRESTLER FUNNIES
STORY AND ART // ANDY KUHN
COLORS // BILL CRABTREE
EL TIGRÉ
TONIGHT'S MATCH
VS:
HOMBRÉ PERFECTO
I DO NOT LIKE YOU, HOMBRÉ PERFECTO!
I DO NOT LIKE YOU, EL TIGRÉ!

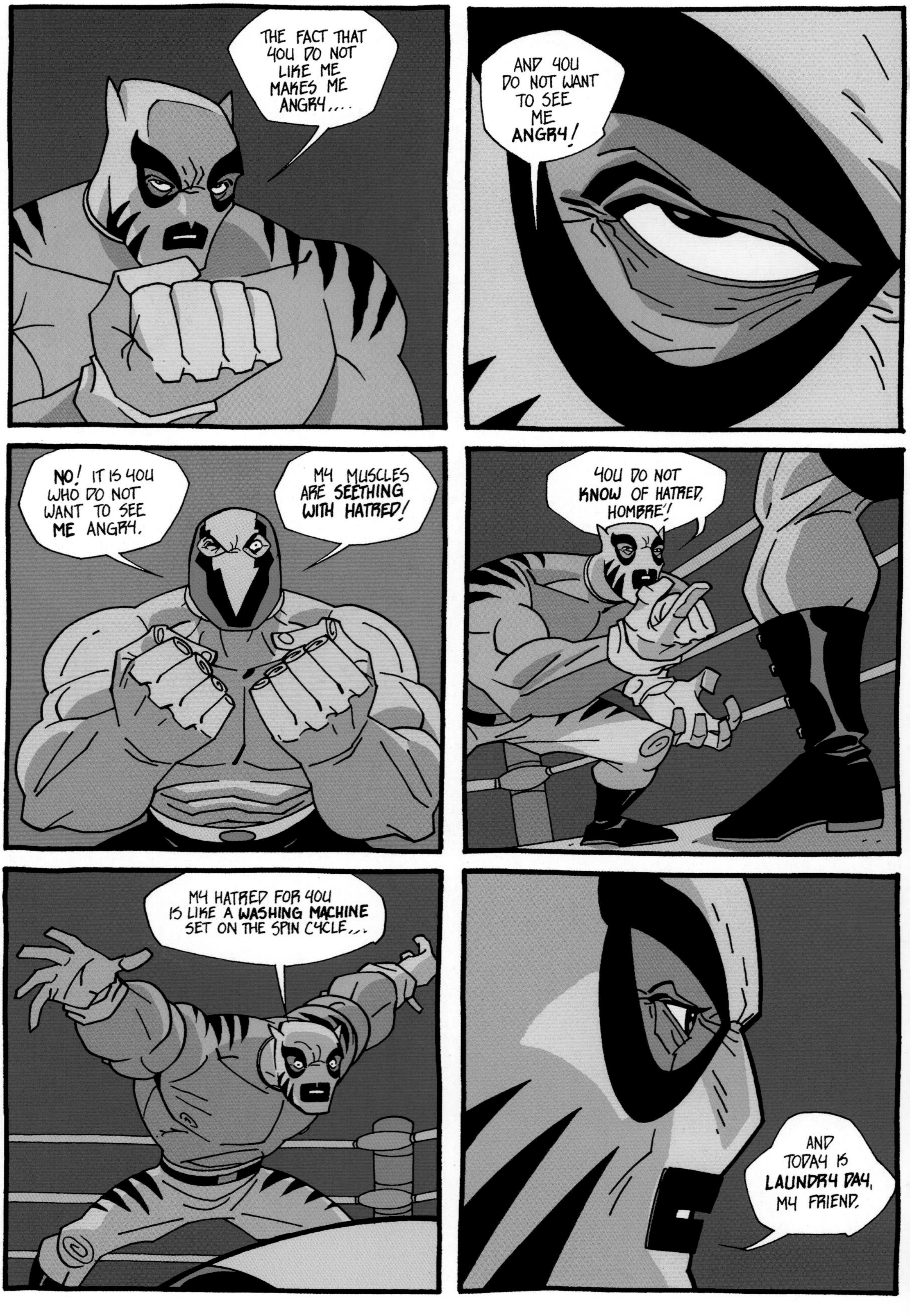
THE FACT THAT YOU DO NOT LIKE ME MAKES ME ANGRY...
AND YOU DO NOT WANT TO SEE ME ANGRY!
NO! IT IS YOU WHO DO NOT WANT TO SEE ME ANGRY.
MY MUSCLES ARE SEETHING WITH HATRED!
YOU DO NOT KNOW OF HATRED, HOMBRE!
MY HATRED FOR YOU IS LIKE A WASHING MACHINE SET ON THE SPIN CYCLE...
AND TODAY IS LAUNDRY DAY, MY FRIEND.

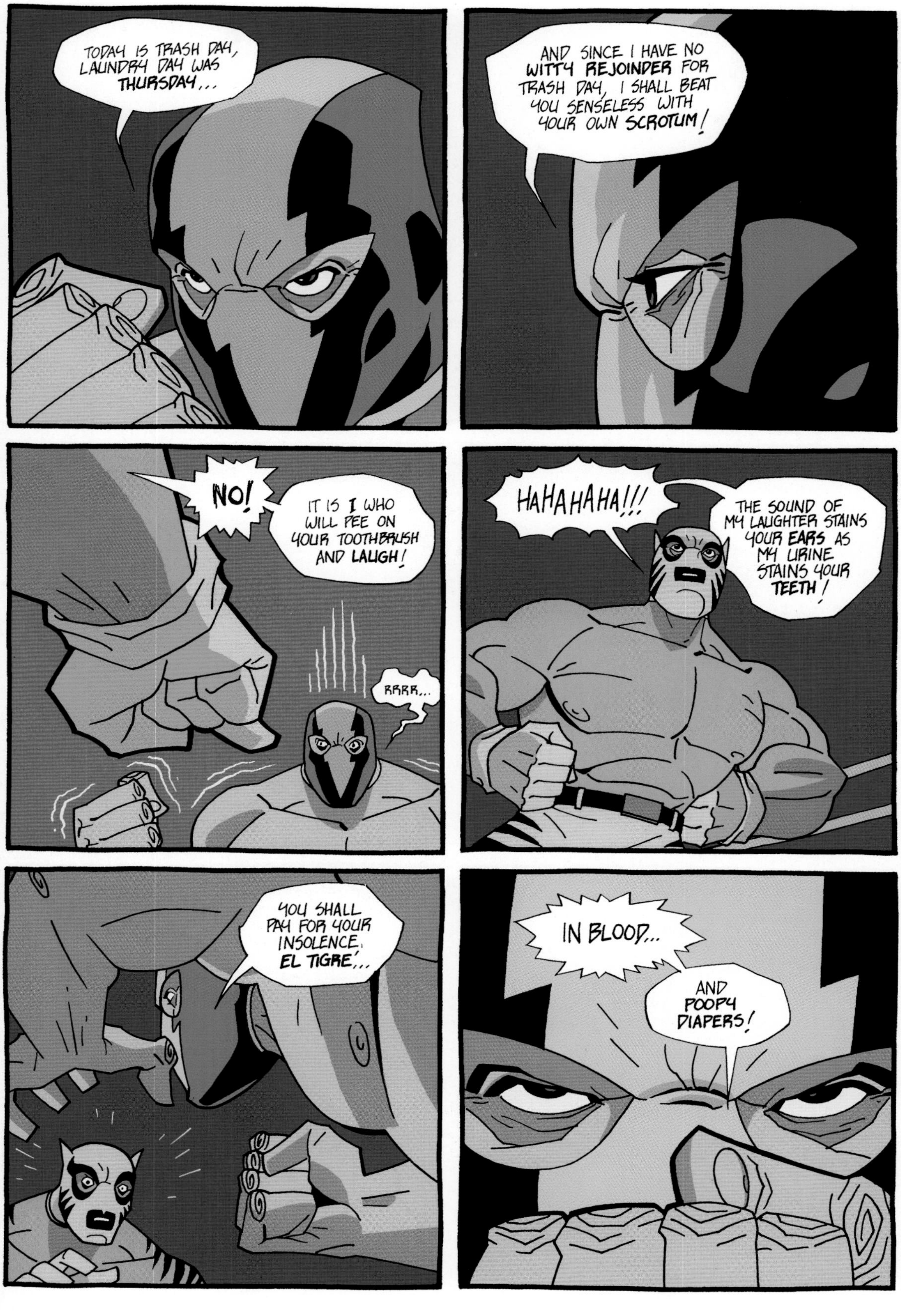
TODAY IS TRASH DAY, LAUNDRY DAY WAS THURSDAY...
AND SINCE I HAVE NO WITTY REJOINDER FOR TRASH DAY, I SHALL BEAT YOU SENSELESS WITH YOUR OWN SCROTUM!
NO!
IT IS I WHO WILL PEE ON YOUR TOOTHBRUSH AND LAUGH!
RRRR...
HAHAHAHA!!!
THE SOUND OF MY LAUGHTER STAINS YOUR EARS AS MY URINE STAINS YOUR TEETH!
YOU SHALL PAY FOR YOUR INSOLENCE, EL TIGRE!...
IN BLOOD...
AND POOPY DIAPERS!

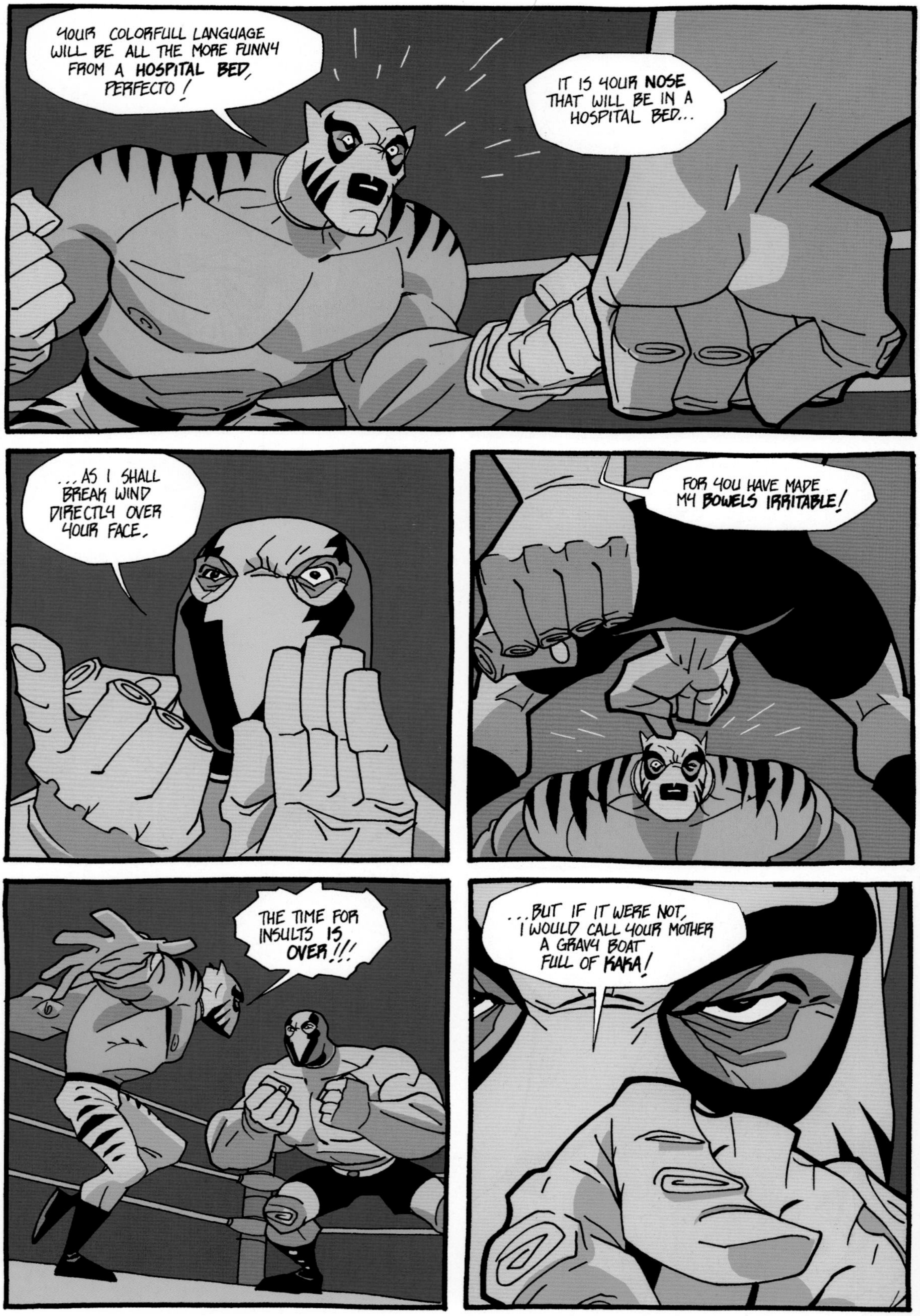
YOUR COLORFULL LANGUAGE WILL BE ALL THE MORE FUNNY FROM A HOSPITAL BED, PERFECTO!
IT IS YOUR NOSE THAT WILL BE IN A HOSPITAL BED...
...AS I SHALL BREAK WIND DIRECTLY OVER YOUR FACE.
FOR YOU HAVE MADE MY BOWELS IRRITABLE!
THE TIME FOR INSULTS IS OVER!!!
...BUT IF IT WERE NOT, I WOULD CALL YOUR MOTHER A GRAVY BOAT FULL OF KAKA!

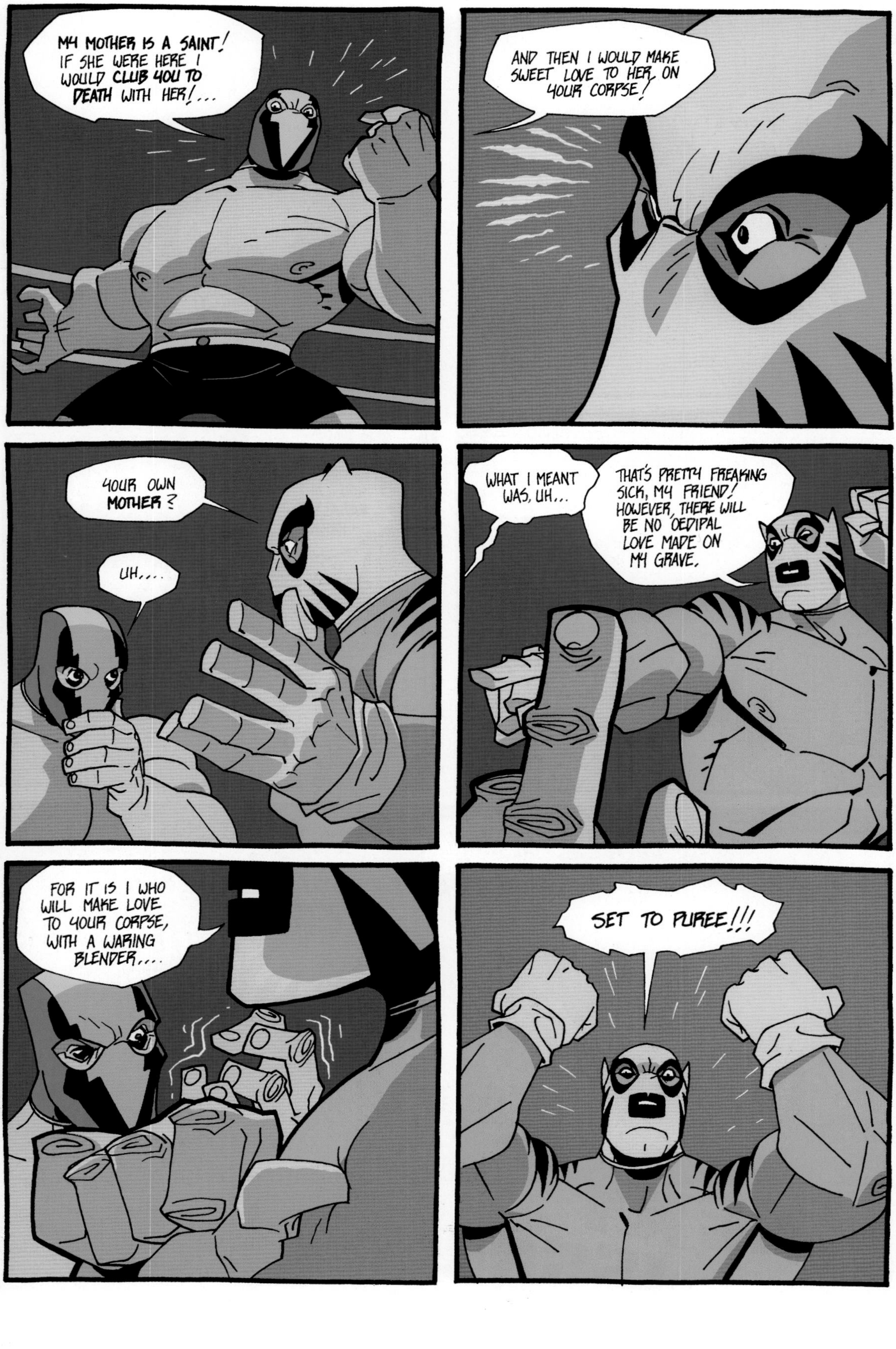
MY MOTHER IS A SAINT! IF SHE WERE HERE I WOULD CLUB YOU TO DEATH WITH HER!...
AND THEN I WOULD MAKE SWEET LOVE TO HER, ON YOUR CORPSE!
YOUR OWN MOTHER?
UH,...
WHAT I MEANT WAS, UH...
THAT'S PRETTY FREAKING SICK, MY FRIEND! HOWEVER, THERE WILL BE NO OEDIPAL LOVE MADE ON MY GRAVE.
FOR IT IS I WHO WILL MAKE LOVE TO YOUR CORPSE, WITH A WARING BLENDER...
SET TO PUREE!!!

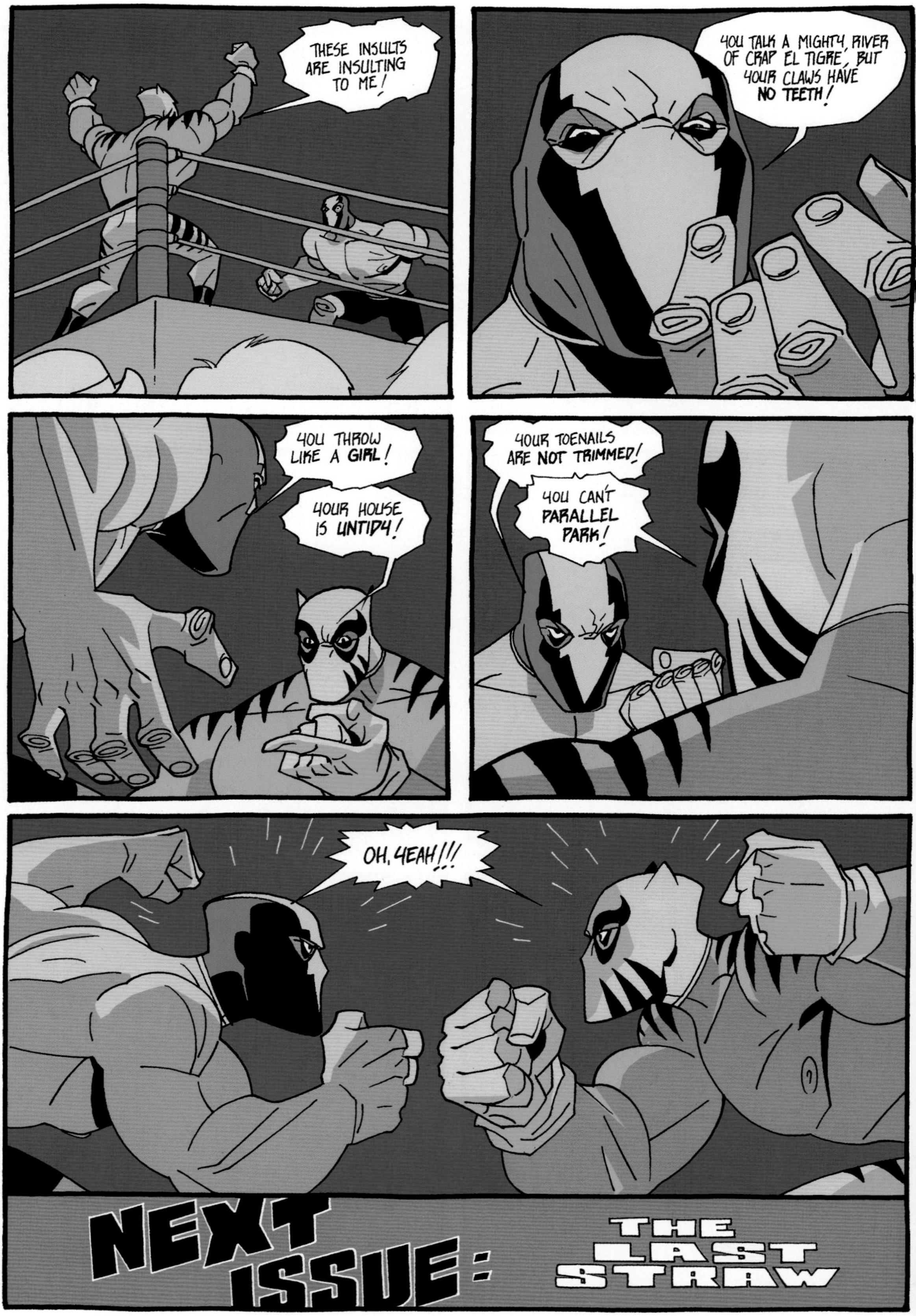
THESE INSULTS ARE INSULTING TO ME!
YOU TALK A MIGHTY RIVER OF CRAP EL TIGRE, BUT YOUR CLAWS HAVE NO TEETH!
YOU THROW LIKE A GIRL!
YOUR HOUSE IS UNTIDY!
YOUR TOENAILS ARE NOT TRIMMED!
YOU CAN'T PARALLEL PARK!
OH, YEAH!!!
NEXT ISSUE: THE LAST STRAW

THE DEATH OF THE MIDNIGHT SKY

WRITTEN BY: RICK REMENDER   ARTWORK BY: JOSH HOYE

FUCK IF I KNOW WHY IT HAPPENED.

NOT A HUMAN ALIVE, NOT ONE COCK-SUCKER, WHO CAN TELL ME I'M CRAZY.

YOU NEVER IN ALL YOUR LIFE CAN IMAGINE IT WILL HAPPEN TO YOU.

CRAZY DON'T SHOP FOR VODKA... AND I SURE AS FUCK DO THAT.

NO MAN IN THE WORLD IMAGINES HE'LL SEE HIS WIFE *DIE* IN FRONT OF HIM.

NO MAN *imagines* THAT. NO, SIR.

I KNOW BECAUSE I'VE FELT MANY DIFFERENT TYPES OF DISTRESS.

FUCK YOU, STONER!!!

IRON MAIDEN

I'LL TELL YOU, THE MAIN DIFFERENCE WAS THAT I LOVED HER.

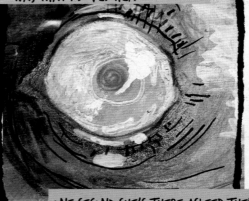

I DEALT WITH ALL THE SHIT THEY COULD DISH OUT.

ONE SECOND SHE'S THERE ASLEEP, THEN...

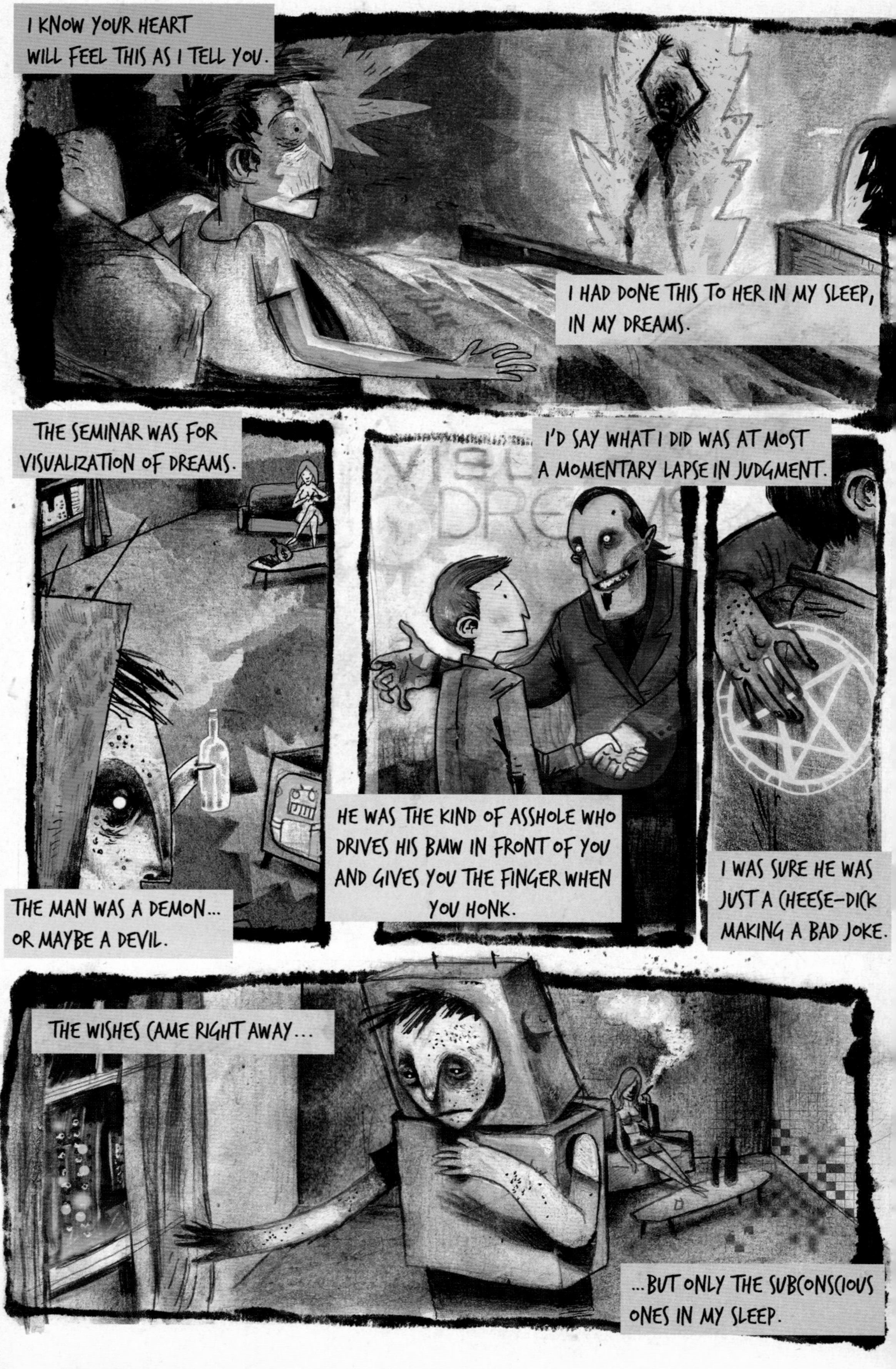
I KNOW YOUR HEART WILL FEEL THIS AS I TELL YOU.
I HAD DONE THIS TO HER IN MY SLEEP, IN MY DREAMS.
THE SEMINAR WAS FOR VISUALIZATION OF DREAMS.
THE MAN WAS A DEMON... OR MAYBE A DEVIL.
I'D SAY WHAT I DID WAS AT MOST A MOMENTARY LAPSE IN JUDGMENT.
HE WAS THE KIND OF ASSHOLE WHO DRIVES HIS BMW IN FRONT OF YOU AND GIVES YOU THE FINGER WHEN YOU HONK.
I WAS SURE HE WAS JUST A CHEESE-DICK MAKING A BAD JOKE.
THE WISHES CAME RIGHT AWAY...
...BUT ONLY THE SUBCONSCIOUS ONES IN MY SLEEP.

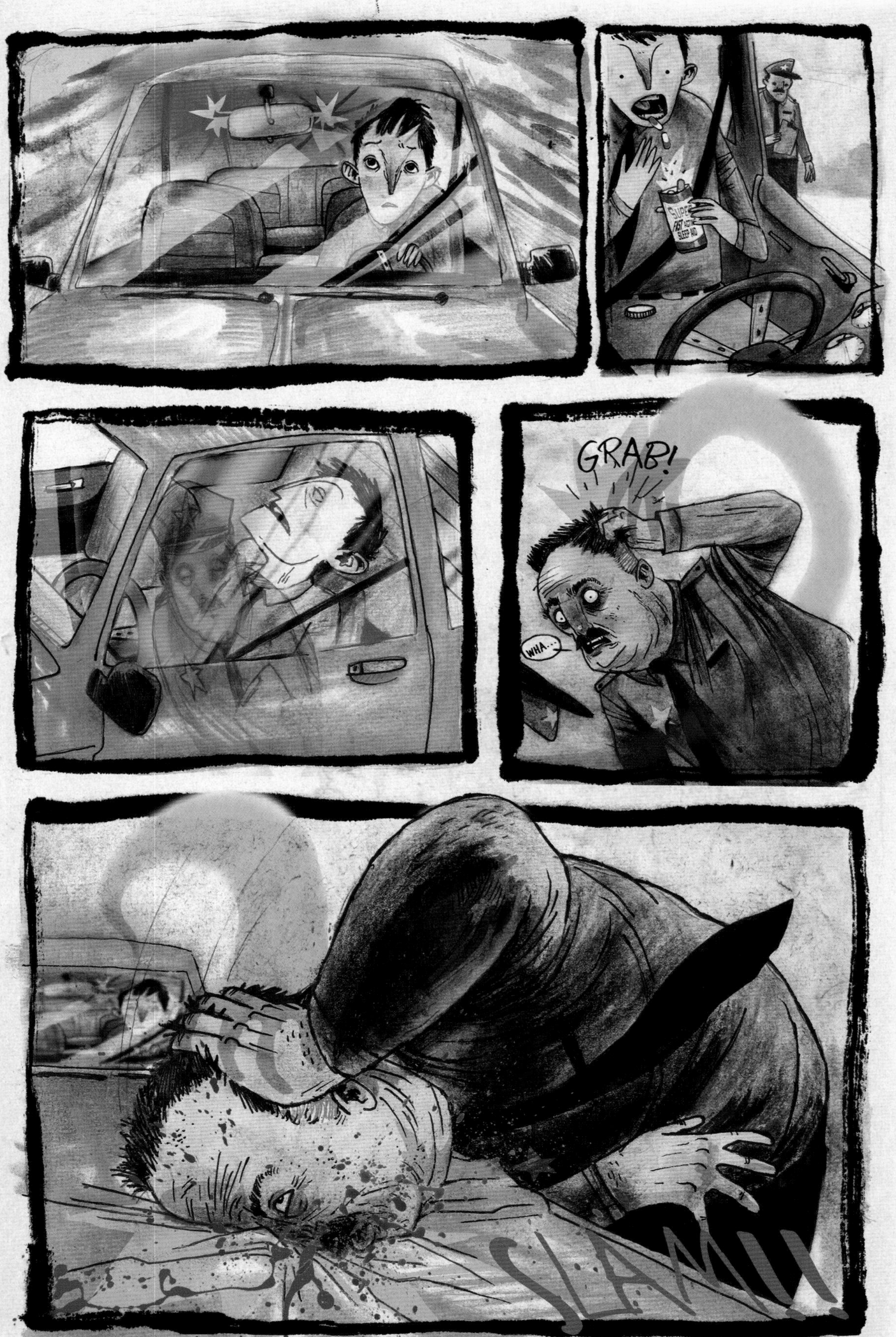
SLEEP AID
GRAB!
WHA...
SLAM!!

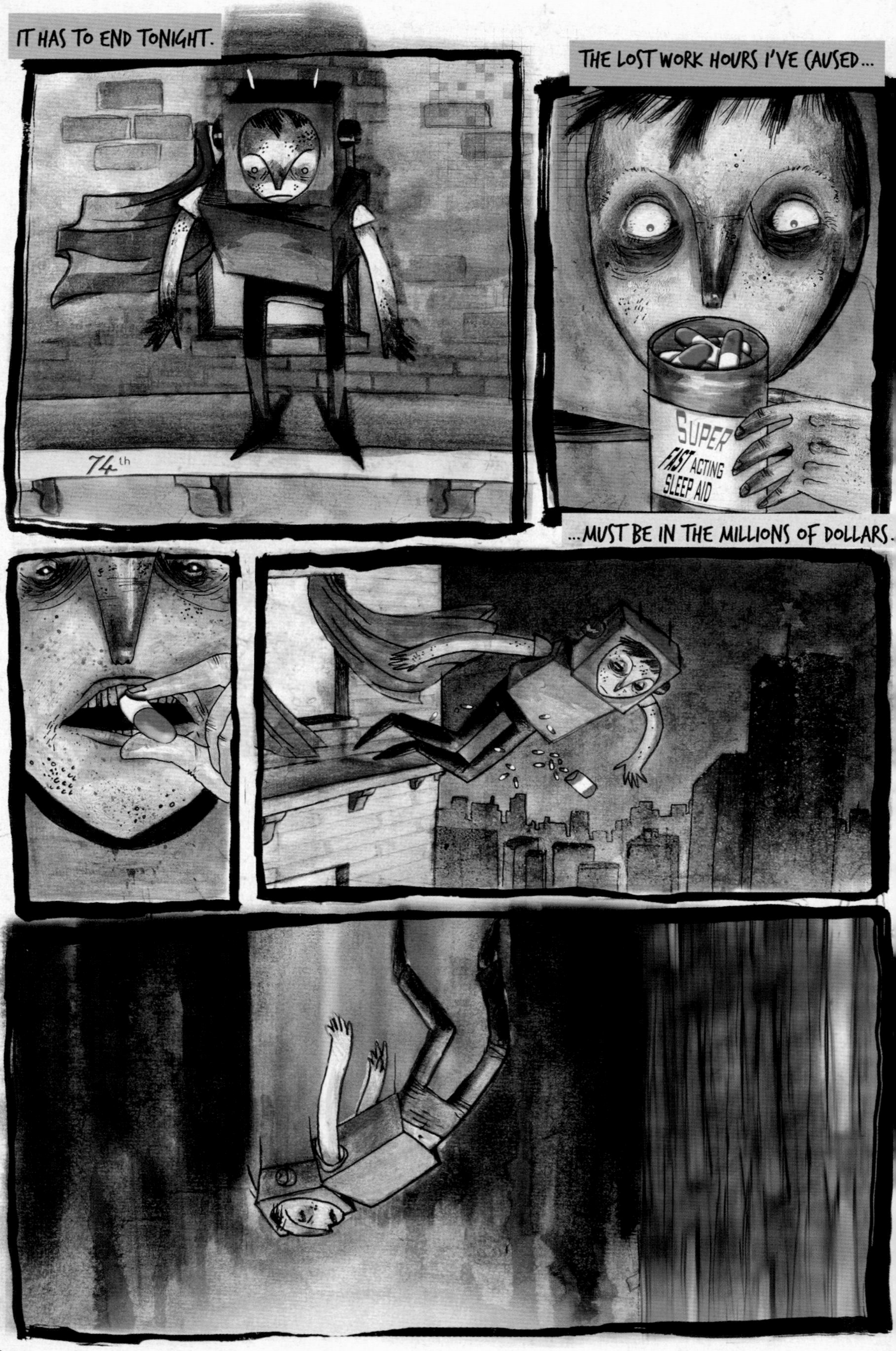
IT HAS TO END TONIGHT.
74th
THE LOST WORK HOURS I'VE CAUSED...
SUPER FAST ACTING SLEEP AID
...MUST BE IN THE MILLIONS OF DOLLARS.

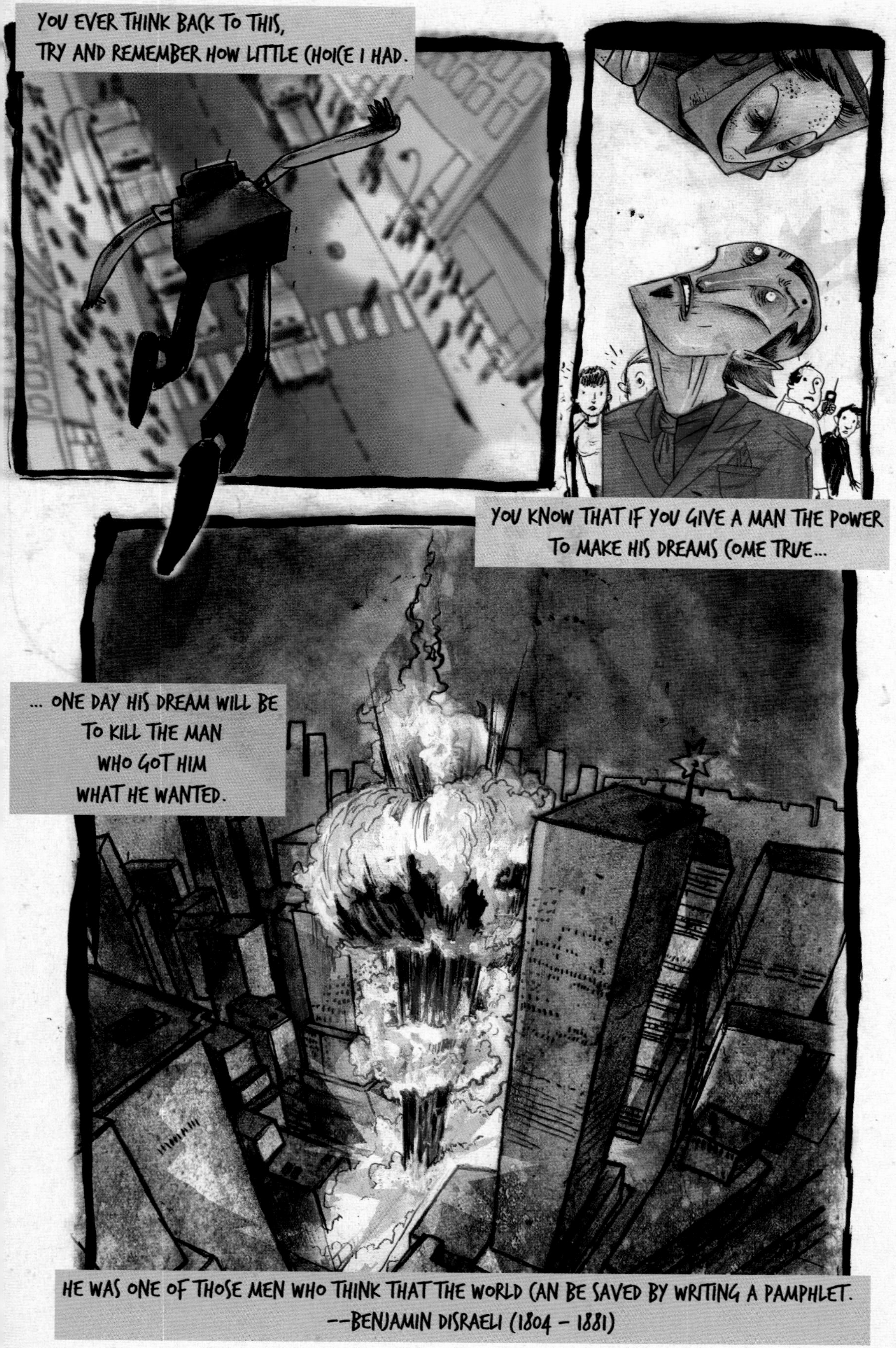
YOU EVER THINK BACK TO THIS, TRY AND REMEMBER HOW LITTLE CHOICE I HAD.
YOU KNOW THAT IF YOU GIVE A MAN THE POWER TO MAKE HIS DREAMS COME TRUE...
... ONE DAY HIS DREAM WILL BE TO KILL THE MAN WHO GOT HIM WHAT HE WANTED.
HE WAS ONE OF THOSE MEN WHO THINK THAT THE WORLD CAN BE SAVED BY WRITING A PAMPHLET.
--BENJAMIN DISRAELI (1804 - 1881)

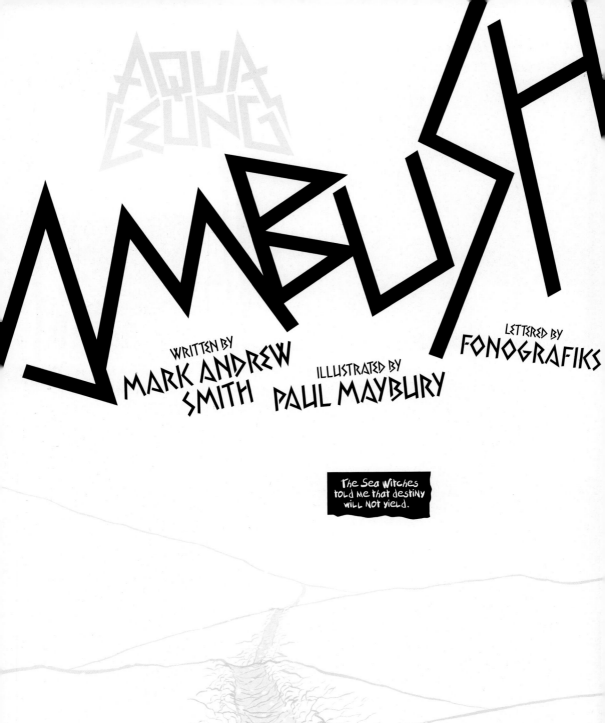

AQUALUNG

AMBUSH

WRITTEN BY
MARK ANDREW
SMITH

ILLUSTRATED BY
PAUL MAYBURY

LETTERED BY
FONOGRAFIKS

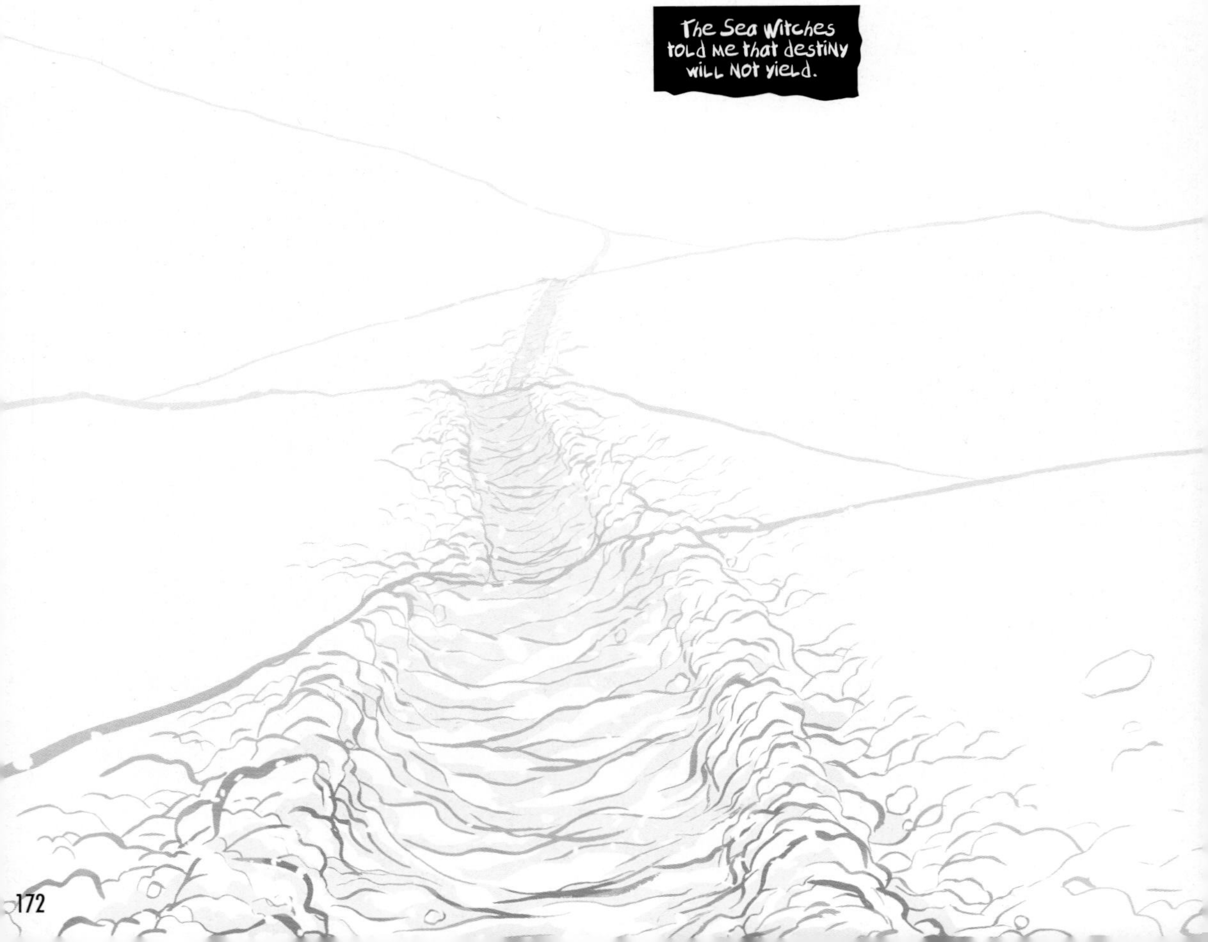

The Sea Witches told me that destiny will not yield.

Especially the destiny of one who has won the favor of the Great Turtle.

Death lies in your wake, Octopus Child.

Flowers wilt as you pass. Mothers mourn their murdered children.

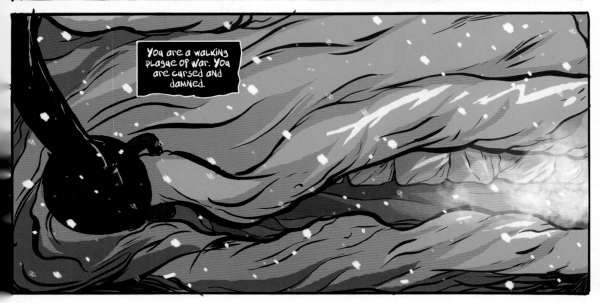

You are a walking plague of war. You are cursed and damned.

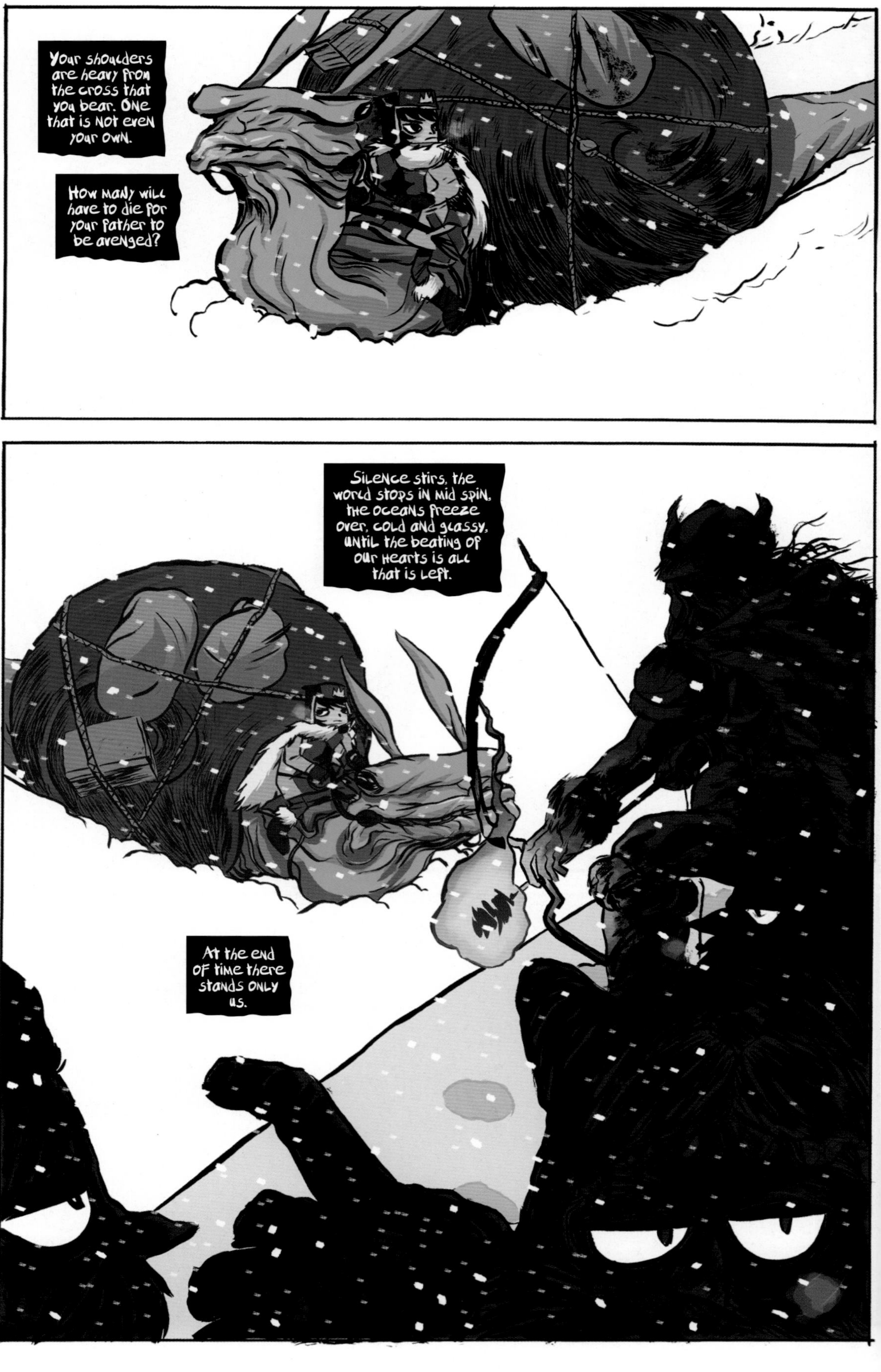
Your shoulders are heavy from the cross that you bear. One that is not even your own.
How many will have to die for your father to be avenged?
Silence stirs, the world stops in mid spin, the oceans freeze over, cold and glassy, until the beating of our hearts is all that is left.
At the end of time there stands only us.

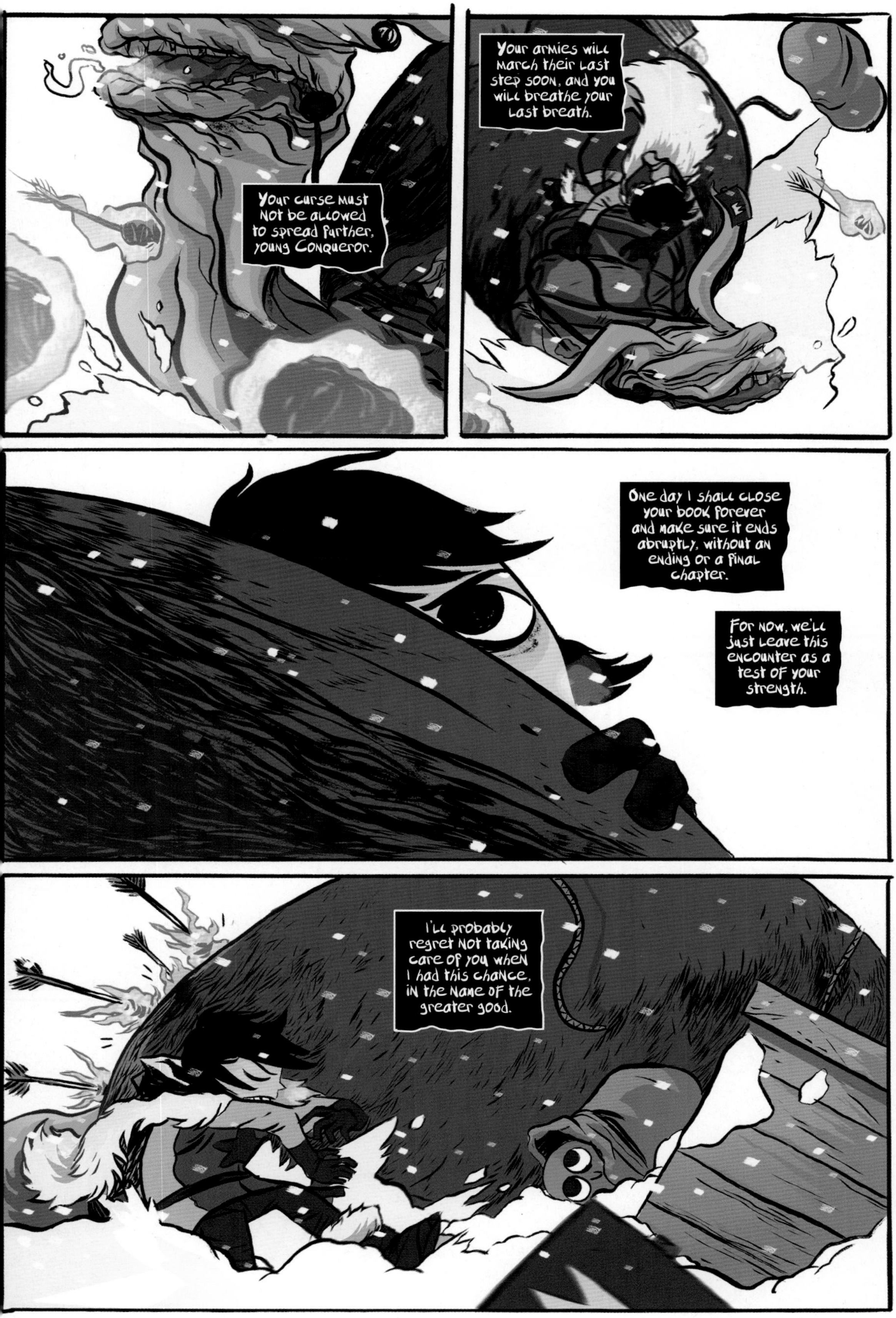
Your curse must not be allowed to spread further, young Conqueror.
Your armies will march their last step soon, and you will breathe your last breath.
One day I shall close your book forever and make sure it ends abruptly, without an ending or a final chapter.
For now, we'll just leave this encounter as a test of your strength.
I'll probably regret not taking care of you when I had this chance, in the name of the greater good.

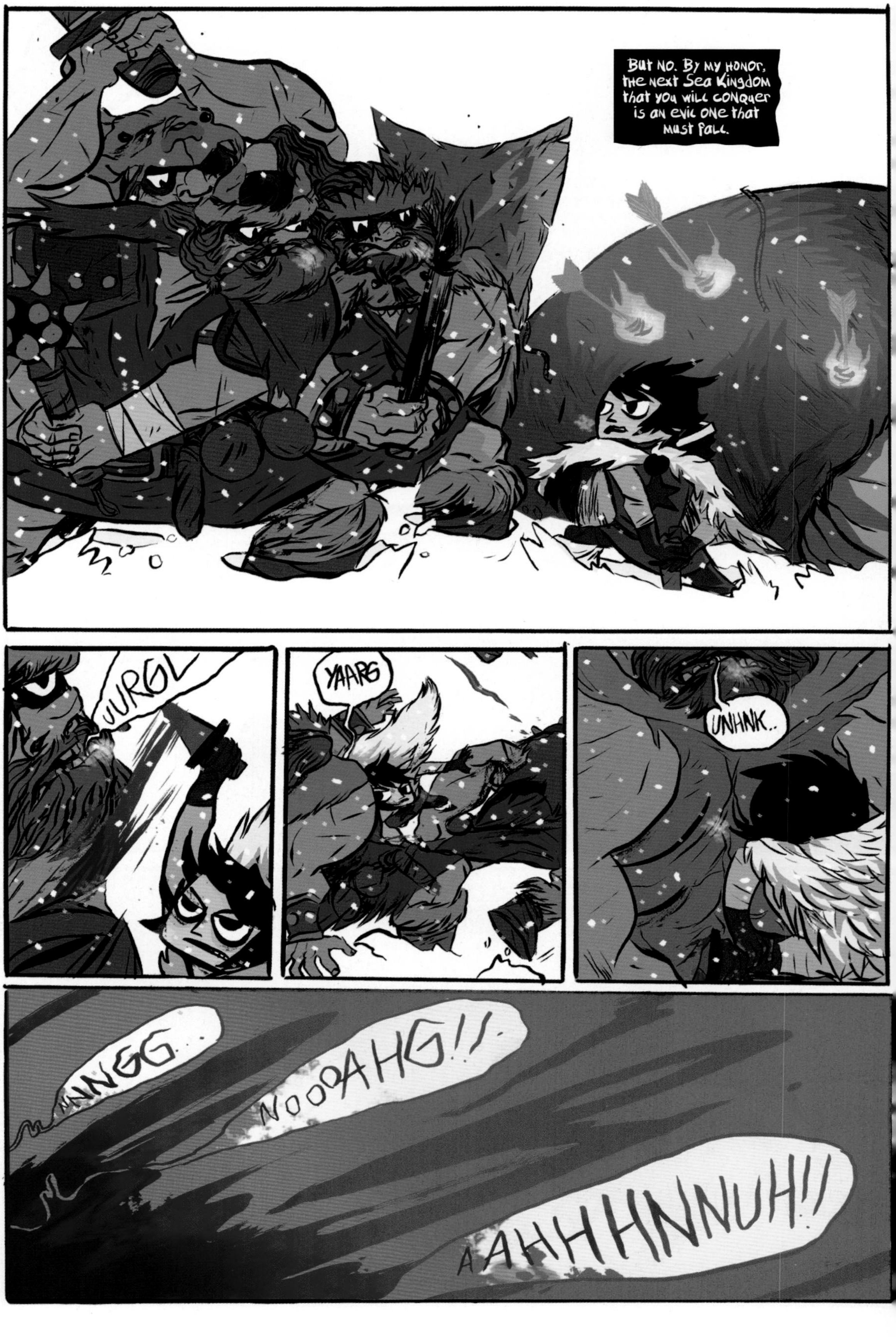
But No. By my honor, the next Sea Kingdom that you will conquer is an evil one that must fall.
UURGL
YAARG
UNHNK..
NNGG..
NOOOAHG!!
AAHHHNNUH!!

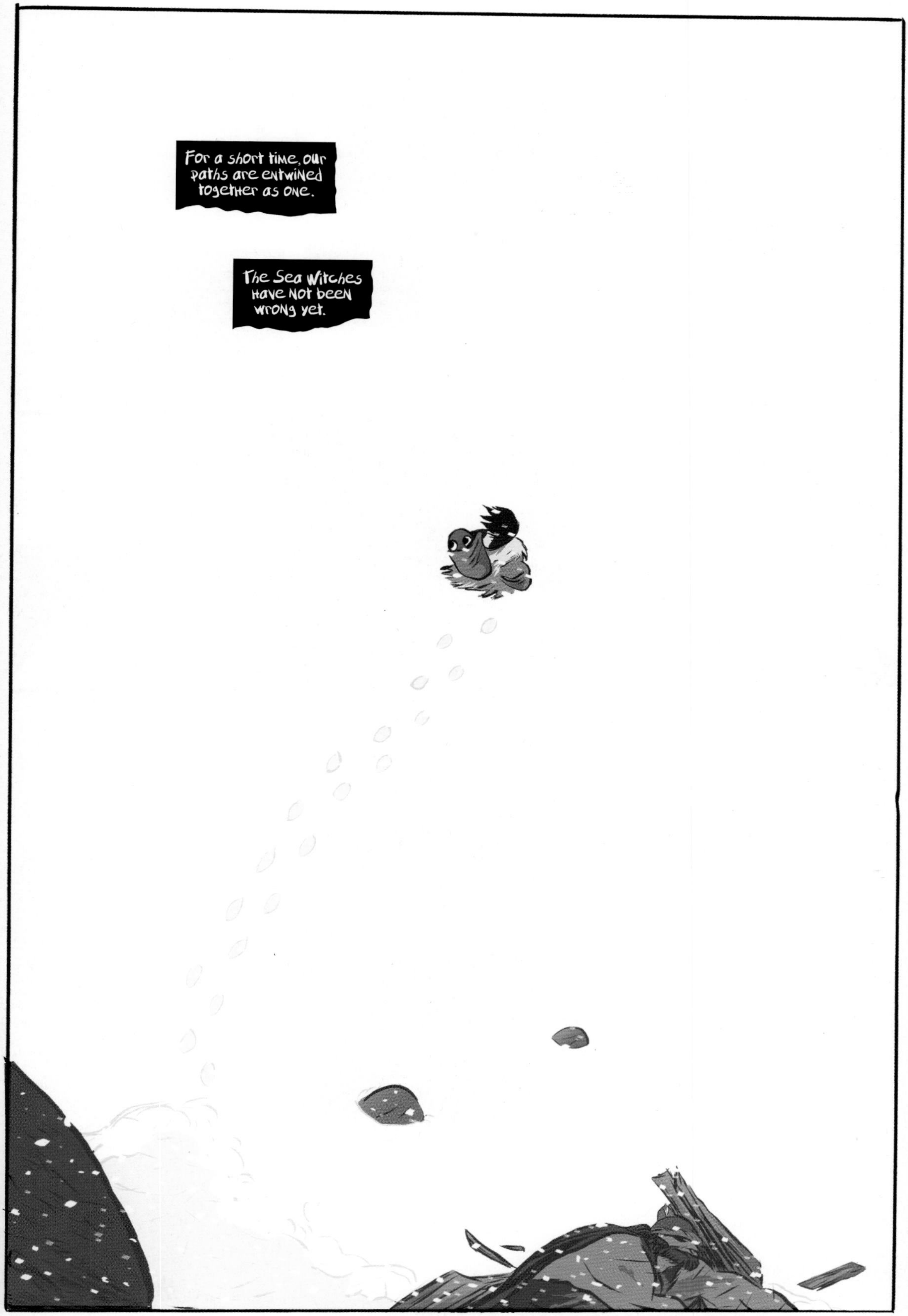
For a short time, our paths are entwined together as one.
The Sea Witches have not been wrong yet.

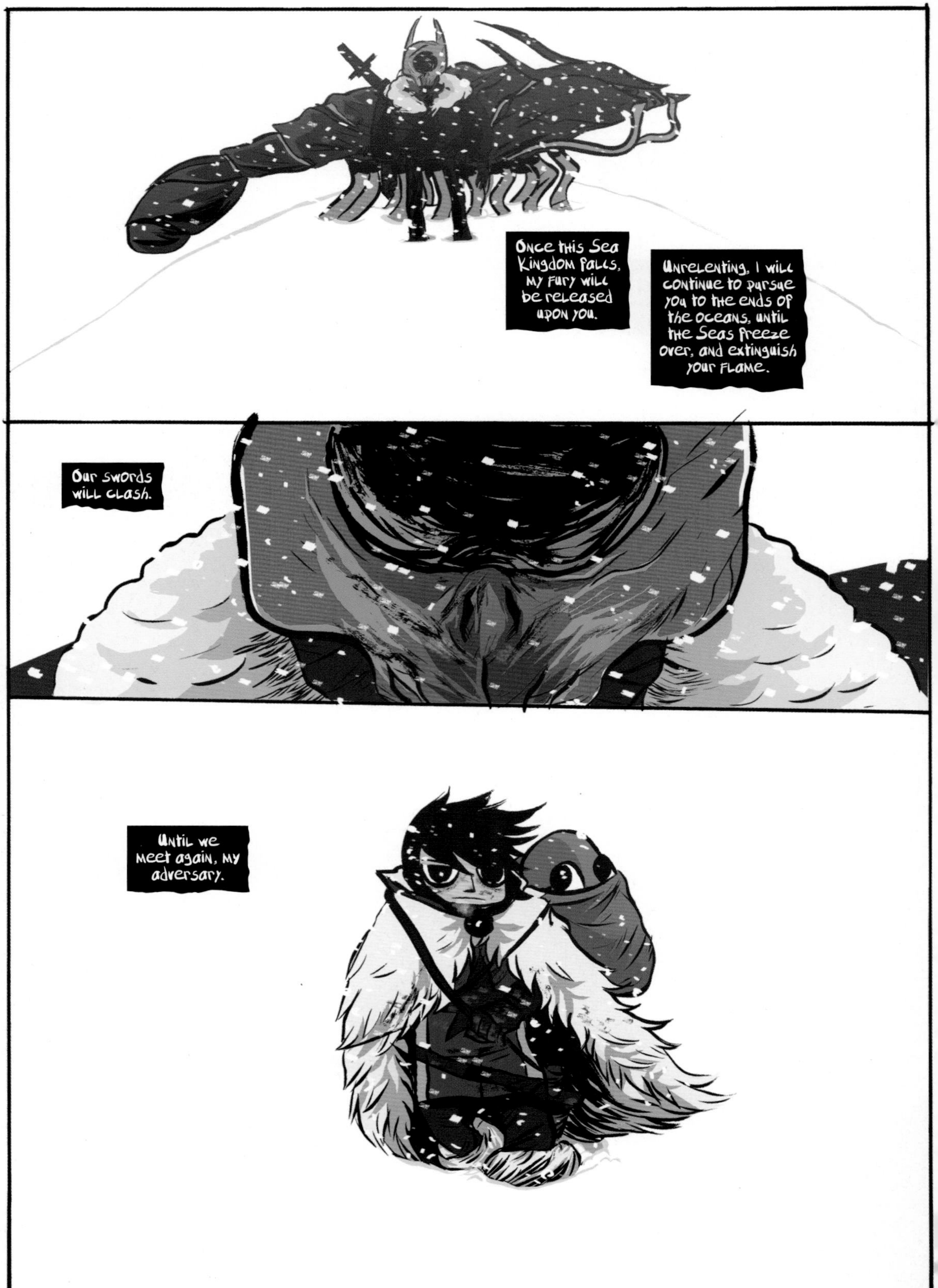
Once this Sea Kingdom falls, my fury will be released upon you.
Unrelenting, I will continue to pursue you to the ends of the oceans, until the Seas freeze over, and extinguish your flame.
Our swords will clash.
Until we meet again, my adversary.
mayburger 2007

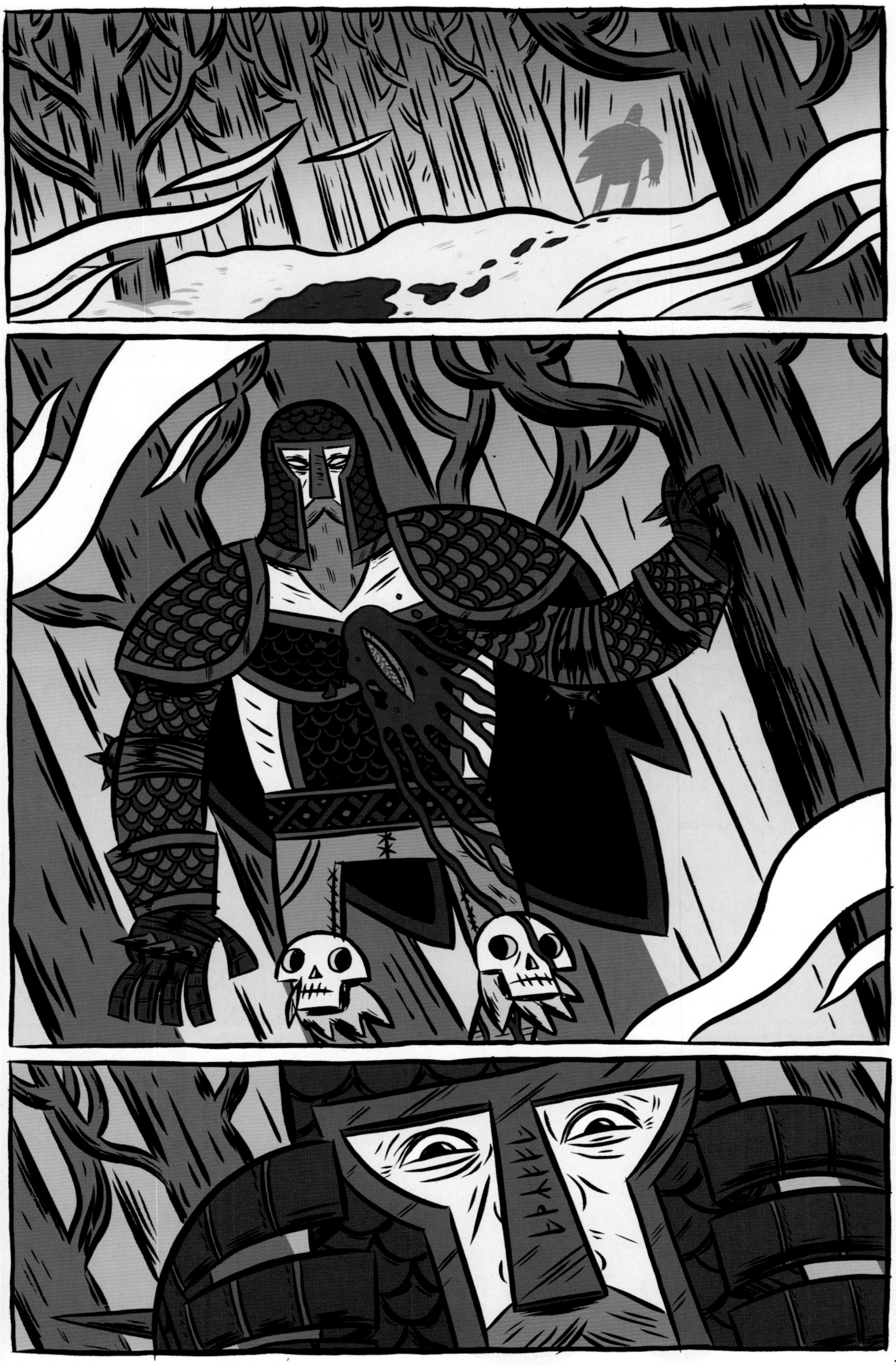

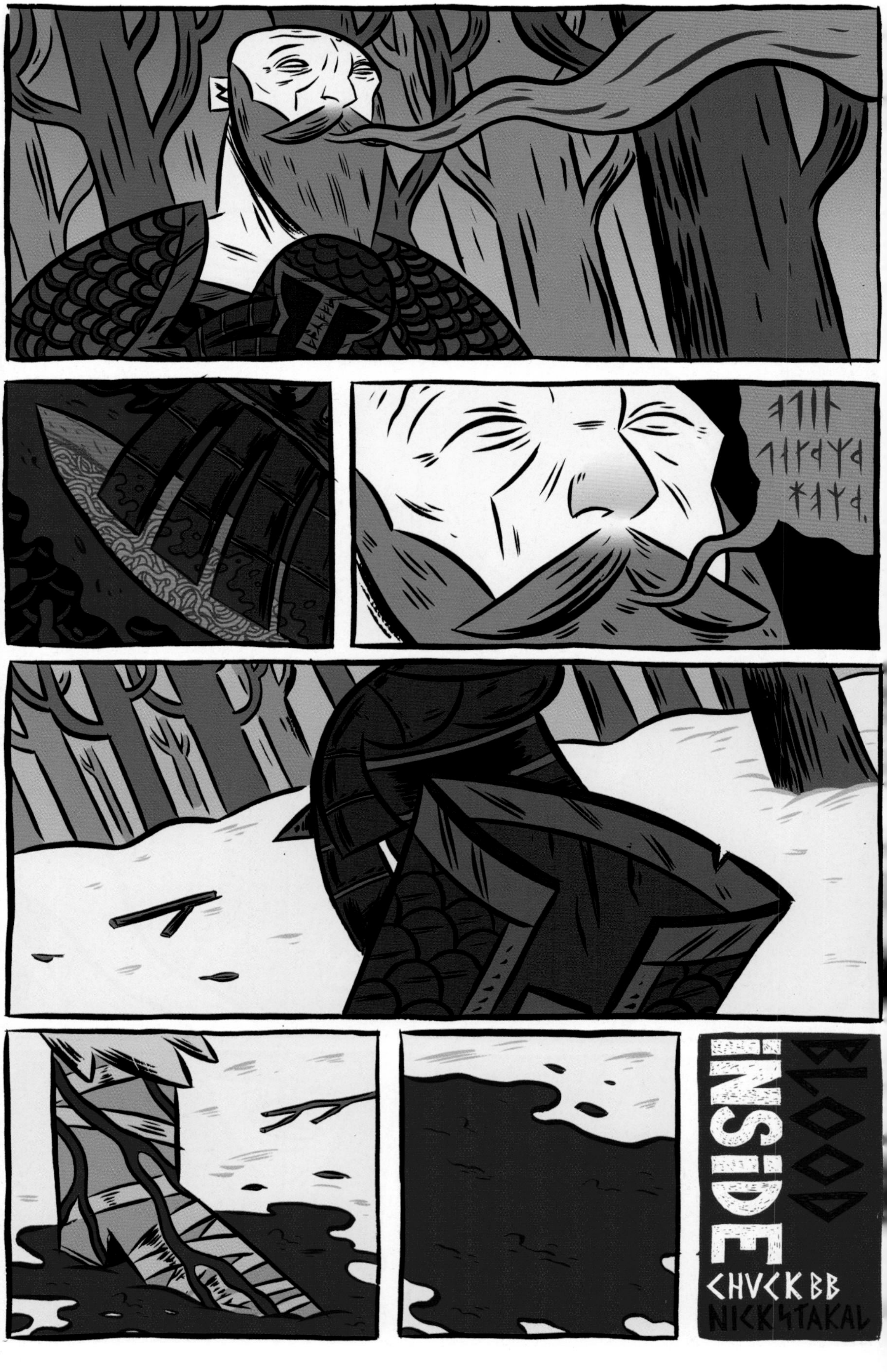
BLOOD
INSIDE
CHVCK BB
NICK STAKAL

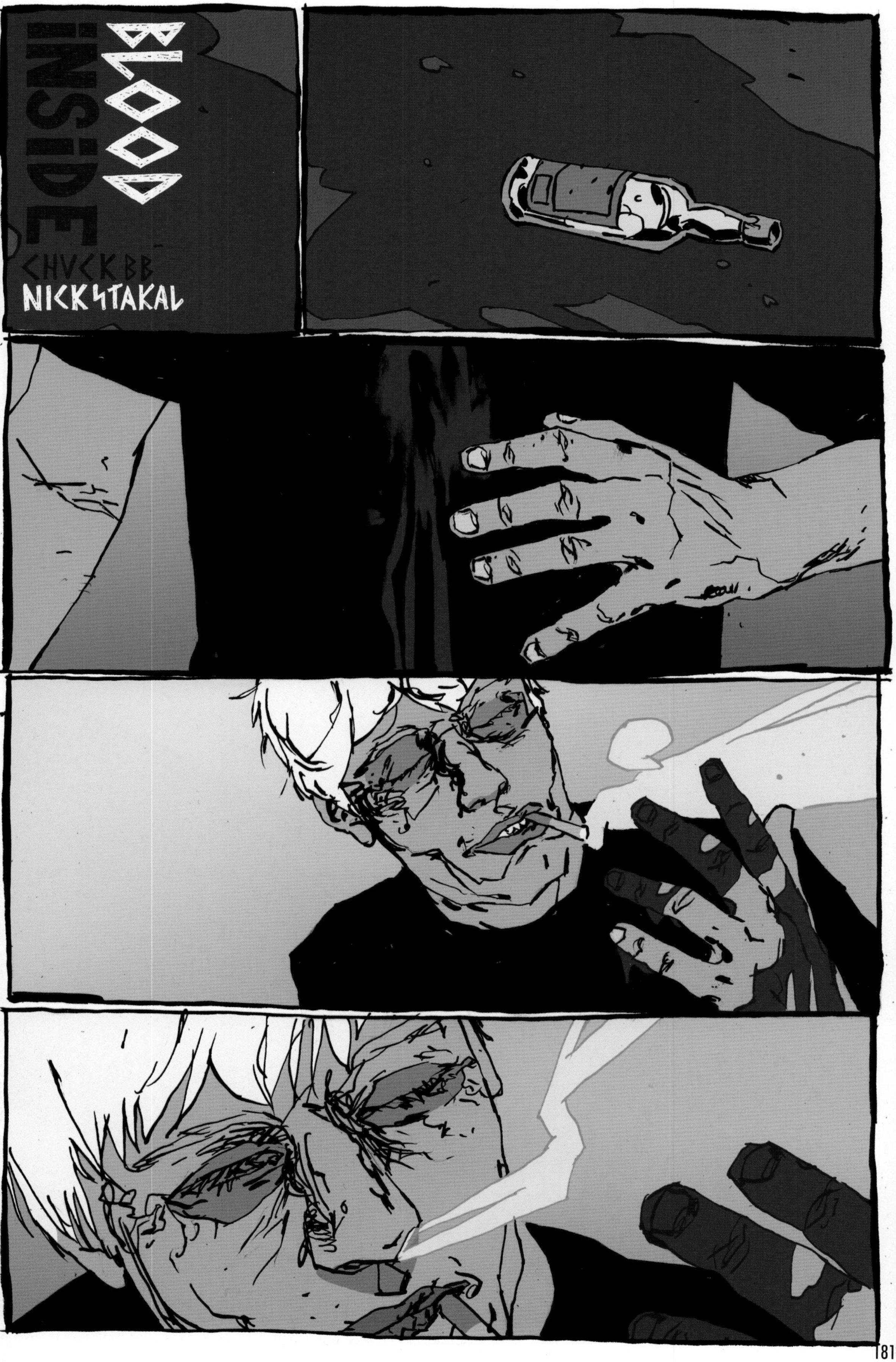
BLOOD
INSIDE
CHUCK BB
NICK STAKAL

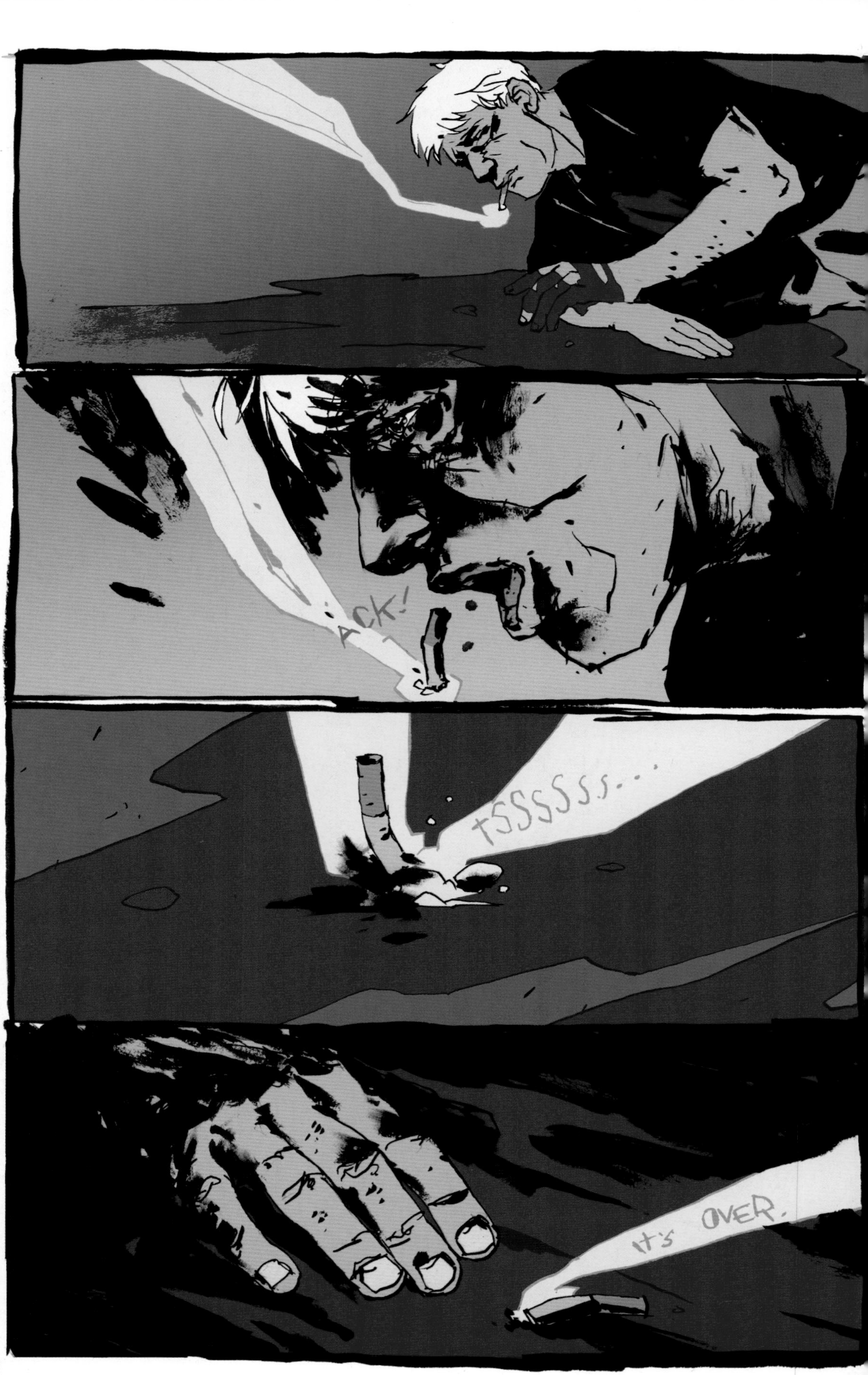
ACK!
tSSSSSS...
it's OVER.

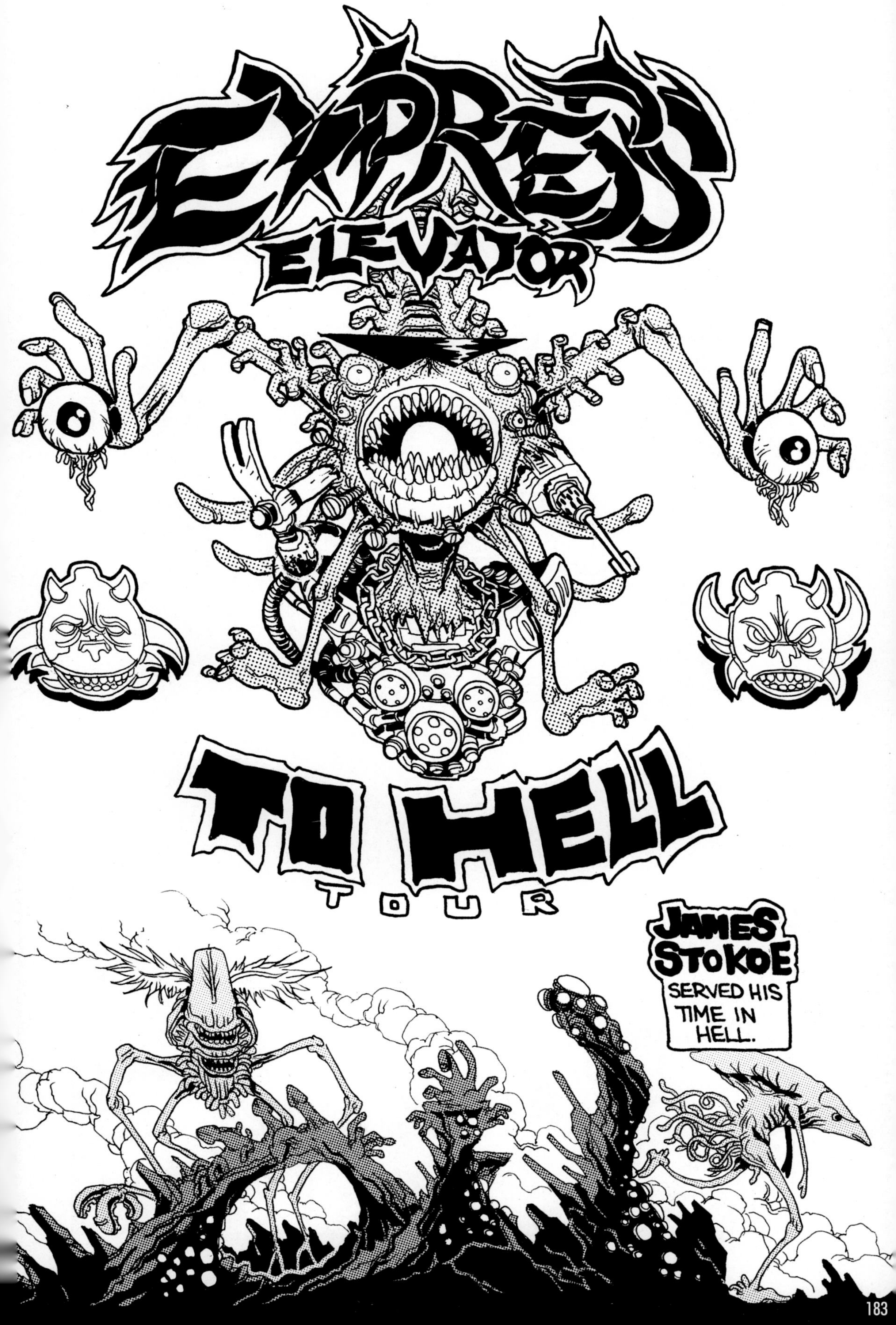
EXPRESS
ELEVATOR
TO HELL
TOUR
JAMES STOKOE
SERVED HIS TIME IN HELL.

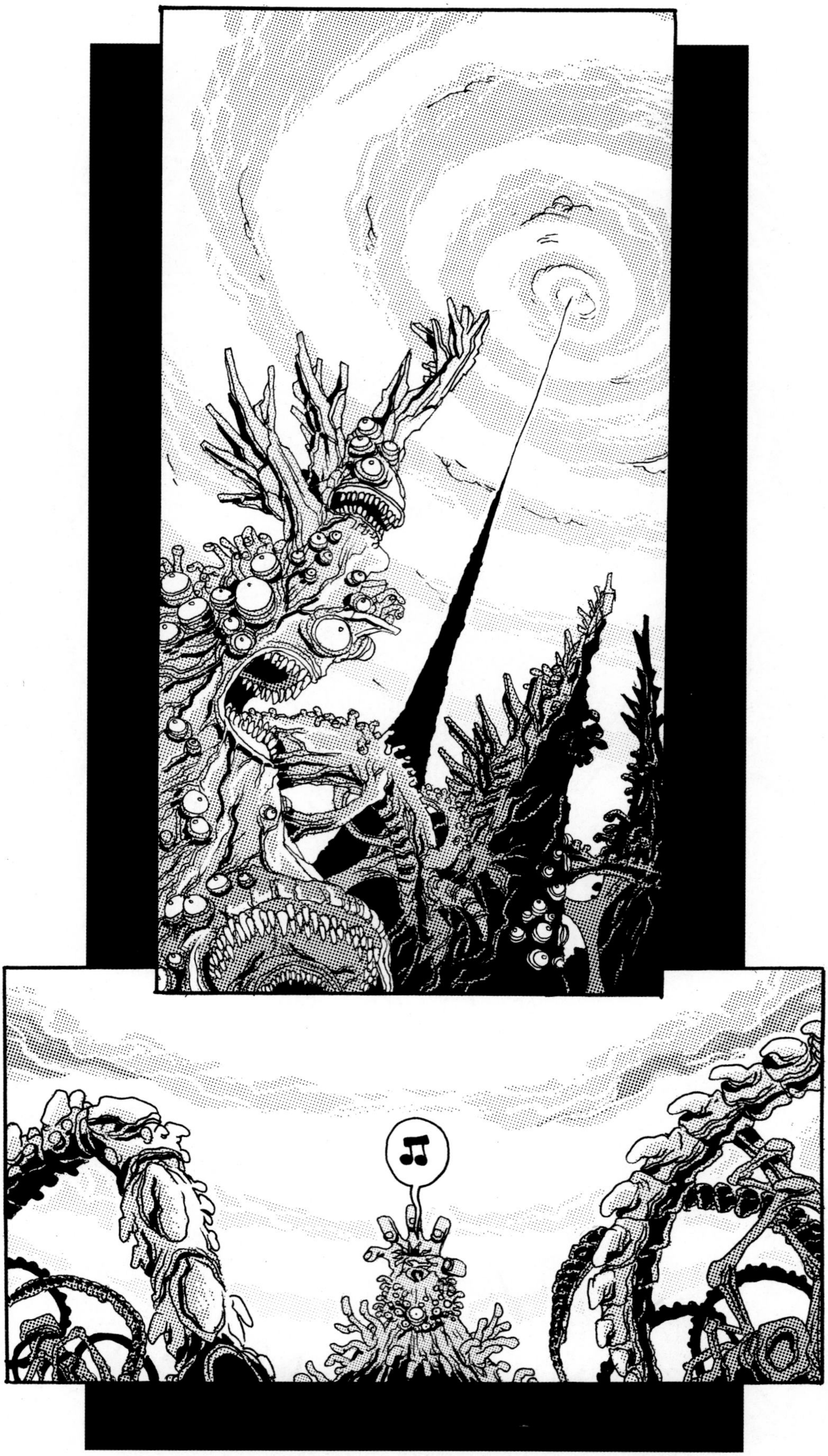

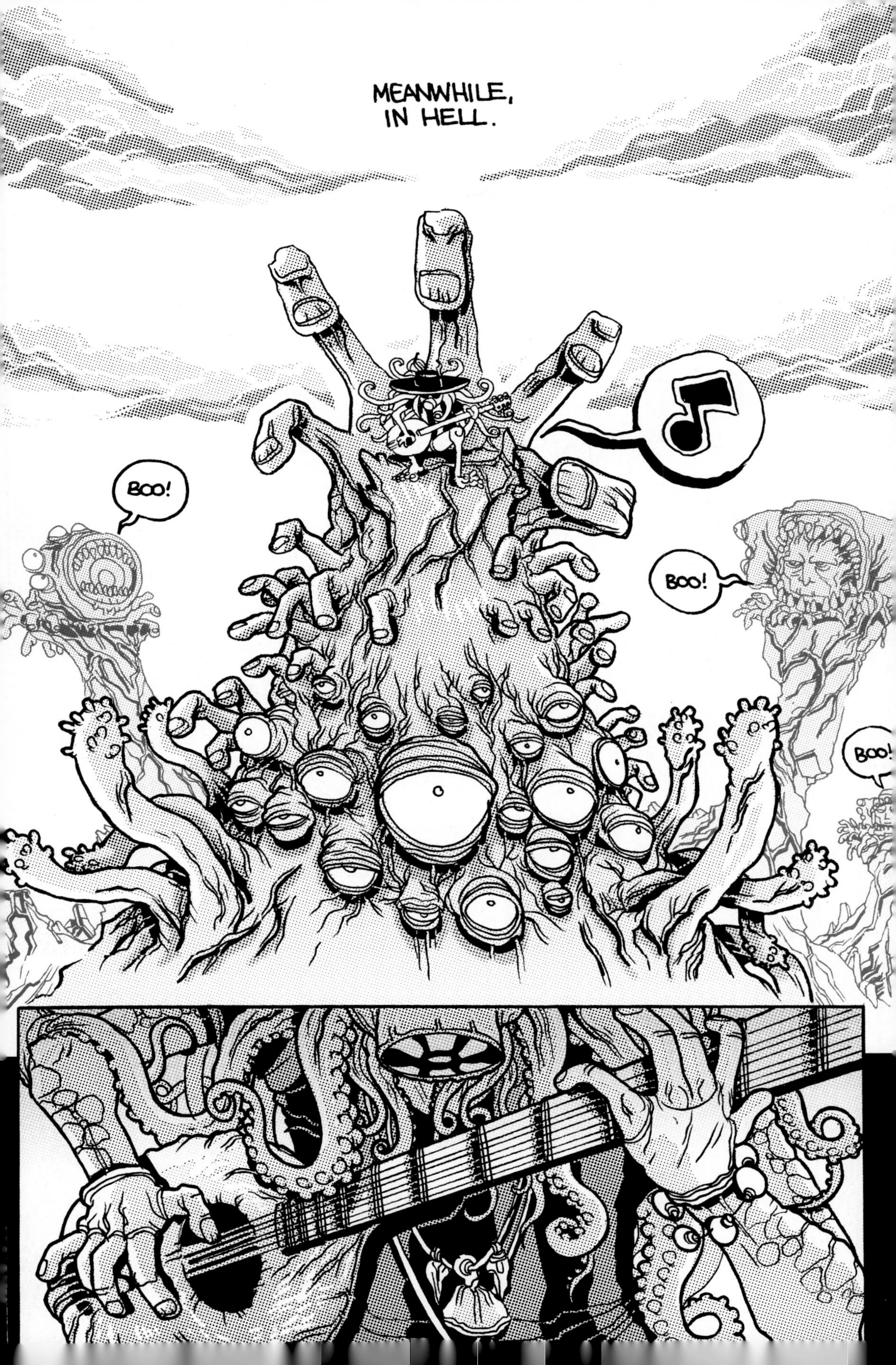
MEANWHILE, IN HELL.
BOO!
BOO!
BOO!

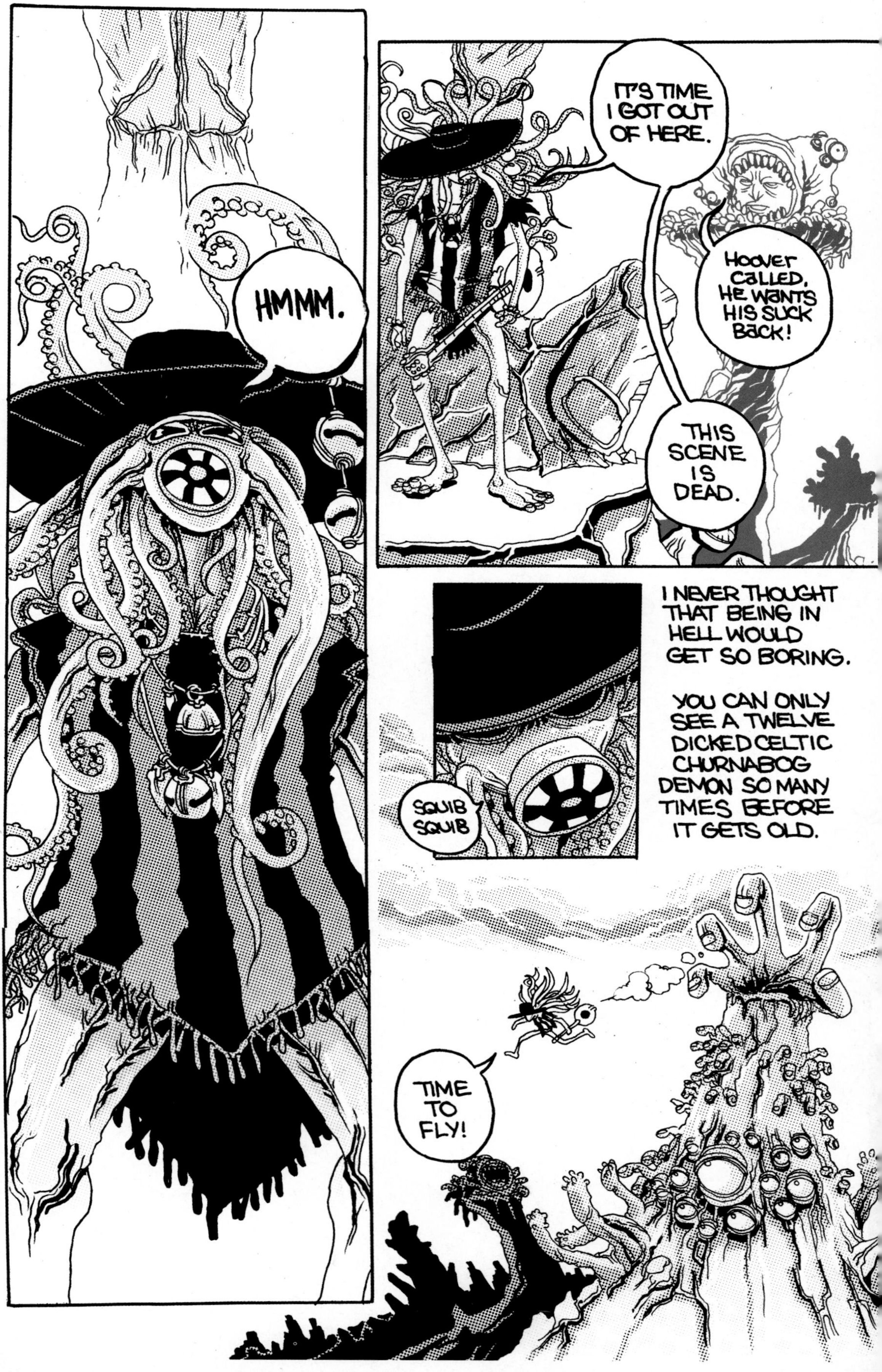
HMMM.
IT'S TIME I GOT OUT OF HERE.
Hoover called. He wants his suck back!
THIS SCENE IS DEAD.
I NEVER THOUGHT THAT BEING IN HELL WOULD GET SO BORING.
YOU CAN ONLY SEE A TWELVE DICKED CELTIC CHURNABOG DEMON SO MANY TIMES BEFORE IT GETS OLD.
SQUIB SQUIB
TIME TO FLY!

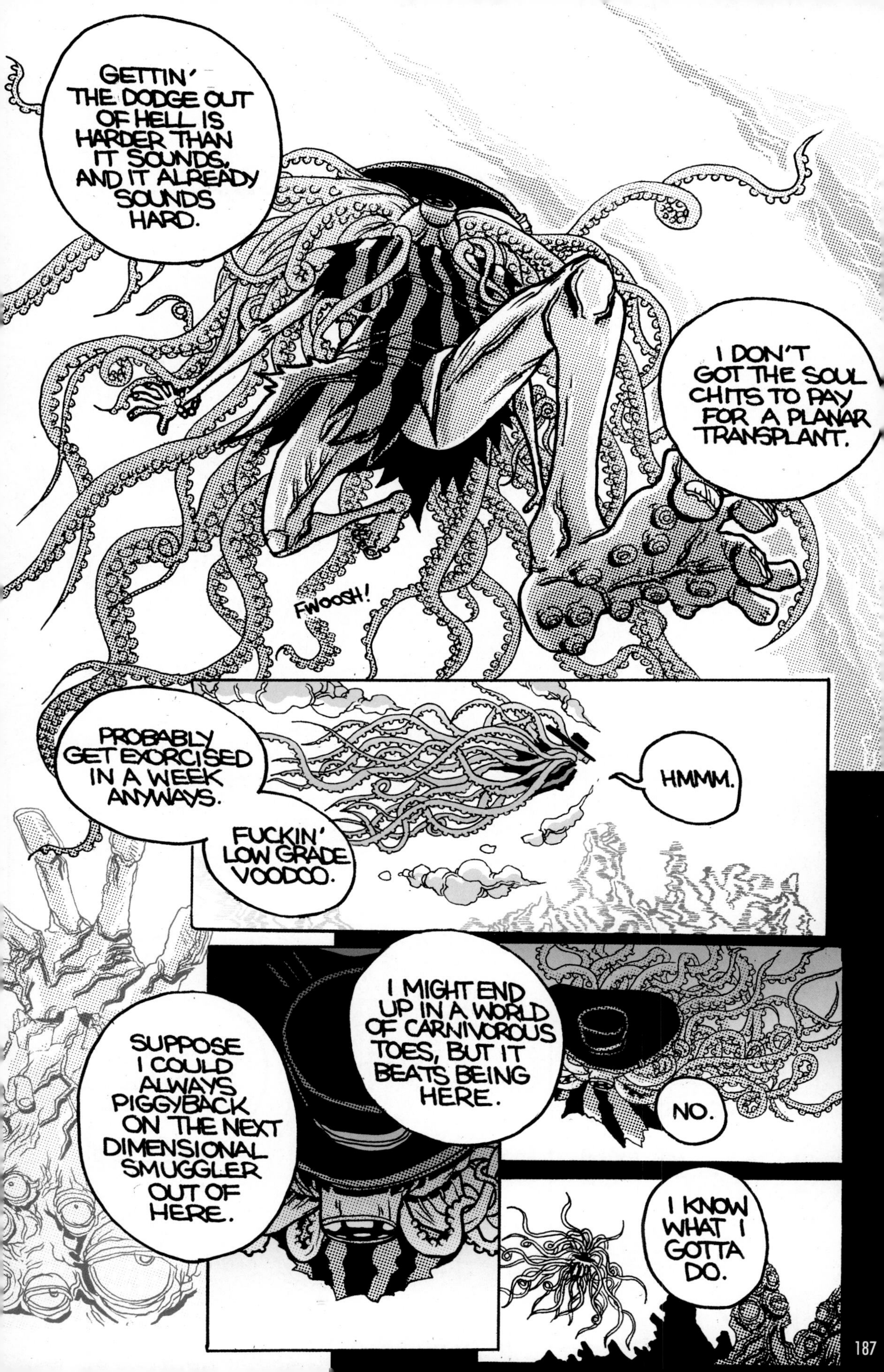

GETTIN' THE DODGE OUT OF HELL IS HARDER THAN IT SOUNDS, AND IT ALREADY SOUNDS HARD.
I DON'T GOT THE SOUL CHITS TO PAY FOR A PLANAR TRANSPLANT.
FWOOSH!
PROBABLY GET EXORCISED IN A WEEK ANYWAYS.
FUCKIN' LOW GRADE VOODOO.
HMMM.
SUPPOSE I COULD ALWAYS PIGGYBACK ON THE NEXT DIMENSIONAL SMUGGLER OUT OF HERE.
I MIGHT END UP IN A WORLD OF CARNIVOROUS TOES, BUT IT BEATS BEING HERE.
NO.
I KNOW WHAT I GOTTA DO.

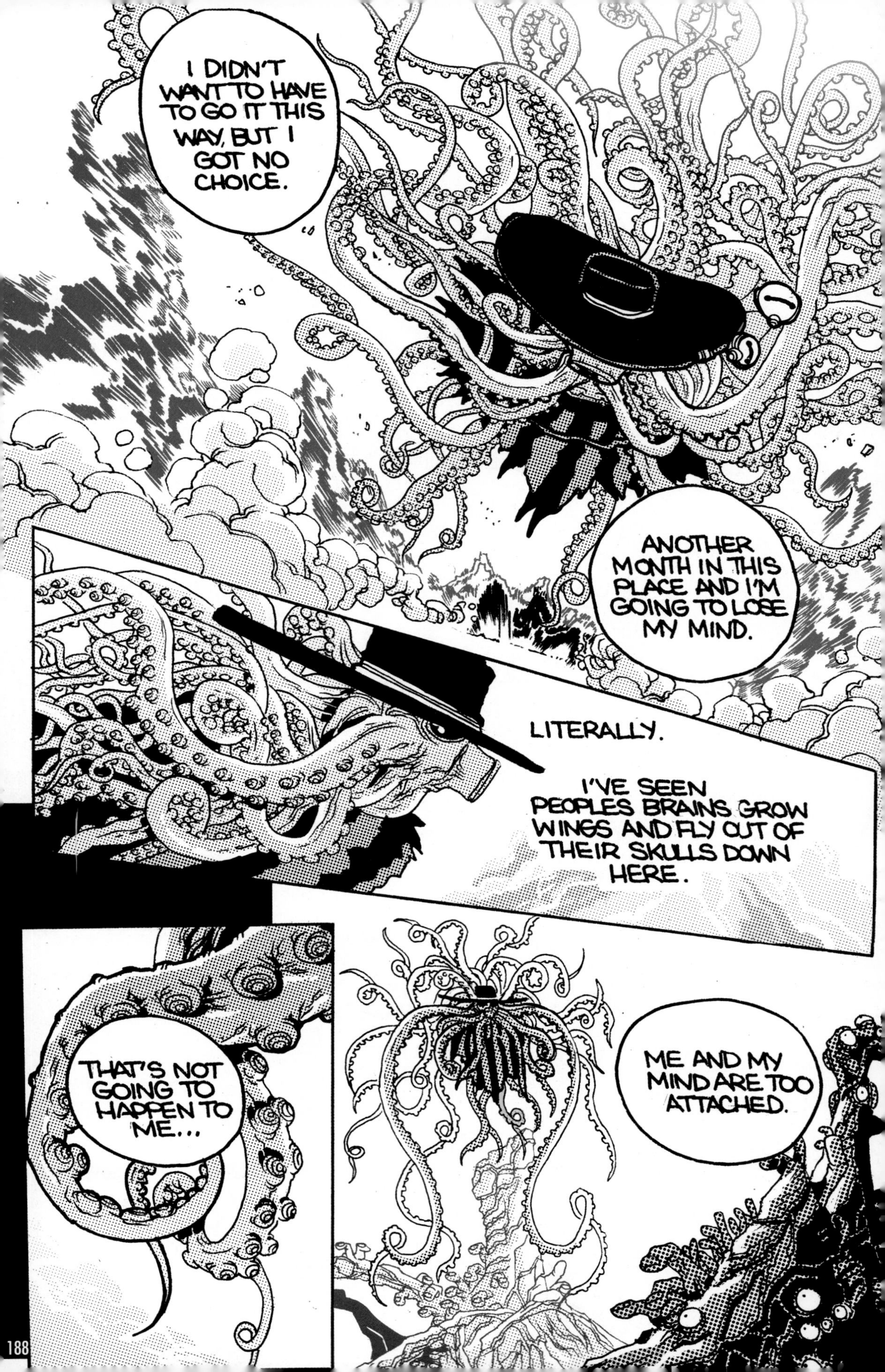
I DIDN'T WANT TO HAVE TO GO IT THIS WAY, BUT I GOT NO CHOICE.
ANOTHER MONTH IN THIS PLACE AND I'M GOING TO LOSE MY MIND.
LITERALLY.
I'VE SEEN PEOPLES BRAINS GROW WINGS AND FLY OUT OF THEIR SKULLS DOWN HERE.
THAT'S NOT GOING TO HAPPEN TO ME...
ME AND MY MIND ARE TOO ATTACHED.

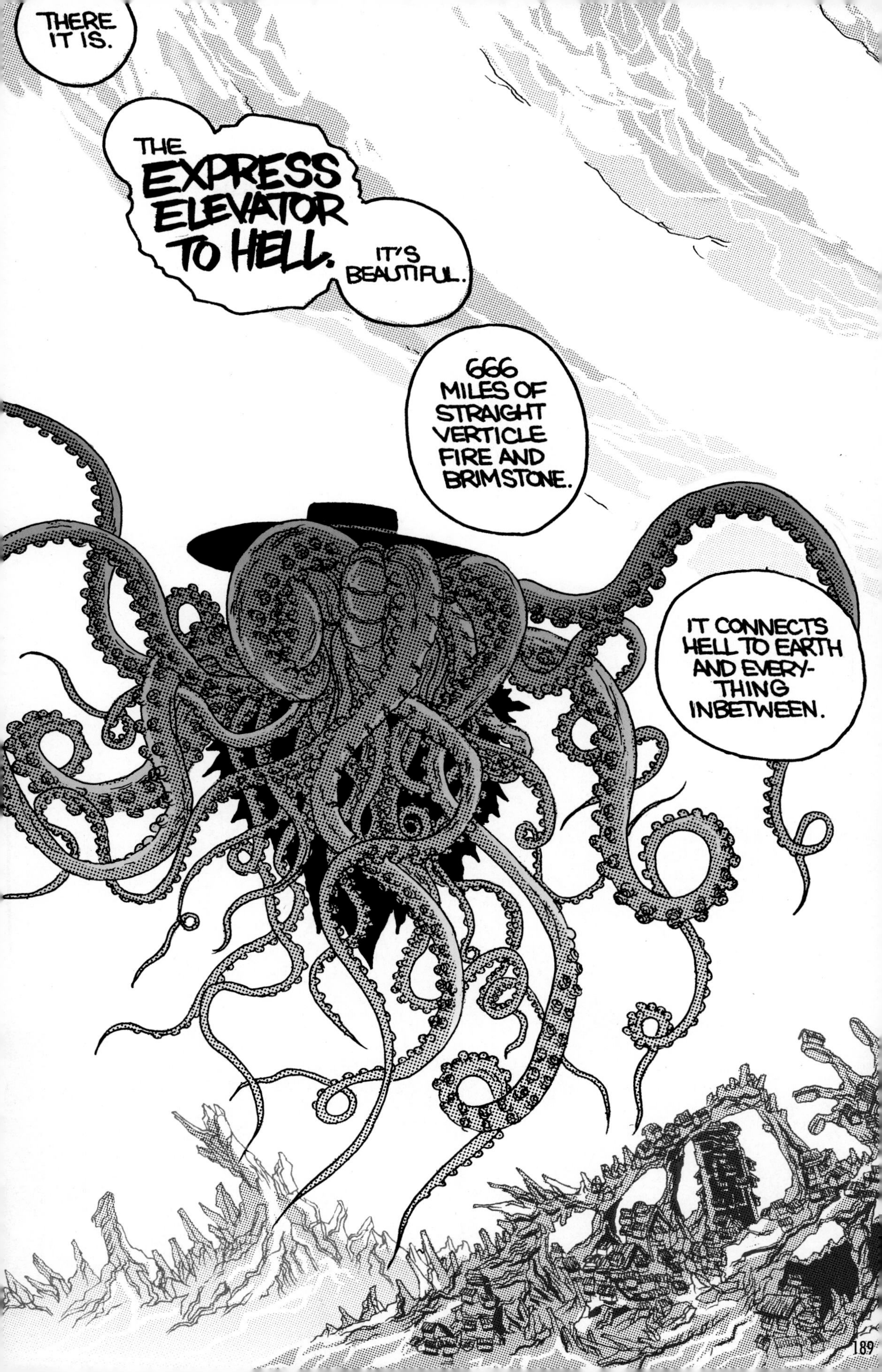
THERE IT IS.
THE EXPRESS ELEVATOR TO HELL.
IT'S BEAUTIFUL.
666 MILES OF STRAIGHT VERTICLE FIRE AND BRIMSTONE.
IT CONNECTS HELL TO EARTH AND EVERY-THING INBETWEEN.

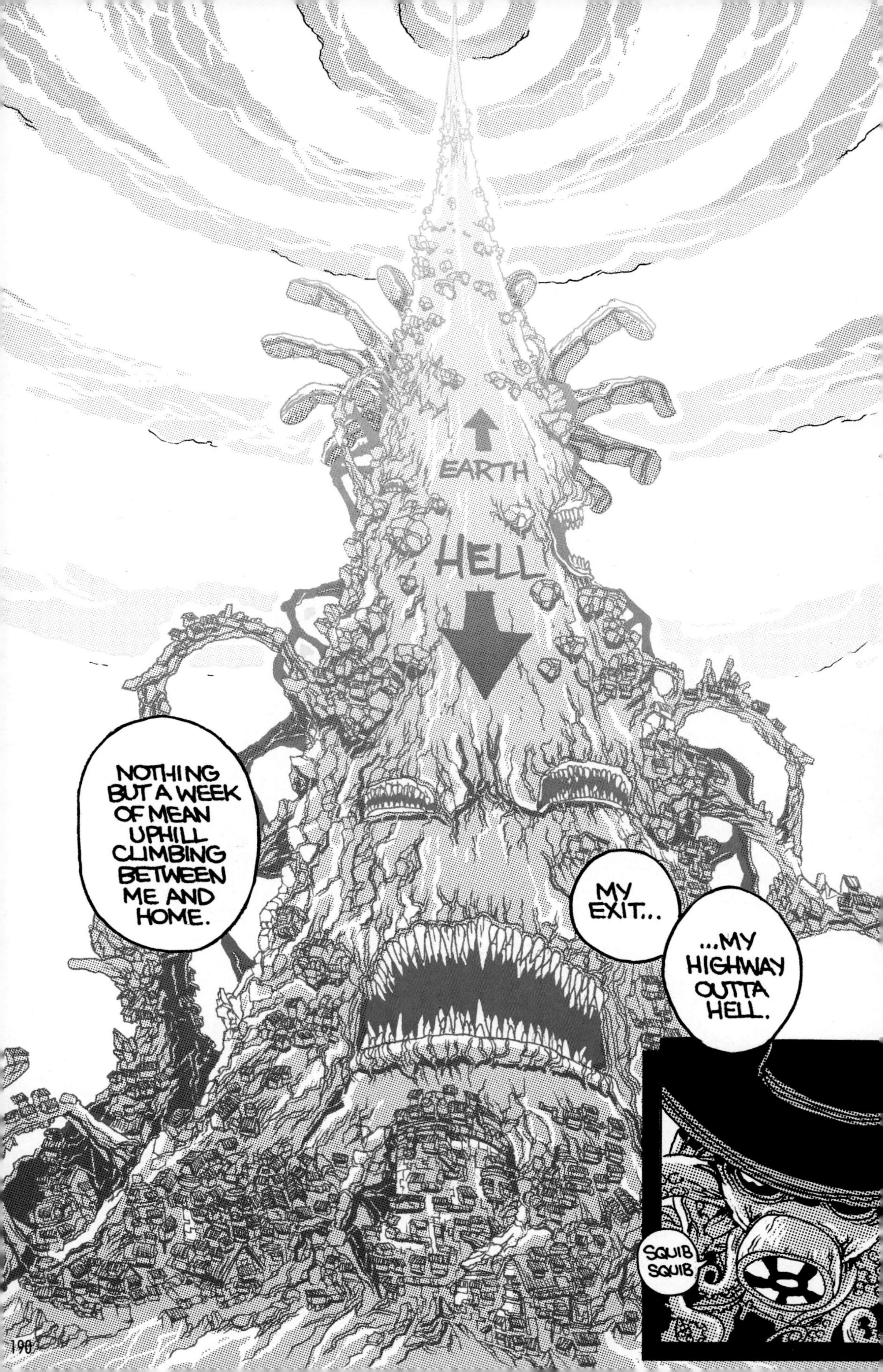
EARTH
HELL
NOTHING BUT A WEEK OF MEAN UPHILL CLIMBING BETWEEN ME AND HOME.
MY EXIT...
...MY HIGHWAY OUTTA HELL.
SQUIB SQUIB

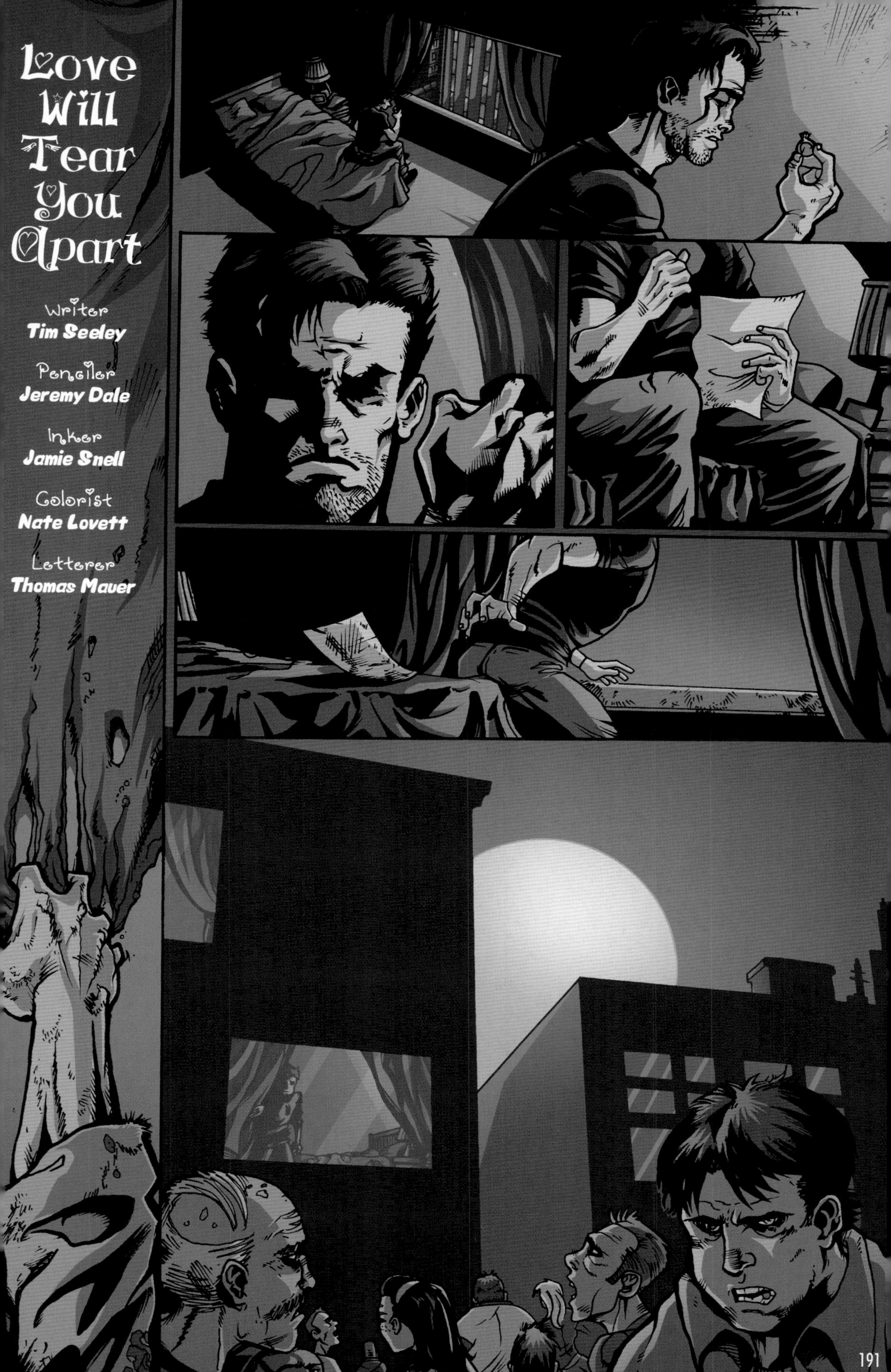
Love Will Tear You Apart
Writer
Tim Seeley
Penciler
Jeremy Dale
Inker
Jamie Snell
Colorist
Nate Lovett
Letterer
Thomas Mauer

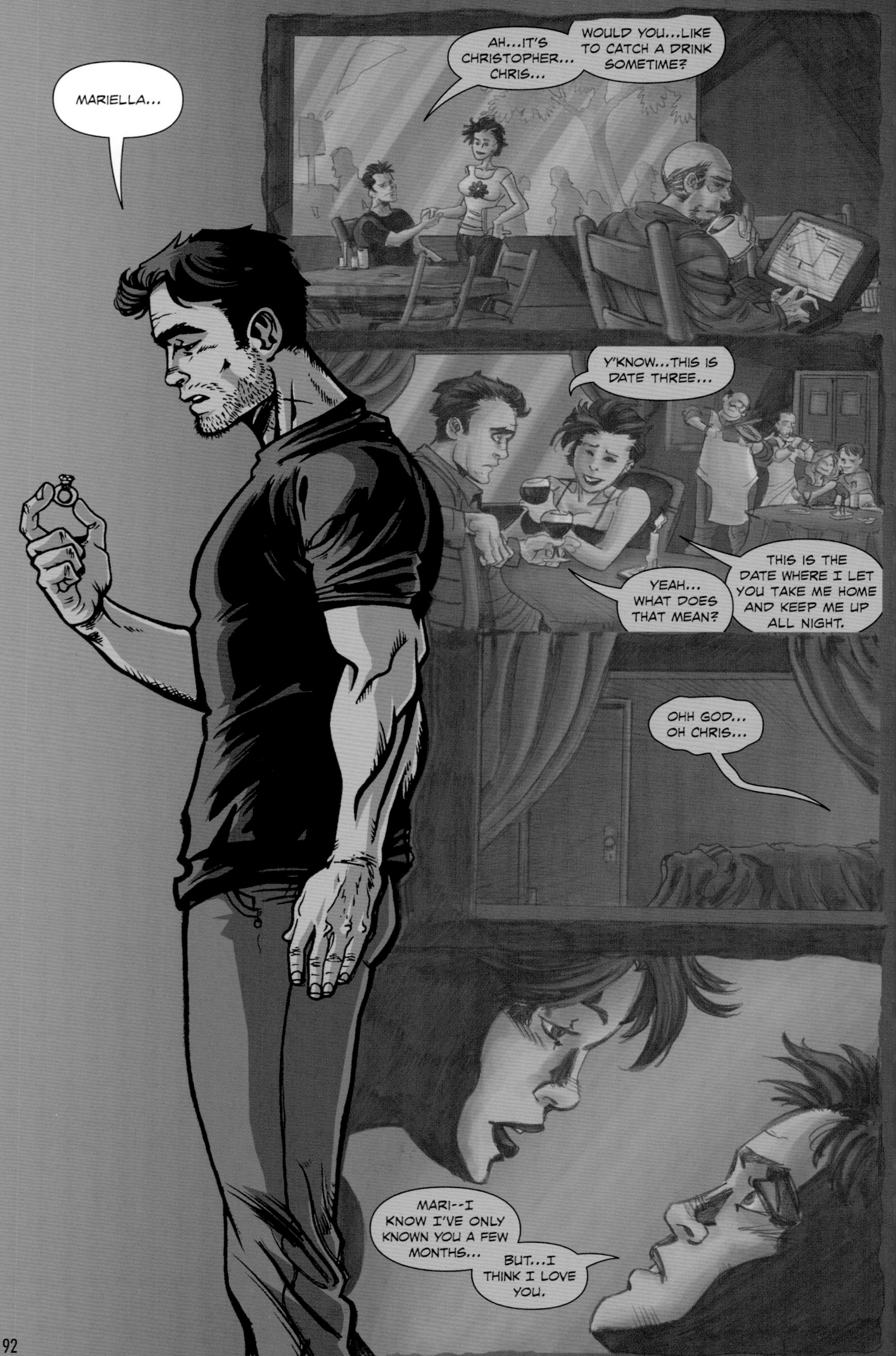
MARIELLA...
AH...IT'S CHRISTOPHER... CHRIS...
WOULD YOU...LIKE TO CATCH A DRINK SOMETIME?
Y'KNOW...THIS IS DATE THREE...
YEAH... WHAT DOES THAT MEAN?
THIS IS THE DATE WHERE I LET YOU TAKE ME HOME AND KEEP ME UP ALL NIGHT.
OHH GOD... OH CHRIS...
MARI--I KNOW I'VE ONLY KNOWN YOU A FEW MONTHS...
BUT...I THINK I LOVE YOU.

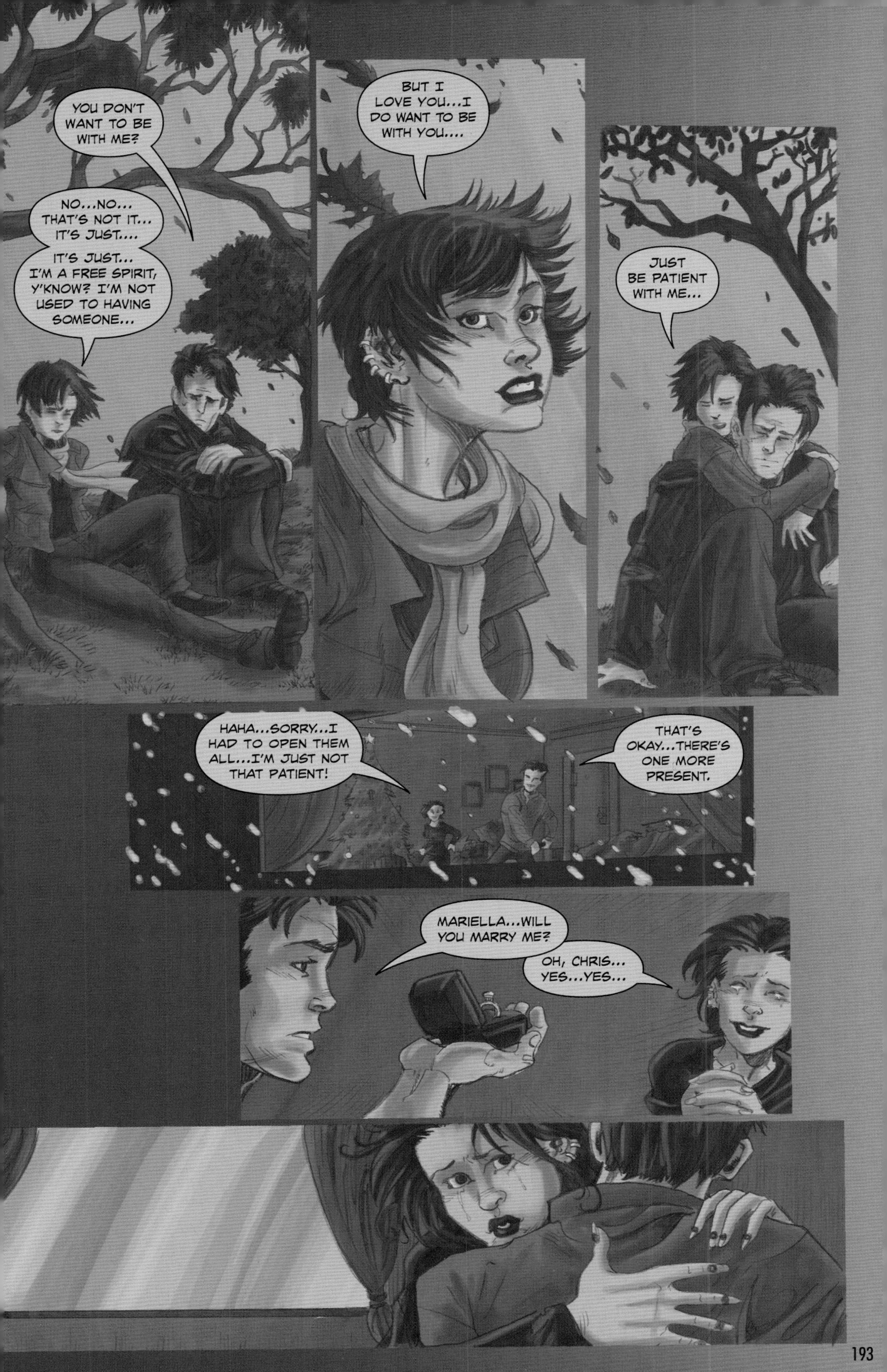
YOU DON'T WANT TO BE WITH ME?
NO...NO... THAT'S NOT IT... IT'S JUST....
IT'S JUST... I'M A FREE SPIRIT, Y'KNOW? I'M NOT USED TO HAVING SOMEONE...
BUT I LOVE YOU...I DO WANT TO BE WITH YOU....
JUST BE PATIENT WITH ME...
HAHA...SORRY...I HAD TO OPEN THEM ALL...I'M JUST NOT THAT PATIENT!
THAT'S OKAY...THERE'S ONE MORE PRESENT.
MARIELLA...WILL YOU MARRY ME?
OH, CHRIS... YES...YES...

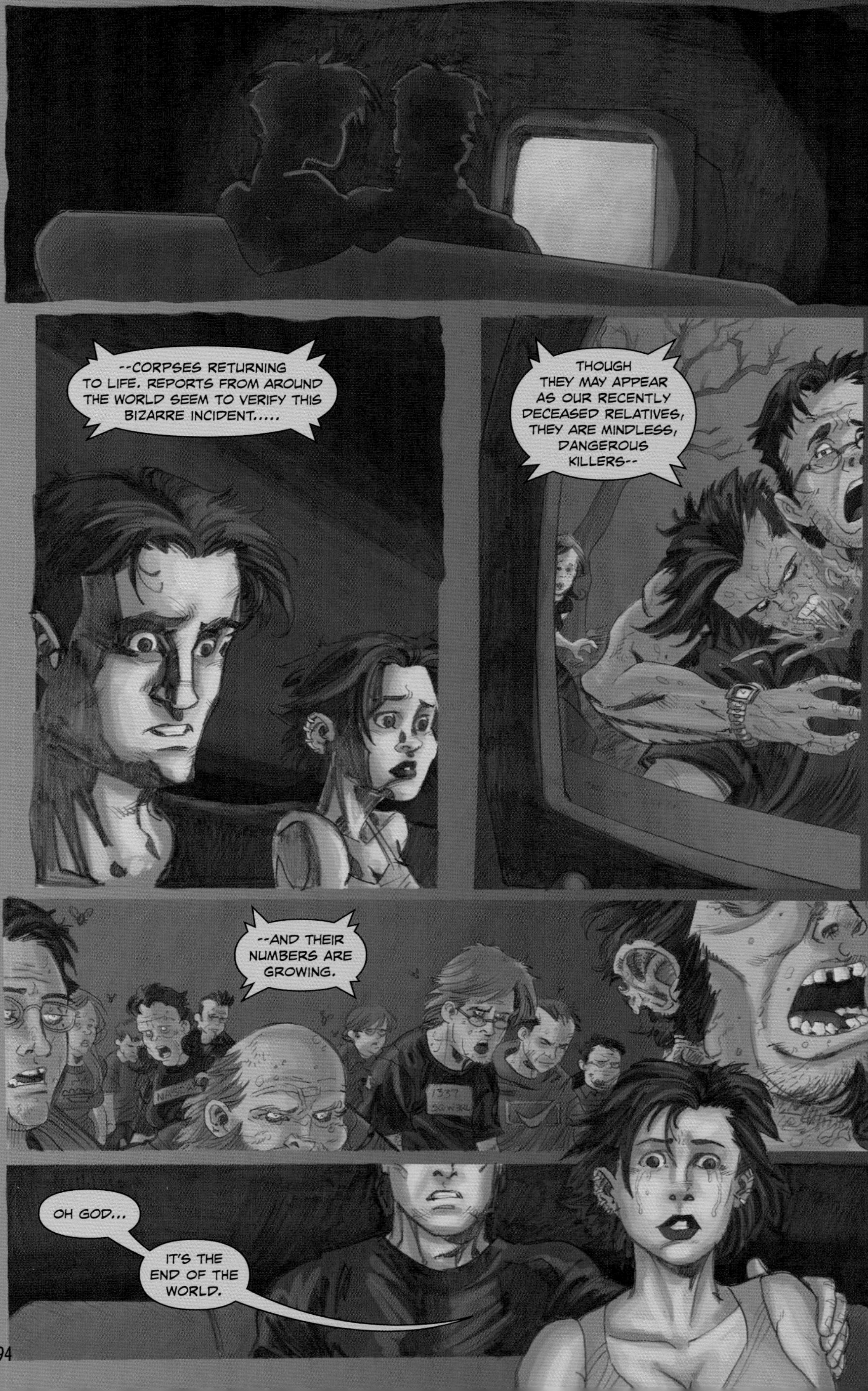
--CORPSES RETURNING TO LIFE. REPORTS FROM AROUND THE WORLD SEEM TO VERIFY THIS BIZARRE INCIDENT.....
THOUGH THEY MAY APPEAR AS OUR RECENTLY DECEASED RELATIVES, THEY ARE MINDLESS, DANGEROUS KILLERS--
--AND THEIR NUMBERS ARE GROWING.
OH GOD...
IT'S THE END OF THE WORLD.

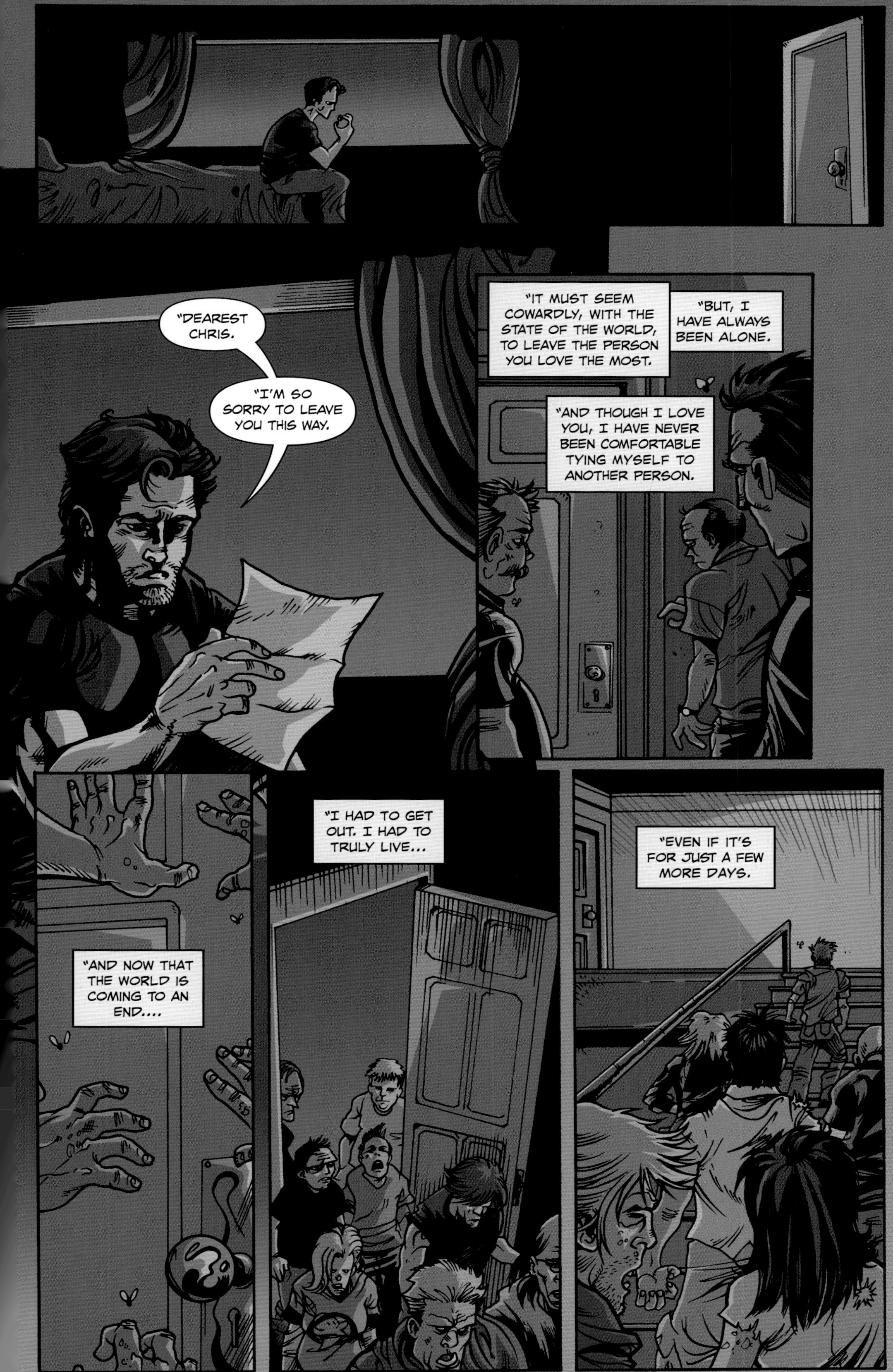
"DEAREST CHRIS.
"I'M SO SORRY TO LEAVE YOU THIS WAY.
"IT MUST SEEM COWARDLY, WITH THE STATE OF THE WORLD, TO LEAVE THE PERSON YOU LOVE THE MOST.
"BUT, I HAVE ALWAYS BEEN ALONE.
"AND THOUGH I LOVE YOU, I HAVE NEVER BEEN COMFORTABLE TYING MYSELF TO ANOTHER PERSON.
"AND NOW THAT THE WORLD IS COMING TO AN END....
"I HAD TO GET OUT. I HAD TO TRULY LIVE...
"EVEN IF IT'S FOR JUST A FEW MORE DAYS.

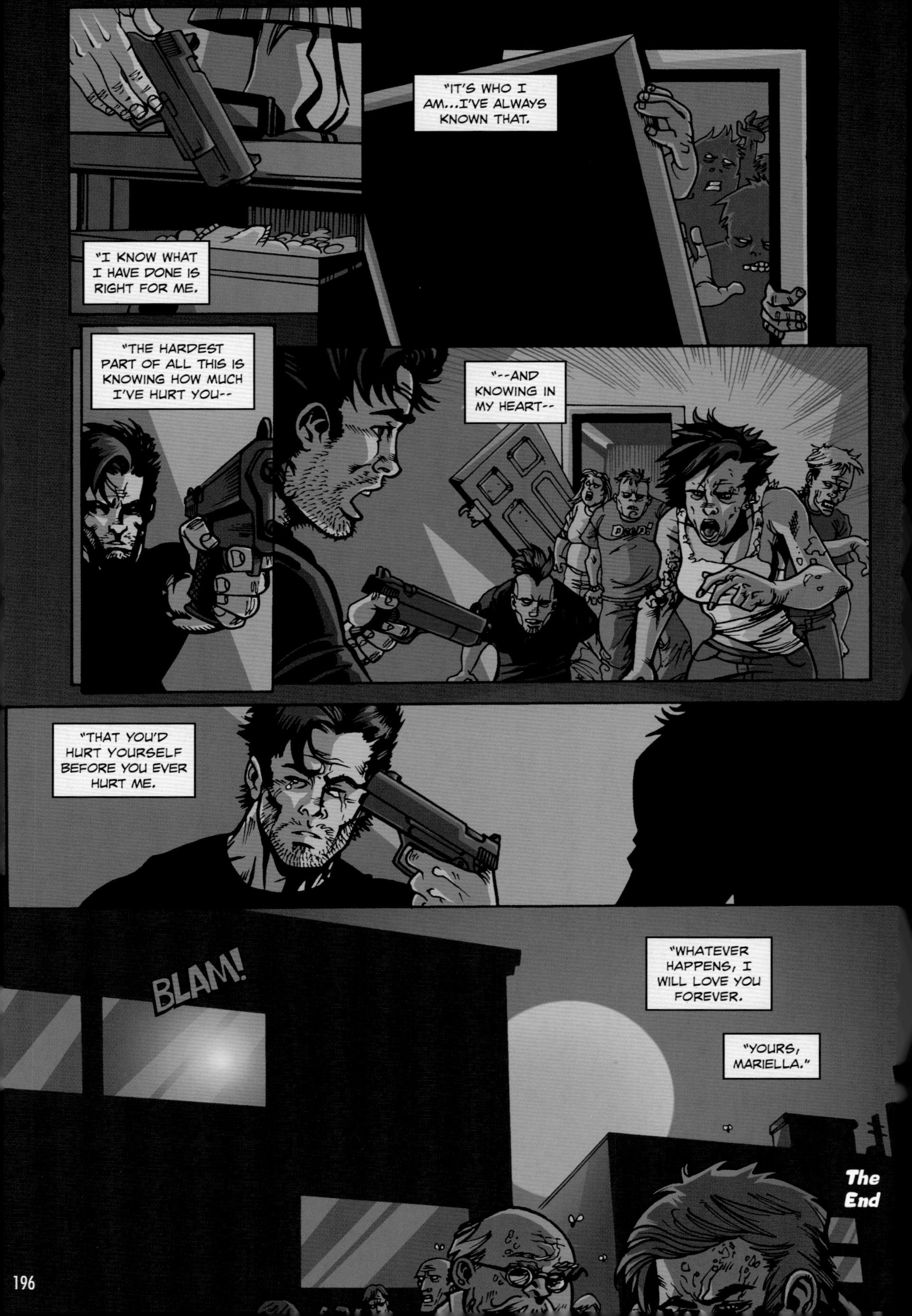
"IT'S WHO I AM...I'VE ALWAYS KNOWN THAT.
"I KNOW WHAT I HAVE DONE IS RIGHT FOR ME.
"THE HARDEST PART OF ALL THIS IS KNOWING HOW MUCH I'VE HURT YOU--
"--AND KNOWING IN MY HEART--
"THAT YOU'D HURT YOURSELF BEFORE YOU EVER HURT ME.
BLAM!
"WHATEVER HAPPENS, I WILL LOVE YOU FOREVER.
"YOURS, MARIELLA."
The End

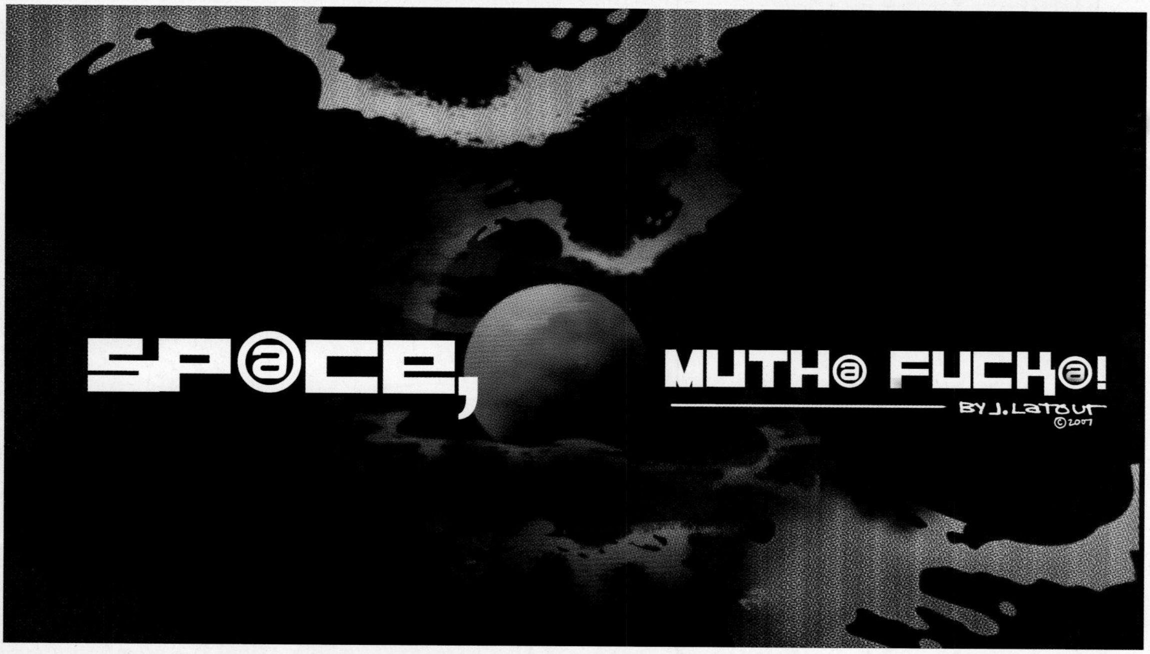
SP@CE, MUTH@ FUCK@!
BY J. LATOUR
©2007

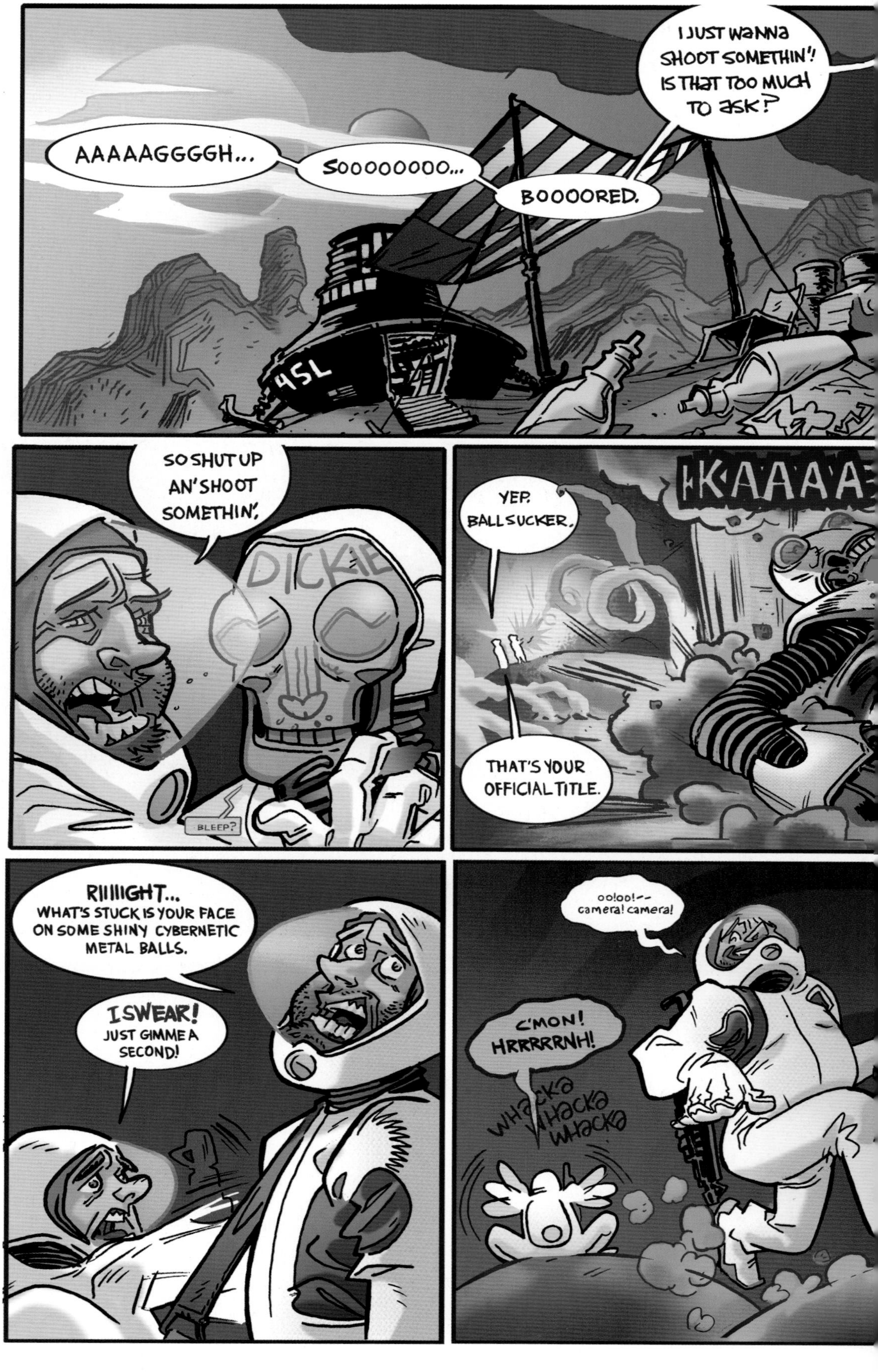

AAAAAGGGGH...
SOOOOOOOO...
BOOOORED.
I JUST WANNA SHOOT SOMETHIN'! IS THAT TOO MUCH TO ASK?
4SL
SO SHUT UP AN' SHOOT SOMETHIN'.
DICKIE
BLEEP?
YEP. BALLSUCKER.
THAT'S YOUR OFFICIAL TITLE.
KAAAA
RIIIIGHT... WHAT'S STUCK IS YOUR FACE ON SOME SHINY CYBERNETIC METAL BALLS.
I SWEAR! JUST GIMME A SECOND!
oo!oo!-- camera! camera!
C'MON! HRRRRRNH!
WHACKA WHACKA WHACKA

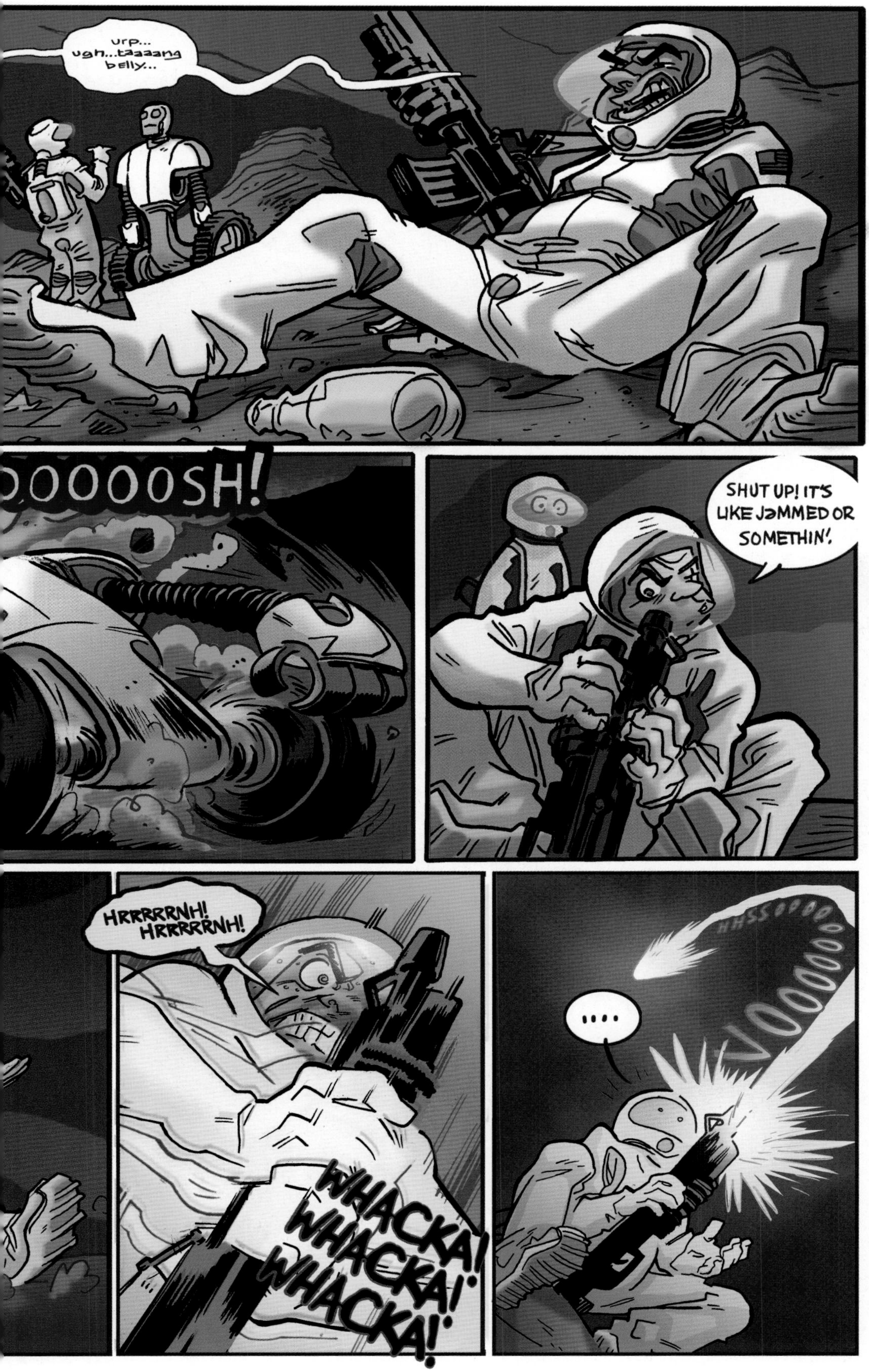
urp... ugh...taaaang belly...
OOOOOOSH!
SHUT UP! IT'S LIKE JAMMED OR SOMETHIN'!
HRRRRRNH! HRRRRRNH!
WHACKA! WHACKA! WHACKA!
....
VOOOOOOOOOOSSHH

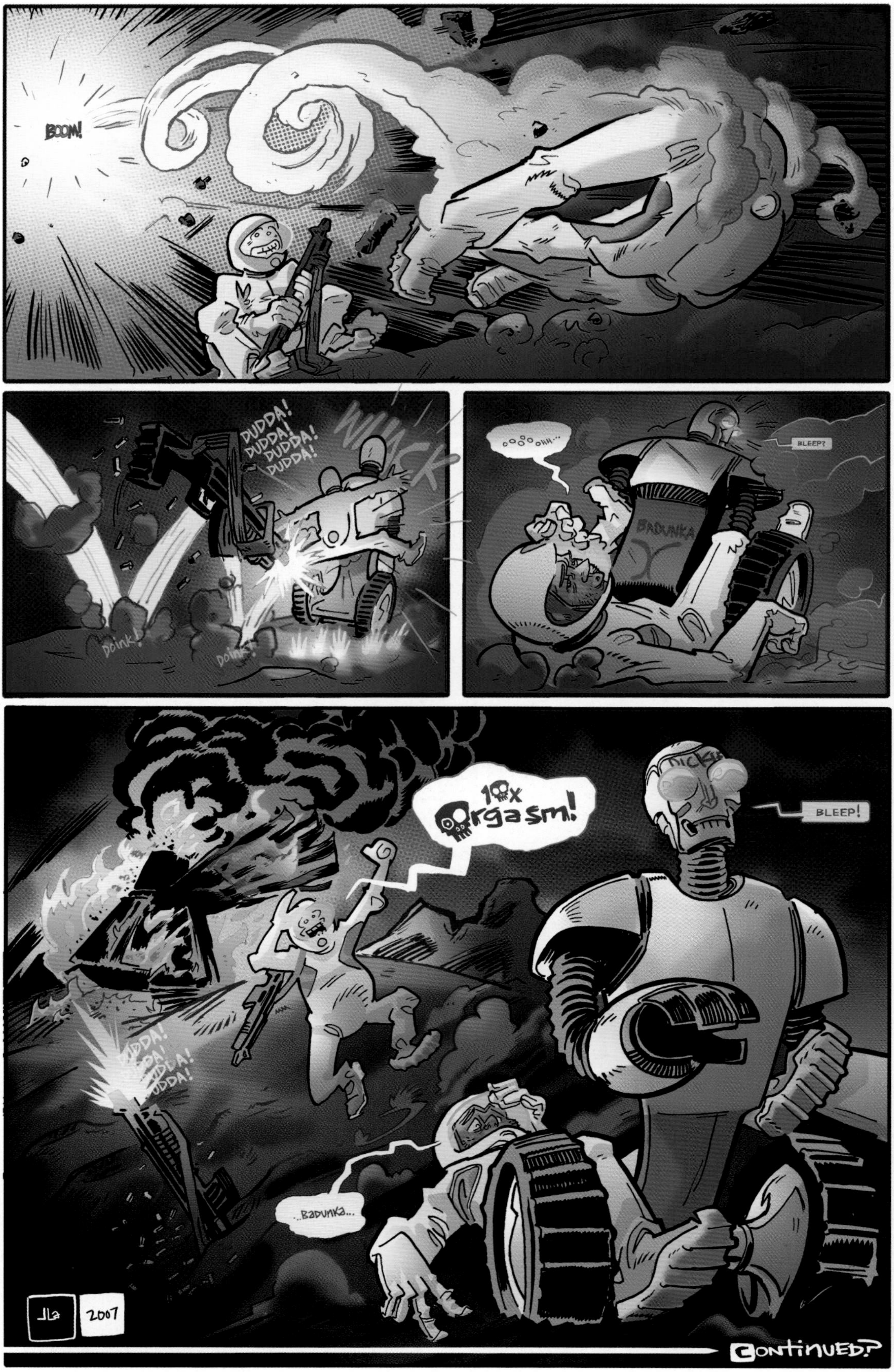
BOOM!
DUDDA! DUDDA! DUDDA! DUDDA!
WHACK
Doink!
Doink!
ooooohh...
BLEEP?
BADUNKA
10x Orgasm!
BLEEP!
DUDDA! DUDDA! DUDDA! DUDDA!
..Badunka...
2007
Continued?

THIS IS:

A COMIC BY
SHELDON VELLA.

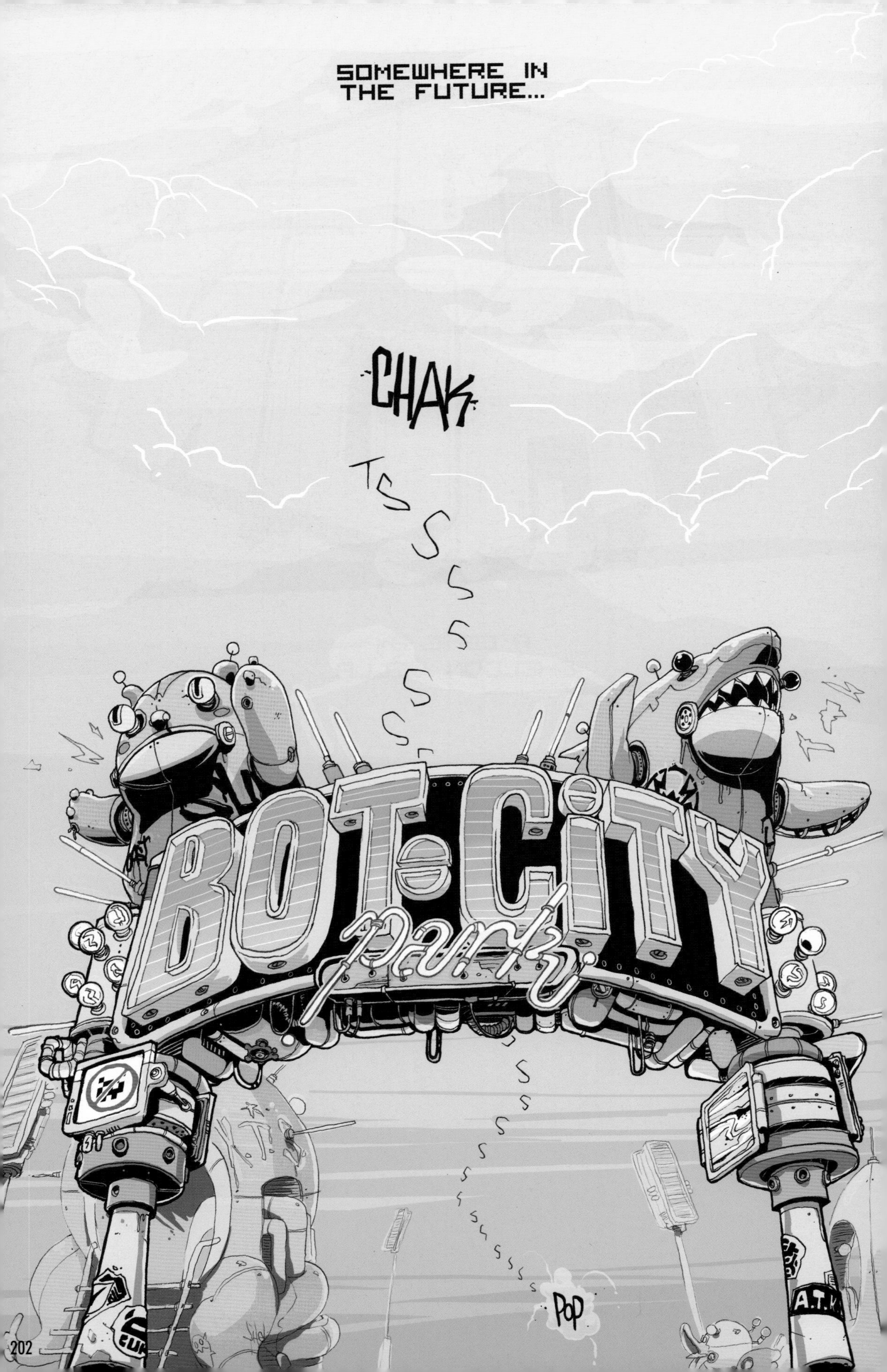
SOMEWHERE IN THE FUTURE...
CHAK
TSSSSSSS
BOT CITY
park
POP
A.T.K.

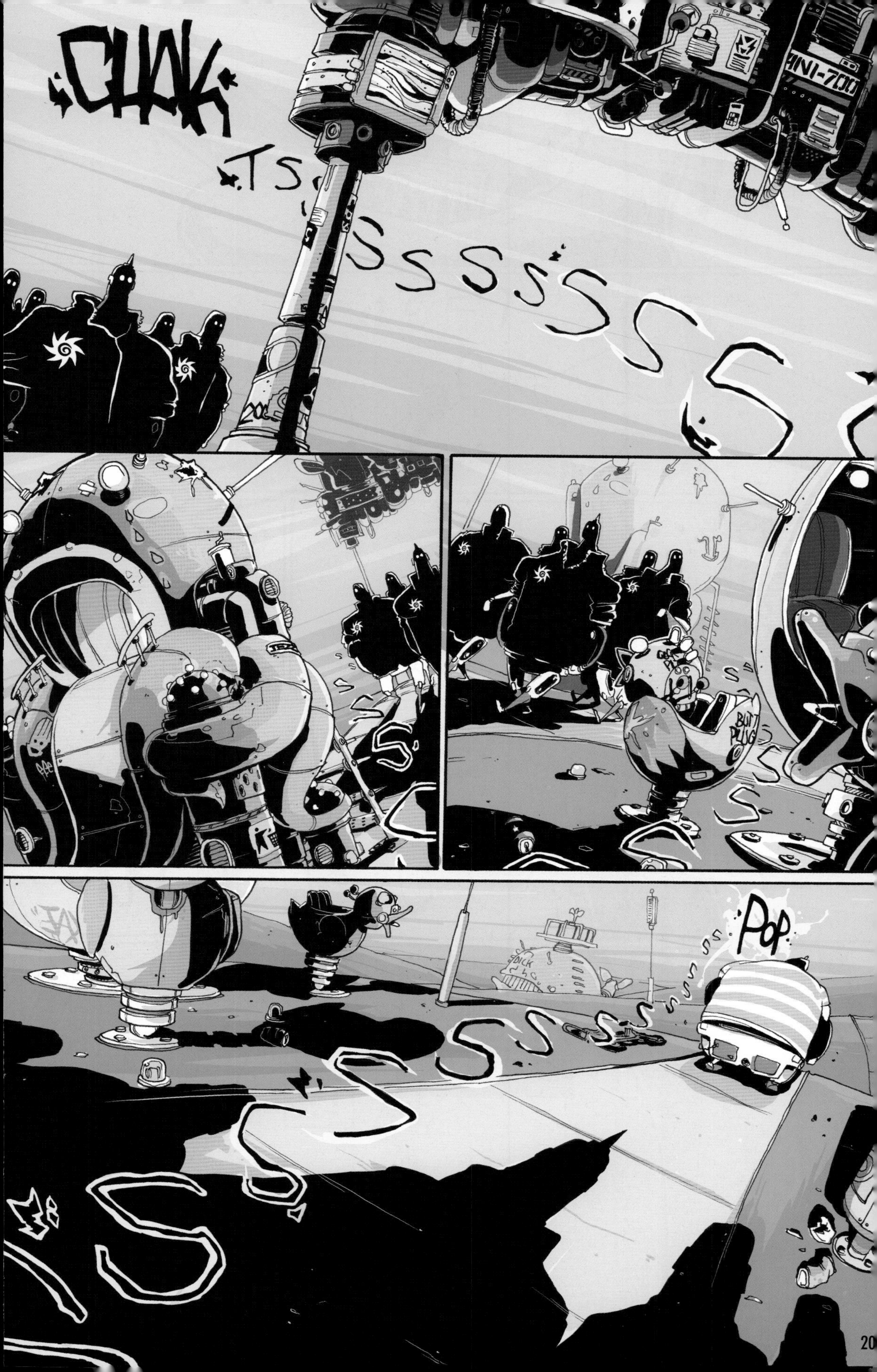
CHUK
TSSSSSSSSS
BUTT PLUG
POP

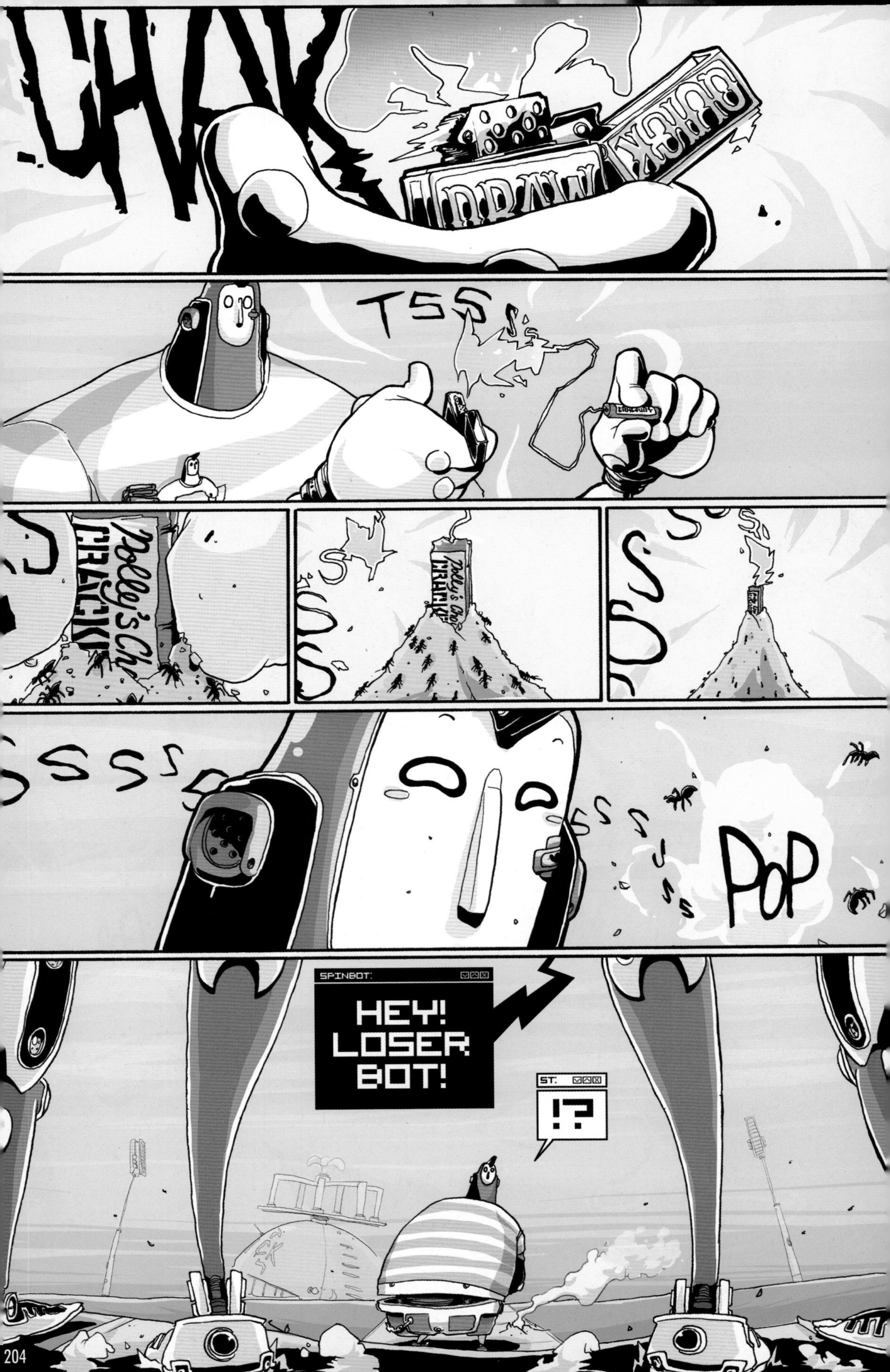
CHAK
QUICK
DRAW
TSSSS
Polly's Cho CRACK
SSSS
POP
SPINBOT:
HEY! LOSER BOT!
ST.
!?

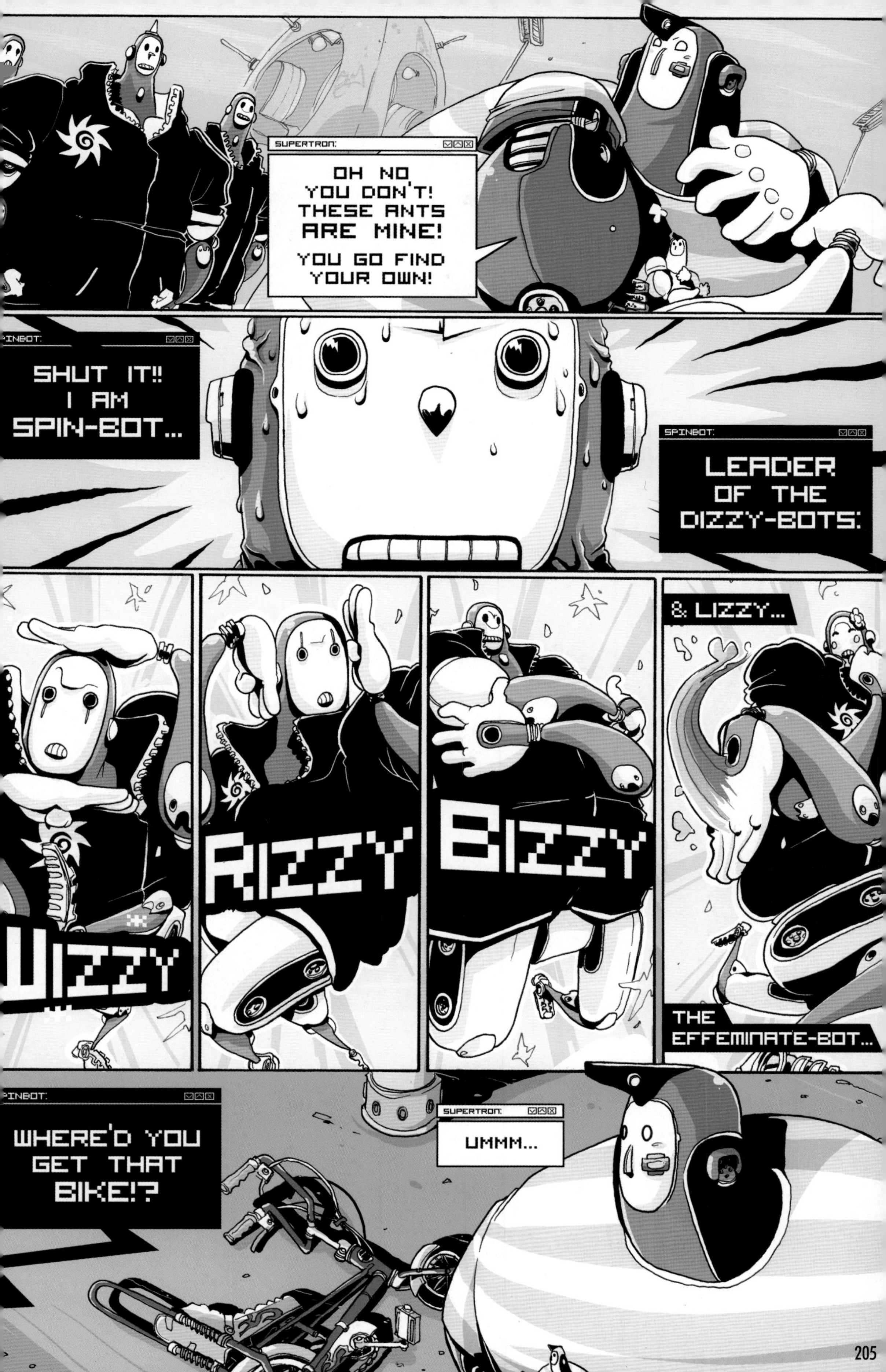
SUPERTRON:
OH NO YOU DON'T! THESE ANTS ARE MINE!
YOU GO FIND YOUR OWN!
SPINBOT:
SHUT IT!! I AM SPIN-BOT...
SPINBOT:
LEADER OF THE DIZZY-BOTS:
WIZZY
RIZZY
BIZZY
& LIZZY...
THE EFFEMINATE-BOT...
SPINBOT:
WHERE'D YOU GET THAT BIKE!?
SUPERTRON:
UMMM...

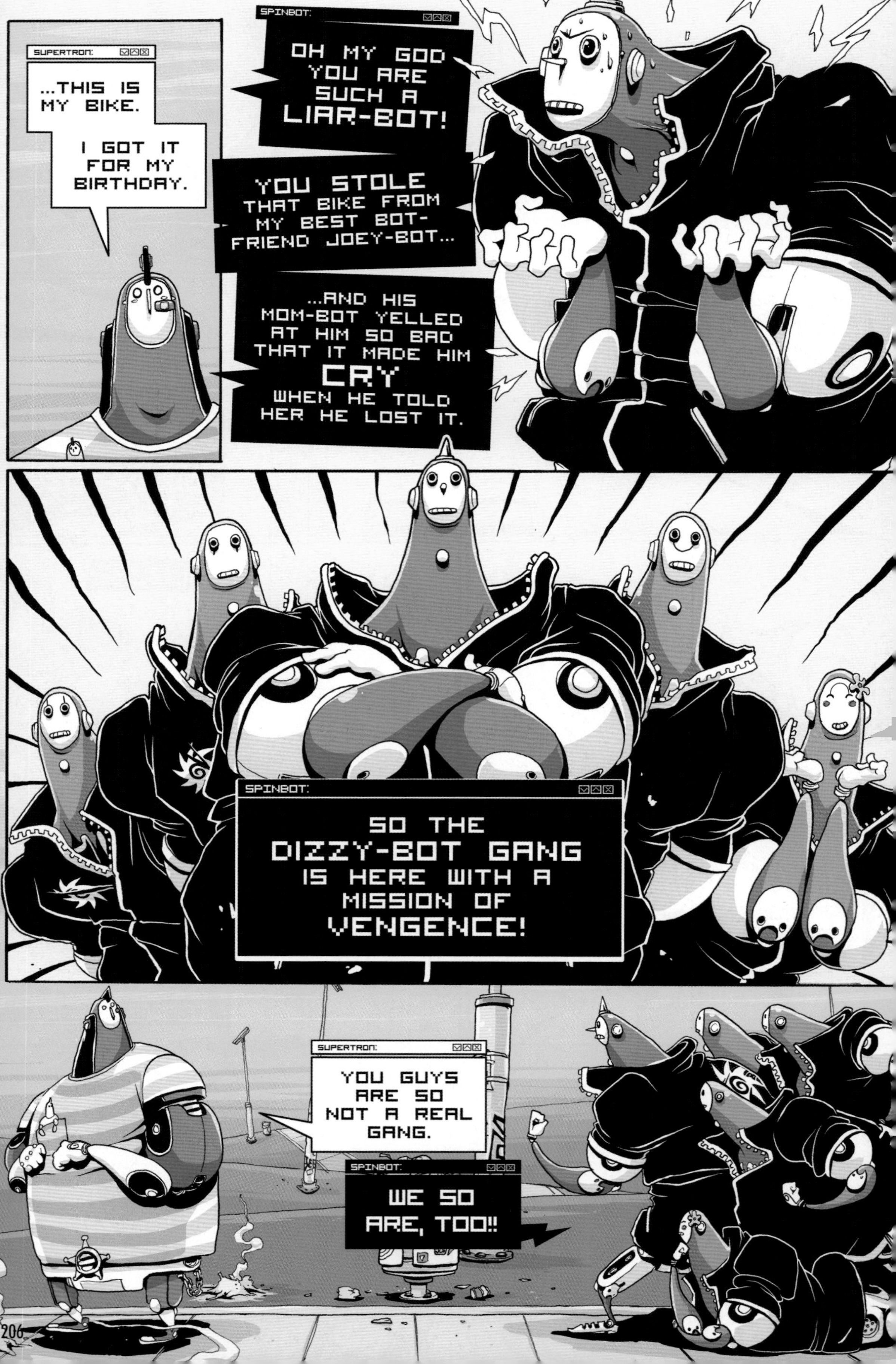
SUPERTRON:
...THIS IS MY BIKE.
I GOT IT FOR MY BIRTHDAY.
SPINBOT:
OH MY GOD YOU ARE SUCH A LIAR-BOT!
YOU STOLE THAT BIKE FROM MY BEST BOT-FRIEND JOEY-BOT...
...AND HIS MOM-BOT YELLED AT HIM SO BAD THAT IT MADE HIM CRY WHEN HE TOLD HER HE LOST IT.
SPINBOT:
SO THE DIZZY-BOT GANG IS HERE WITH A MISSION OF VENGENCE!
SUPERTRON:
YOU GUYS ARE SO NOT A REAL GANG.
SPINBOT:
WE SO ARE, TOO!!

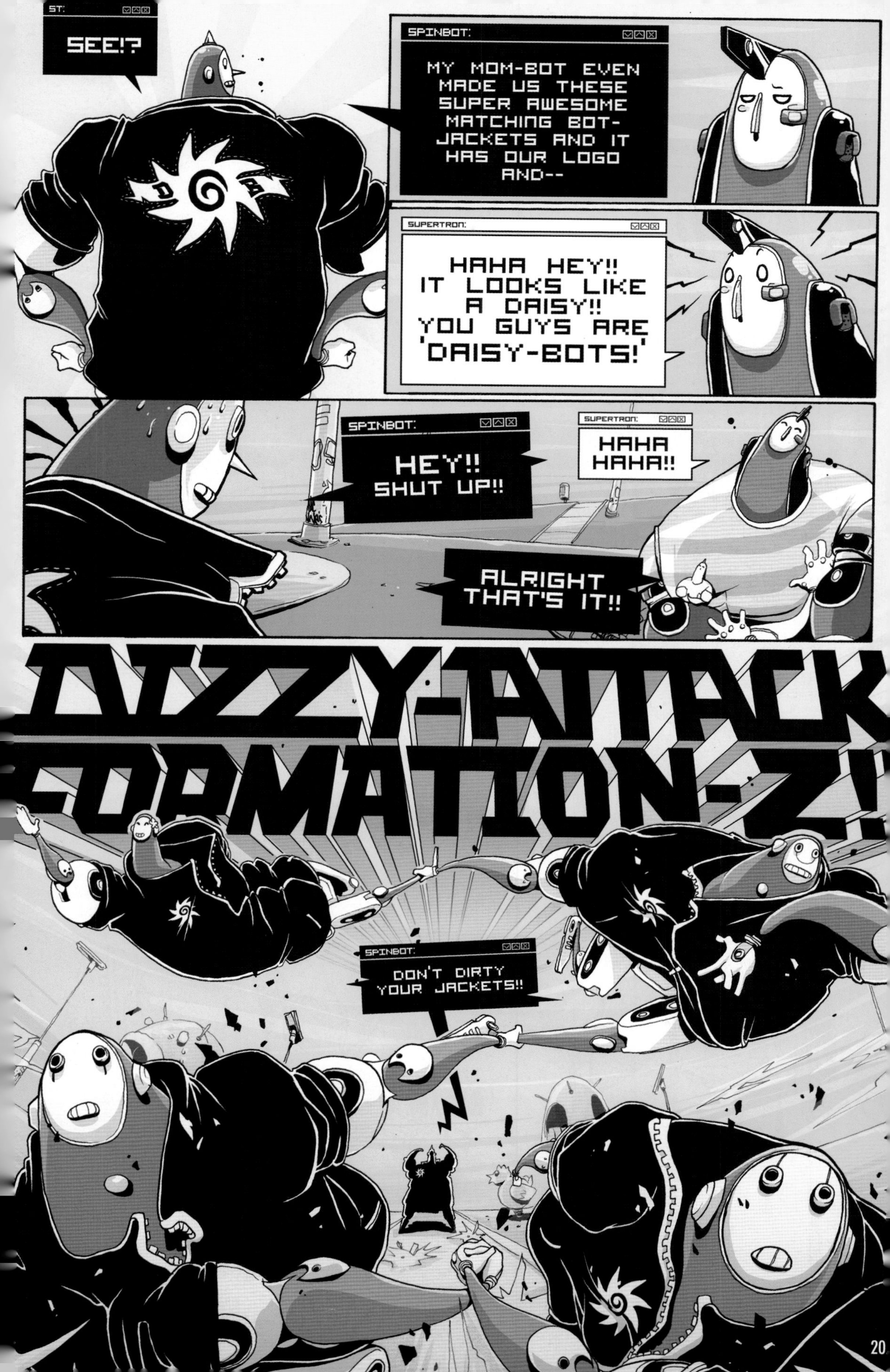
ST:
SEE!?
SPINBOT:
MY MOM-BOT EVEN MADE US THESE SUPER AWESOME MATCHING BOT-JACKETS AND IT HAS OUR LOGO AND--
SUPERTRON:
HAHA HEY!! IT LOOKS LIKE A DAISY!! YOU GUYS ARE 'DAISY-BOTS!'
SPINBOT:
HEY!! SHUT UP!!
SUPERTRON:
HAHA HAHA!!
ALRIGHT THAT'S IT!!
DIZZY-ATTACK FORMATION-Z!
SPINBOT:
DON'T DIRTY YOUR JACKETS!!

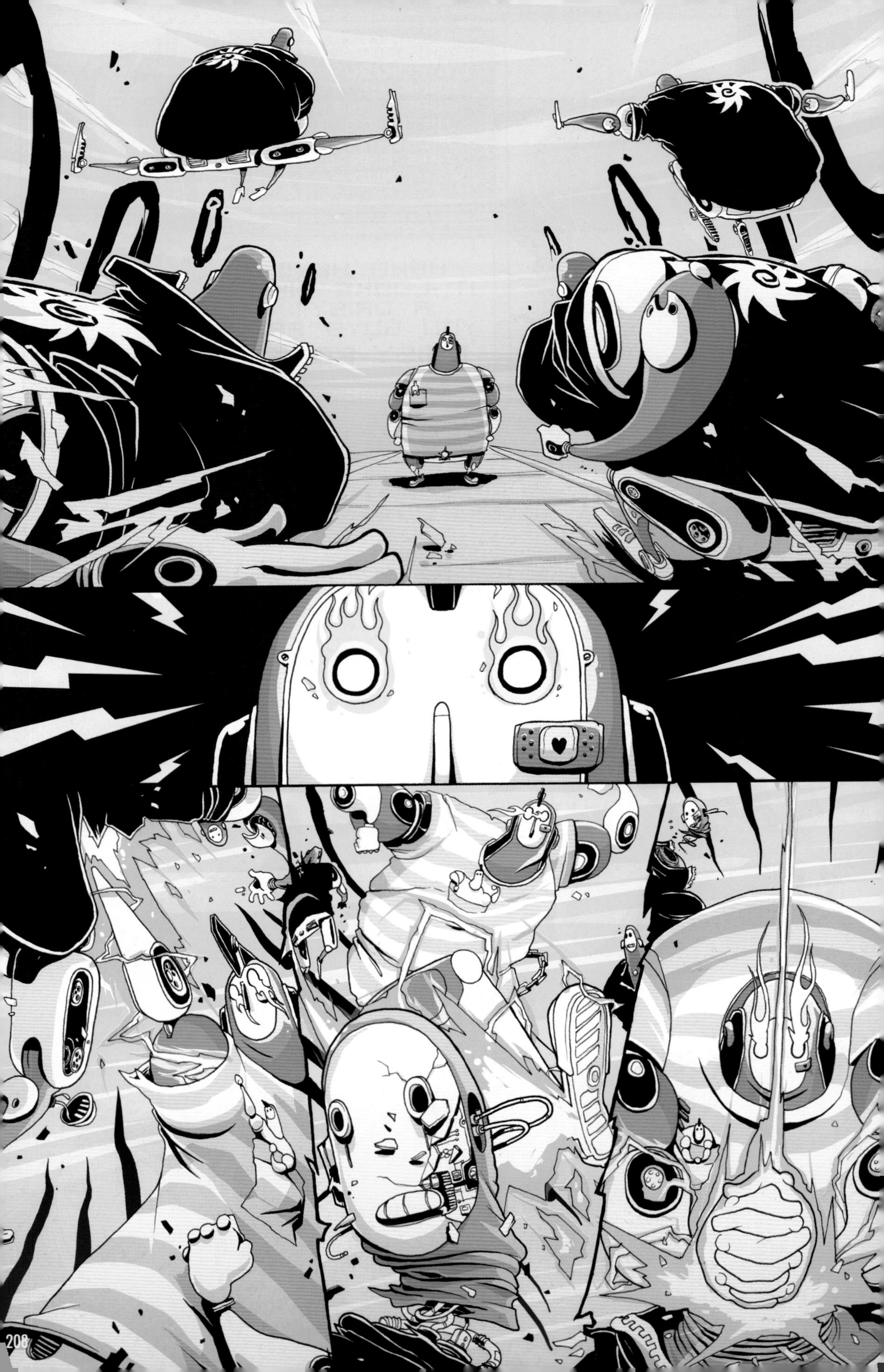

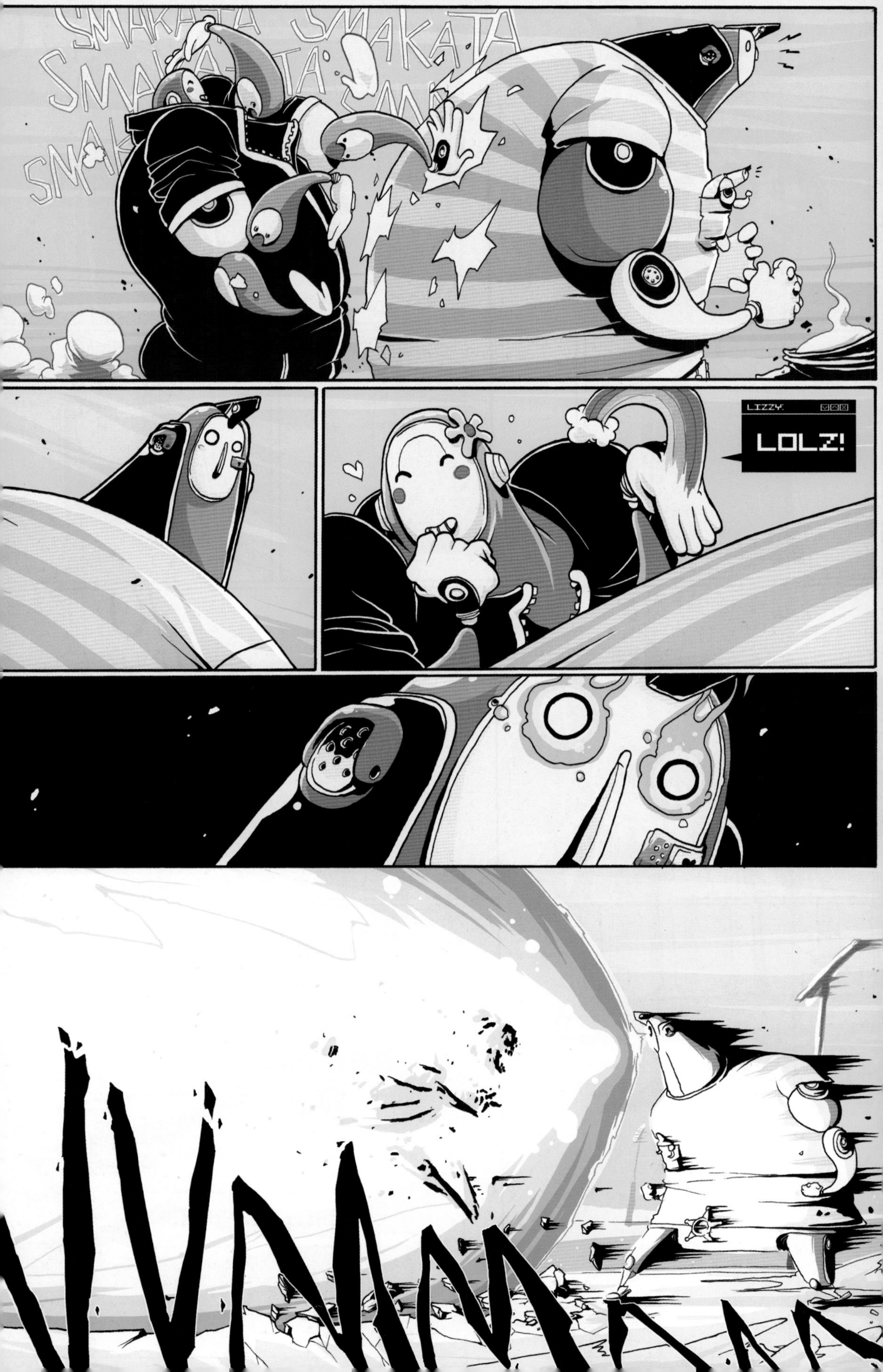
SMAKATA SMAKATA
SMAKATA
LIZZY:
LOLZ!

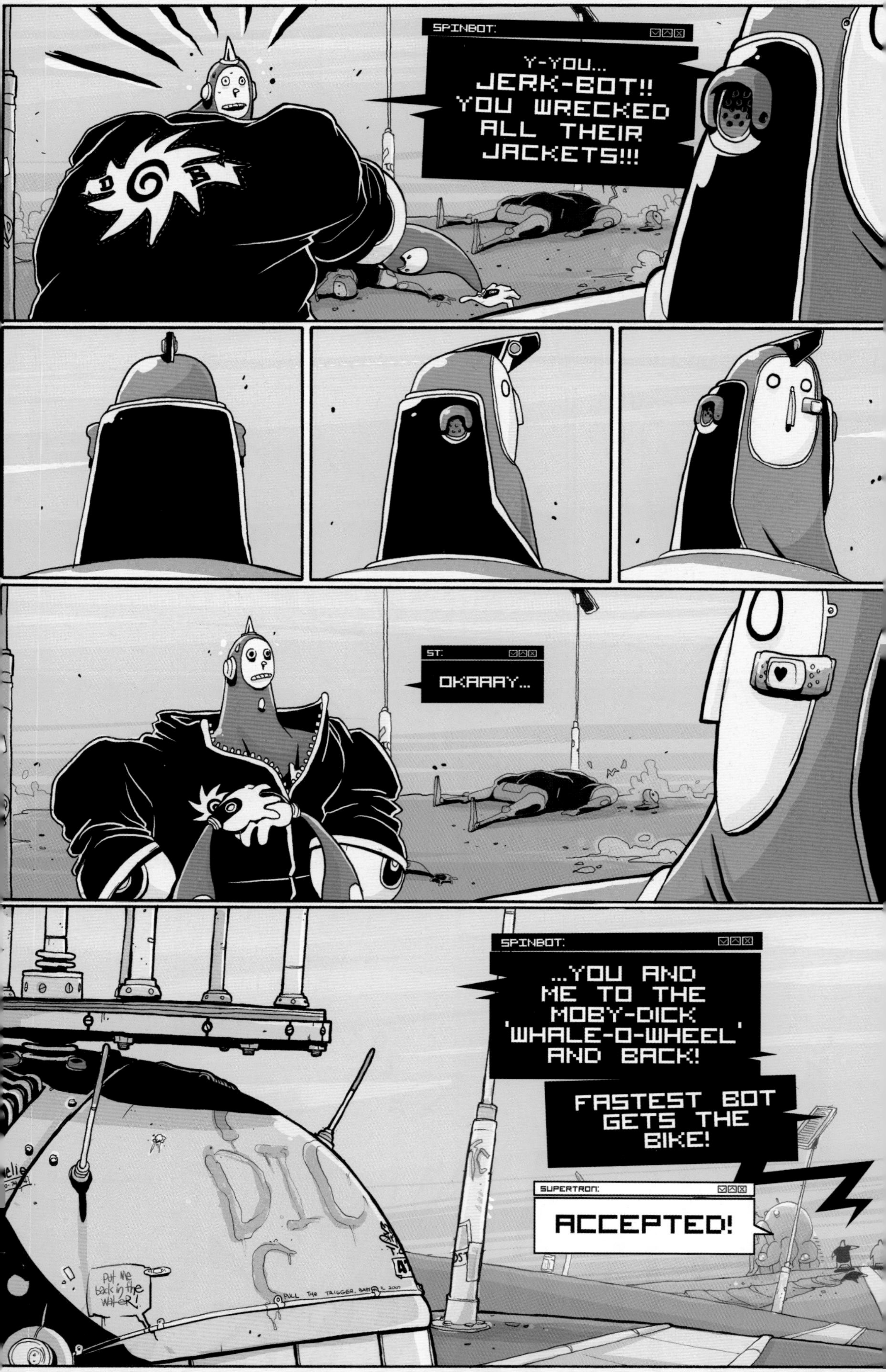
SPINBOT:
Y-YOU... JERK-BOT!! YOU WRECKED ALL THEIR JACKETS!!!
ST:
OKAAAY...
SPINBOT:
...YOU AND ME TO THE MOBY-DICK 'WHALE-O-WHEEL' AND BACK!
FASTEST BOT GETS THE BIKE!
SUPERTRON:
ACCEPTED!
Put me back in the water!

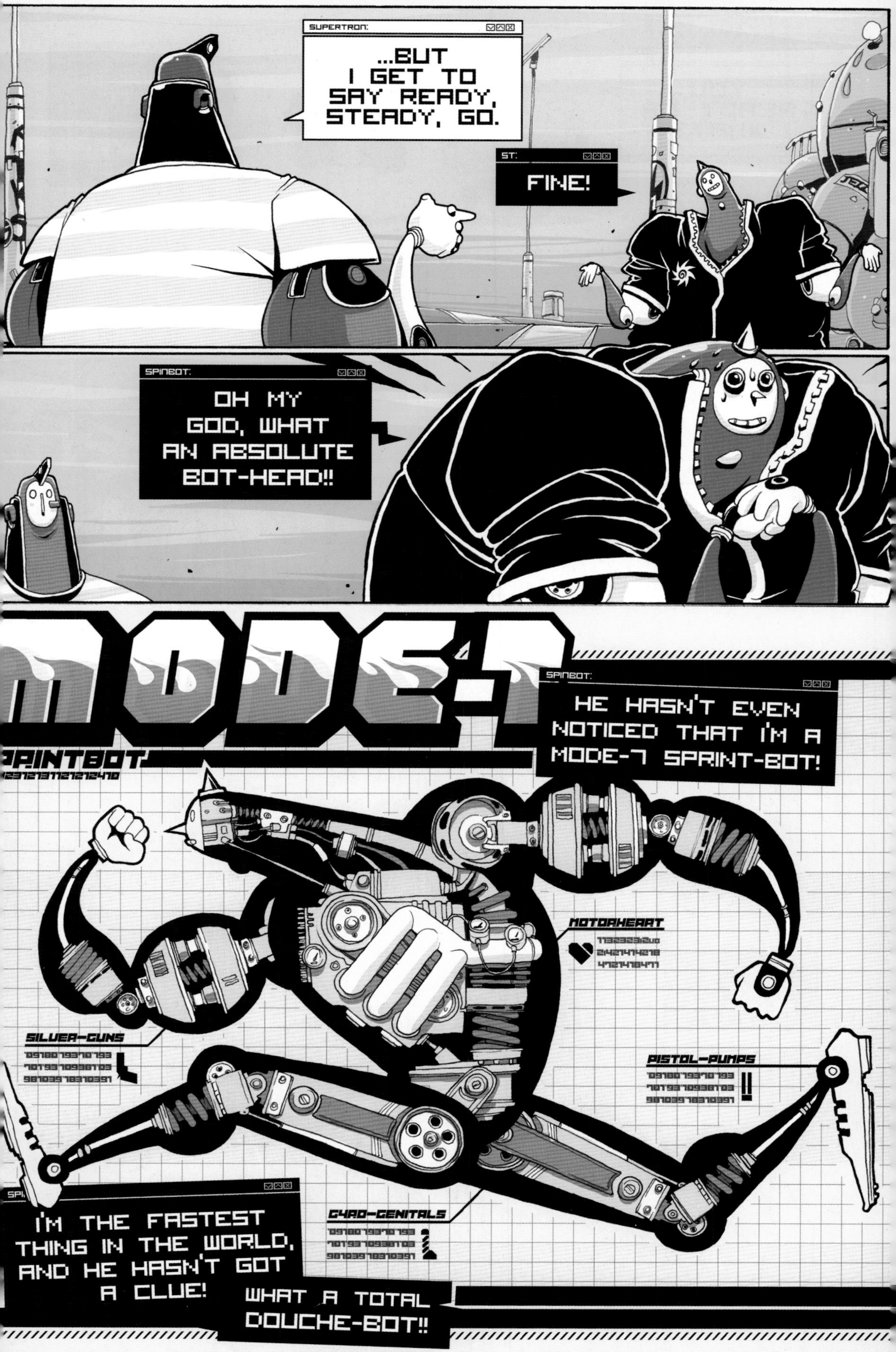
SUPERTRON:
...BUT I GET TO SAY READY, STEADY, GO.
ST:
FINE!
SPINBOT:
OH MY GOD, WHAT AN ABSOLUTE BOT-HEAD!!
MODE-7
SPRINTBOT
SPINBOT:
HE HASN'T EVEN NOTICED THAT I'M A MODE-7 SPRINT-BOT!
MOTORHEART
SILVER-GUNS
PISTOL-PUMPS
G4RD-GENITALS
I'M THE FASTEST THING IN THE WORLD, AND HE HASN'T GOT A CLUE!
WHAT A TOTAL DOUCHE-BOT!!

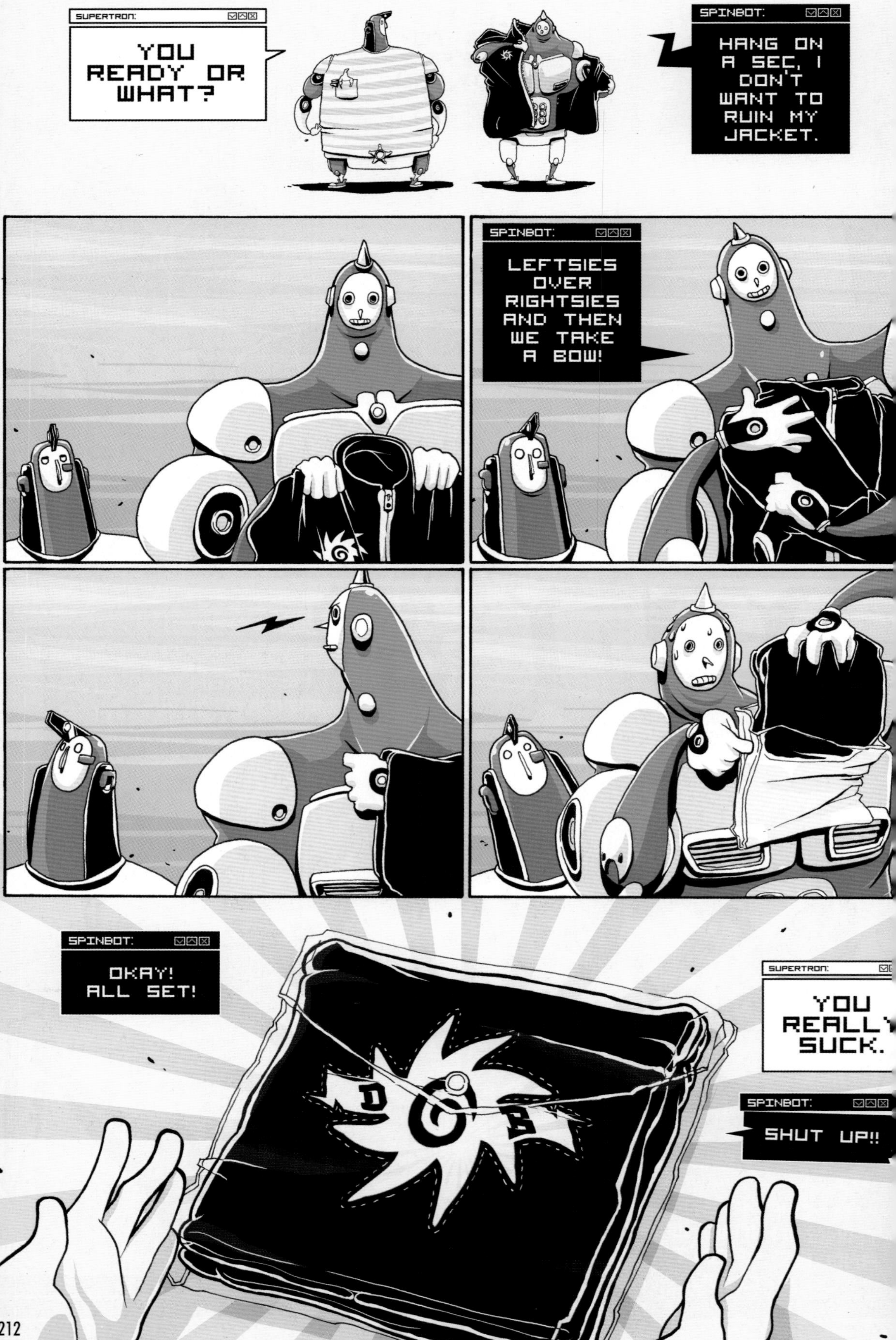
SUPERTRON:
YOU READY OR WHAT?
SPINBOT:
HANG ON A SEC, I DON'T WANT TO RUIN MY JACKET.
SPINBOT:
LEFTSIES OVER RIGHTSIES AND THEN WE TAKE A BOW!
SPINBOT:
OKAY! ALL SET!
SUPERTRON:
YOU REALLY SUCK.
SPINBOT:
SHUT UP!!

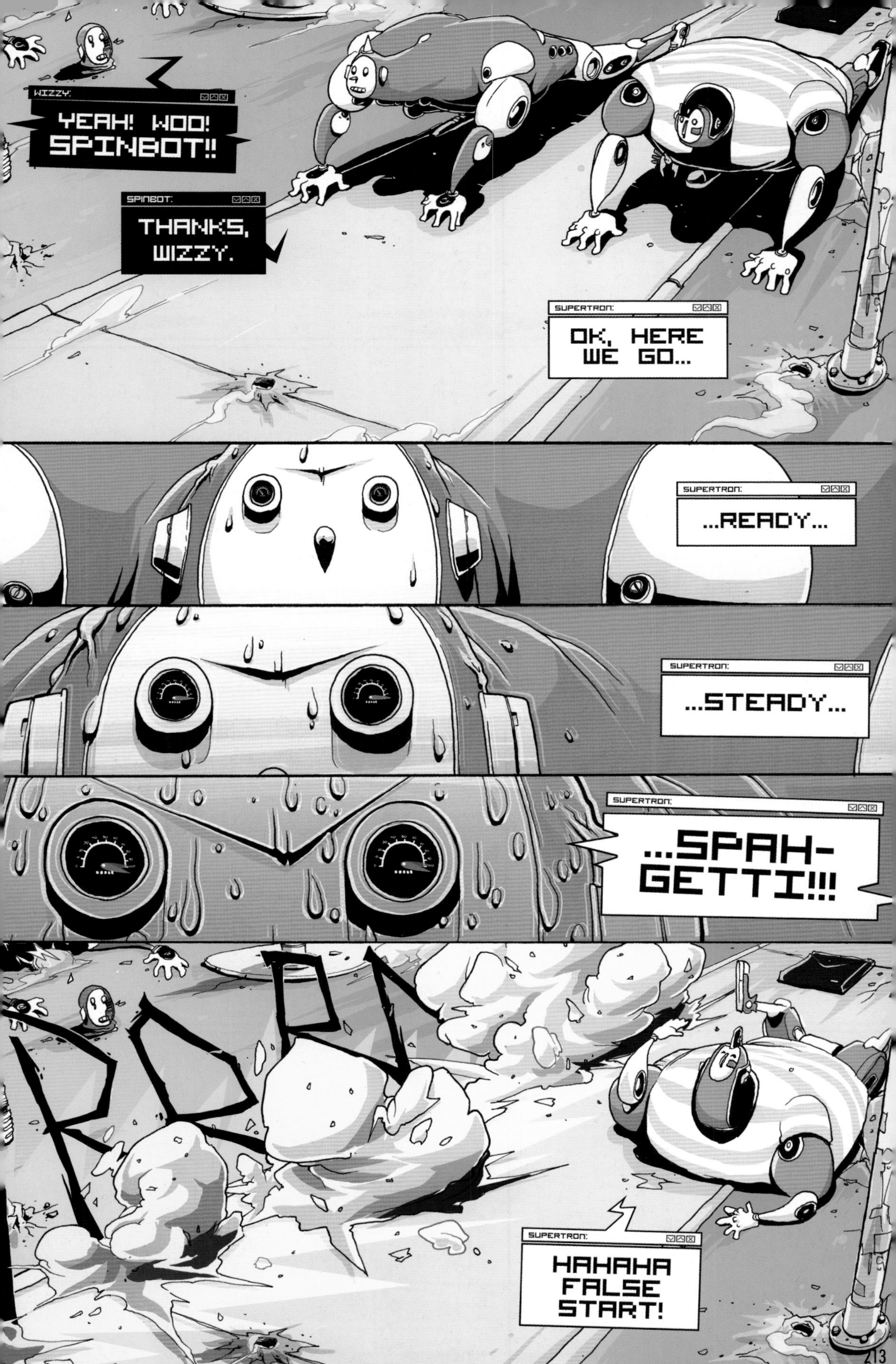
WIZZY:
YEAH! WOO! SPINBOT!!
SPINBOT:
THANKS, WIZZY.
SUPERTRON:
OK, HERE WE GO...
SUPERTRON:
...READY...
SUPERTRON:
...STEADY...
SUPERTRON:
...SPAH-GETTI!!!
SUPERTRON:
HAHAHA FALSE START!

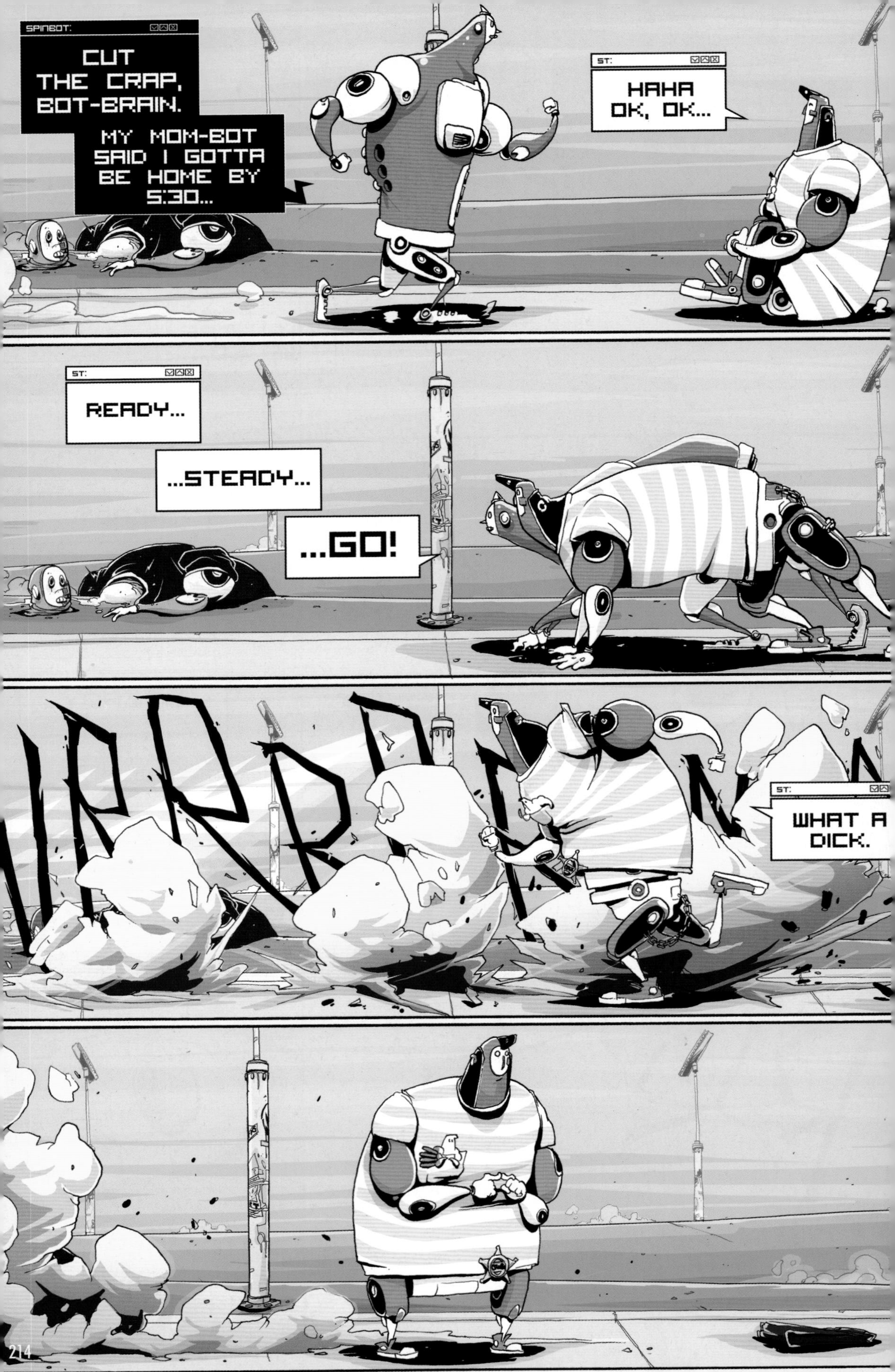
SPINBOT:
CUT THE CRAP, BOT-BRAIN.
MY MOM-BOT SAID I GOTTA BE HOME BY 5:30...
ST:
HAHA OK, OK...
ST:
READY...
...STEADY...
...GO!
ST:
WHAT A DICK.

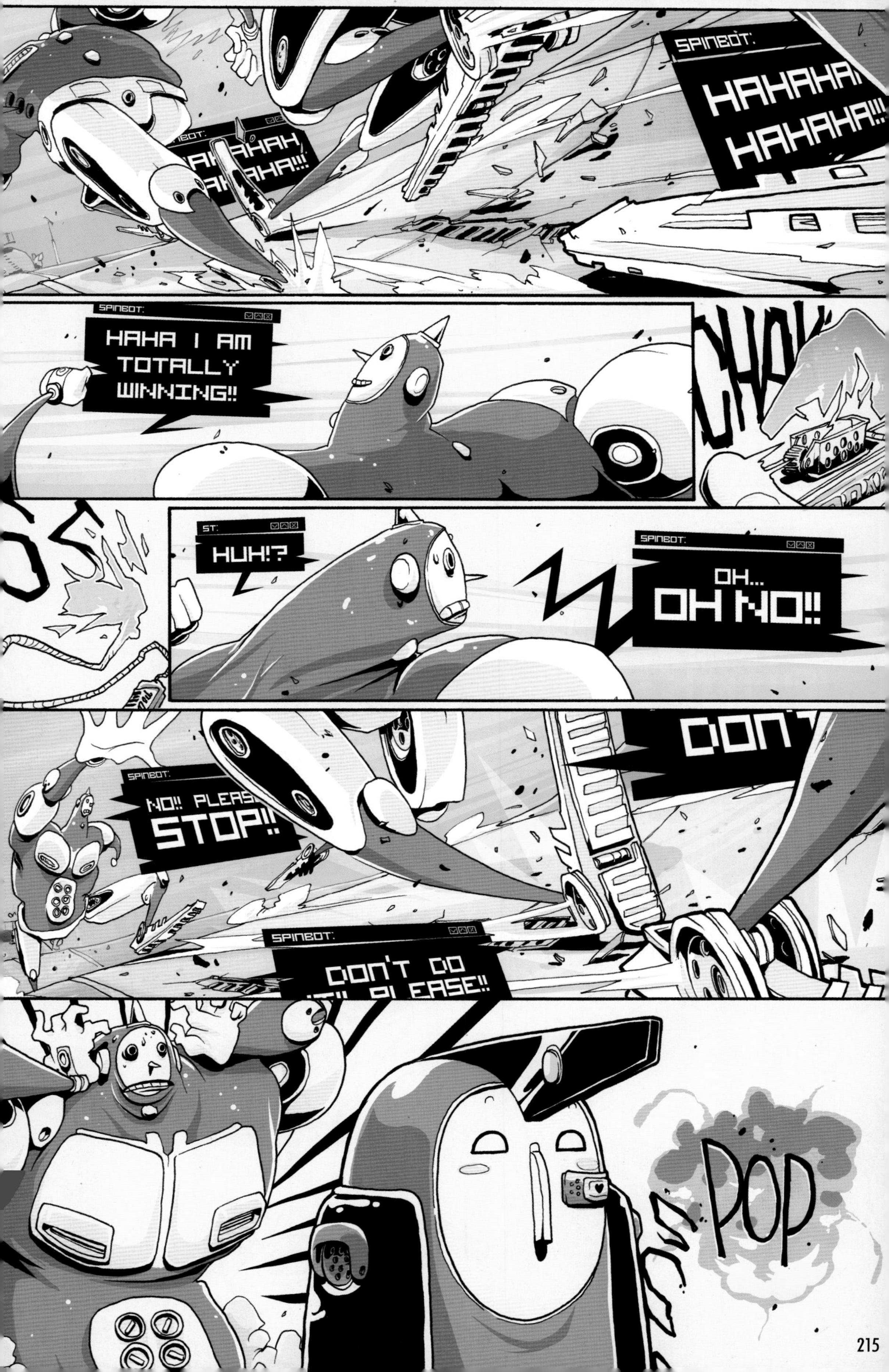
SPINBOT:
HAHAHA! HAHAHA!!!
SPINBOT:
HAHA I AM TOTALLY WINNING!!
ST:
HUH!?
SPINBOT:
OH... OH NO!!
SPINBOT:
STOP!!
SPINBOT:
DON'T DO
POP

NOOOOOOOOOOOOOOOOII!!

SPINBOT:

YOU...YOU FFF-⚡⚡⚡⚡ING PUNK-BOT!!

SPINBOT:

OH MAN, I'M GONNA BE IN SO MUCH TROUBLE WHEN MY MOM-BOT FINDS OUT ABOUT THIS!!

SUPERTRON:

AND IT'S GONNA BE **DOUBLE TROUBLE** WHEN I SQUEAL ON YOU FOR SWEARING!!

ST:

GASP!

END

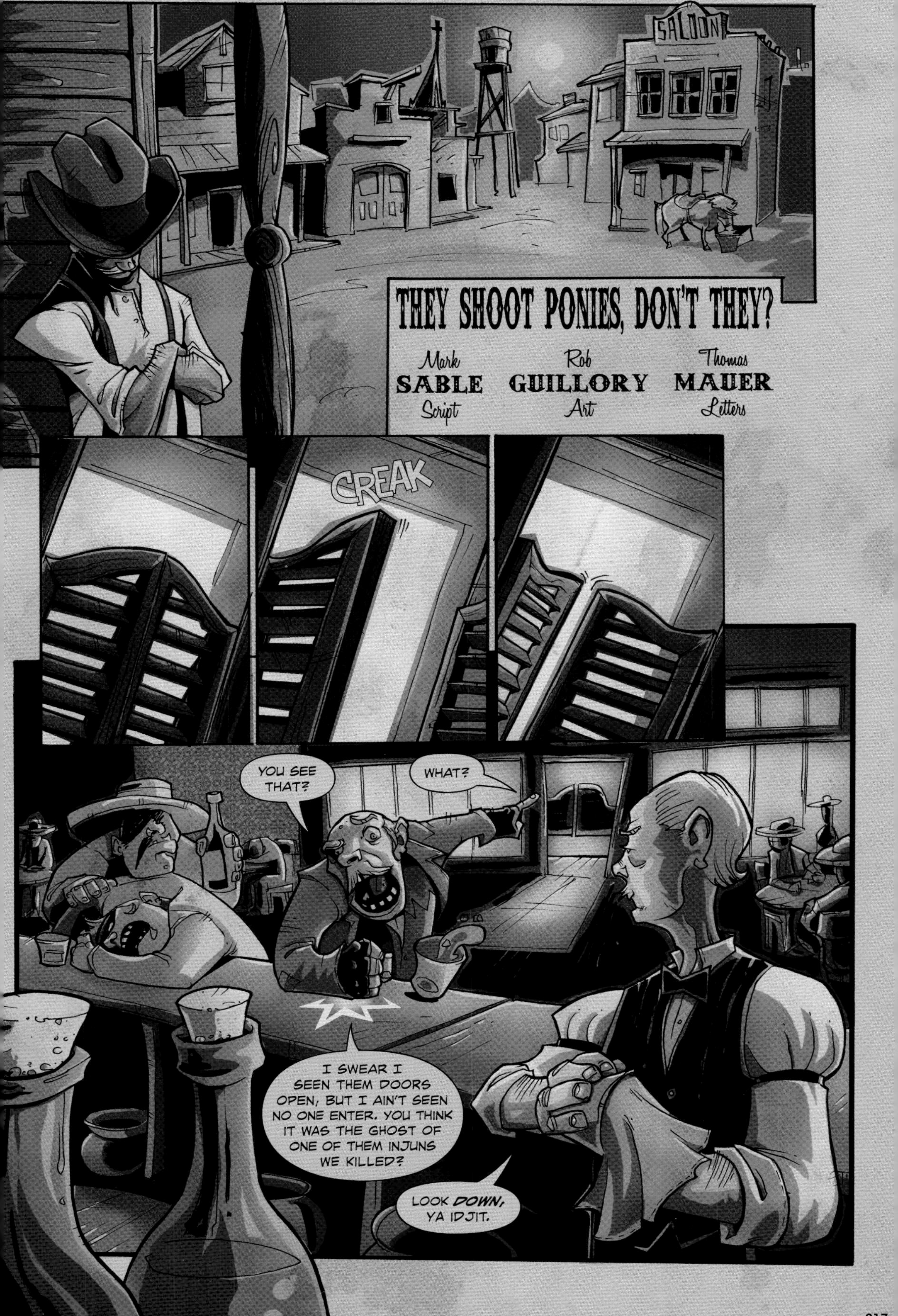
SALOON
THEY SHOOT PONIES, DON'T THEY?
Mark SABLE Script
Rob GUILLORY Art
Thomas MAUER Letters
CREAK
YOU SEE THAT?
WHAT?
I SWEAR I SEEN THEM DOORS OPEN, BUT I AIN'T SEEN NO ONE ENTER. YOU THINK IT WAS THE GHOST OF ONE OF THEM INJUNS WE KILLED?
LOOK *DOWN,* YA IDJIT.

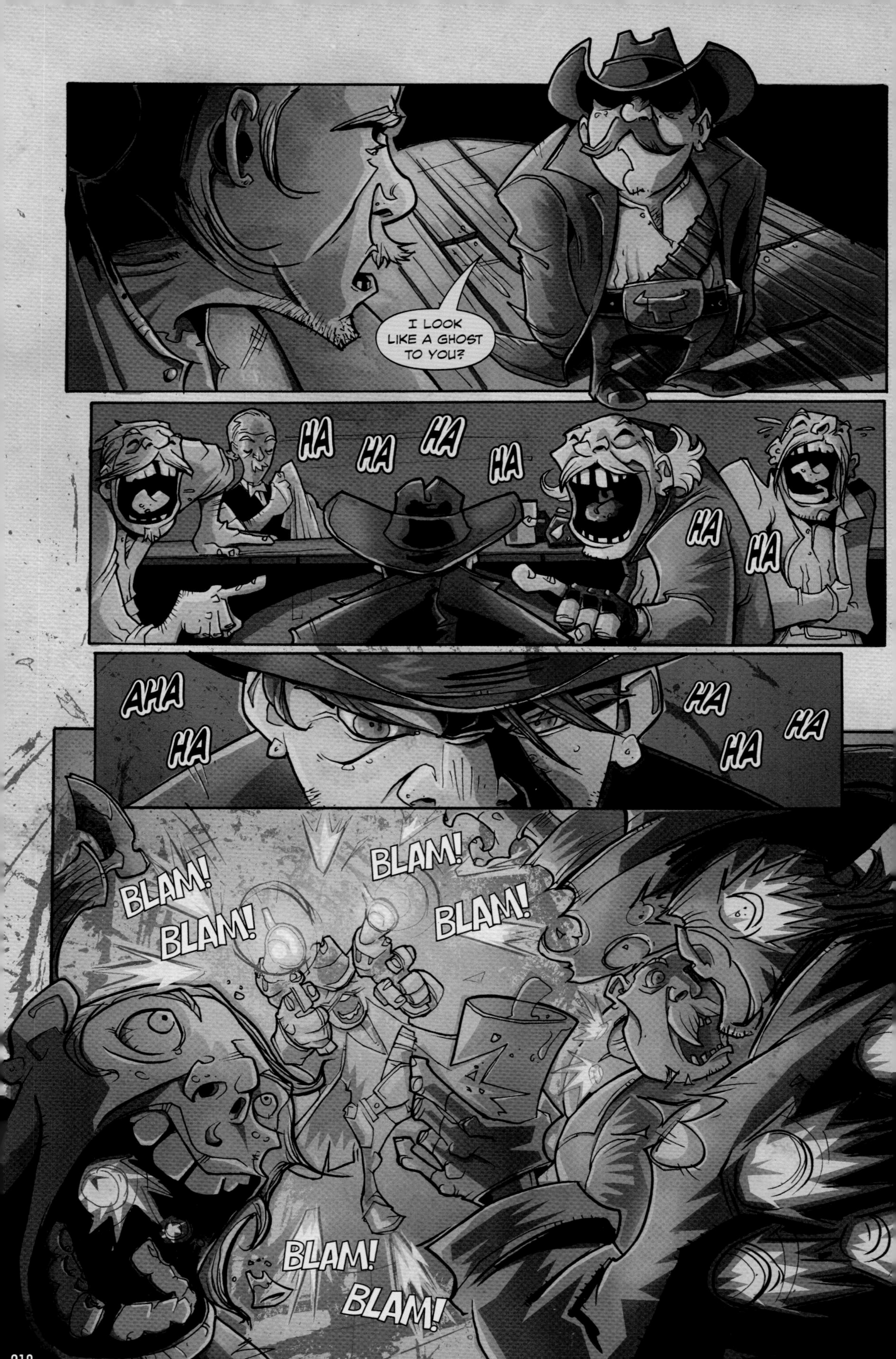
I LOOK LIKE A GHOST TO YOU?
HA
HA
HA
HA
HA
HA
AHA
HA
HA
HA
HA
BLAM!
BLAM!
BLAM!
BLAM!
BLAM!
BLAM!

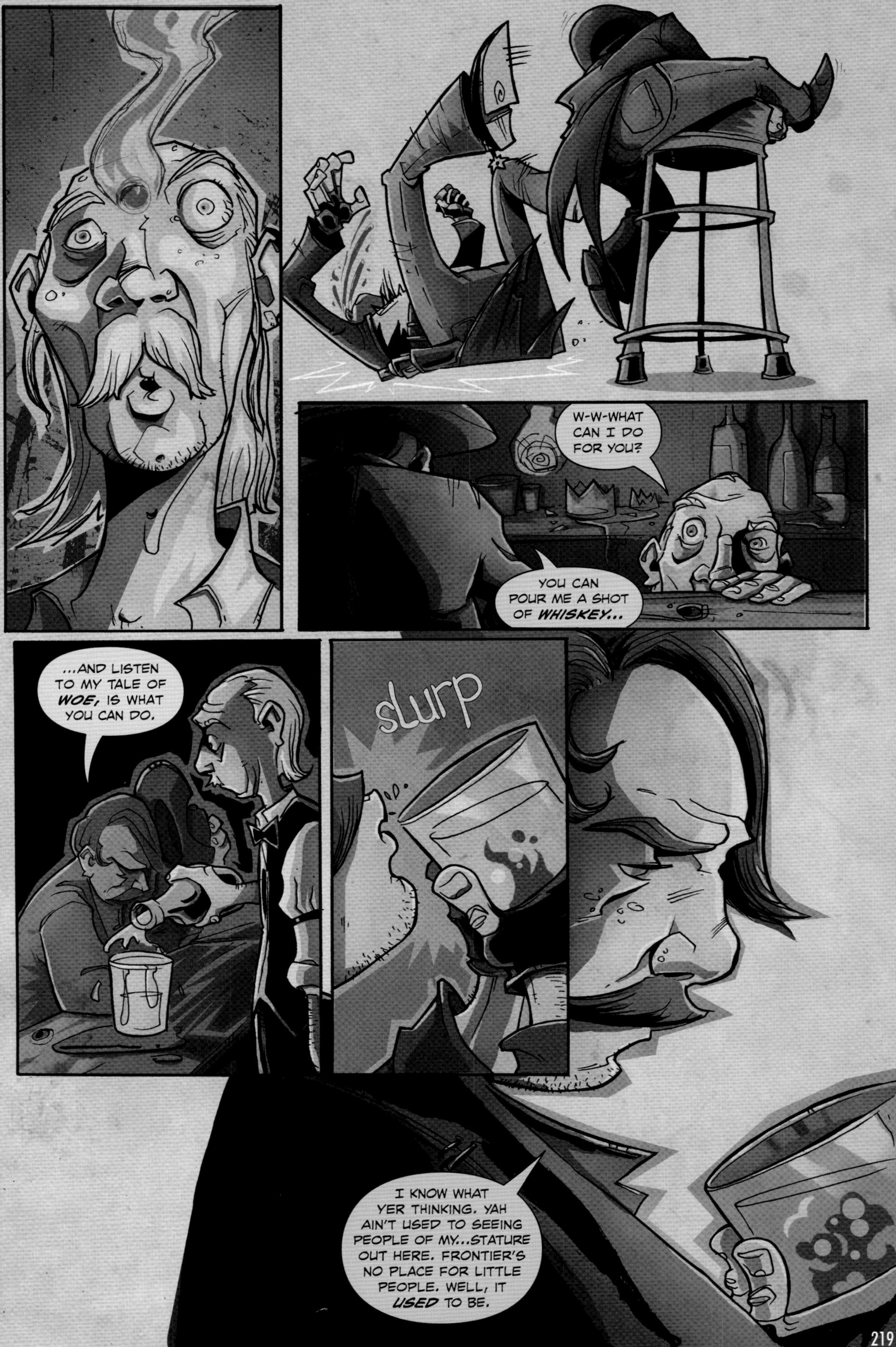
W-W-WHAT CAN I DO FOR YOU?
YOU CAN POUR ME A SHOT OF WHISKEY...
...AND LISTEN TO MY TALE OF WOE, IS WHAT YOU CAN DO.
slurp
I KNOW WHAT YER THINKING. YAH AIN'T USED TO SEEING PEOPLE OF MY...STATURE OUT HERE. FRONTIER'S NO PLACE FOR LITTLE PEOPLE. WELL, IT USED TO BE.

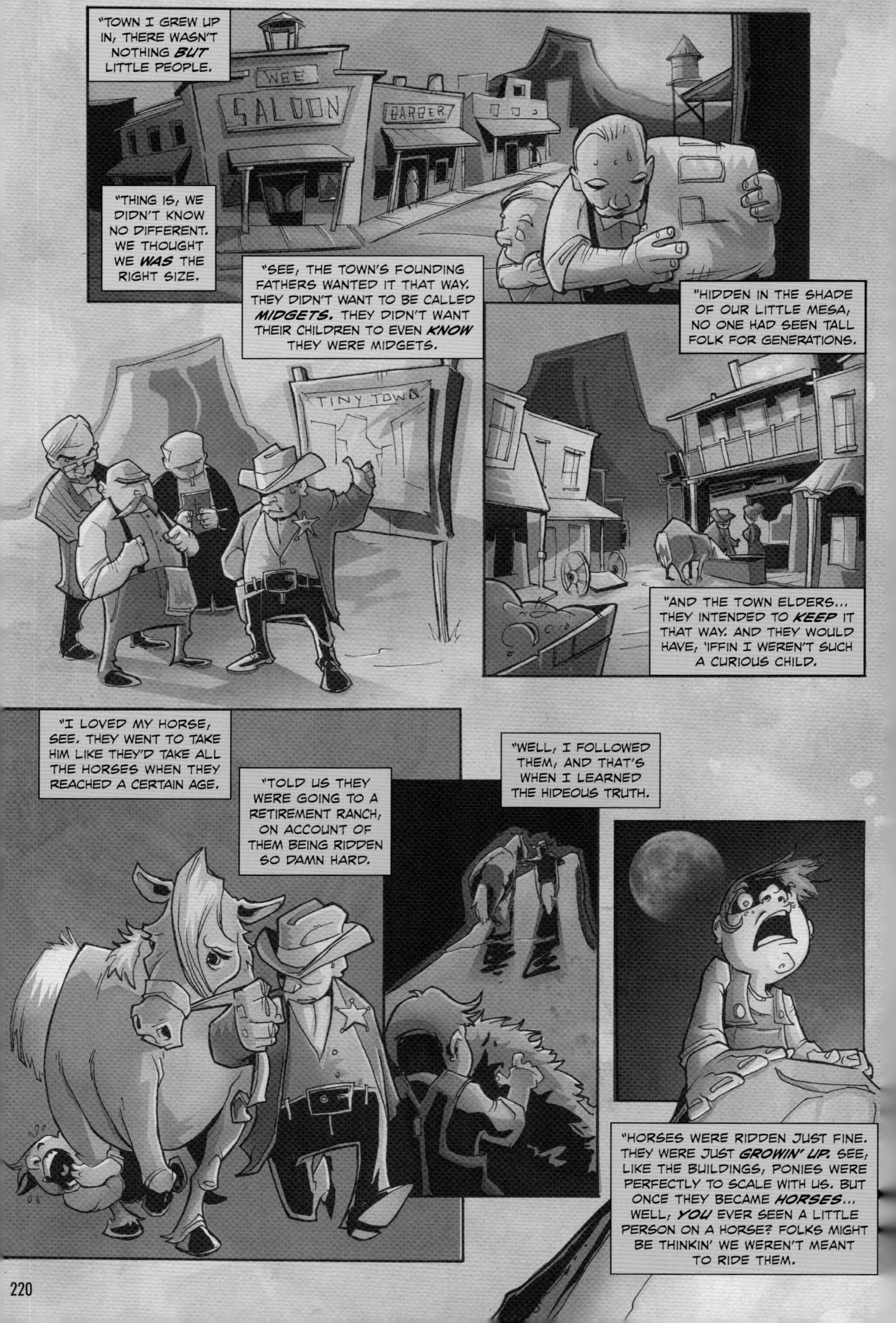
"TOWN I GREW UP IN, THERE WASN'T NOTHING *BUT* LITTLE PEOPLE.
WEE
SALOON
BARBER
"THING IS, WE DIDN'T KNOW NO DIFFERENT. WE THOUGHT WE *WAS* THE RIGHT SIZE.
"SEE, THE TOWN'S FOUNDING FATHERS WANTED IT THAT WAY. THEY DIDN'T WANT TO BE CALLED *MIDGETS.* THEY DIDN'T WANT THEIR CHILDREN TO EVEN *KNOW* THEY WERE MIDGETS.
TINY TOWN
"HIDDEN IN THE SHADE OF OUR LITTLE MESA, NO ONE HAD SEEN TALL FOLK FOR GENERATIONS.
"AND THE TOWN ELDERS... THEY INTENDED TO *KEEP* IT THAT WAY. AND THEY WOULD HAVE, 'IFFIN I WEREN'T SUCH A CURIOUS CHILD.
"I LOVED MY HORSE, SEE. THEY WENT TO TAKE HIM LIKE THEY'D TAKE ALL THE HORSES WHEN THEY REACHED A CERTAIN AGE.
"TOLD US THEY WERE GOING TO A RETIREMENT RANCH, ON ACCOUNT OF THEM BEING RIDDEN SO DAMN HARD.
"WELL, I FOLLOWED THEM, AND THAT'S WHEN I LEARNED THE HIDEOUS TRUTH.
"HORSES WERE RIDDEN JUST FINE. THEY WERE JUST *GROWIN' UP.* SEE, LIKE THE BUILDINGS, PONIES WERE PERFECTLY TO SCALE WITH US. BUT ONCE THEY BECAME *HORSES*... WELL, *YOU* EVER SEEN A LITTLE PERSON ON A HORSE? FOLKS MIGHT BE THINKIN' WE WEREN'T MEANT TO RIDE THEM.

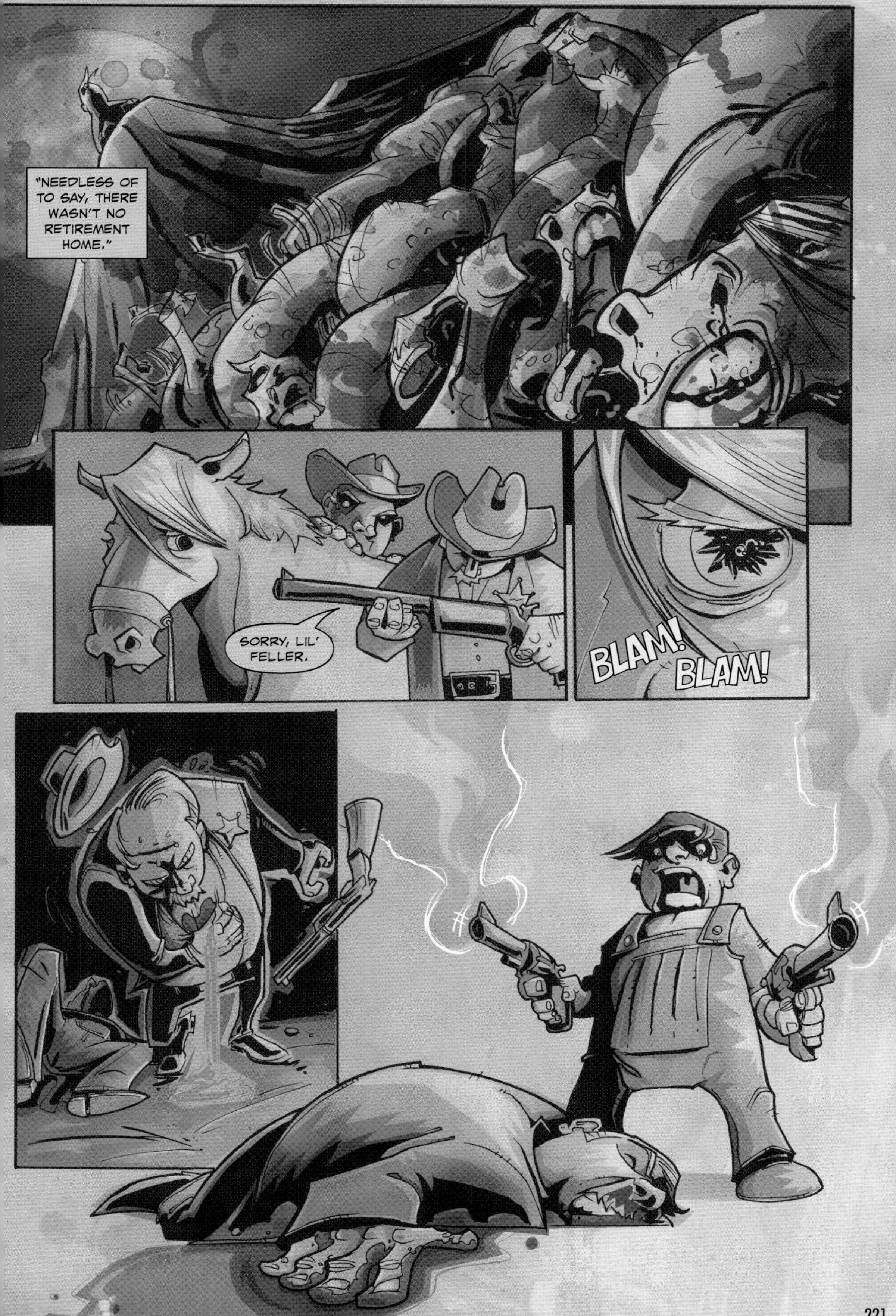
"NEEDLESS OF TO SAY, THERE WASN'T NO RETIREMENT HOME."
SORRY, LIL' FELLER.
BLAM! BLAM!

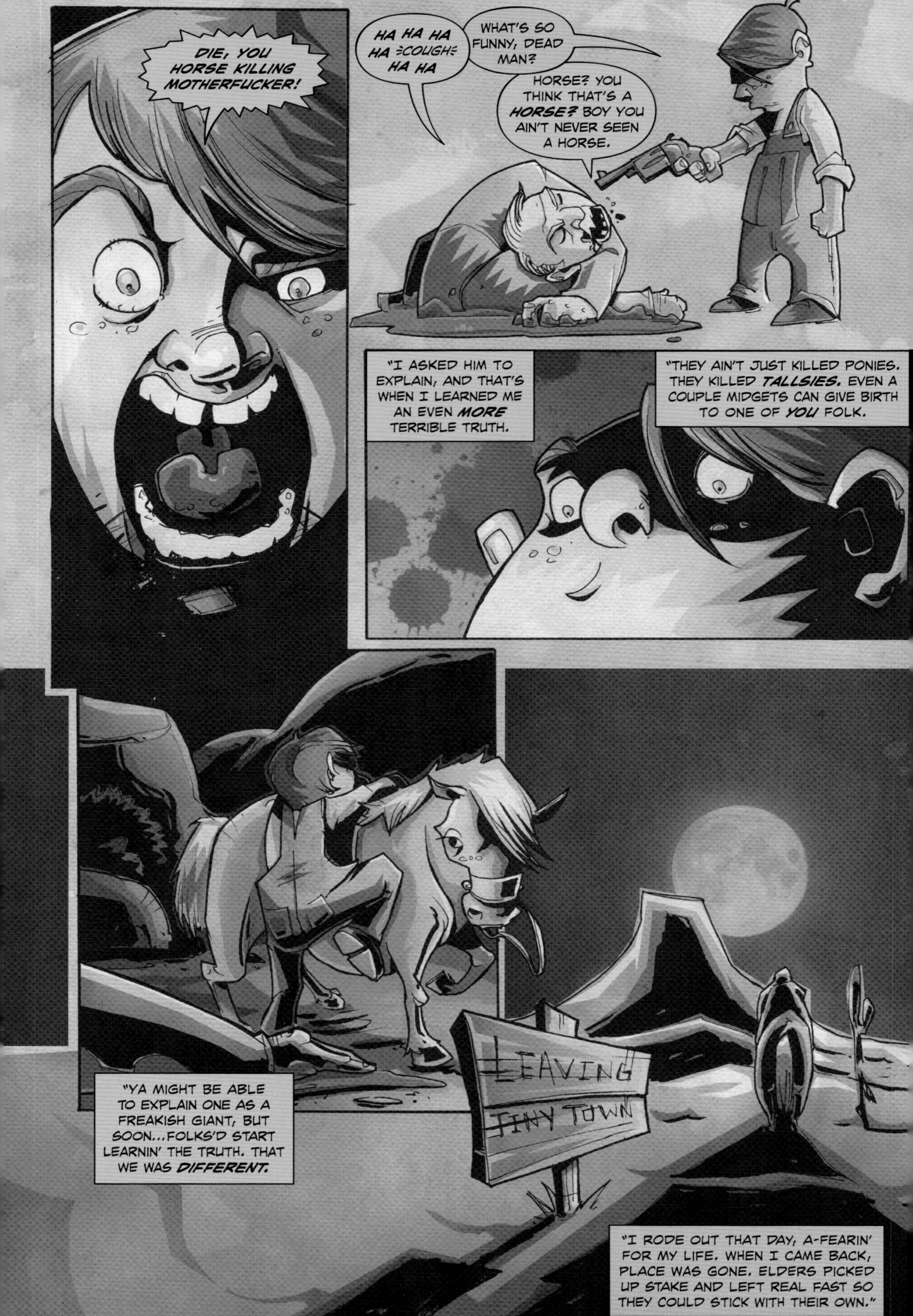

DIE, YOU HORSE KILLING MOTHERFUCKER!
HA HA HA HA =COUGH= HA HA
WHAT'S SO FUNNY, DEAD MAN?
HORSE? YOU THINK THAT'S A HORSE? BOY YOU AIN'T NEVER SEEN A HORSE.
"I ASKED HIM TO EXPLAIN, AND THAT'S WHEN I LEARNED ME AN EVEN MORE TERRIBLE TRUTH.
"THEY AIN'T JUST KILLED PONIES. THEY KILLED TALLSIES. EVEN A COUPLE MIDGETS CAN GIVE BIRTH TO ONE OF YOU FOLK.
"YA MIGHT BE ABLE TO EXPLAIN ONE AS A FREAKISH GIANT, BUT SOON...FOLKS'D START LEARNIN' THE TRUTH. THAT WE WAS DIFFERENT.
LEAVING TINY TOWN
"I RODE OUT THAT DAY, A-FEARIN' FOR MY LIFE. WHEN I CAME BACK, PLACE WAS GONE. ELDERS PICKED UP STAKE AND LEFT REAL FAST SO THEY COULD STICK WITH THEIR OWN."

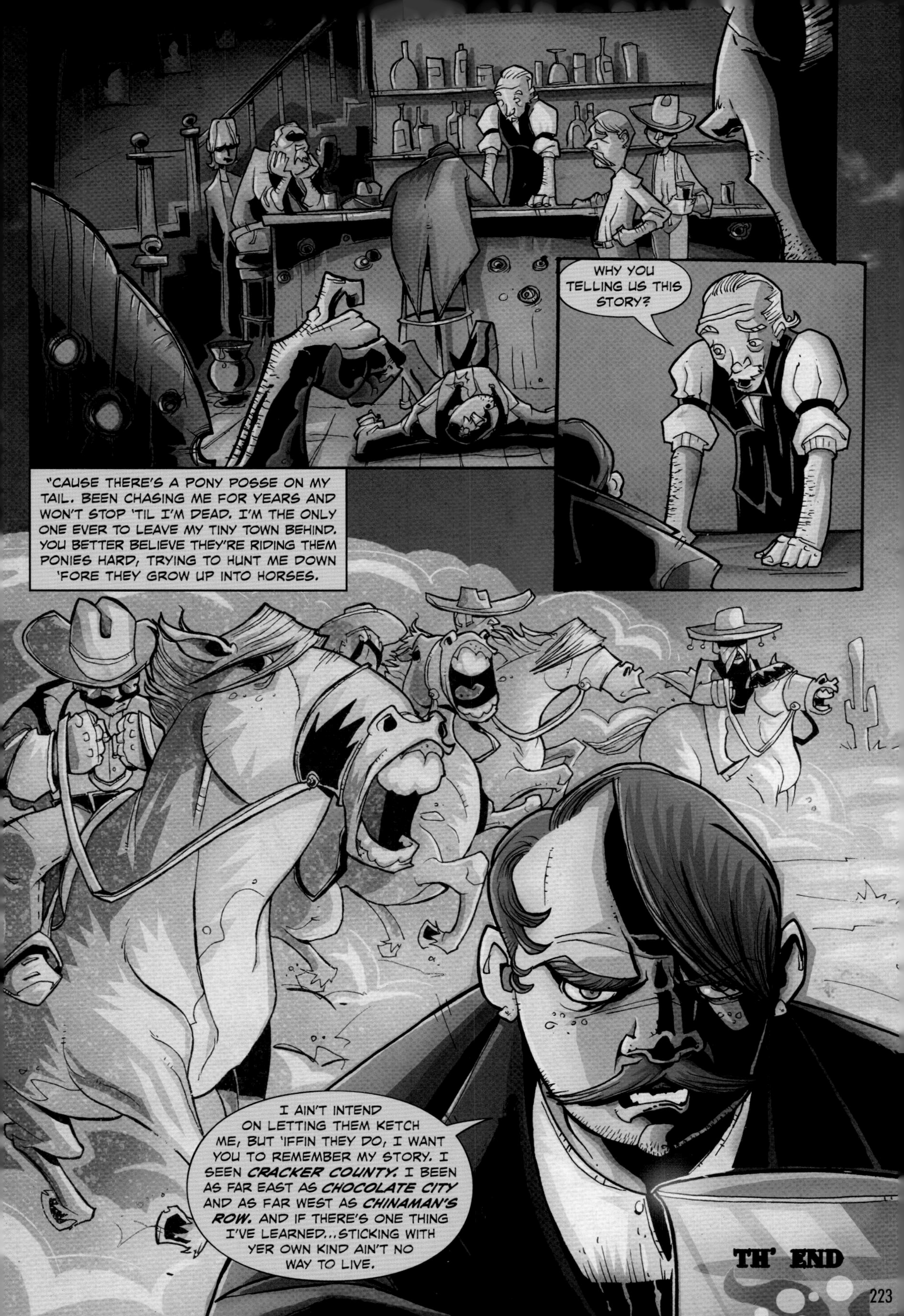
WHY YOU TELLING US THIS STORY?
'CAUSE THERE'S A PONY POSSE ON MY TAIL. BEEN CHASING ME FOR YEARS AND WON'T STOP 'TIL I'M DEAD. I'M THE ONLY ONE EVER TO LEAVE MY TINY TOWN BEHIND. YOU BETTER BELIEVE THEY'RE RIDING THEM PONIES HARD, TRYING TO HUNT ME DOWN 'FORE THEY GROW UP INTO HORSES.
I AIN'T INTEND ON LETTING THEM KETCH ME, BUT 'IFFIN THEY DO, I WANT YOU TO REMEMBER MY STORY. I SEEN *CRACKER COUNTY.* I BEEN AS FAR EAST AS *CHOCOLATE CITY* AND AS FAR WEST AS *CHINAMAN'S ROW.* AND IF THERE'S ONE THING I'VE LEARNED...STICKING WITH YER OWN KIND AIN'T NO WAY TO LIVE.
TH' END

FOR JUST SEVENTY-FIVE CENTS, WATCH YOUR ENEMIES FLEE IN TERROR AS YOU UNLEASH THE POWER OF MONSTERS!

You like monsters, don't you? Of course you do! Weak, pitiful child that you are, it's only natural that you fantasize about huge, hideous creatures with razor-sharp fangs. You dream of drooling, mindless beasts that hunger for the chance to chew the heads off of your parents, siblings, schoolyard bullies, and all others who dare to thwart your wishes.

Then you discover this advertisement; you begin to tremble excitedly and ask, "can you sell me real monsters that I may send them forth against my enemies?" Our answer is, "of course not. There are strict Federal laws that prohibit the shipment of monsters through the mail, and besides, we're in the business of selling seeds." Your eyes become moist, and you start to whimper, "but you promised me monsters! What does a bunch of dumb seeds have to do with monsters? Will your seeds eventually turn into monsters?" Our reply comes like a hard slap against your tender cheek, "silly boy, don't be stupid."

For the low price of seventy-five cents, you will receive almost nothing; the seeds that will arrive at your door in six to ten weeks are old, dried-out, and almost certainly inviable. A grim realization will hit you like an elbow to the stomach; we took your seventy-five cents and shipped you a worthless packet of seeds, leaving you to wallow in the knowledge that you are a helpless chump. The only thing we guarantee is disappointment, but remember: there's power in disappointment. Given the proper stimulus, today's helpless chump becomes tomorrow's mass murderer, and the seeds from which true monsters grow are already inside you.

Nurture these seeds, and one day, you'll unleash a fearsome, ravenous thing that might consume the world.

Wow, that sounds like a great offer! Here's my seventy-five cents; please send me worthless seeds so that I can transform my lifelong frustration into murderous rage!

________________________ (your name)

____

________________________ (your address)

send money to: DIRTCO
c/o D.D.L.D.F.
P.O. Box 901
Old Chelsea Station
New York, NY 10113

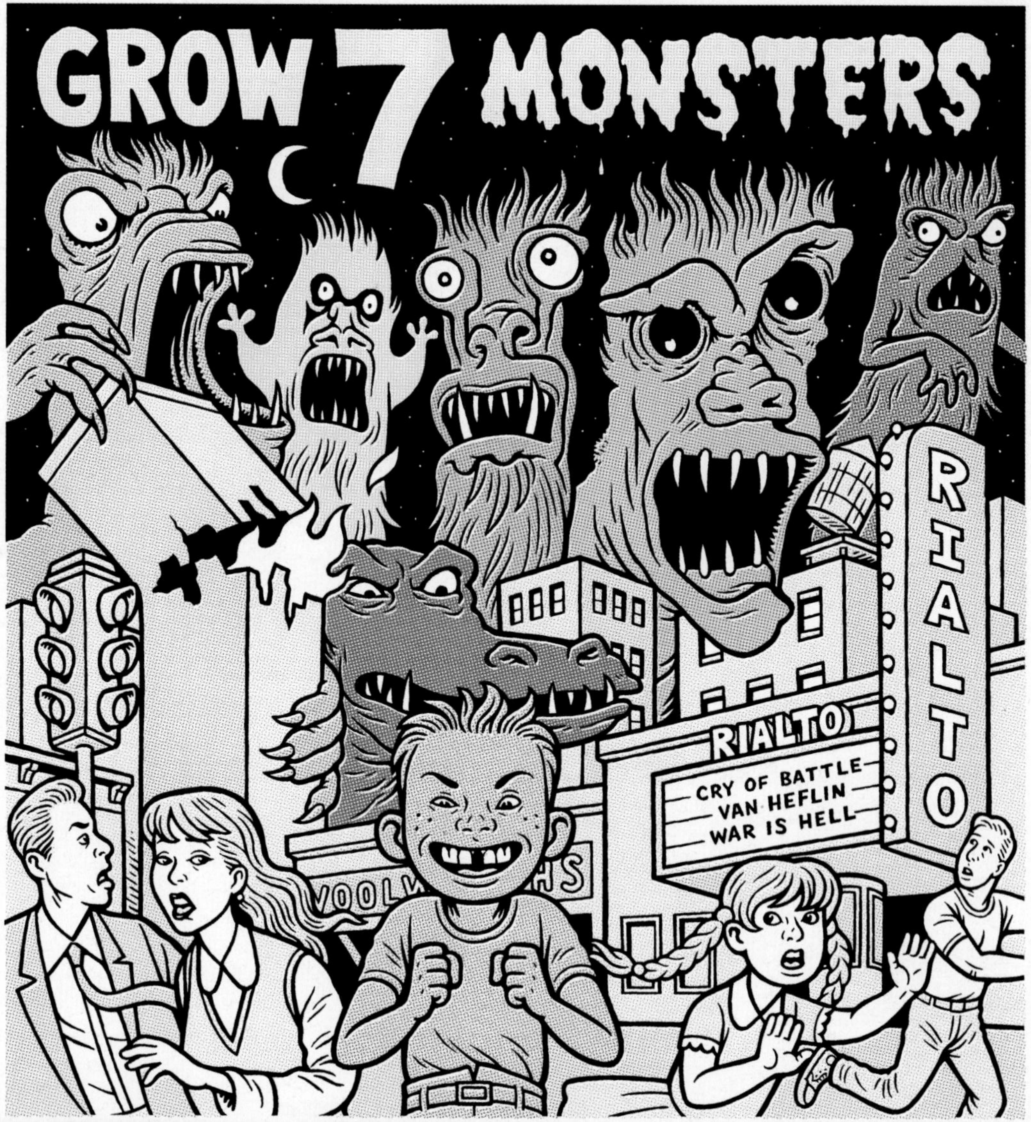
GROW 7 MONSTERS
RIALTO
RIALTO
CRY OF BATTLE
VAN HEFLIN
WAR IS HELL

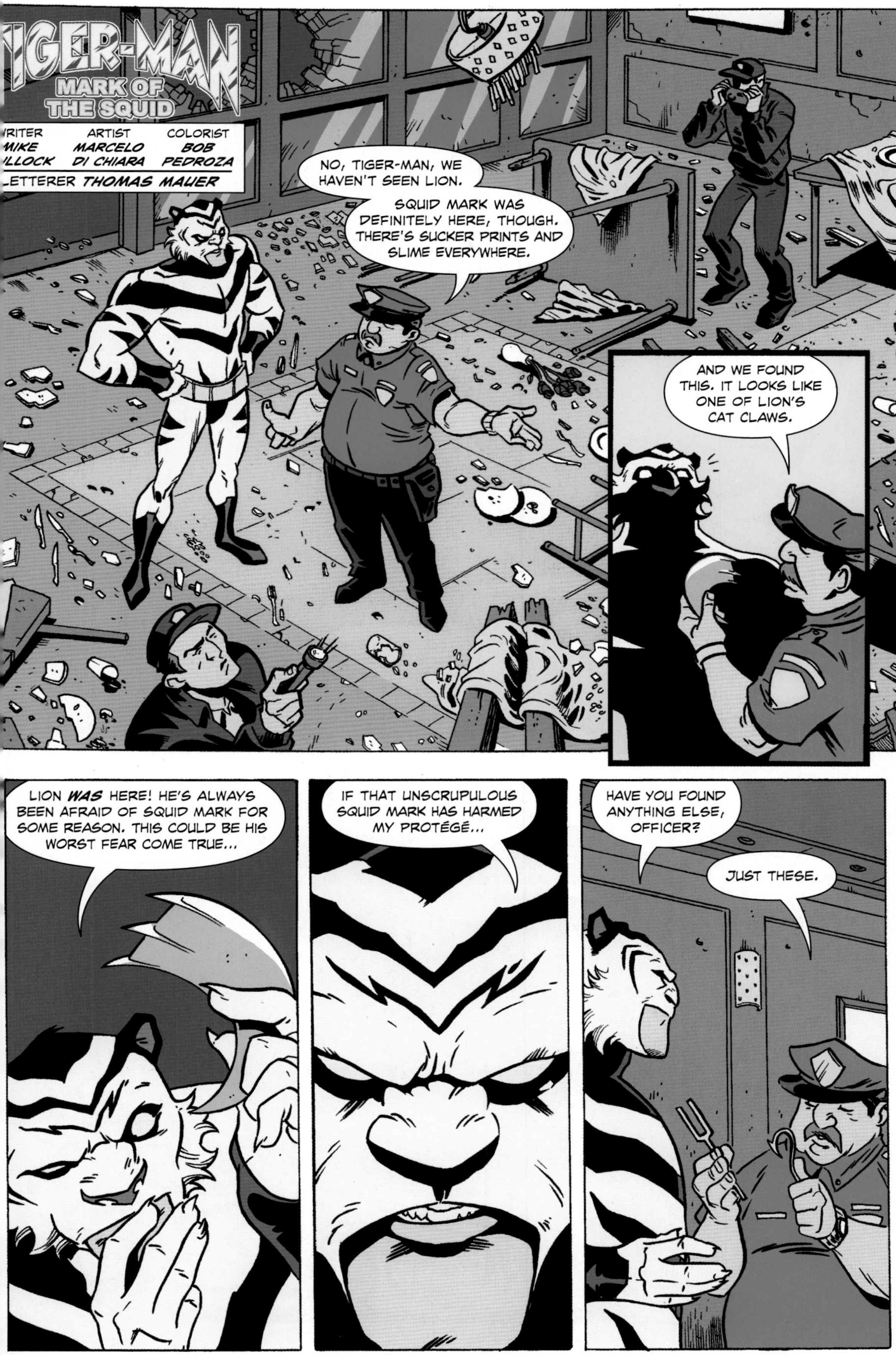
TIGER-MAN
MARK OF THE SQUID
WRITER MIKE ULLOCK ARTIST MARCELO DI CHIARA COLORIST BOB PEDROZA
LETTERER THOMAS MAUER
NO, TIGER-MAN, WE HAVEN'T SEEN LION.
SQUID MARK WAS DEFINITELY HERE, THOUGH. THERE'S SUCKER PRINTS AND SLIME EVERYWHERE.
AND WE FOUND THIS. IT LOOKS LIKE ONE OF LION'S CAT CLAWS.
LION WAS HERE! HE'S ALWAYS BEEN AFRAID OF SQUID MARK FOR SOME REASON. THIS COULD BE HIS WORST FEAR COME TRUE...
IF THAT UNSCRUPULOUS SQUID MARK HAS HARMED MY PROTÉGÉ...
HAVE YOU FOUND ANYTHING ELSE, OFFICER?
JUST THESE.

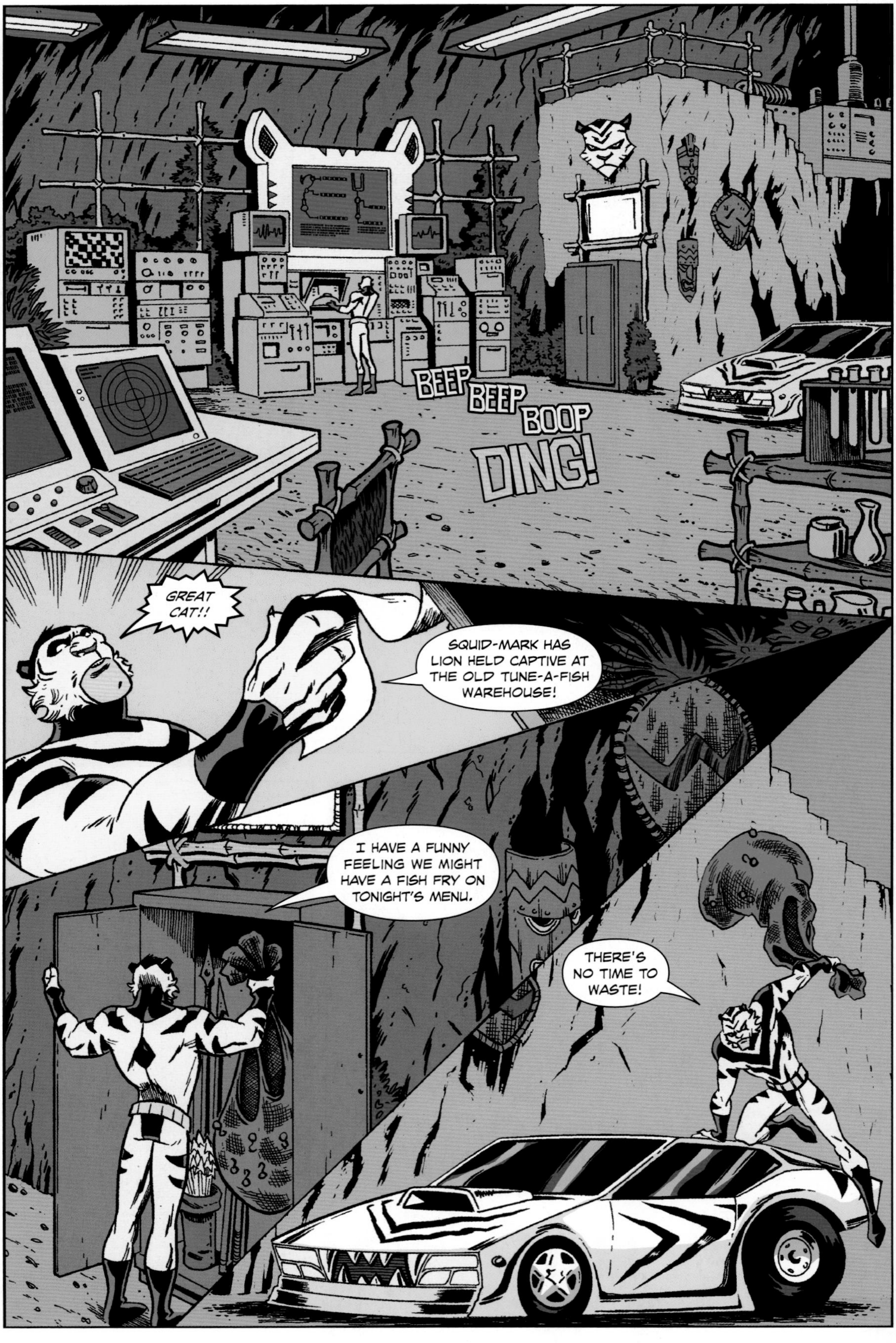
BEEP BEEP BOOP
DING!
GREAT CAT!!
SQUID-MARK HAS LION HELD CAPTIVE AT THE OLD TUNE-A-FISH WAREHOUSE!
I HAVE A FUNNY FEELING WE MIGHT HAVE A FISH FRY ON TONIGHT'S MENU.
THERE'S NO TIME TO WASTE!

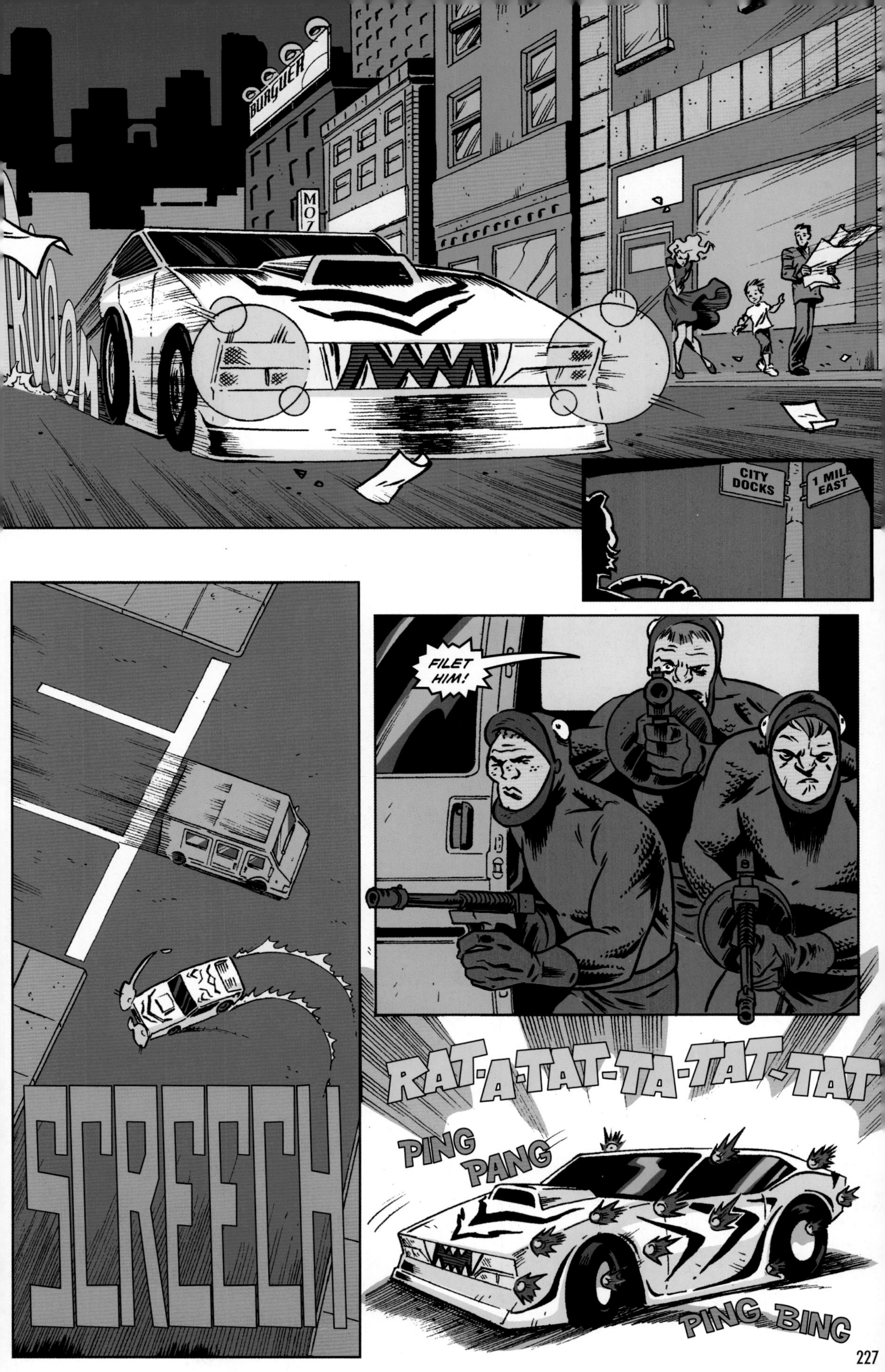
RROOOOM
BURGUER
MOT
CITY DOCKS
1 MIL EAST
SCREECH
FILET HIM!
RAT-A-TAT-TA-TAT-TAT
PING
PANG
PING
BING

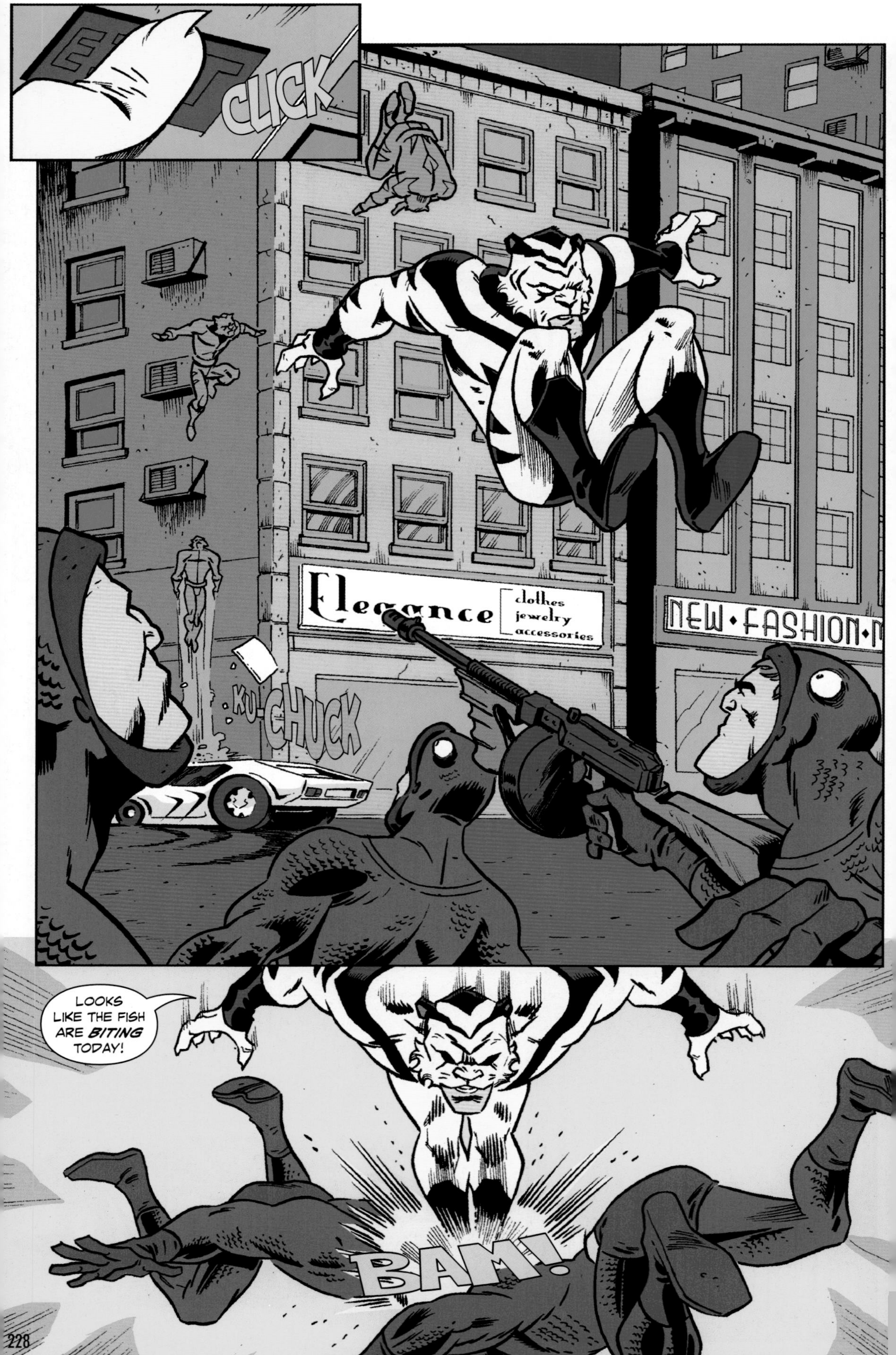
CLICK
Elegance clothes jewelry accessories
NEW • FASHION • M
KU-CHUCK
LOOKS LIKE THE FISH ARE *BITING* TODAY!
BAM!

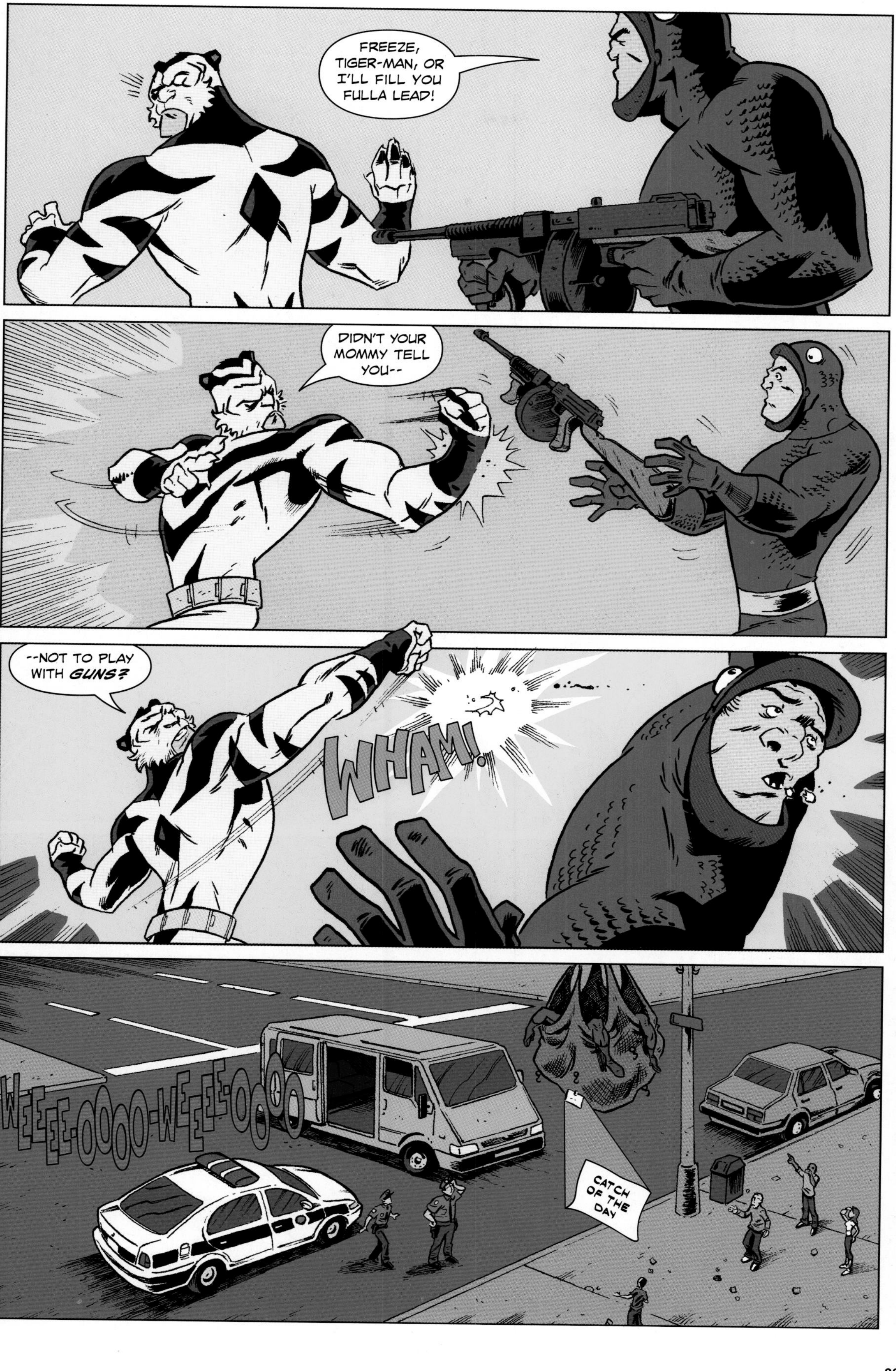
FREEZE, TIGER-MAN, OR I'LL FILL YOU FULLA LEAD!
DIDN'T YOUR MOMMY TELL YOU--
--NOT TO PLAY WITH GUNS?
WHAM!
WEEEE-OOOO-WEEEE-OOOO
CATCH OF THE DAY

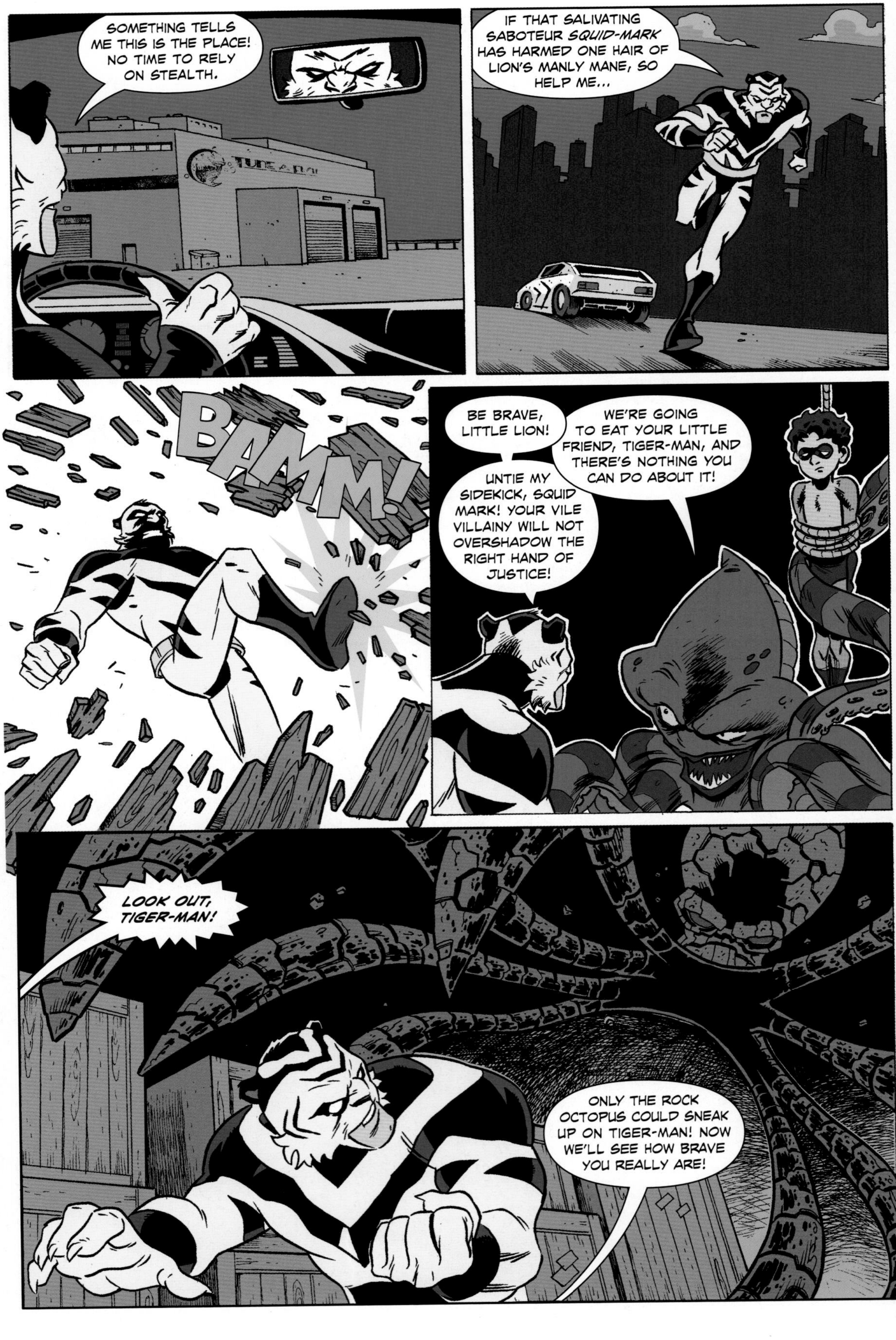
SOMETHING TELLS ME THIS IS THE PLACE! NO TIME TO RELY ON STEALTH.
IF THAT SALIVATING SABOTEUR SQUID-MARK HAS HARMED ONE HAIR OF LION'S MANLY MANE, SO HELP ME...
BAMM!
BE BRAVE, LITTLE LION!
WE'RE GOING TO EAT YOUR LITTLE FRIEND, TIGER-MAN, AND THERE'S NOTHING YOU CAN DO ABOUT IT!
UNTIE MY SIDEKICK, SQUID MARK! YOUR VILE VILLAINY WILL NOT OVERSHADOW THE RIGHT HAND OF JUSTICE!
LOOK OUT, TIGER-MAN!
ONLY THE ROCK OCTOPUS COULD SNEAK UP ON TIGER-MAN! NOW WE'LL SEE HOW BRAVE YOU REALLY ARE!

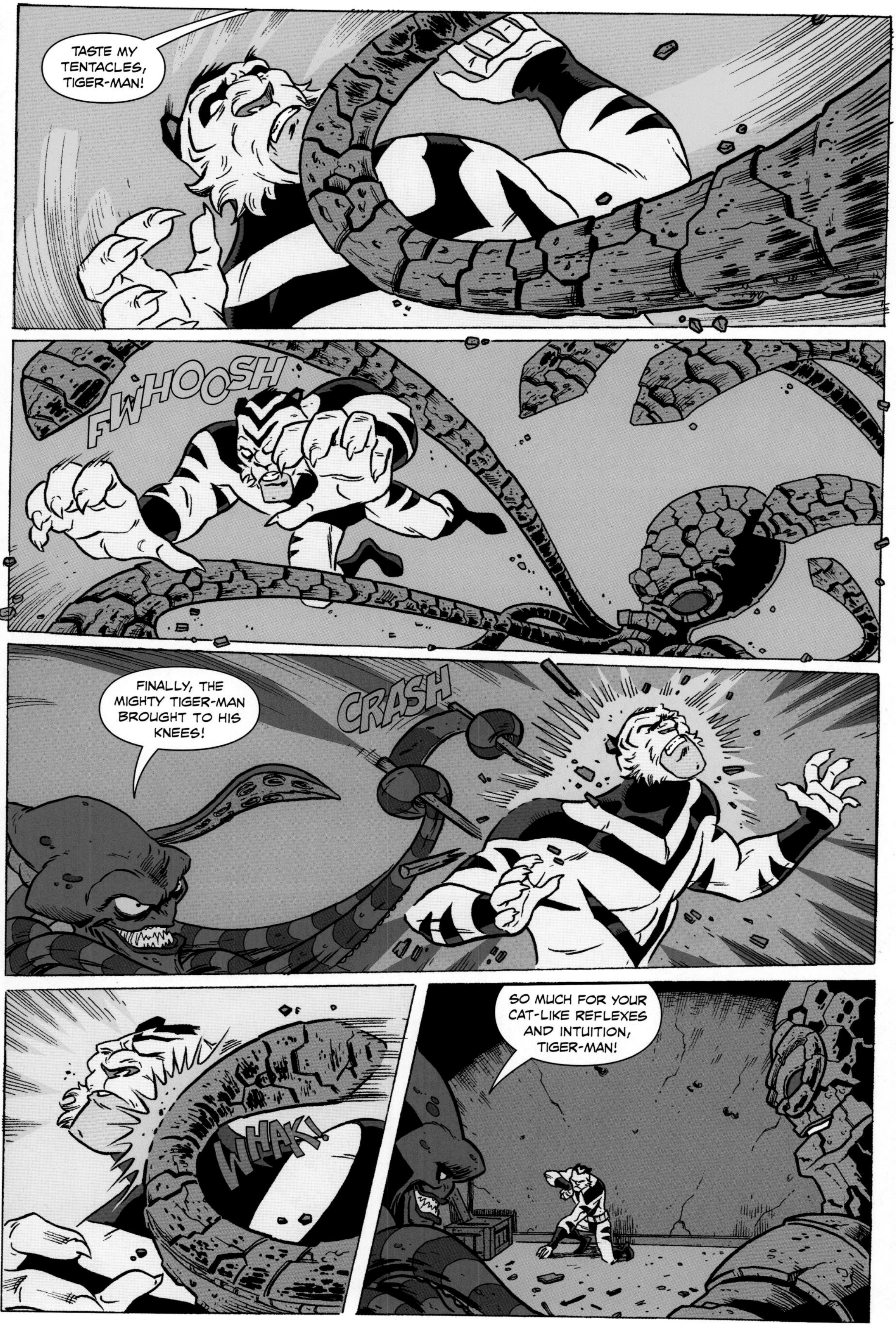
TASTE MY TENTACLES, TIGER-MAN!
FWHOOSH
FINALLY, THE MIGHTY TIGER-MAN BROUGHT TO HIS KNEES!
CRASH
WHAK!
SO MUCH FOR YOUR CAT-LIKE REFLEXES AND INTUITION, TIGER-MAN!

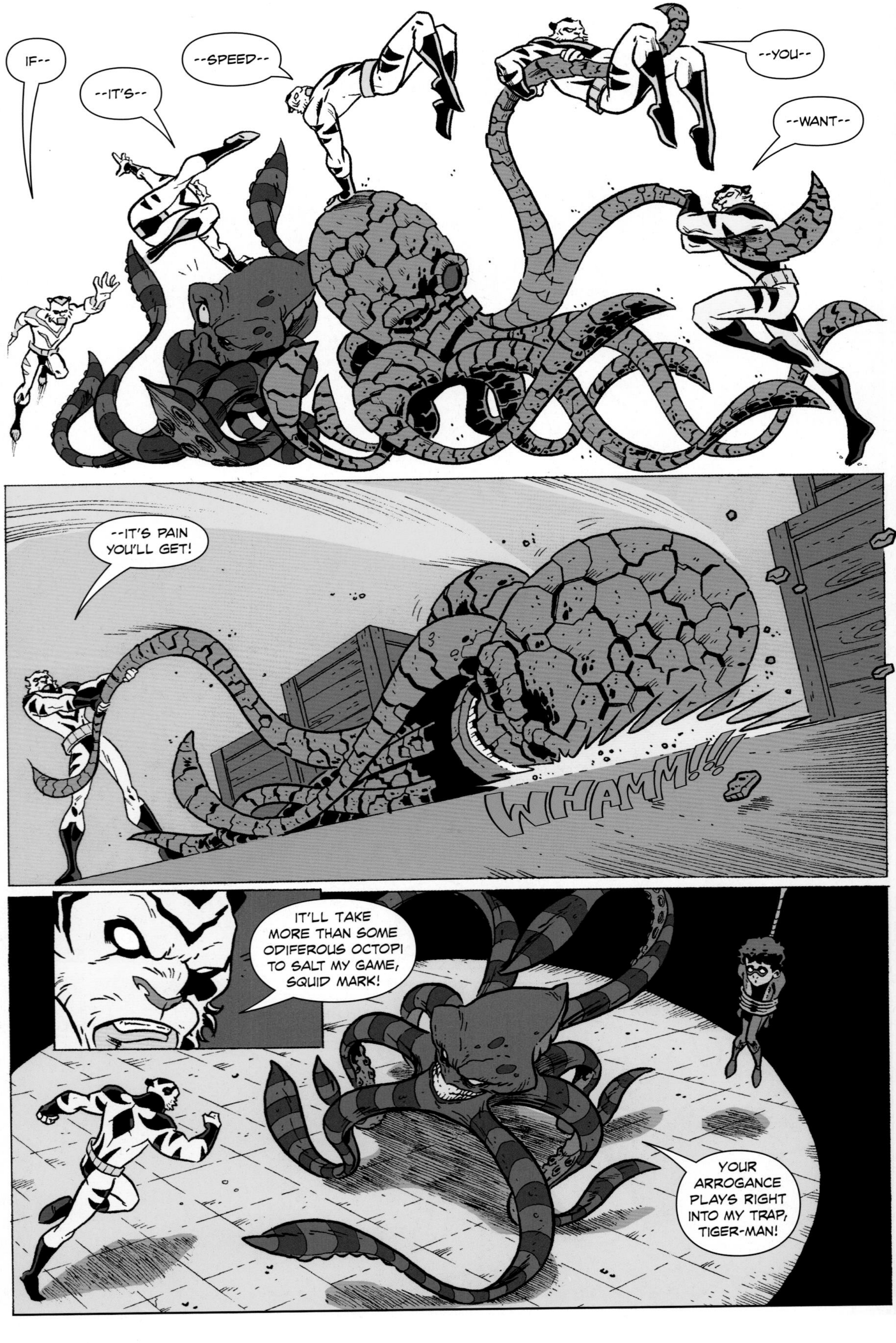
IF--
--IT'S--
--SPEED--
--YOU--
--WANT--
--IT'S PAIN YOU'LL GET!
WHAMM!!!
IT'LL TAKE MORE THAN SOME ODIFEROUS OCTOPI TO SALT MY GAME, SQUID MARK!
YOUR ARROGANCE PLAYS RIGHT INTO MY TRAP, TIGER-MAN!

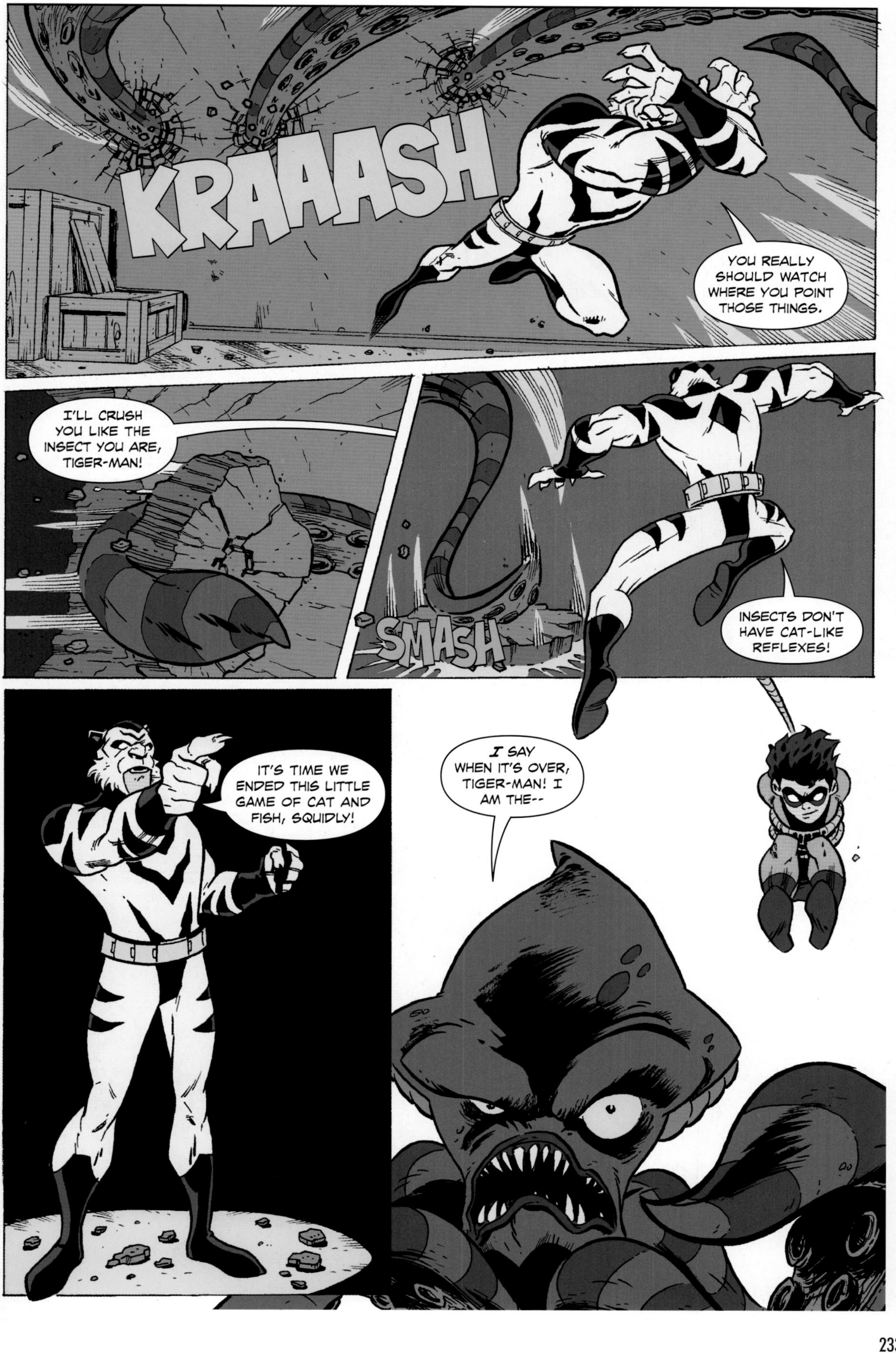
KRAAASH
YOU REALLY SHOULD WATCH WHERE YOU POINT THOSE THINGS.
I'LL CRUSH YOU LIKE THE INSECT YOU ARE, TIGER-MAN!
SMASH
INSECTS DON'T HAVE CAT-LIKE REFLEXES!
IT'S TIME WE ENDED THIS LITTLE GAME OF CAT AND FISH, SQUIDLY!
I SAY WHEN IT'S OVER, TIGER-MAN! I AM THE--

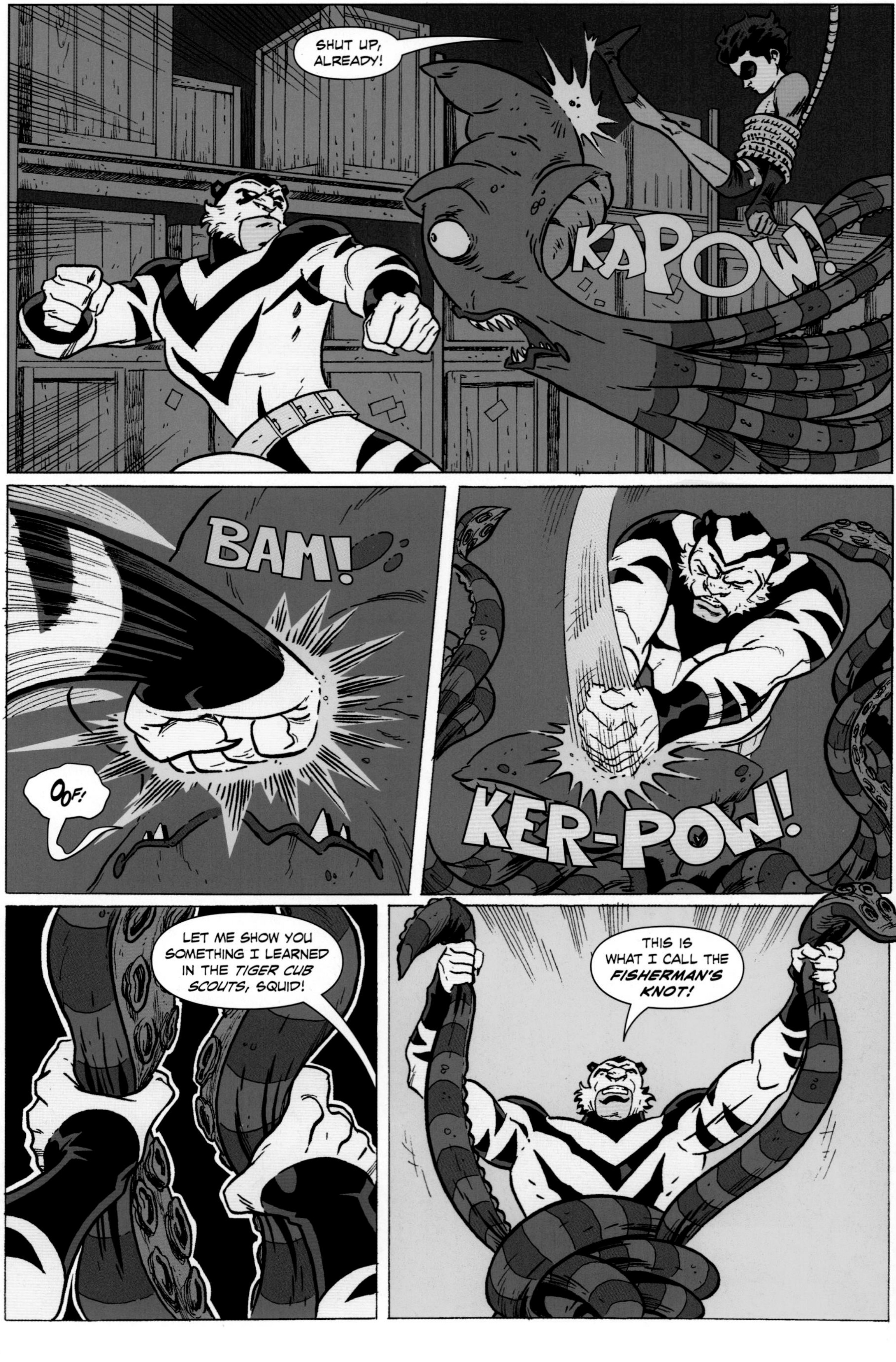
SHUT UP, ALREADY!
KAPOW!
BAM!
OOF!
KER-POW!
LET ME SHOW YOU SOMETHING I LEARNED IN THE *TIGER CUB SCOUTS*, SQUID!
THIS IS WHAT I CALL THE *FISHERMAN'S KNOT!*

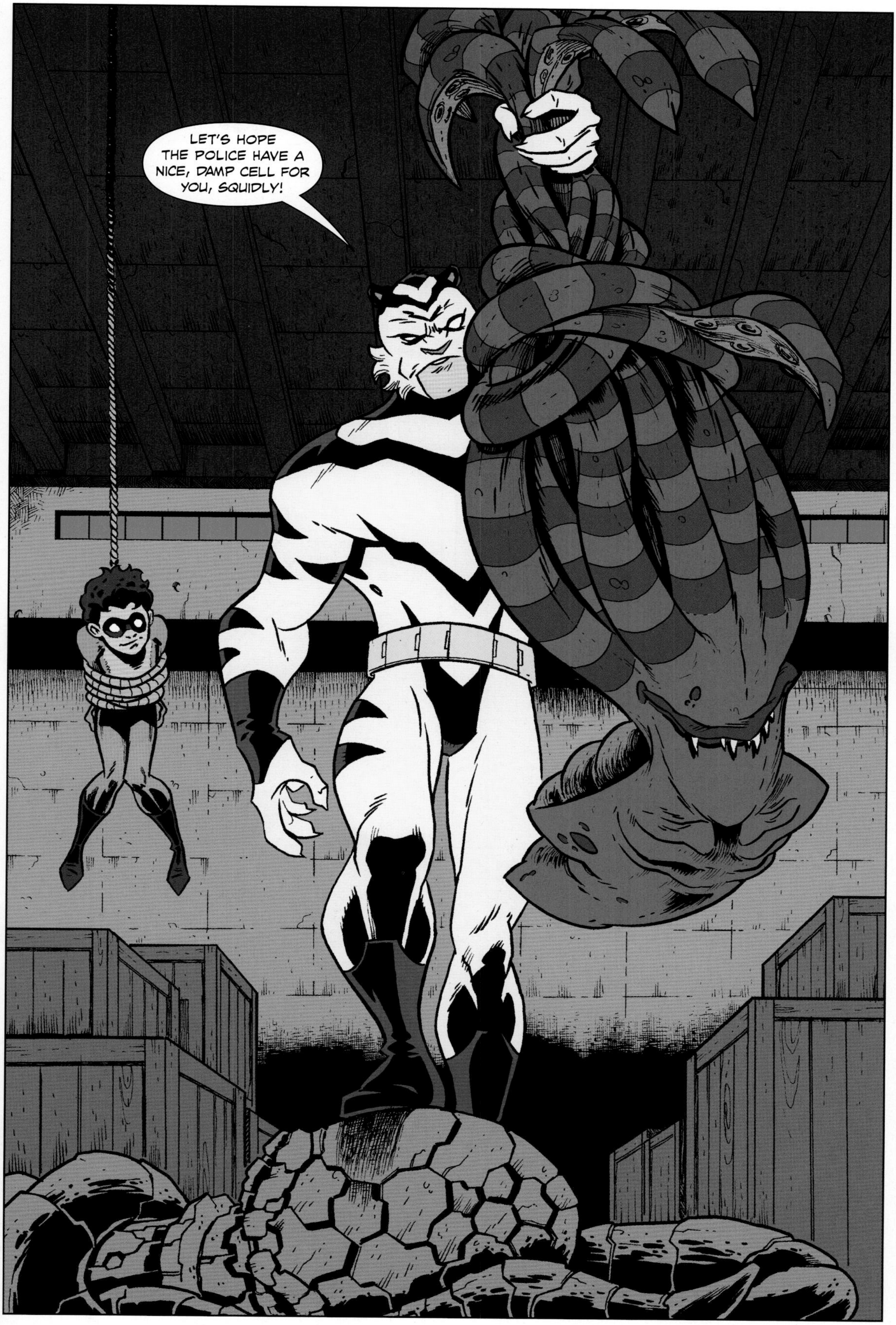
LET'S HOPE THE POLICE HAVE A NICE, DAMP CELL FOR YOU, SQUIDLY!

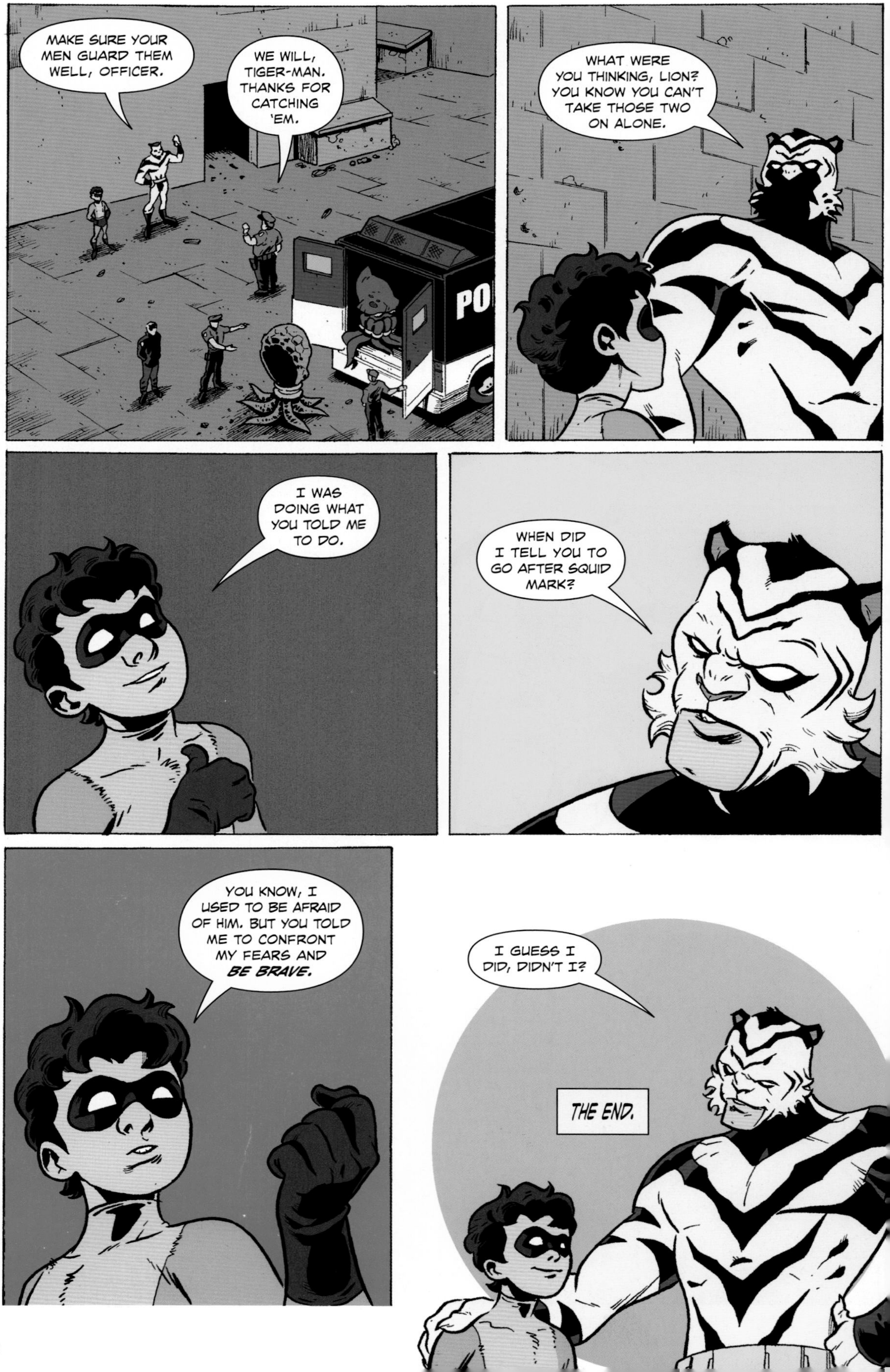
MAKE SURE YOUR MEN GUARD THEM WELL, OFFICER.
WE WILL, TIGER-MAN. THANKS FOR CATCHING 'EM.
POL
WHAT WERE YOU THINKING, LION? YOU KNOW YOU CAN'T TAKE THOSE TWO ON ALONE.
I WAS DOING WHAT YOU TOLD ME TO DO.
WHEN DID I TELL YOU TO GO AFTER SQUID MARK?
YOU KNOW, I USED TO BE AFRAID OF HIM. BUT YOU TOLD ME TO CONFRONT MY FEARS AND *BE BRAVE.*
I GUESS I DID, DIDN'T I?
THE END.

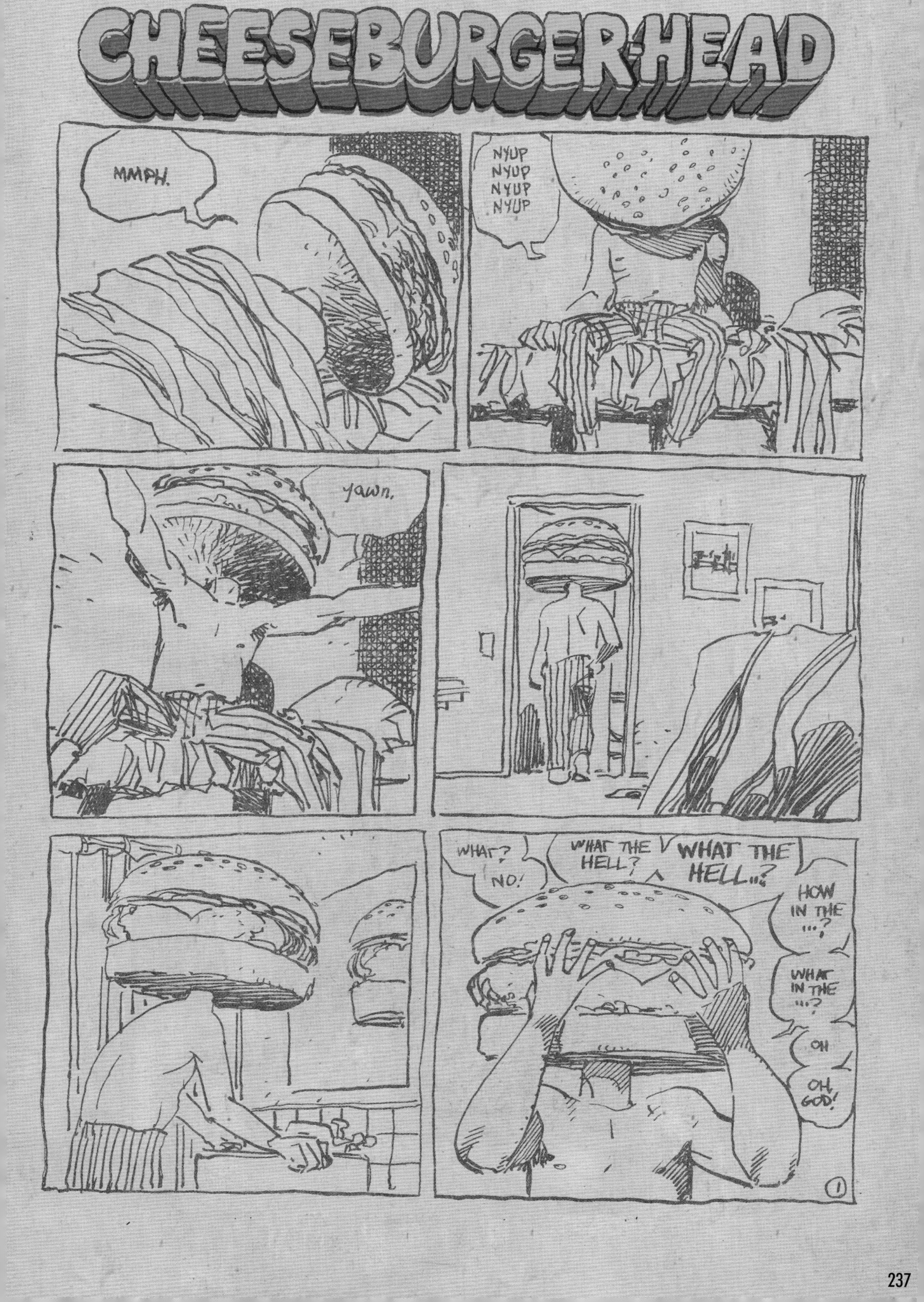
CHEESEBURGER-HEAD
MMPH.
NYUP
NYUP
NYUP
NYUP
yawn.
WHAT?
NO!
WHAT THE HELL?
WHAT THE HELL...?
HOW IN THE ...?
WHAT IN THE ...?
OH
OH, GOD!
1

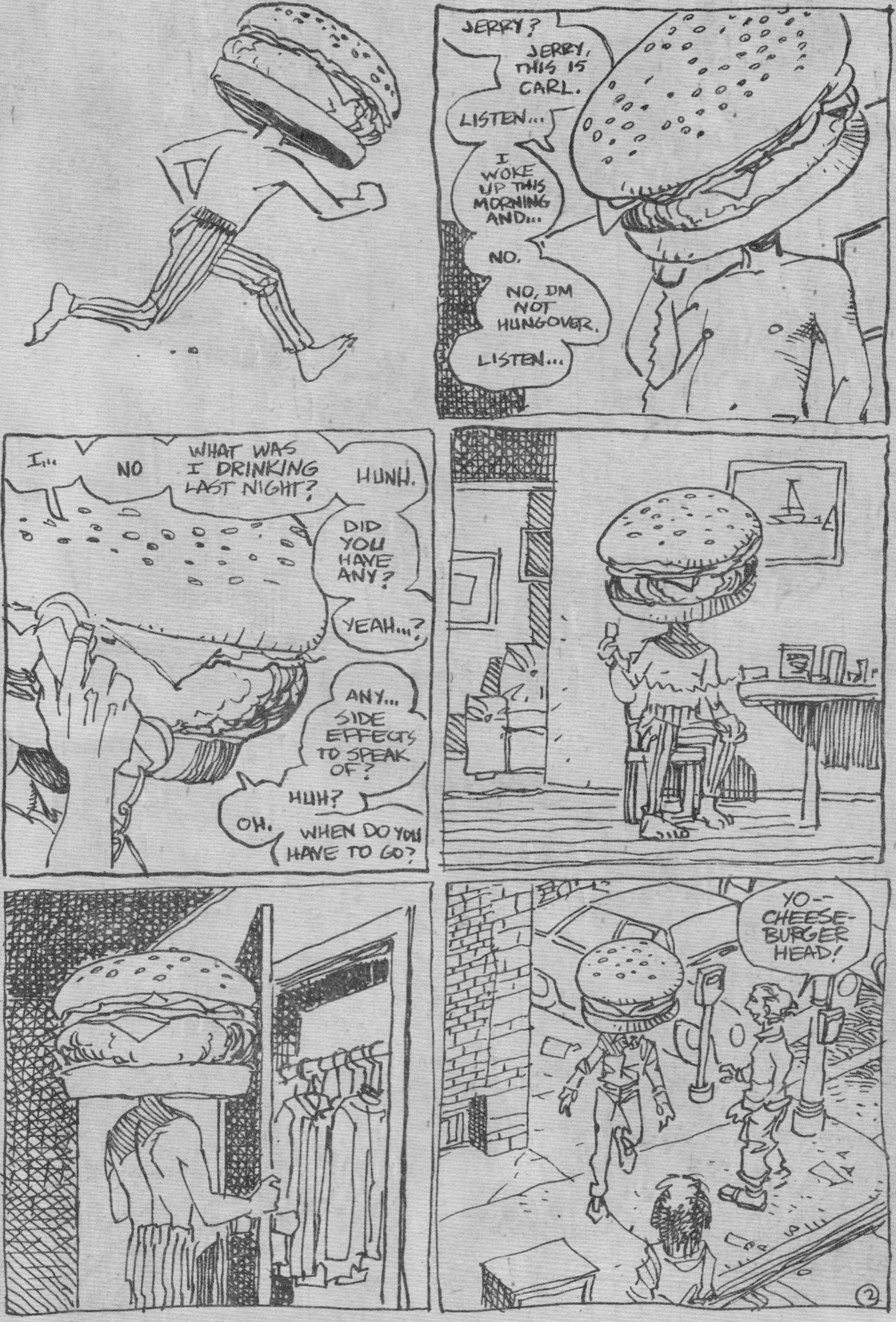
JERRY?
JERRY, THIS IS CARL.
LISTEN...
I WOKE UP THIS MORNING AND...
NO.
NO, I'M NOT HUNGOVER.
LISTEN...
I...
NO
WHAT WAS I DRINKING LAST NIGHT?
HUNH.
DID YOU HAVE ANY?
YEAH...?
ANY... SIDE EFFECTS TO SPEAK OF?
HUH?
OH.
WHEN DO YOU HAVE TO GO?
YO--CHEESE-BURGER HEAD!
2

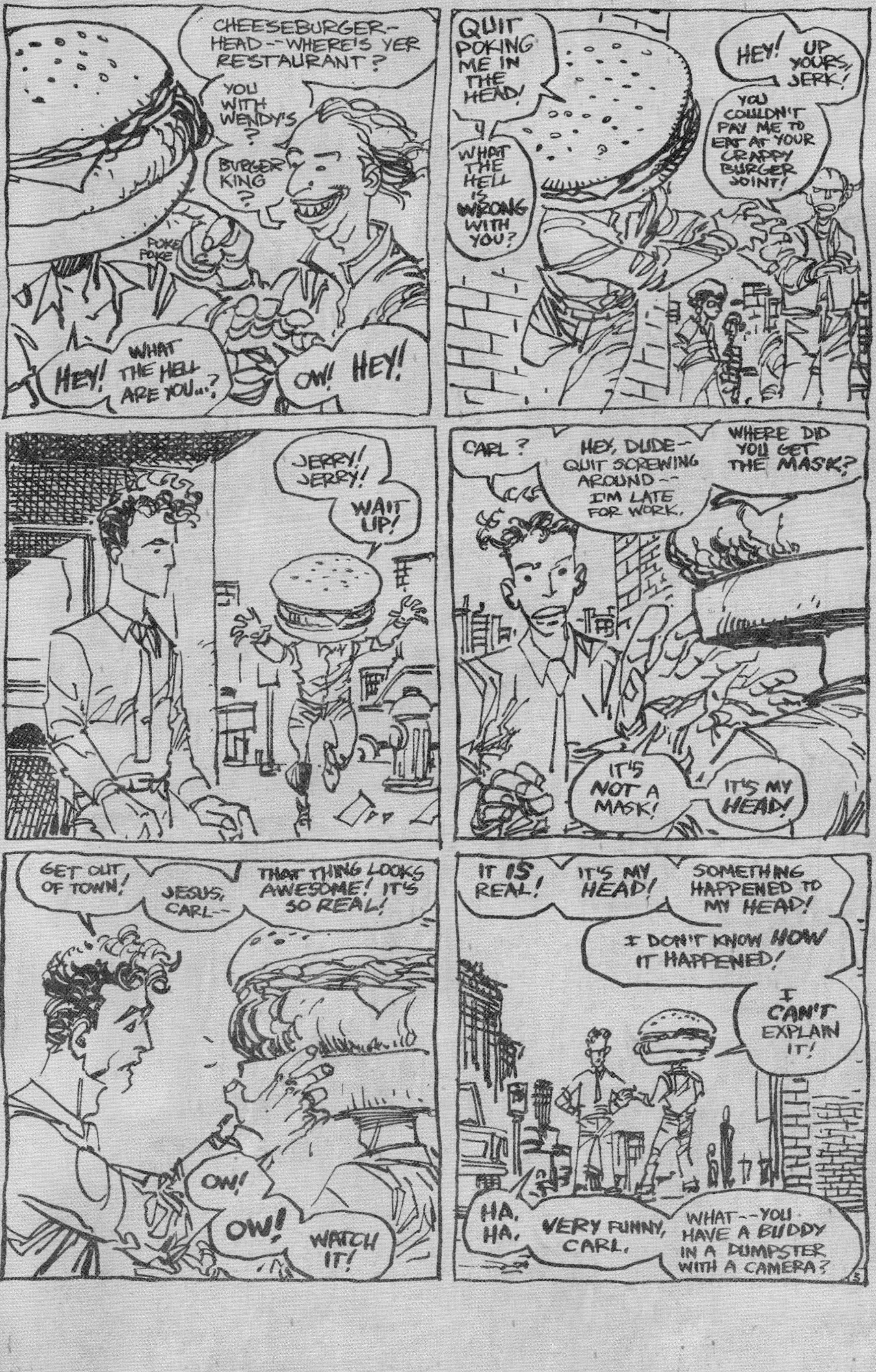
CHEESEBURGER-HEAD--WHERE'S YER RESTAURANT?
YOU WITH WENDY'S?
BURGER KING?
POKE POKE
HEY!
WHAT THE HELL ARE YOU...?
OW!
HEY!
QUIT POKING ME IN THE HEAD!
WHAT THE HELL IS WRONG WITH YOU?
HEY! UP YOURS, JERK!
YOU COULDN'T PAY ME TO EAT AT YOUR CRAPPY BURGER JOINT!
JERRY! JERRY!
WAIT UP!
CARL?
HEY, DUDE-- QUIT SCREWING AROUND-- I'M LATE FOR WORK.
WHERE DID YOU GET THE MASK?
IT'S NOT A MASK!
IT'S MY HEAD!
GET OUT OF TOWN!
JESUS, CARL--
THAT THING LOOKS AWESOME! IT'S SO REAL!
OW!
OW!
WATCH IT!
IT IS REAL!
IT'S MY HEAD!
SOMETHING HAPPENED TO MY HEAD!
I DON'T KNOW HOW IT HAPPENED!
I CAN'T EXPLAIN IT!
HA, HA.
VERY FUNNY, CARL.
WHAT--YOU HAVE A BUDDY IN A DUMPSTER WITH A CAMERA?
5

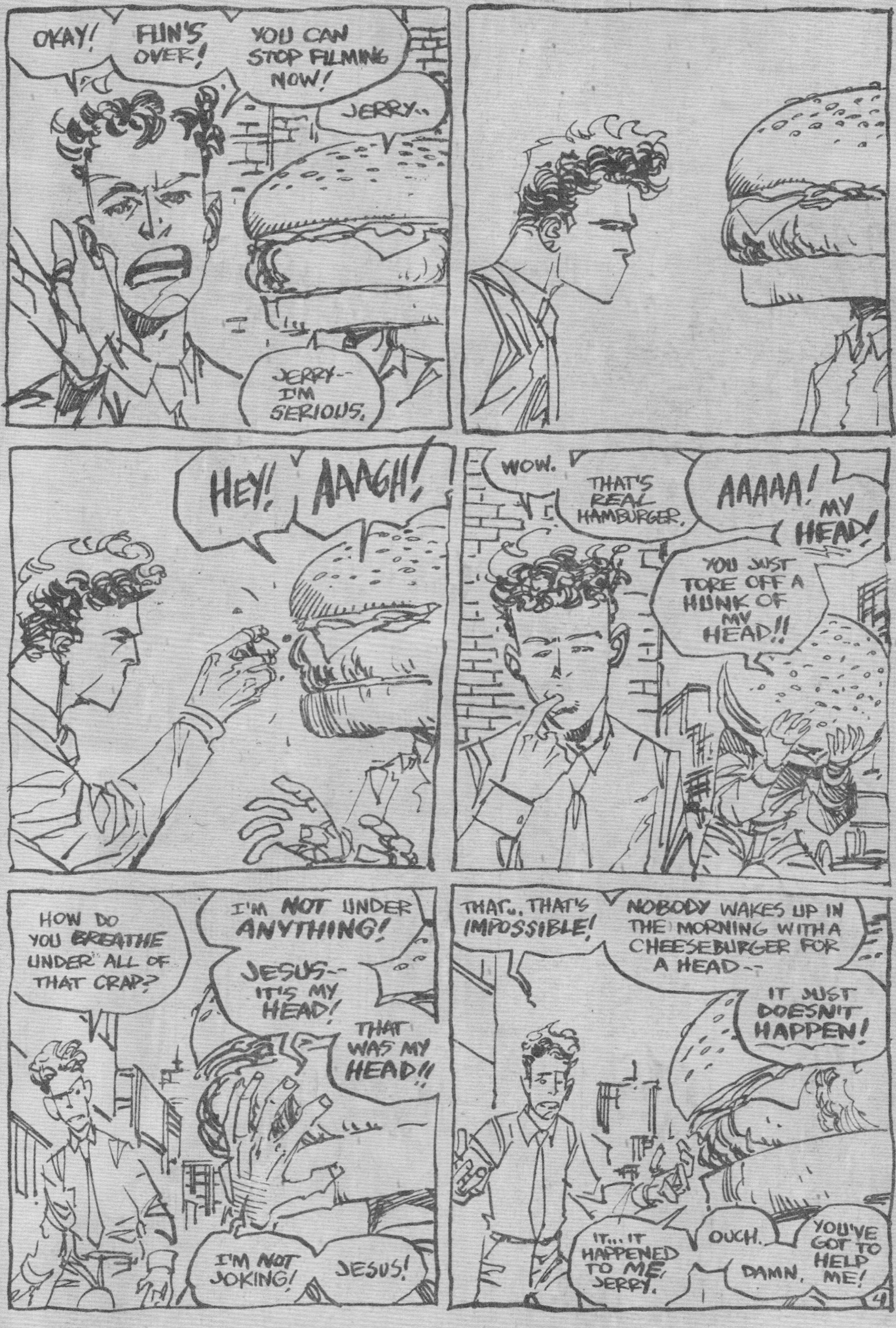

OKAY!
FUN'S OVER!
YOU CAN STOP FILMING NOW!
JERRY..
JERRY-- I'M SERIOUS.
HEY!
AAAGH!
WOW.
THAT'S REAL HAMBURGER.
AAAAA!
MY HEAD!
YOU JUST TORE OFF A HUNK OF MY HEAD!!
HOW DO YOU BREATHE UNDER ALL OF THAT CRAP?
I'M NOT UNDER ANYTHING!
JESUS-- IT'S MY HEAD!
THAT WAS MY HEAD!!
I'M NOT JOKING!
JESUS!
THAT.. THAT'S IMPOSSIBLE!
NOBODY WAKES UP IN THE MORNING WITH A CHEESEBURGER FOR A HEAD--
IT JUST DOESN'T HAPPEN!
IT... IT HAPPENED TO ME, JERRY.
OUCH.
DAMN.
YOU'VE GOT TO HELP ME!
4

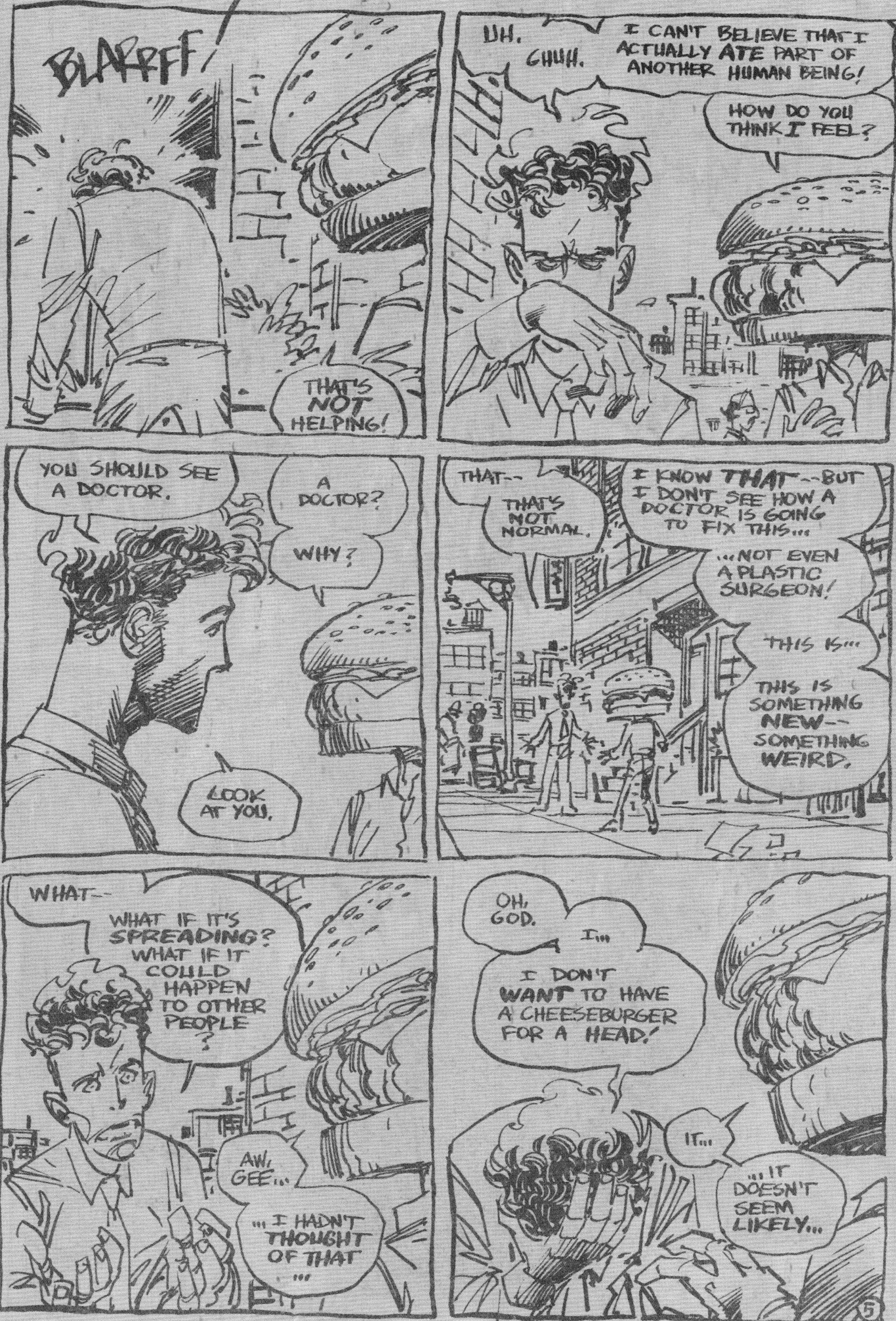
BLARRFF!
THAT'S NOT HELPING!
UH.
GHUH.
I CAN'T BELIEVE THAT I ACTUALLY ATE PART OF ANOTHER HUMAN BEING!
HOW DO YOU THINK I FEEL?
YOU SHOULD SEE A DOCTOR.
A DOCTOR?
WHY?
LOOK AT YOU.
THAT--
THAT'S NOT NORMAL.
I KNOW THAT--BUT I DON'T SEE HOW A DOCTOR IS GOING TO FIX THIS...
...NOT EVEN A PLASTIC SURGEON!
THIS IS...
THIS IS SOMETHING NEW--SOMETHING WEIRD.
WHAT--
WHAT IF IT'S SPREADING? WHAT IF IT COULD HAPPEN TO OTHER PEOPLE?
AW, GEE...
...I HADN'T THOUGHT OF THAT...
OH, GOD.
I...
I DON'T WANT TO HAVE A CHEESEBURGER FOR A HEAD!
IT...
...IT DOESN'T SEEM LIKELY...
5

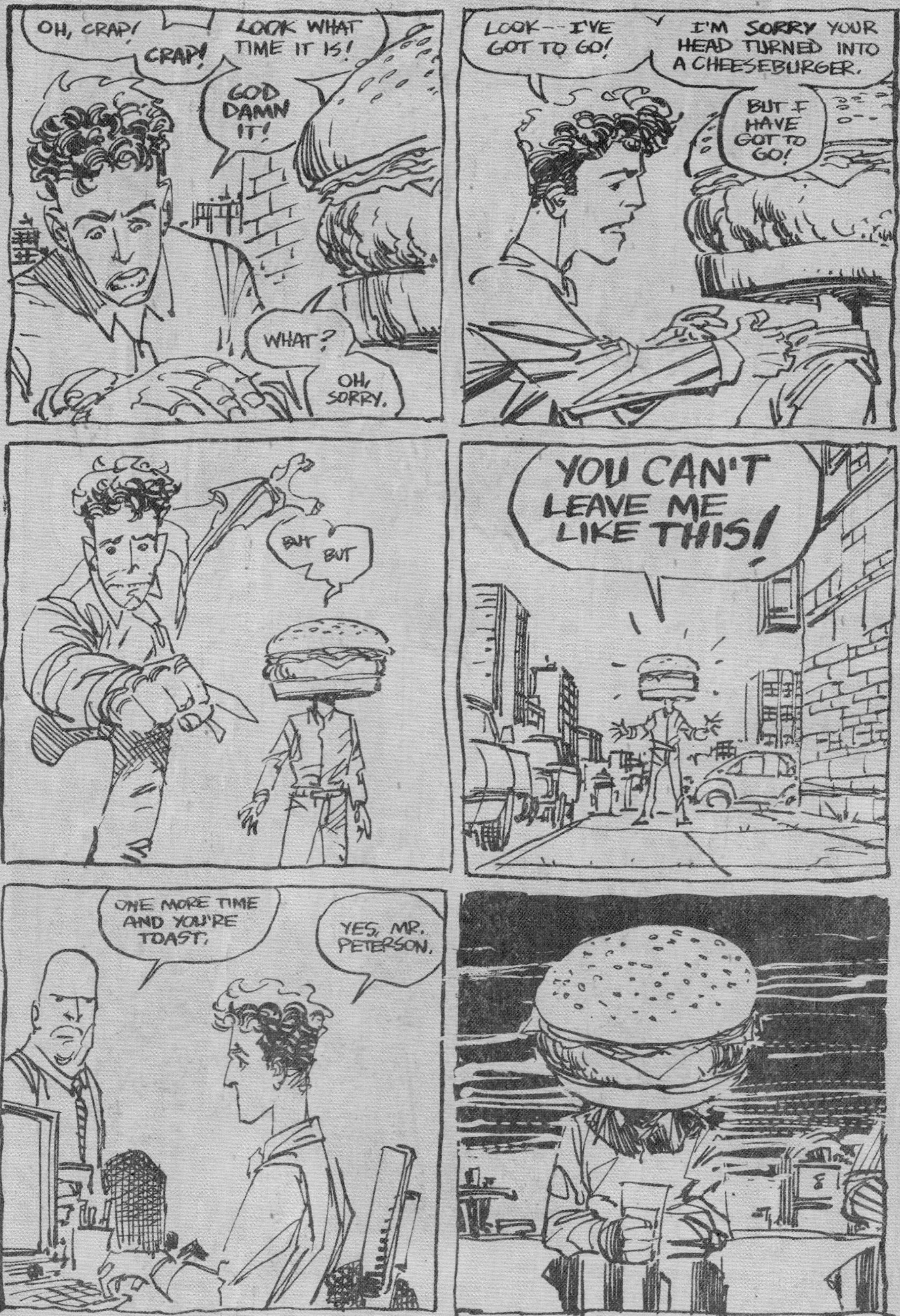
OH, CRAP!
CRAP!
LOOK WHAT TIME IT IS!
GOD DAMN IT!
WHAT?
OH, SORRY.
LOOK--I'VE GOT TO GO!
I'M SORRY YOUR HEAD TURNED INTO A CHEESEBURGER.
BUT I HAVE GOT TO GO!
BUT BUT
YOU CAN'T LEAVE ME LIKE THIS!
ONE MORE TIME AND YOU'RE TOAST.
YES, MR. PETERSON.

Black **Circle** White

The Recycle Soul Project

{ This five-page story is not commentary supporting a singular belief system, but is simply the bored exploration of a layman… Dabbling. }

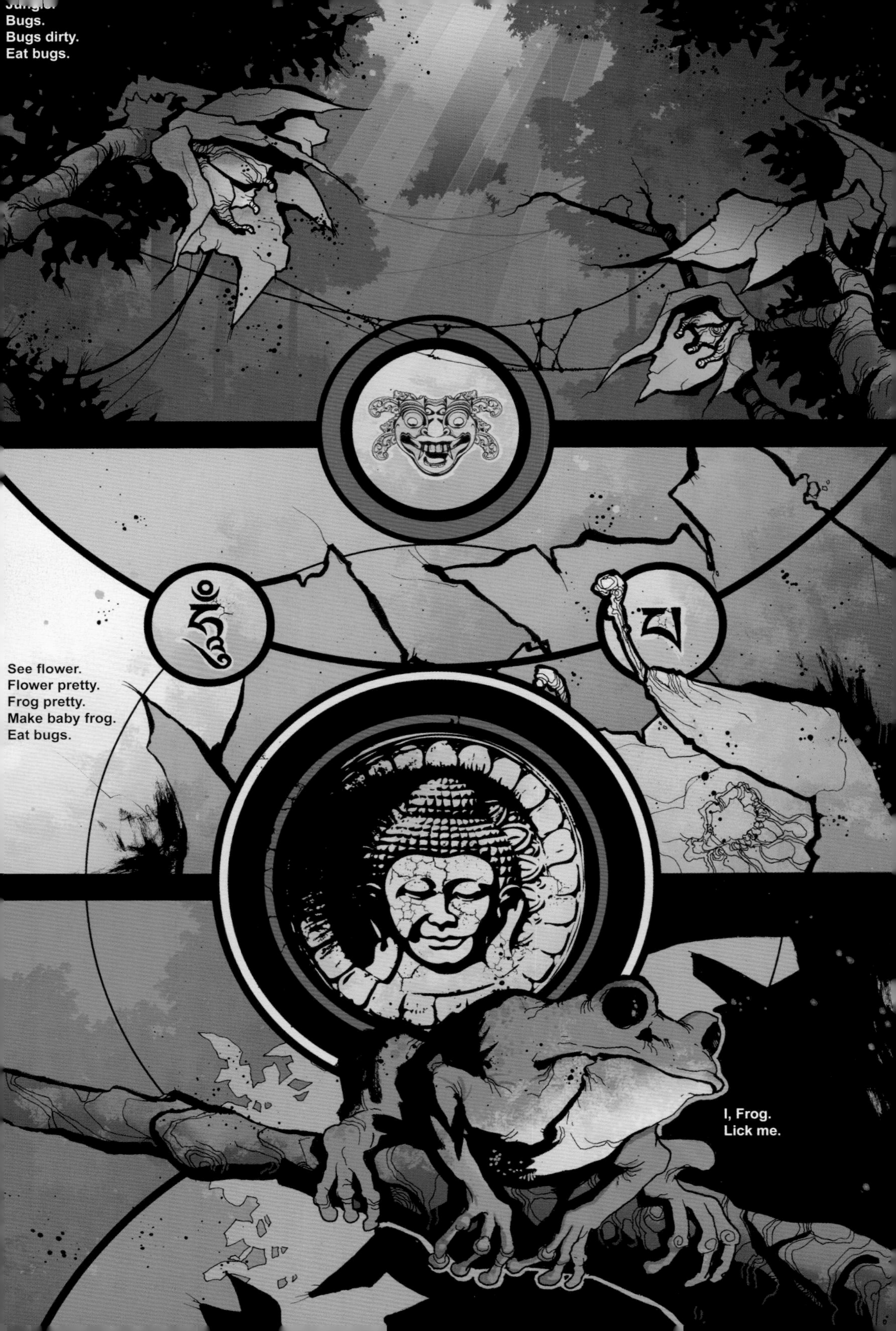
Bugs.
Bugs dirty.
Eat bugs.
See flower.
Flower pretty.
Frog pretty.
Make baby frog.
Eat bugs.
I, Frog.
Lick me.

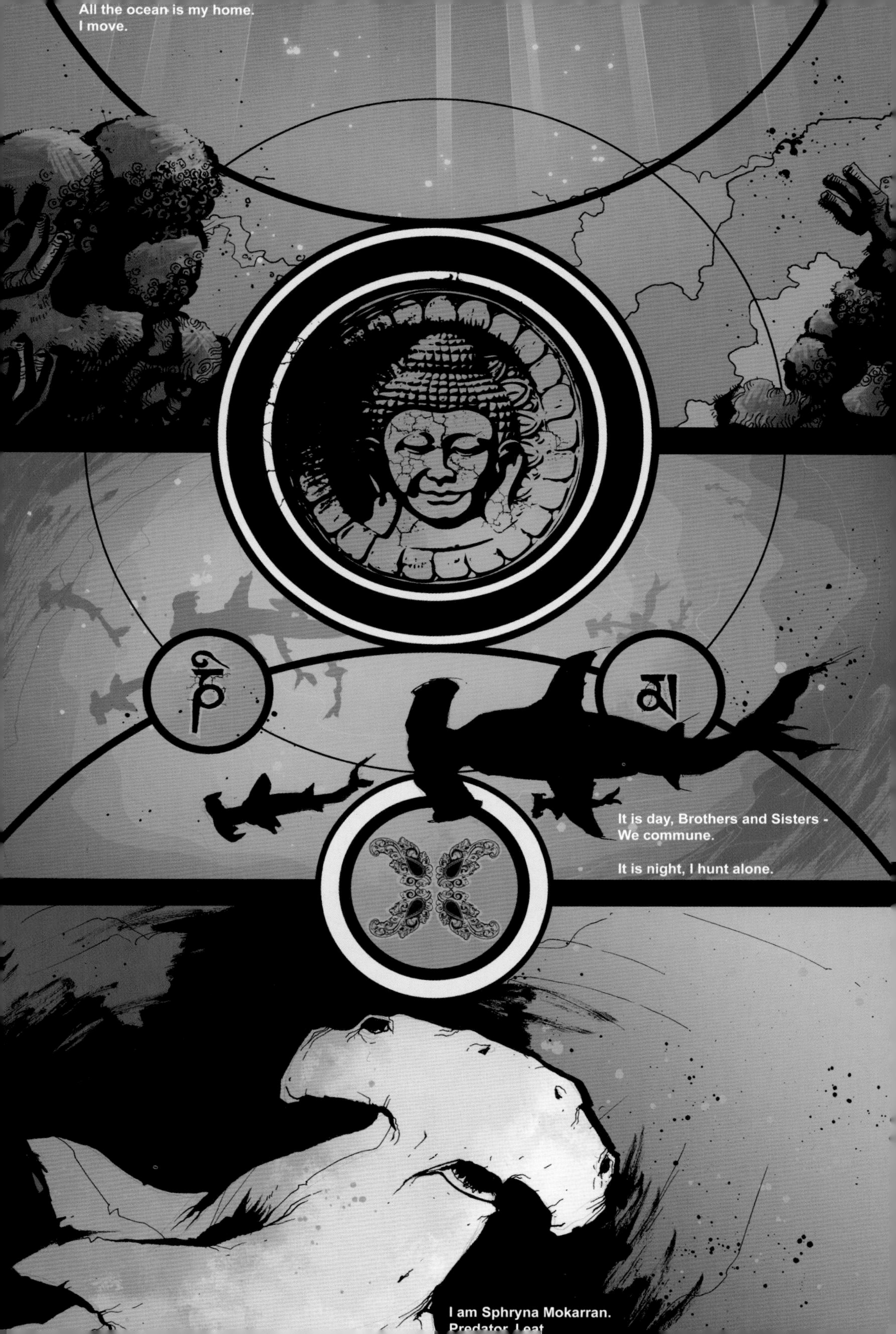
All the ocean is my home.
I move.
It is day, Brothers and Sisters -
We commune.
It is night, I hunt alone.
I am Sphryna Mokarran.
Predator. I eat

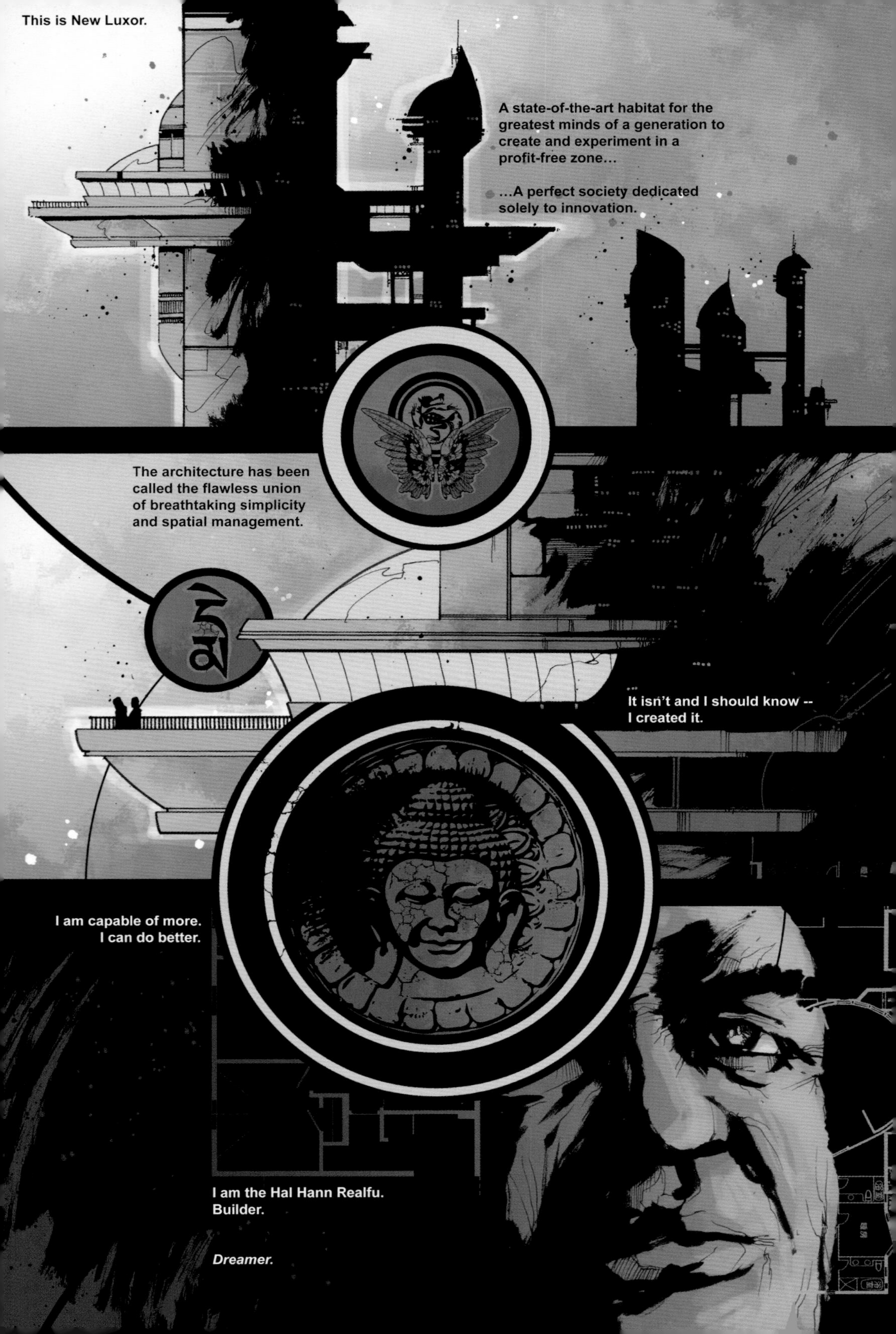
This is New Luxor.
A state-of-the-art habitat for the greatest minds of a generation to create and experiment in a profit-free zone...
...A perfect society dedicated solely to innovation.
The architecture has been called the flawless union of breathtaking simplicity and spatial management.
It isn't and I should know -- I created it.
I am capable of more. I can do better.
I am the Hal Hann Realfu. Builder.
Dreamer.

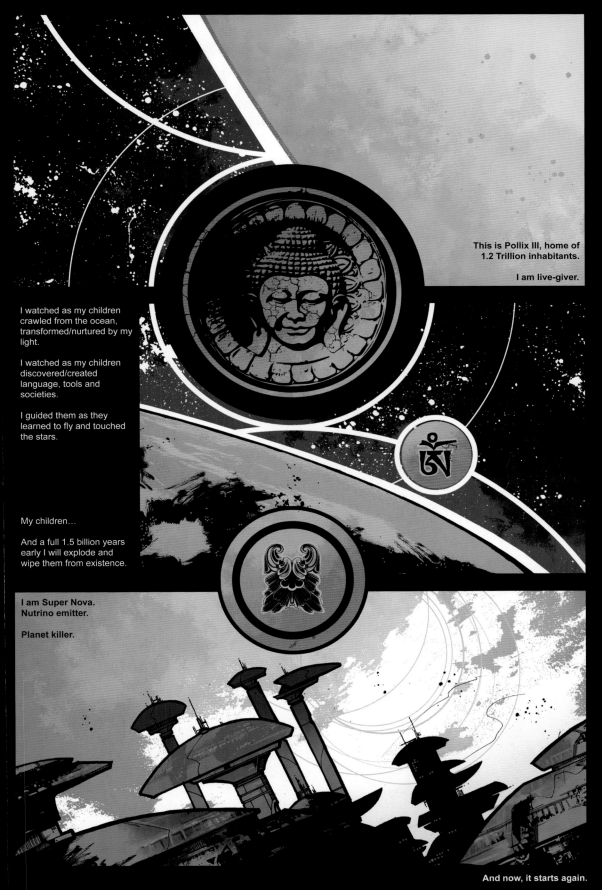

This is Pollix III, home of 1.2 Trillion inhabitants.

I am live-giver.

I watched as my children crawled from the ocean, transformed/nurtured by my light.

I watched as my children discovered/created language, tools and societies.

I guided them as they learned to fly and touched the stars.

My children…

And a full 1.5 billion years early I will explode and wipe them from existence.

I am Super Nova. Nutrino emitter.

Planet killer.

And now, it starts again.

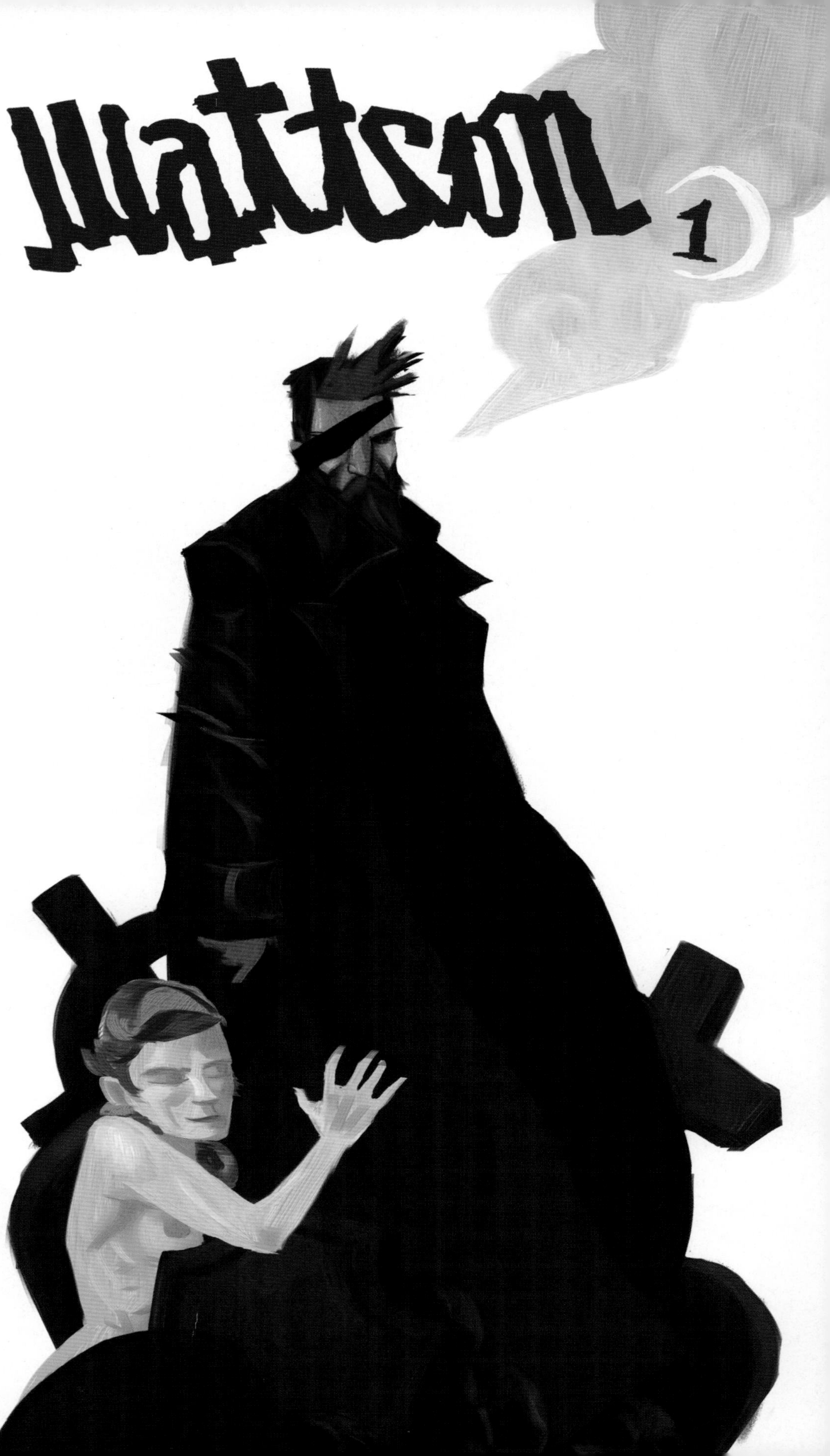
Wattson
1

a tale for popgun

what originally started as a way for
me to be suave with the dames
(you'll notice I use that one a lot)
eventually turned into a way for
me to have poptarts, without the tart

to
samuel spade
philip marlowe
and the great
sherlock holmes

adapted from my head

A MAN NAMED WATTSON

STORY & ART
KRIS ANKA

LOGO
SHANE LONG

A HEAD AMONG SKULLS

for
robots
heroes
monsters
and the damsels
they kidnap

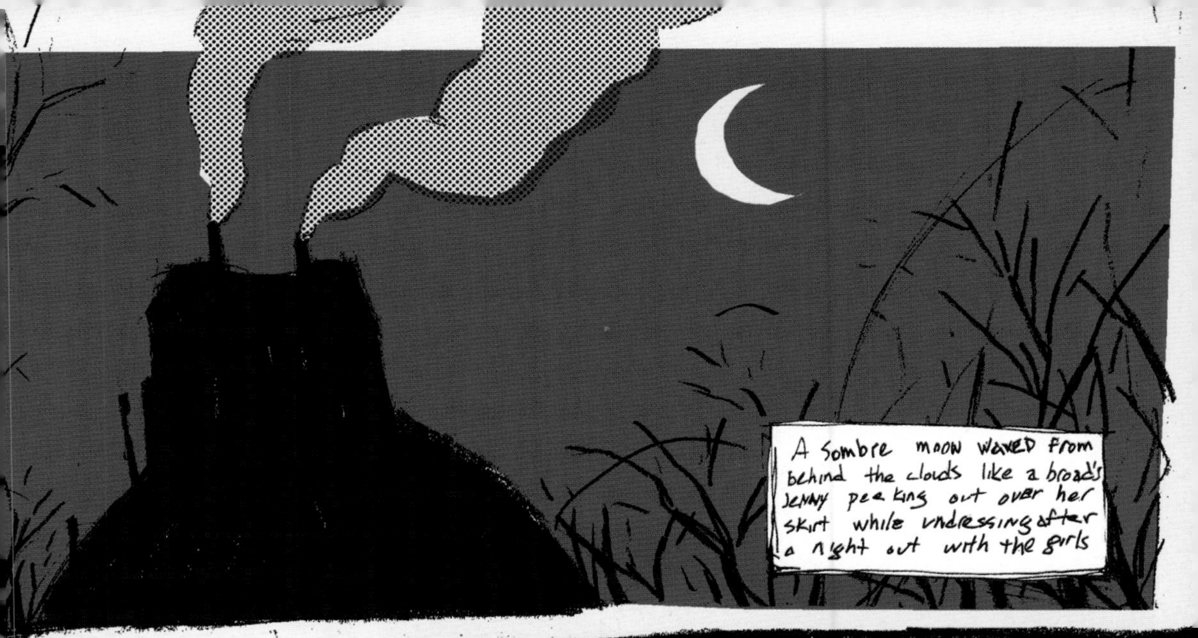
A Sombre moon waved from behind the clouds like a broad's jenny peaking out over her skirt while undressing after a night out with the girls

A head among Skulls

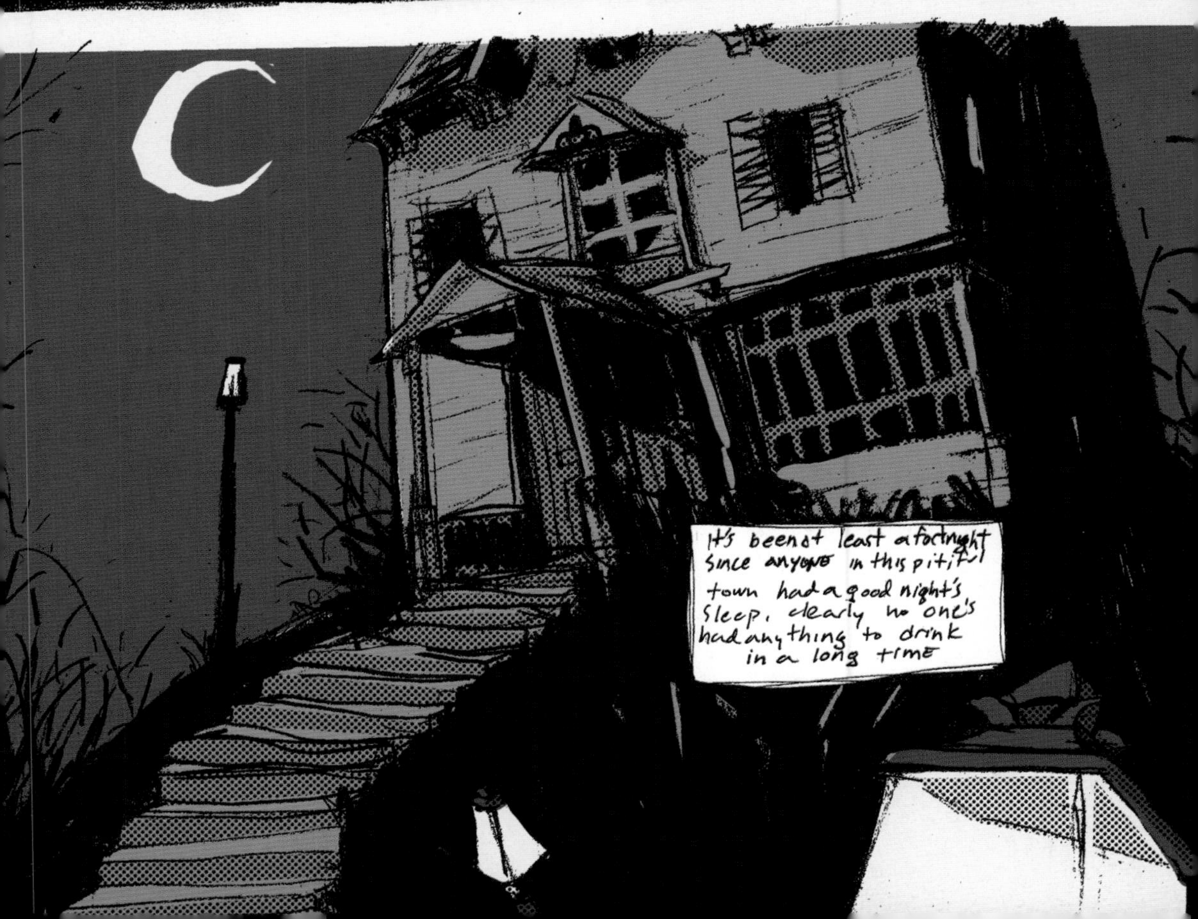
It's been at least a fortnight since anyone in this pitiful town had a good night's sleep. clearly no one's had anything to drink in a long time

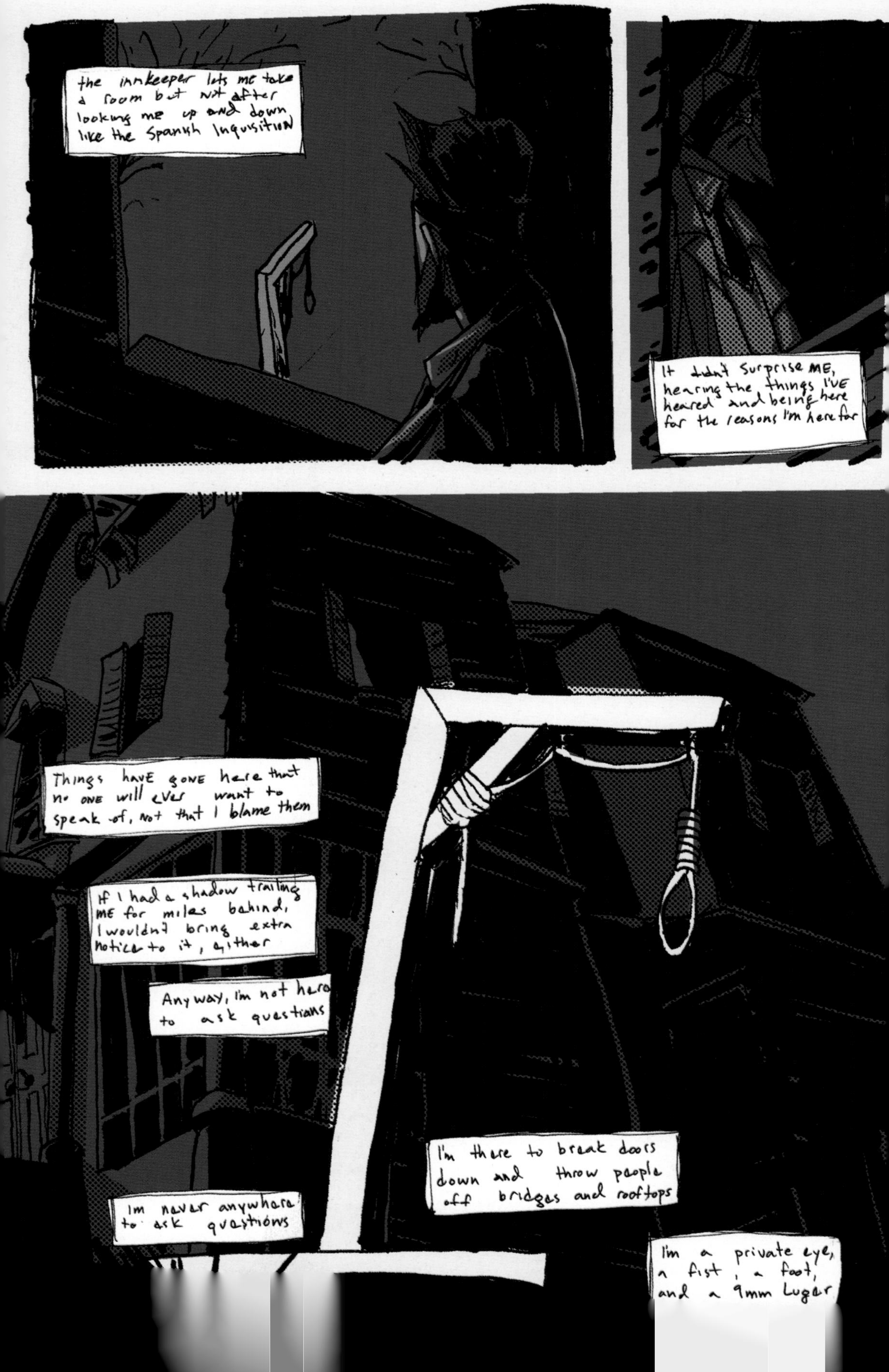
the innkeeper lets me take a room but not after looking me up and down like the Spanish Inquisition
It didn't surprise ME, hearing the things I'VE heared and being here for the reasons I'm here for
Things have gone here that no one will ever want to speak of, not that I blame them
If I had a shadow trailing ME for miles behind, I wouldn't bring extra notice to it, either
Anyway, I'm not here to ask questions
I'm never anywhere to ask questions
I'm there to break doors down and throw people off bridges and rooftops
I'm a private eye, a fist, a foot, and a 9mm Luger

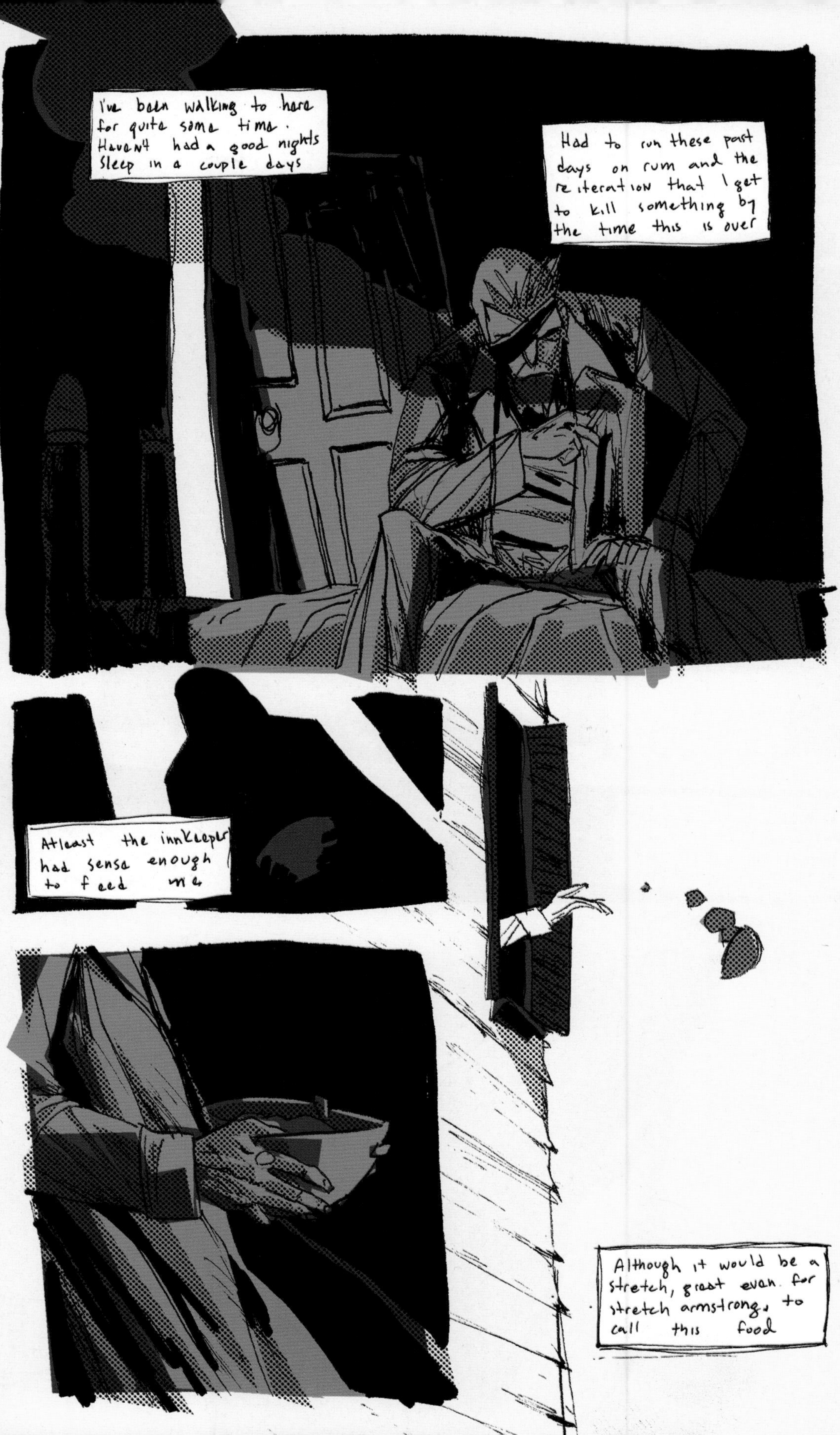
I've been walking to here for quite some time. Haven't had a good nights Sleep in a couple days
Had to run these past days on rum and the reiteration that I get to kill something by the time this is over
Atleast the innKeeper had sense enough to feed me
Although it would be a stretch, great even, for stretch armstrong, to call this food

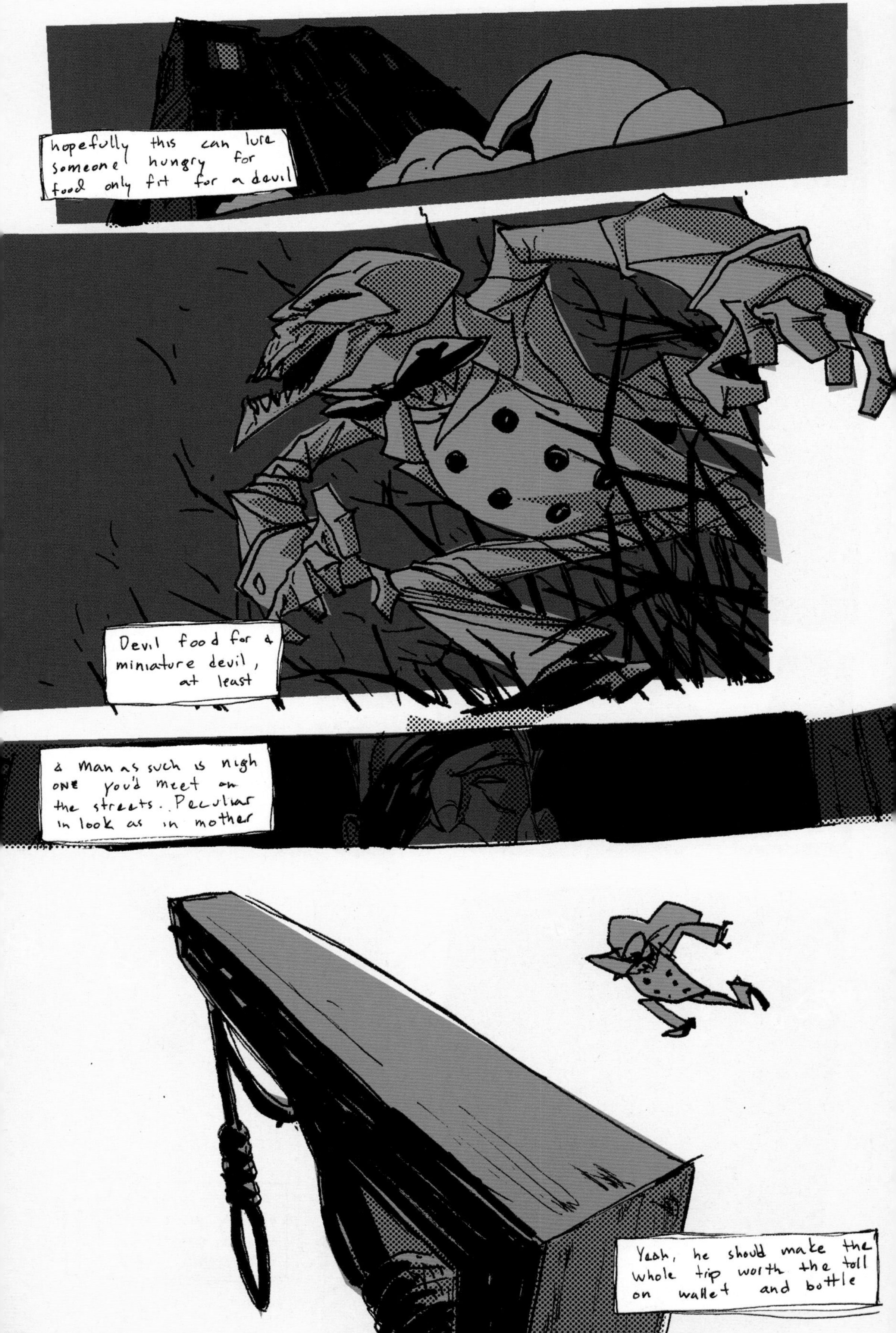
hopefully this can lure someone hungry for food only fit for a devil
Devil food for a miniature devil, at least
a man as such is nigh one you'd meet on the streets. Peculiar in look as in mother
Yeah, he should make the whole trip worth the toll on wallet and bottle

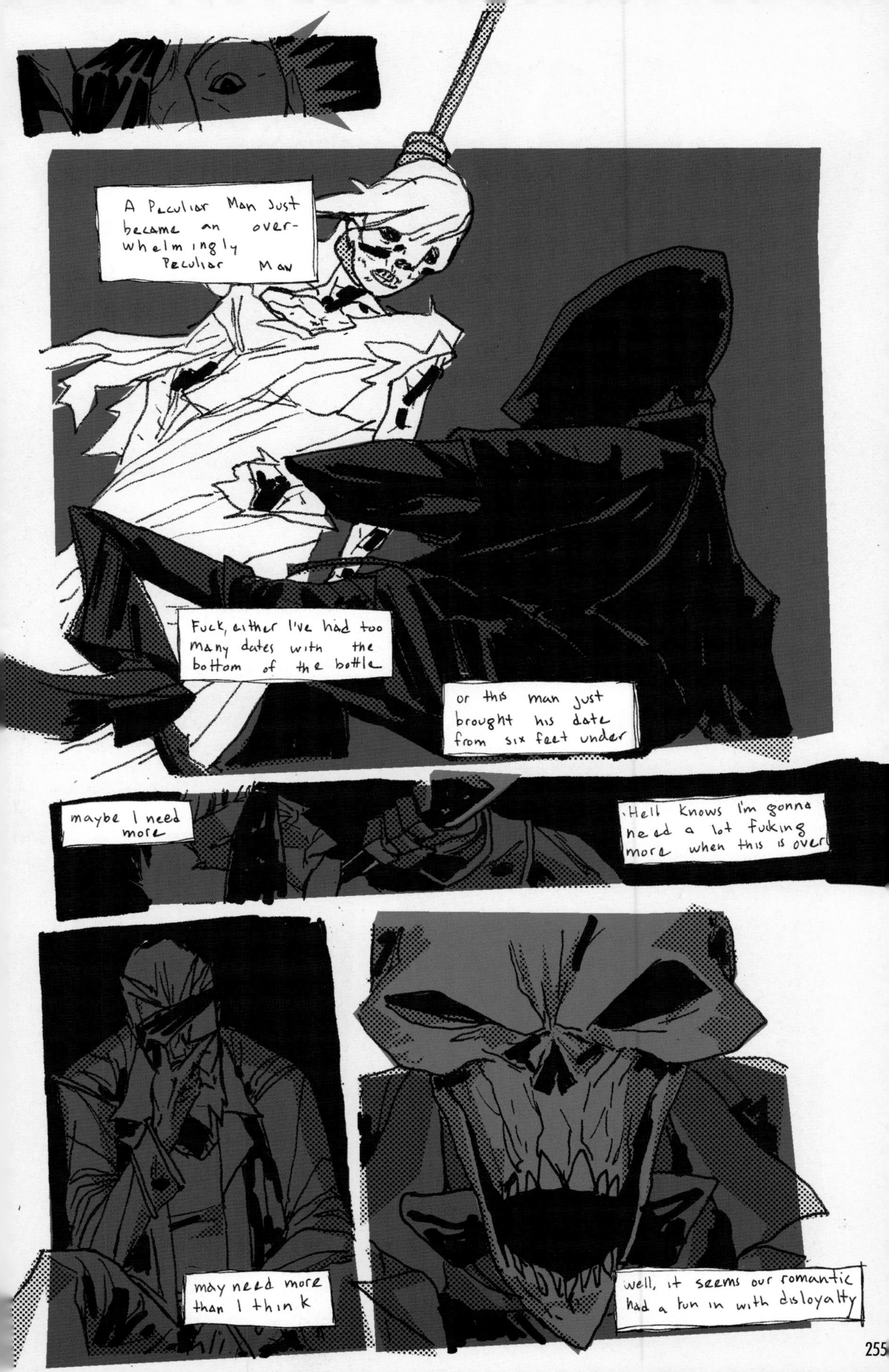
A Peculiar Man Just became an over-whelmingly Peculiar Man
Fuck, either I've had too many dates with the bottom of the bottle
or this man just brought his date from six feet under
maybe I need more
Hell knows I'm gonna need a lot fucking more when this is over
may need more than I think
well, it seems our romantic had a run in with disloyalty

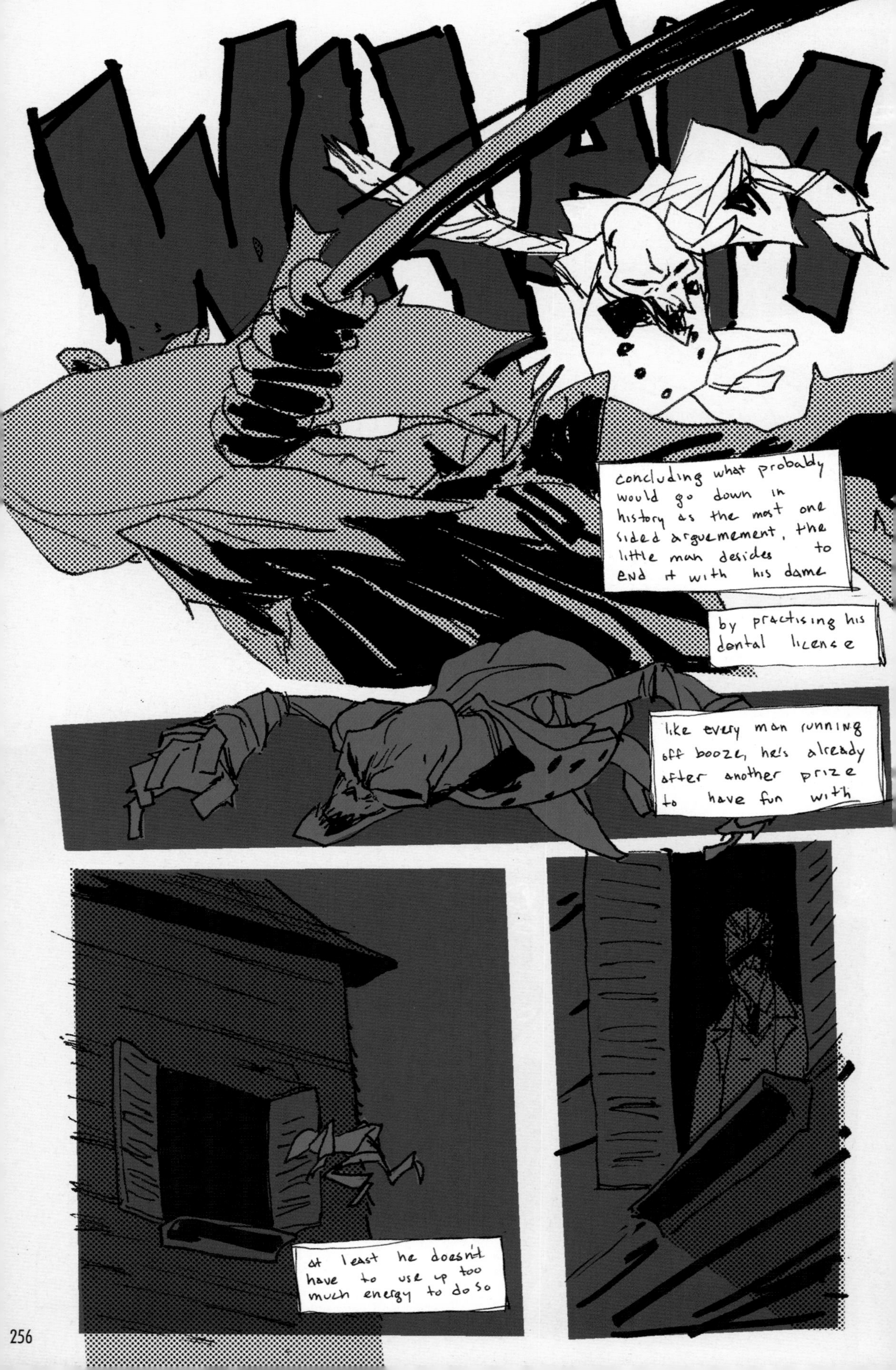
concluding what probably would go down in history as the most one sided arguement, the little man desides to end it with his dame
by practising his dental license
like every man running off booze, he's already after another prize to have fun with
at least he doesn't have to use up too much energy to do so

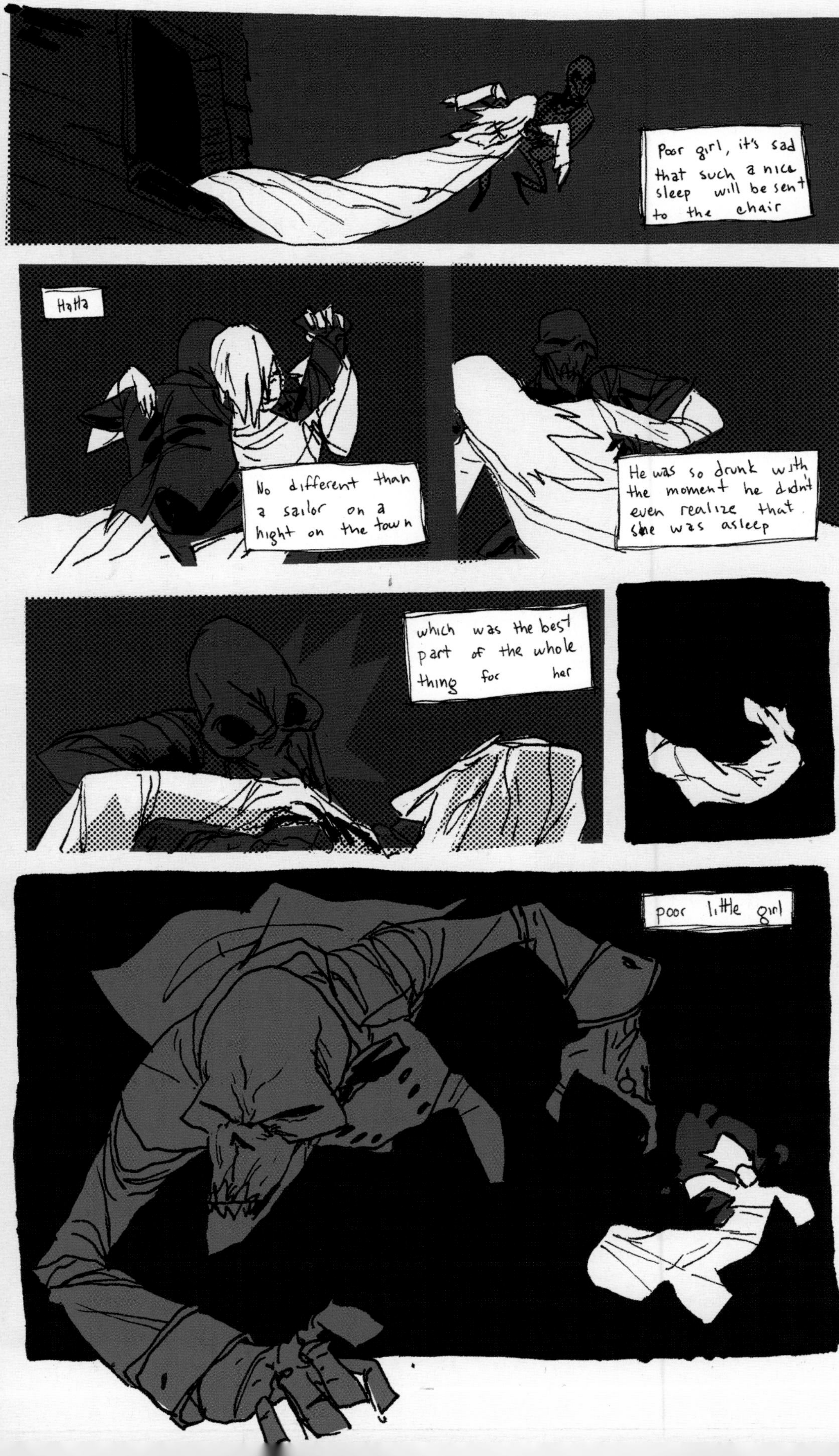
Poor girl, it's sad that such a nice sleep will be sent to the chair
Hatta
No different than a sailor on a night on the town
He was so drunk with the moment he didn't even realize that she was asleep
which was the best part of the whole thing for her
poor little girl

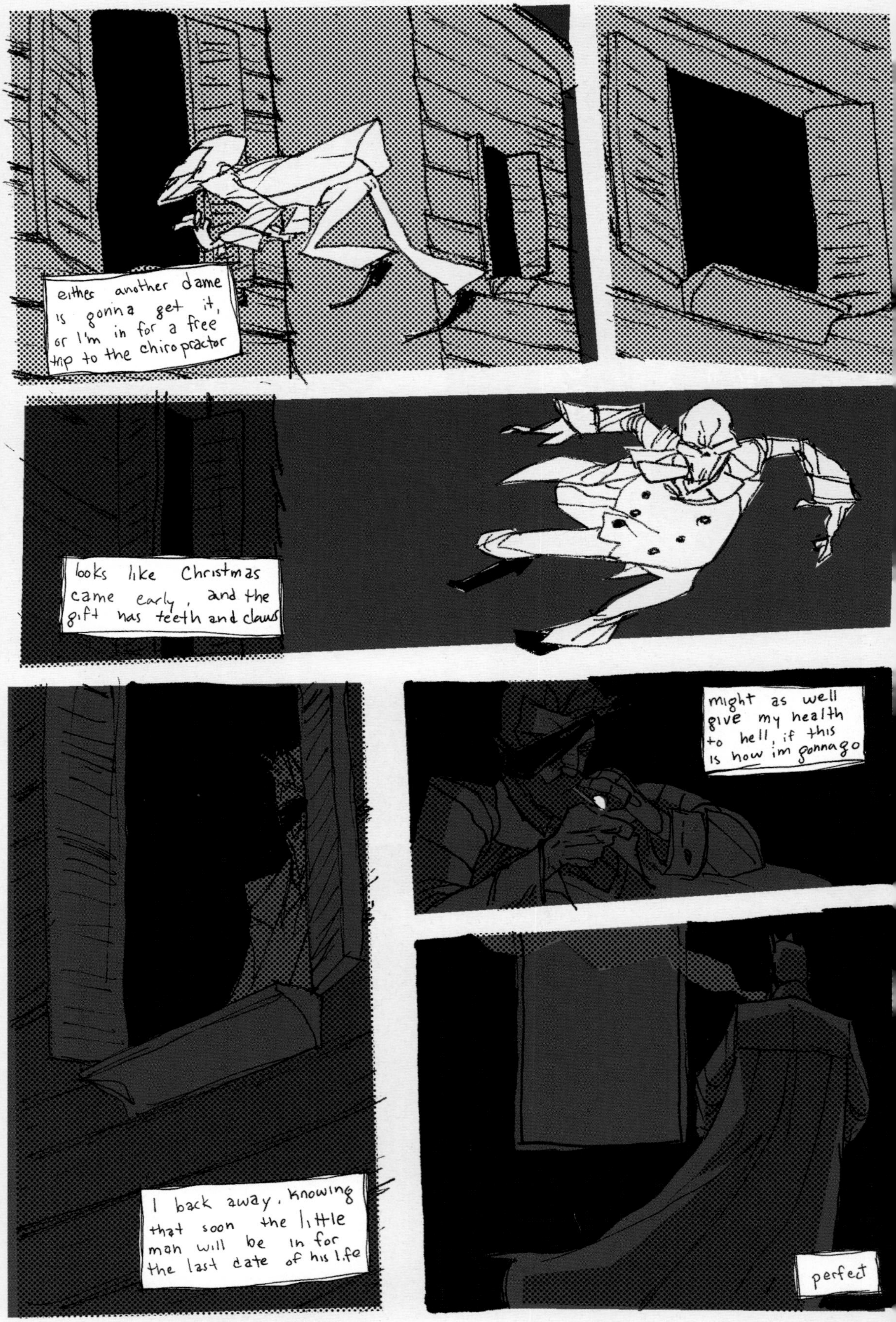
either another dame is gonna get it, or I'm in for a free trip to the chiropractor
looks like Christmas came early, and the gift has teeth and claws
I back away, knowing that soon the little man will be in for the last date of his life
might as well give my health to hell, if this is how im gonna go
perfect

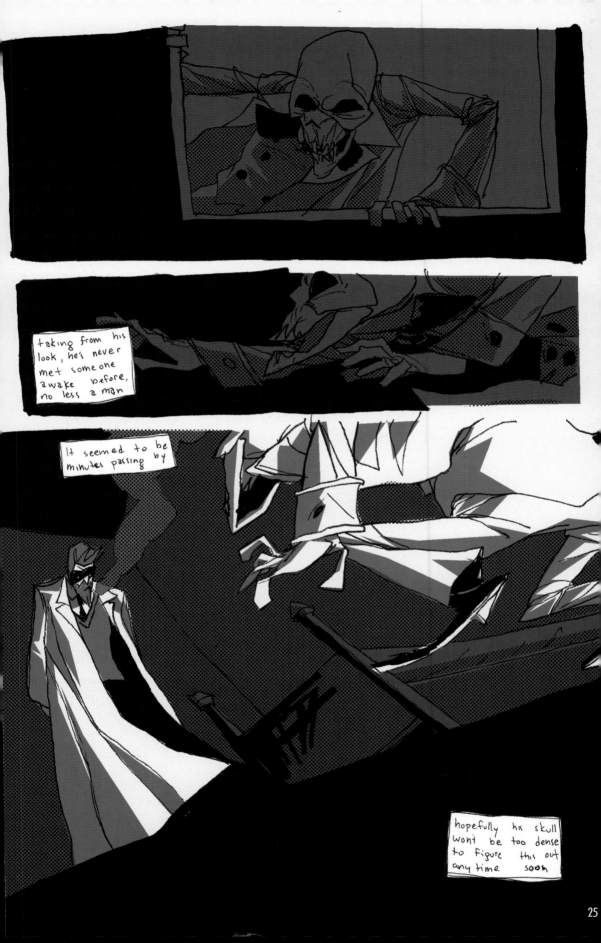

taking from his look, he's never met someone awake before, no less a man

It seemed to be minutes passing by

hopefully his skull wont be too dense to figure this out any time soon

25

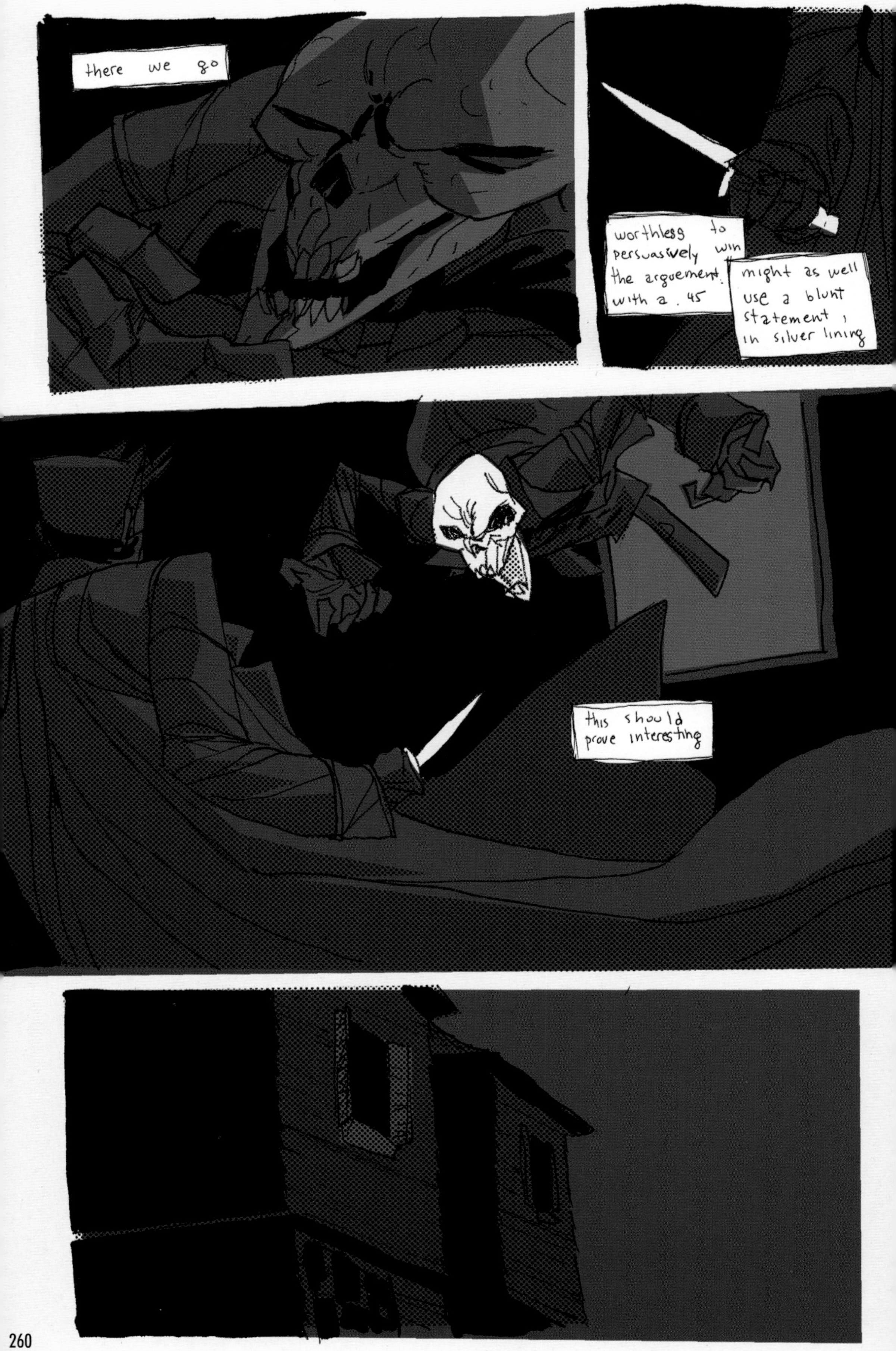
there we go
worthless to persuasively win the arguement with a .45
might as well use a blunt statement, in silver lining
this should prove interesting

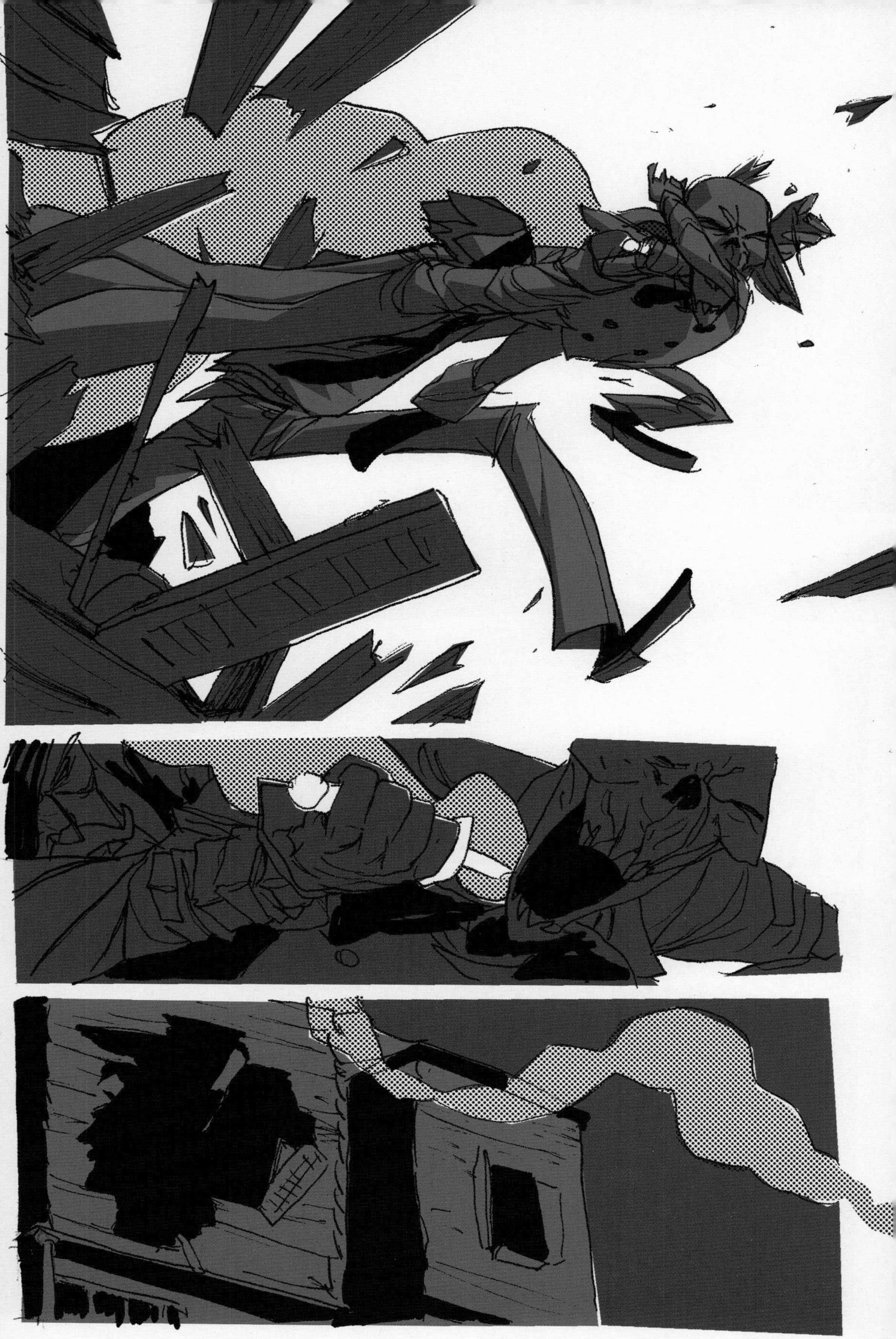

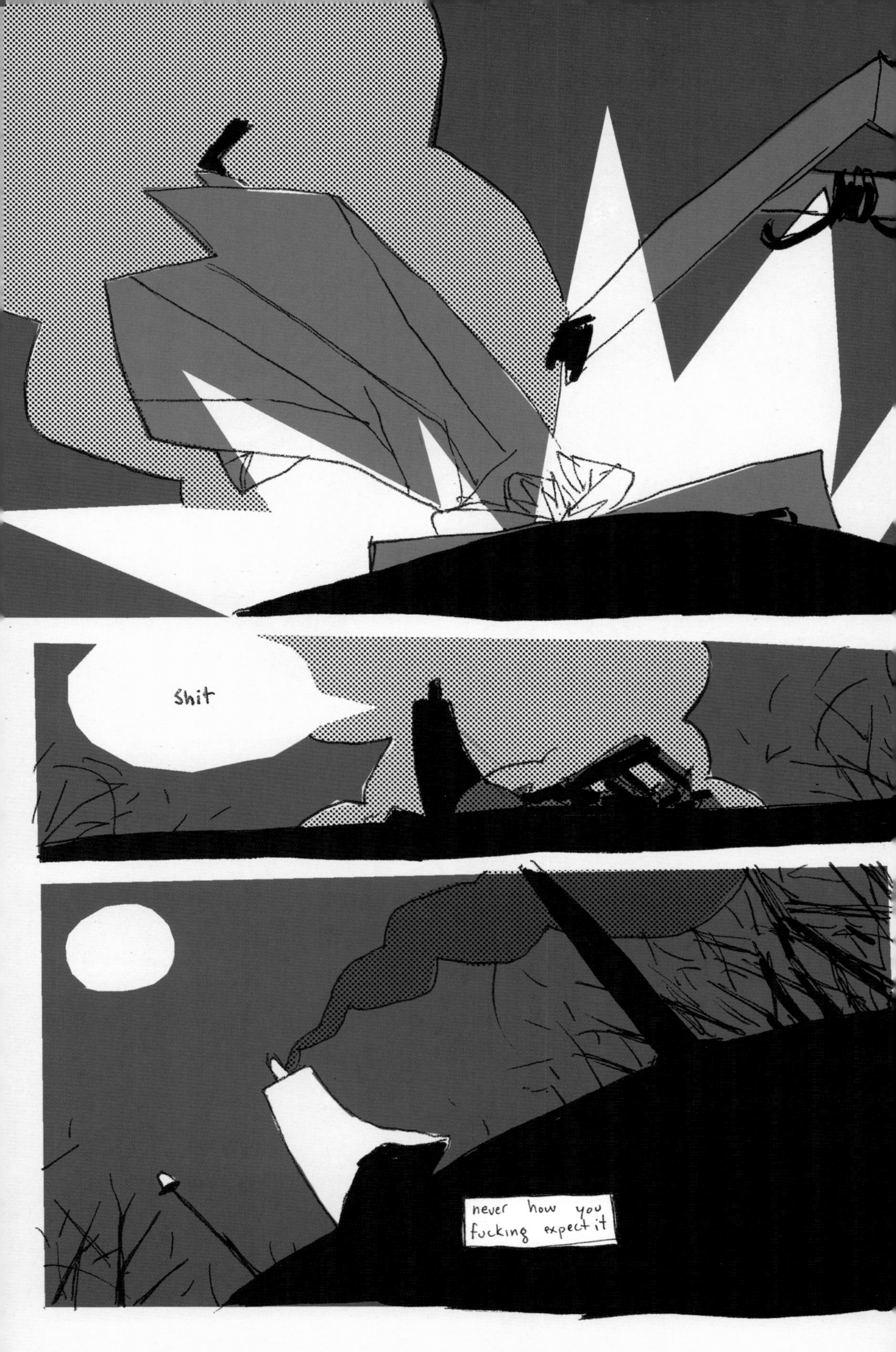
shit
never how you fucking expect it

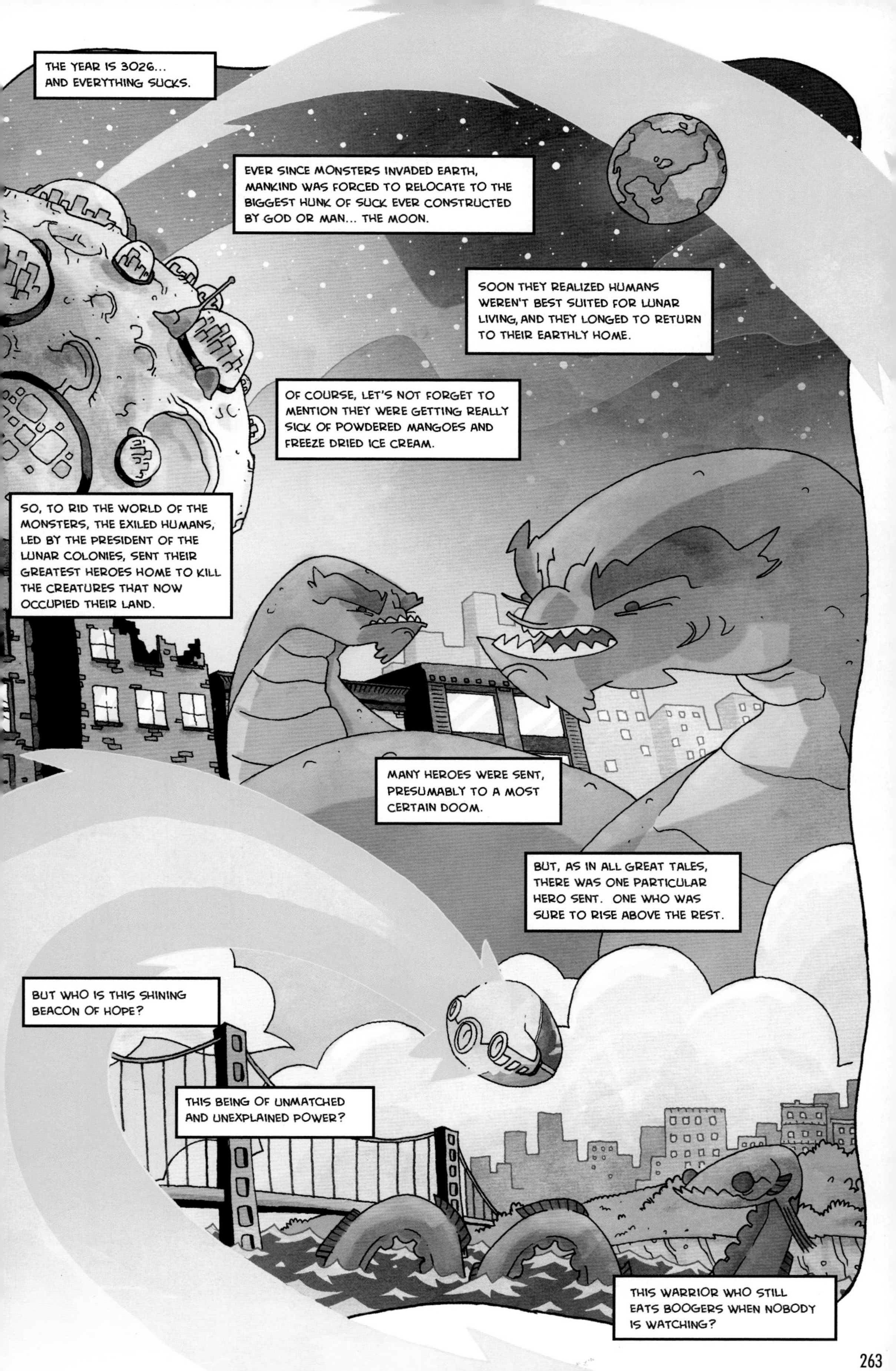
THE YEAR IS 3026...
AND EVERYTHING SUCKS.
EVER SINCE MONSTERS INVADED EARTH, MANKIND WAS FORCED TO RELOCATE TO THE BIGGEST HUNK OF SUCK EVER CONSTRUCTED BY GOD OR MAN... THE MOON.
SOON THEY REALIZED HUMANS WEREN'T BEST SUITED FOR LUNAR LIVING, AND THEY LONGED TO RETURN TO THEIR EARTHLY HOME.
OF COURSE, LET'S NOT FORGET TO MENTION THEY WERE GETTING REALLY SICK OF POWDERED MANGOES AND FREEZE DRIED ICE CREAM.
SO, TO RID THE WORLD OF THE MONSTERS, THE EXILED HUMANS, LED BY THE PRESIDENT OF THE LUNAR COLONIES, SENT THEIR GREATEST HEROES HOME TO KILL THE CREATURES THAT NOW OCCUPIED THEIR LAND.
MANY HEROES WERE SENT, PRESUMABLY TO A MOST CERTAIN DOOM.
BUT, AS IN ALL GREAT TALES, THERE WAS ONE PARTICULAR HERO SENT. ONE WHO WAS SURE TO RISE ABOVE THE REST.
BUT WHO IS THIS SHINING BEACON OF HOPE?
THIS BEING OF UNMATCHED AND UNEXPLAINED POWER?
THIS WARRIOR WHO STILL EATS BOOGERS WHEN NOBODY IS WATCHING?

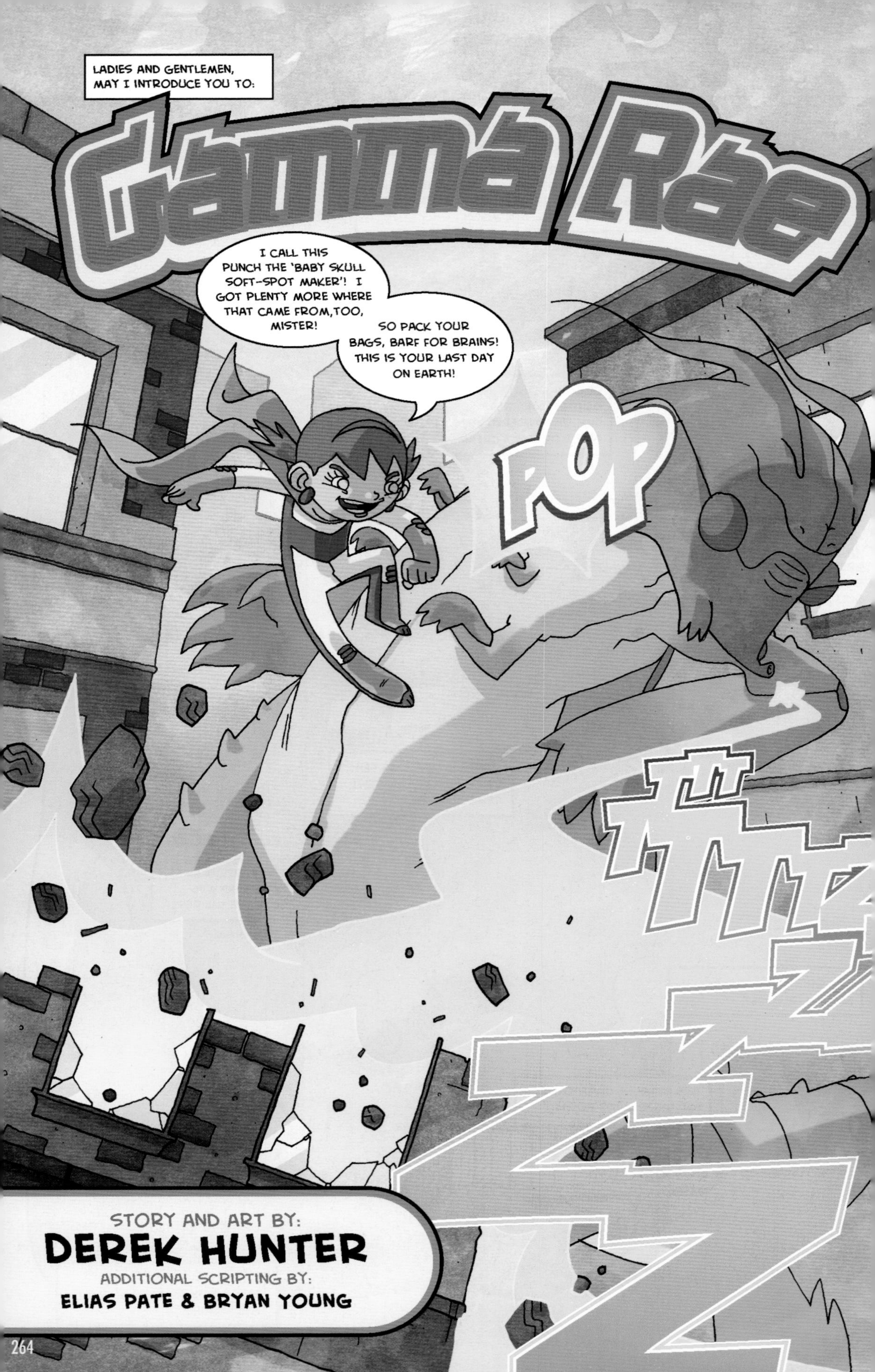
LADIES AND GENTLEMEN, MAY I INTRODUCE YOU TO:
Gamma Rae
I CALL THIS PUNCH THE 'BABY SKULL SOFT-SPOT MAKER'! I GOT PLENTY MORE WHERE THAT CAME FROM,TOO, MISTER!
SO PACK YOUR BAGS, BARF FOR BRAINS! THIS IS YOUR LAST DAY ON EARTH!
POP
STORY AND ART BY:
DEREK HUNTER
ADDITIONAL SCRIPTING BY:
ELIAS PATE & BRYAN YOUNG

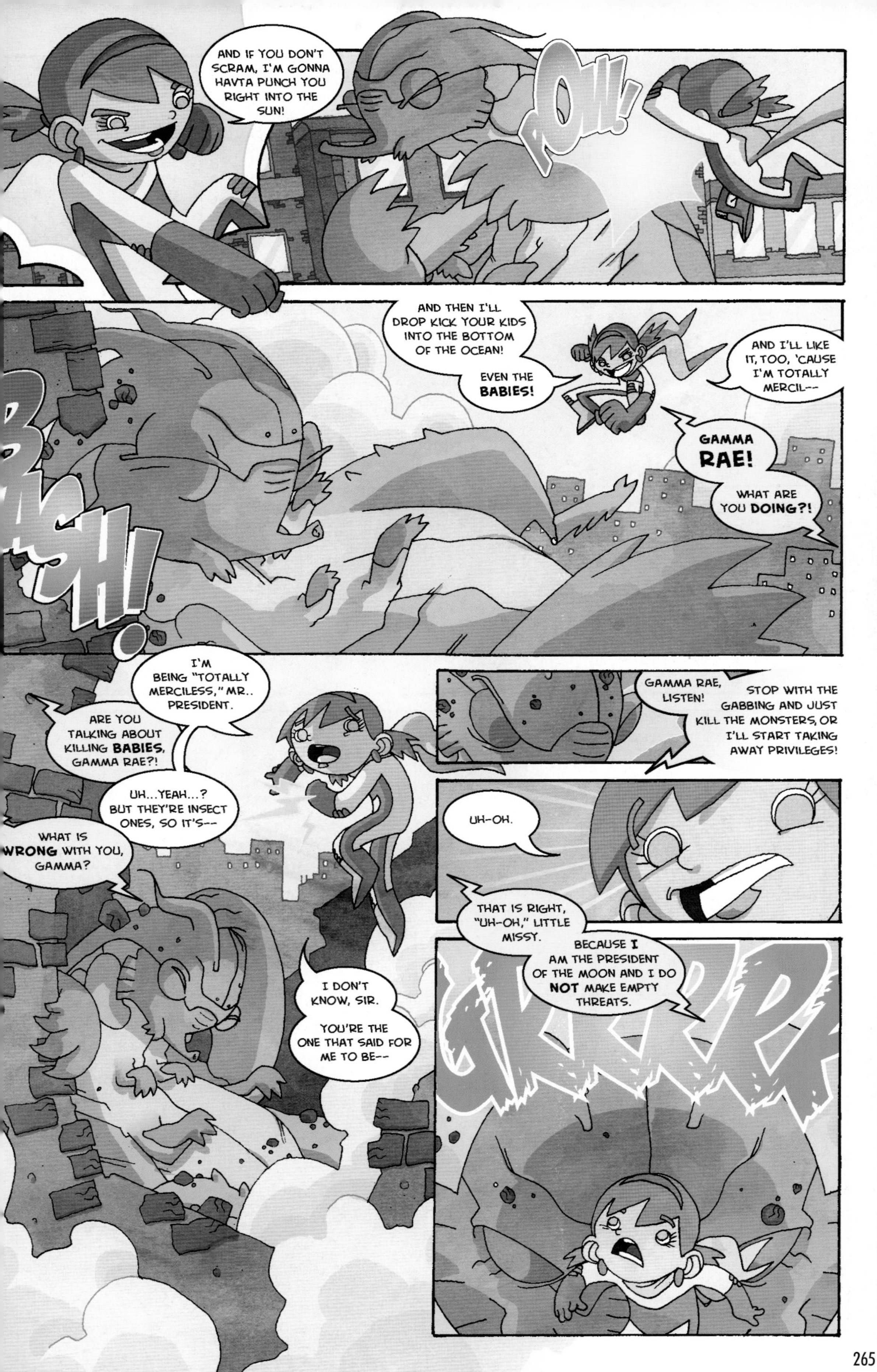
AND IF YOU DON'T SCRAM, I'M GONNA HAVTA PUNCH YOU RIGHT INTO THE SUN!
POW!
AND THEN I'LL DROP KICK YOUR KIDS INTO THE BOTTOM OF THE OCEAN!
EVEN THE BABIES!
AND I'LL LIKE IT, TOO, 'CAUSE I'M TOTALLY MERCIL--
GAMMA RAE!
WHAT ARE YOU DOING?!
I'M BEING "TOTALLY MERCILESS," MR.. PRESIDENT.
ARE YOU TALKING ABOUT KILLING BABIES, GAMMA RAE?!
UH...YEAH...? BUT THEY'RE INSECT ONES, SO IT'S--
WHAT IS WRONG WITH YOU, GAMMA?
I DON'T KNOW, SIR.
YOU'RE THE ONE THAT SAID FOR ME TO BE--
GAMMA RAE, LISTEN!
STOP WITH THE GABBING AND JUST KILL THE MONSTERS, OR I'LL START TAKING AWAY PRIVILEGES!
UH-OH.
THAT IS RIGHT, "UH-OH," LITTLE MISSY.
BECAUSE I AM THE PRESIDENT OF THE MOON AND I DO NOT MAKE EMPTY THREATS.

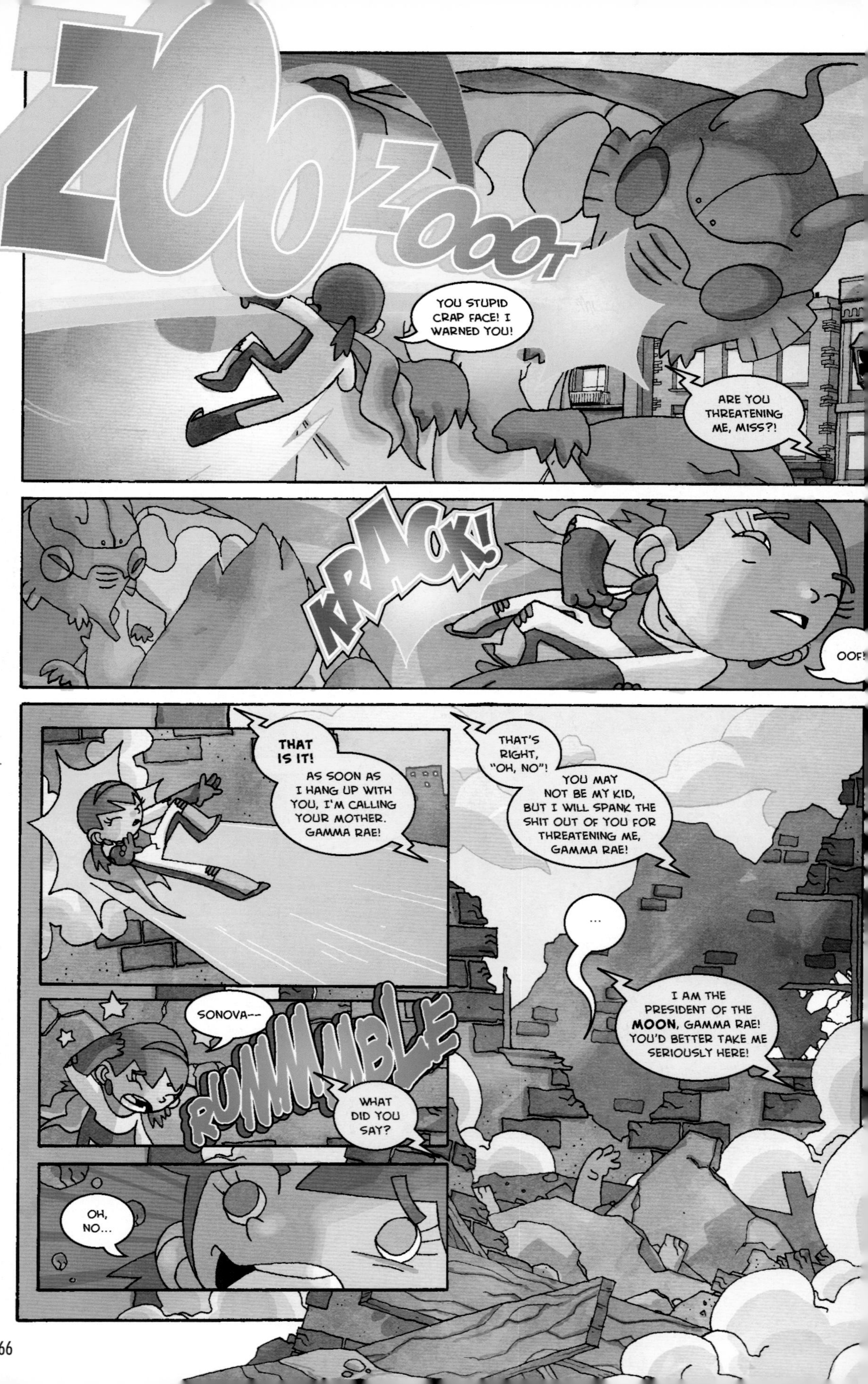
ZOOOZOOOT
YOU STUPID CRAP FACE! I WARNED YOU!
ARE YOU THREATENING ME, MISS?!
KRACK!
OOF!
THAT IS IT!
AS SOON AS I HANG UP WITH YOU, I'M CALLING YOUR MOTHER. GAMMA RAE!
THAT'S RIGHT, "OH, NO"!
YOU MAY NOT BE MY KID, BUT I WILL SPANK THE SHIT OUT OF YOU FOR THREATENING ME, GAMMA RAE!
...
I AM THE PRESIDENT OF THE MOON, GAMMA RAE! YOU'D BETTER TAKE ME SERIOUSLY HERE!
SONOVA--
RUMMMBLE
WHAT DID YOU SAY?
OH, NO...

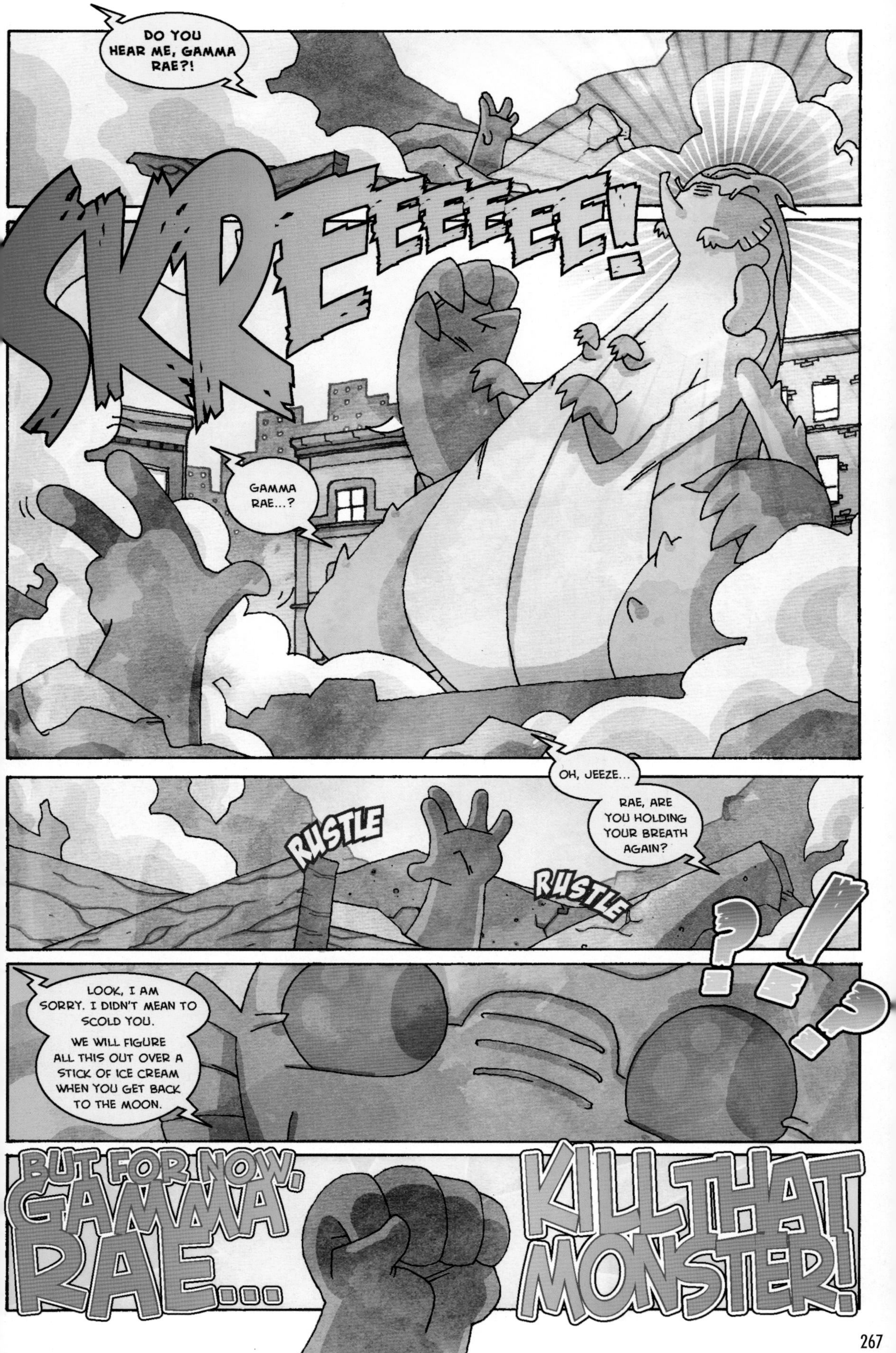
DO YOU HEAR ME, GAMMA RAE?!
SKREEEEEEE!
GAMMA RAE...?
OH, JEEZE...
RAE, ARE YOU HOLDING YOUR BREATH AGAIN?
RUSTLE
RUSTLE
?!
LOOK, I AM SORRY. I DIDN'T MEAN TO SCOLD YOU.
WE WILL FIGURE ALL THIS OUT OVER A STICK OF ICE CREAM WHEN YOU GET BACK TO THE MOON.
?!?
BUT FOR NOW, GAMMA RAE...
KILL THAT MONSTER!

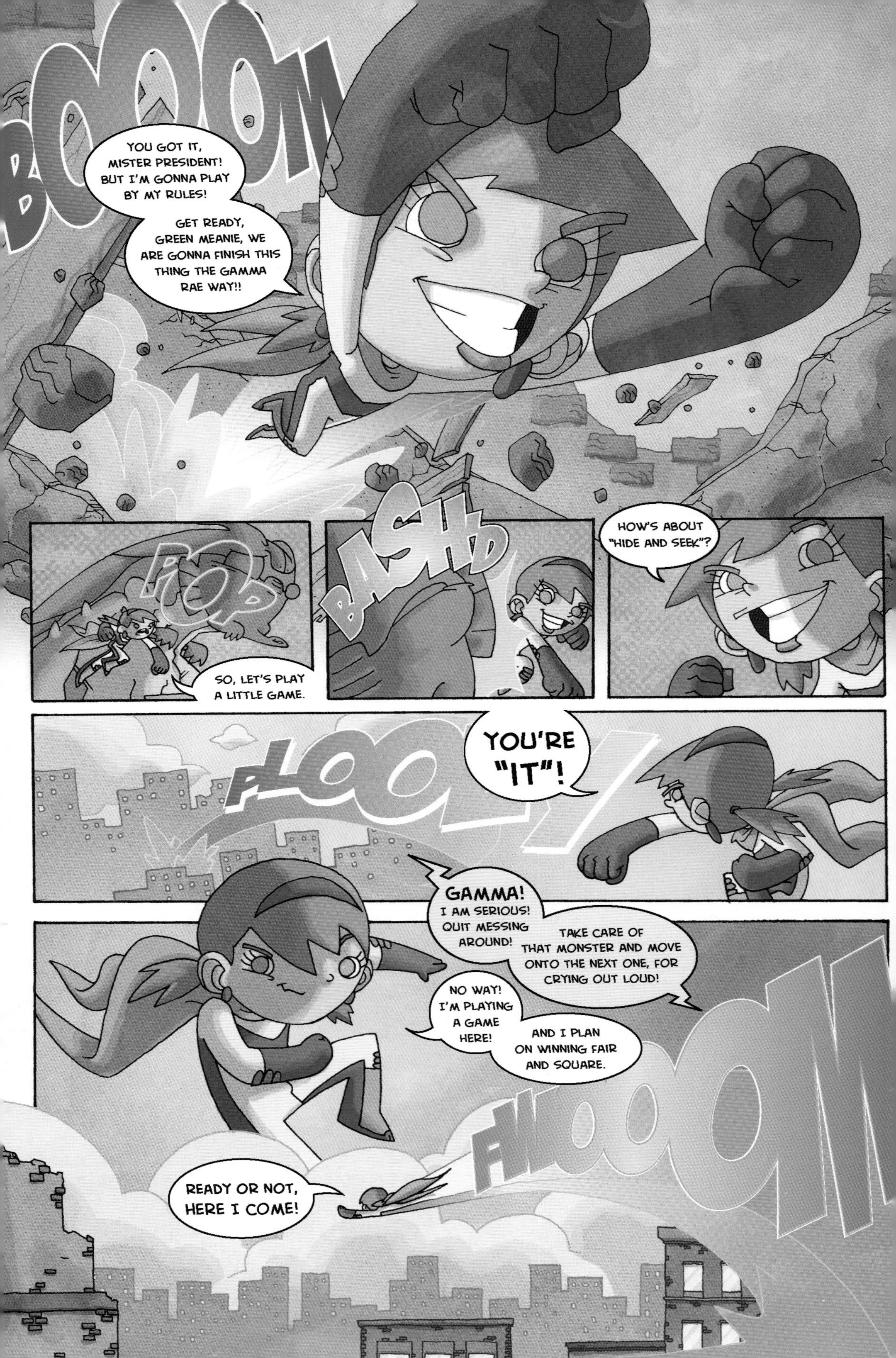
BOOOM
YOU GOT IT, MISTER PRESIDENT! BUT I'M GONNA PLAY BY MY RULES!
GET READY, GREEN MEANIE, WE ARE GONNA FINISH THIS THING THE GAMMA RAE WAY!!
POP
SO, LET'S PLAY A LITTLE GAME.
BASHD
HOW'S ABOUT "HIDE AND SEEK"?
YOU'RE "IT"!
GAMMA! I AM SERIOUS! QUIT MESSING AROUND!
TAKE CARE OF THAT MONSTER AND MOVE ONTO THE NEXT ONE, FOR CRYING OUT LOUD!
NO WAY! I'M PLAYING A GAME HERE!
AND I PLAN ON WINNING FAIR AND SQUARE.
READY OR NOT, HERE I COME!

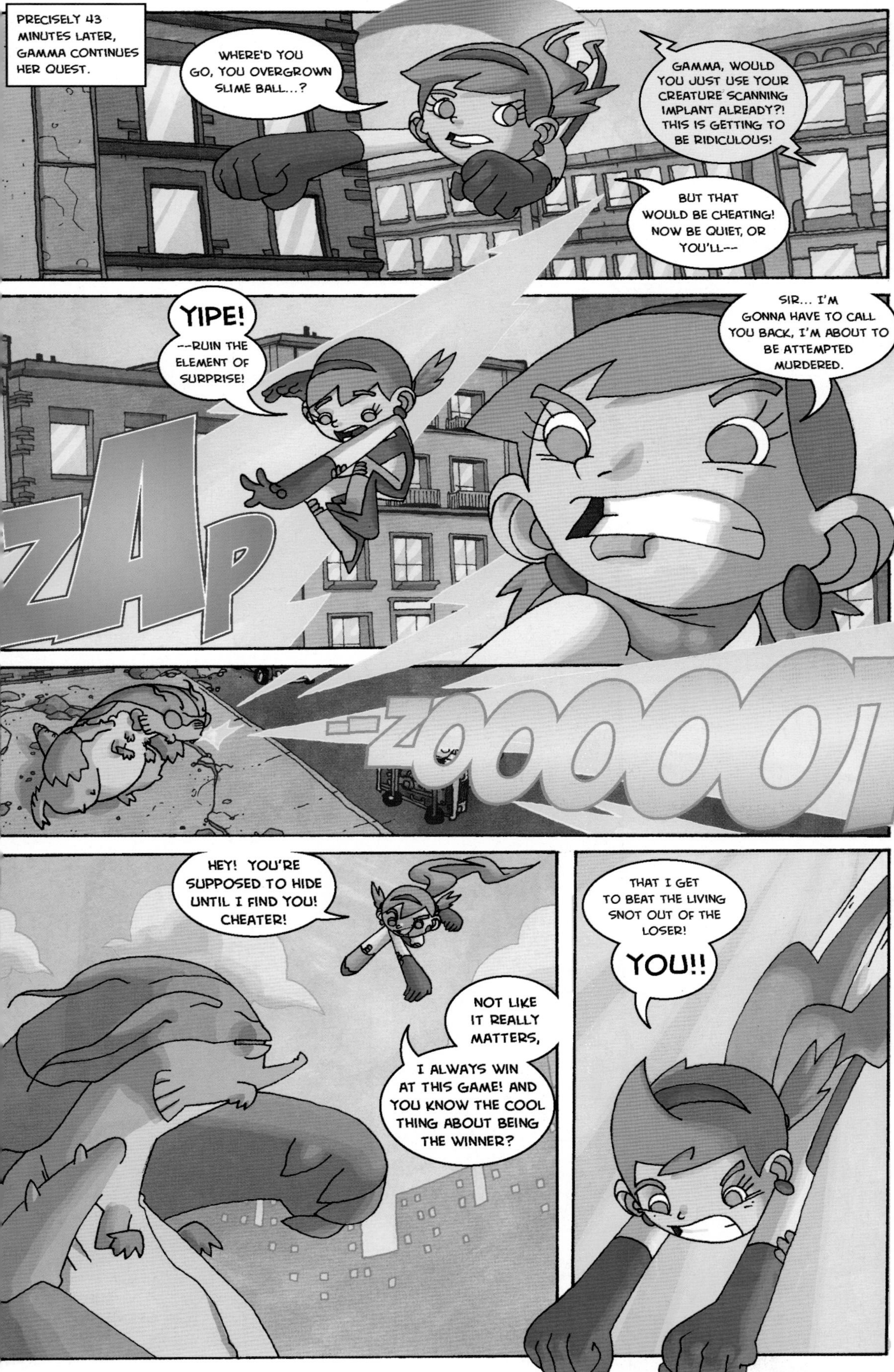
PRECISELY 43 MINUTES LATER, GAMMA CONTINUES HER QUEST.
WHERE'D YOU GO, YOU OVERGROWN SLIME BALL...?
GAMMA, WOULD YOU JUST USE YOUR CREATURE SCANNING IMPLANT ALREADY?! THIS IS GETTING TO BE RIDICULOUS!
BUT THAT WOULD BE CHEATING! NOW BE QUIET, OR YOU'LL--
YIPE!
--RUIN THE ELEMENT OF SURPRISE!
SIR... I'M GONNA HAVE TO CALL YOU BACK, I'M ABOUT TO BE ATTEMPTED MURDERED.
ZAP
ZOOOOOT
HEY! YOU'RE SUPPOSED TO HIDE UNTIL I FIND YOU! CHEATER!
NOT LIKE IT REALLY MATTERS,
I ALWAYS WIN AT THIS GAME! AND YOU KNOW THE COOL THING ABOUT BEING THE WINNER?
THAT I GET TO BEAT THE LIVING SNOT OUT OF THE LOSER!
YOU!!

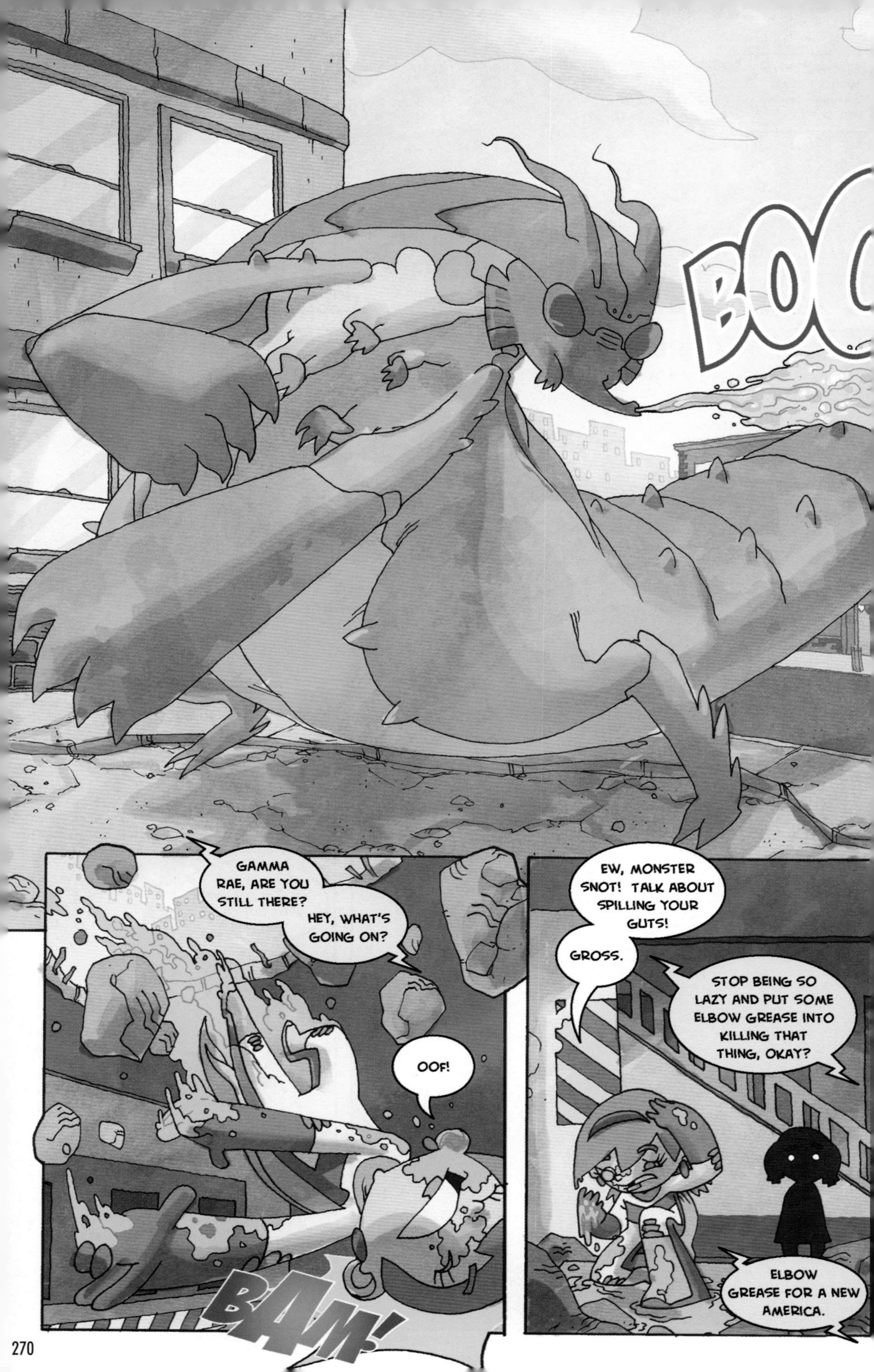
BOO
GAMMA RAE, ARE YOU STILL THERE?
HEY, WHAT'S GOING ON?
OOF!
BAM!
EW, MONSTER SNOT! TALK ABOUT SPILLING YOUR GUTS!
GROSS.
STOP BEING SO LAZY AND PUT SOME ELBOW GREASE INTO KILLING THAT THING, OKAY?
ELBOW GREASE FOR A NEW AMERICA.

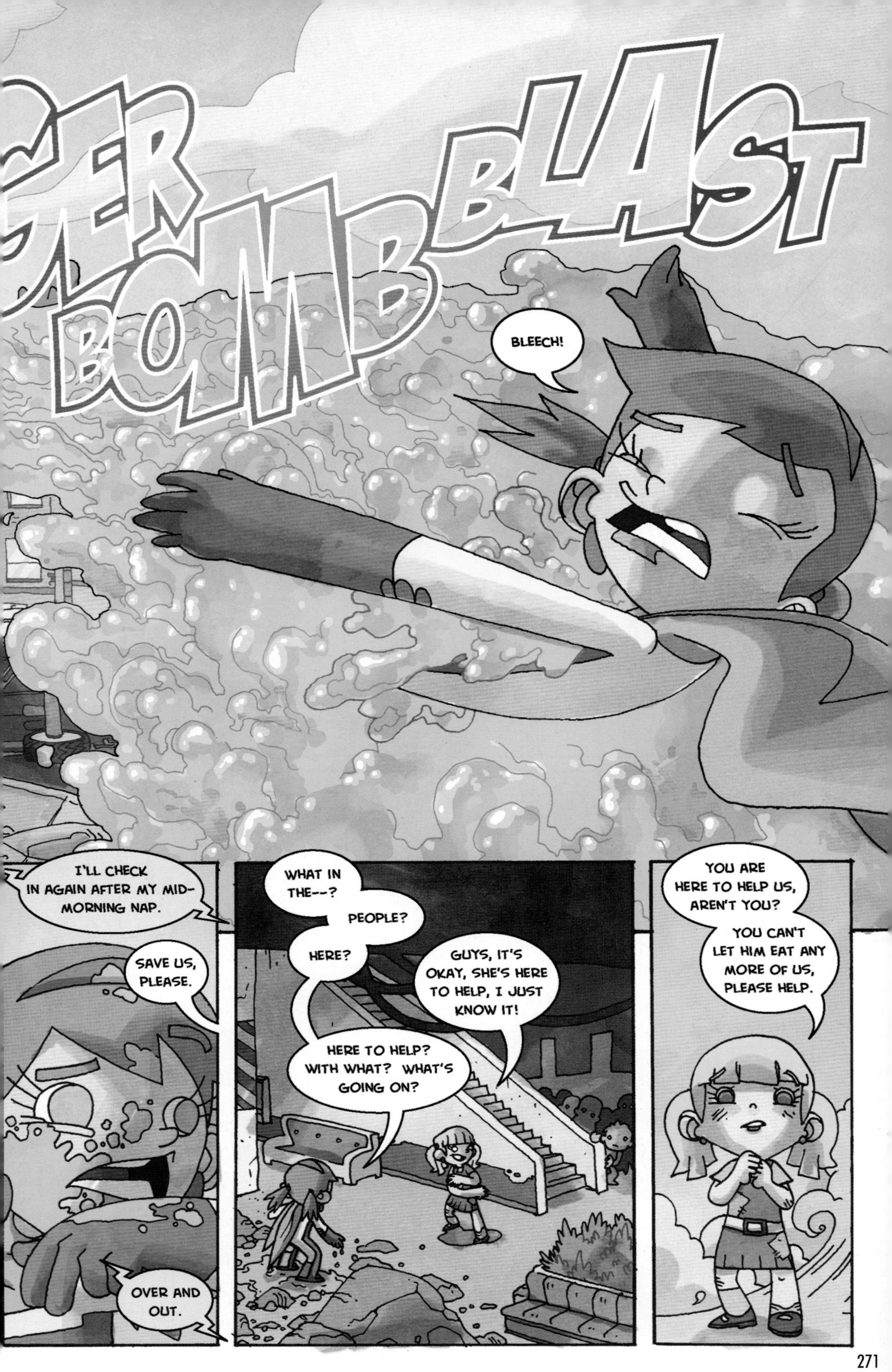

GER BOMBBLAST
BLEECH!
I'LL CHECK IN AGAIN AFTER MY MID-MORNING NAP.
SAVE US, PLEASE.
OVER AND OUT.
WHAT IN THE--?
PEOPLE?
HERE?
GUYS, IT'S OKAY, SHE'S HERE TO HELP, I JUST KNOW IT!
HERE TO HELP? WITH WHAT? WHAT'S GOING ON?
YOU ARE HERE TO HELP US, AREN'T YOU?
YOU CAN'T LET HIM EAT ANY MORE OF US, PLEASE HELP.

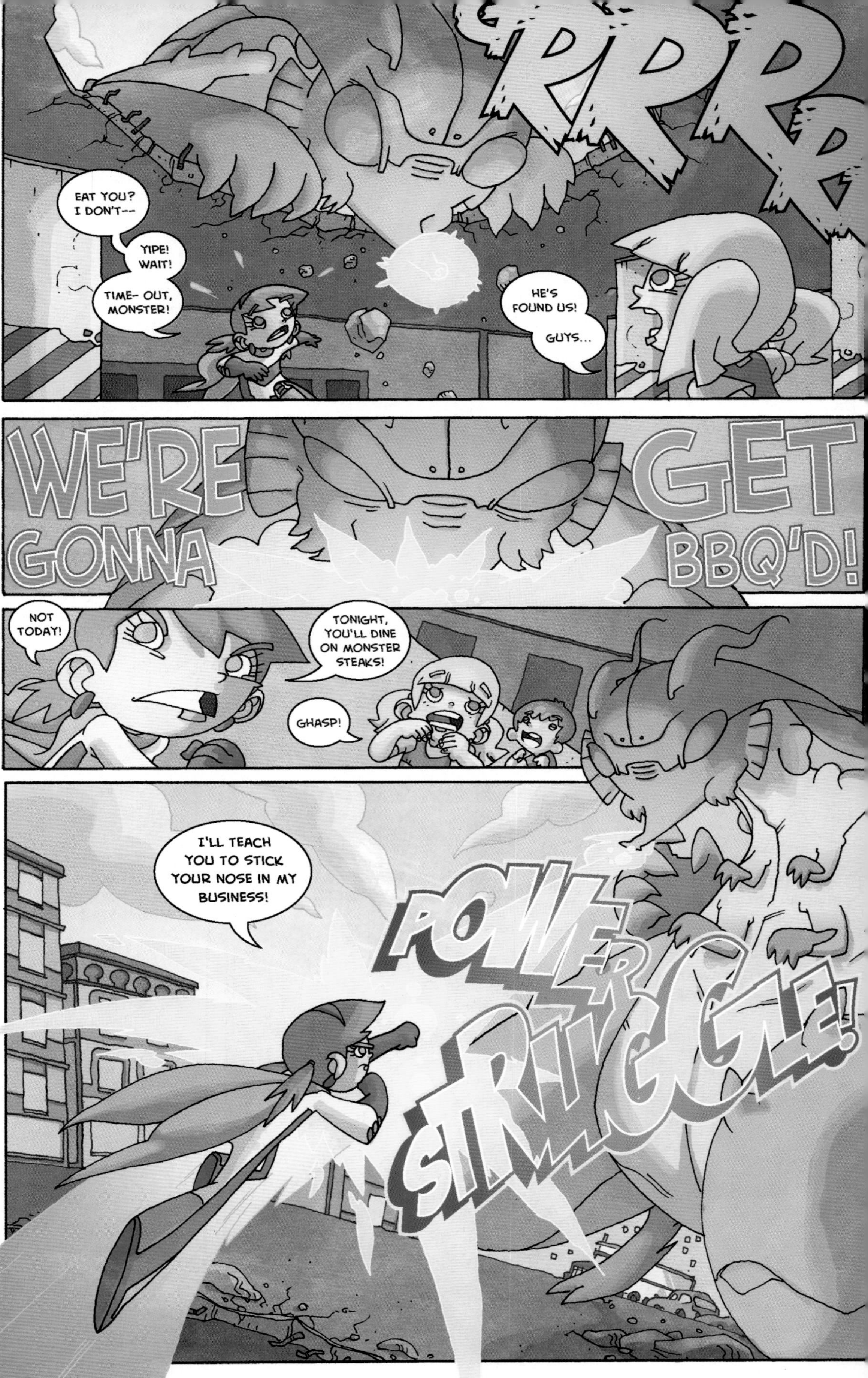
RRRR
EAT YOU? I DON'T--
YIPE! WAIT!
TIME- OUT, MONSTER!
HE'S FOUND US!
GUYS...
WE'RE GONNA GET BBQ'D!
NOT TODAY!
TONIGHT, YOU'LL DINE ON MONSTER STEAKS!
GHASP!
I'LL TEACH YOU TO STICK YOUR NOSE IN MY BUSINESS!
POWER STRUGGLE!

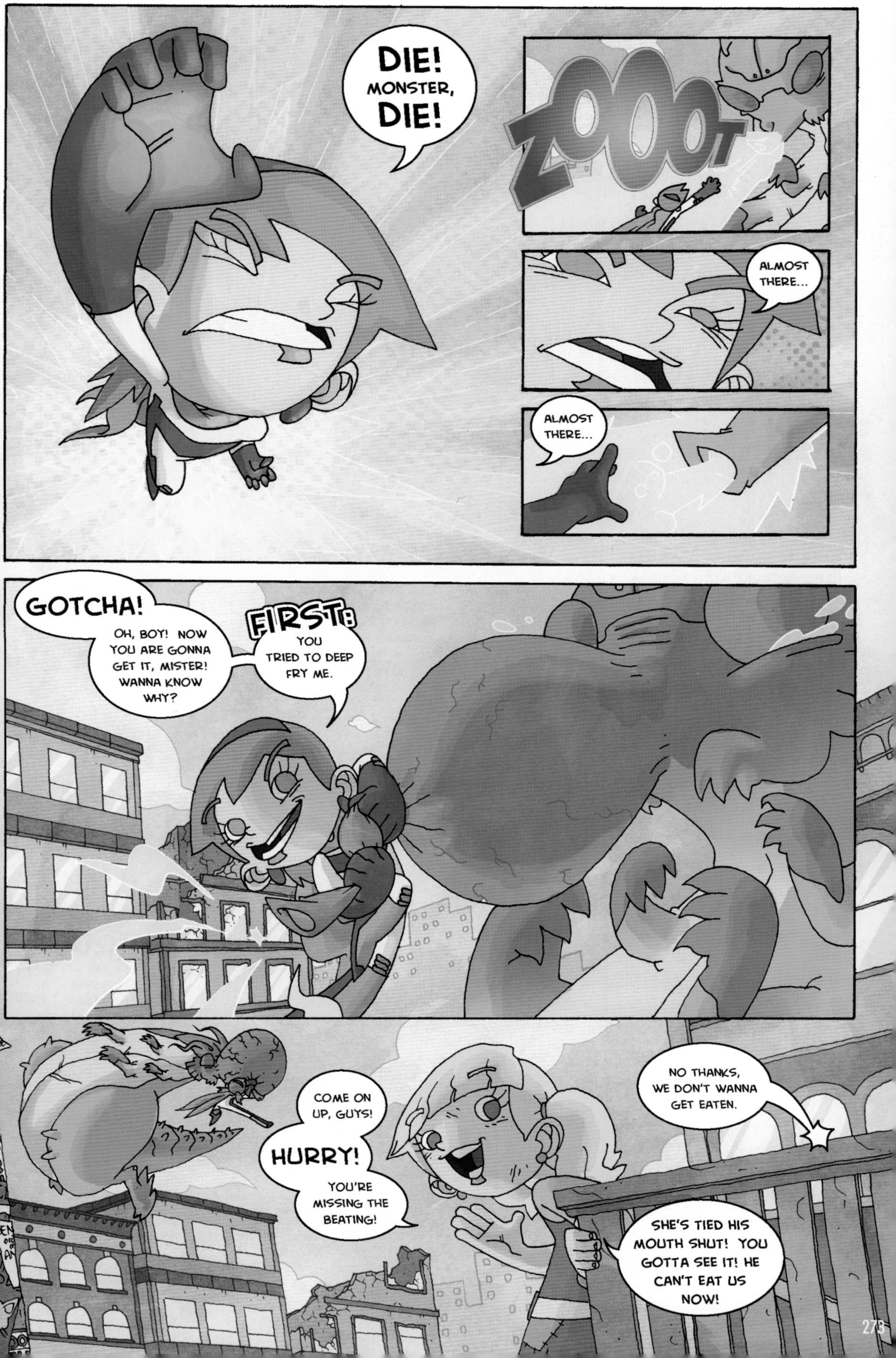
DIE! MONSTER, DIE!
ZOOOT
ALMOST THERE...
ALMOST THERE...
GOTCHA!
OH, BOY! NOW YOU ARE GONNA GET IT, MISTER! WANNA KNOW WHY?
FIRST:
YOU TRIED TO DEEP FRY ME.
COME ON UP, GUYS!
HURRY!
YOU'RE MISSING THE BEATING!
NO THANKS, WE DON'T WANNA GET EATEN.
SHE'S TIED HIS MOUTH SHUT! YOU GOTTA SEE IT! HE CAN'T EAT US NOW!

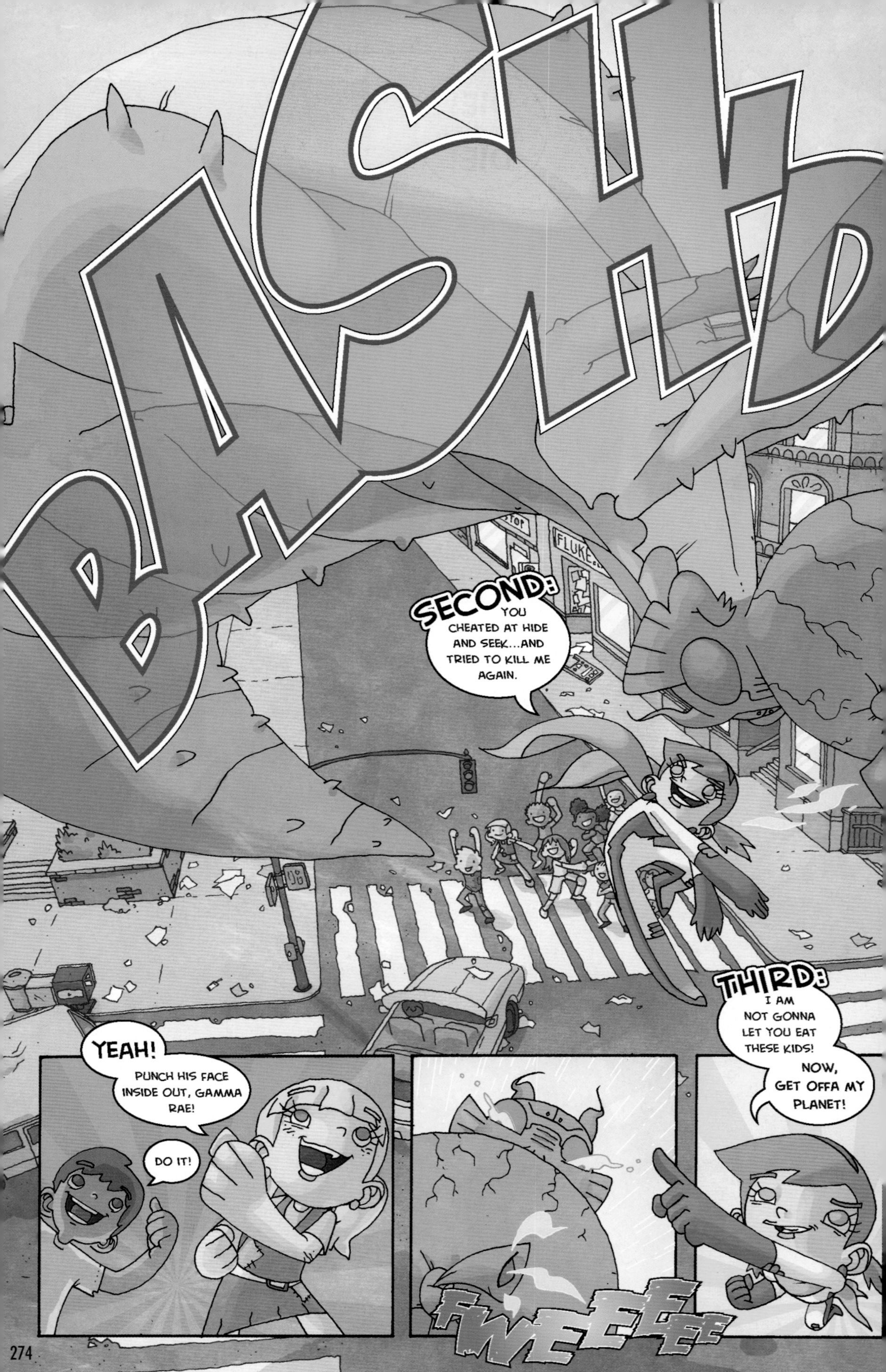
BASHHD
SECOND: YOU CHEATED AT HIDE AND SEEK...AND TRIED TO KILL ME AGAIN.
STOP
FLUKE
THIRD: I AM NOT GONNA LET YOU EAT THESE KIDS!
YEAH! PUNCH HIS FACE INSIDE OUT, GAMMA RAE!
DO IT!
NOW, GET OFFA MY PLANET!
FWEEEEE

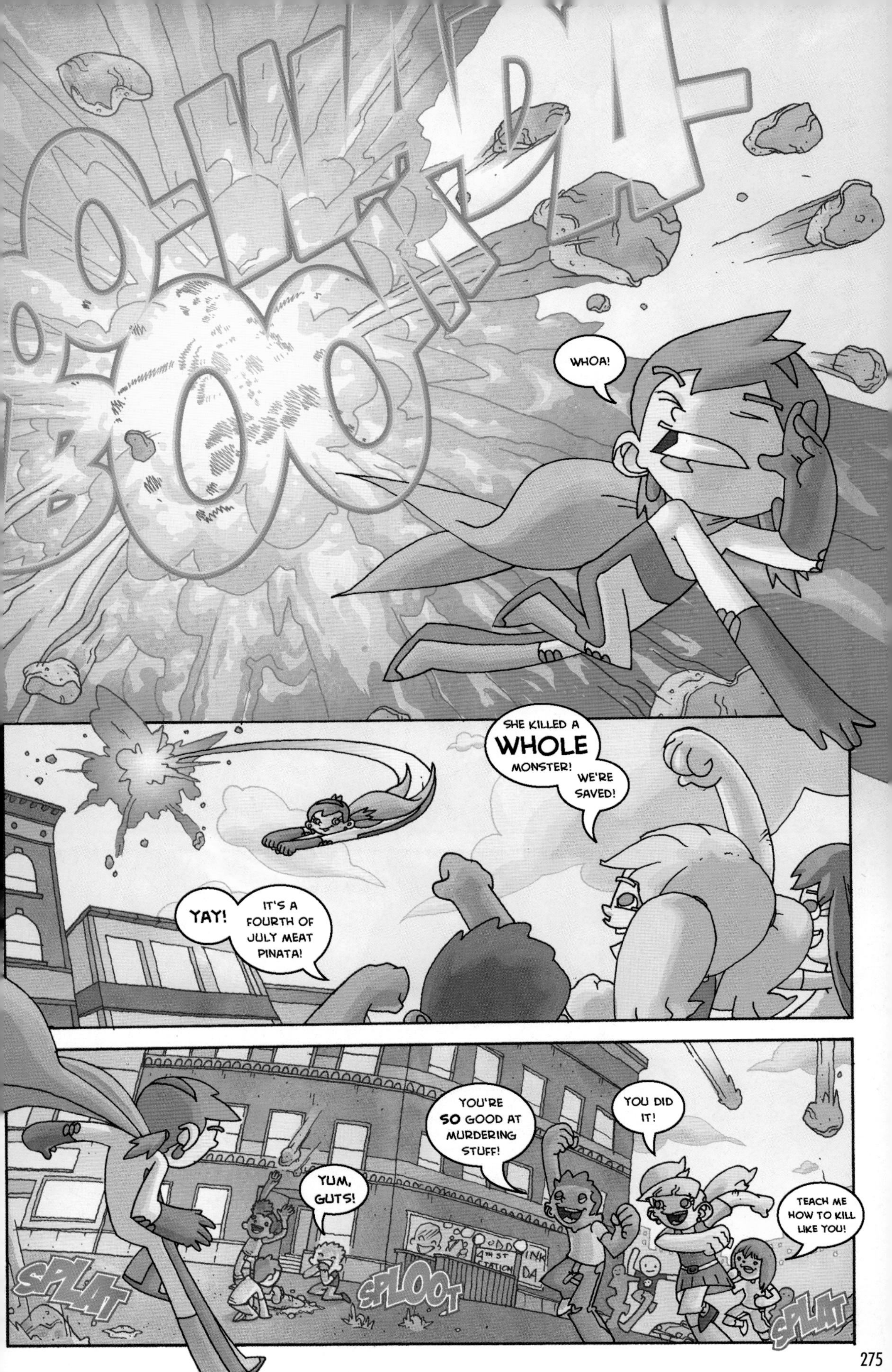
WHOA!
SHE KILLED A WHOLE MONSTER!
WE'RE SAVED!
YAY!
IT'S A FOURTH OF JULY MEAT PINATA!
SPLAT
YUM, GUTS!
SPLOOT
YOU'RE SO GOOD AT MURDERING STUFF!
YOU DID IT!
TEACH ME HOW TO KILL LIKE YOU!
SPLAT

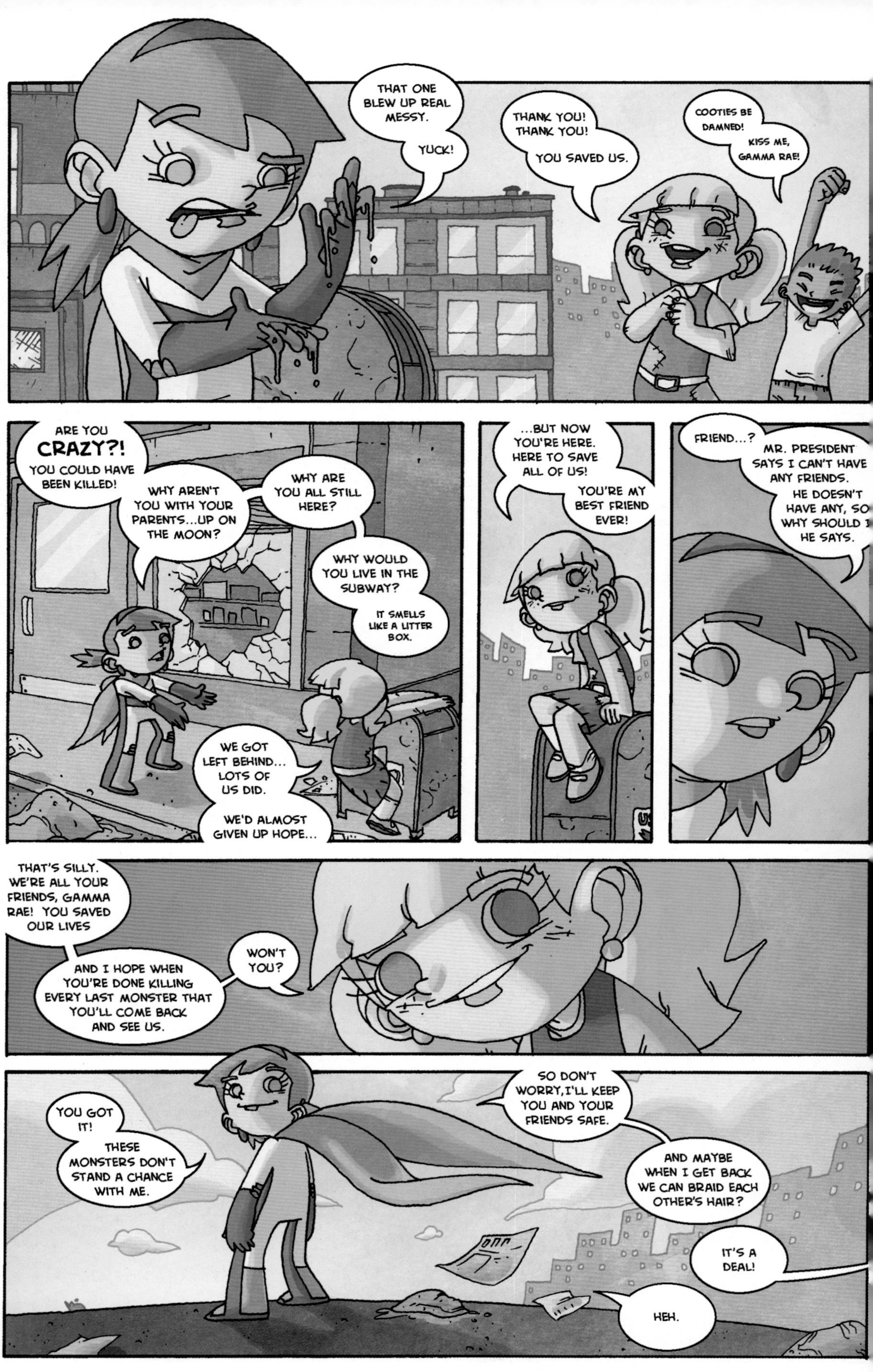
THAT ONE BLEW UP REAL MESSY.
YUCK!
THANK YOU! THANK YOU!
YOU SAVED US.
COOTIES BE DAMNED!
KISS ME, GAMMA RAE!
ARE YOU CRAZY?!
YOU COULD HAVE BEEN KILLED!
WHY AREN'T YOU WITH YOUR PARENTS...UP ON THE MOON?
WHY ARE YOU ALL STILL HERE?
WHY WOULD YOU LIVE IN THE SUBWAY?
IT SMELLS LIKE A LITTER BOX.
WE GOT LEFT BEHIND... LOTS OF US DID.
WE'D ALMOST GIVEN UP HOPE...
...BUT NOW YOU'RE HERE. HERE TO SAVE ALL OF US!
YOU'RE MY BEST FRIEND EVER!
FRIEND...?
MR. PRESIDENT SAYS I CAN'T HAVE ANY FRIENDS.
HE DOESN'T HAVE ANY, SO WHY SHOULD I HE SAYS.
THAT'S SILLY. WE'RE ALL YOUR FRIENDS, GAMMA RAE! YOU SAVED OUR LIVES
AND I HOPE WHEN YOU'RE DONE KILLING EVERY LAST MONSTER THAT YOU'LL COME BACK AND SEE US.
WON'T YOU?
YOU GOT IT!
THESE MONSTERS DON'T STAND A CHANCE WITH ME.
SO DON'T WORRY, I'LL KEEP YOU AND YOUR FRIENDS SAFE.
AND MAYBE WHEN I GET BACK WE CAN BRAID EACH OTHER'S HAIR?
IT'S A DEAL!
HEH.

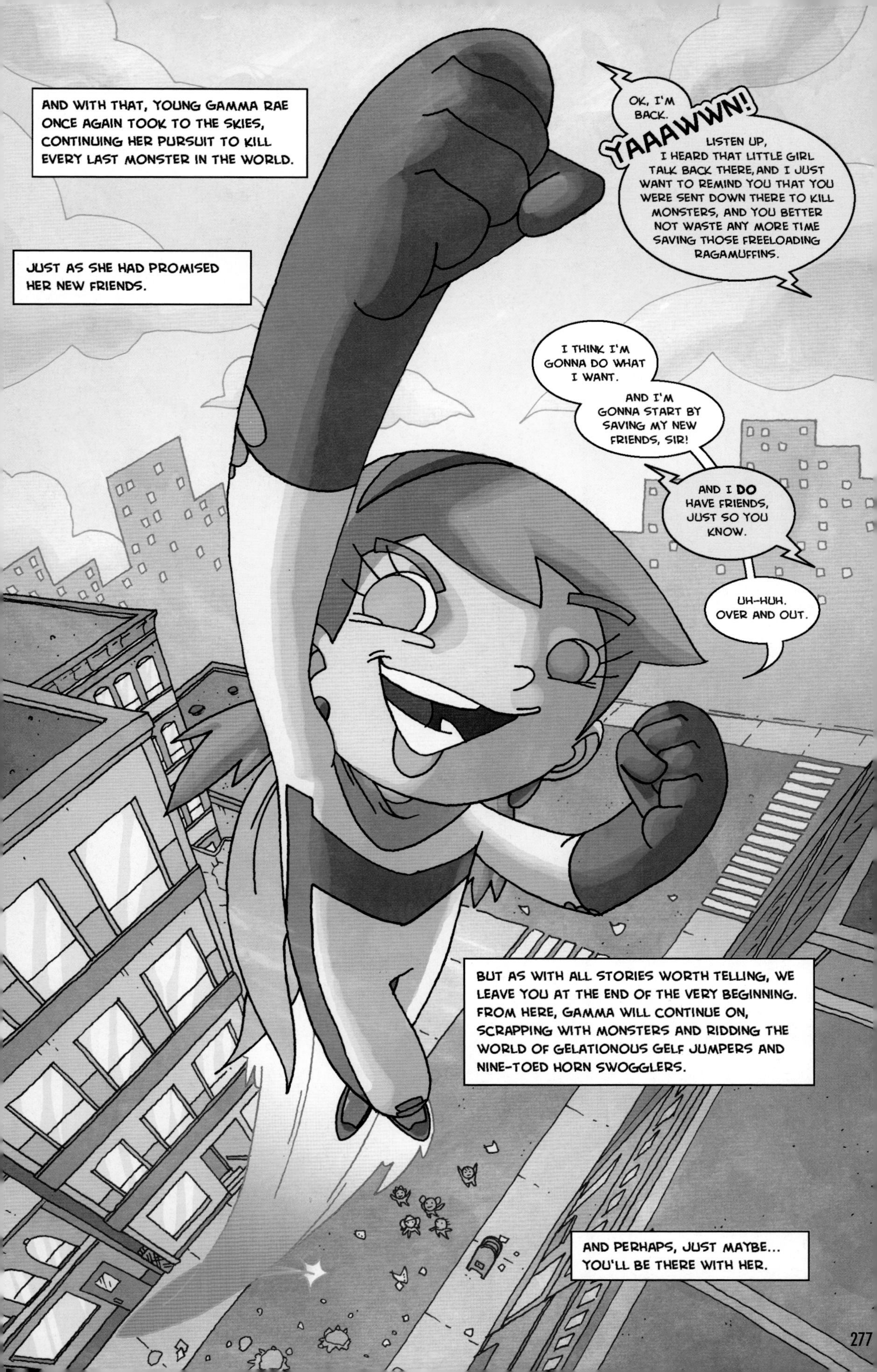
AND WITH THAT, YOUNG GAMMA RAE ONCE AGAIN TOOK TO THE SKIES, CONTINUING HER PURSUIT TO KILL EVERY LAST MONSTER IN THE WORLD.
OK, I'M BACK.
YAAAWWN!
LISTEN UP, I HEARD THAT LITTLE GIRL TALK BACK THERE, AND I JUST WANT TO REMIND YOU THAT YOU WERE SENT DOWN THERE TO KILL MONSTERS, AND YOU BETTER NOT WASTE ANY MORE TIME SAVING THOSE FREELOADING RAGAMUFFINS.
JUST AS SHE HAD PROMISED HER NEW FRIENDS.
I THINK I'M GONNA DO WHAT I WANT.
AND I'M GONNA START BY SAVING MY NEW FRIENDS, SIR!
AND I **DO** HAVE FRIENDS, JUST SO YOU KNOW.
UH-HUH. OVER AND OUT.
BUT AS WITH ALL STORIES WORTH TELLING, WE LEAVE YOU AT THE END OF THE VERY BEGINNING. FROM HERE, GAMMA WILL CONTINUE ON, SCRAPPING WITH MONSTERS AND RIDDING THE WORLD OF GELATIONOUS GELF JUMPERS AND NINE-TOED HORN SWOGGLERS.
AND PERHAPS, JUST MAYBE... YOU'LL BE THERE WITH HER.

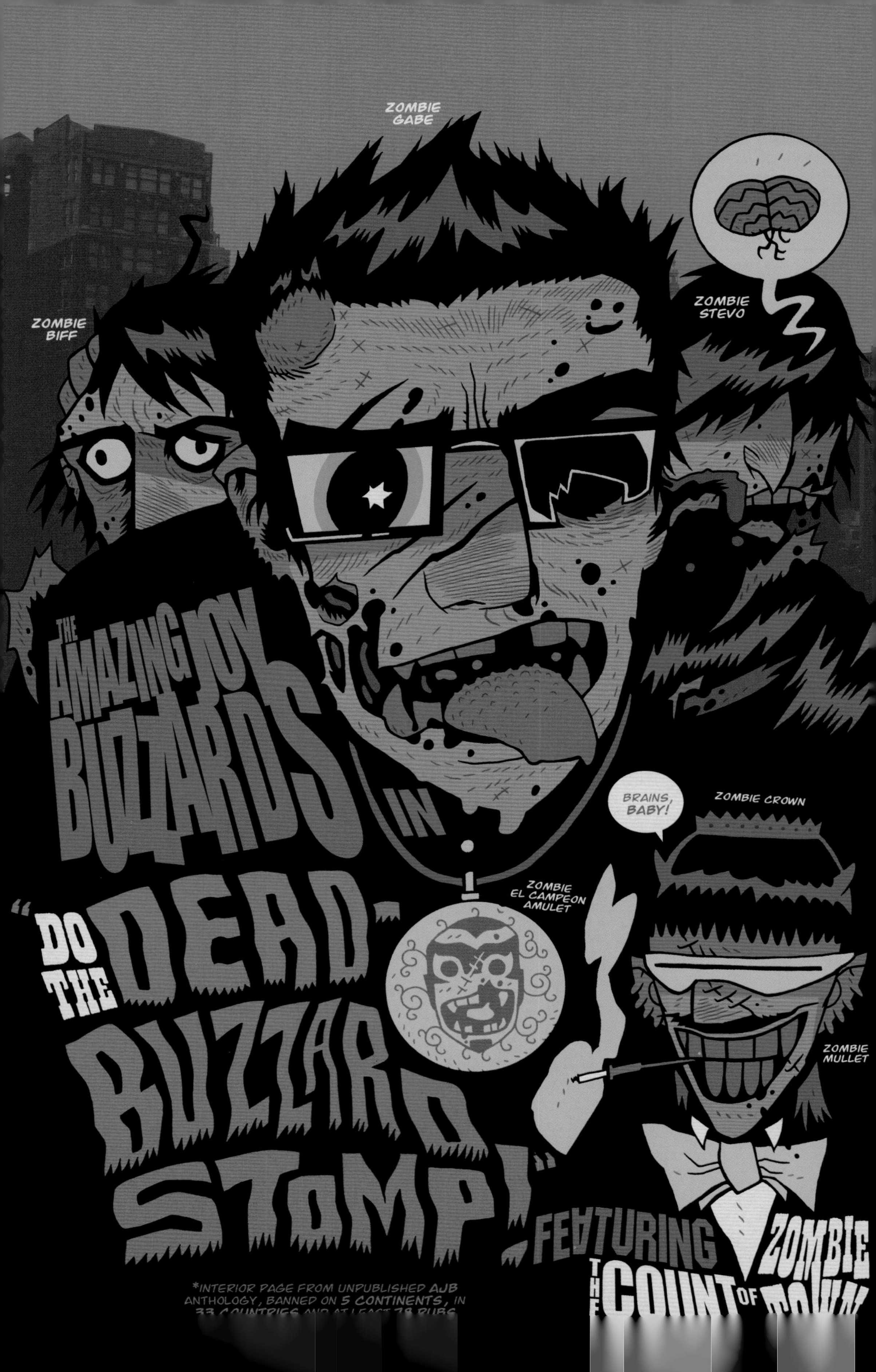
ZOMBIE GABE
ZOMBIE BIFF
ZOMBIE STEVO
THE AMAZING JOY BUZZARDS IN
BRAINS, BABY!
ZOMBIE CROWN
ZOMBIE EL CAMPEON AMULET
"DO THE DEAD-BUZZARD STOMP!"
ZOMBIE MULLET
FEATURING THE COUNT OF ZOMBIE TOWN
*INTERIOR PAGE FROM UNPUBLISHED AJB ANTHOLOGY, BANNED ON 5 CONTINENTS, IN

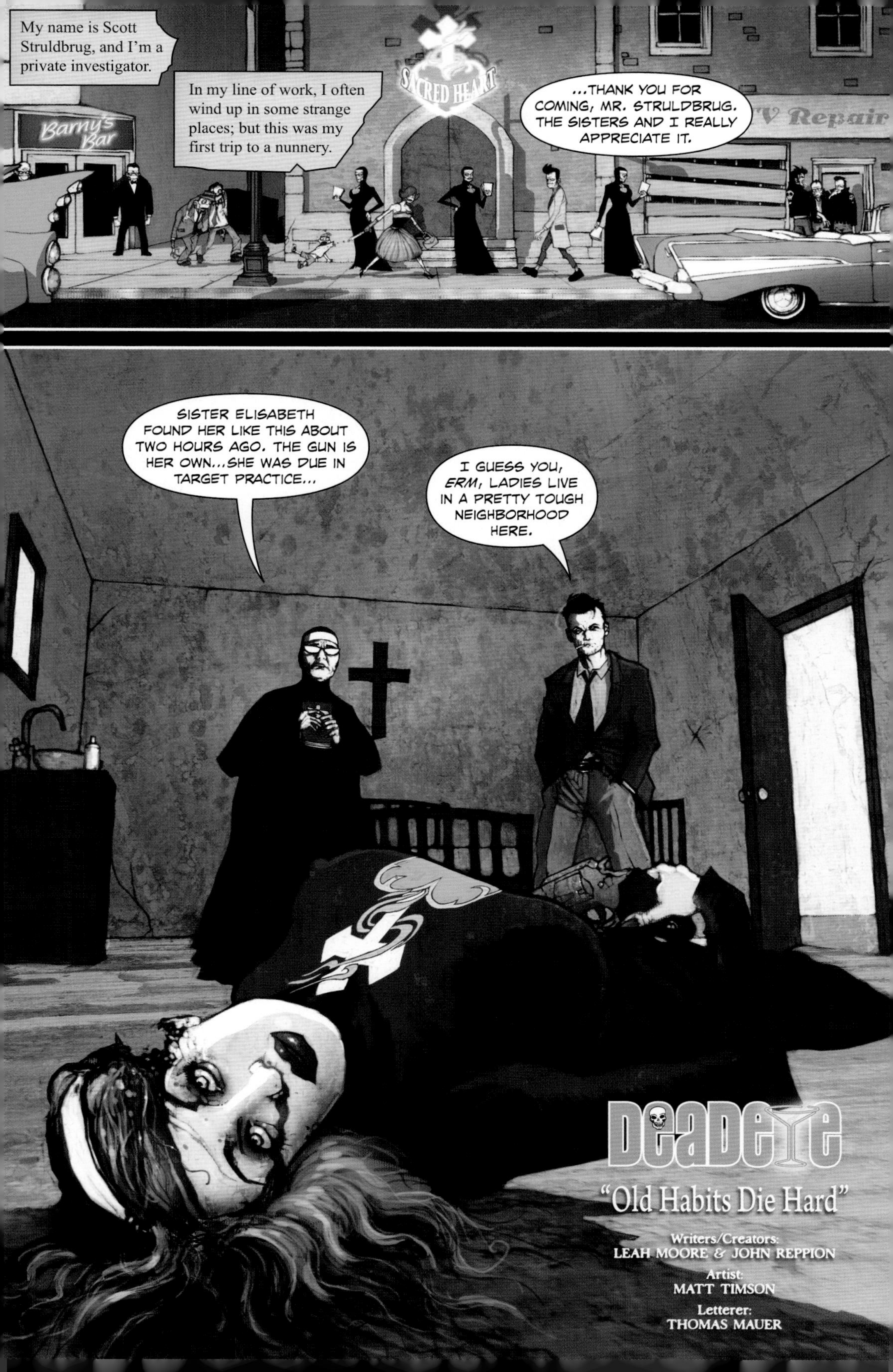
My name is Scott Struldbrug, and I'm a private investigator.
In my line of work, I often wind up in some strange places; but this was my first trip to a nunnery.
Barny's Bar
SACRED HEART
TV Repair
...THANK YOU FOR COMING, MR. STRULDBRUG. THE SISTERS AND I REALLY APPRECIATE IT.
SISTER ELISABETH FOUND HER LIKE THIS ABOUT TWO HOURS AGO. THE GUN IS HER OWN...SHE WAS DUE IN TARGET PRACTICE...
I GUESS YOU, *ERM*, LADIES LIVE IN A PRETTY TOUGH NEIGHBORHOOD HERE.
DeadEye
"Old Habits Die Hard"
Writers/Creators:
LEAH MOORE & JOHN REPPION
Artist:
MATT TIMSON
Letterer:
THOMAS MAUER

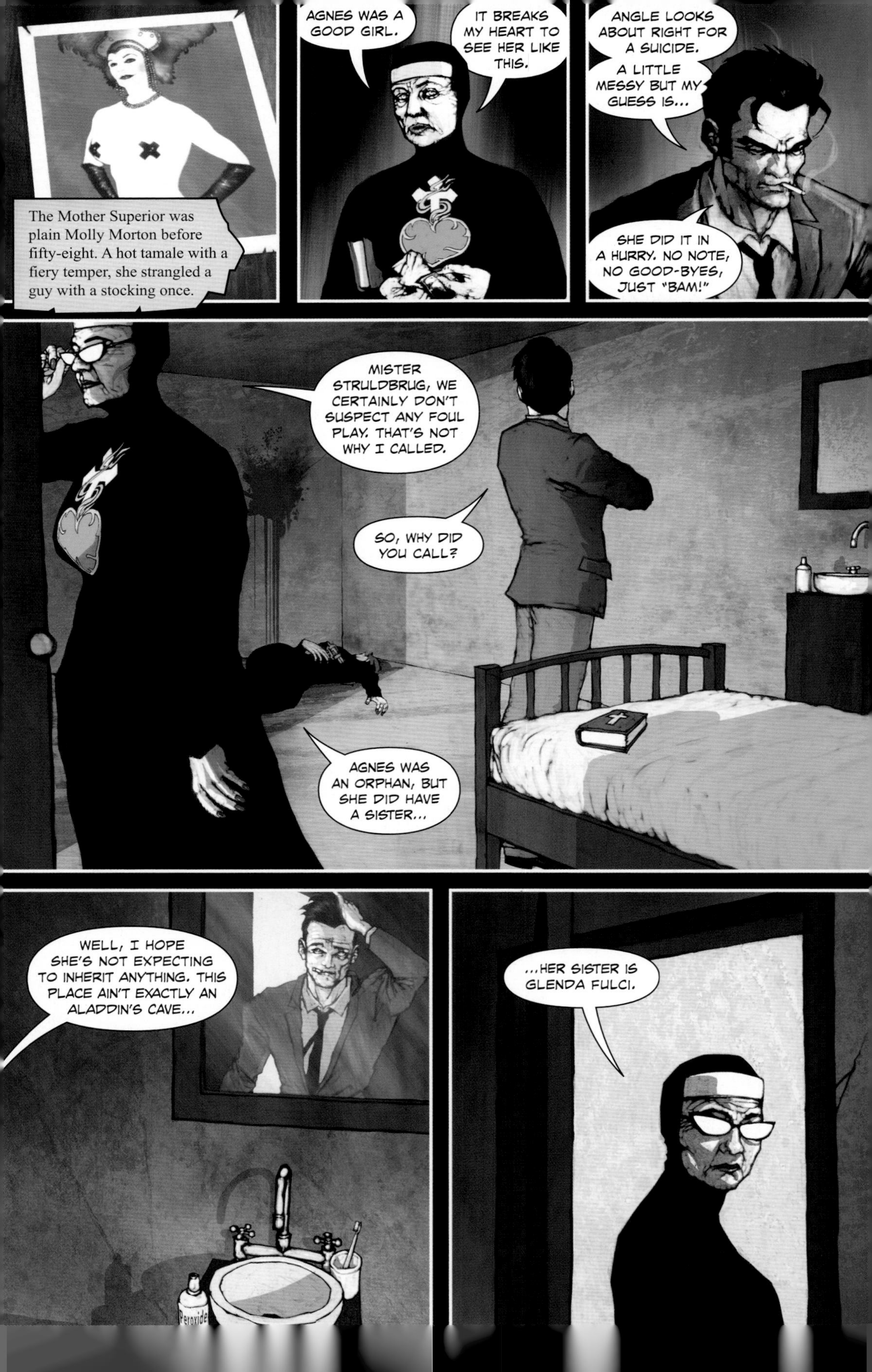
The Mother Superior was plain Molly Morton before fifty-eight. A hot tamale with a fiery temper, she strangled a guy with a stocking once.
AGNES WAS A GOOD GIRL.
IT BREAKS MY HEART TO SEE HER LIKE THIS.
ANGLE LOOKS ABOUT RIGHT FOR A SUICIDE.
A LITTLE MESSY BUT MY GUESS IS...
SHE DID IT IN A HURRY. NO NOTE, NO GOOD-BYES, JUST "BAM!"
MISTER STRULDBRUG, WE CERTAINLY DON'T SUSPECT ANY FOUL PLAY. THAT'S NOT WHY I CALLED.
SO, WHY DID YOU CALL?
AGNES WAS AN ORPHAN, BUT SHE DID HAVE A SISTER...
WELL, I HOPE SHE'S NOT EXPECTING TO INHERIT ANYTHING. THIS PLACE AIN'T EXACTLY AN ALADDIN'S CAVE...
Peroxide
...HER SISTER IS GLENDA FULCI.

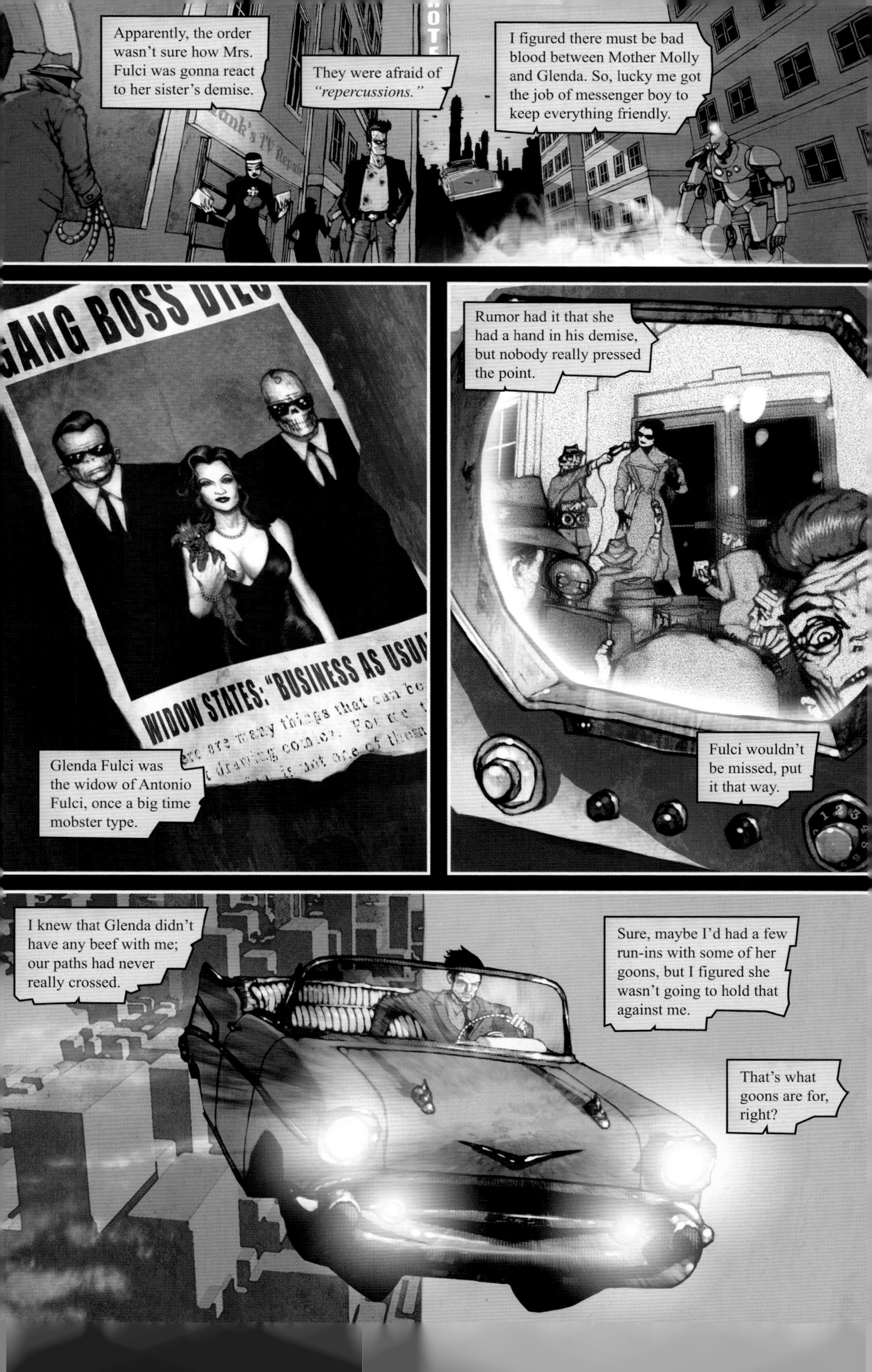

Apparently, the order wasn't sure how Mrs. Fulci was gonna react to her sister's demise.
They were afraid of *"repercussions."*
I figured there must be bad blood between Mother Molly and Glenda. So, lucky me got the job of messenger boy to keep everything friendly.
GANG BOSS DIES
WIDOW STATES: "BUSINESS AS USUAL
Glenda Fulci was the widow of Antonio Fulci, once a big time mobster type.
Rumor had it that she had a hand in his demise, but nobody really pressed the point.
Fulci wouldn't be missed, put it that way.
I knew that Glenda didn't have any beef with me; our paths had never really crossed.
Sure, maybe I'd had a few run-ins with some of her goons, but I figured she wasn't going to hold that against me.
That's what goons are for, right?

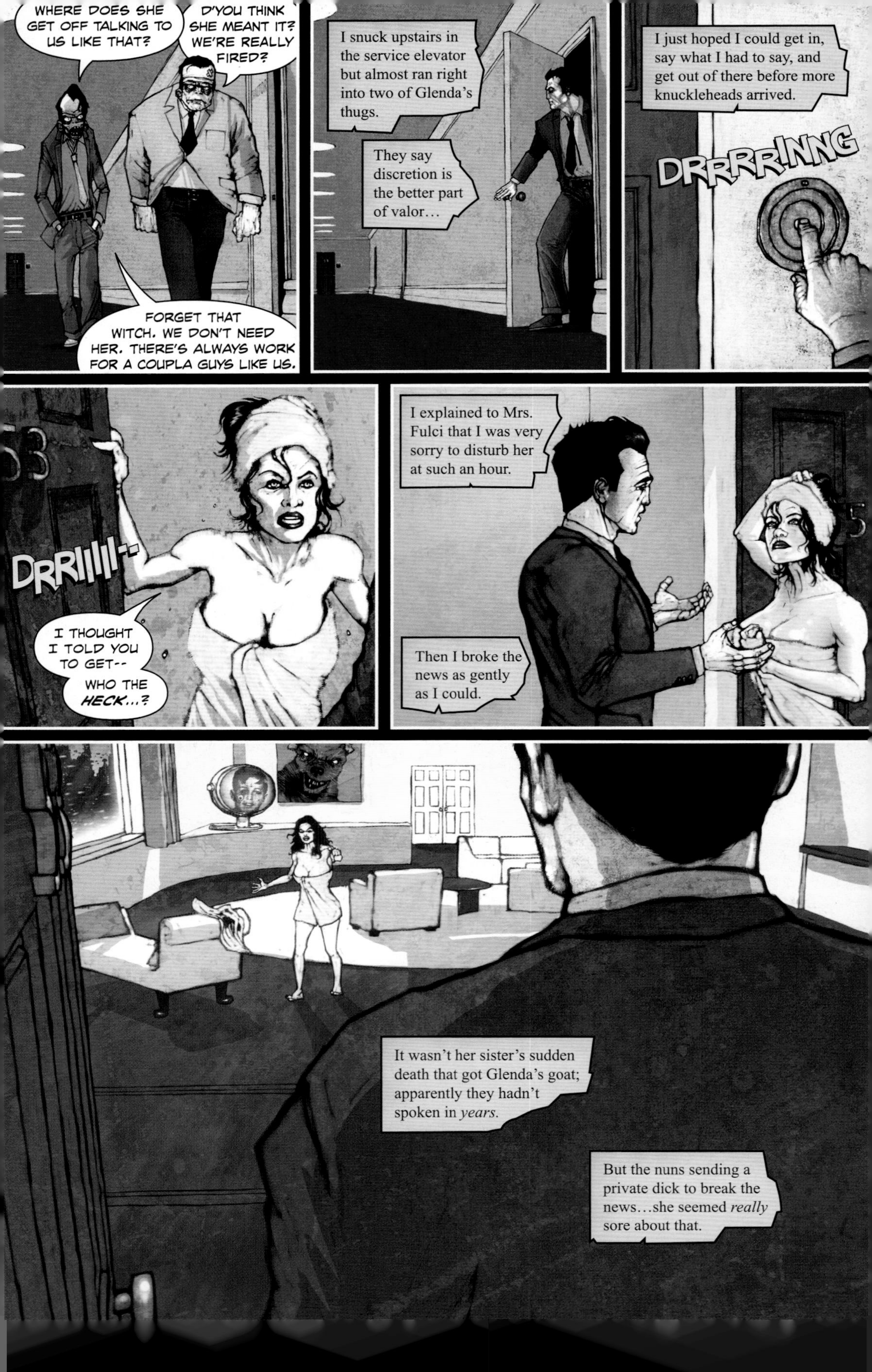
WHERE DOES SHE GET OFF TALKING TO US LIKE THAT?
D'YOU THINK SHE MEANT IT? WE'RE REALLY FIRED?
FORGET THAT WITCH. WE DON'T NEED HER. THERE'S ALWAYS WORK FOR A COUPLA GUYS LIKE US.
I snuck upstairs in the service elevator but almost ran right into two of Glenda's thugs.
They say discretion is the better part of valor…
I just hoped I could get in, say what I had to say, and get out of there before more knuckleheads arrived.
DRRRRINNG
DRRIIIII--
I THOUGHT I TOLD YOU TO GET--
WHO THE *HECK*…?
I explained to Mrs. Fulci that I was very sorry to disturb her at such an hour.
Then I broke the news as gently as I could.
It wasn't her sister's sudden death that got Glenda's goat; apparently they hadn't spoken in *years*.
But the nuns sending a private dick to break the news…she seemed *really* sore about that.

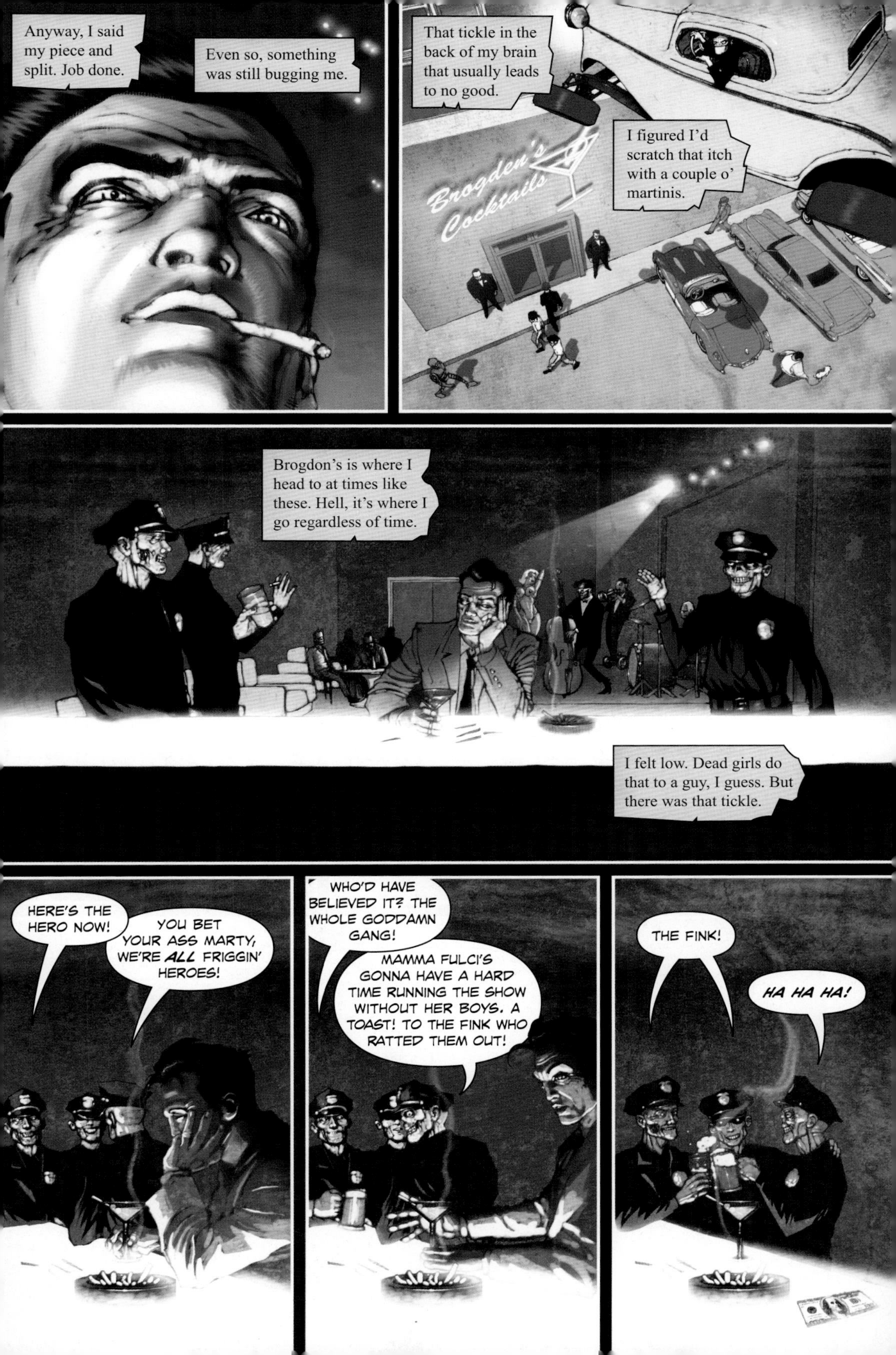
Anyway, I said my piece and split. Job done.
Even so, something was still bugging me.
That tickle in the back of my brain that usually leads to no good.
Brogden's Cocktails
I figured I'd scratch that itch with a couple o' martinis.
Brogdon's is where I head to at times like these. Hell, it's where I go regardless of time.
I felt low. Dead girls do that to a guy, I guess. But there was that tickle.
HERE'S THE HERO NOW!
YOU BET YOUR ASS MARTY, WE'RE ALL FRIGGIN' HEROES!
WHO'D HAVE BELIEVED IT? THE WHOLE GODDAMN GANG!
MAMMA FULCI'S GONNA HAVE A HARD TIME RUNNING THE SHOW WITHOUT HER BOYS. A TOAST! TO THE FINK WHO RATTED THEM OUT!
THE FINK!
HA HA HA!

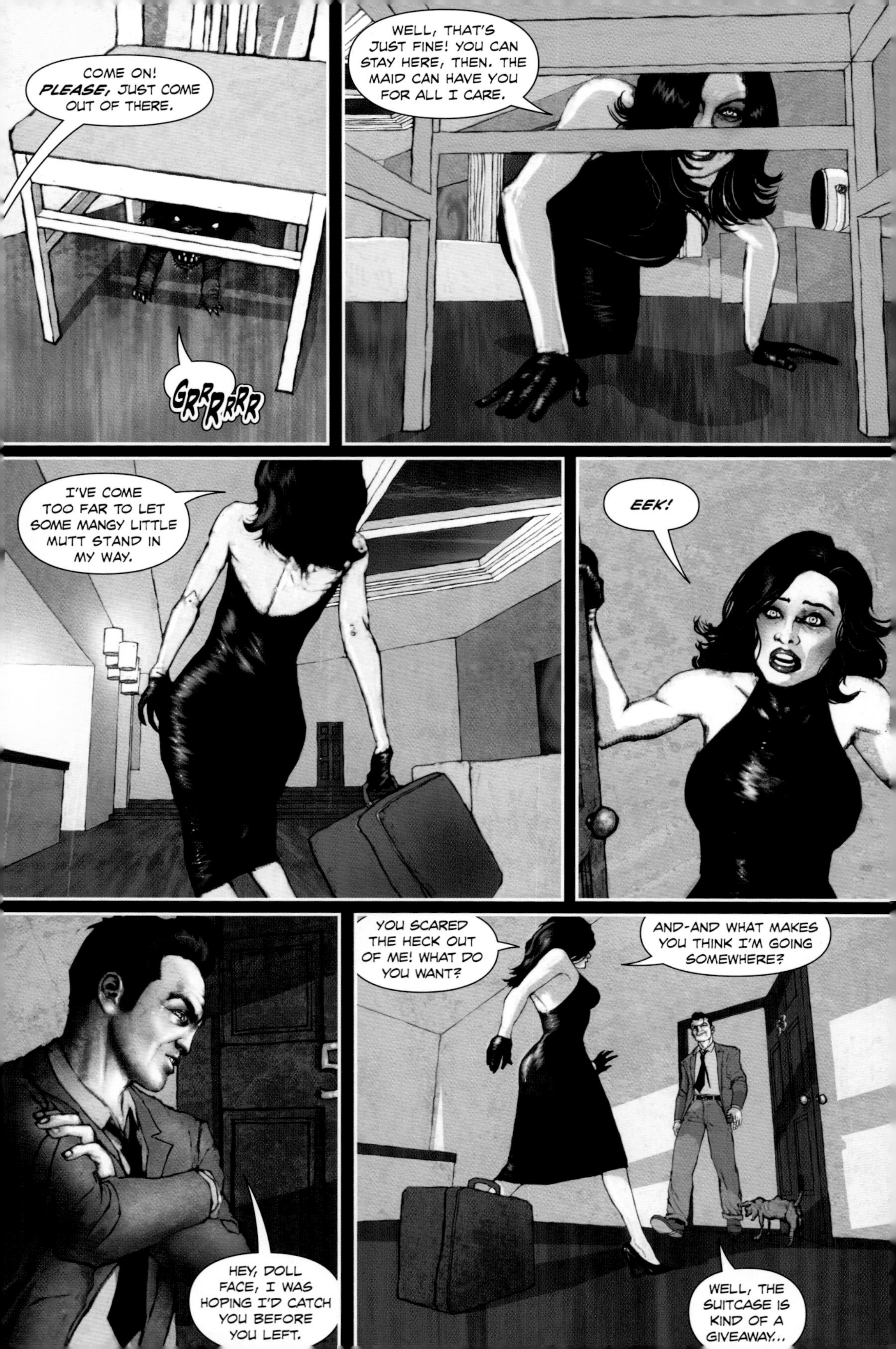
COME ON! *PLEASE,* JUST COME OUT OF THERE.
GRRRRRR
WELL, THAT'S JUST FINE! YOU CAN STAY HERE, THEN. THE MAID CAN HAVE YOU FOR ALL I CARE.
I'VE COME TOO FAR TO LET SOME MANGY LITTLE MUTT STAND IN MY WAY.
EEK!
HEY, DOLL FACE, I WAS HOPING I'D CATCH YOU BEFORE YOU LEFT.
YOU SCARED THE HECK OUT OF ME! WHAT DO YOU WANT?
AND-AND WHAT MAKES YOU THINK I'M GOING SOMEWHERE?
WELL, THE SUITCASE IS KIND OF A GIVEAWAY...

BESIDES, *AGNES,* WE BOTH KNOW YOU NEVER INTENDED ON HANGING AROUND.

"The first thing that bothered me was the peroxide in your room. Yeah, the body was a blonde, so it kinda made sense."

EXCEPT THAT YOU'RE A NUN WHO, OF COURSE, WEARS A WIMPLE MOST OF THE TIME. NUNS AREN'T NORMALLY CONCERNED ABOUT HAIR COLOR.

"Then, inside the closet avoiding Flotsam and Jetsam, I heard them bitching about you giving them a ticking off and letting 'em go."

I-I ≷SNIFF≷ I DIDN'T WANT TO HAVE ANYTHING TO DO WITH ALL THAT. I'M... I'M NOT A CRIMINAL.

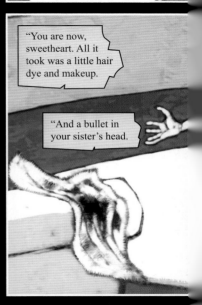

"You are now, sweetheart. All it took was a little hair dye and makeup."

"And a bullet in your sister's head."

BUT SHE DESERVED IT, RIGHT? SHE HAD ALL THIS, AND THERE YOU WERE LIVING LIKE A SAINT WITH NOTHING BUT BARE, PLASTERED WALLS.

"You thought you'd do good things with the money, didn't you? And squealing to the cops just guaranteed you a fresh start."

I KNOW YOU'RE A GOOD PERSON, AGNES. YOU JUST GOT A LITTLE... CONFUSED.

I CALLED THE SISTERS--

NO! THEY CAN'T KNOW!

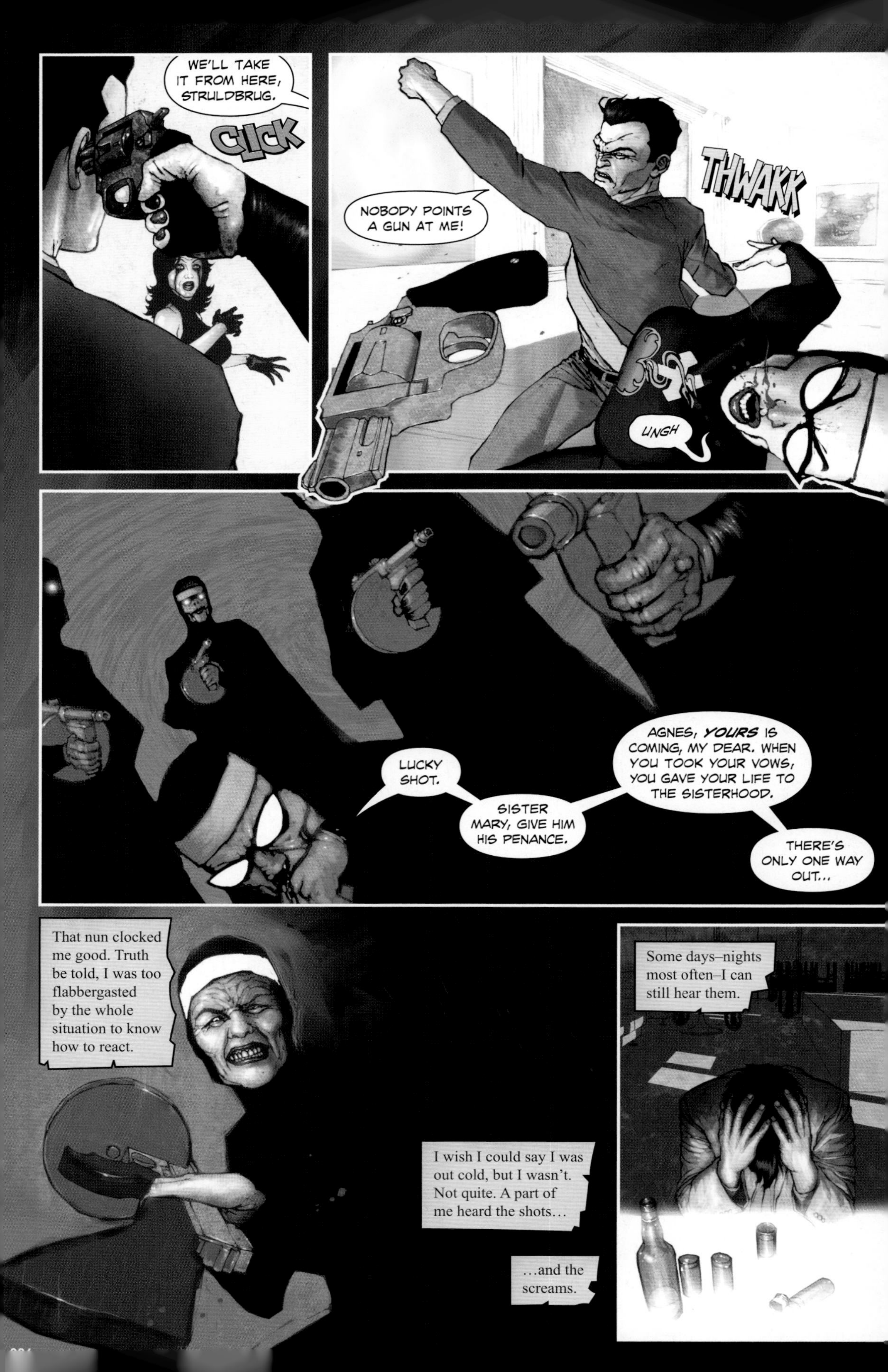
WE'LL TAKE IT FROM HERE, STRULDBRUG.
CLICK
NOBODY POINTS A GUN AT ME!
THWAKK
UNGH
LUCKY SHOT.
SISTER MARY, GIVE HIM HIS PENANCE.
AGNES, YOURS IS COMING, MY DEAR. WHEN YOU TOOK YOUR VOWS, YOU GAVE YOUR LIFE TO THE SISTERHOOD.
THERE'S ONLY ONE WAY OUT...
That nun clocked me good. Truth be told, I was too flabbergasted by the whole situation to know how to react.
I wish I could say I was out cold, but I wasn't. Not quite. A part of me heard the shots...
...and the screams.
Some days–nights most often–I can still hear them.

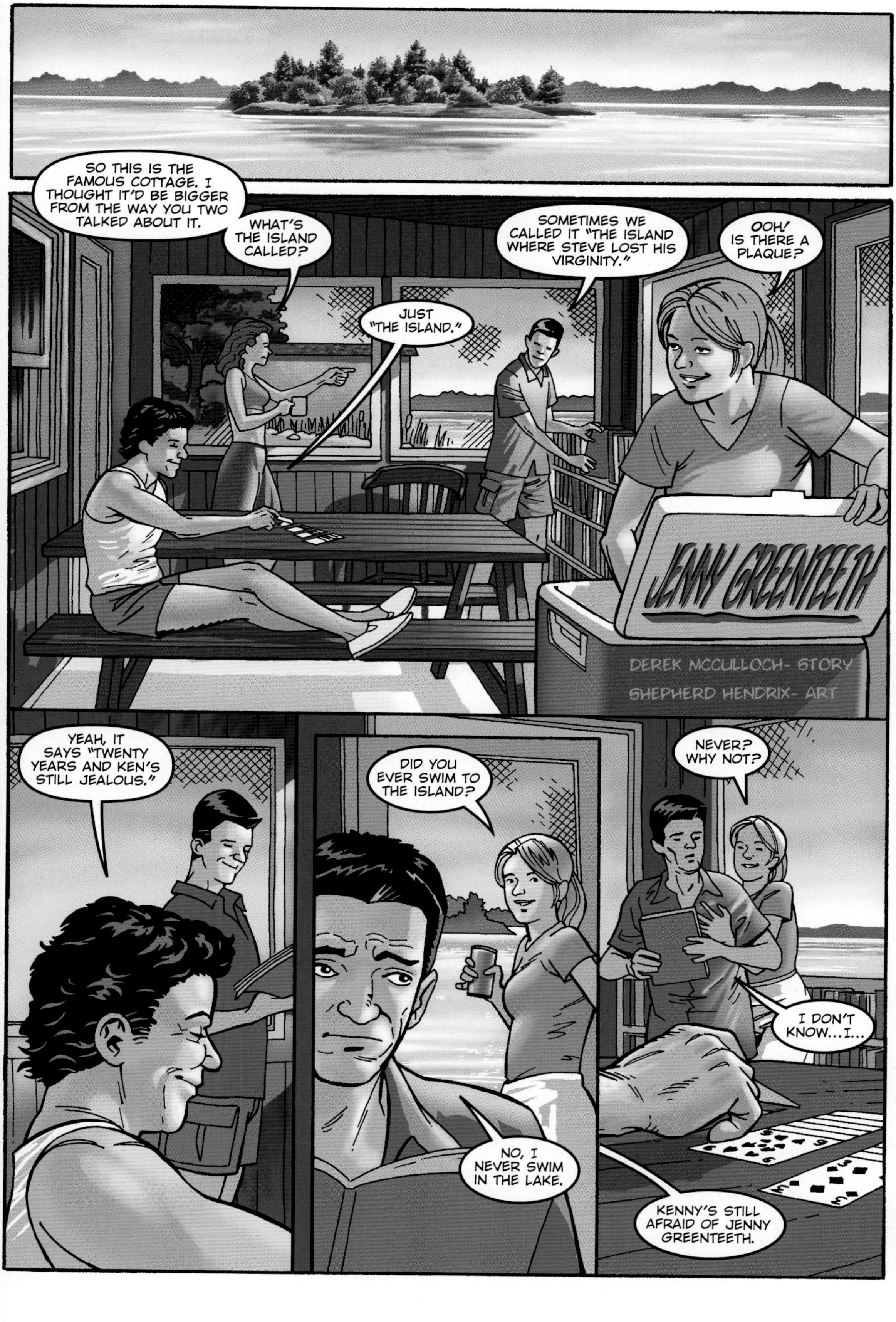

SO THIS IS THE FAMOUS COTTAGE. I THOUGHT IT'D BE BIGGER FROM THE WAY YOU TWO TALKED ABOUT IT.
WHAT'S THE ISLAND CALLED?
JUST "THE ISLAND."
SOMETIMES WE CALLED IT "THE ISLAND WHERE STEVE LOST HIS VIRGINITY."
OOH! IS THERE A PLAQUE?
JENNY GREENTEETH
DEREK MCCULLOCH- STORY
SHEPHERD HENDRIX- ART
YEAH, IT SAYS "TWENTY YEARS AND KEN'S STILL JEALOUS."
DID YOU EVER SWIM TO THE ISLAND?
NO, I NEVER SWIM IN THE LAKE.
NEVER? WHY NOT?
I DON'T KNOW... I...
KENNY'S STILL AFRAID OF JENNY GREENTEETH.

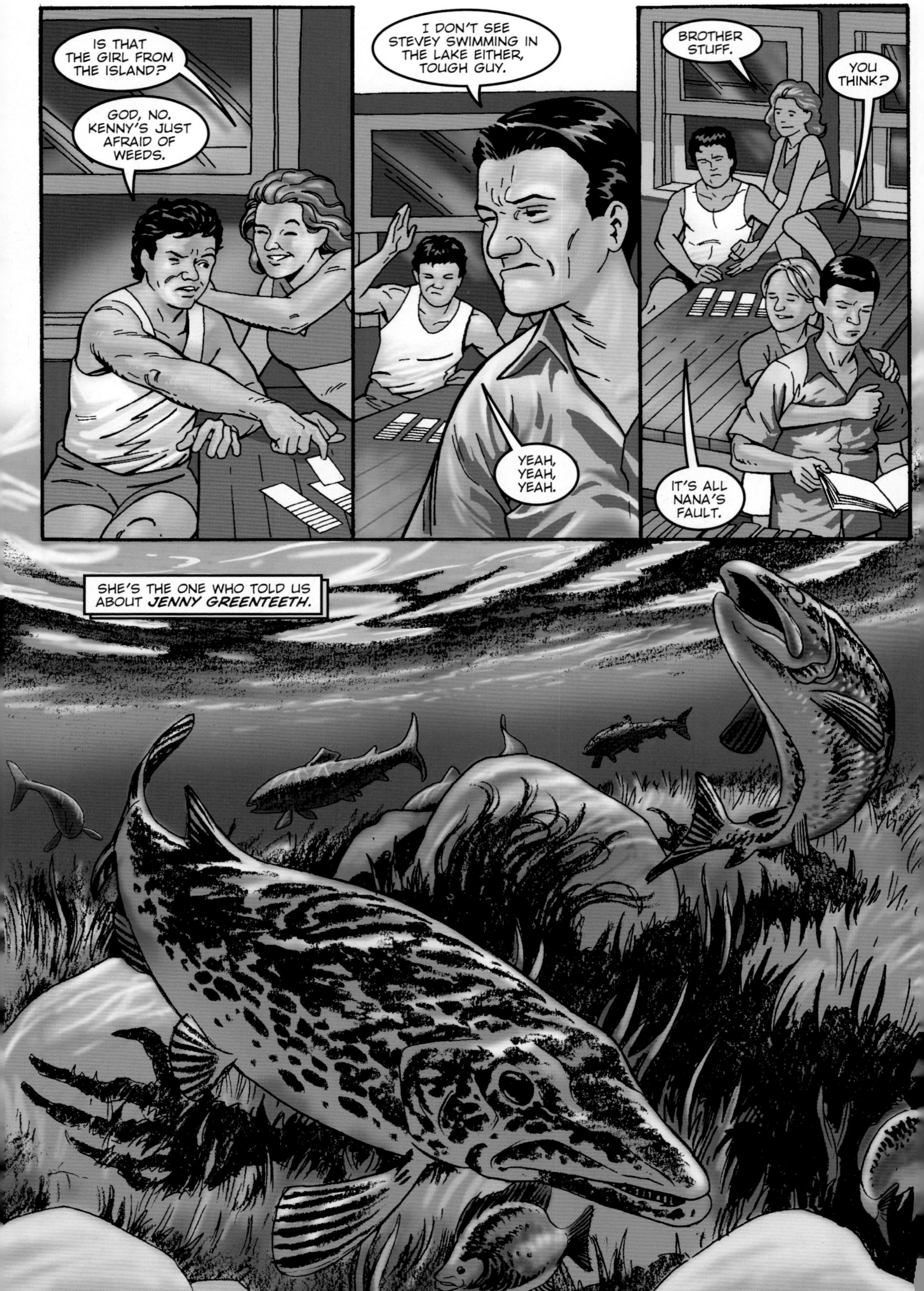
IS THAT THE GIRL FROM THE ISLAND?
GOD, NO. KENNY'S JUST AFRAID OF WEEDS.
I DON'T SEE STEVEY SWIMMING IN THE LAKE EITHER, TOUGH GUY.
YEAH, YEAH, YEAH.
BROTHER STUFF.
YOU THINK?
IT'S ALL NANA'S FAULT.
SHE'S THE ONE WHO TOLD US ABOUT *JENNY GREENTEETH*.

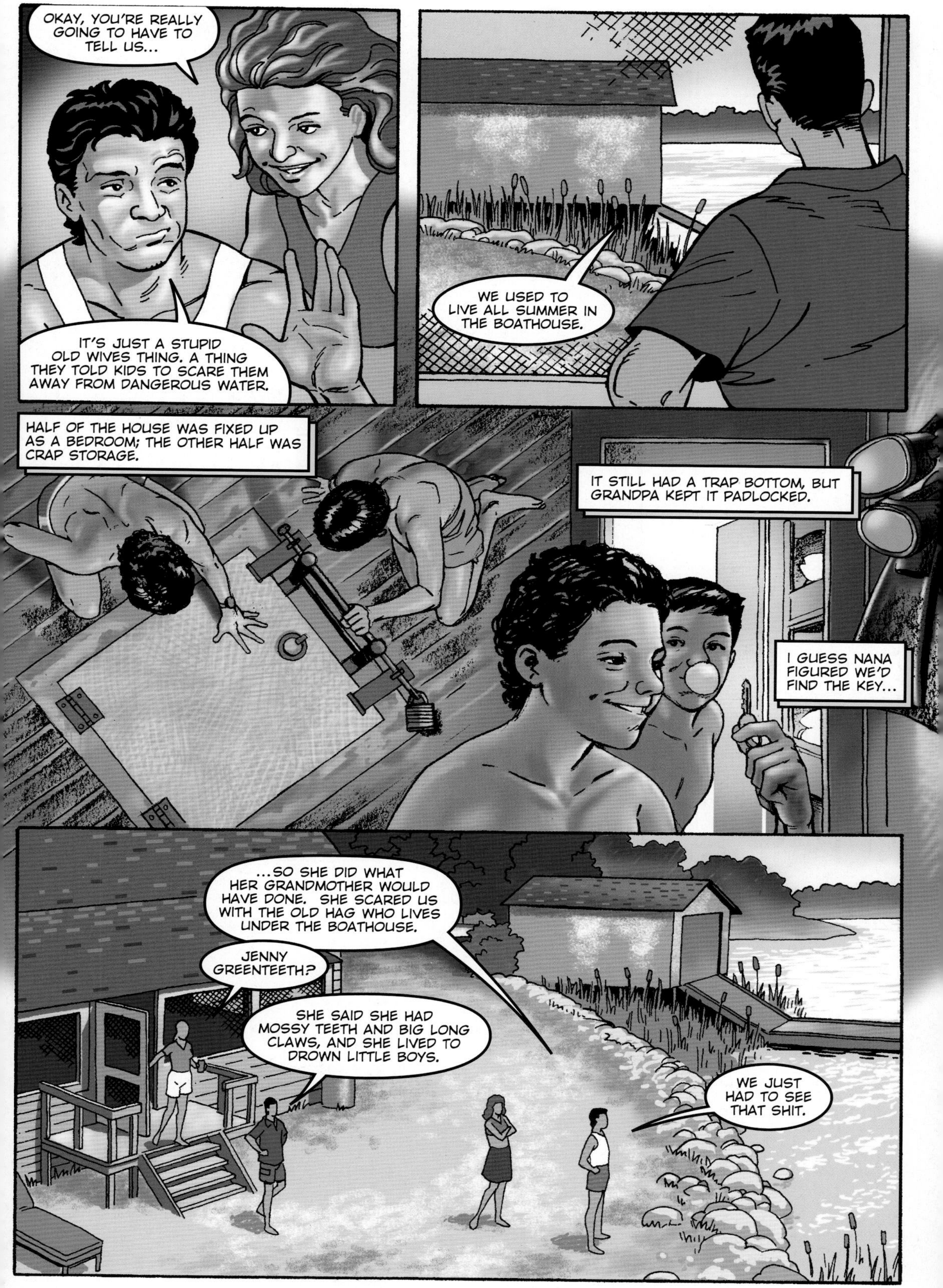
OKAY, YOU'RE REALLY GOING TO HAVE TO TELL US...
IT'S JUST A STUPID OLD WIVES THING. A THING THEY TOLD KIDS TO SCARE THEM AWAY FROM DANGEROUS WATER.
WE USED TO LIVE ALL SUMMER IN THE BOATHOUSE.
HALF OF THE HOUSE WAS FIXED UP AS A BEDROOM; THE OTHER HALF WAS CRAP STORAGE.
IT STILL HAD A TRAP BOTTOM, BUT GRANDPA KEPT IT PADLOCKED.
I GUESS NANA FIGURED WE'D FIND THE KEY...
...SO SHE DID WHAT HER GRANDMOTHER WOULD HAVE DONE. SHE SCARED US WITH THE OLD HAG WHO LIVES UNDER THE BOATHOUSE.
JENNY GREENTEETH?
SHE SAID SHE HAD MOSSY TEETH AND BIG LONG CLAWS, AND SHE LIVED TO DROWN LITTLE BOYS.
WE JUST HAD TO SEE THAT SHIT.

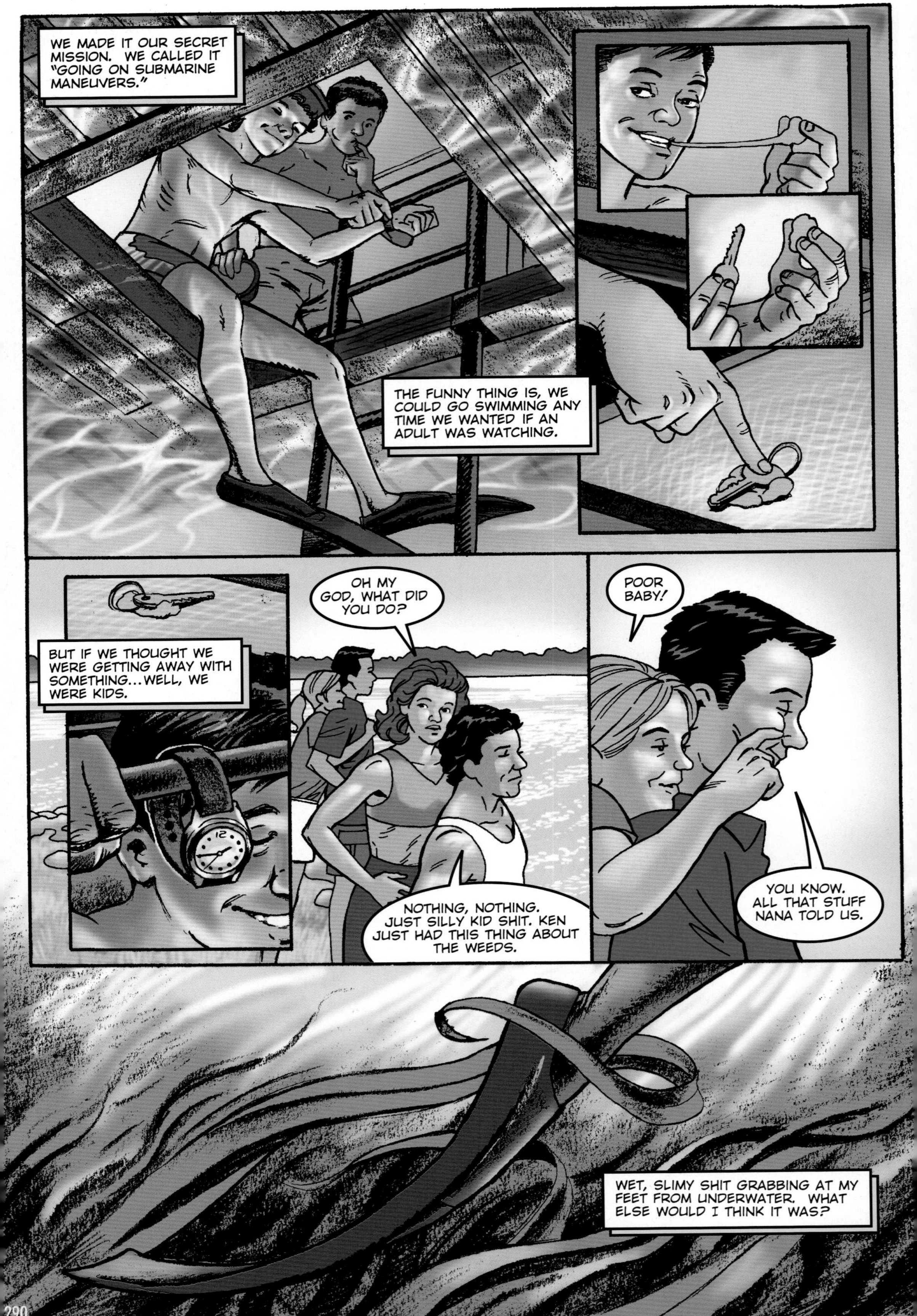
WE MADE IT OUR SECRET MISSION. WE CALLED IT "GOING ON SUBMARINE MANEUVERS."
THE FUNNY THING IS, WE COULD GO SWIMMING ANY TIME WE WANTED IF AN ADULT WAS WATCHING.
BUT IF WE THOUGHT WE WERE GETTING AWAY WITH SOMETHING...WELL, WE WERE KIDS.
OH MY GOD, WHAT DID YOU DO?
NOTHING, NOTHING. JUST SILLY KID SHIT. KEN JUST HAD THIS THING ABOUT THE WEEDS.
POOR BABY!
YOU KNOW. ALL THAT STUFF NANA TOLD US.
WET, SLIMY SHIT GRABBING AT MY FEET FROM UNDERWATER. WHAT ELSE WOULD I THINK IT WAS?

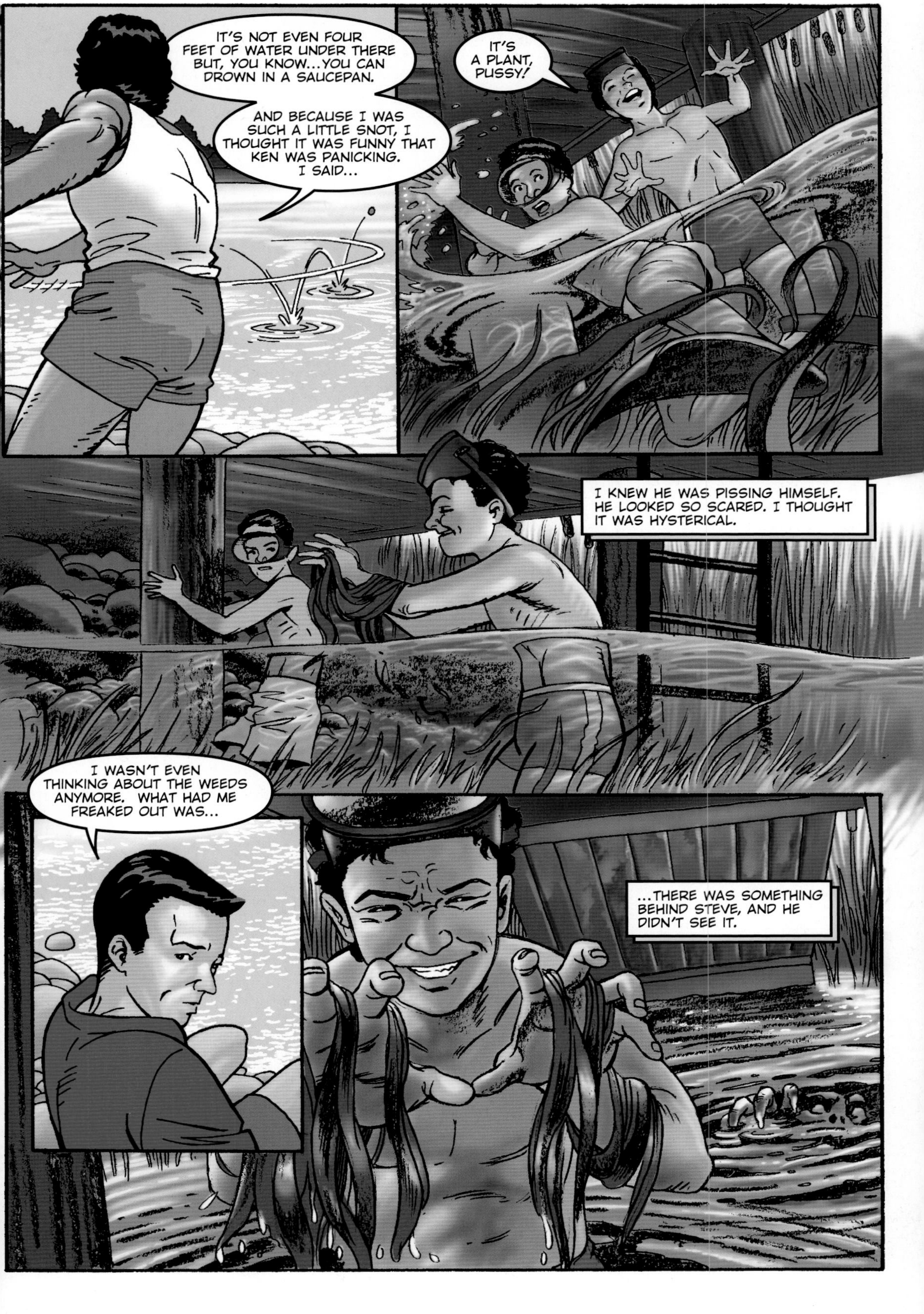
IT'S NOT EVEN FOUR FEET OF WATER UNDER THERE BUT, YOU KNOW...YOU CAN DROWN IN A SAUCEPAN.
AND BECAUSE I WAS SUCH A LITTLE SNOT, I THOUGHT IT WAS FUNNY THAT KEN WAS PANICKING. I SAID...
IT'S A PLANT, PUSSY!
I KNEW HE WAS PISSING HIMSELF. HE LOOKED SO SCARED. I THOUGHT IT WAS HYSTERICAL.
I WASN'T EVEN THINKING ABOUT THE WEEDS ANYMORE. WHAT HAD ME FREAKED OUT WAS...
...THERE WAS SOMETHING BEHIND STEVE, AND HE DIDN'T SEE IT.

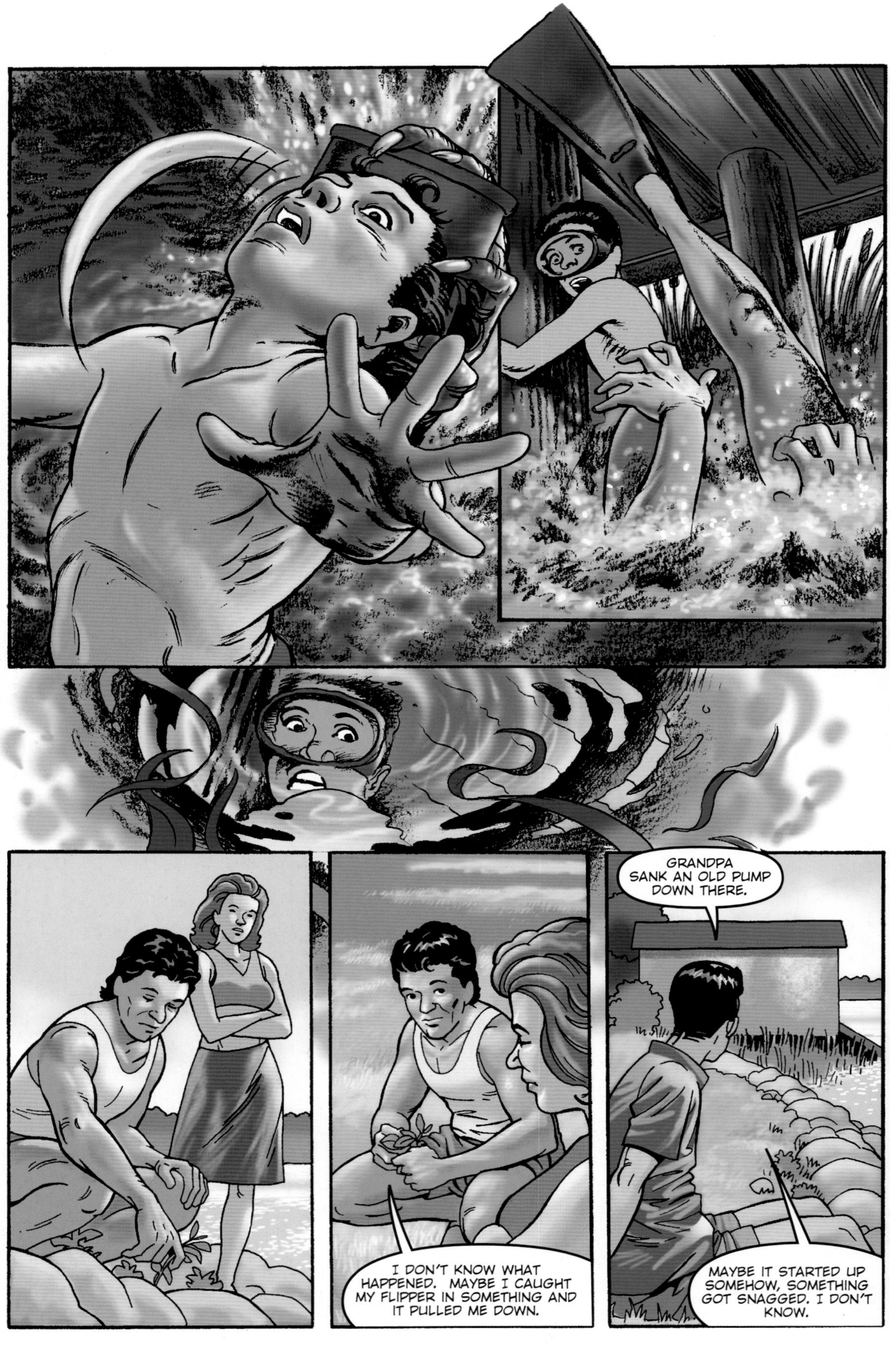
GRANDPA SANK AN OLD PUMP DOWN THERE.
I DON'T KNOW WHAT HAPPENED. MAYBE I CAUGHT MY FLIPPER IN SOMETHING AND IT PULLED ME DOWN.
MAYBE IT STARTED UP SOMEHOW, SOMETHING GOT SNAGGED. I DON'T KNOW.

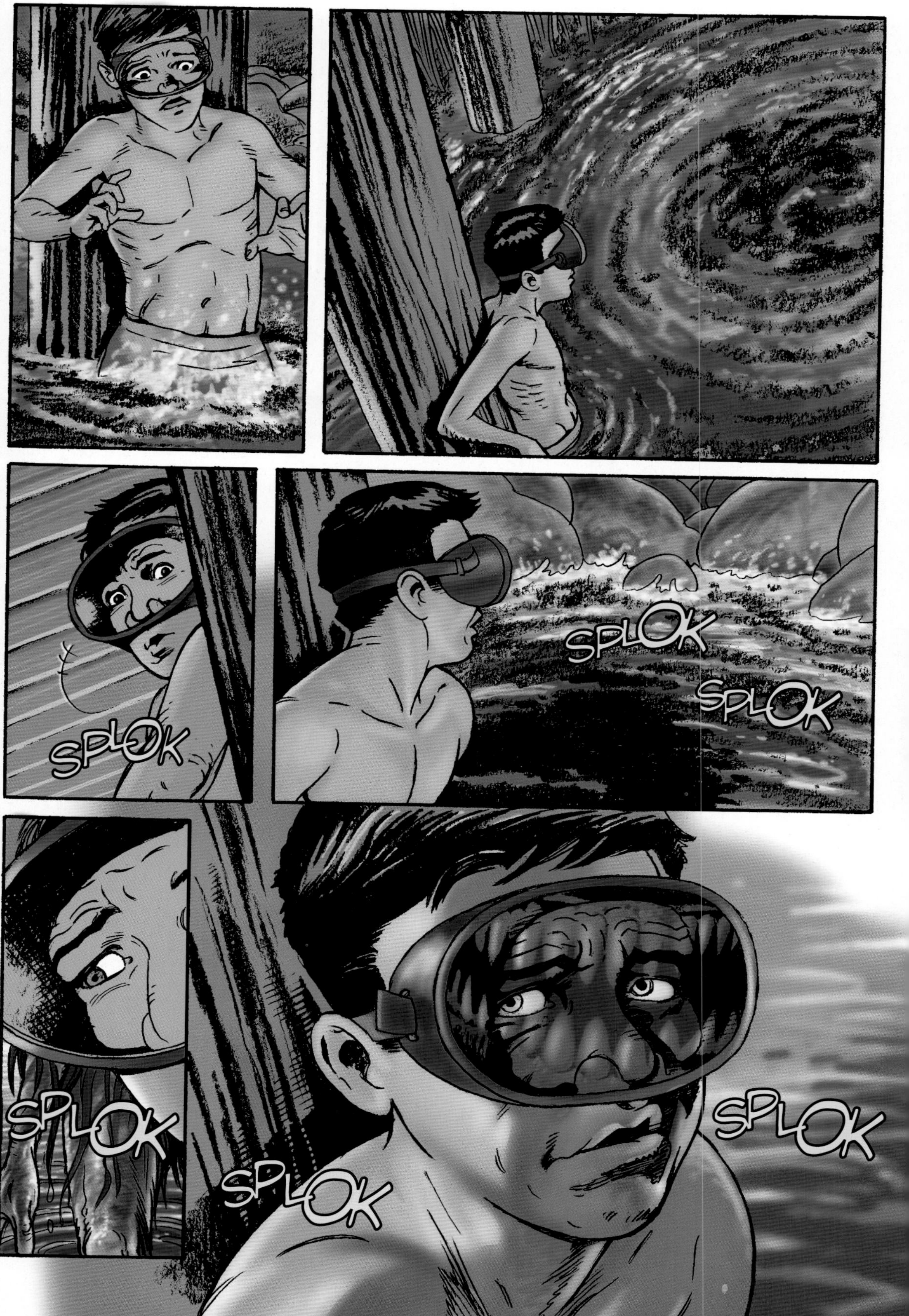
SPLOK
SPLOK
SPLOK
SPLOK
SPLOK
SPLOK

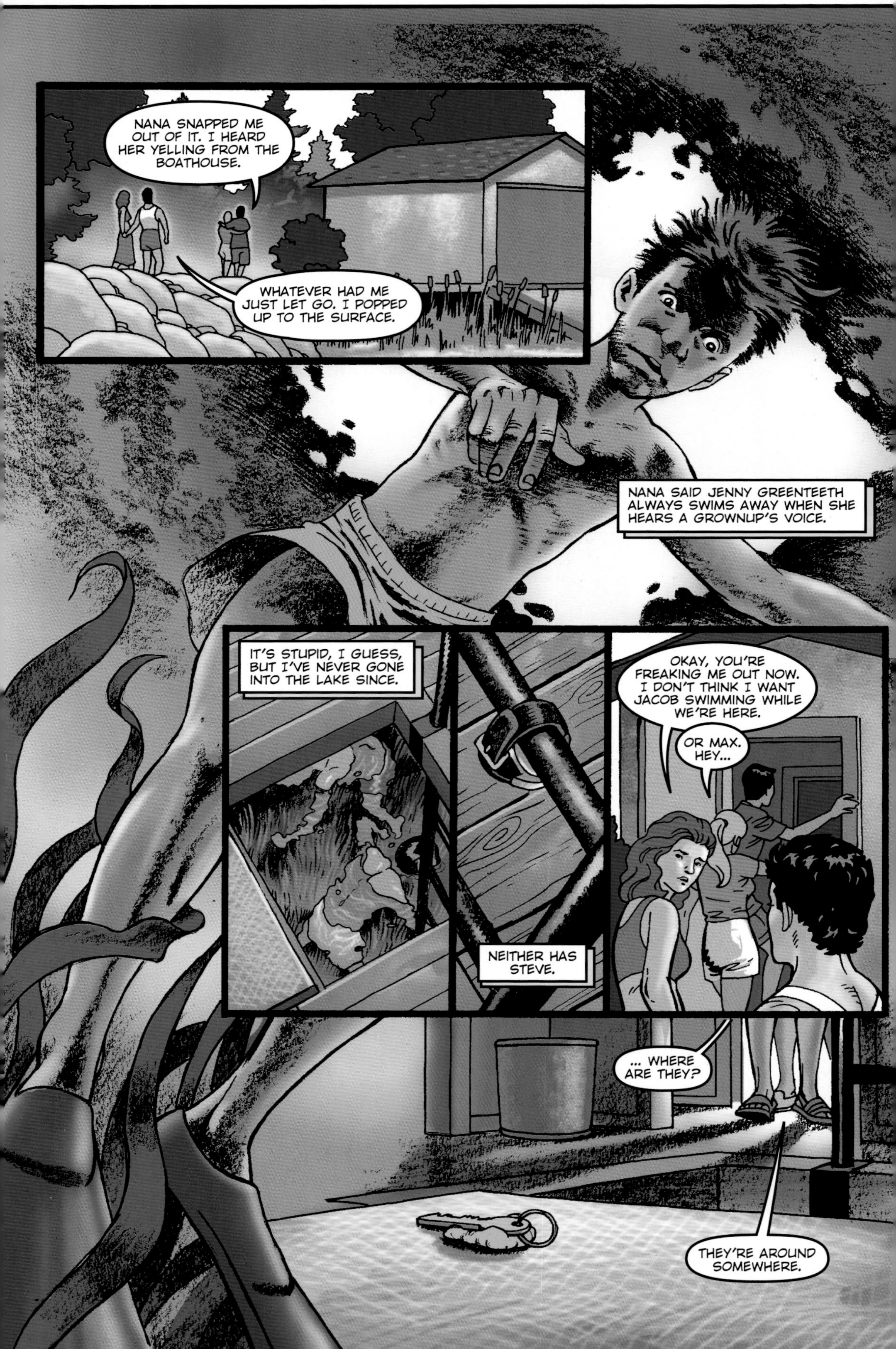

NANA SNAPPED ME OUT OF IT. I HEARD HER YELLING FROM THE BOATHOUSE.
WHATEVER HAD ME JUST LET GO. I POPPED UP TO THE SURFACE.
NANA SAID JENNY GREENTEETH ALWAYS SWIMS AWAY WHEN SHE HEARS A GROWNUP'S VOICE.
IT'S STUPID, I GUESS, BUT I'VE NEVER GONE INTO THE LAKE SINCE.
NEITHER HAS STEVE.
OKAY, YOU'RE FREAKING ME OUT NOW. I DON'T THINK I WANT JACOB SWIMMING WHILE WE'RE HERE.
OR MAX. HEY...
... WHERE ARE THEY?
THEY'RE AROUND SOMEWHERE.

IT WAS THE SUMMER OF FORTY-EIGHT WHEN I FIRST GOT THE NOTION IN MY HEAD.

I WAS OUT VISITING MY GRANDPARENTS AT THEIR PLACE IN THE COUNTRY.

I HAD SEEN IT IN A NEWSREEL THE DAY BEFORE--THE ROCKET MAN FROM THE SERIALS HAD COME TO LIFE THANKS TO A SCIENTIST NAMED WERNER SCHLÖNDORFF.

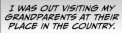

IT WAS THAT MAN WHO MADE MY FLIGHTS OF FANCY AN HONEST TO GOD REALITY.

HE MADE ME BELIEVE I COULD FLY.

SO, THERE I WAS, ON THE ROOF OF MY GRANDPARENT'S BARN, WITH ALL THE AMERICAN INGENUITY A SEVEN YEAR-OLD COULD MUSTER, DETERMINED TO BE THE FIRST BOY TO FLY.

I BROKE BOTH LEGS THAT DAY.

295

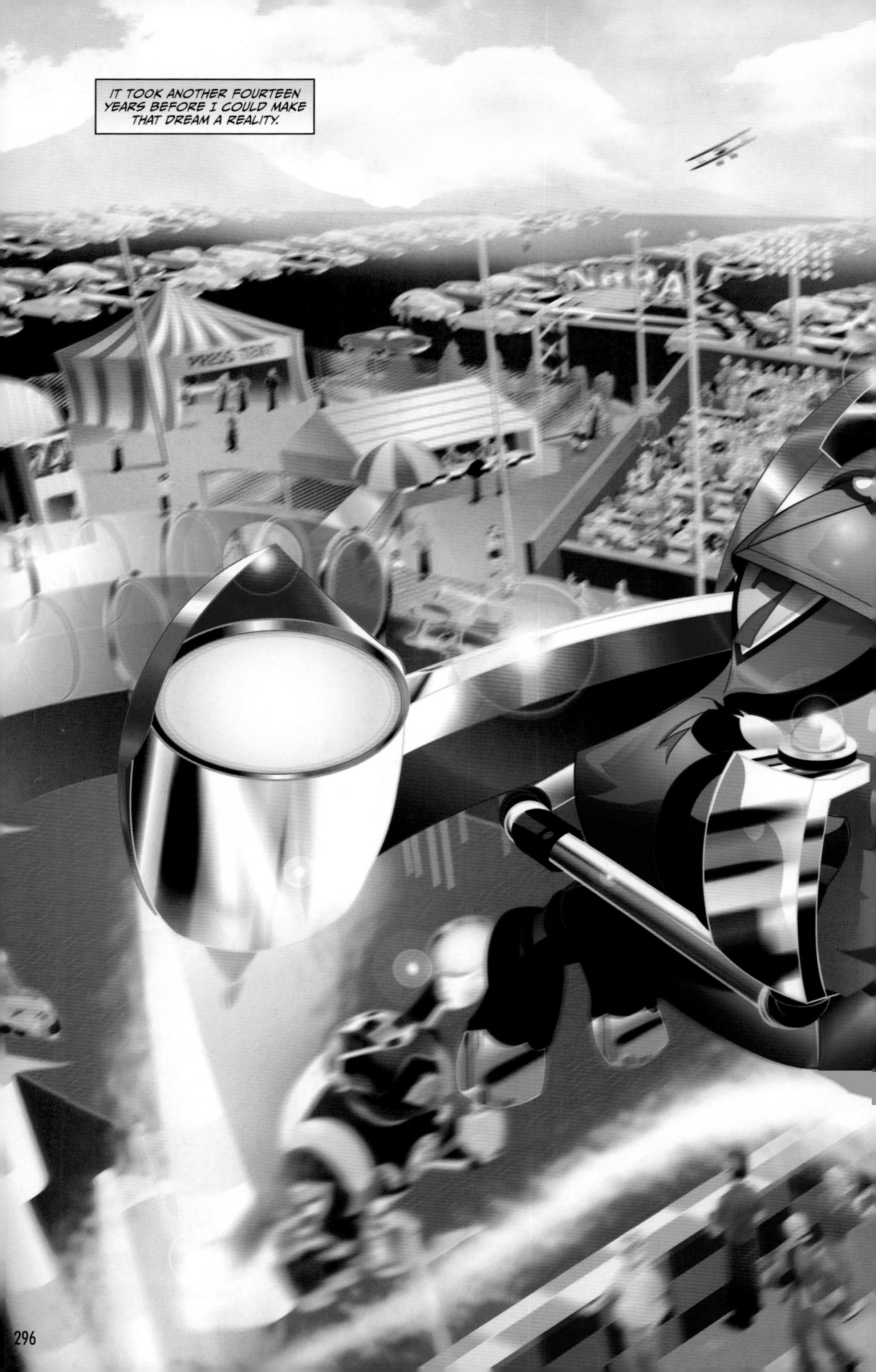
IT TOOK ANOTHER FOURTEEN YEARS BEFORE I COULD MAKE THAT DREAM A REALITY.
PRESS TENT

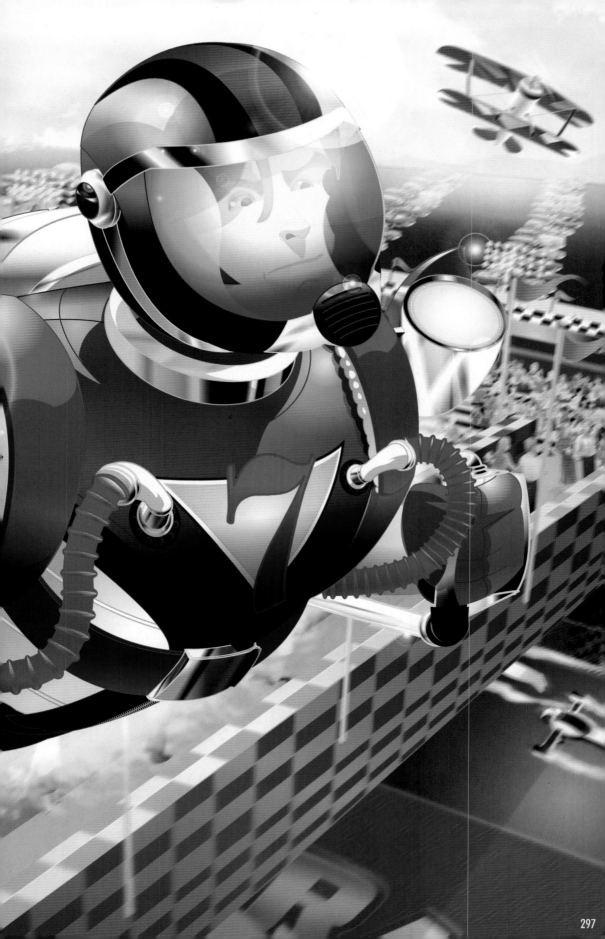

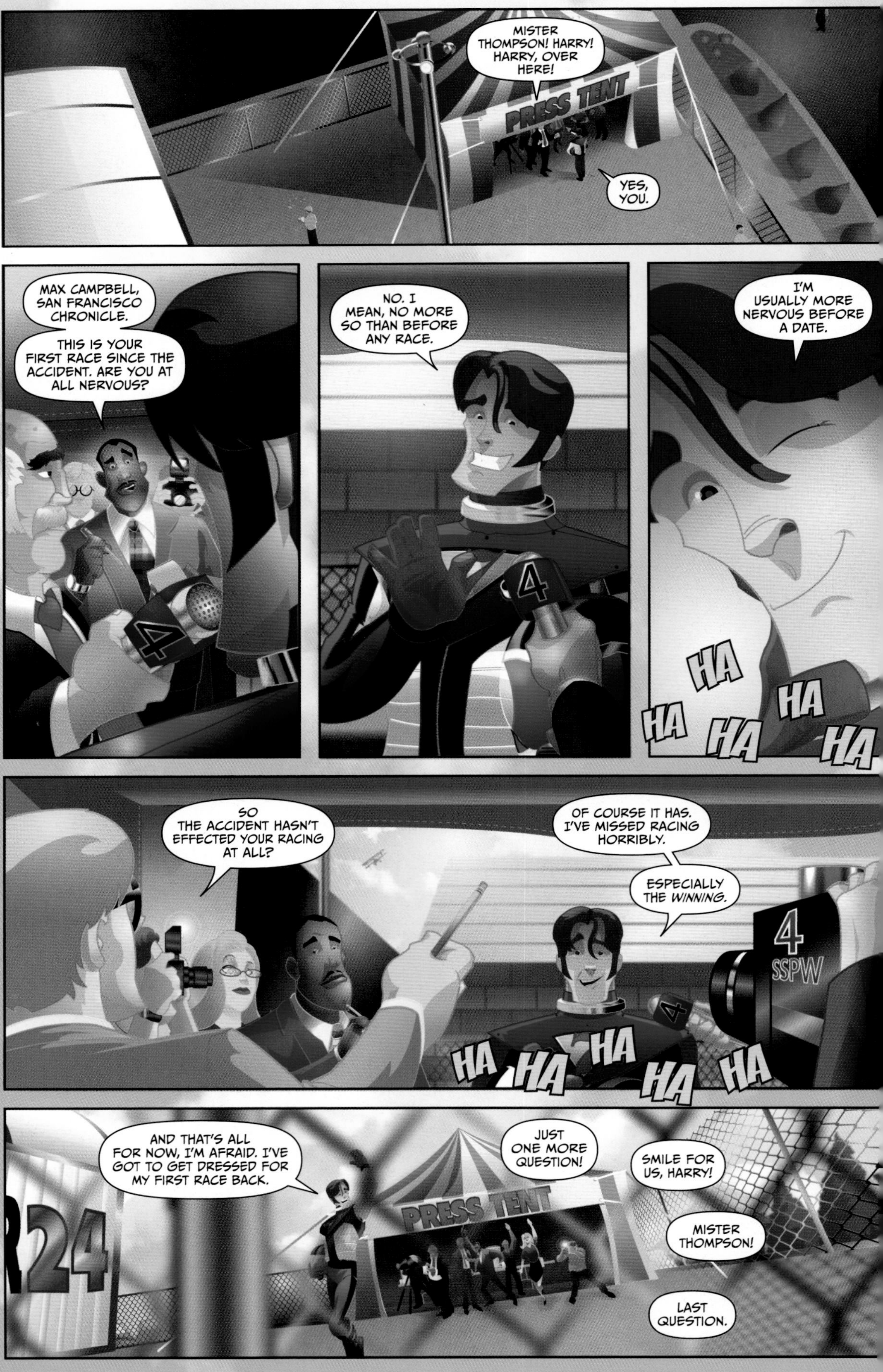
MISTER THOMPSON! HARRY! HARRY, OVER HERE!
PRESS TENT
YES, YOU.
MAX CAMPBELL, SAN FRANCISCO CHRONICLE.
THIS IS YOUR FIRST RACE SINCE THE ACCIDENT. ARE YOU AT ALL NERVOUS?
NO. I MEAN, NO MORE SO THAN BEFORE ANY RACE.
I'M USUALLY MORE NERVOUS BEFORE A DATE.
HA HA HA HA HA HA
SO THE ACCIDENT HASN'T EFFECTED YOUR RACING AT ALL?
OF COURSE IT HAS. I'VE MISSED RACING HORRIBLY.
ESPECIALLY THE *WINNING.*
4 SSPW
HA HA HA HA HA HA
AND THAT'S ALL FOR NOW, I'M AFRAID. I'VE GOT TO GET DRESSED FOR MY FIRST RACE BACK.
JUST ONE MORE QUESTION!
SMILE FOR US, HARRY!
MISTER THOMPSON!
LAST QUESTION.
PRESS TENT
R24

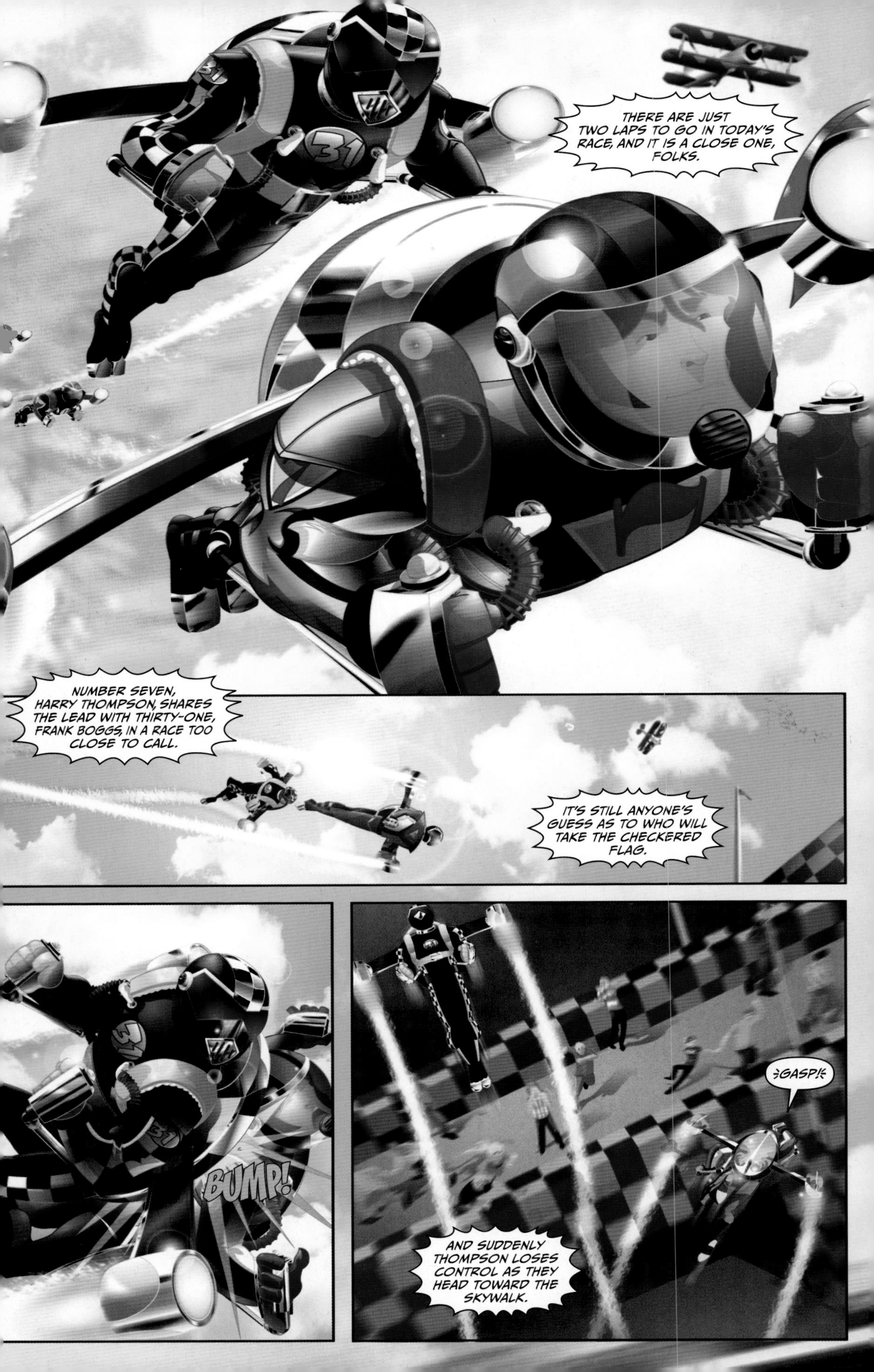
THERE ARE JUST TWO LAPS TO GO IN TODAY'S RACE, AND IT IS A CLOSE ONE, FOLKS.
NUMBER SEVEN, HARRY THOMPSON, SHARES THE LEAD WITH THIRTY-ONE, FRANK BOGGS, IN A RACE TOO CLOSE TO CALL.
IT'S STILL ANYONE'S GUESS AS TO WHO WILL TAKE THE CHECKERED FLAG.
BUMP!
GASP!
AND SUDDENLY THOMPSON LOSES CONTROL AS THEY HEAD TOWARD THE SKYWALK.

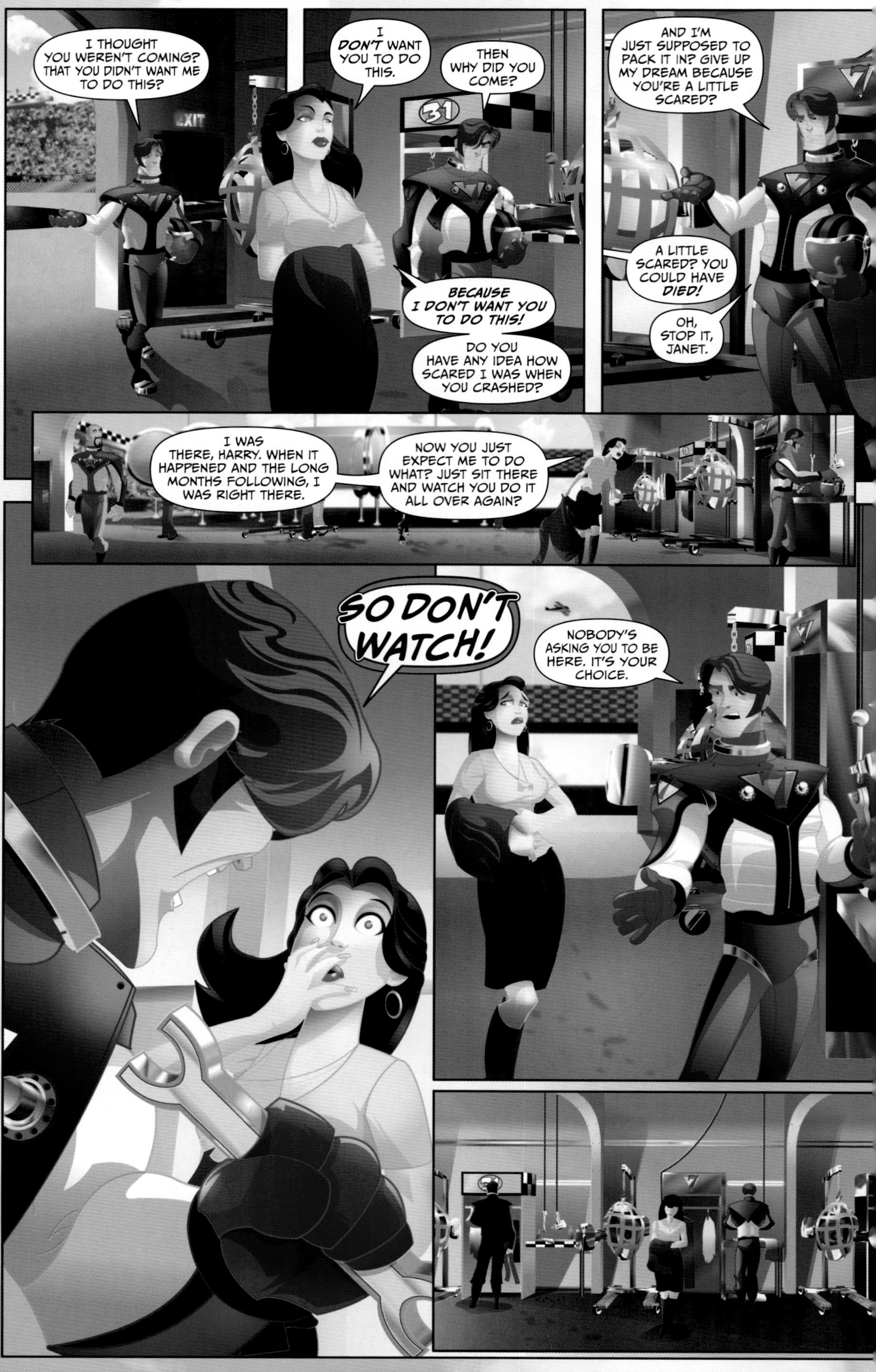
I THOUGHT YOU WEREN'T COMING? THAT YOU DIDN'T WANT ME TO DO THIS?
EXIT
I *DON'T* WANT YOU TO DO THIS.
THEN WHY DID YOU COME?
31
BECAUSE I DON'T WANT YOU TO DO THIS!
DO YOU HAVE ANY IDEA HOW SCARED I WAS WHEN YOU CRASHED?
AND I'M JUST SUPPOSED TO PACK IT IN? GIVE UP MY DREAM BECAUSE YOU'RE A LITTLE SCARED?
A LITTLE SCARED? YOU COULD HAVE *DIED!*
OH, STOP IT, JANET.
I WAS THERE, HARRY. WHEN IT HAPPENED AND THE LONG MONTHS FOLLOWING, I WAS RIGHT THERE.
NOW YOU JUST EXPECT ME TO DO WHAT? JUST SIT THERE AND WATCH YOU DO IT ALL OVER AGAIN?
SO DON'T WATCH!
NOBODY'S ASKING YOU TO BE HERE. IT'S YOUR CHOICE.

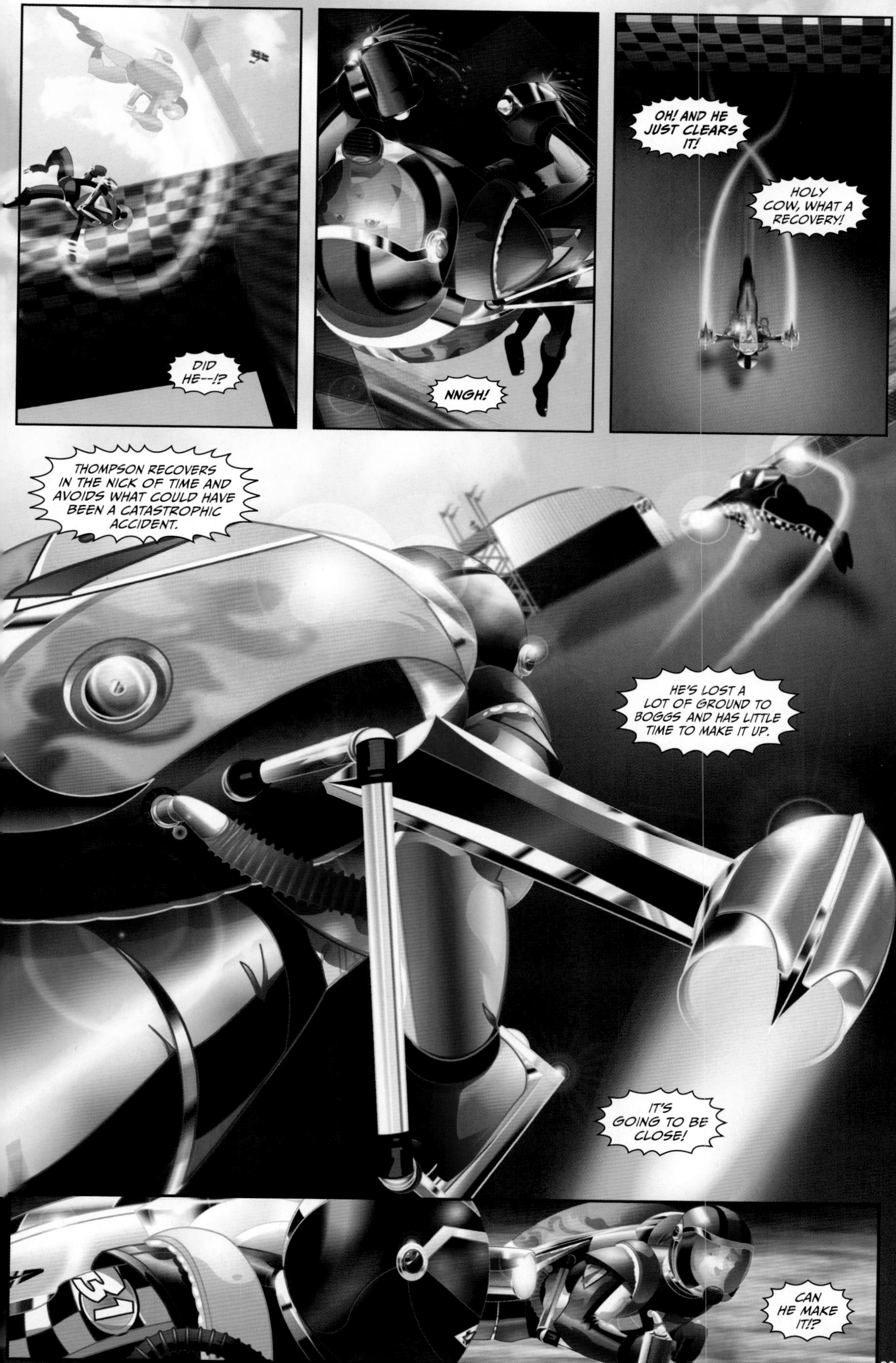
DID HE--!?
NNGH!
OH! AND HE JUST CLEARS IT!
HOLY COW, WHAT A RECOVERY!
THOMPSON RECOVERS IN THE NICK OF TIME AND AVOIDS WHAT COULD HAVE BEEN A CATASTROPHIC ACCIDENT.
HE'S LOST A LOT OF GROUND TO BOGGS AND HAS LITTLE TIME TO MAKE IT UP.
IT'S GOING TO BE CLOSE!
CAN HE MAKE IT!?

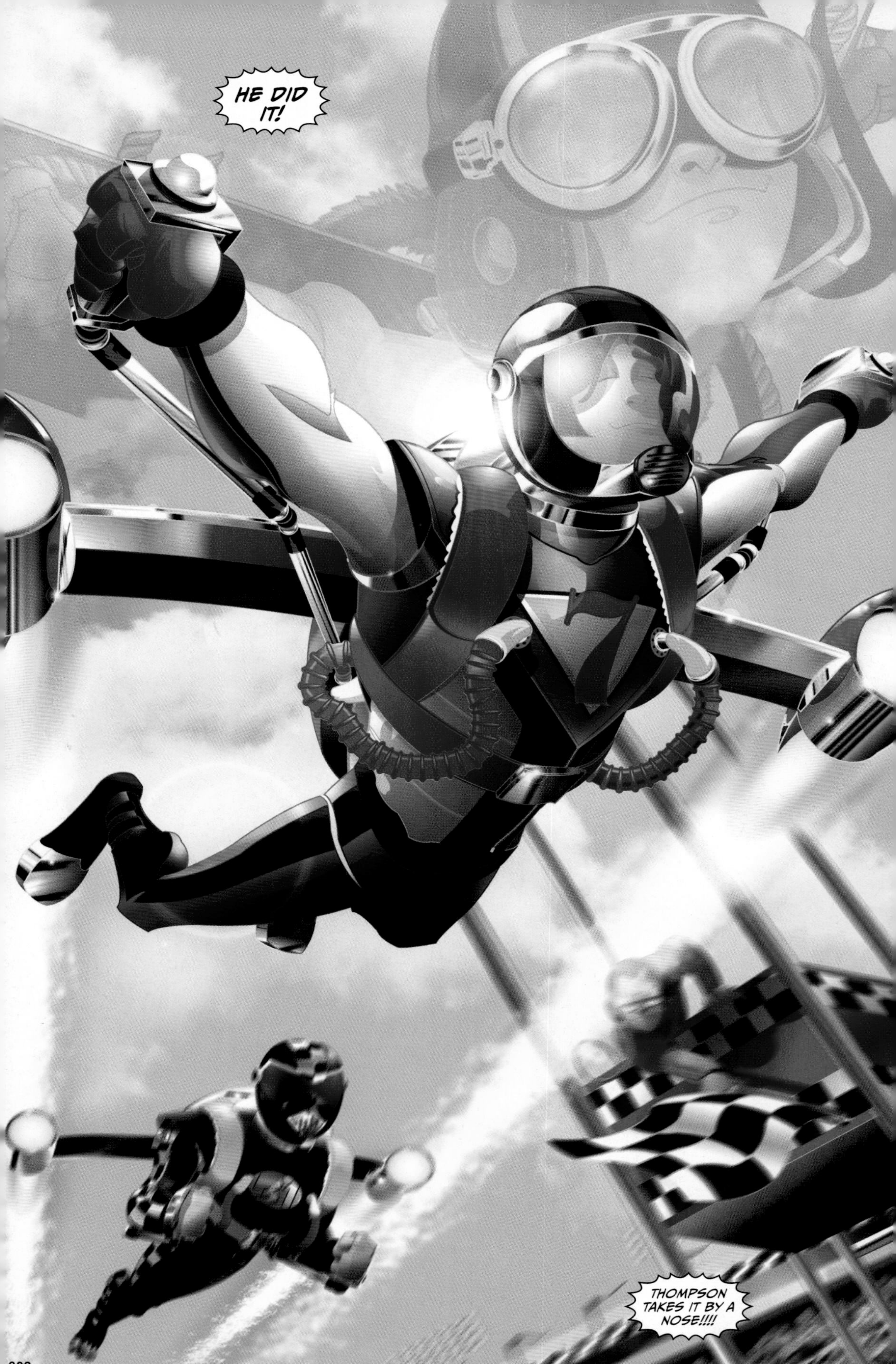
HE DID IT!
THOMPSON TAKES IT BY A NOSE!!!!

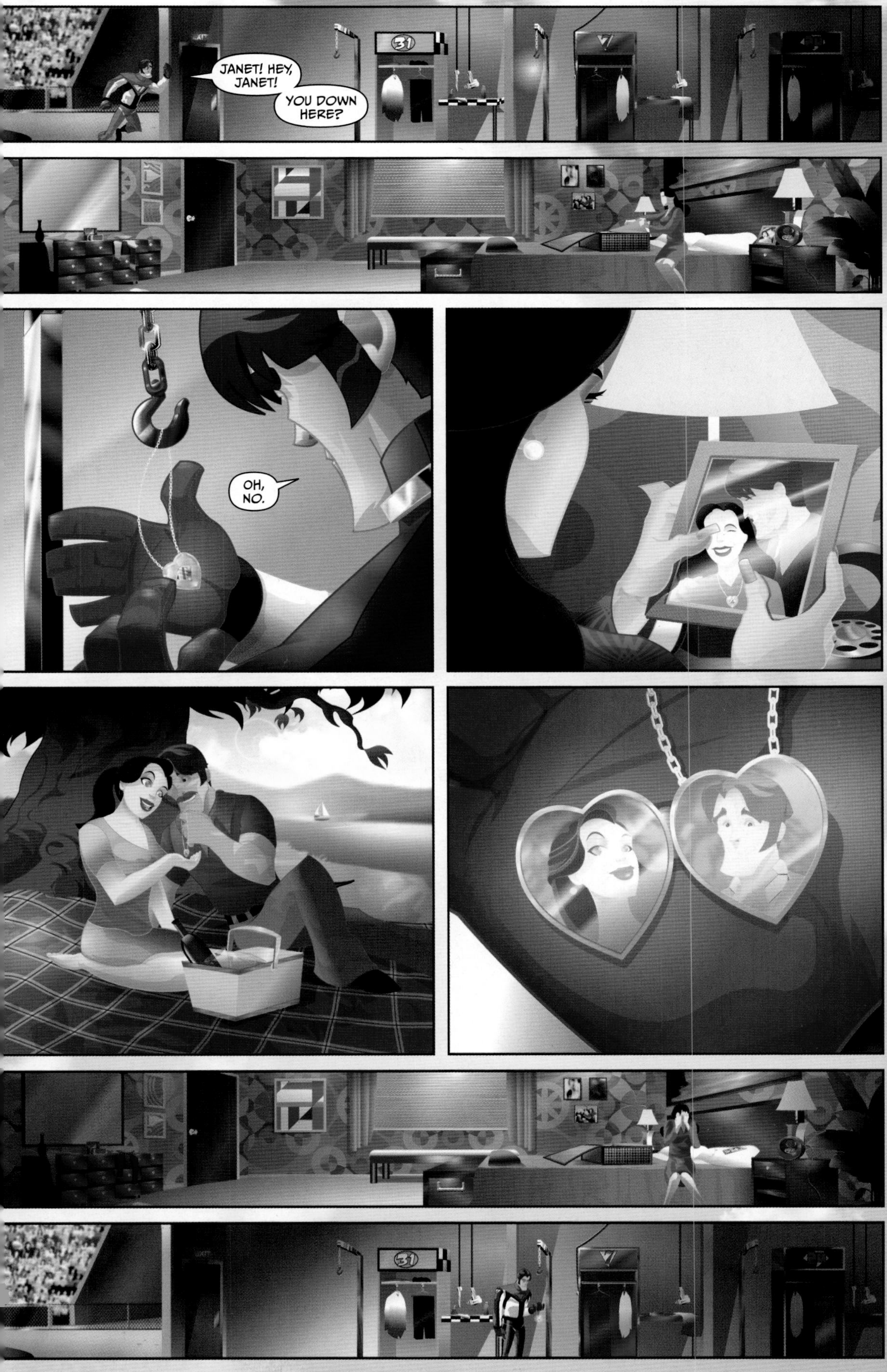
JANET! HEY, JANET!
YOU DOWN HERE?
OH, NO.

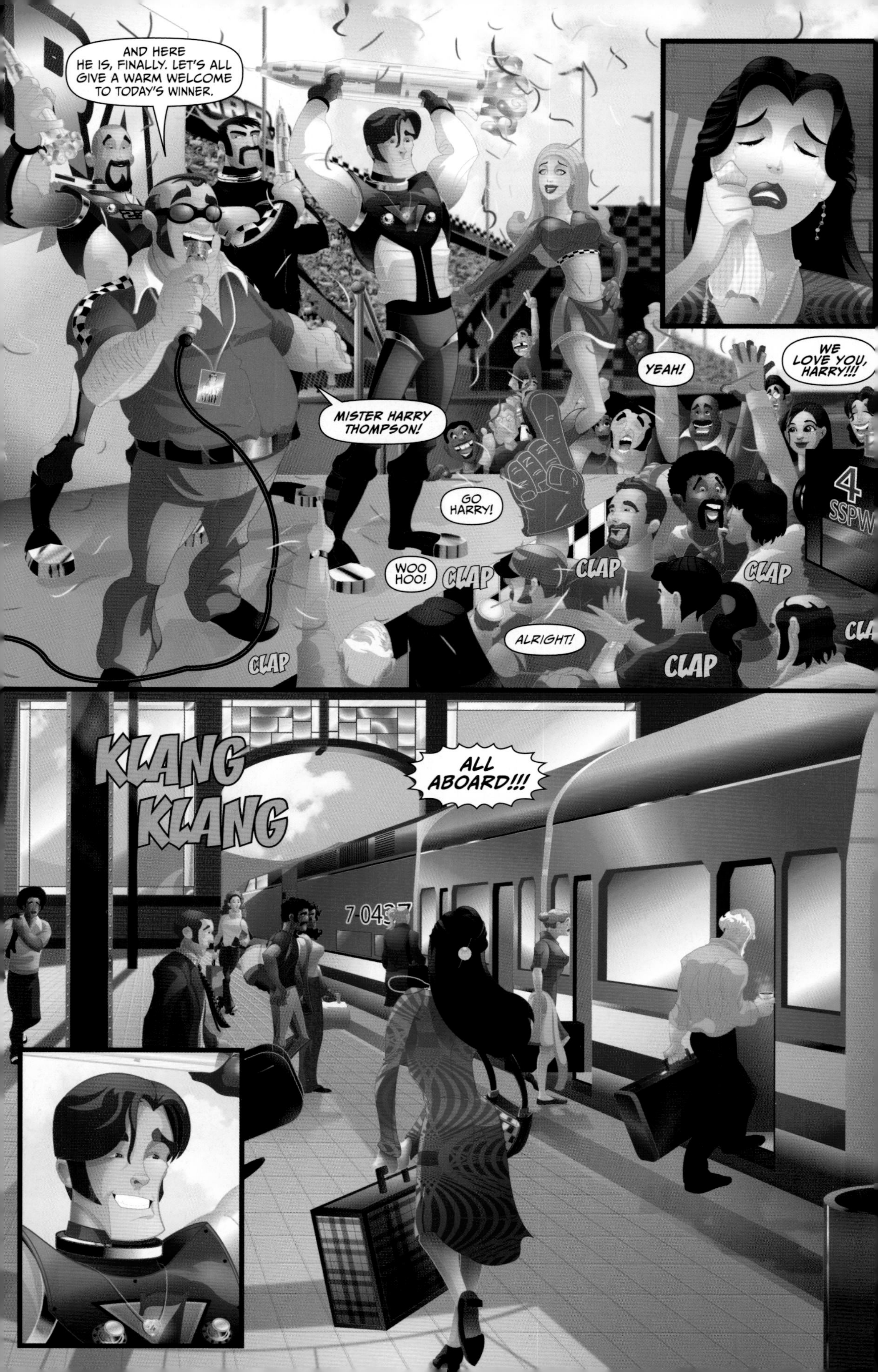
AND HERE HE IS, FINALLY. LET'S ALL GIVE A WARM WELCOME TO TODAY'S WINNER.
MISTER HARRY THOMPSON!
YEAH!
WE LOVE YOU, HARRY!!!
GO HARRY!
WOO HOO!
CLAP
CLAP
CLAP
ALRIGHT!
CLAP
CLAP
KLANG KLANG
ALL ABOARD!!!

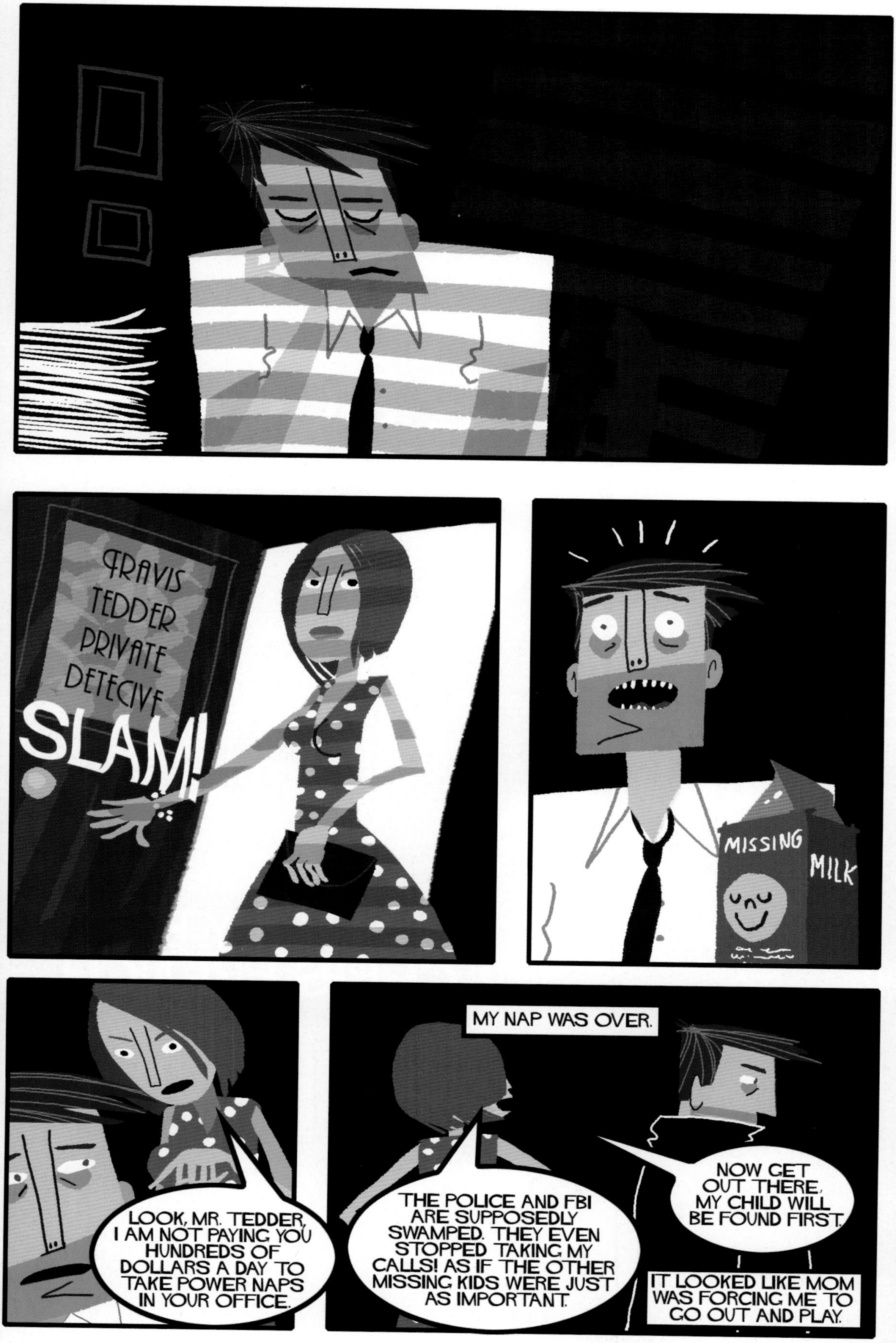
TRAVIS
TEDDER
PRIVATE
DETECTIVE
SLAM!
MISSING
MILK
LOOK, MR. TEDDER, I AM NOT PAYING YOU HUNDREDS OF DOLLARS A DAY TO TAKE POWER NAPS IN YOUR OFFICE.
MY NAP WAS OVER.
THE POLICE AND FBI ARE SUPPOSEDLY SWAMPED. THEY EVEN STOPPED TAKING MY CALLS! AS IF THE OTHER MISSING KIDS WERE JUST AS IMPORTANT.
NOW GET OUT THERE. MY CHILD WILL BE FOUND FIRST.
IT LOOKED LIKE MOM WAS FORCING ME TO GO OUT AND PLAY.

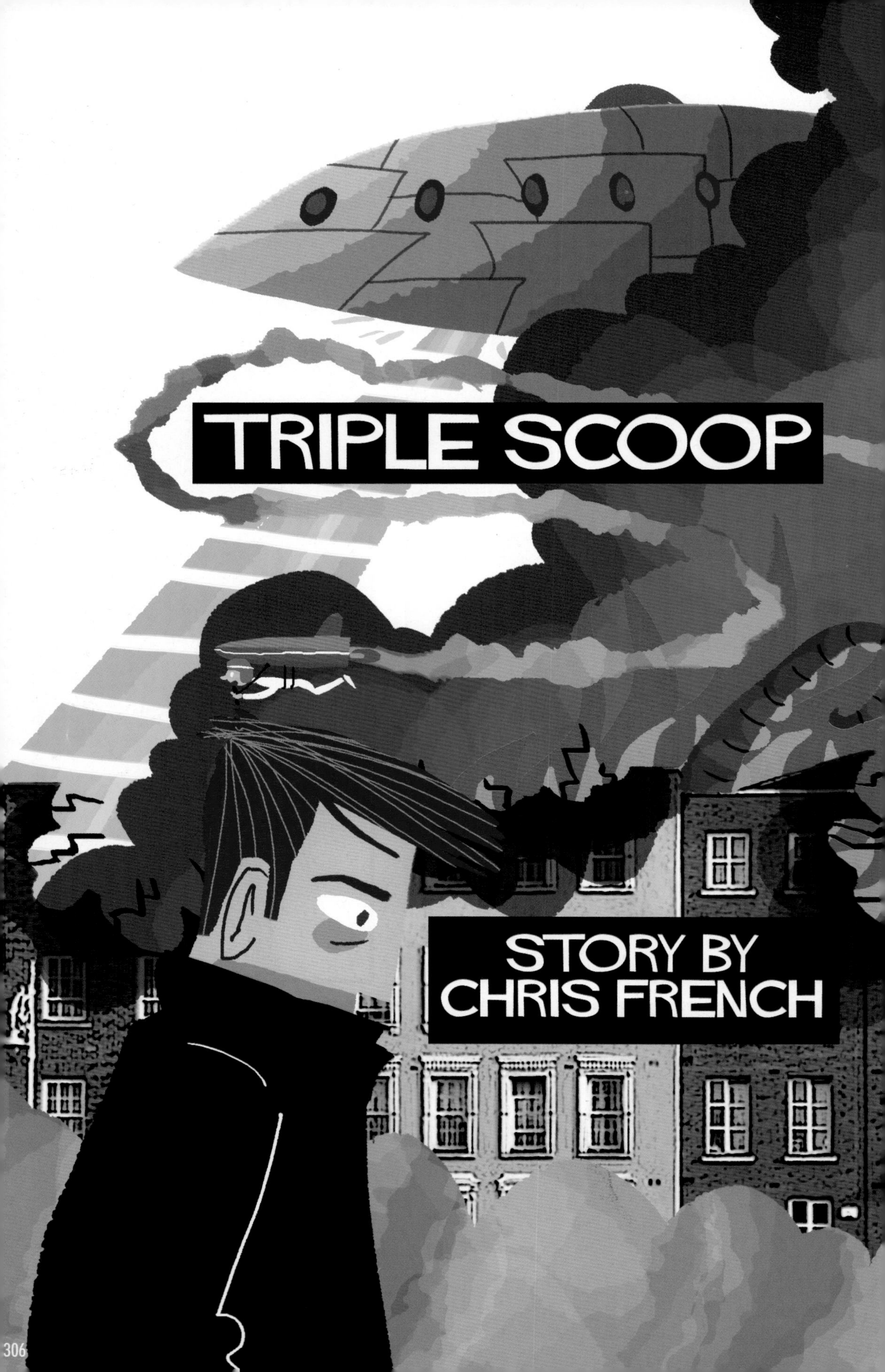
TRIPLE SCOOP
STORY BY
CHRIS FRENCH

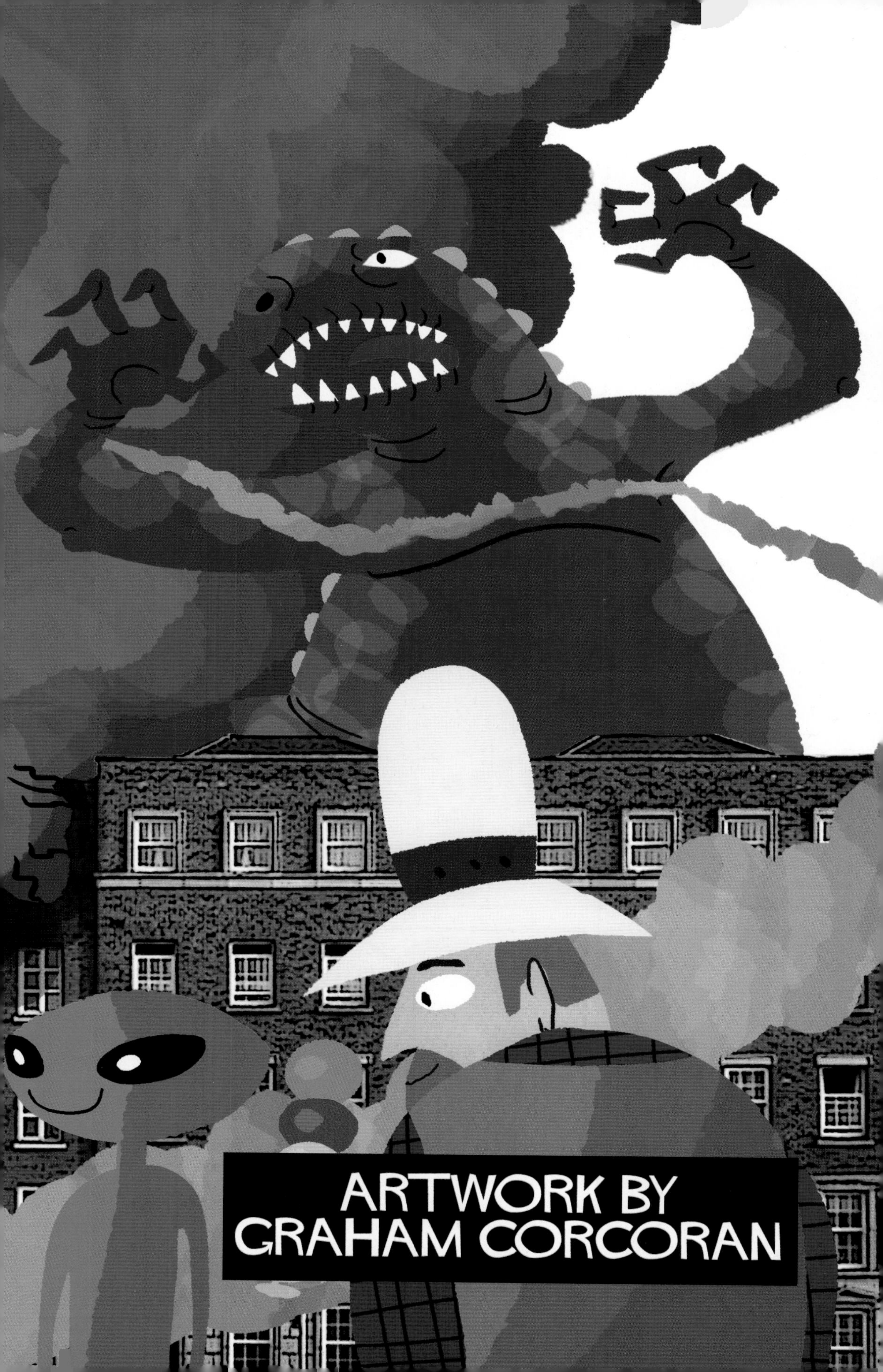
ARTWORK BY
GRAHAM CORCORAN

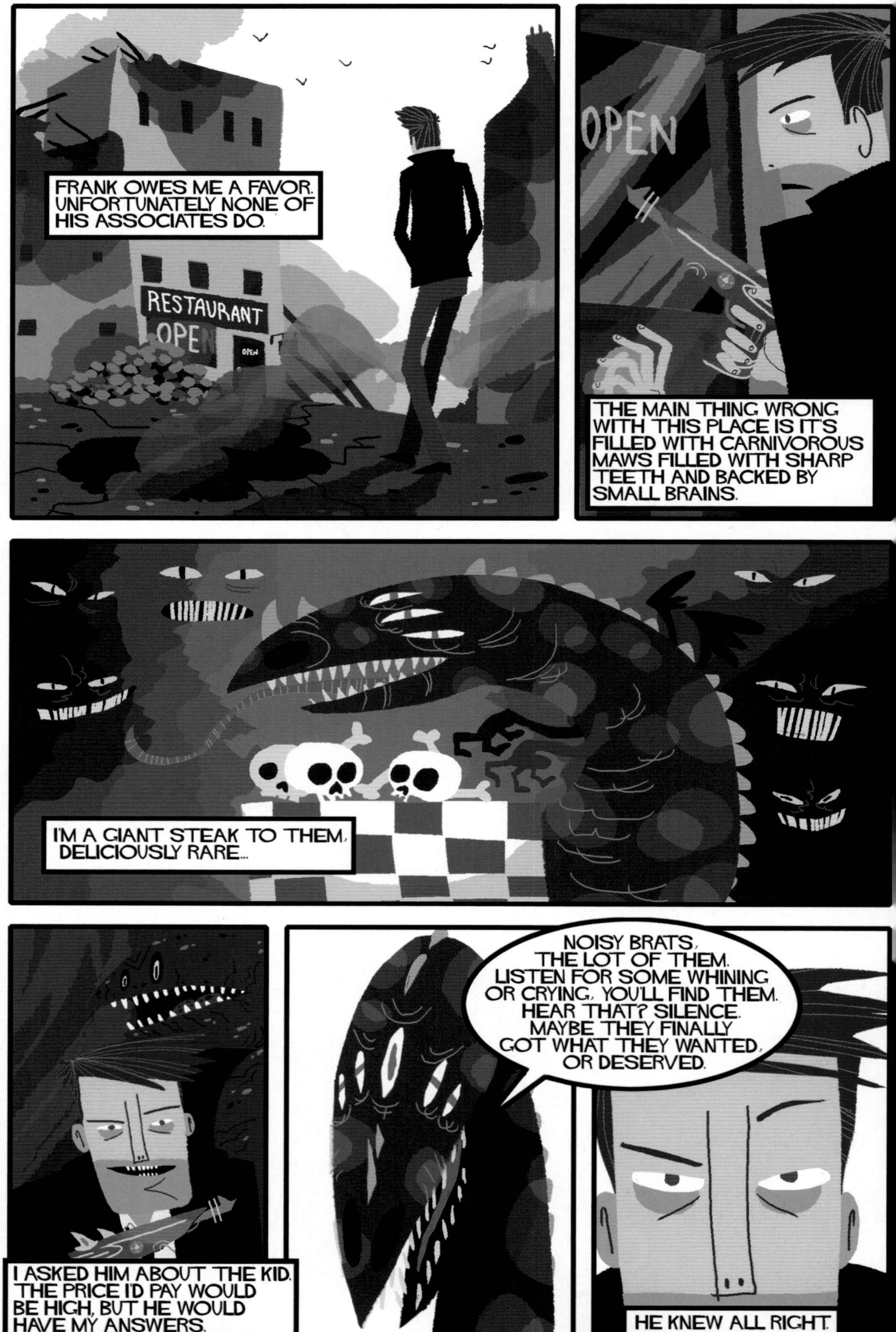
FRANK OWES ME A FAVOR. UNFORTUNATELY NONE OF HIS ASSOCIATES DO.
RESTAURANT
OPE
OPEN
OPEN
THE MAIN THING WRONG WITH THIS PLACE IS IT'S FILLED WITH CARNIVOROUS MAWS FILLED WITH SHARP TEETH AND BACKED BY SMALL BRAINS.
I'M A GIANT STEAK TO THEM, DELICIOUSLY RARE...
I ASKED HIM ABOUT THE KID. THE PRICE I'D PAY WOULD BE HIGH, BUT HE WOULD HAVE MY ANSWERS.
NOISY BRATS, THE LOT OF THEM. LISTEN FOR SOME WHINING OR CRYING, YOU'LL FIND THEM. HEAR THAT? SILENCE. MAYBE THEY FINALLY GOT WHAT THEY WANTED, OR DESERVED.
HE KNEW ALL RIGHT.

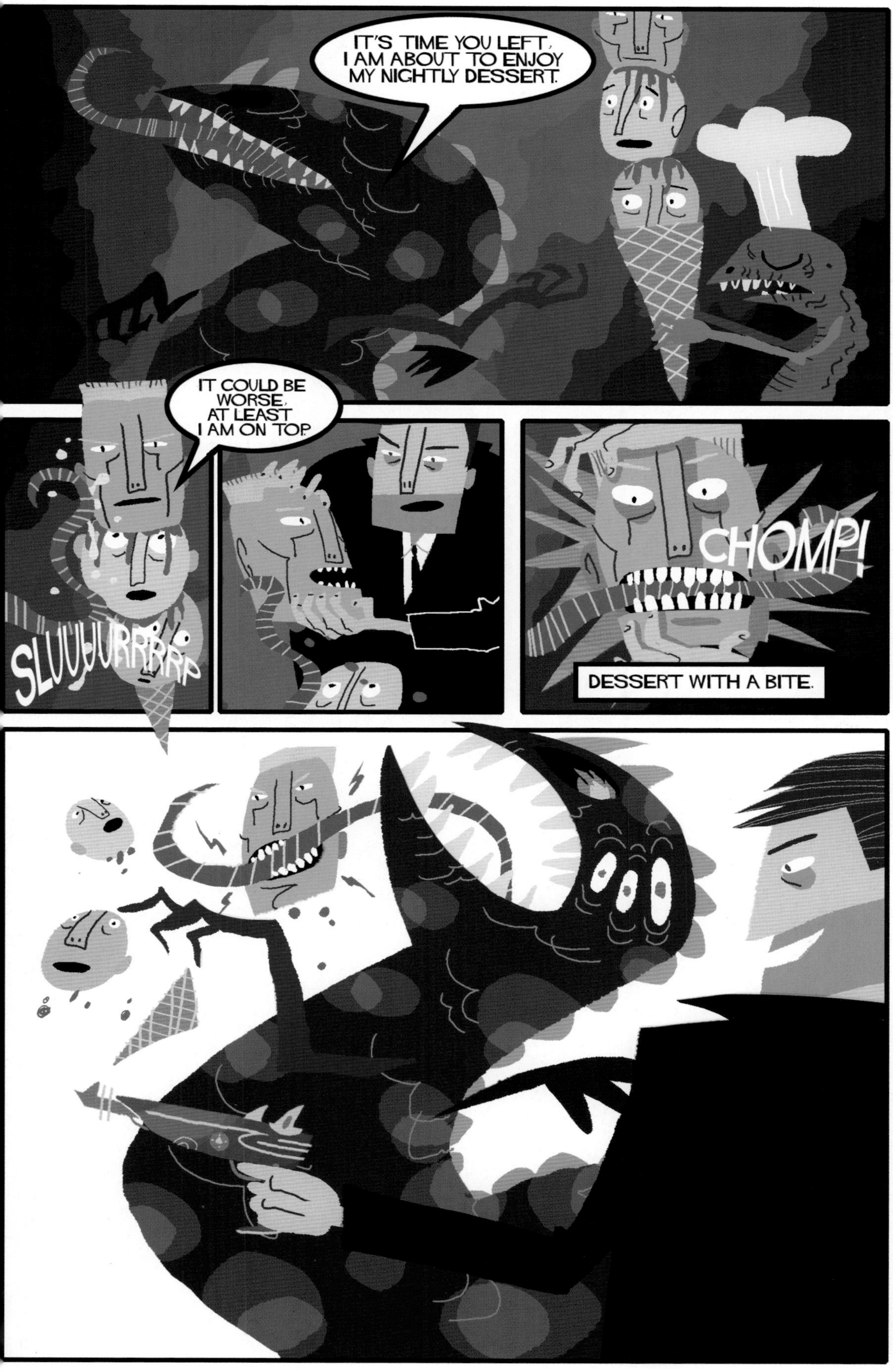
IT'S TIME YOU LEFT, I AM ABOUT TO ENJOY MY NIGHTLY DESSERT.
IT COULD BE WORSE, AT LEAST I AM ON TOP.
SLUUUURRRRP
CHOMP!
DESSERT WITH A BITE.

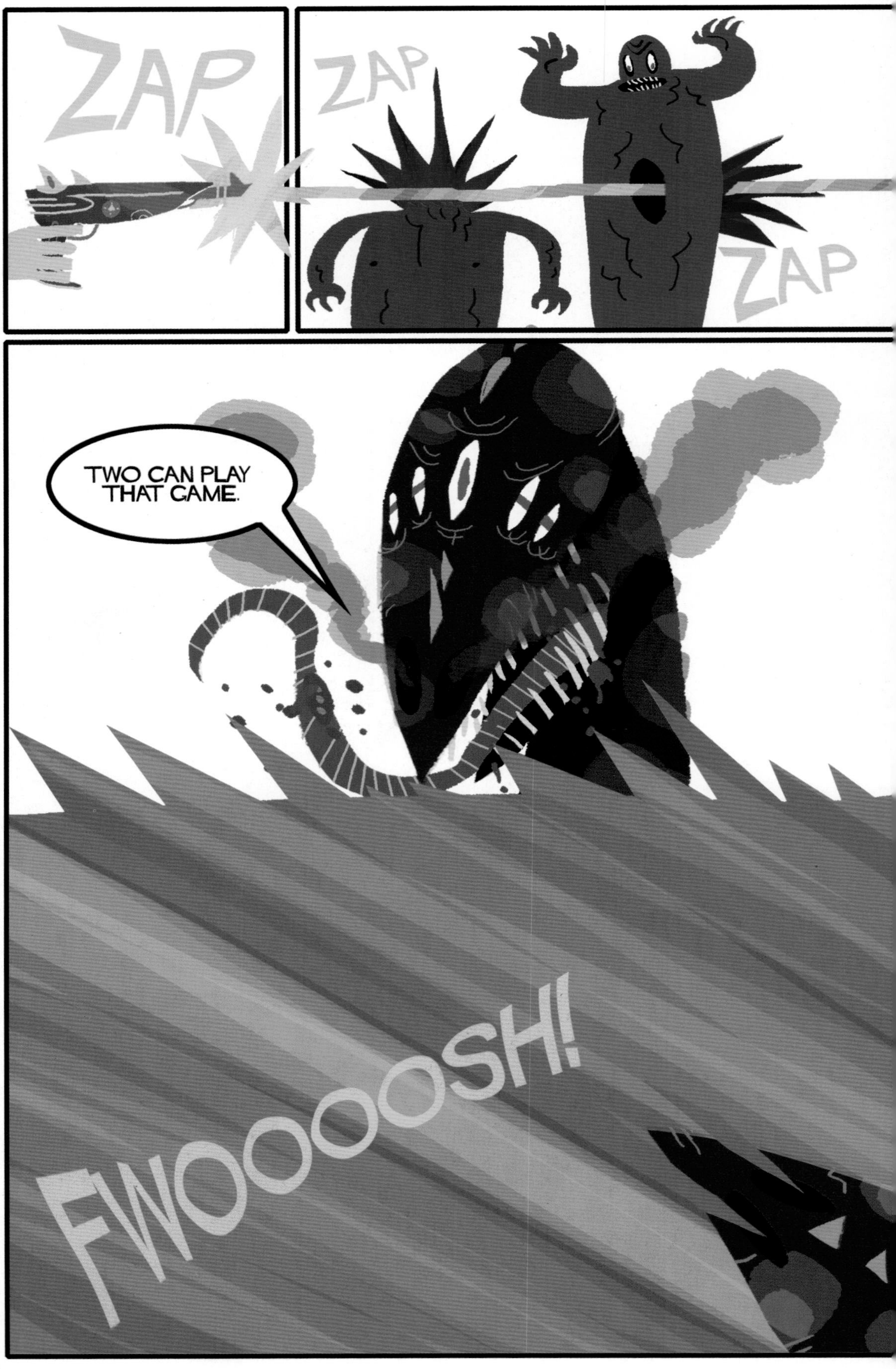
ZAP
ZAP
ZAP
TWO CAN PLAY THAT GAME.
FWOOOOSH!

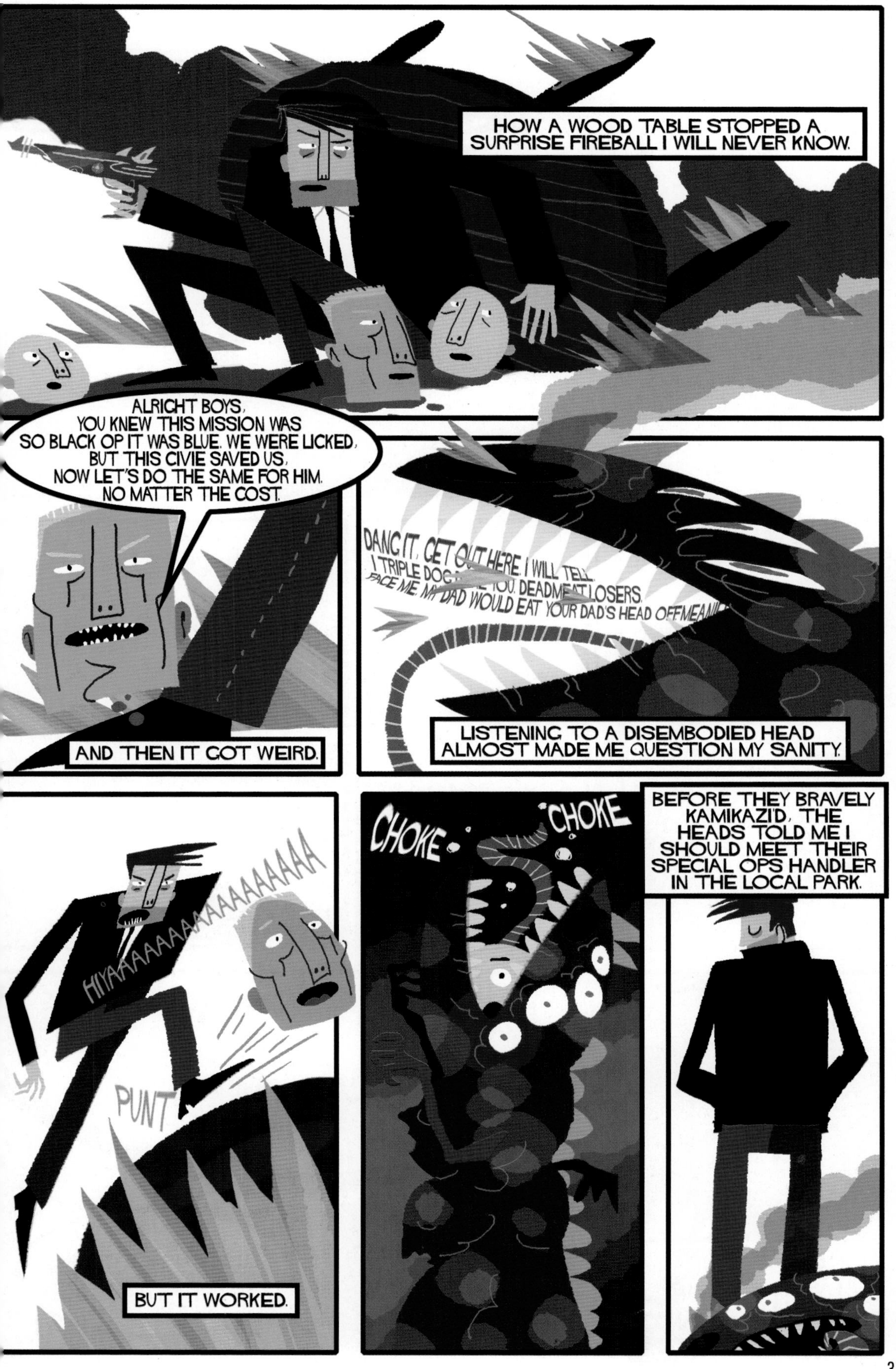
HOW A WOOD TABLE STOPPED A SURPRISE FIREBALL I WILL NEVER KNOW.
ALRIGHT BOYS, YOU KNEW THIS MISSION WAS SO BLACK OP IT WAS BLUE. WE WERE LICKED, BUT THIS CIVIE SAVED US, NOW LET'S DO THE SAME FOR HIM. NO MATTER THE COST.
AND THEN IT GOT WEIRD.
DANG IT. GET OUT HERE. I WILL TELL.
I TRIPLE DOG
YOU. DEADMEAT LOSERS.
FACE ME. MY DAD WOULD EAT YOUR DAD'S HEAD OFF.
LISTENING TO A DISEMBODIED HEAD ALMOST MADE ME QUESTION MY SANITY.
HIYAAAAAAAAAAAAAAAAAAAAA
PUNT
BUT IT WORKED.
CHOKE
CHOKE
BEFORE THEY BRAVELY KAMIKAZI'D, THE HEADS TOLD ME I SHOULD MEET THEIR SPECIAL OPS HANDLER IN THE LOCAL PARK.

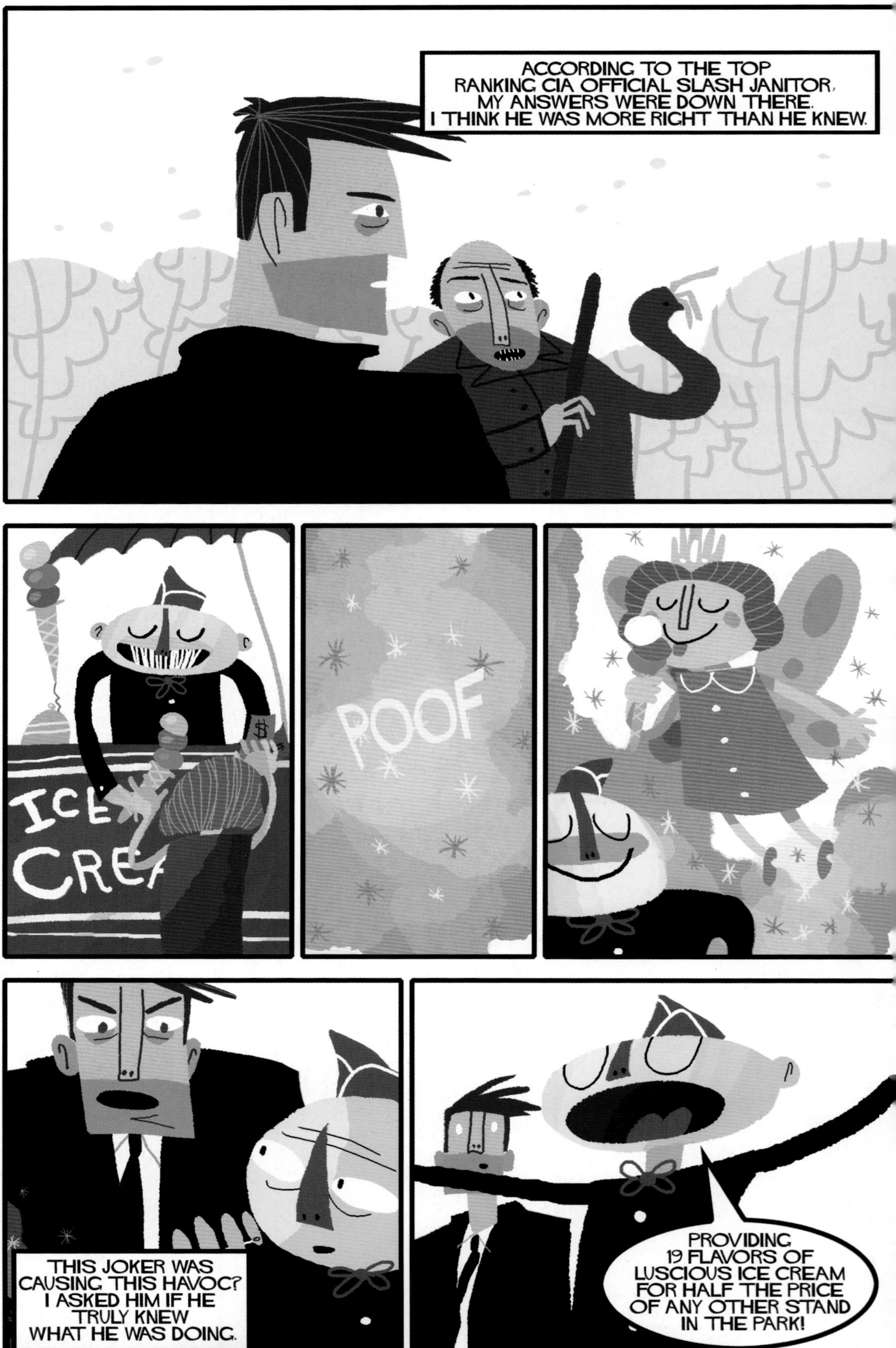
ACCORDING TO THE TOP RANKING CIA OFFICIAL SLASH JANITOR, MY ANSWERS WERE DOWN THERE. I THINK HE WAS MORE RIGHT THAN HE KNEW.
ICE CREA
POOF
THIS JOKER WAS CAUSING THIS HAVOC? I ASKED HIM IF HE TRULY KNEW WHAT HE WAS DOING.
PROVIDING 19 FLAVORS OF LUSCIOUS ICE CREAM FOR HALF THE PRICE OF ANY OTHER STAND IN THE PARK!

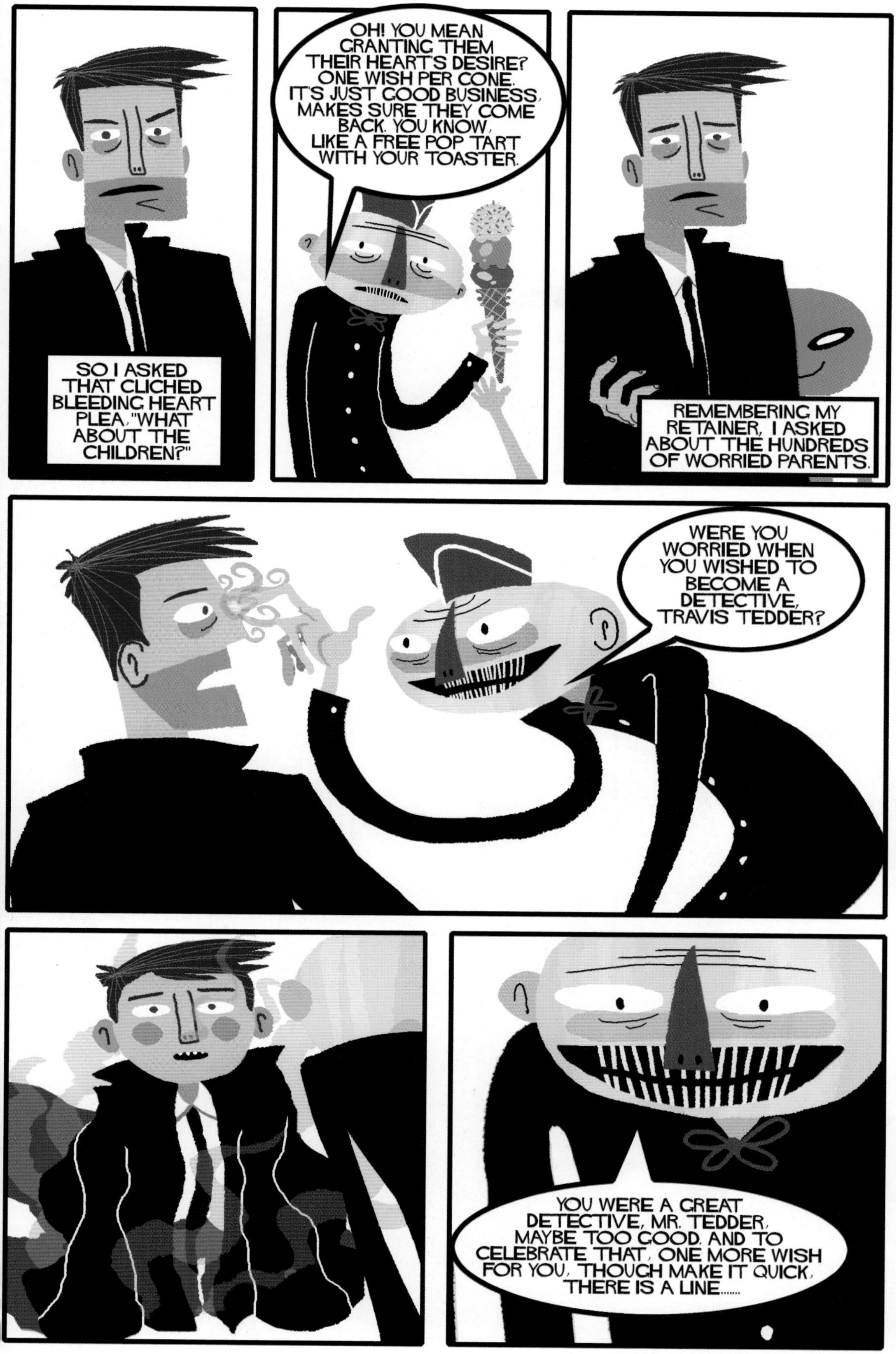
SO I ASKED THAT CLICHED BLEEDING HEART PLEA, "WHAT ABOUT THE CHILDREN?"
OH! YOU MEAN GRANTING THEM THEIR HEART'S DESIRE? ONE WISH PER CONE. IT'S JUST GOOD BUSINESS, MAKES SURE THEY COME BACK. YOU KNOW, LIKE A FREE POP TART WITH YOUR TOASTER.
REMEMBERING MY RETAINER, I ASKED ABOUT THE HUNDREDS OF WORRIED PARENTS.
WERE YOU WORRIED WHEN YOU WISHED TO BECOME A DETECTIVE, TRAVIS TEDDER?
YOU WERE A GREAT DETECTIVE, MR. TEDDER, MAYBE TOO GOOD. AND TO CELEBRATE THAT, ONE MORE WISH FOR YOU, THOUGH MAKE IT QUICK, THERE IS A LINE......

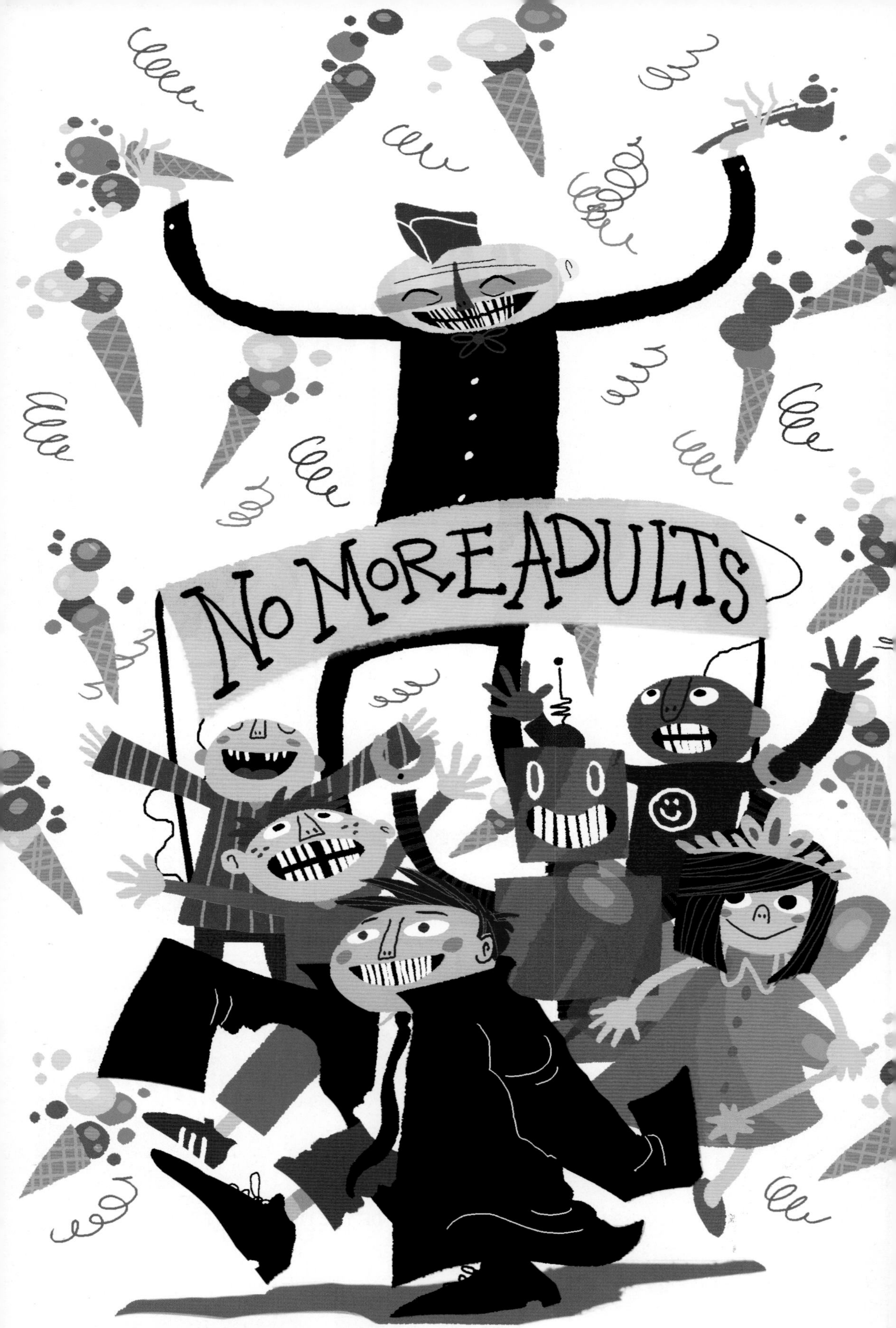
NO MORE ADULTS

AND THEN MY TRUE WISH WAS FULFILLED.

FIN.

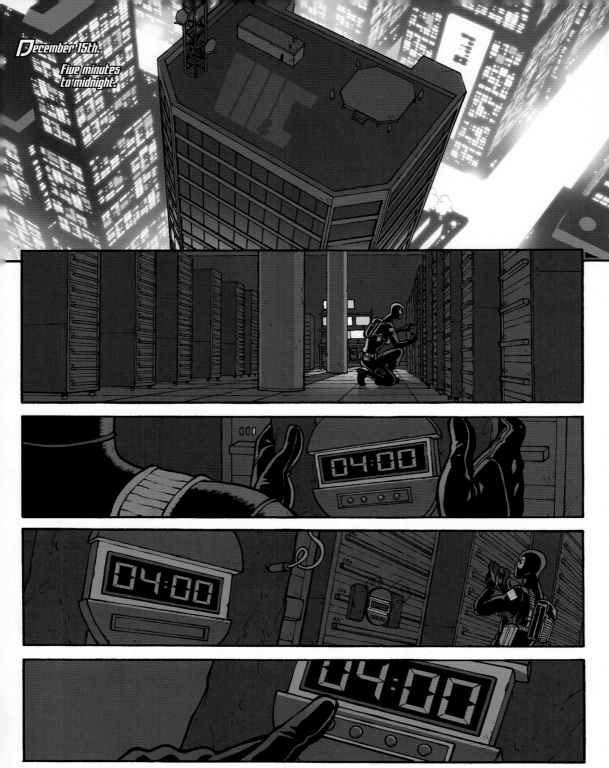

December 15th.
Five minutes to midnight.

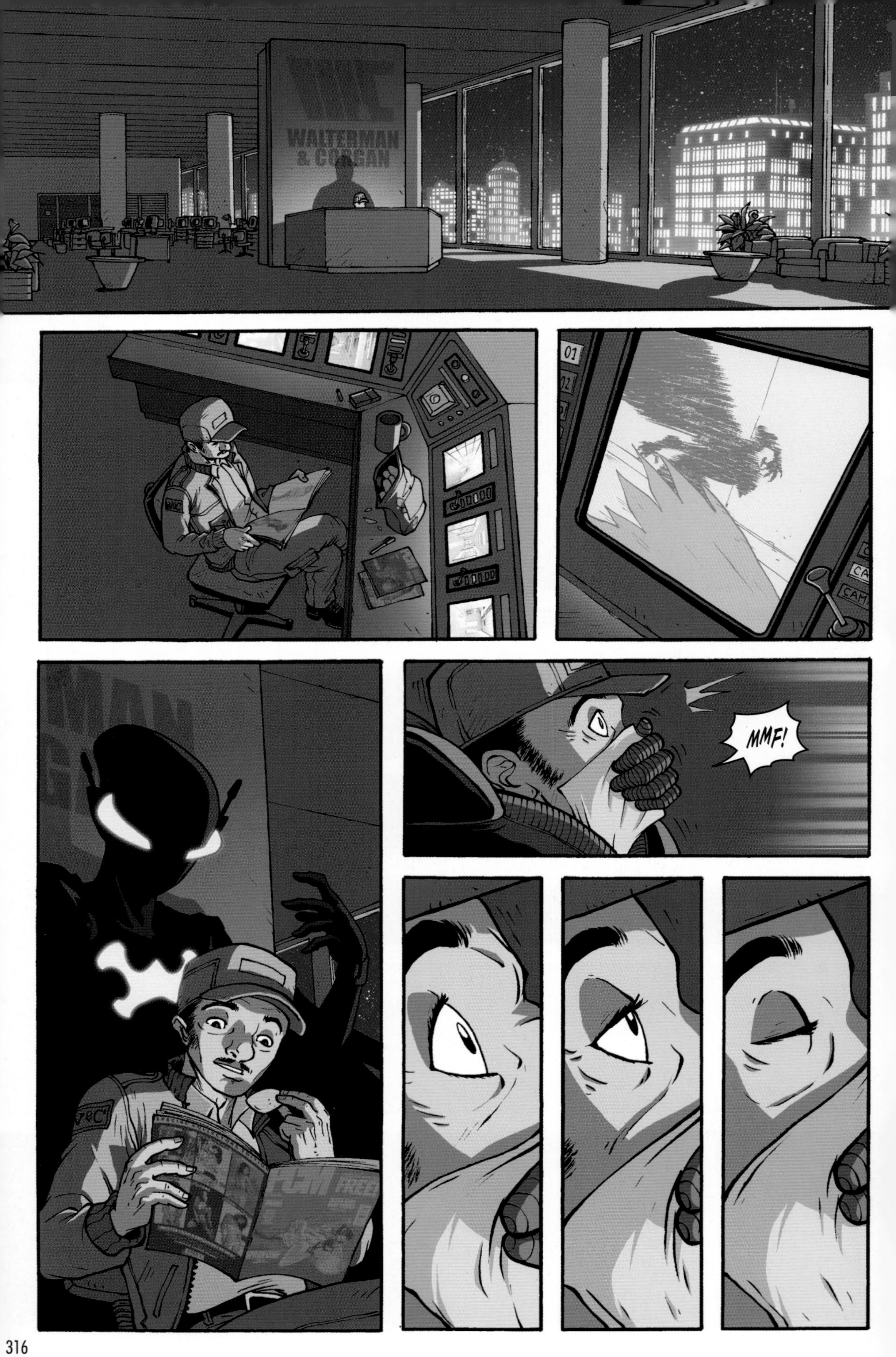
WALTERMAN
& CORGAN
MMF!

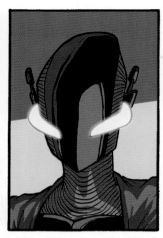

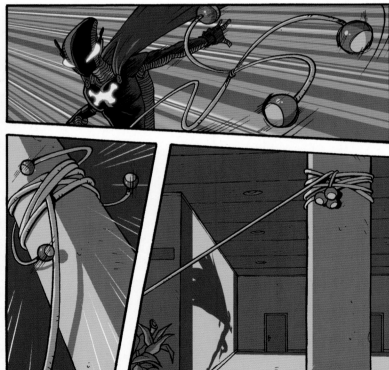

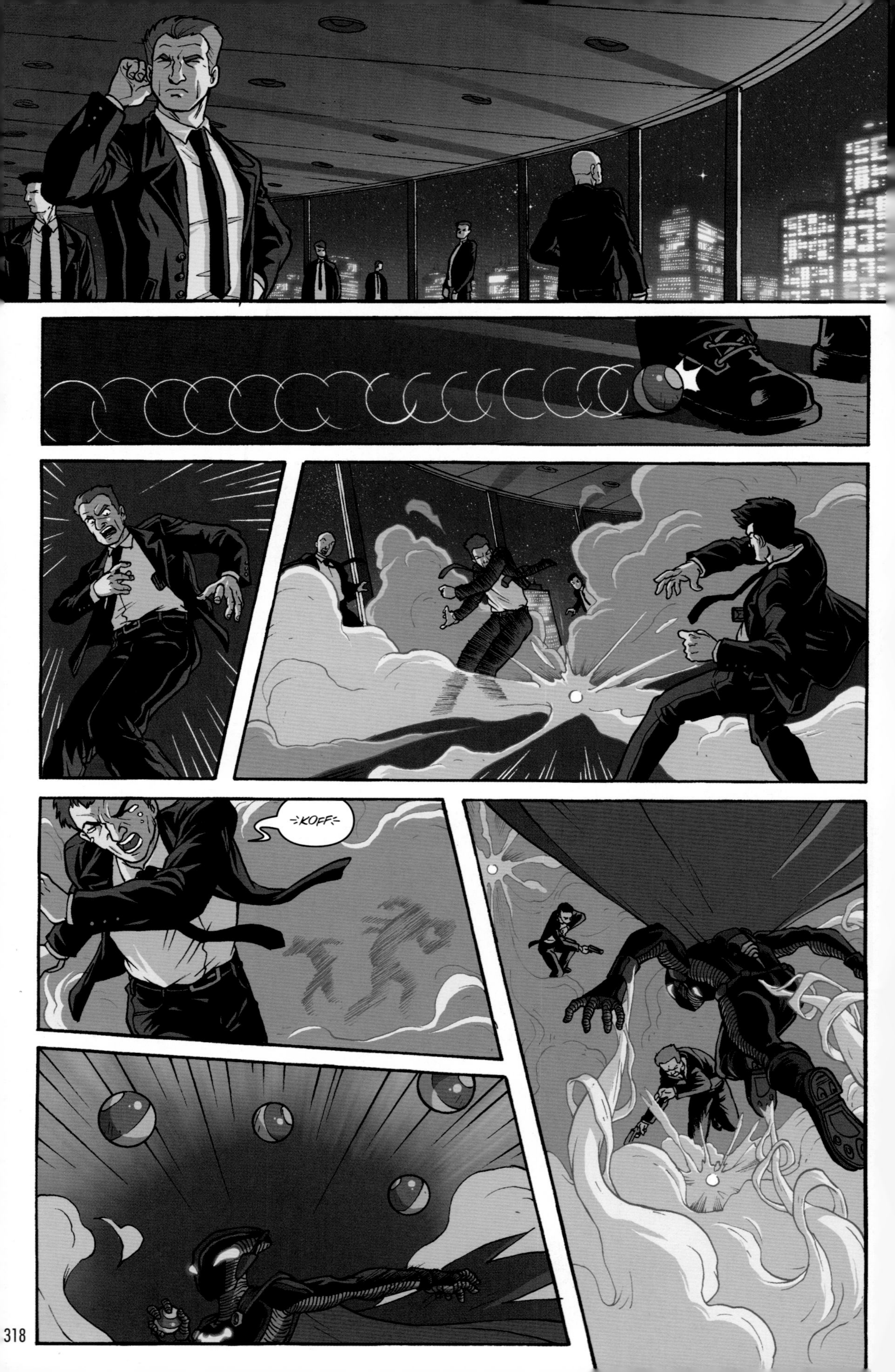
=KOFF=

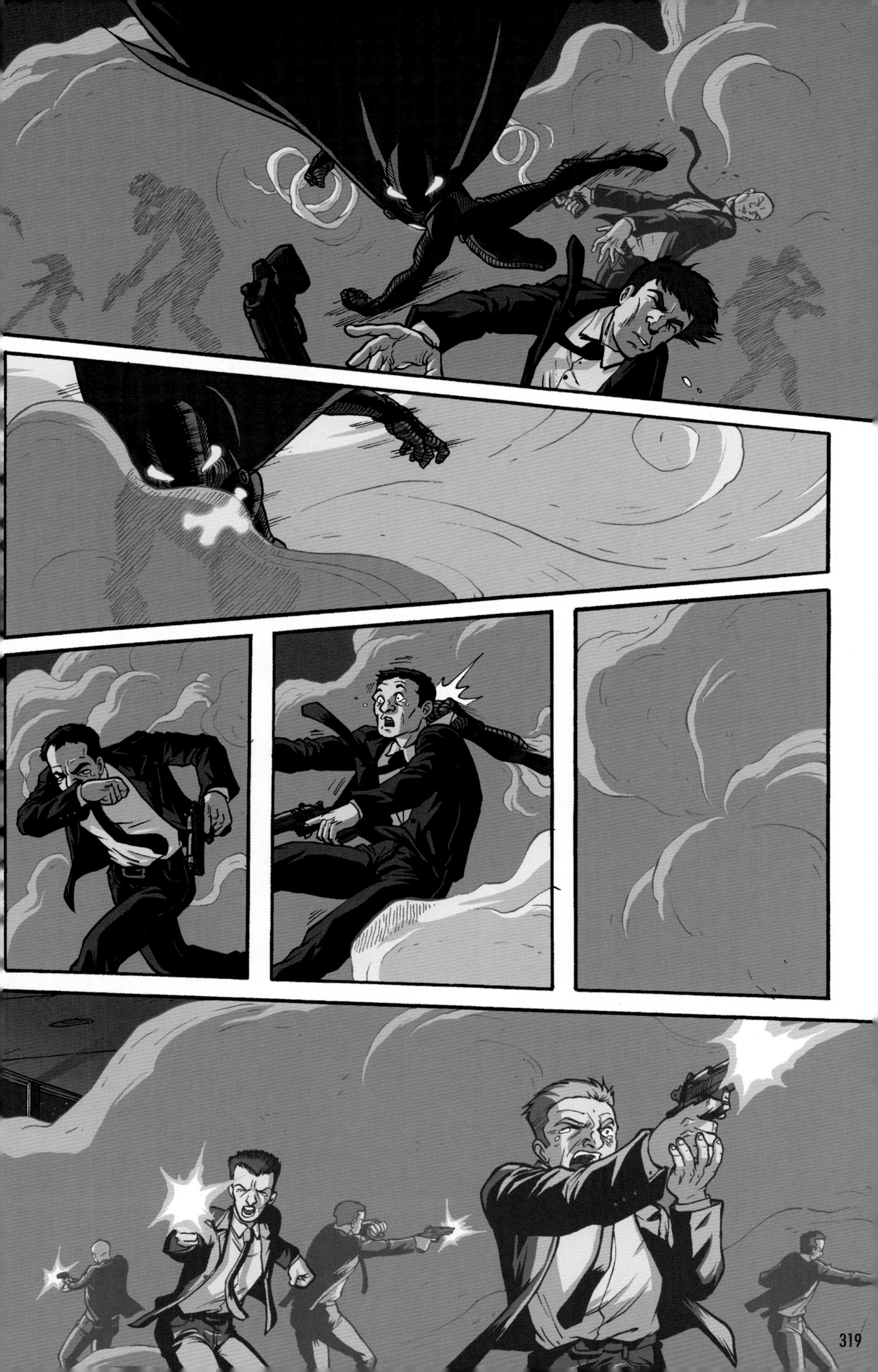

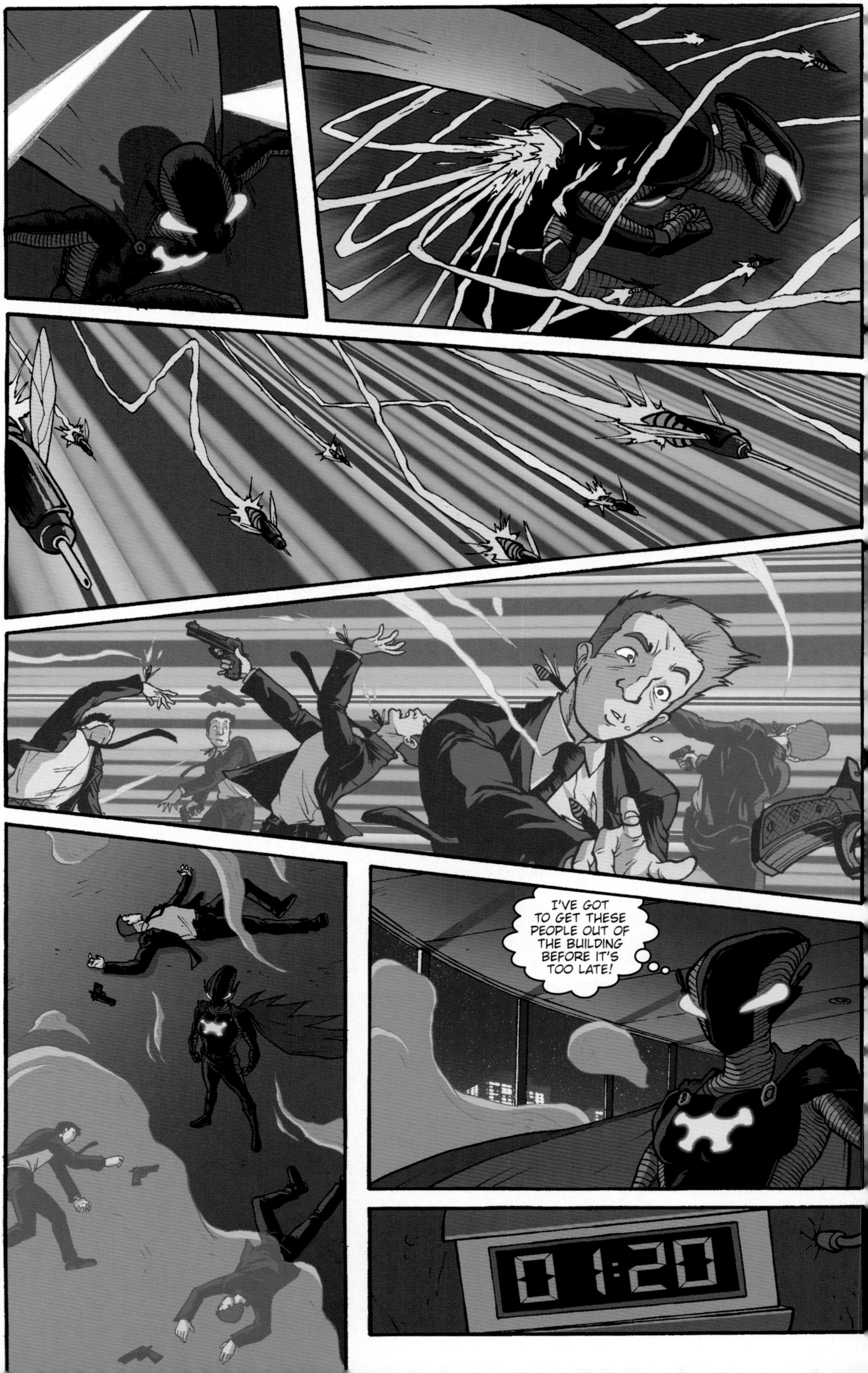
I'VE GOT TO GET THESE PEOPLE OUT OF THE BUILDING BEFORE IT'S TOO LATE!
01:20

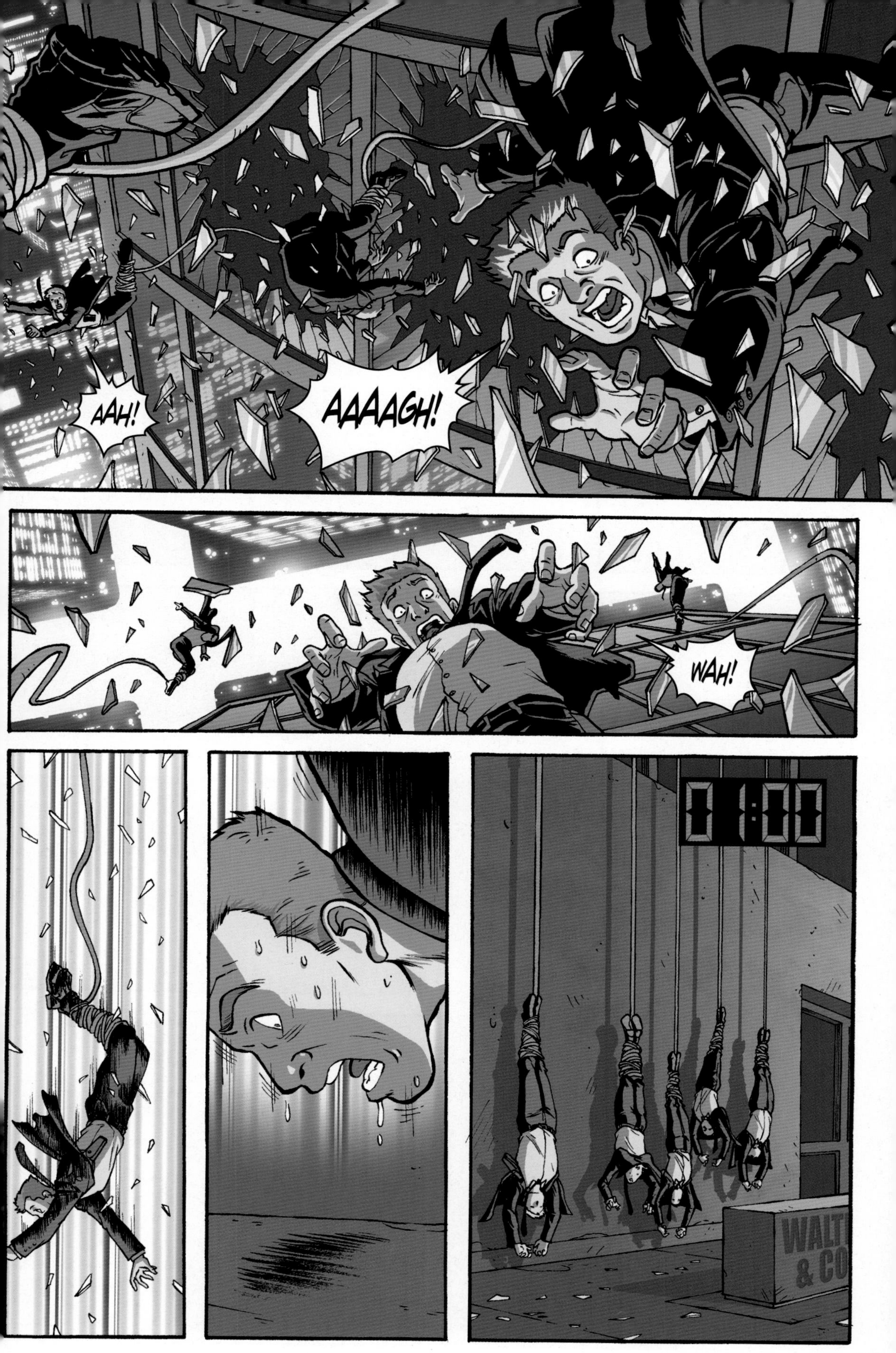
AAH!
AAAAGH!
WAH!
01:00
WALT
& CO

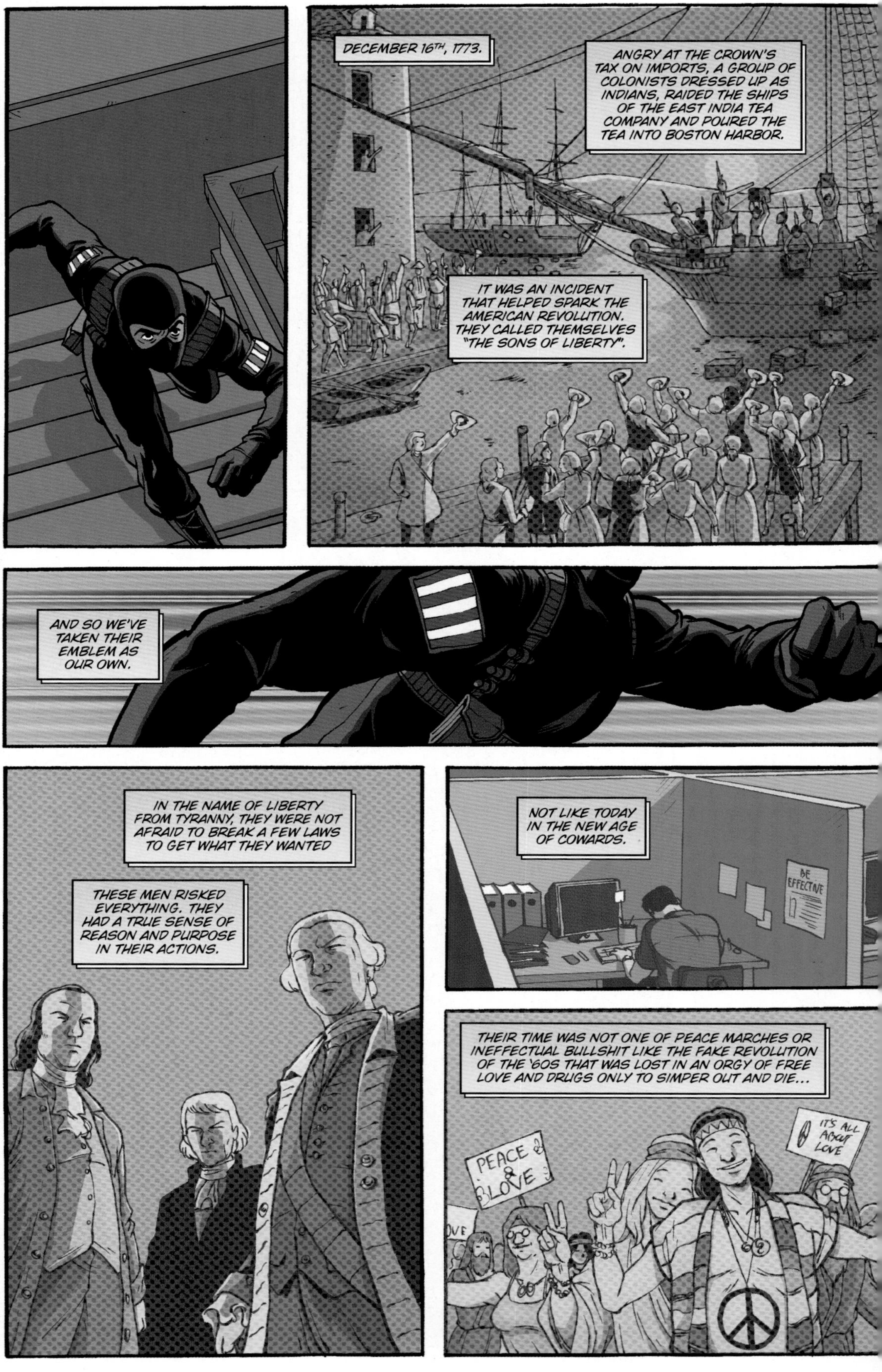
DECEMBER 16TH, 1773.
ANGRY AT THE CROWN'S TAX ON IMPORTS, A GROUP OF COLONISTS DRESSED UP AS INDIANS, RAIDED THE SHIPS OF THE EAST INDIA TEA COMPANY AND POURED THE TEA INTO BOSTON HARBOR.
IT WAS AN INCIDENT THAT HELPED SPARK THE AMERICAN REVOLUTION. THEY CALLED THEMSELVES "THE SONS OF LIBERTY".
AND SO WE'VE TAKEN THEIR EMBLEM AS OUR OWN.
IN THE NAME OF LIBERTY FROM TYRANNY, THEY WERE NOT AFRAID TO BREAK A FEW LAWS TO GET WHAT THEY WANTED
THESE MEN RISKED EVERYTHING. THEY HAD A TRUE SENSE OF REASON AND PURPOSE IN THEIR ACTIONS.
NOT LIKE TODAY IN THE NEW AGE OF COWARDS.
BE EFFECTIVE
THEIR TIME WAS NOT ONE OF PEACE MARCHES OR INEFFECTUAL BULLSHIT LIKE THE FAKE REVOLUTION OF THE '60S THAT WAS LOST IN AN ORGY OF FREE LOVE AND DRUGS ONLY TO SIMPER OUT AND DIE...
PEACE & LOVE
IT'S ALL ABOUT LOVE

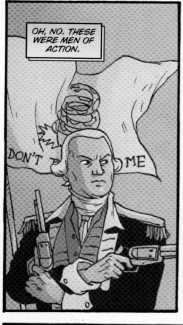

OH, NO. THESE WERE MEN OF ACTION.
DON'T ME
VIOLENT OPPRESSION SHOULD BE MET WITH STRONG RETALIATION.
IN CONGRESS
A DECLARATION
UNITED STATES OF AMERICA.
IN THE DECLARATION OF INDEPENDENCE IT STATES THAT IF A GOVERNMENT BECOMES OPPRESSIVE IT IS THE DUTY OF THE PEOPLE TO RISE UP AND CHANGE THAT GOVERNMENT.
AS CITIZENS, WE HAVE A CONTRACT WITH THE GOVERNMENT BY WAY OF THE CONSTITUTION --
-- NOT WITH PRIVATE COMPANIES WHO HAVE TAKEN EVERYTHING OVER AND CREATED A SYSTEM TO KEEP PEOPLE IN BONDAGE.
THE GOVERNMENT IS NOW RUN BY GANGSTERS AND YAKUZA -- MEN THAT BOUGHT AND PAID FOR AMERICA.
WHEN THOSE COMPANIES BECOME MORE IMPORTANT THAN THE PEOPLE, THEY BECOME THE NEW KINGS AND DESPOTS THAT MUST BE OVERTHROWN.
THE OCTOPUS'S HANDS ARE EVERYWHERE.
BILL OF RIGHTS
THERE'S A NEW KING GEORGE IN TOWN.
I'M NOT AN EVIL MAN. I JUST DO WHAT EVERYONE ELSE IS TOO SCARED TO DO -- MY CIVIC DUTY.
FOR TRUE FREEDOM, IT TAKES BALLS AND RISK. IT TAKES ACTION.

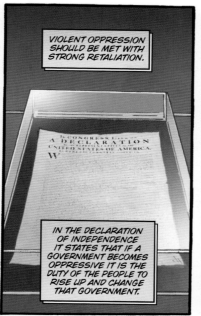

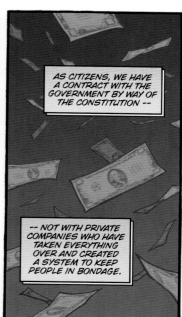

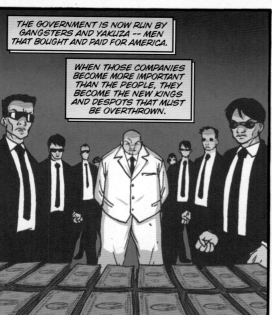

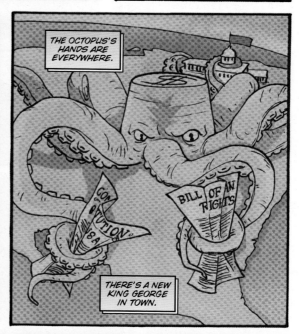

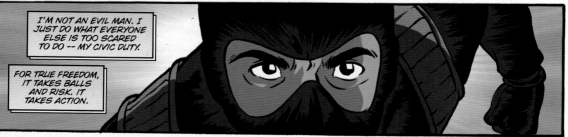

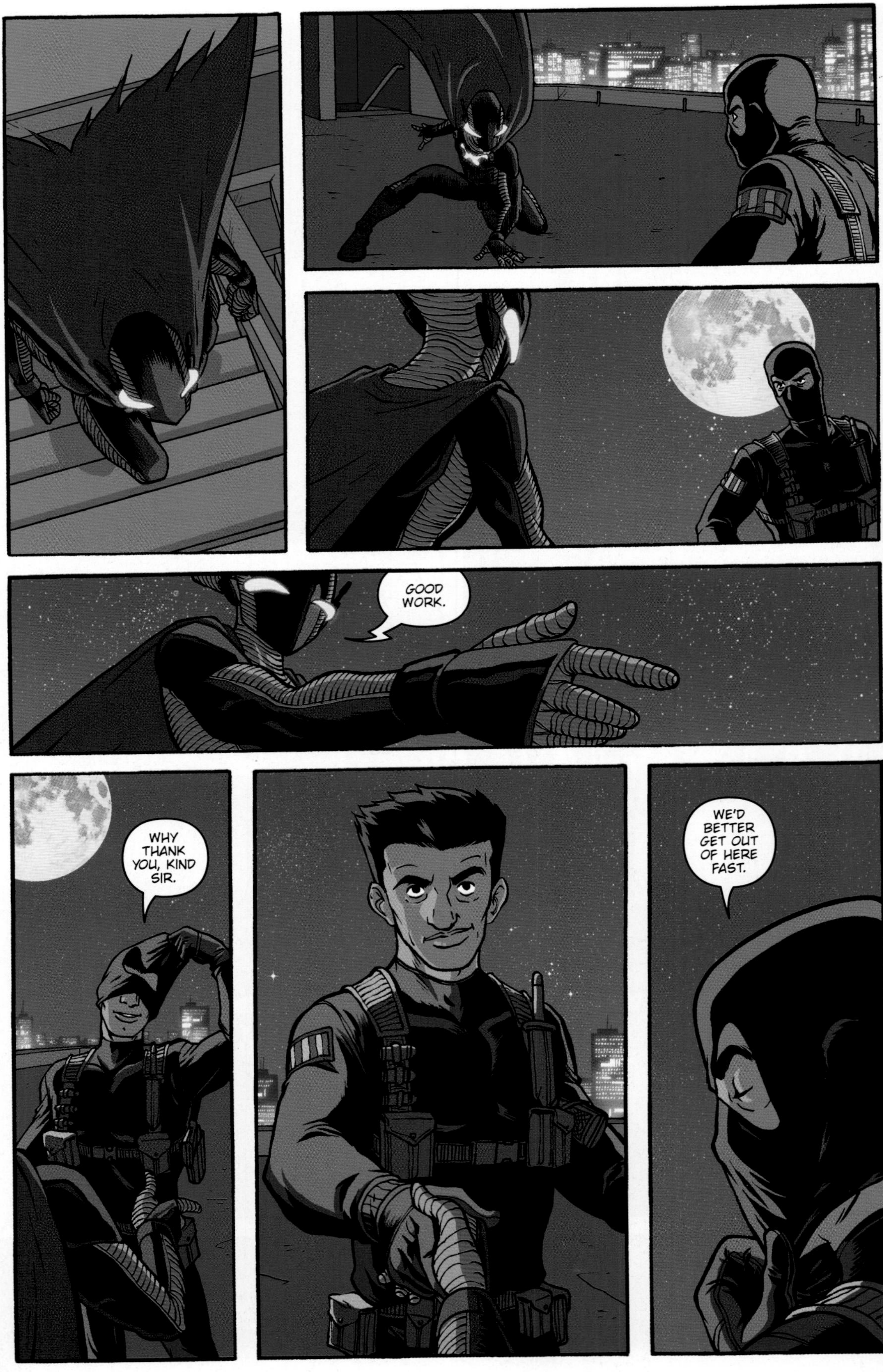
GOOD WORK.
WHY THANK YOU, KIND SIR.
WE'D BETTER GET OUT OF HERE FAST.

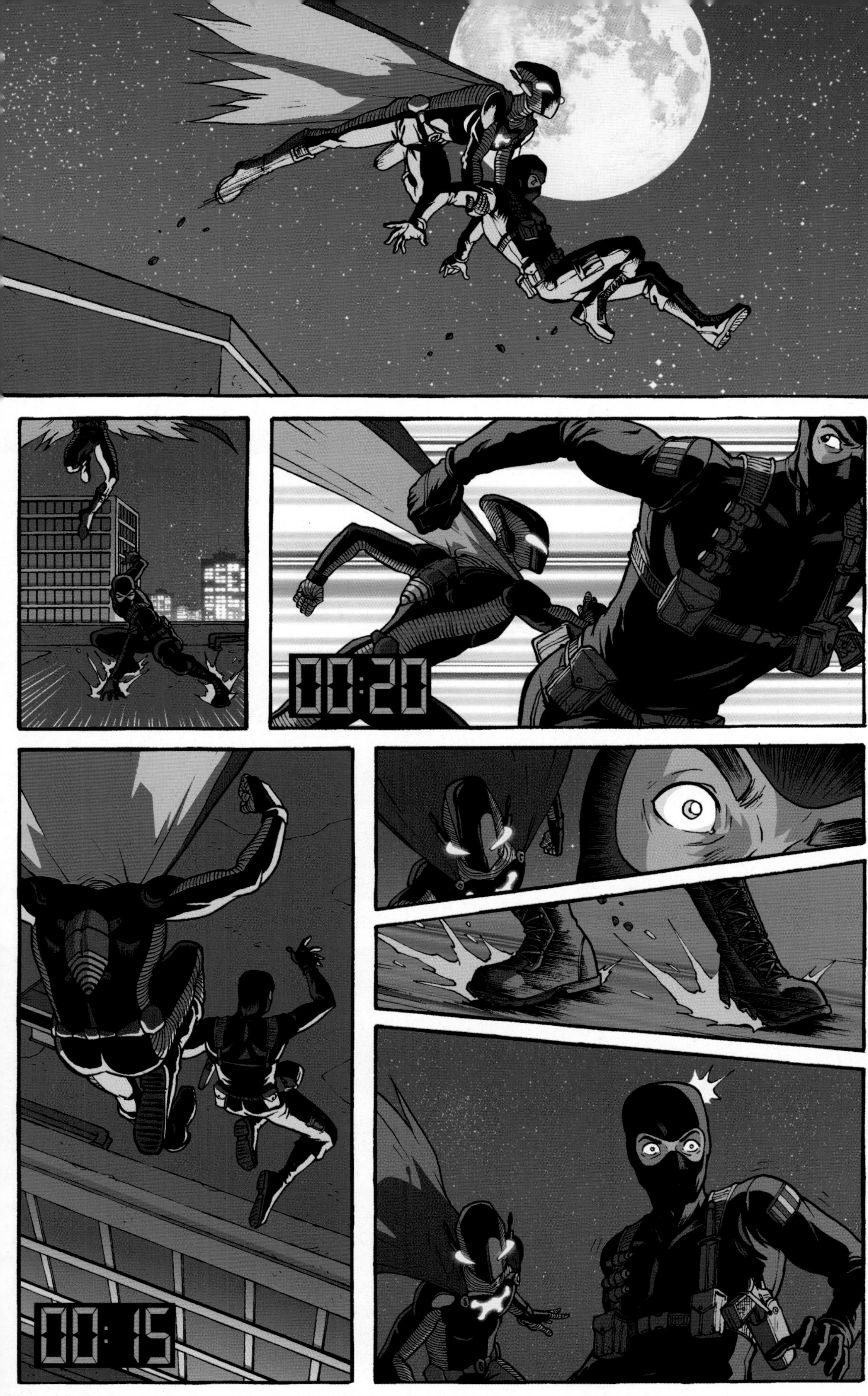
00:20
00:15

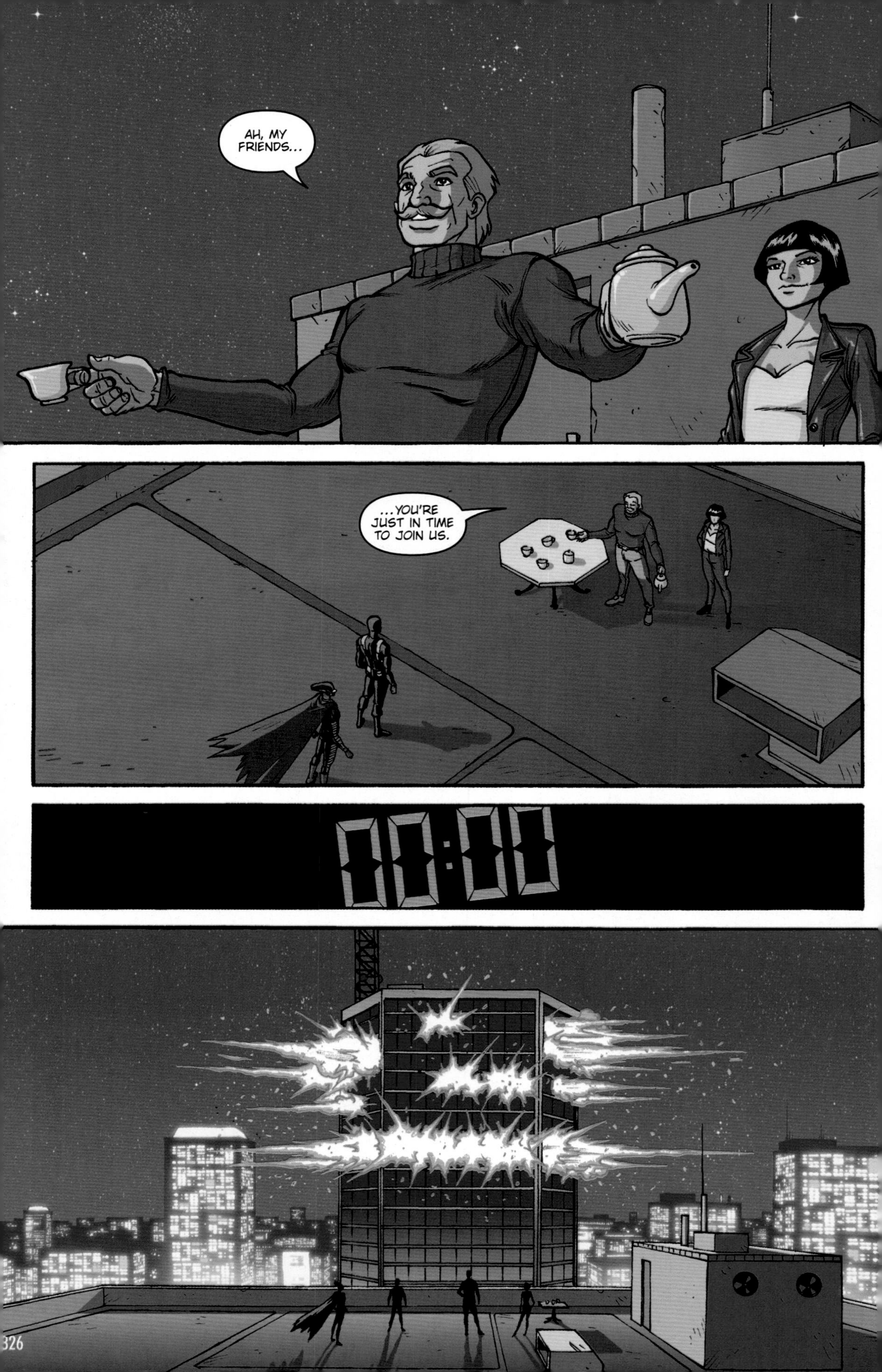
AH, MY FRIENDS...
...YOU'RE JUST IN TIME TO JOIN US.
00:00

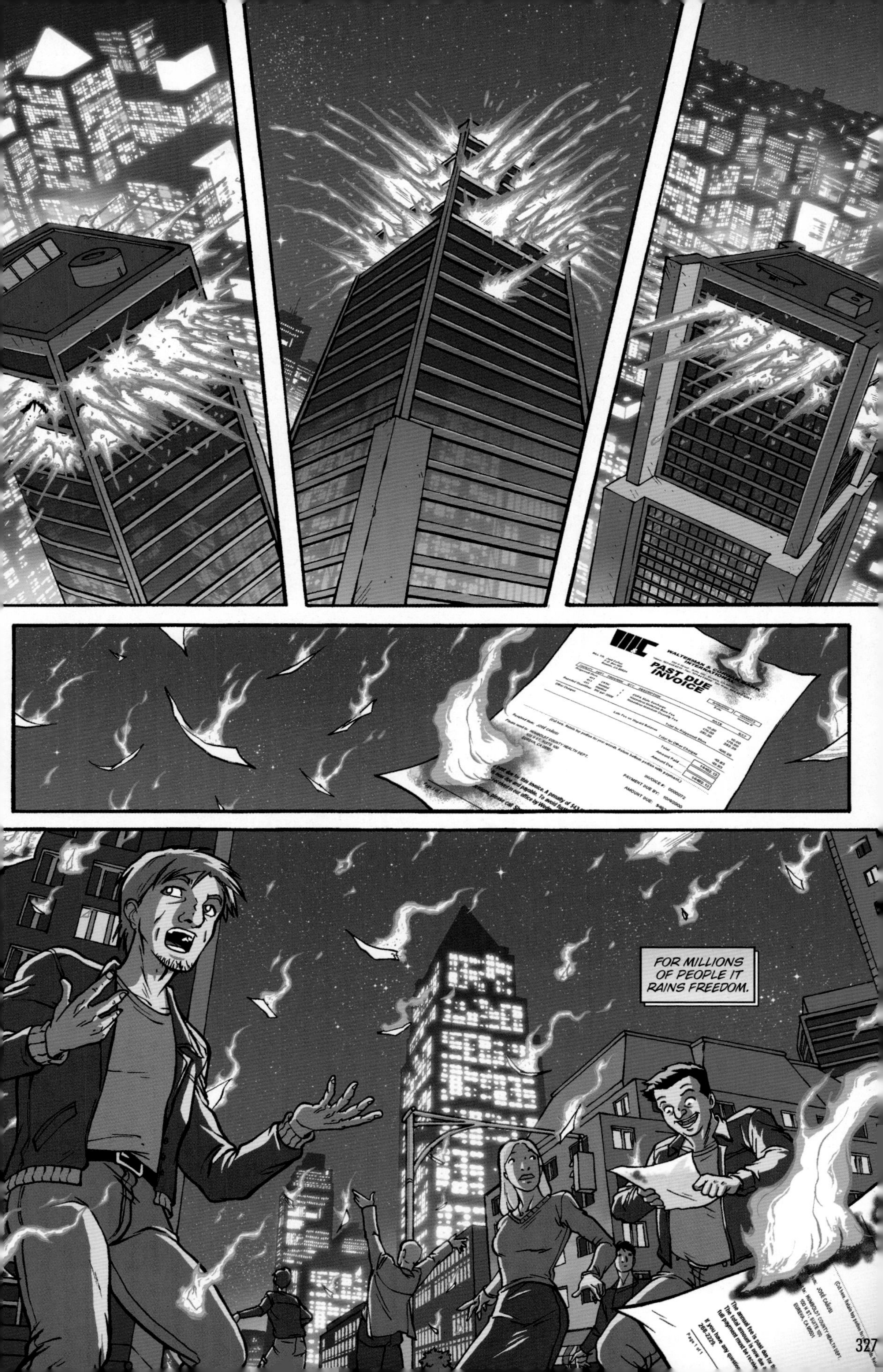
PAST DUE
INVOICE
FOR MILLIONS OF PEOPLE IT RAINS FREEDOM.

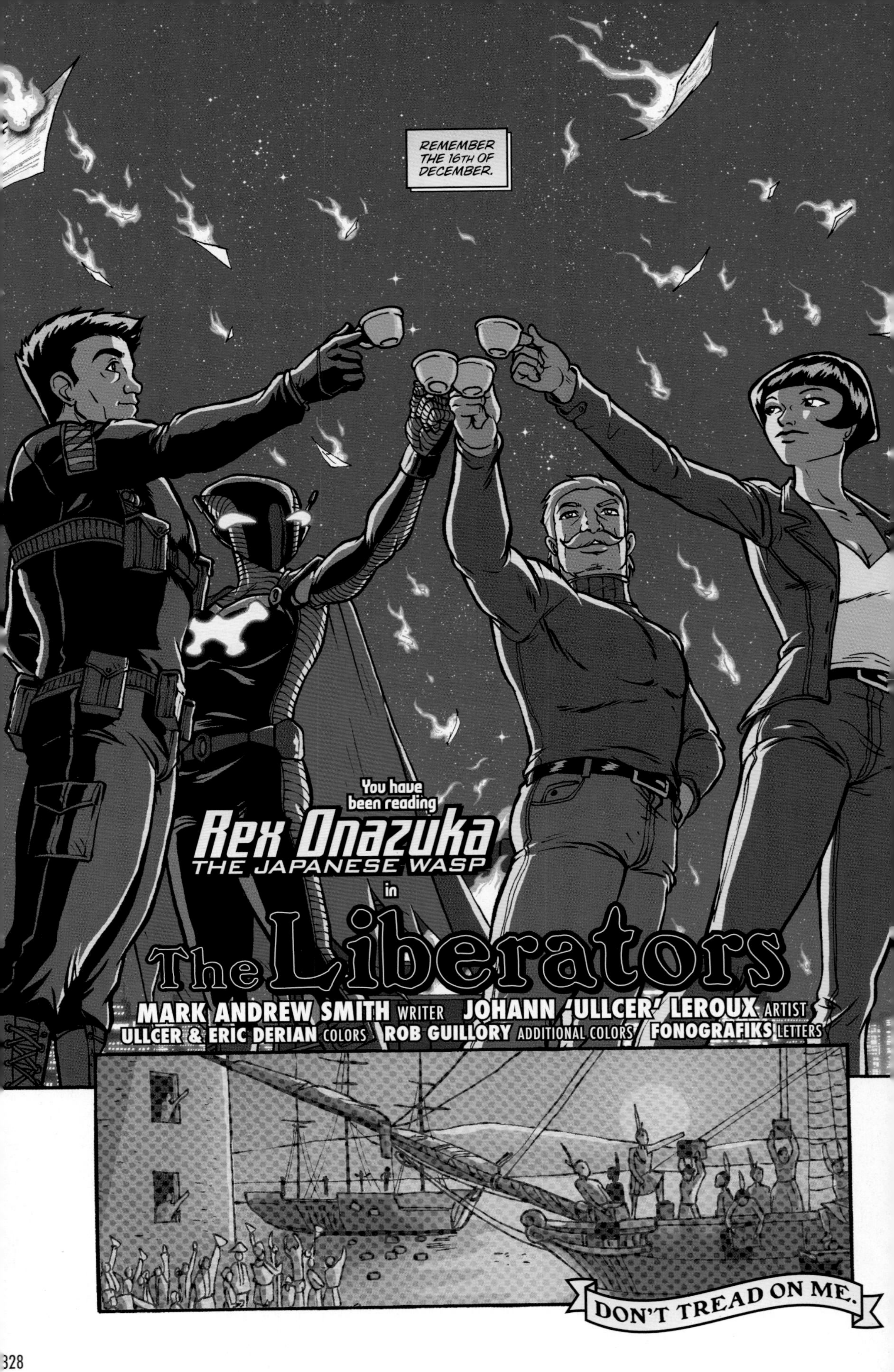
REMEMBER THE 16TH OF DECEMBER.
You have been reading
Rex Onazuka
THE JAPANESE WASP
in
The Liberators
MARK ANDREW SMITH WRITER JOHANN 'ULLCER' LEROUX ARTIST
ULLCER & ERIC DERIAN COLORS ROB GUILLORY ADDITIONAL COLORS FONOGRAFIKS LETTERS
DON'T TREAD ON ME.

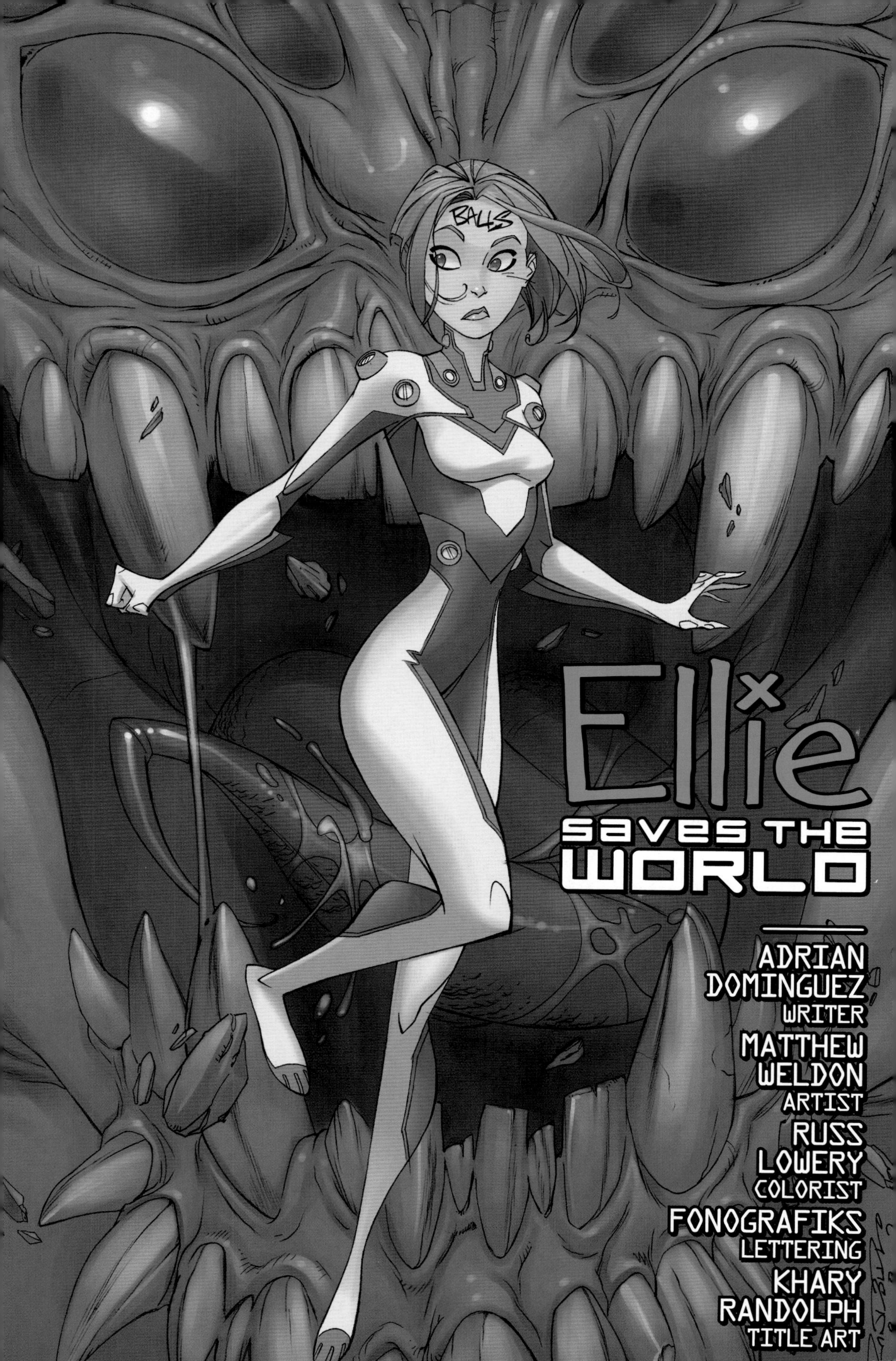
BALLS
Ellie
saves the
WORLD
ADRIAN DOMINGUEZ
WRITER
MATTHEW WELDON
ARTIST
RUSS LOWERY
COLORIST
FONOGRAFIKS
LETTERING
KHARY RANDOLPH
TITLE ART

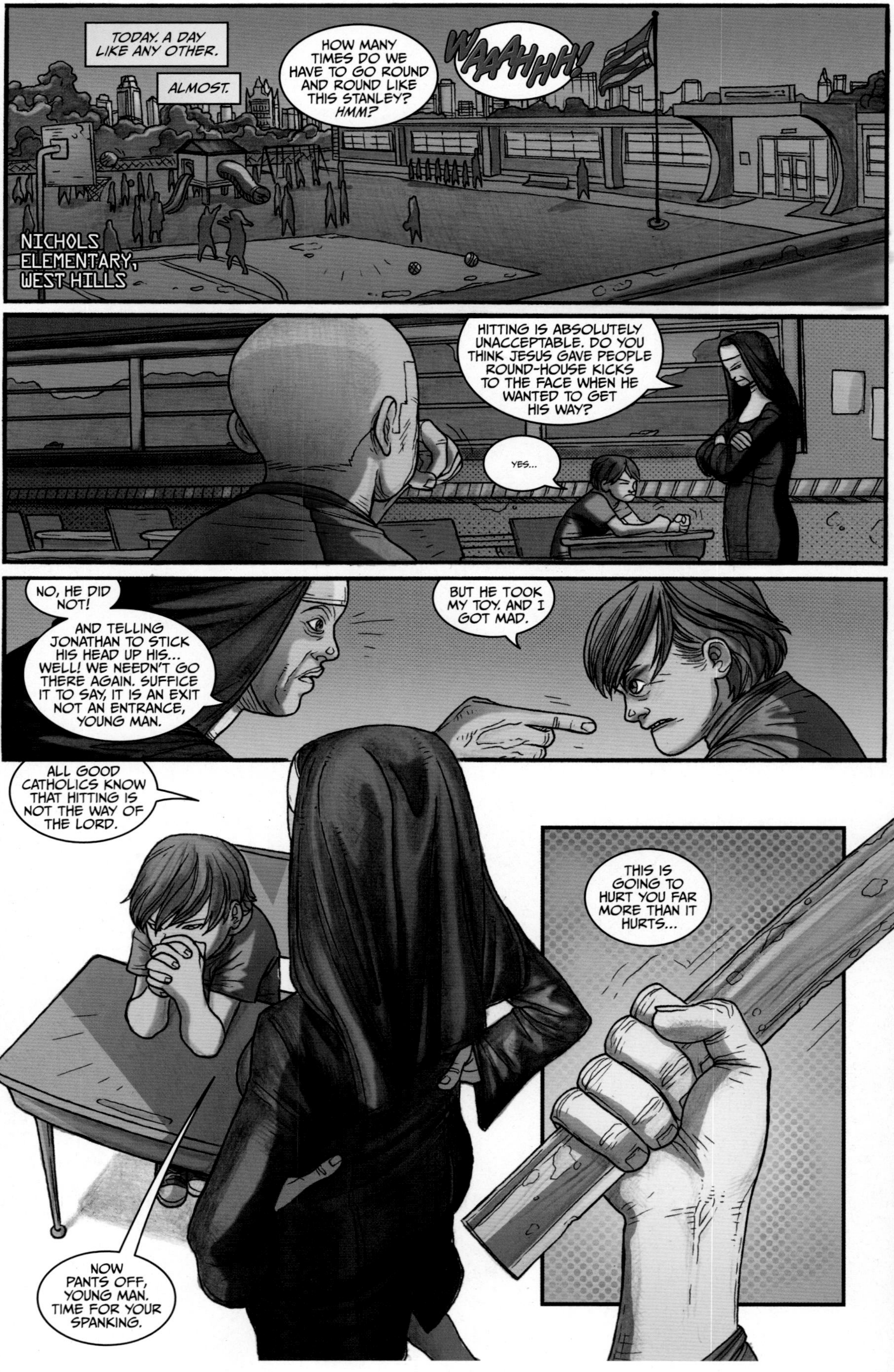
TODAY. A DAY LIKE ANY OTHER.
ALMOST.
HOW MANY TIMES DO WE HAVE TO GO ROUND AND ROUND LIKE THIS STANLEY? HMM?
WAAAHHH!
NICHOLS ELEMENTARY, WEST HILLS
HITTING IS ABSOLUTELY UNACCEPTABLE. DO YOU THINK JESUS GAVE PEOPLE ROUND-HOUSE KICKS TO THE FACE WHEN HE WANTED TO GET HIS WAY?
YES...
NO, HE DID NOT!
AND TELLING JONATHAN TO STICK HIS HEAD UP HIS... WELL! WE NEEDN'T GO THERE AGAIN. SUFFICE IT TO SAY, IT IS AN EXIT NOT AN ENTRANCE, YOUNG MAN.
BUT HE TOOK MY TOY. AND I GOT MAD.
ALL GOOD CATHOLICS KNOW THAT HITTING IS NOT THE WAY OF THE LORD.
THIS IS GOING TO HURT YOU FAR MORE THAN IT HURTS...
NOW PANTS OFF, YOUNG MAN. TIME FOR YOUR SPANKING.

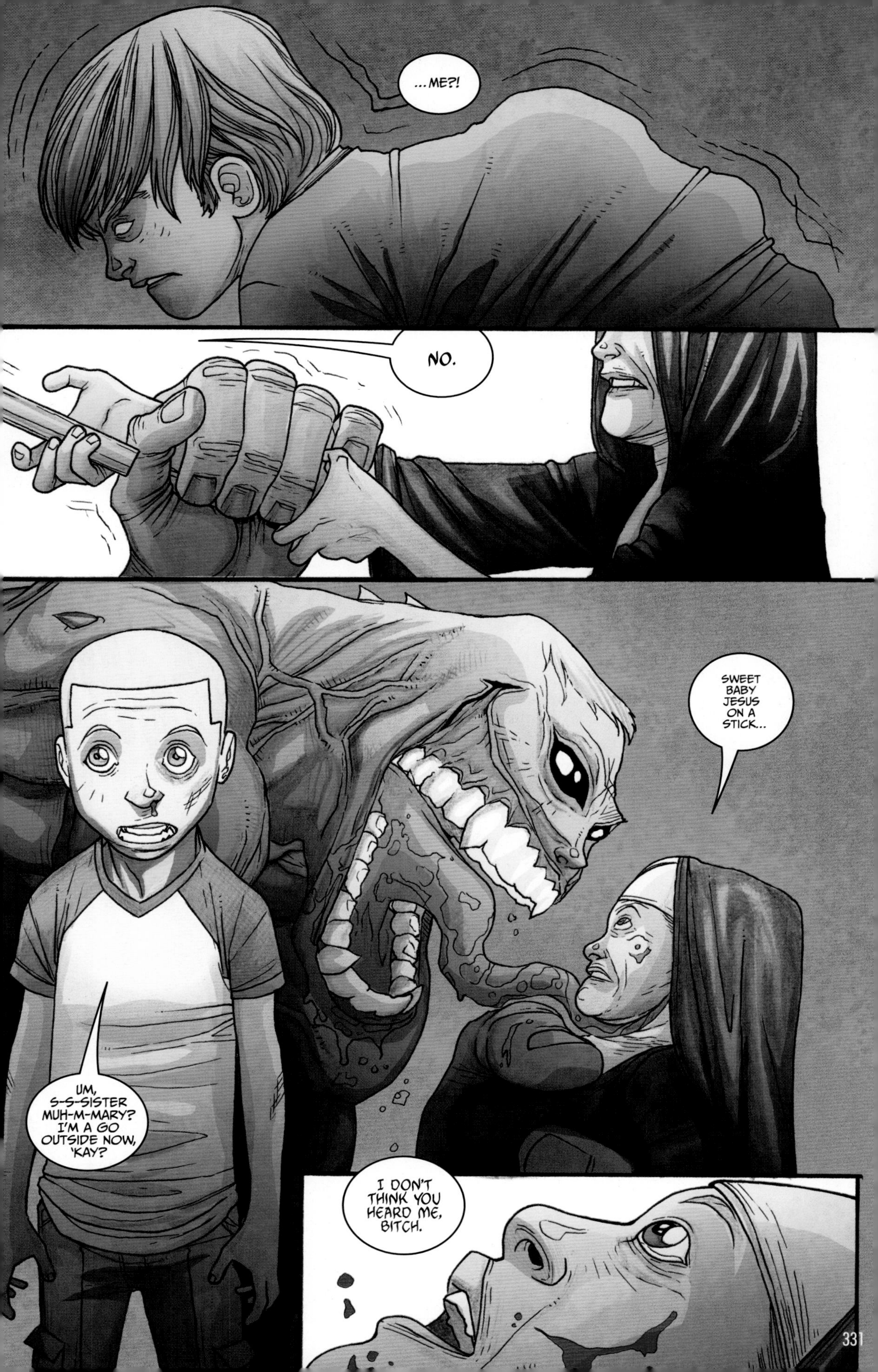
...ME?!
NO.
SWEET BABY JESUS ON A STICK...
UM, S-S-SISTER MUH-M-MARY? I'M A GO OUTSIDE NOW, 'KAY?
I DON'T THINK YOU HEARD ME, BITCH.

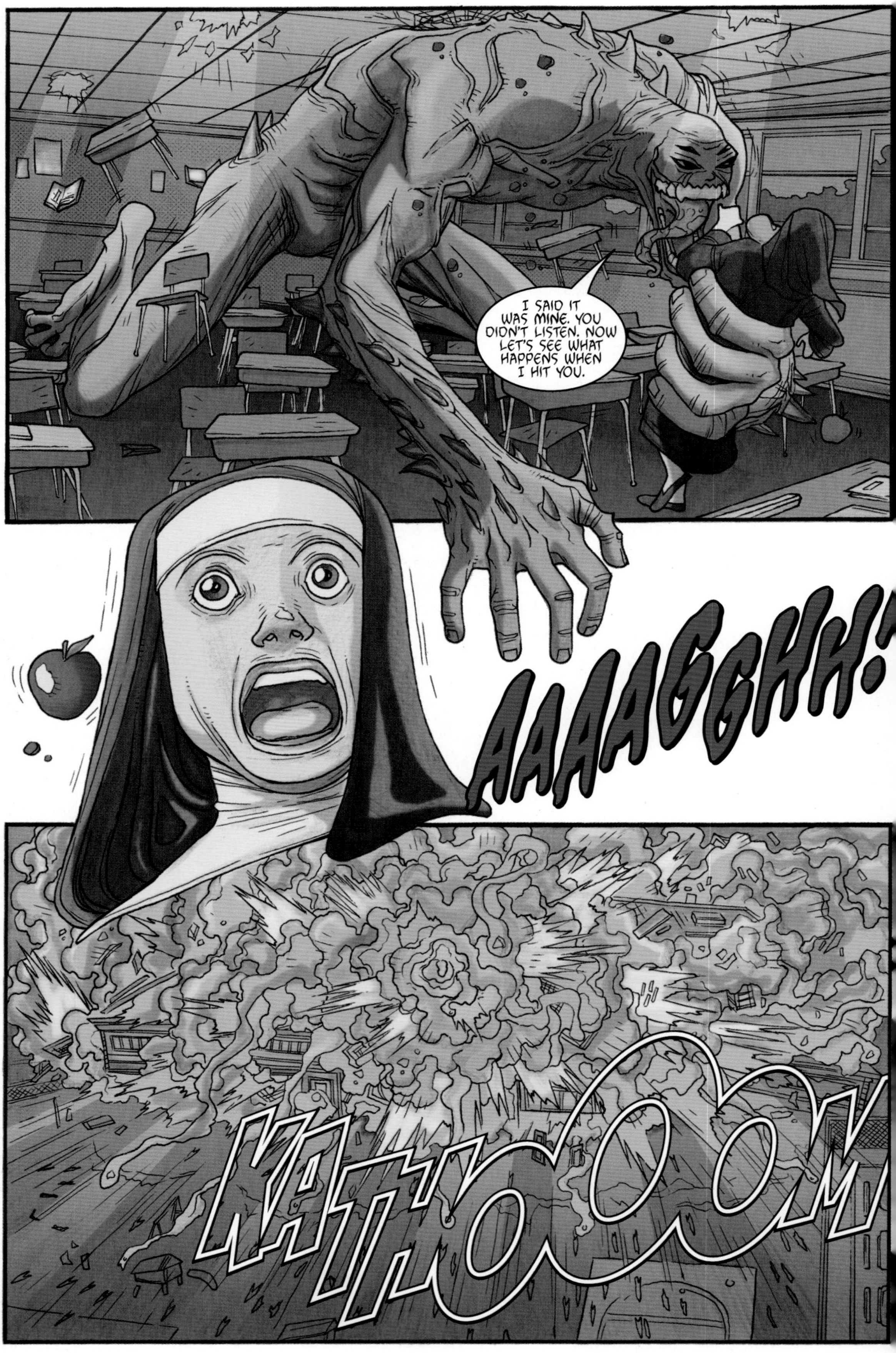
I SAID IT WAS MINE. YOU DIDN'T LISTEN. NOW LET'S SEE WHAT HAPPENS WHEN I HIT YOU.
AAAAGGHH!
KATHOOOM

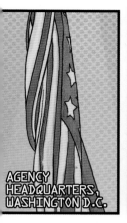

AGENCY
HEADQUARTERS,
WASHINGTON D.C.

THIS JUST IN. EXPLOSIONS ARE BEING REPORTED IN THE WEST HILLS AREA. POSSIBLY THE RESULT OF SUPERHUMAN ACTIVITY. OUR LIVE 5 CHOPPER IS ON THE SCENE. CHUCK, WHAT CAN YOU TELL US --

BZZT BZZT

THIS IS GRIFFIN.

DIRECTOR GRIFFIN, SIR... I'M CALLING ON BEHALF OF THE PRESIDENT. I TRUST THAT YOU'RE AWARE OF OUR SITUATION?

IT'S ONLY ON EVERY CHANNEL, MORGAN. A ROGUE SUPER TAKES OUT A SCHOOL OF LITTLE KIDS AND PEOPLE TEND TO TAKE NOTICE. WHAT CLASS ARE WE DEALING WITH?

ULTIMATE, UNREGISTERED. NAME'S STANLEY CLAY. A DAMN TEN YEAR OLD!

WE'VE HIT HIM WITH EVERYTHING WE'VE GOT AND NOTHING'S SLOWING HIM DOWN. THE PRESIDENT DOESN'T LIKE IT, BUT YOU'RE ALL WE'VE GOT.

TELL HIM NOT TO WORRY. HE'S IN GOOD HANDS. TAKE THE REST OF TODAY OFF AND READ ABOUT IT IN TOMORROW'S PAPER. WE'VE GOT OUR OWN LITTLE DETERRENT.

SIR?

FIRE UP THE NERVE CENTER AND GO GET ELLIE. THERE'S A PISSED OFF TEN YEAR OLD WITH A GOD COMPLEX READY TO TAKE OUT THE WEST COAST.

LET'S PUT HIM IN A CORNER.

TIME TO SAVE THE WORLD AGAIN, ELLIE. HOPE YOU'RE UP TO IT.

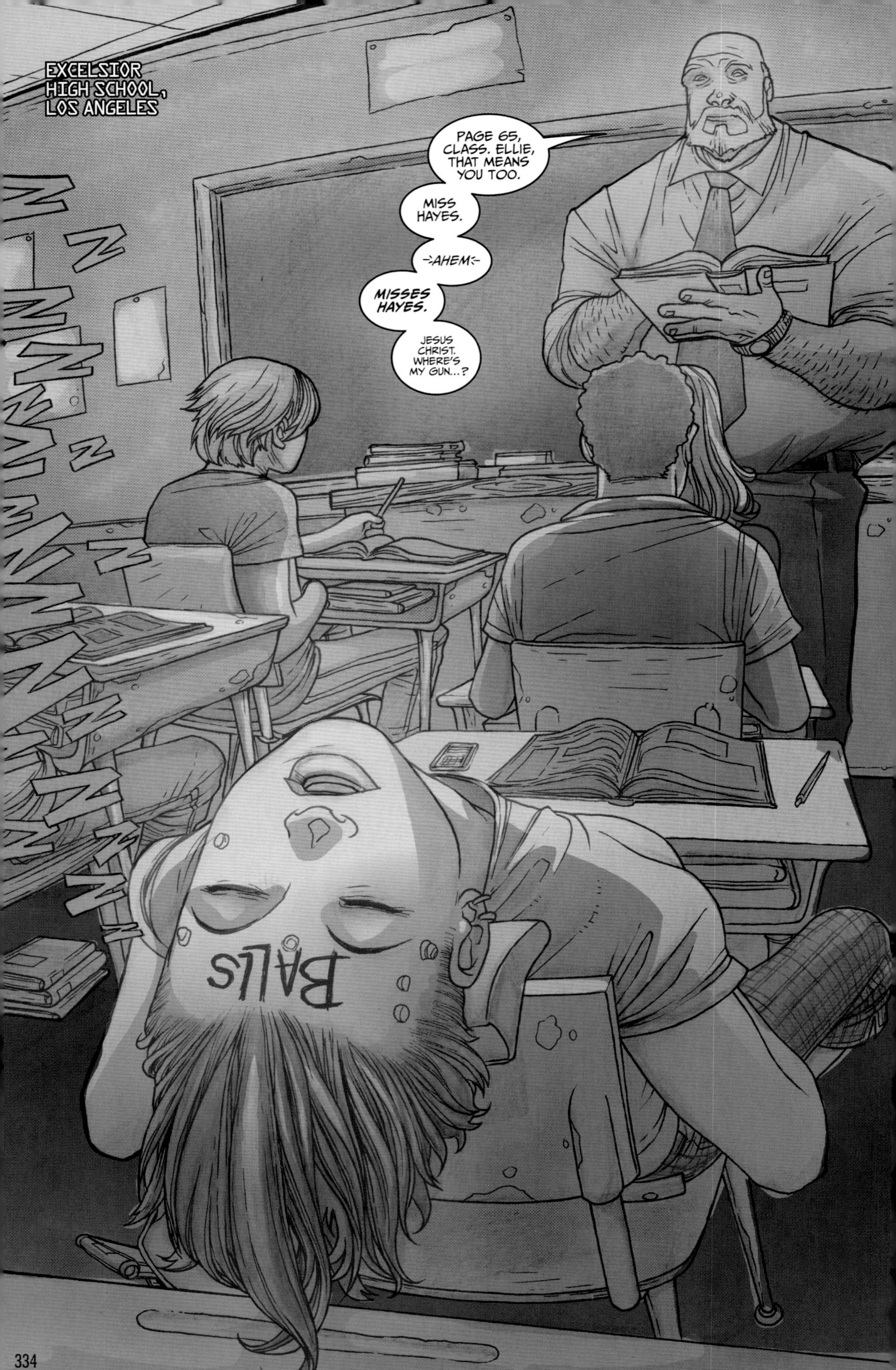

EXCELSIOR HIGH SCHOOL, LOS ANGELES
PAGE 65, CLASS. ELLIE, THAT MEANS YOU TOO.
MISS HAYES.
AHEM
MISSES HAYES.
JESUS CHRIST. WHERE'S MY GUN...?
ZZZZZZZZZZZZZZZZZZ
BALLS

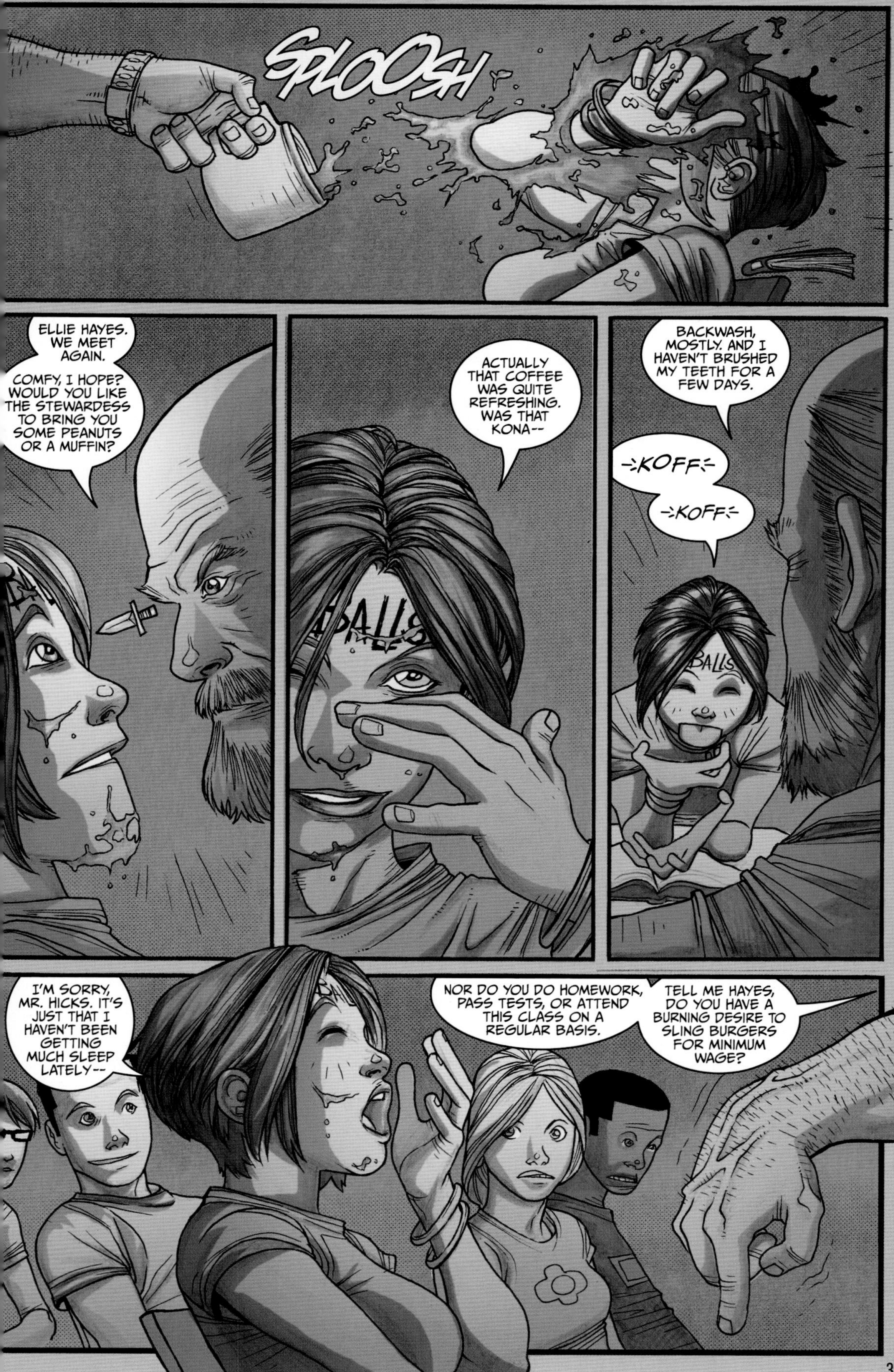
SPLOOSH
ELLIE HAYES. WE MEET AGAIN.
COMFY, I HOPE? WOULD YOU LIKE THE STEWARDESS TO BRING YOU SOME PEANUTS OR A MUFFIN?
ACTUALLY THAT COFFEE WAS QUITE REFRESHING. WAS THAT KONA--
BALLS
BACKWASH, MOSTLY. AND I HAVEN'T BRUSHED MY TEETH FOR A FEW DAYS.
KOFF
KOFF
BALLS
I'M SORRY, MR. HICKS. IT'S JUST THAT I HAVEN'T BEEN GETTING MUCH SLEEP LATELY--
NOR DO YOU DO HOMEWORK, PASS TESTS, OR ATTEND THIS CLASS ON A REGULAR BASIS.
TELL ME HAYES, DO YOU HAVE A BURNING DESIRE TO SLING BURGERS FOR MINIMUM WAGE?

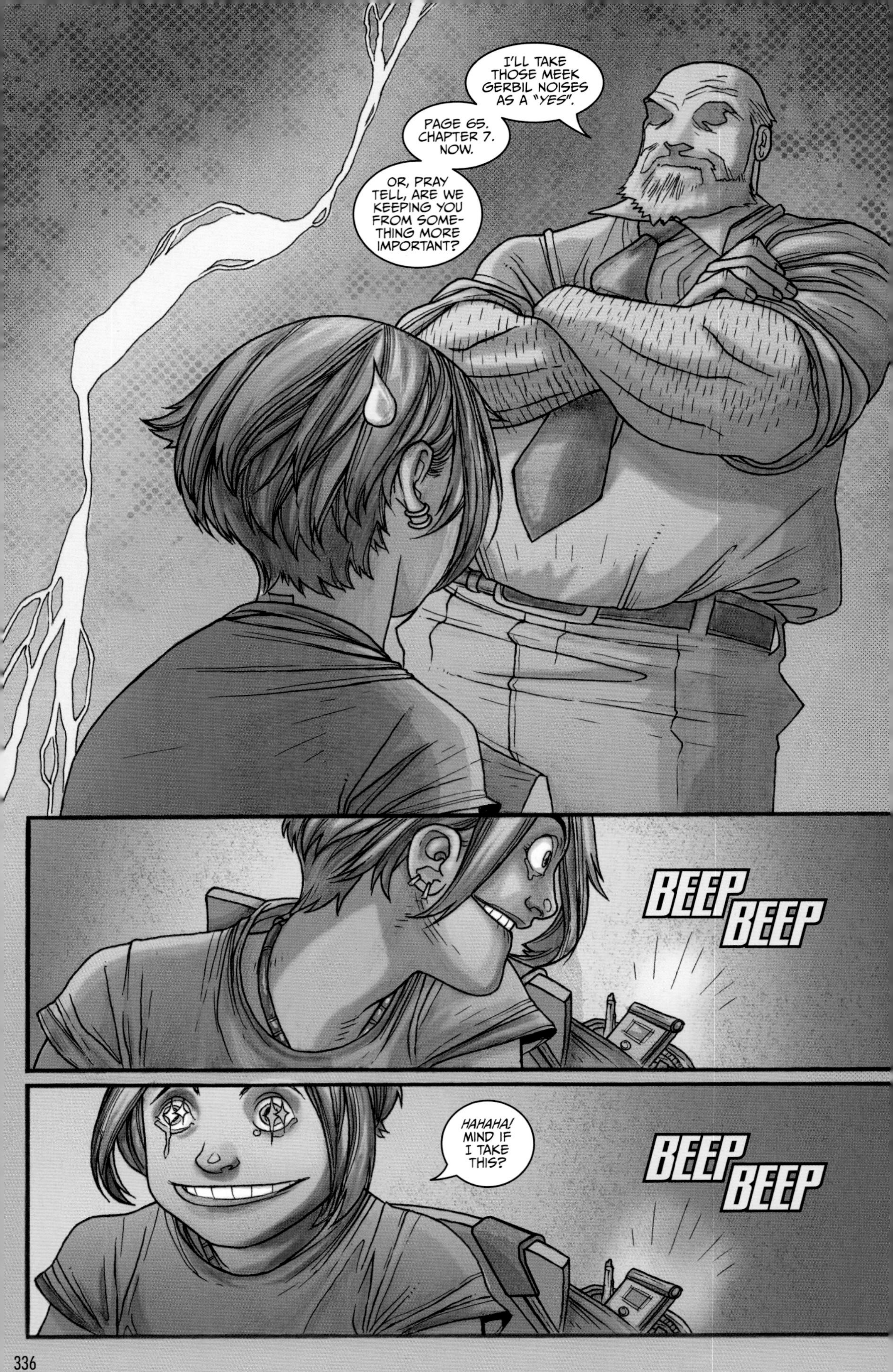
I'LL TAKE THOSE MEEK GERBIL NOISES AS A "YES".
PAGE 65. CHAPTER 7. NOW.
OR, PRAY TELL, ARE WE KEEPING YOU FROM SOME-THING MORE IMPORTANT?
BEEP BEEP
HAHAHA! MIND IF I TAKE THIS?
BEEP BEEP

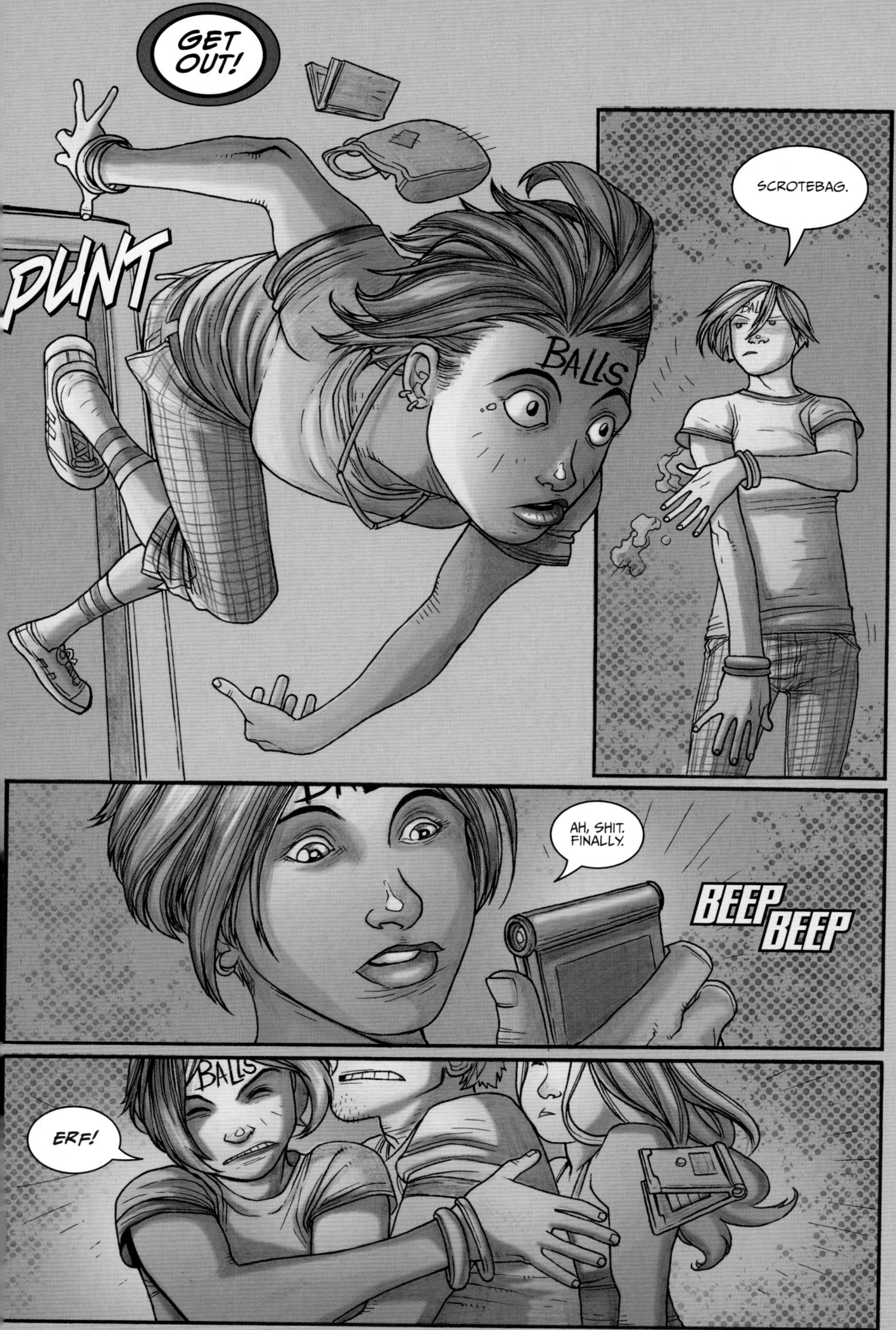
GET OUT!
PUNT
BALLS
SCROTEBAG.
AH, SHIT. FINALLY.
BEEP BEEP
BALLS
ERF!

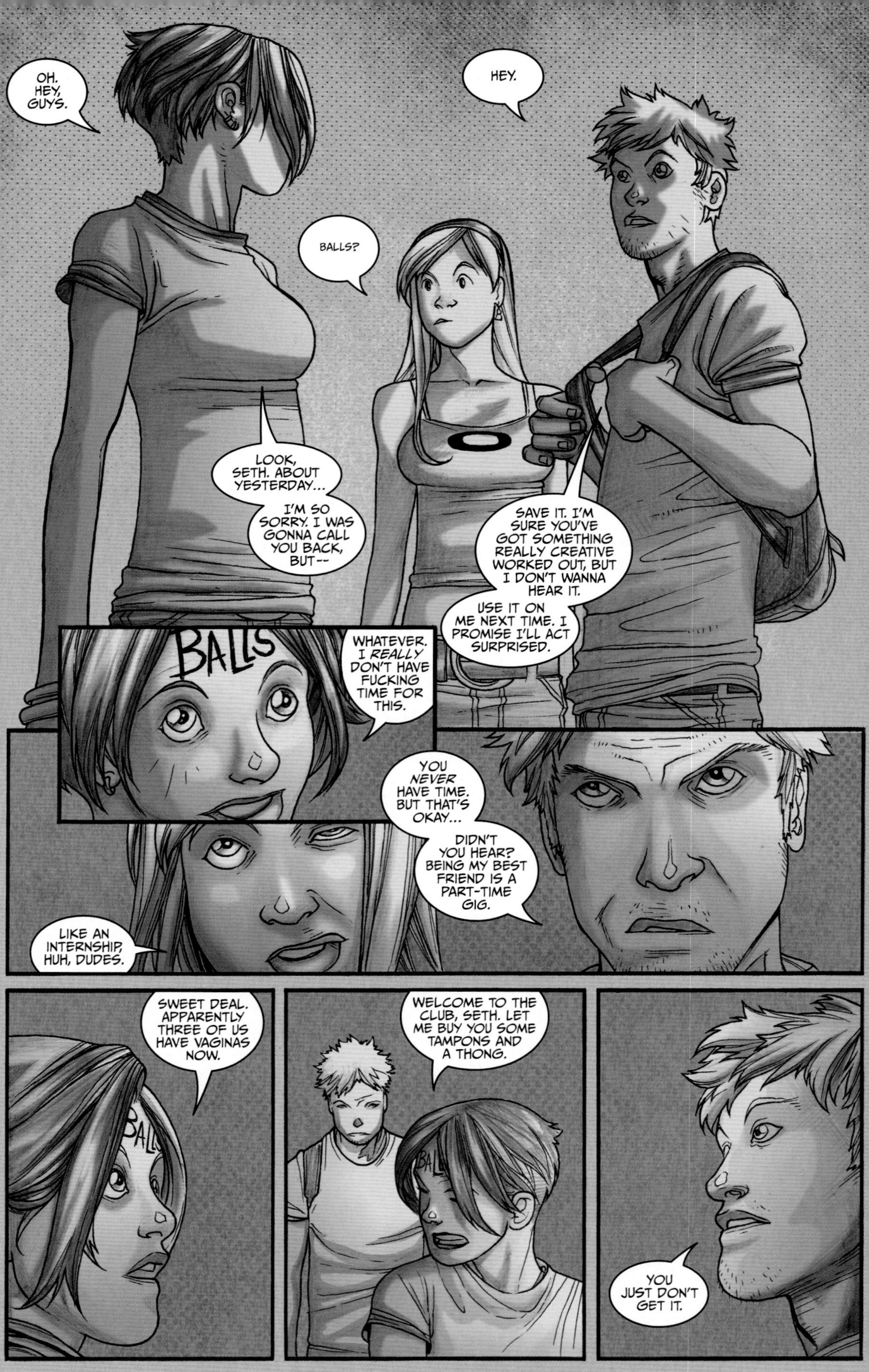
OH. HEY, GUYS.
HEY.
BALLS?
LOOK, SETH. ABOUT YESTERDAY...
I'M SO SORRY. I WAS GONNA CALL YOU BACK, BUT--
SAVE IT. I'M SURE YOU'VE GOT SOMETHING REALLY CREATIVE WORKED OUT, BUT I DON'T WANNA HEAR IT.
USE IT ON ME NEXT TIME. I PROMISE I'LL ACT SURPRISED.
BALLS
WHATEVER. I *REALLY* DON'T HAVE FUCKING TIME FOR THIS.
YOU *NEVER* HAVE TIME. BUT THAT'S OKAY...
DIDN'T YOU HEAR? BEING MY BEST FRIEND IS A PART-TIME GIG.
LIKE AN INTERNSHIP, HUH, DUDES.
SWEET DEAL. APPARENTLY THREE OF US HAVE VAGINAS NOW.
WELCOME TO THE CLUB, SETH. LET ME BUY YOU SOME TAMPONS AND A THONG.
YOU JUST DON'T GET IT.

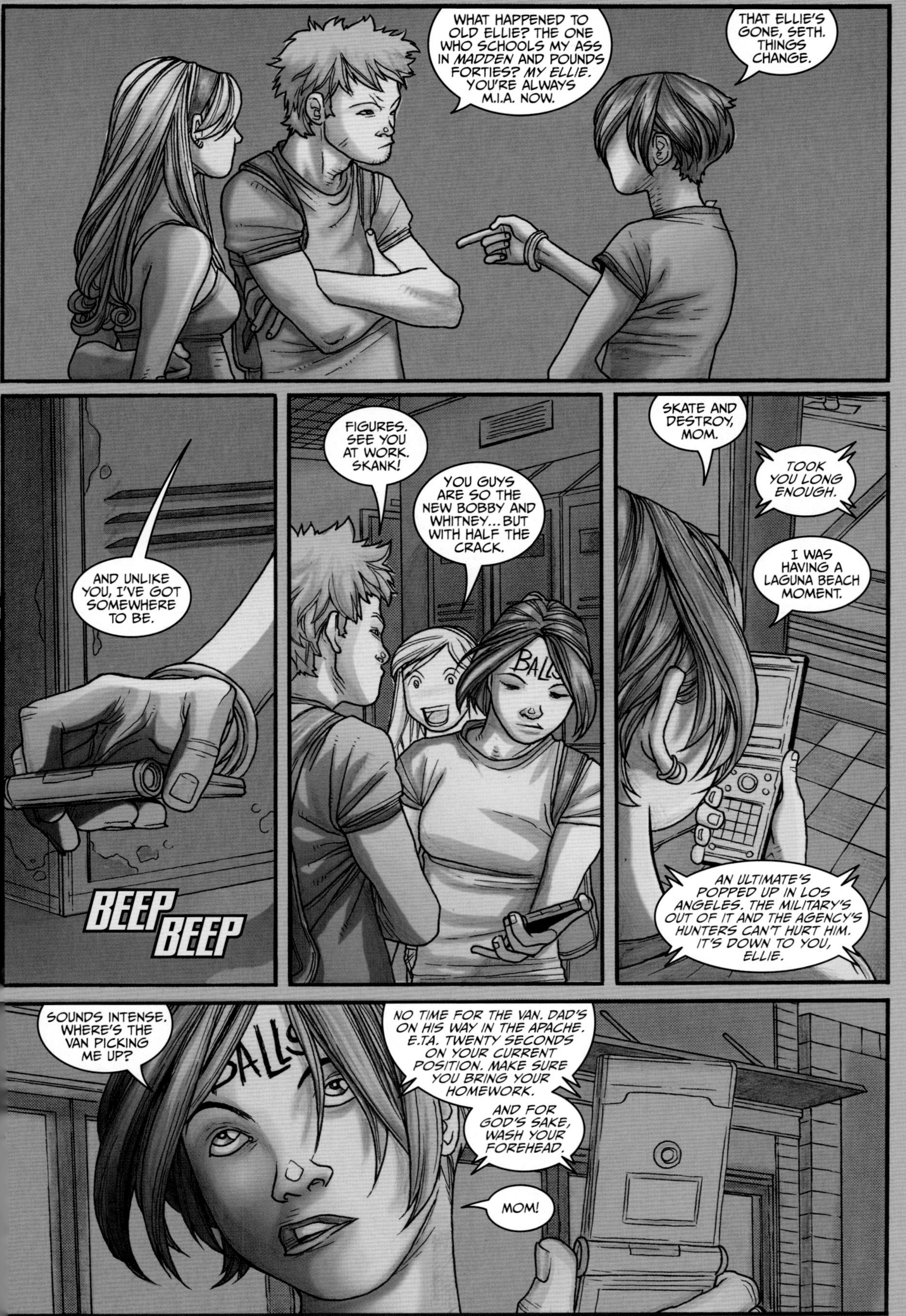
WHAT HAPPENED TO OLD ELLIE? THE ONE WHO SCHOOLS MY ASS IN *MADDEN* AND POUNDS FORTIES? *MY ELLIE.* YOU'RE ALWAYS M.I.A. NOW.
THAT ELLIE'S GONE, SETH. THINGS CHANGE.
AND UNLIKE YOU, I'VE GOT SOMEWHERE TO BE.
BEEP BEEP
FIGURES. SEE YOU AT WORK. SKANK!
YOU GUYS ARE SO THE NEW BOBBY AND WHITNEY... BUT WITH HALF THE CRACK.
BALLS
SKATE AND DESTROY, MOM.
TOOK YOU LONG ENOUGH.
I WAS HAVING A LAGUNA BEACH MOMENT.
AN ULTIMATE'S POPPED UP IN LOS ANGELES. THE MILITARY'S OUT OF IT AND THE AGENCY'S HUNTERS CAN'T HURT HIM. IT'S DOWN TO YOU, ELLIE.
SOUNDS INTENSE. WHERE'S THE VAN PICKING ME UP?
NO TIME FOR THE VAN. DAD'S ON HIS WAY IN THE APACHE. E.T.A. TWENTY SECONDS ON YOUR CURRENT POSITION. MAKE SURE YOU BRING YOUR HOMEWORK.
AND FOR GOD'S SAKE, WASH YOUR FOREHEAD.
MOM!

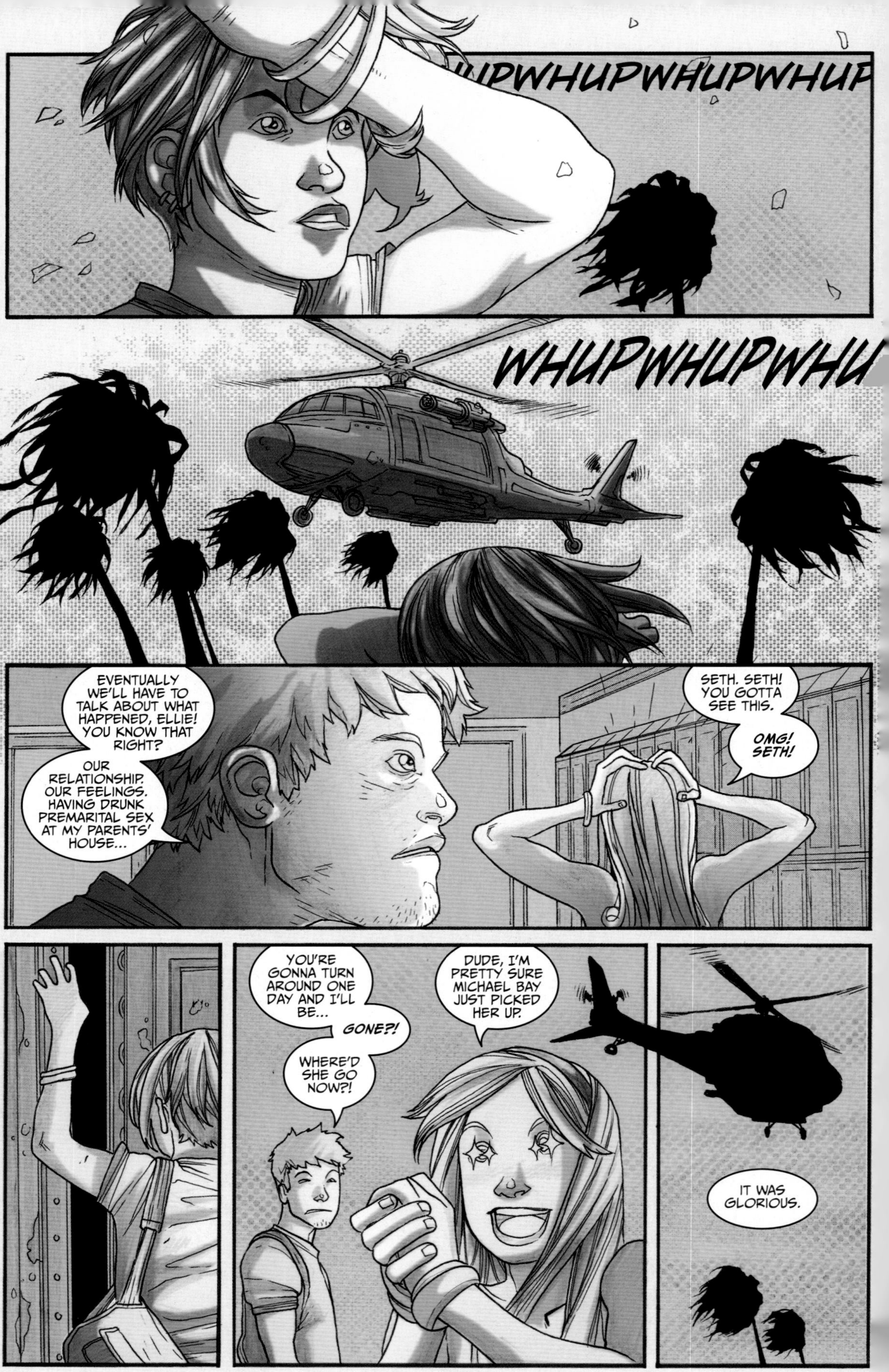
WHUPWHUPWHUPWHUP
WHUPWHUPWHU
EVENTUALLY WE'LL HAVE TO TALK ABOUT WHAT HAPPENED, ELLIE! YOU KNOW THAT RIGHT?
OUR RELATIONSHIP. OUR FEELINGS. HAVING DRUNK PREMARITAL SEX AT MY PARENTS' HOUSE...
SETH. SETH! YOU GOTTA SEE THIS.
OMG! SETH!
YOU'RE GONNA TURN AROUND ONE DAY AND I'LL BE...
GONE?!
WHERE'D SHE GO NOW?!
DUDE, I'M PRETTY SURE MICHAEL BAY JUST PICKED HER UP.
IT WAS GLORIOUS.

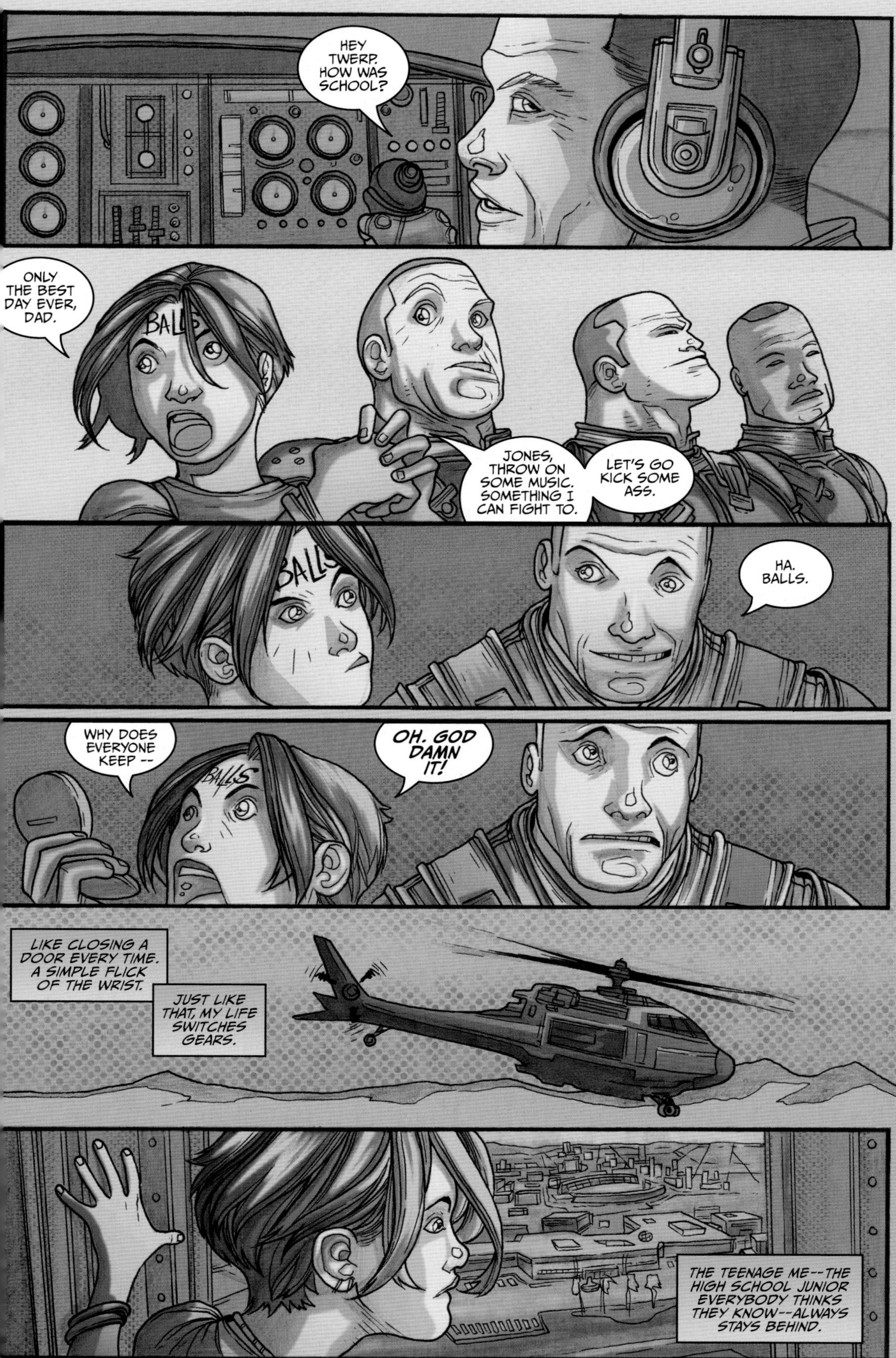
HEY TWERP. HOW WAS SCHOOL?
ONLY THE BEST DAY EVER, DAD.
BALLS
JONES, THROW ON SOME MUSIC. SOMETHING I CAN FIGHT TO.
LET'S GO KICK SOME ASS.
BALLS
HA. BALLS.
WHY DOES EVERYONE KEEP --
BALLS
OH. GOD DAMN IT!
LIKE CLOSING A DOOR EVERY TIME. A SIMPLE FLICK OF THE WRIST.
JUST LIKE THAT, MY LIFE SWITCHES GEARS.
THE TEENAGE ME--THE HIGH SCHOOL JUNIOR EVERYBODY THINKS THEY KNOW--ALWAYS STAYS BEHIND.

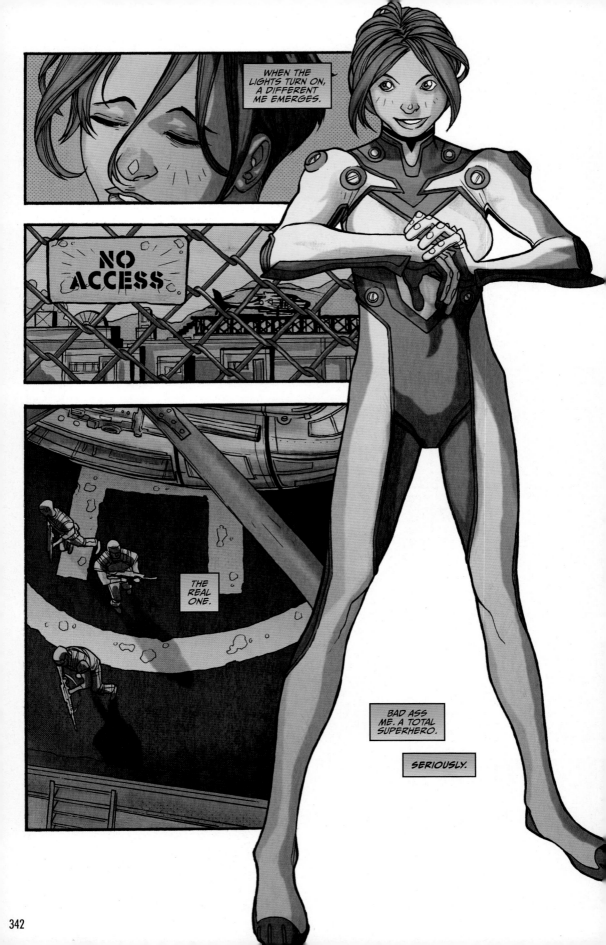

WHEN THE LIGHTS TURN ON, A DIFFERENT ME EMERGES.

NO ACCESS

THE REAL ONE.

BAD ASS ME. A TOTAL SUPERHERO.

SERIOUSLY.

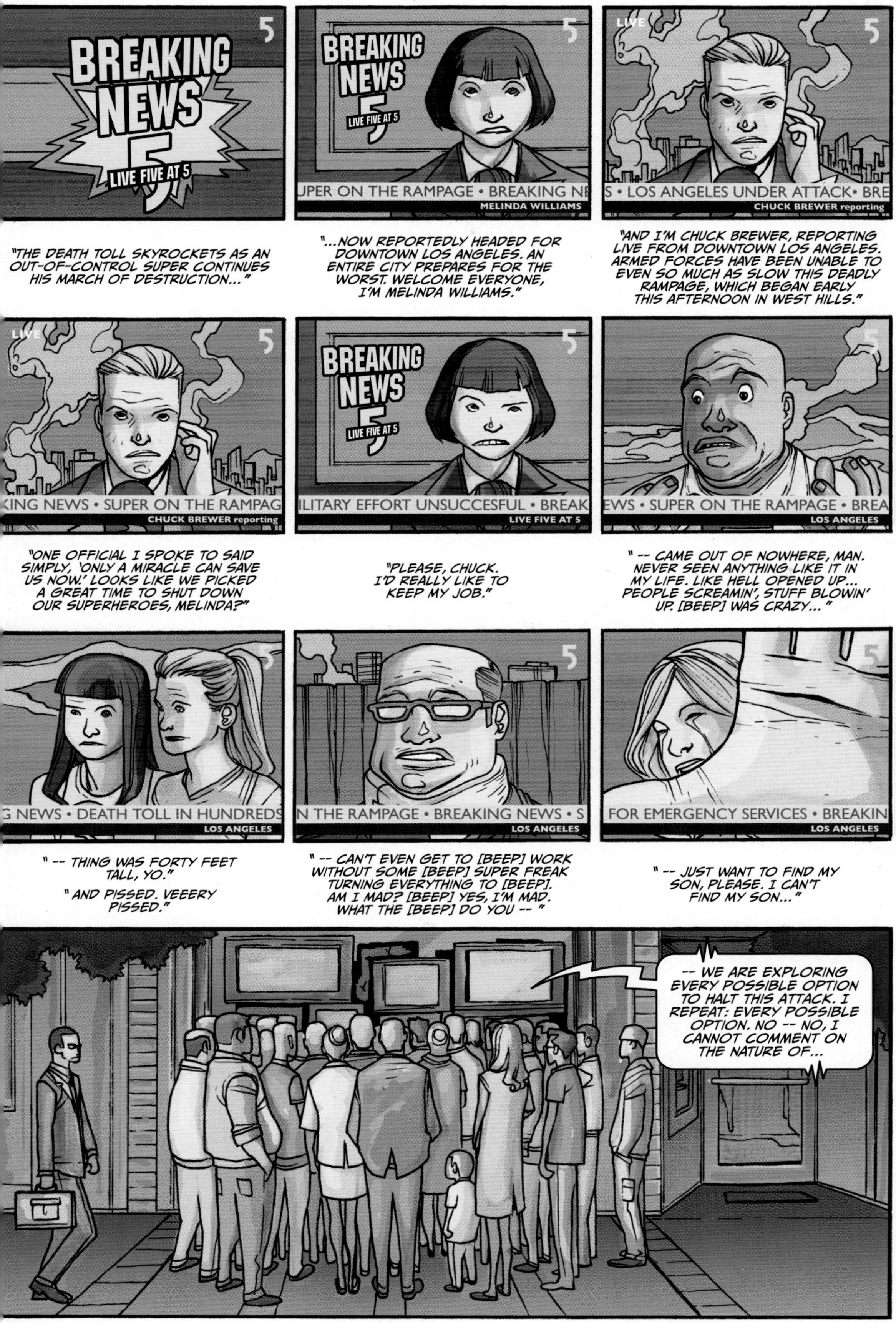

BREAKING NEWS 5 LIVE FIVE AT 5
"THE DEATH TOLL SKYROCKETS AS AN OUT-OF-CONTROL SUPER CONTINUES HIS MARCH OF DESTRUCTION..."
BREAKING NEWS 5 LIVE FIVE AT 5
UPER ON THE RAMPAGE • BREAKING NE
MELINDA WILLIAMS
"...NOW REPORTEDLY HEADED FOR DOWNTOWN LOS ANGELES. AN ENTIRE CITY PREPARES FOR THE WORST. WELCOME EVERYONE, I'M MELINDA WILLIAMS."
LIVE
S • LOS ANGELES UNDER ATTACK • BRE
CHUCK BREWER reporting
"AND I'M CHUCK BREWER, REPORTING LIVE FROM DOWNTOWN LOS ANGELES. ARMED FORCES HAVE BEEN UNABLE TO EVEN SO MUCH AS SLOW THIS DEADLY RAMPAGE, WHICH BEGAN EARLY THIS AFTERNOON IN WEST HILLS."
LIVE
KING NEWS • SUPER ON THE RAMPAG
CHUCK BREWER reporting
"ONE OFFICIAL I SPOKE TO SAID SIMPLY, 'ONLY A MIRACLE CAN SAVE US NOW.' LOOKS LIKE WE PICKED A GREAT TIME TO SHUT DOWN OUR SUPERHEROES, MELINDA?"
BREAKING NEWS 5 LIVE FIVE AT 5
ILITARY EFFORT UNSUCCESFUL • BREAK
LIVE FIVE AT 5
"PLEASE, CHUCK. I'D REALLY LIKE TO KEEP MY JOB."
EWS • SUPER ON THE RAMPAGE • BREA
LOS ANGELES
" -- CAME OUT OF NOWHERE, MAN. NEVER SEEN ANYTHING LIKE IT IN MY LIFE. LIKE HELL OPENED UP... PEOPLE SCREAMIN', STUFF BLOWIN' UP. [BEEP] WAS CRAZY... "
G NEWS • DEATH TOLL IN HUNDREDS
LOS ANGELES
" -- THING WAS FORTY FEET TALL, YO."
" AND PISSED. VEEERY PISSED."
N THE RAMPAGE • BREAKING NEWS • S
LOS ANGELES
" -- CAN'T EVEN GET TO [BEEP] WORK WITHOUT SOME [BEEP] SUPER FREAK TURNING EVERYTHING TO [BEEP]. AM I MAD? [BEEP] YES, I'M MAD. WHAT THE [BEEP] DO YOU -- "
FOR EMERGENCY SERVICES • BREAKIN
LOS ANGELES
" -- JUST WANT TO FIND MY SON, PLEASE. I CAN'T FIND MY SON..."
-- WE ARE EXPLORING EVERY POSSIBLE OPTION TO HALT THIS ATTACK. I REPEAT: EVERY POSSIBLE OPTION. NO -- NO, I CANNOT COMMENT ON THE NATURE OF...

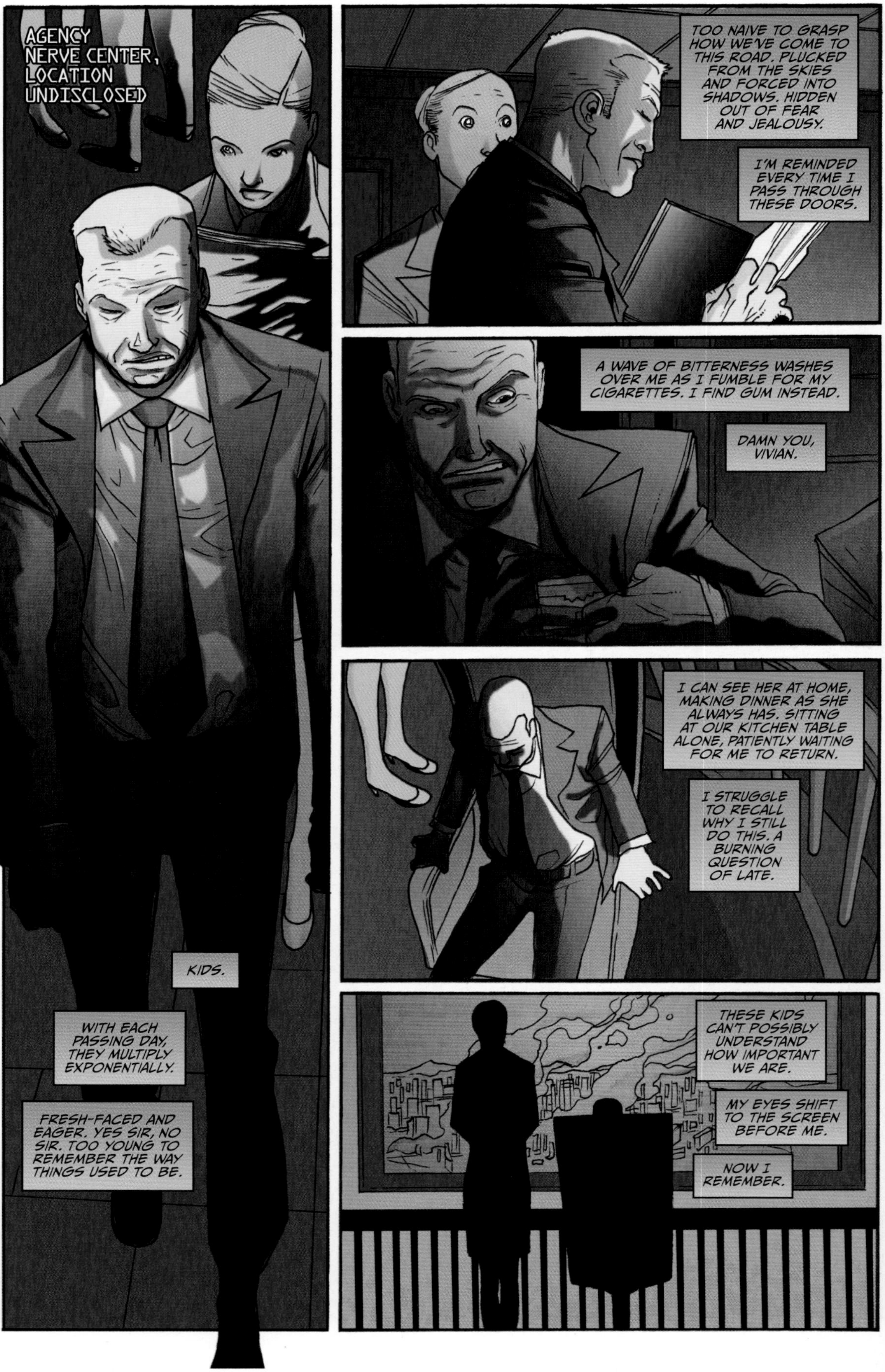
AGENCY NERVE CENTER, LOCATION UNDISCLOSED
KIDS.
WITH EACH PASSING DAY, THEY MULTIPLY EXPONENTIALLY.
FRESH-FACED AND EAGER. YES SIR, NO SIR. TOO YOUNG TO REMEMBER THE WAY THINGS USED TO BE.
TOO NAIVE TO GRASP HOW WE'VE COME TO THIS ROAD. PLUCKED FROM THE SKIES AND FORCED INTO SHADOWS. HIDDEN OUT OF FEAR AND JEALOUSY.
I'M REMINDED EVERY TIME I PASS THROUGH THESE DOORS.
A WAVE OF BITTERNESS WASHES OVER ME AS I FUMBLE FOR MY CIGARETTES. I FIND GUM INSTEAD.
DAMN YOU, VIVIAN.
I CAN SEE HER AT HOME, MAKING DINNER AS SHE ALWAYS HAS. SITTING AT OUR KITCHEN TABLE ALONE, PATIENTLY WAITING FOR ME TO RETURN.
I STRUGGLE TO RECALL WHY I STILL DO THIS. A BURNING QUESTION OF LATE.
THESE KIDS CAN'T POSSIBLY UNDERSTAND HOW IMPORTANT WE ARE.
MY EYES SHIFT TO THE SCREEN BEFORE ME.
NOW I REMEMBER.

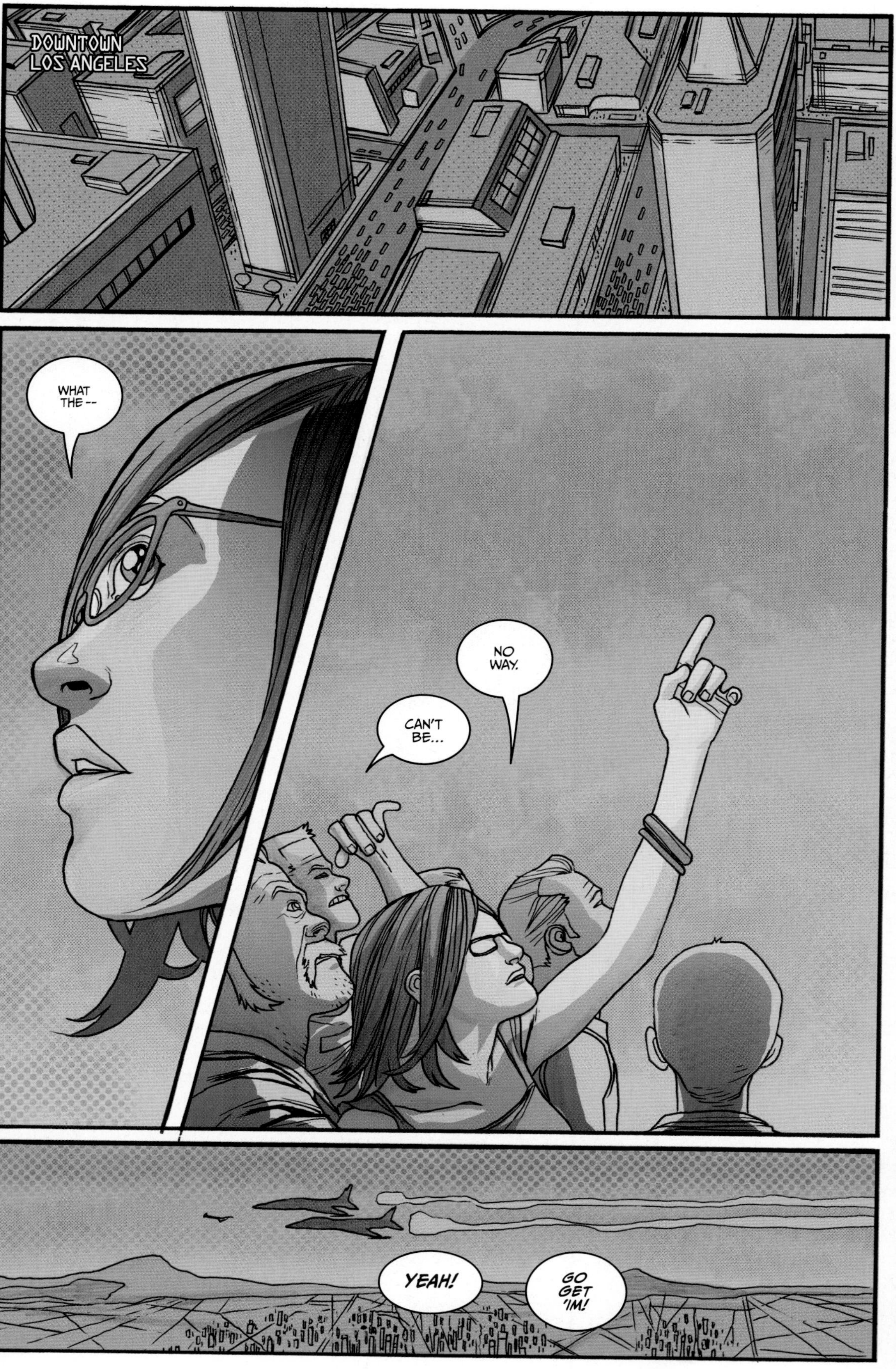
DOWNTOWN LOS ANGELES
WHAT THE --
NO WAY.
CAN'T BE...
YEAH!
GO GET 'IM!

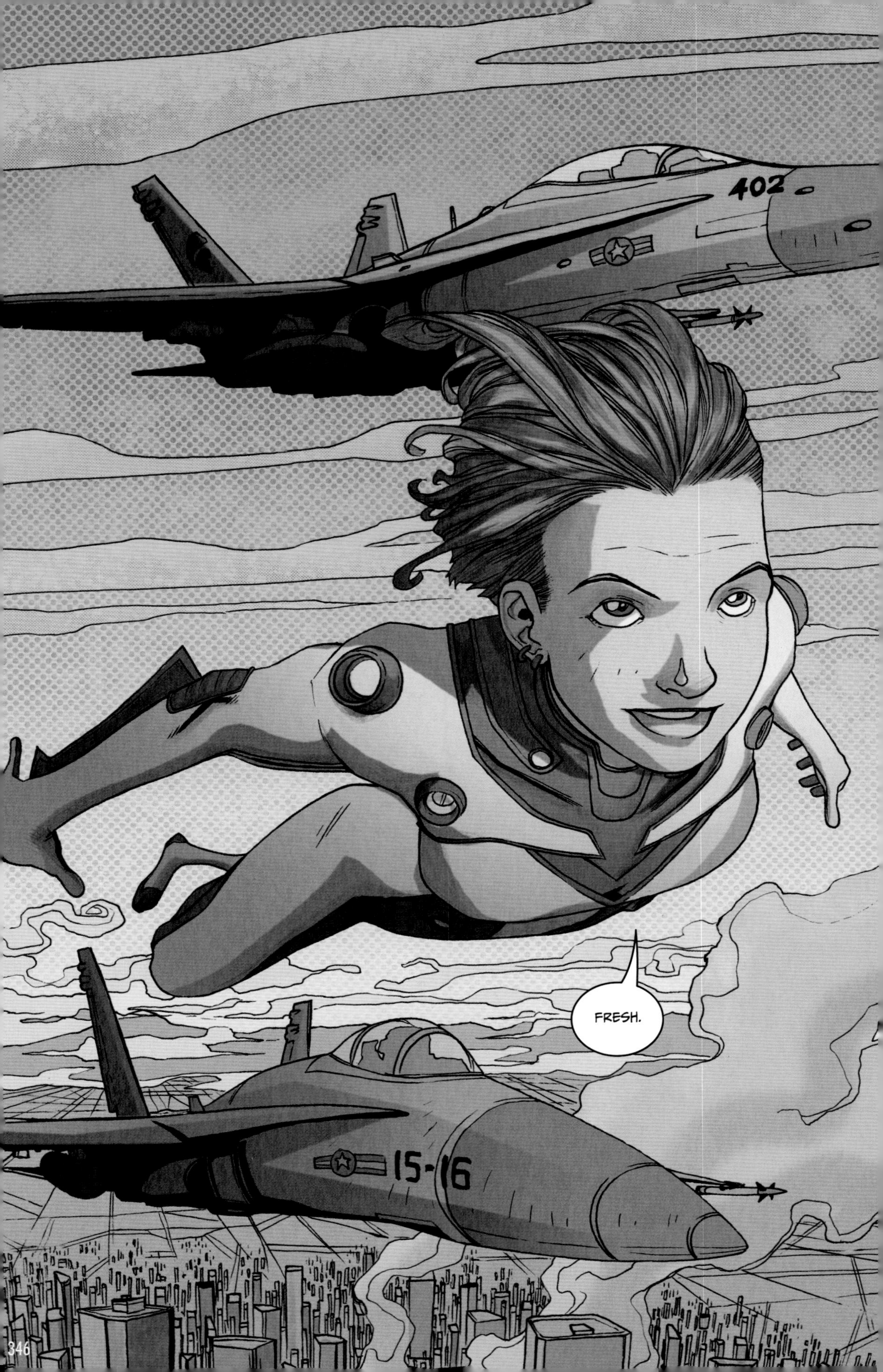
402
FRESH.
15-16

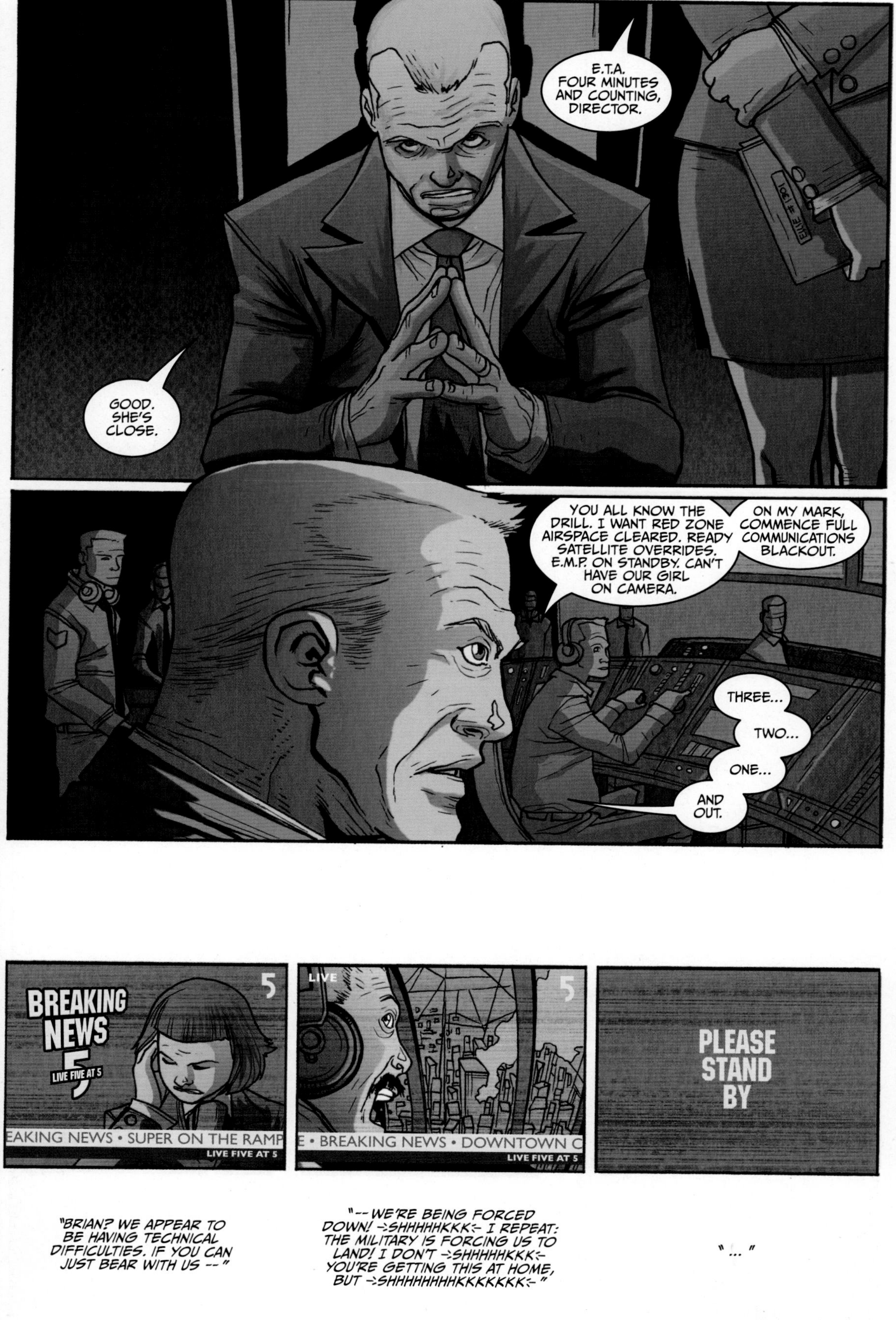
E.T.A. FOUR MINUTES AND COUNTING, DIRECTOR.
GOOD. SHE'S CLOSE.
YOU ALL KNOW THE DRILL. I WANT RED ZONE AIRSPACE CLEARED. READY SATELLITE OVERRIDES. E.M.P. ON STANDBY. CAN'T HAVE OUR GIRL ON CAMERA.
ON MY MARK, COMMENCE FULL COMMUNICATIONS BLACKOUT.
THREE...
TWO...
ONE...
AND OUT.
BREAKING NEWS
5
LIVE FIVE AT 5
EAKING NEWS • SUPER ON THE RAMP
LIVE FIVE AT 5
LIVE
5
E • BREAKING NEWS • DOWNTOWN C
LIVE FIVE AT 5
PLEASE STAND BY
"BRIAN? WE APPEAR TO BE HAVING TECHNICAL DIFFICULTIES. IF YOU CAN JUST BEAR WITH US --"
"--WE'RE BEING FORCED DOWN! ->SHHHHHKKK<- I REPEAT: THE MILITARY IS FORCING US TO LAND! I DON'T ->SHHHHHKKK<- YOU'RE GETTING THIS AT HOME, BUT ->SHHHHHHHHKKKKKKK<-"
"..."

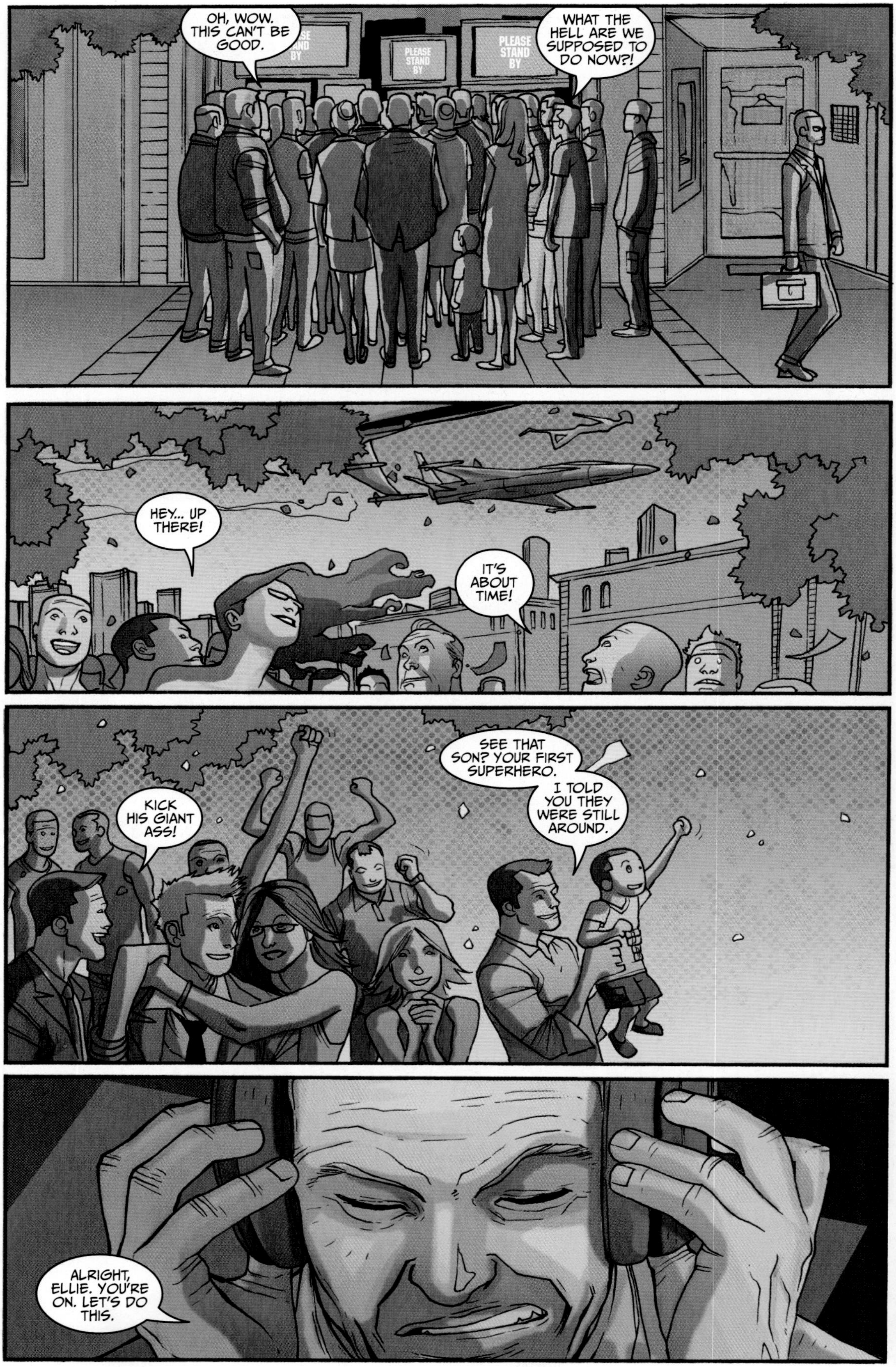
OH, WOW. THIS CAN'T BE GOOD.
PLEASE STAND BY
WHAT THE HELL ARE WE SUPPOSED TO DO NOW?!
HEY... UP THERE!
IT'S ABOUT TIME!
KICK HIS GIANT ASS!
SEE THAT SON? YOUR FIRST SUPERHERO.
I TOLD YOU THEY WERE STILL AROUND.
ALRIGHT, ELLIE. YOU'RE ON. LET'S DO THIS.

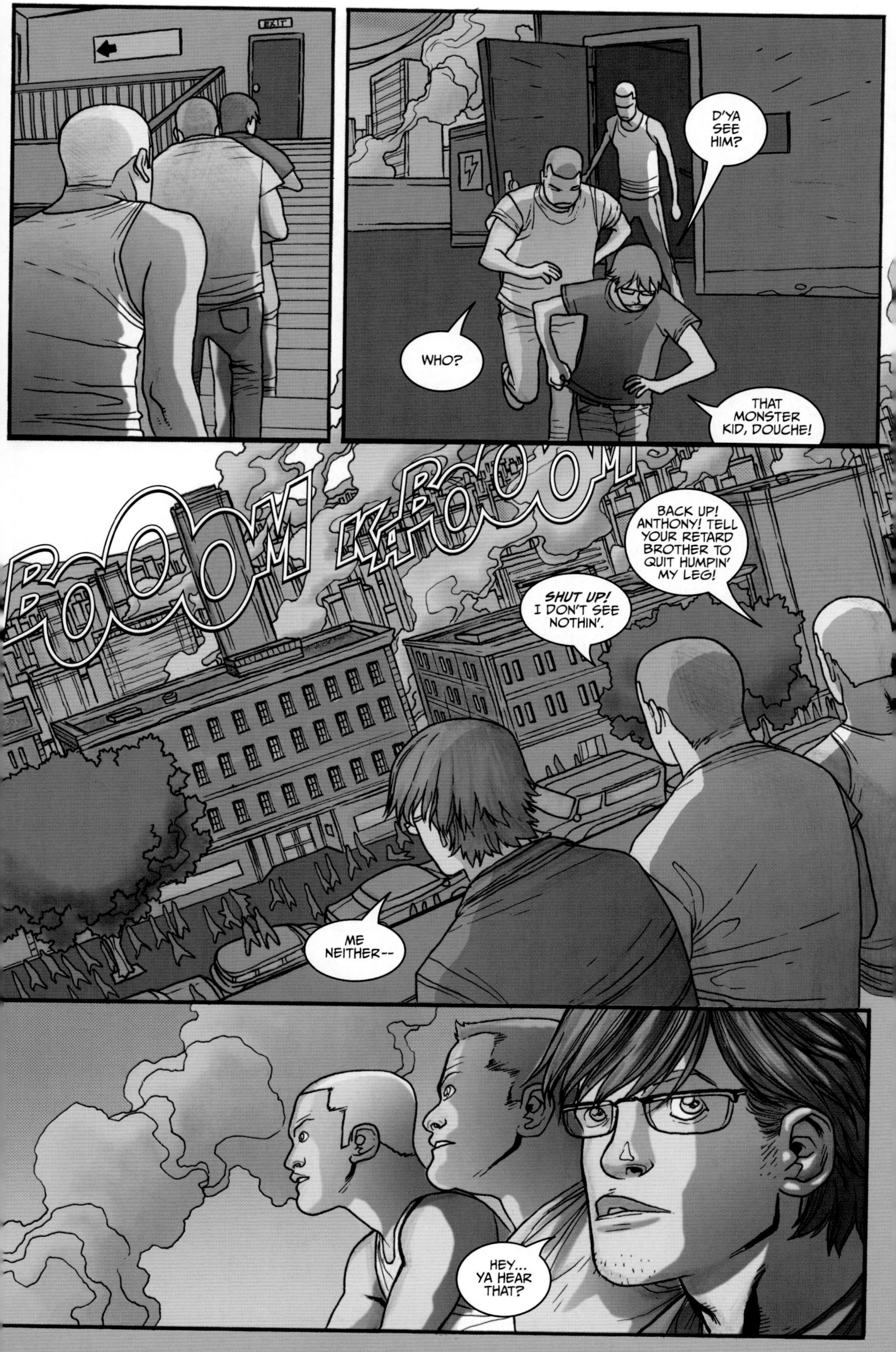
EXIT
D'YA SEE HIM?
WHO?
THAT MONSTER KID, DOUCHE!
BOOOOM KA-BOOOM
BACK UP! ANTHONY! TELL YOUR RETARD BROTHER TO QUIT HUMPIN' MY LEG!
SHUT UP! I DON'T SEE NOTHIN'.
ME NEITHER--
HEY... YA HEAR THAT?

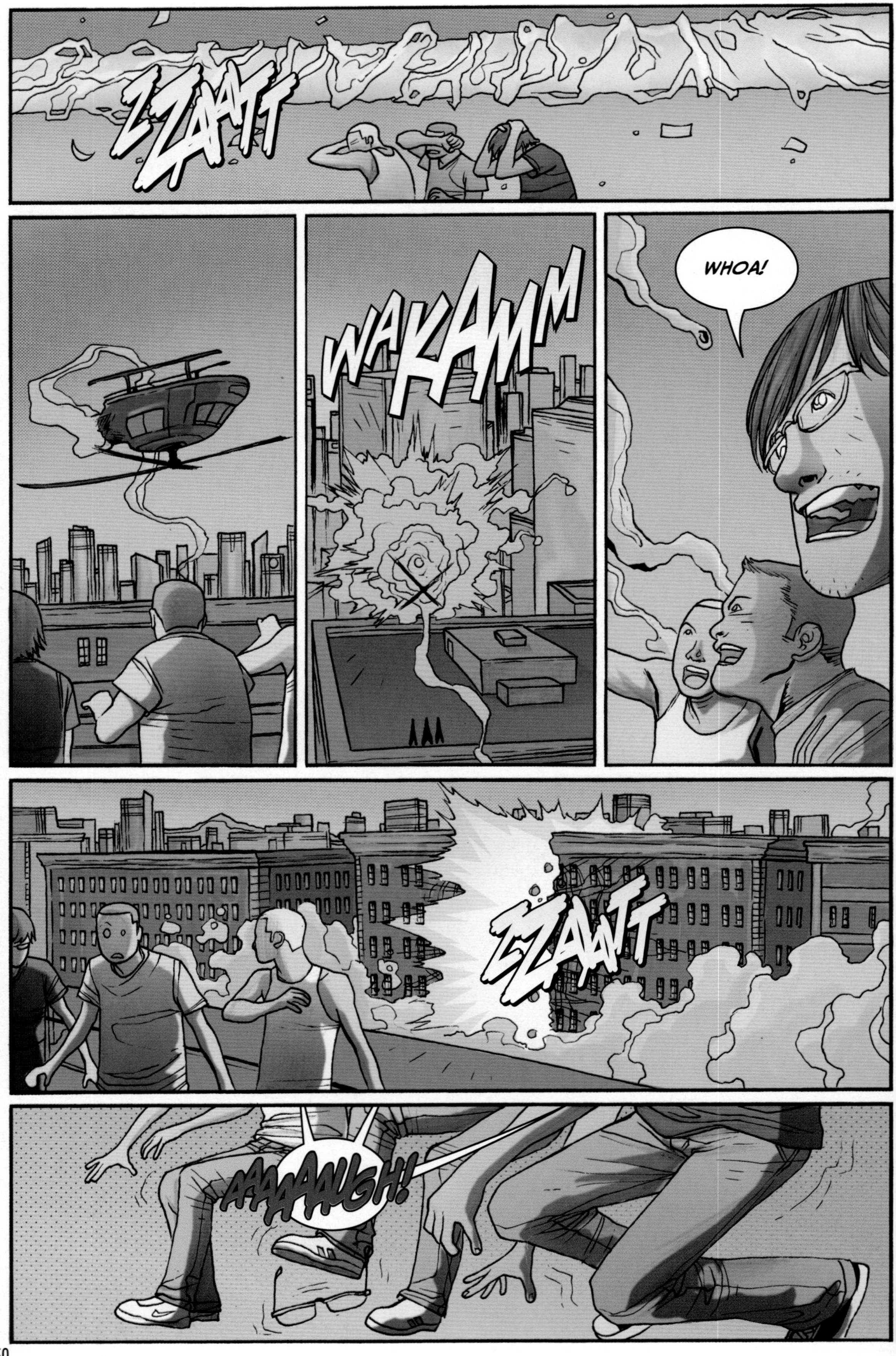
ZZAATT
WAKAMM
WHOA!
ZZAATT
AAAAAAUGH!

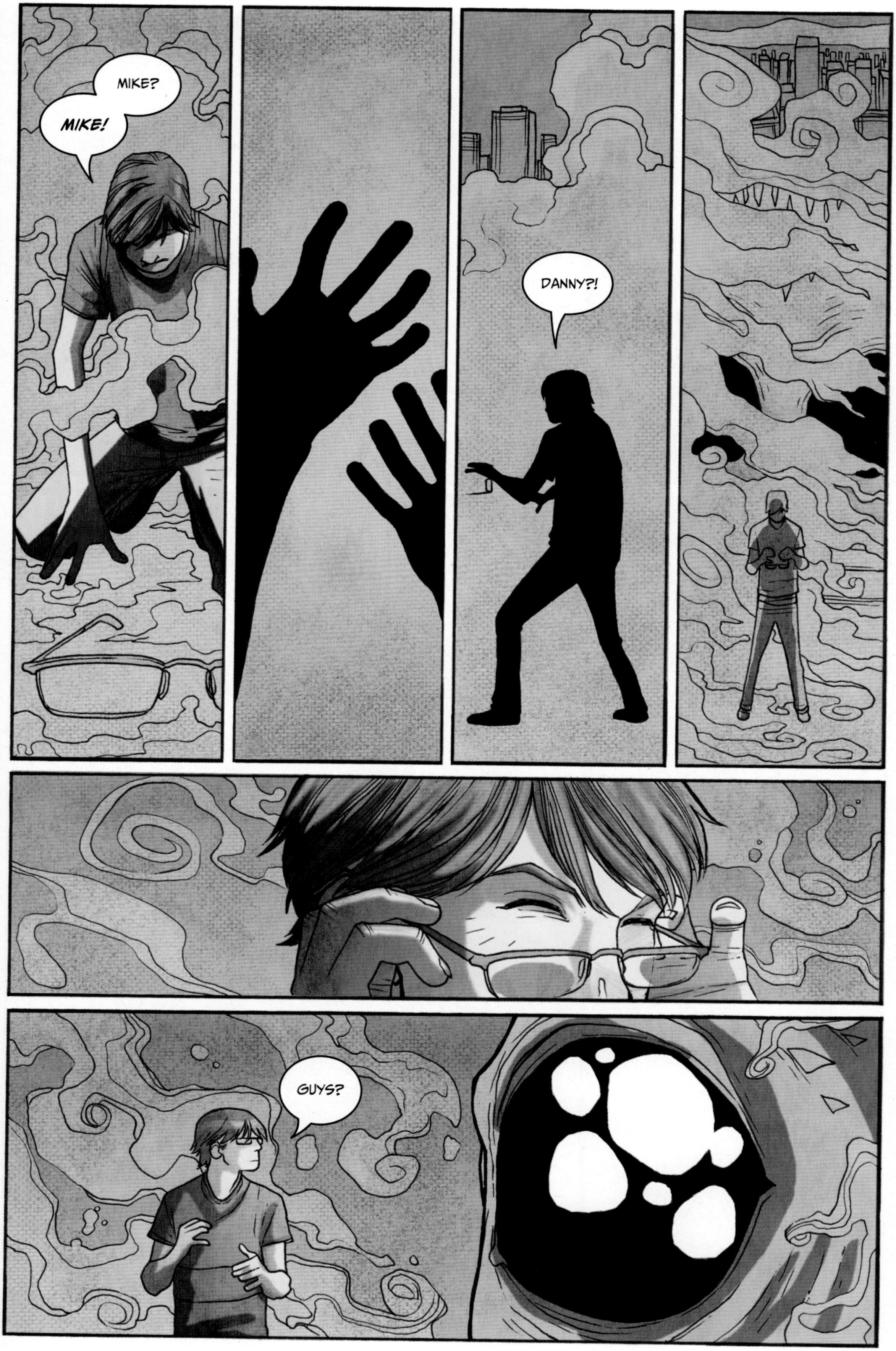
MIKE?
MIKE!
DANNY?!
GUYS?

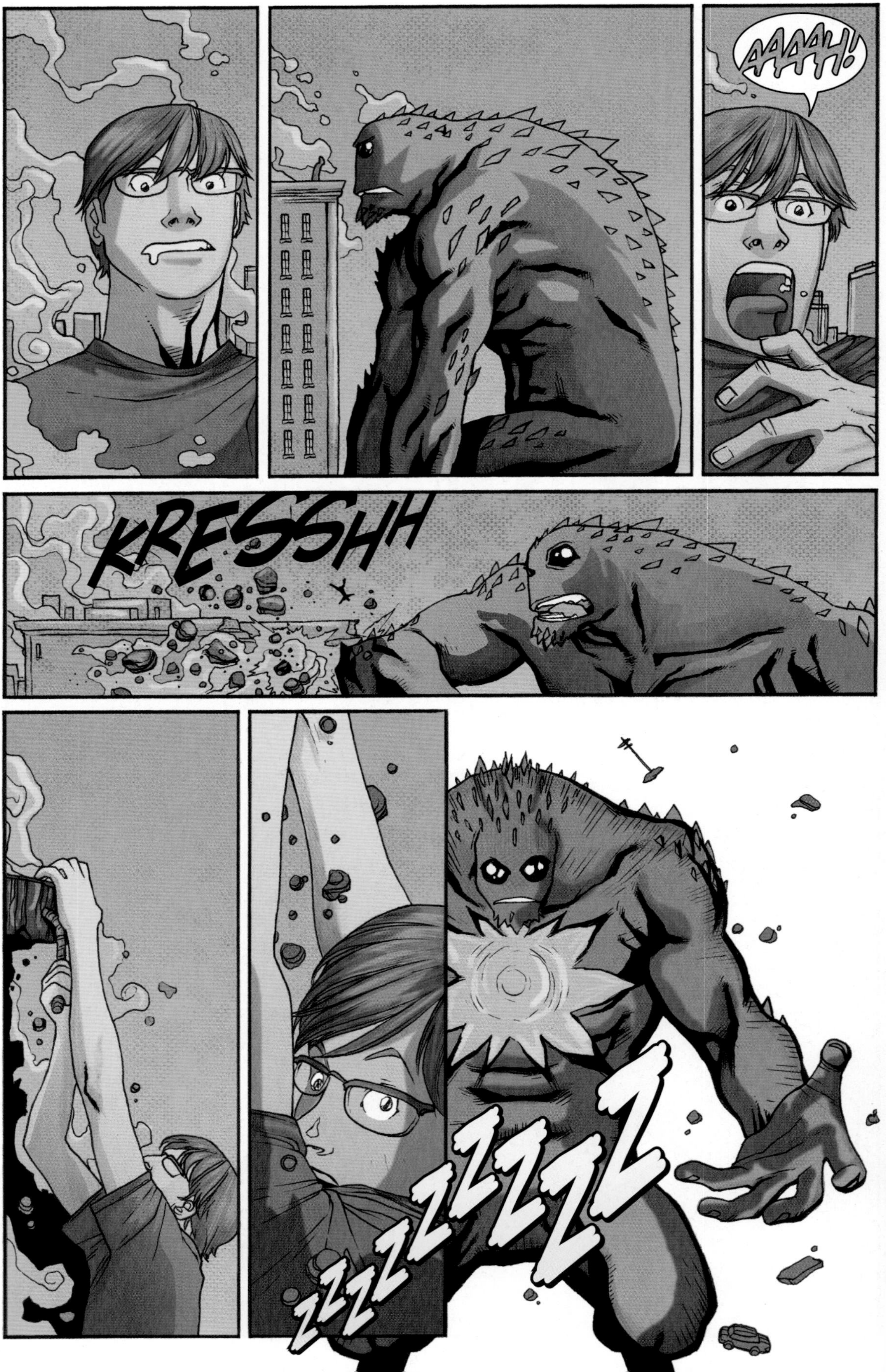
AAAAH!
KRESSHH
ZZZZZZZZZZZ

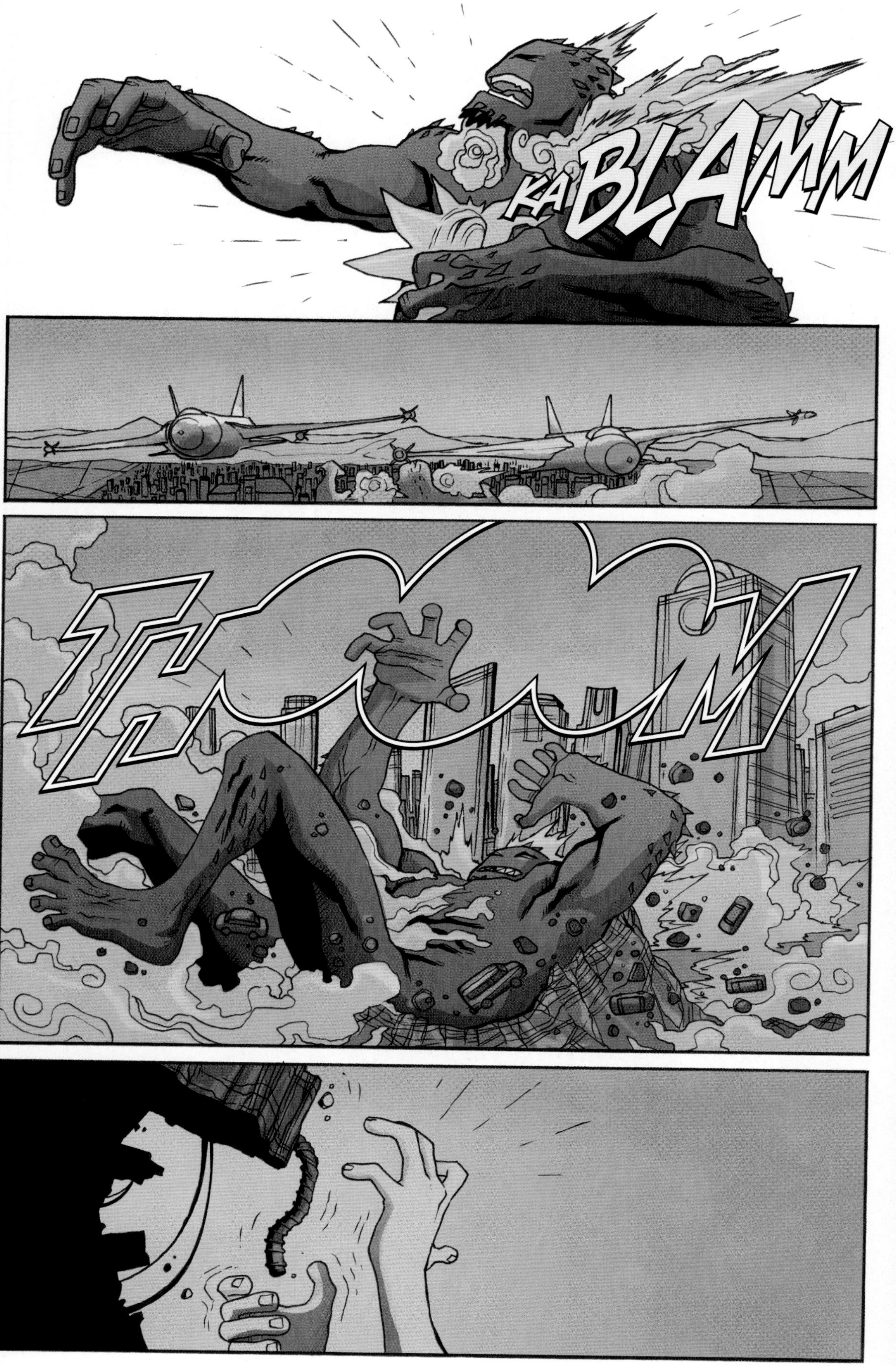
KA BLAMM
THOOM

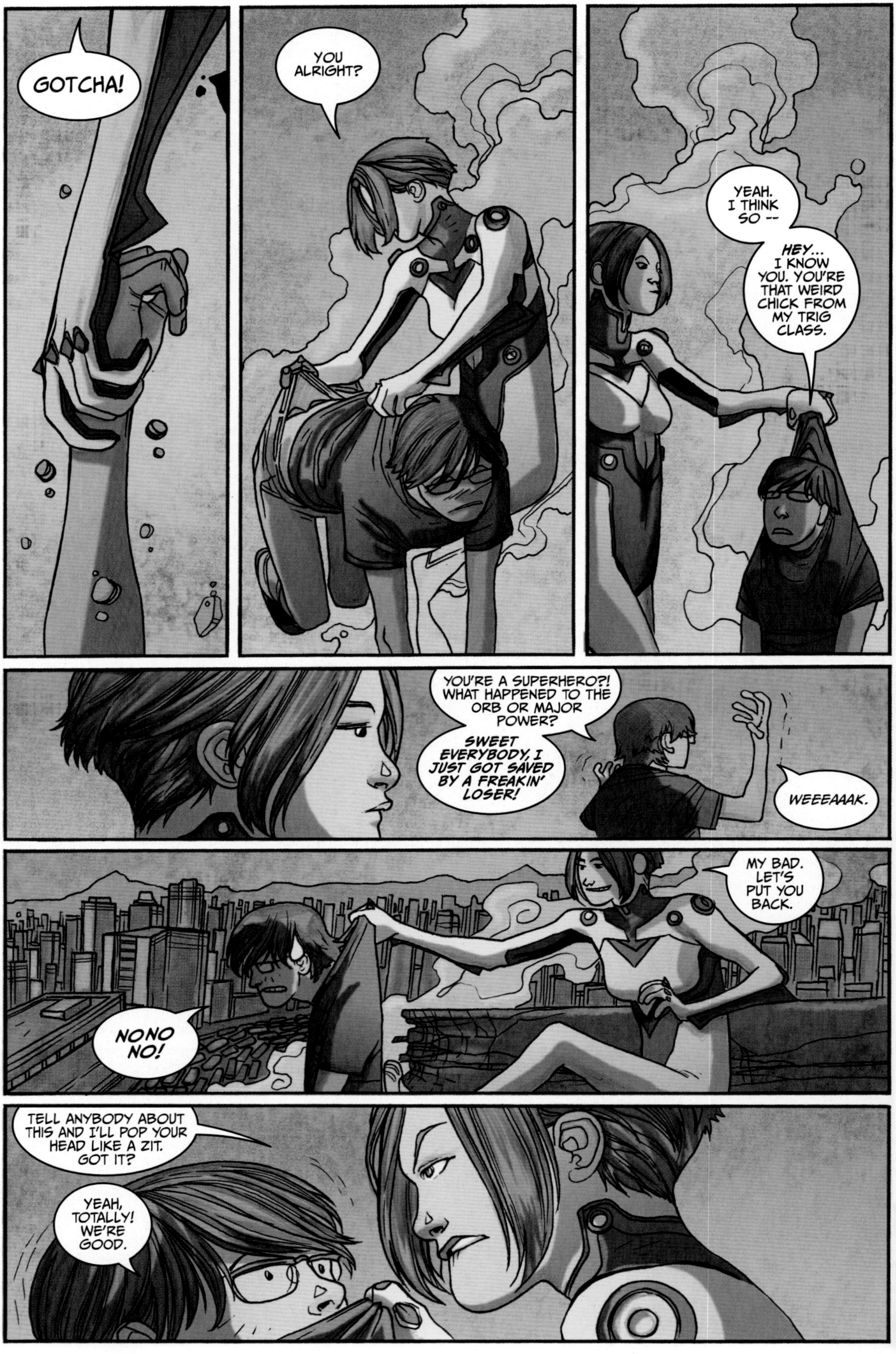
GOTCHA!
YOU ALRIGHT?
YEAH. I THINK SO --
HEY... I KNOW YOU. YOU'RE THAT WEIRD CHICK FROM MY TRIG CLASS.
YOU'RE A SUPERHERO?! WHAT HAPPENED TO THE ORB OR MAJOR POWER?
SWEET EVERYBODY, I JUST GOT SAVED BY A FREAKIN' LOSER!
WEEEAAAK.
MY BAD. LET'S PUT YOU BACK.
NONO NO!
TELL ANYBODY ABOUT THIS AND I'LL POP YOUR HEAD LIKE A ZIT. GOT IT?
YEAH, TOTALLY! WE'RE GOOD.

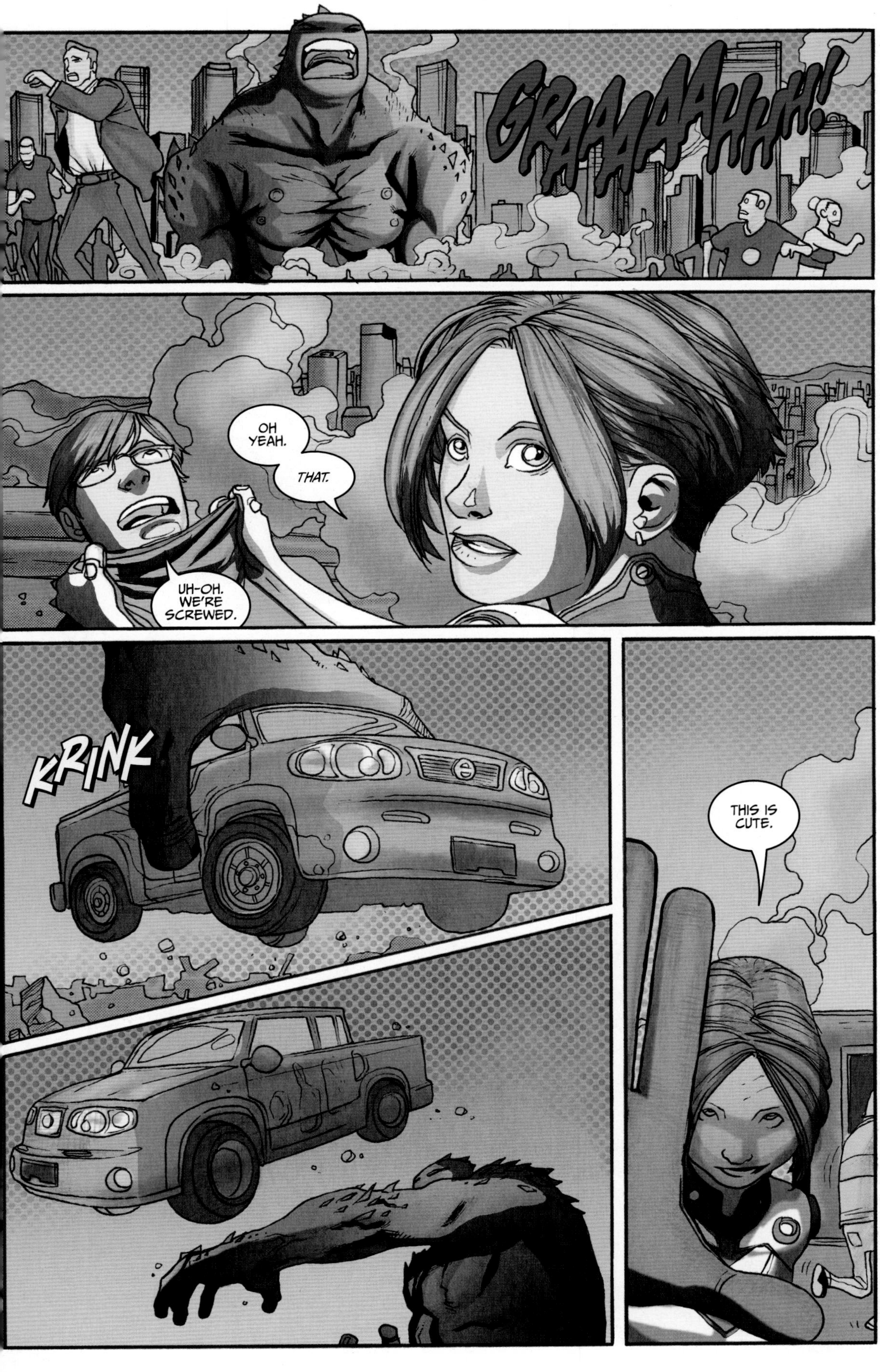
GRAAAAAHHH!
OH YEAH.
THAT.
UH-OH. WE'RE SCREWED.
KRINK
THIS IS CUTE.

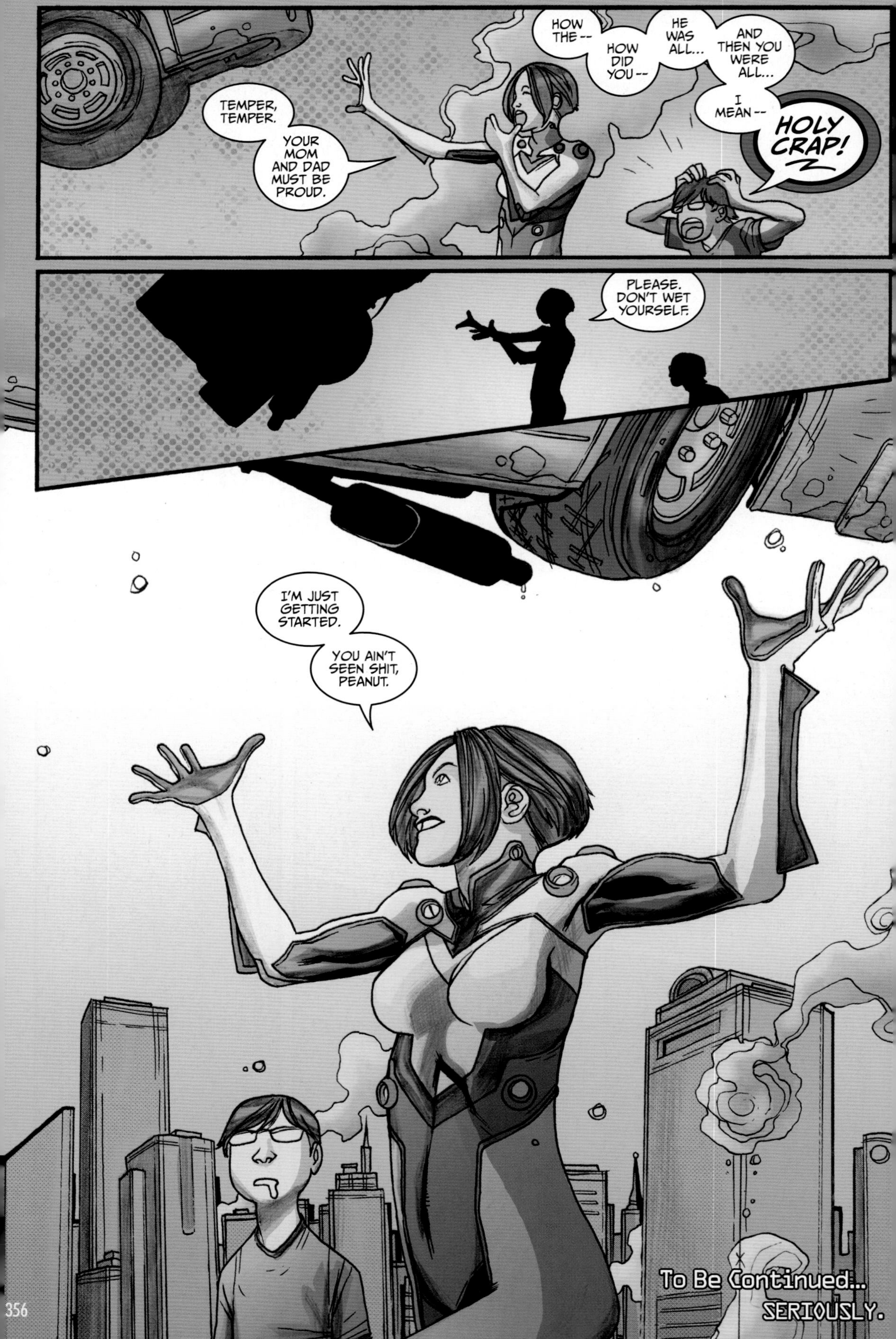
TEMPER, TEMPER.
YOUR MOM AND DAD MUST BE PROUD.
HOW THE --
HOW DID YOU --
HE WAS ALL...
AND THEN YOU WERE ALL...
I MEAN --
HOLY CRAP!
PLEASE. DON'T WET YOURSELF.
I'M JUST GETTING STARTED.
YOU AIN'T SEEN SHIT, PEANUT.
To Be Continued...
SERIOUSLY.

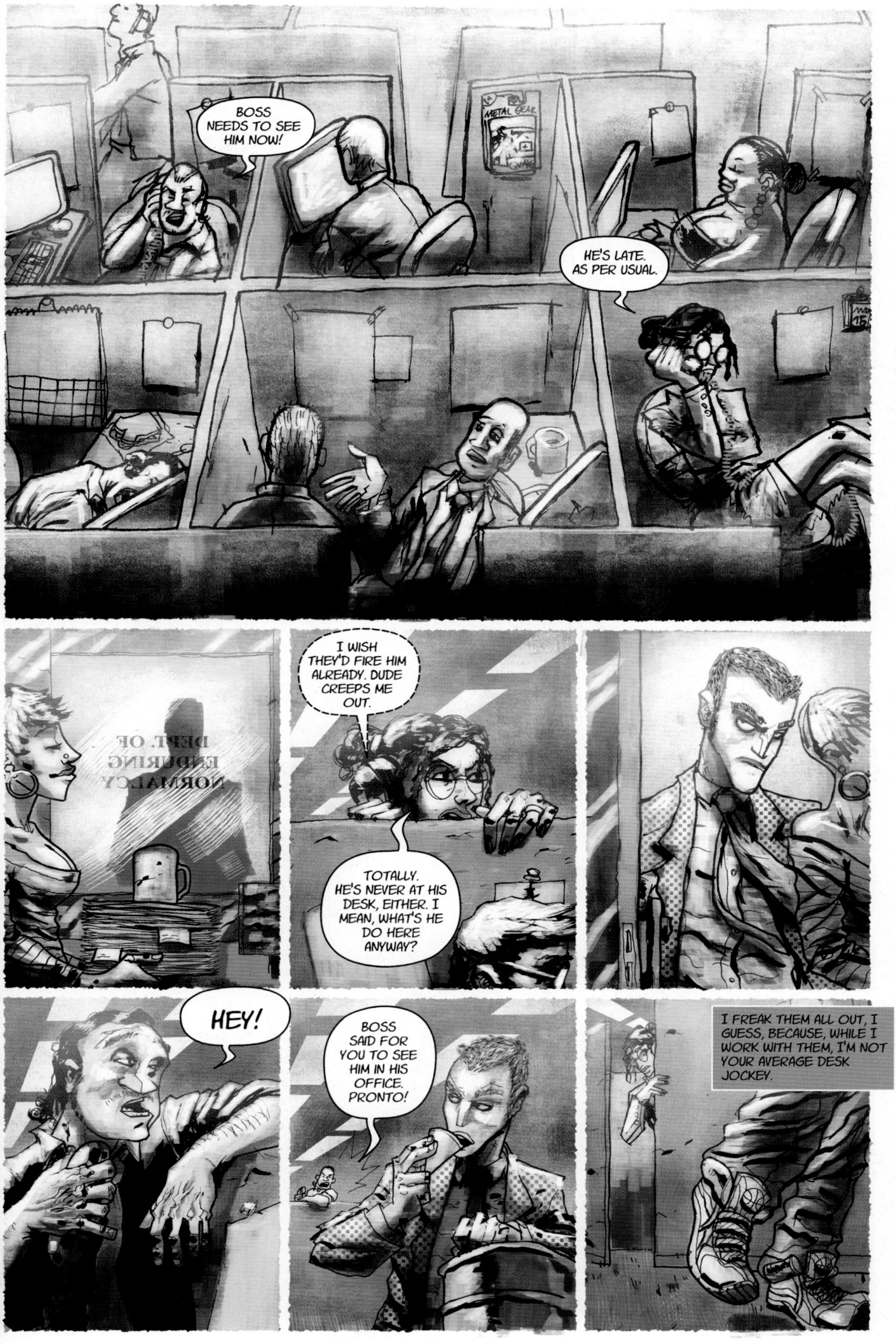
BOSS NEEDS TO SEE HIM NOW!
METAL GEAR
HE'S LATE. AS PER USUAL.
DEPT. OF ENDURING NORMALCY
I WISH THEY'D FIRE HIM ALREADY. DUDE CREEPS ME OUT.
TOTALLY. HE'S NEVER AT HIS DESK, EITHER. I MEAN, WHAT'S HE DO HERE ANYWAY?
HEY!
BOSS SAID FOR YOU TO SEE HIM IN HIS OFFICE. PRONTO!
I FREAK THEM ALL OUT, I GUESS, BECAUSE, WHILE I WORK WITH THEM, I'M NOT YOUR AVERAGE DESK JOCKEY.

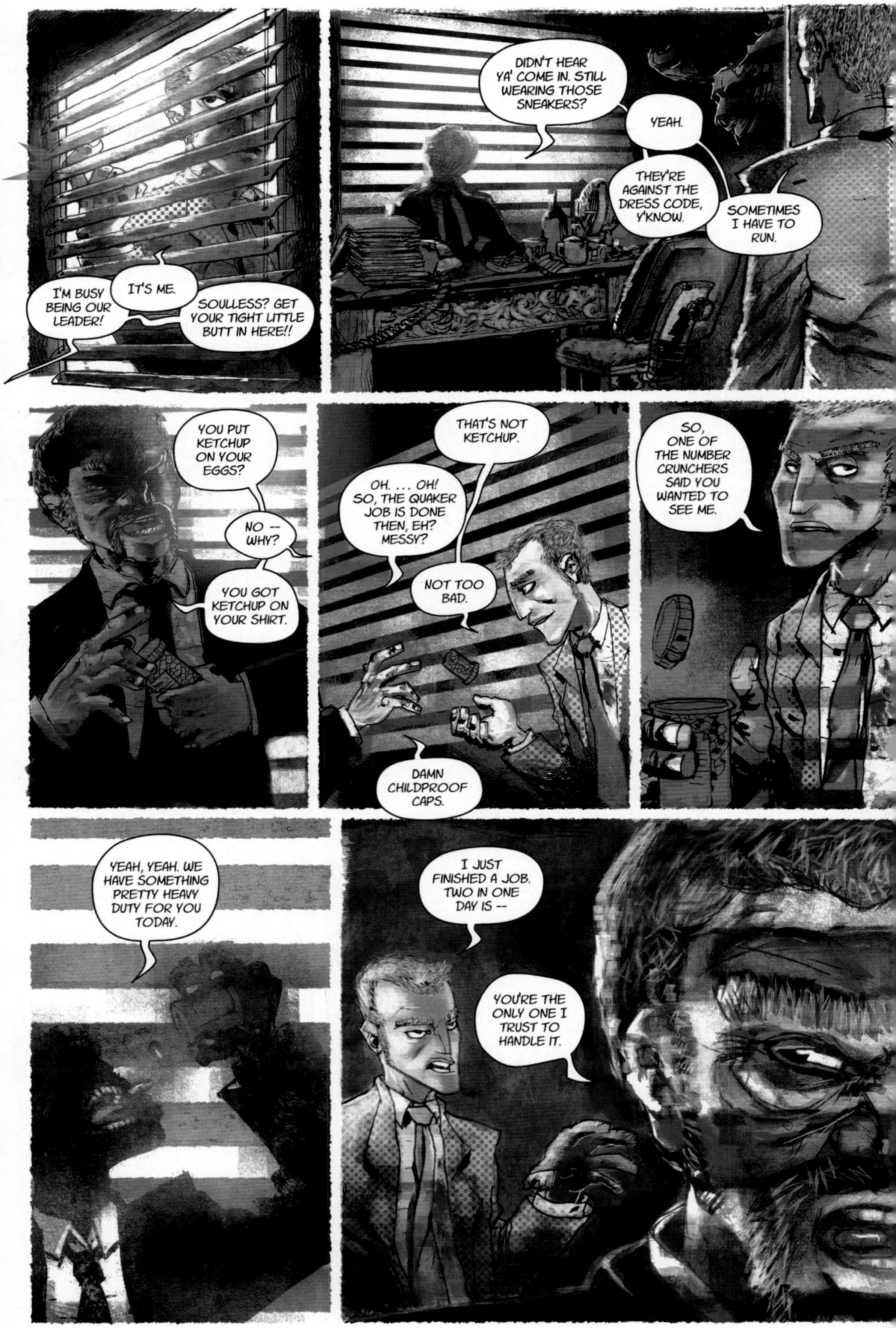
SOULLESS? GET YOUR TIGHT LITTLE BUTT IN HERE!!
IT'S ME.
I'M BUSY BEING OUR LEADER!
DIDN'T HEAR YA' COME IN. STILL WEARING THOSE SNEAKERS?
YEAH.
THEY'RE AGAINST THE DRESS CODE, Y'KNOW.
SOMETIMES I HAVE TO RUN.
YOU PUT KETCHUP ON YOUR EGGS?
NO -- WHY?
YOU GOT KETCHUP ON YOUR SHIRT.
THAT'S NOT KETCHUP.
OH. ... OH! SO, THE QUAKER JOB IS DONE THEN, EH? MESSY?
NOT TOO BAD.
DAMN CHILDPROOF CAPS.
SO, ONE OF THE NUMBER CRUNCHERS SAID YOU WANTED TO SEE ME.
YEAH, YEAH. WE HAVE SOMETHING PRETTY HEAVY DUTY FOR YOU TODAY.
I JUST FINISHED A JOB. TWO IN ONE DAY IS --
YOU'RE THE ONLY ONE I TRUST TO HANDLE IT.

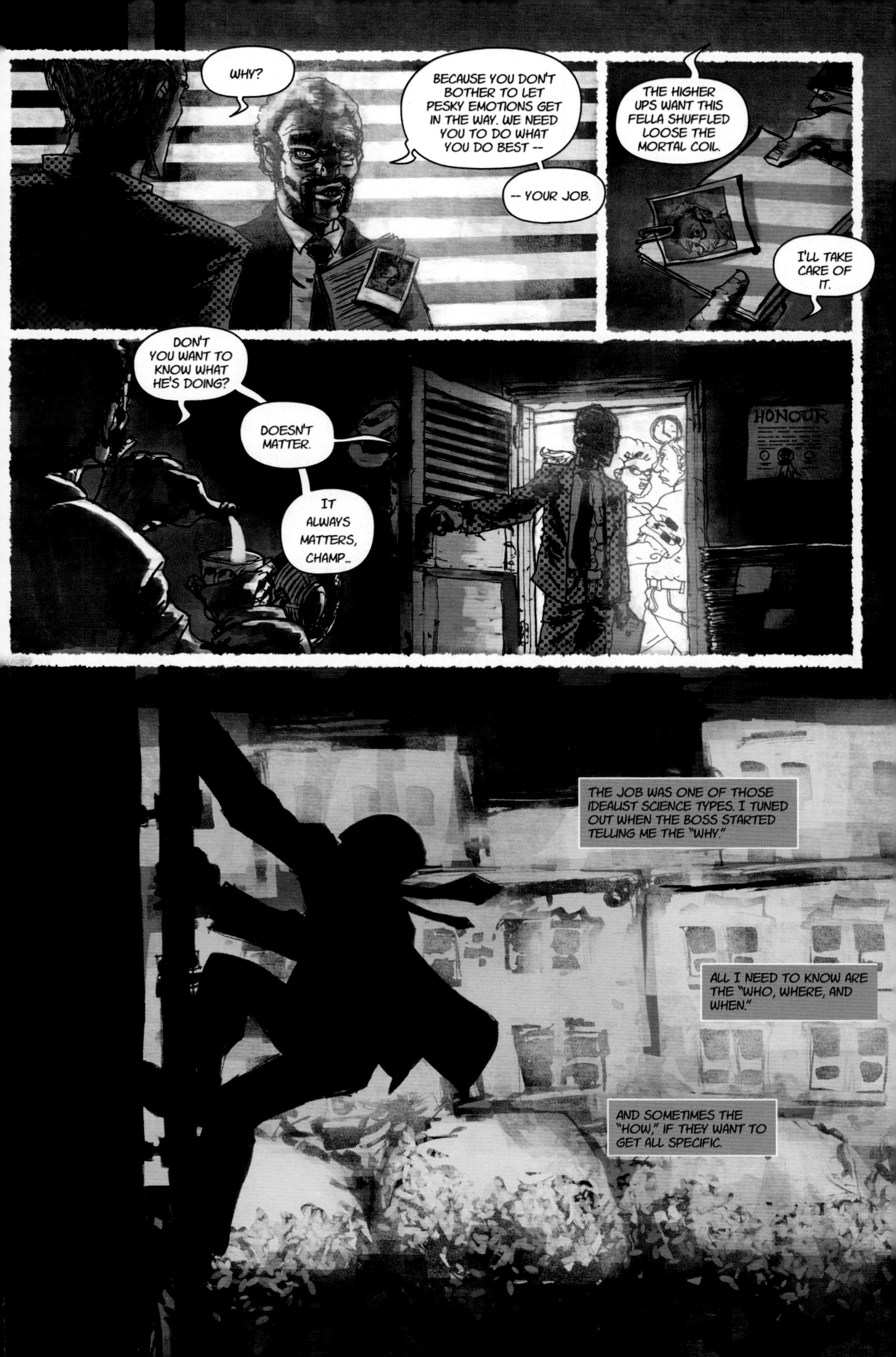
WHY?
BECAUSE YOU DON'T BOTHER TO LET PESKY EMOTIONS GET IN THE WAY. WE NEED YOU TO DO WHAT YOU DO BEST --
-- YOUR JOB.
THE HIGHER UPS WANT THIS FELLA SHUFFLED LOOSE THE MORTAL COIL.
I'LL TAKE CARE OF IT.
DON'T YOU WANT TO KNOW WHAT HE'S DOING?
DOESN'T MATTER.
IT ALWAYS MATTERS, CHAMP...
HONOUR
THE JOB WAS ONE OF THOSE IDEALIST SCIENCE TYPES. I TUNED OUT WHEN THE BOSS STARTED TELLING ME THE "WHY."
ALL I NEED TO KNOW ARE THE "WHO, WHERE, AND WHEN."
AND SOMETIMES THE "HOW," IF THEY WANT TO GET ALL SPECIFIC.

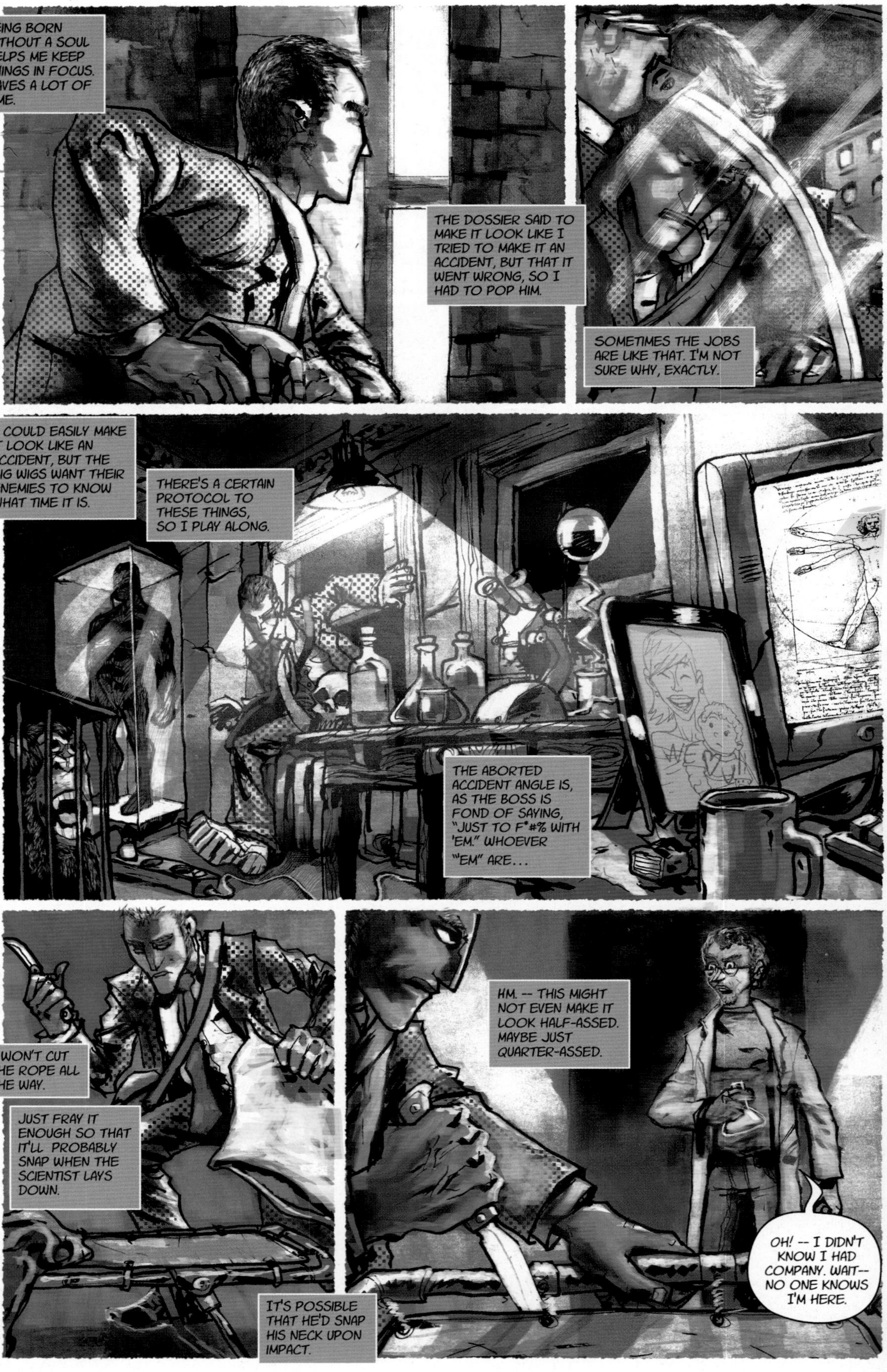
BEING BORN WITHOUT A SOUL HELPS ME KEEP THINGS IN FOCUS. SAVES A LOT OF TIME.
THE DOSSIER SAID TO MAKE IT LOOK LIKE I TRIED TO MAKE IT AN ACCIDENT, BUT THAT IT WENT WRONG, SO I HAD TO POP HIM.
SOMETIMES THE JOBS ARE LIKE THAT. I'M NOT SURE WHY, EXACTLY.
I COULD EASILY MAKE IT LOOK LIKE AN ACCIDENT, BUT THE BIG WIGS WANT THEIR ENEMIES TO KNOW WHAT TIME IT IS.
THERE'S A CERTAIN PROTOCOL TO THESE THINGS, SO I PLAY ALONG.
THE ABORTED ACCIDENT ANGLE IS, AS THE BOSS IS FOND OF SAYING, "JUST TO F*#% WITH 'EM." WHOEVER "EM" ARE...
I WON'T CUT THE ROPE ALL THE WAY.
JUST FRAY IT ENOUGH SO THAT IT'LL PROBABLY SNAP WHEN THE SCIENTIST LAYS DOWN.
IT'S POSSIBLE THAT HE'D SNAP HIS NECK UPON IMPACT.
HM. -- THIS MIGHT NOT EVEN MAKE IT LOOK HALF-ASSED. MAYBE JUST QUARTER-ASSED.
OH! -- I DIDN'T KNOW I HAD COMPANY. WAIT-- NO ONE KNOWS I'M HERE.

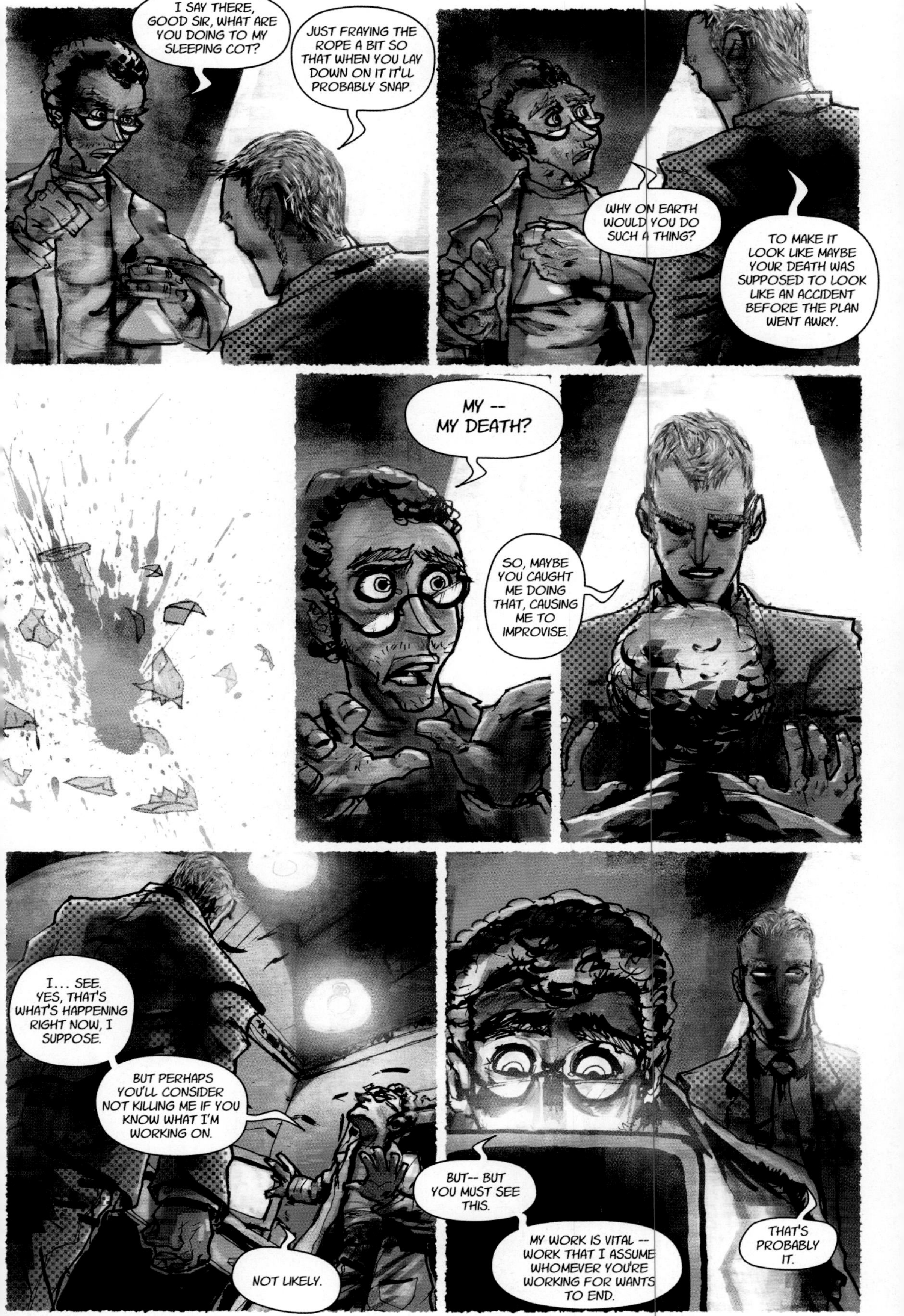
I SAY THERE, GOOD SIR, WHAT ARE YOU DOING TO MY SLEEPING COT?
JUST FRAYING THE ROPE A BIT SO THAT WHEN YOU LAY DOWN ON IT IT'LL PROBABLY SNAP.
WHY ON EARTH WOULD YOU DO SUCH A THING?
TO MAKE IT LOOK LIKE MAYBE YOUR DEATH WAS SUPPOSED TO LOOK LIKE AN ACCIDENT BEFORE THE PLAN WENT AWRY.
MY -- MY DEATH?
SO, MAYBE YOU CAUGHT ME DOING THAT, CAUSING ME TO IMPROVISE.
I... SEE. YES, THAT'S WHAT'S HAPPENING RIGHT NOW, I SUPPOSE.
BUT PERHAPS YOU'LL CONSIDER NOT KILLING ME IF YOU KNOW WHAT I'M WORKING ON.
NOT LIKELY.
BUT-- BUT YOU MUST SEE THIS.
MY WORK IS VITAL -- WORK THAT I ASSUME WHOMEVER YOU'RE WORKING FOR WANTS TO END.
THAT'S PROBABLY IT.

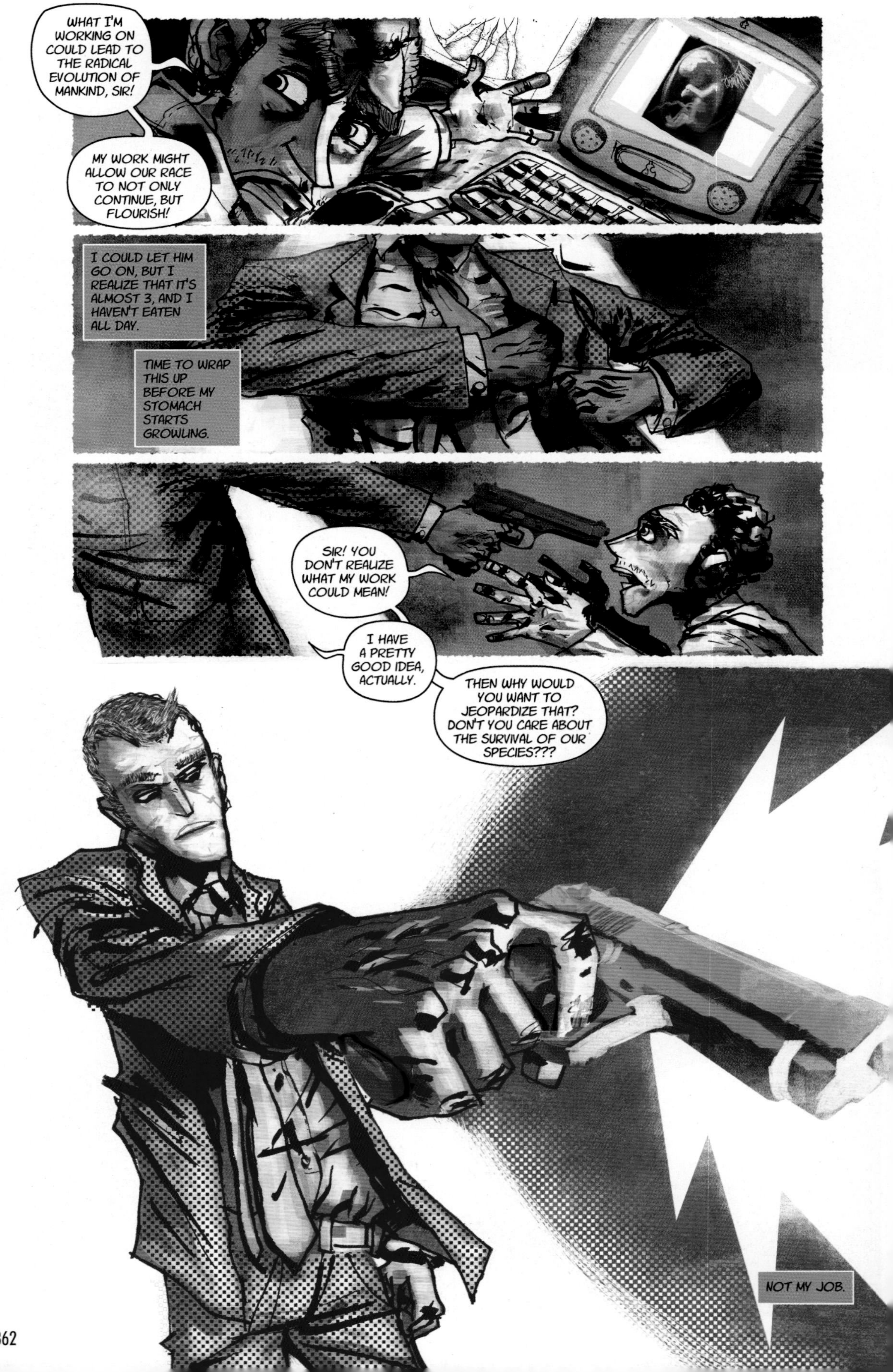
WHAT I'M WORKING ON COULD LEAD TO THE RADICAL EVOLUTION OF MANKIND, SIR!
MY WORK MIGHT ALLOW OUR RACE TO NOT ONLY CONTINUE, BUT FLOURISH!
I COULD LET HIM GO ON, BUT I REALIZE THAT IT'S ALMOST 3, AND I HAVEN'T EATEN ALL DAY.
TIME TO WRAP THIS UP BEFORE MY STOMACH STARTS GROWLING.
SIR! YOU DON'T REALIZE WHAT MY WORK COULD MEAN!
I HAVE A PRETTY GOOD IDEA, ACTUALLY.
THEN WHY WOULD YOU WANT TO JEOPARDIZE THAT? DON'T YOU CARE ABOUT THE SURVIVAL OF OUR SPECIES???
NOT MY JOB.

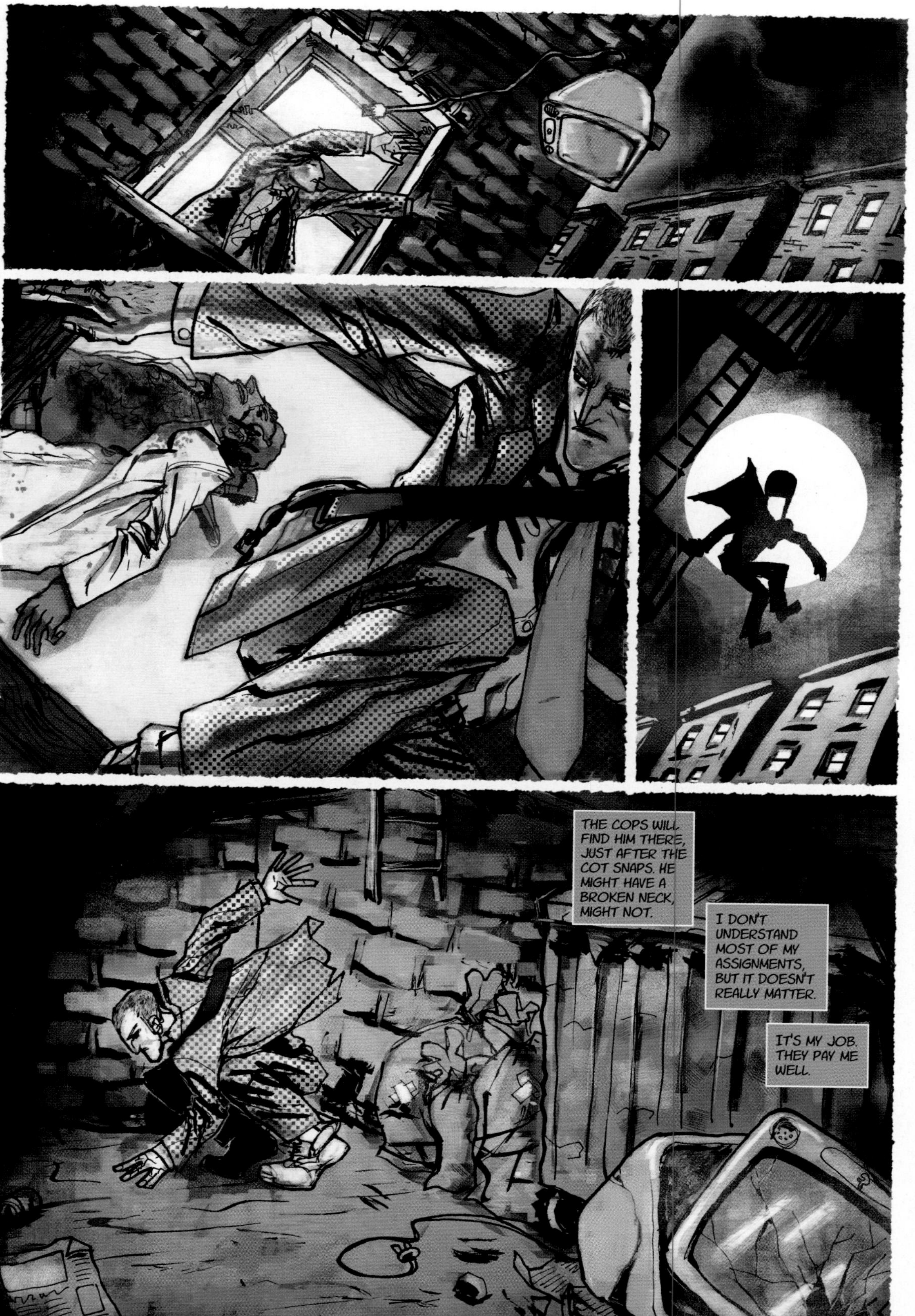
THE COPS WILL FIND HIM THERE, JUST AFTER THE COT SNAPS. HE MIGHT HAVE A BROKEN NECK, MIGHT NOT.
I DON'T UNDERSTAND MOST OF MY ASSIGNMENTS, BUT IT DOESN'T REALLY MATTER.
IT'S MY JOB. THEY PAY ME WELL.

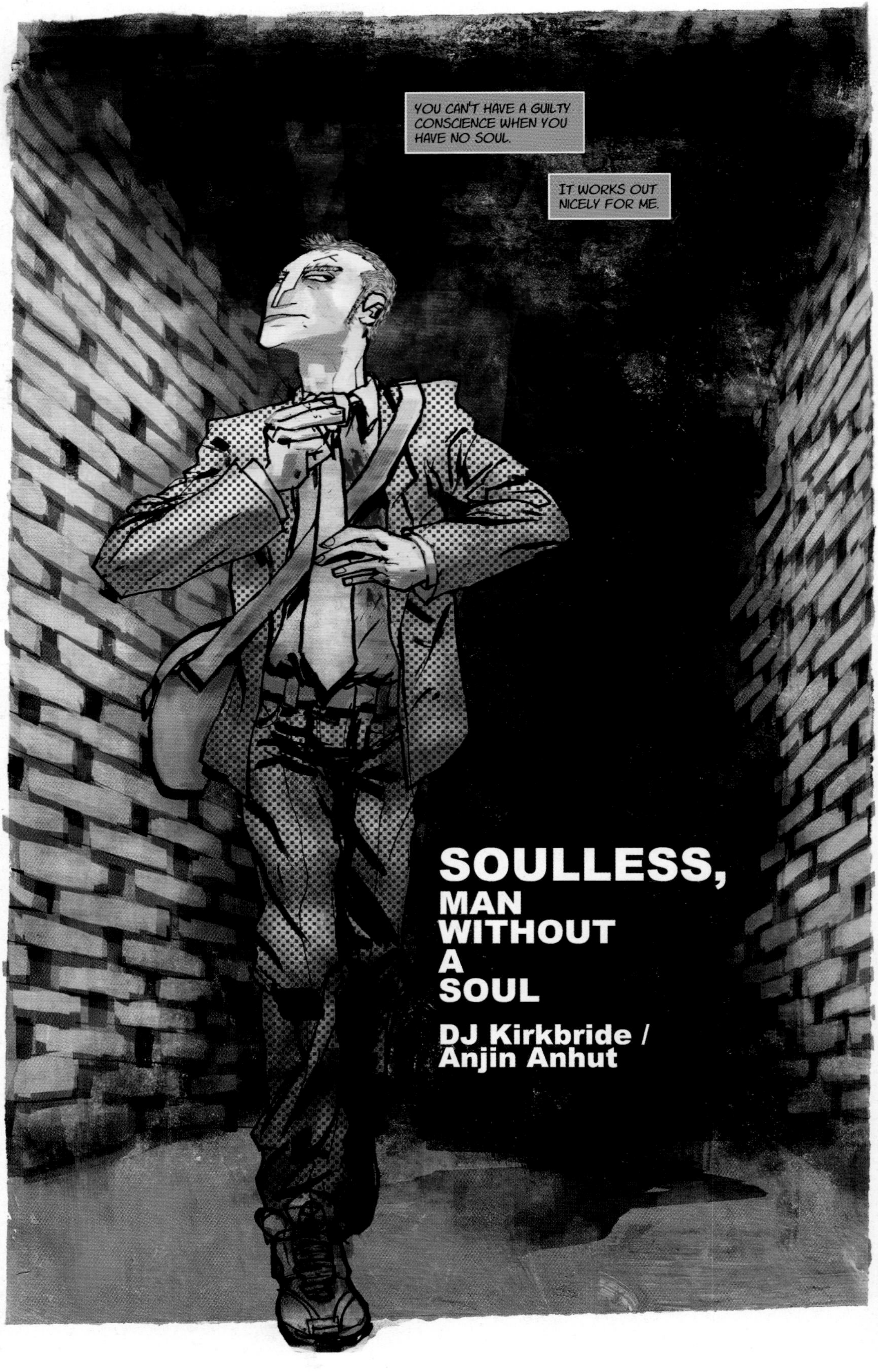
YOU CAN'T HAVE A GUILTY CONSCIENCE WHEN YOU HAVE NO SOUL.
IT WORKS OUT NICELY FOR ME.
SOULLESS, MAN WITHOUT A SOUL
DJ Kirkbride / Anjin Anhut

Deep within the bowels of the dilapidated Citadel lies a vast network of ancient catacombs.

The subterranean resting place for the damned and forgotten.

EUREKA!

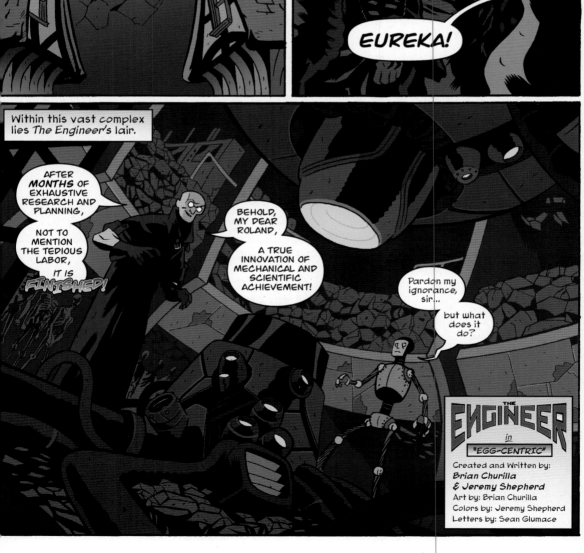

Within this vast complex lies *The Engineer's* lair.

AFTER **MONTHS** OF EXHAUSTIVE RESEARCH AND PLANNING,

NOT TO MENTION THE TEDIOUS LABOR, IT IS *FINISHED!*

BEHOLD, MY DEAR ROLAND,

A TRUE INNOVATION OF MECHANICAL AND SCIENTIFIC ACHIEVEMENT!

Pardon my ignorance, sir...

but what does it do?

THE ENGINEER in "EGG-CENTRIC"

Created and Written by:
Brian Churilla
& Jeremy Shepherd
Art by: Brian Churilla
Colors by: Jeremy Shepherd
Letters by: Sean Glumace

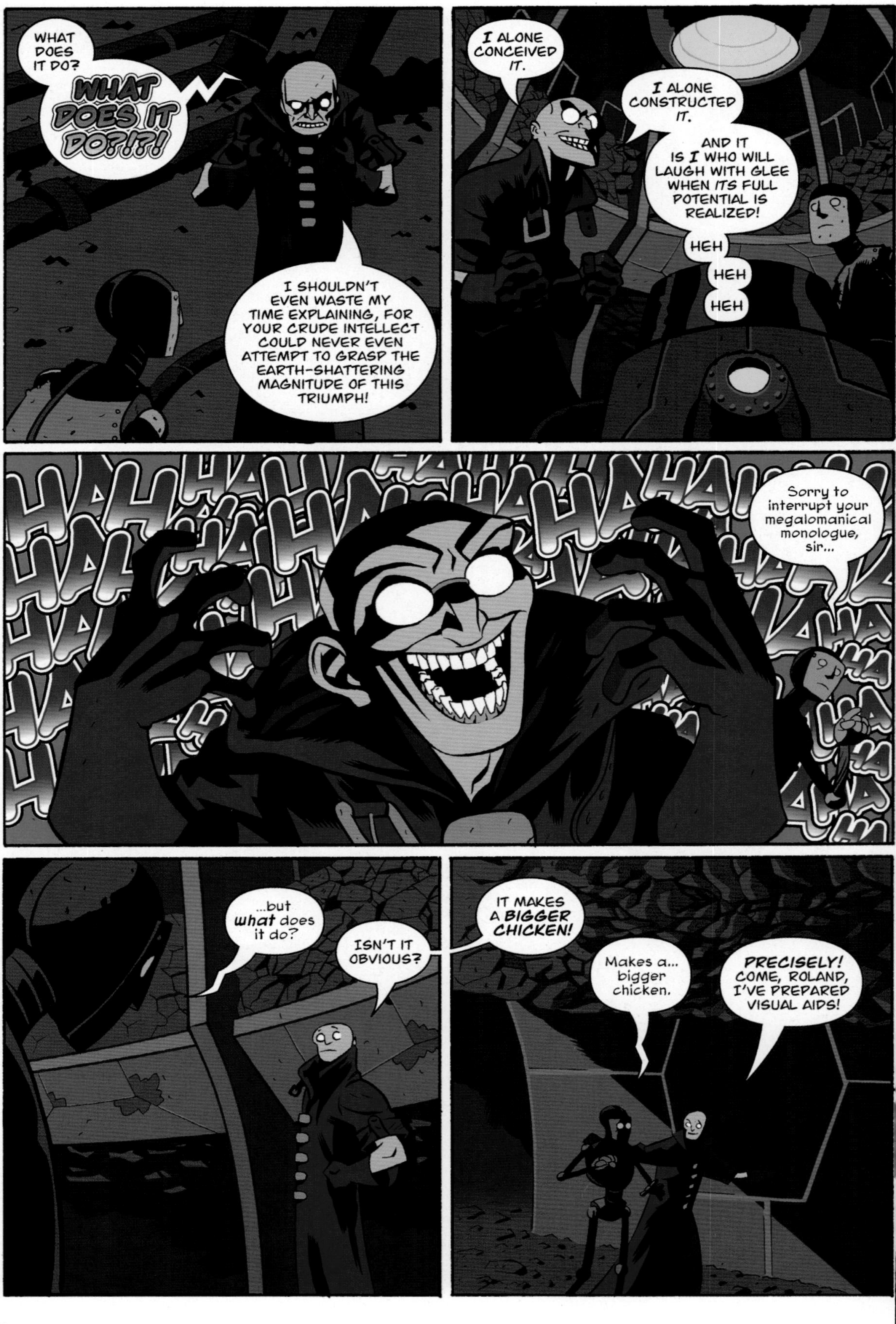

WHAT DOES IT DO?
WHAT DOES IT DO?!?!
I SHOULDN'T EVEN WASTE MY TIME EXPLAINING, FOR YOUR CRUDE INTELLECT COULD NEVER EVEN ATTEMPT TO GRASP THE EARTH-SHATTERING MAGNITUDE OF THIS TRIUMPH!
I ALONE CONCEIVED IT.
I ALONE CONSTRUCTED IT.
AND IT IS I WHO WILL LAUGH WITH GLEE WHEN ITS FULL POTENTIAL IS REALIZED!
HEH
HEH
HEH
Sorry to interrupt your megalomanical monologue, sir...
...but what does it do?
ISN'T IT OBVIOUS?
IT MAKES A BIGGER CHICKEN!
Makes a... bigger chicken.
PRECISELY! COME, ROLAND, I'VE PREPARED VISUAL AIDS!

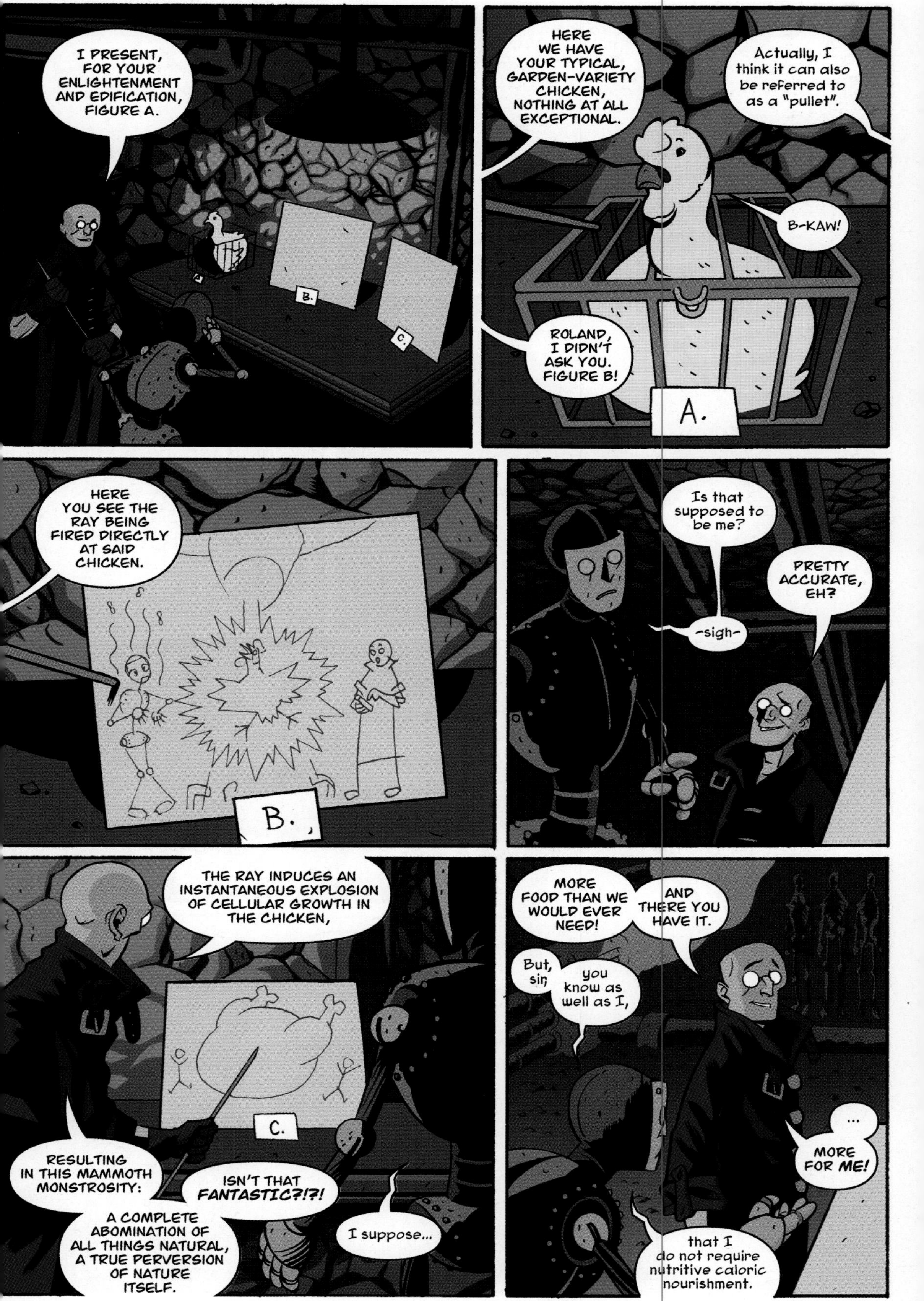
I PRESENT, FOR YOUR ENLIGHTENMENT AND EDIFICATION, FIGURE A.
B.
C.
HERE WE HAVE YOUR TYPICAL, GARDEN-VARIETY CHICKEN, NOTHING AT ALL EXCEPTIONAL.
Actually, I think it can also be referred to as a "pullet".
B-KAW!
ROLAND, I DIDN'T ASK YOU. FIGURE B!
A.
HERE YOU SEE THE RAY BEING FIRED DIRECTLY AT SAID CHICKEN.
B.
Is that supposed to be me?
PRETTY ACCURATE, EH?
-sigh-
THE RAY INDUCES AN INSTANTANEOUS EXPLOSION OF CELLULAR GROWTH IN THE CHICKEN,
C.
RESULTING IN THIS MAMMOTH MONSTROSITY:
ISN'T THAT FANTASTIC?!?!
A COMPLETE ABOMINATION OF ALL THINGS NATURAL, A TRUE PERVERSION OF NATURE ITSELF.
I suppose...
MORE FOOD THAN WE WOULD EVER NEED!
AND THERE YOU HAVE IT.
But, sir,
you know as well as I,
that I do not require nutritive caloric nourishment.
...
MORE FOR ME!

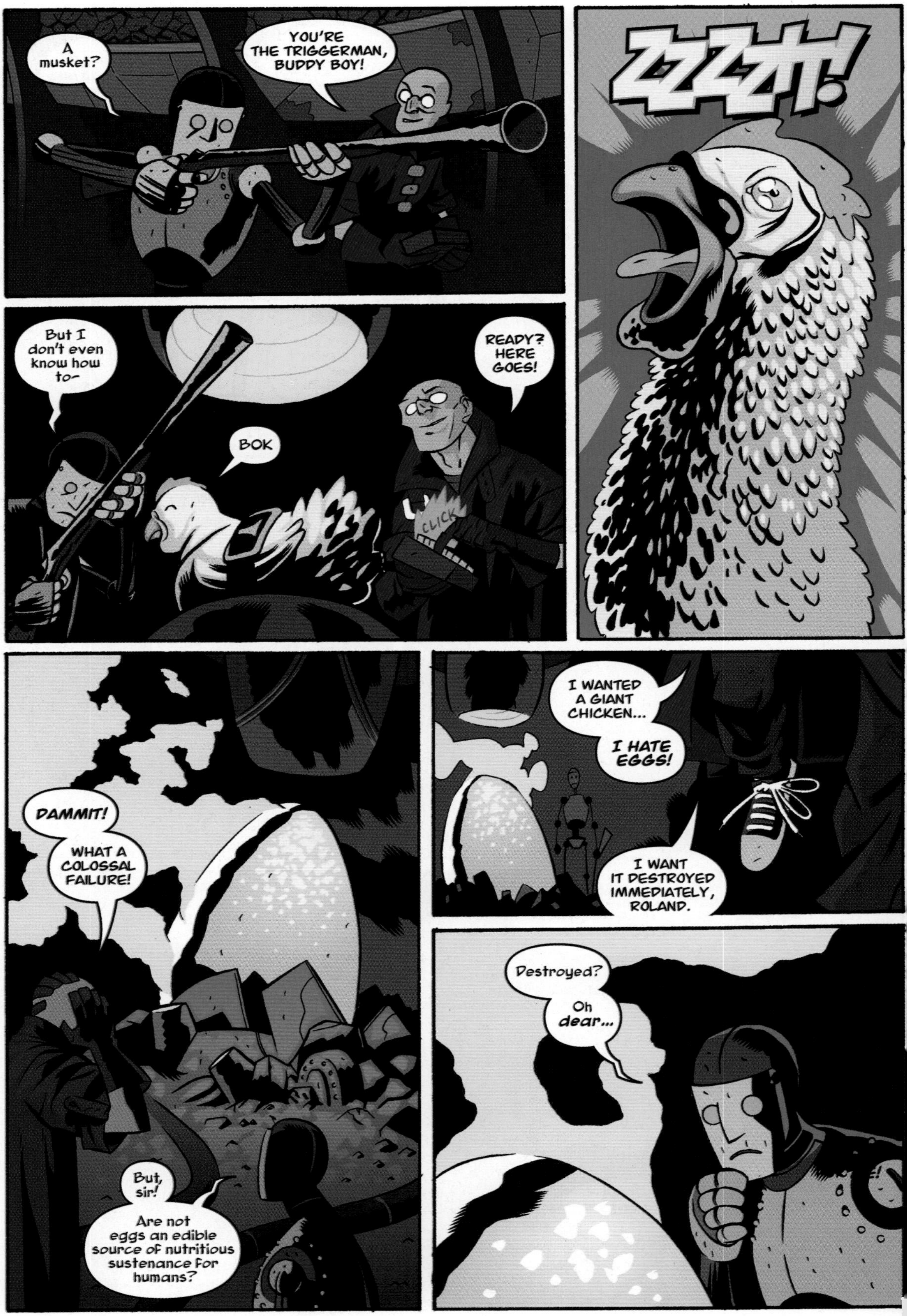

A musket?
YOU'RE THE TRIGGERMAN, BUDDY BOY!
ZZZZAT!
But I don't even know how to-
READY? HERE GOES!
BOK
CLICK
DAMMIT!
WHAT A COLOSSAL FAILURE!
But, sir!
Are not eggs an edible source of nutritious sustenance for humans?
I WANTED A GIANT CHICKEN...
I HATE EGGS!
I WANT IT DESTROYED IMMEDIATELY, ROLAND.
Destroyed?
Oh dear...

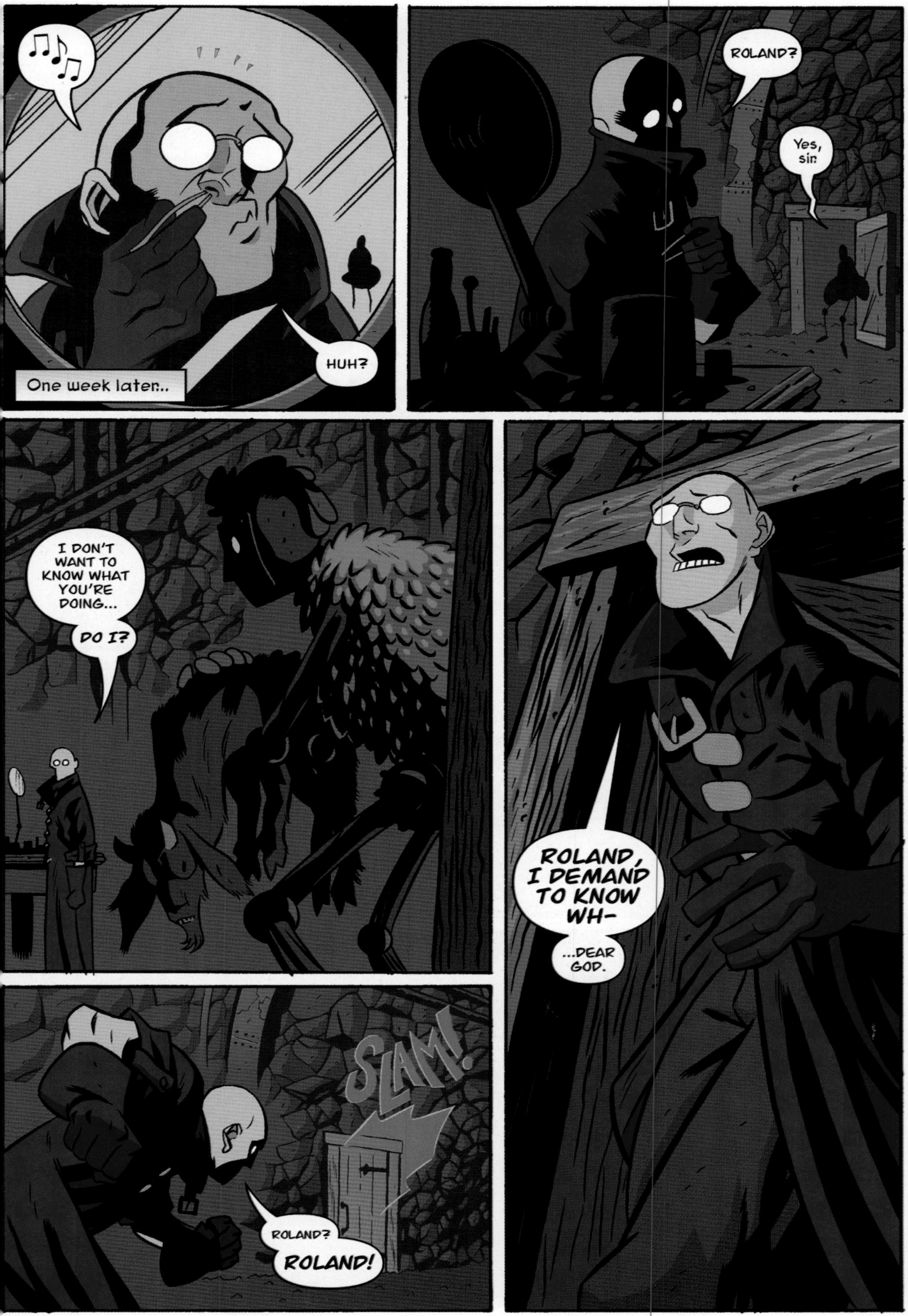

♫♪♫
HUH?
One week later...
ROLAND?
Yes, sir.
I DON'T WANT TO KNOW WHAT YOU'RE DOING...
DO I?
ROLAND, I DEMAND TO KNOW WH-
...DEAR GOD.
SLAM!
ROLAND?
ROLAND!

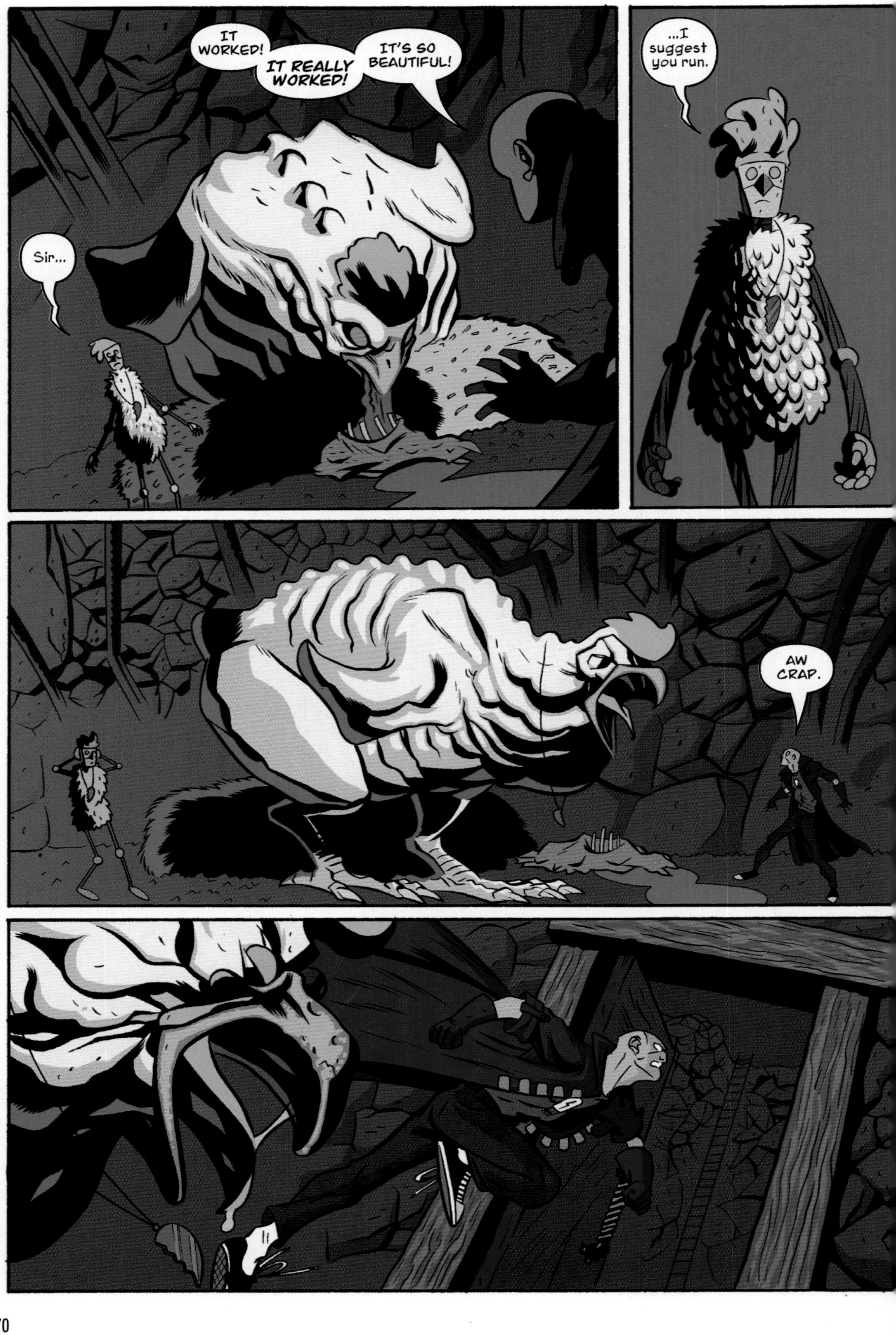
IT WORKED!
IT REALLY WORKED!
IT'S SO BEAUTIFUL!
Sir...
...I suggest you run.
AW CRAP.

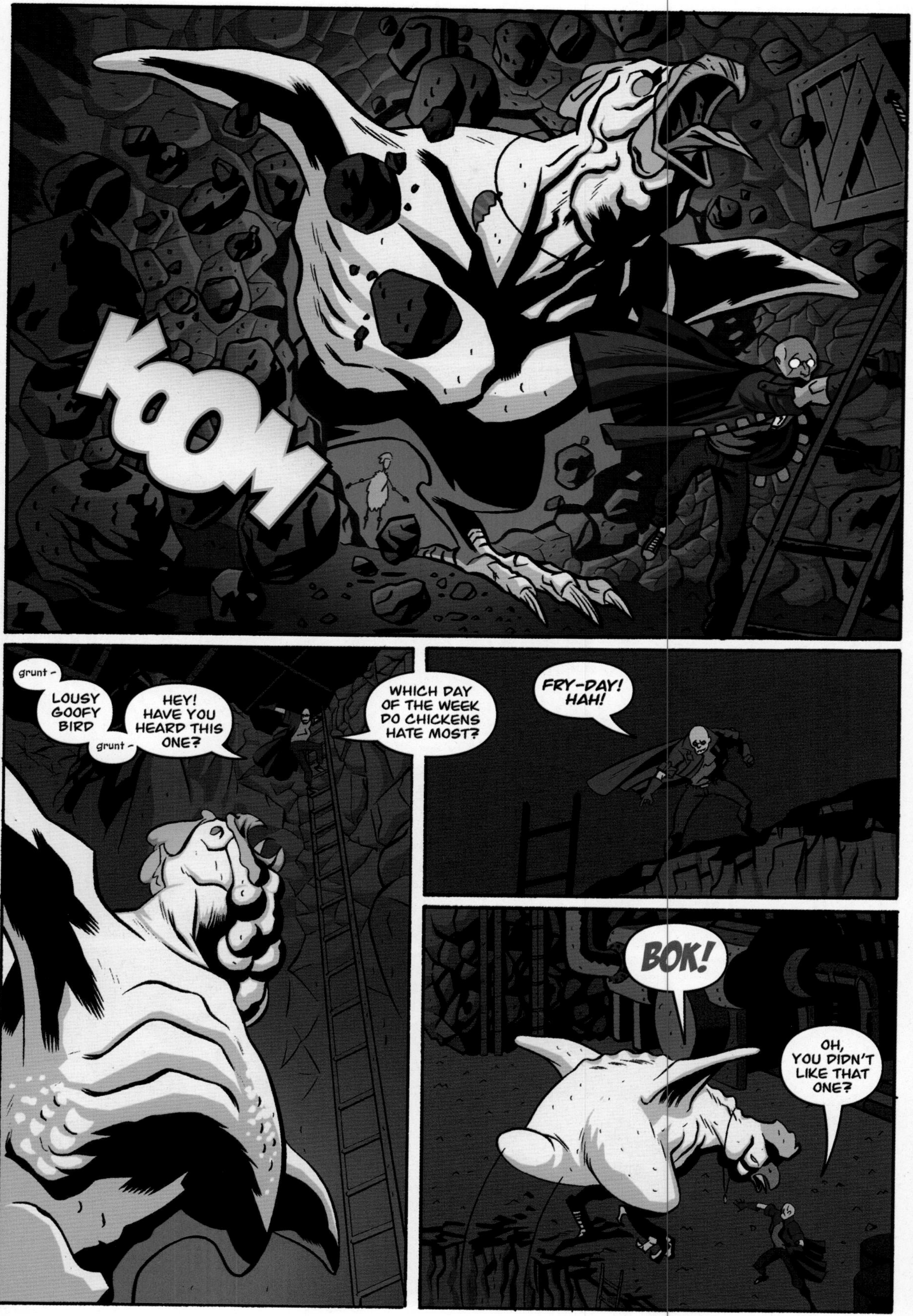
TOOM
grunt -
LOUSY GOOFY BIRD
grunt -
HEY! HAVE YOU HEARD THIS ONE?
WHICH DAY OF THE WEEK DO CHICKENS HATE MOST?
FRY-DAY! HAH!
BOK!
OH, YOU DIDN'T LIKE THAT ONE?

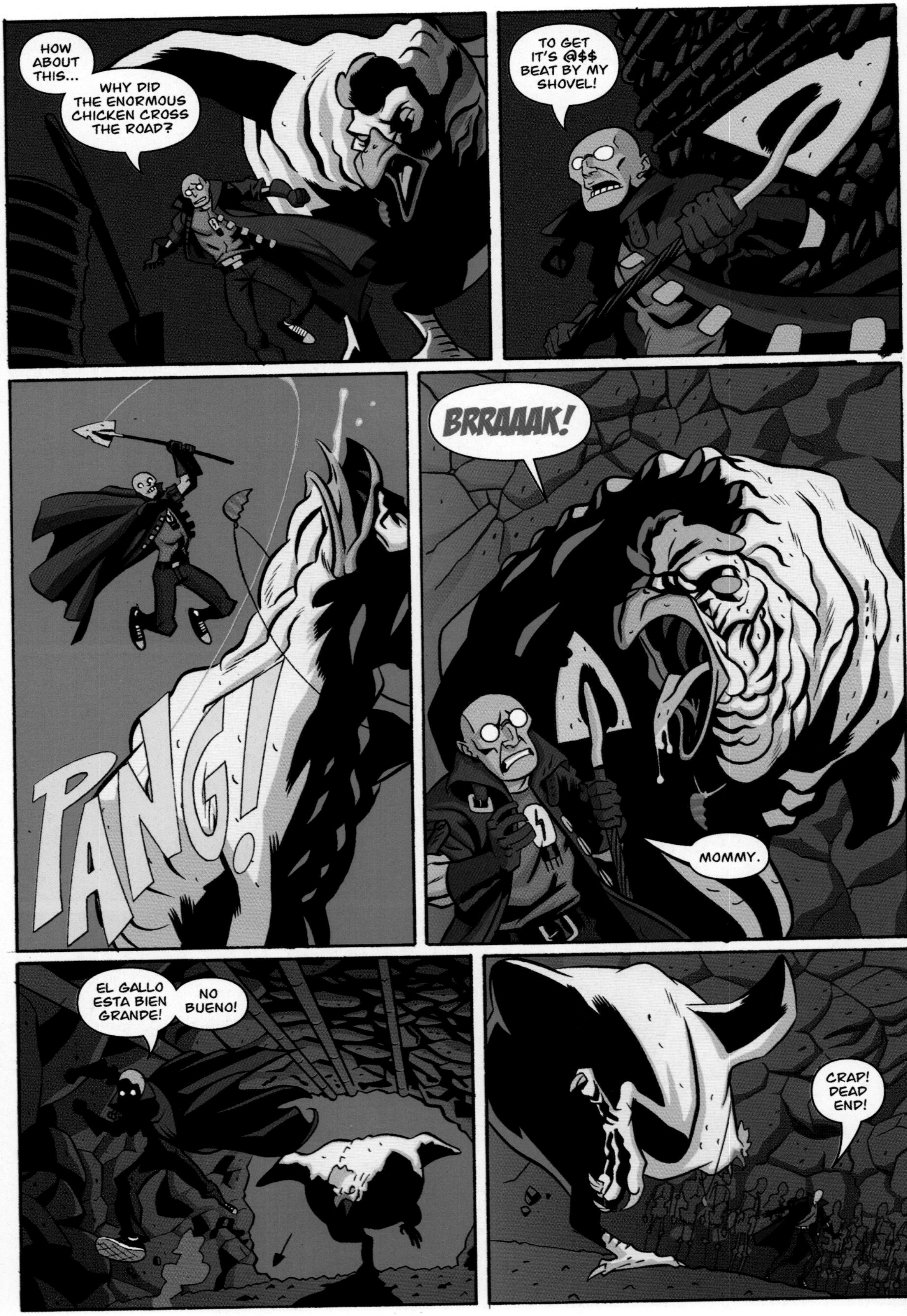

HOW ABOUT THIS...
WHY DID THE ENORMOUS CHICKEN CROSS THE ROAD?
TO GET IT'S @$$ BEAT BY MY SHOVEL!
PANG!
BRRAAAK!
MOMMY.
EL GALLO ESTA BIEN GRANDE!
NO BUENO!
CRAP! DEAD END!

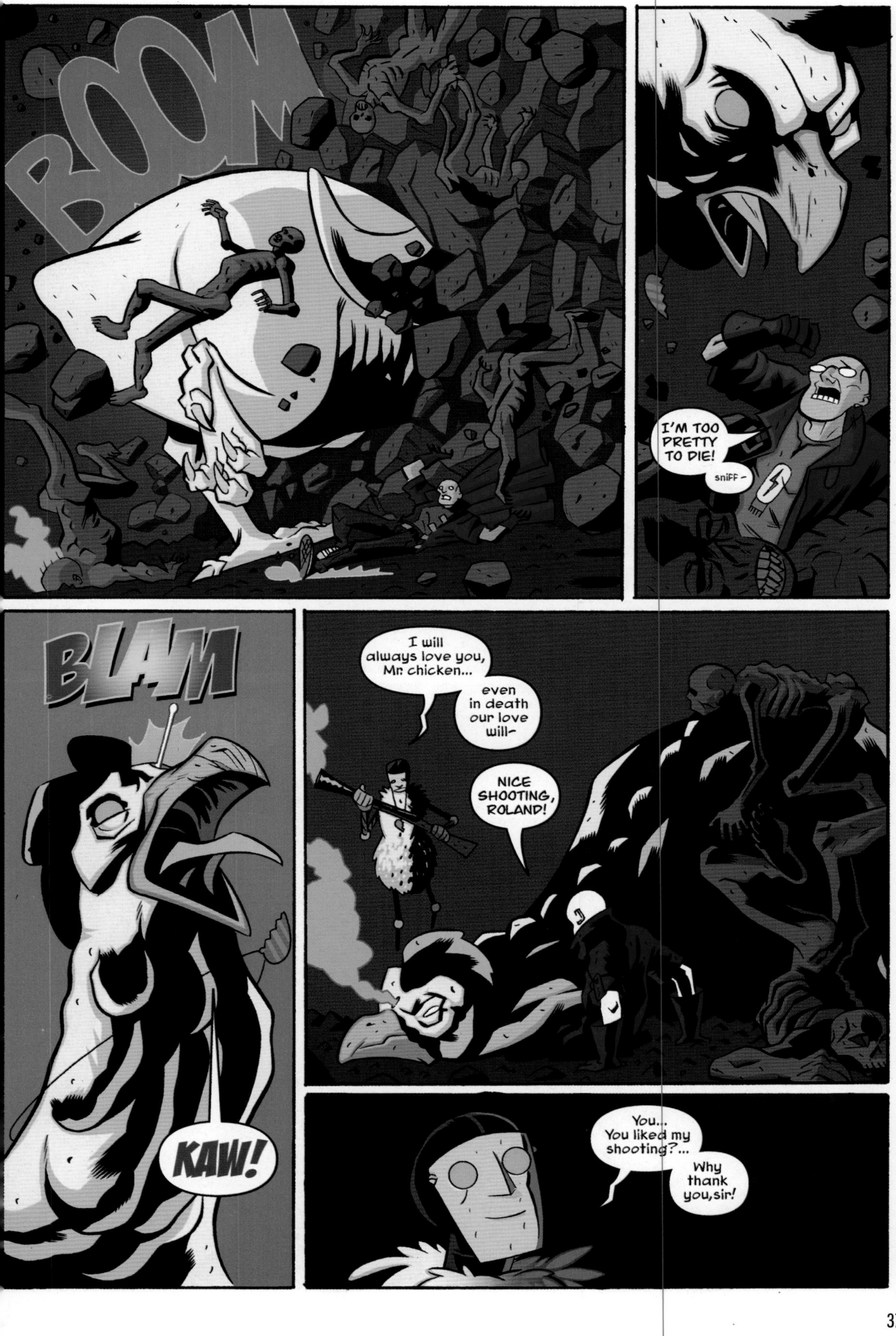
BOOM
I'M TOO PRETTY TO DIE!
sniff -
BLAM
KAW!
I will always love you, Mr. chicken...
even in death our love will-
NICE SHOOTING, ROLAND!
You... You liked my shooting?...
Why thank you, sir!

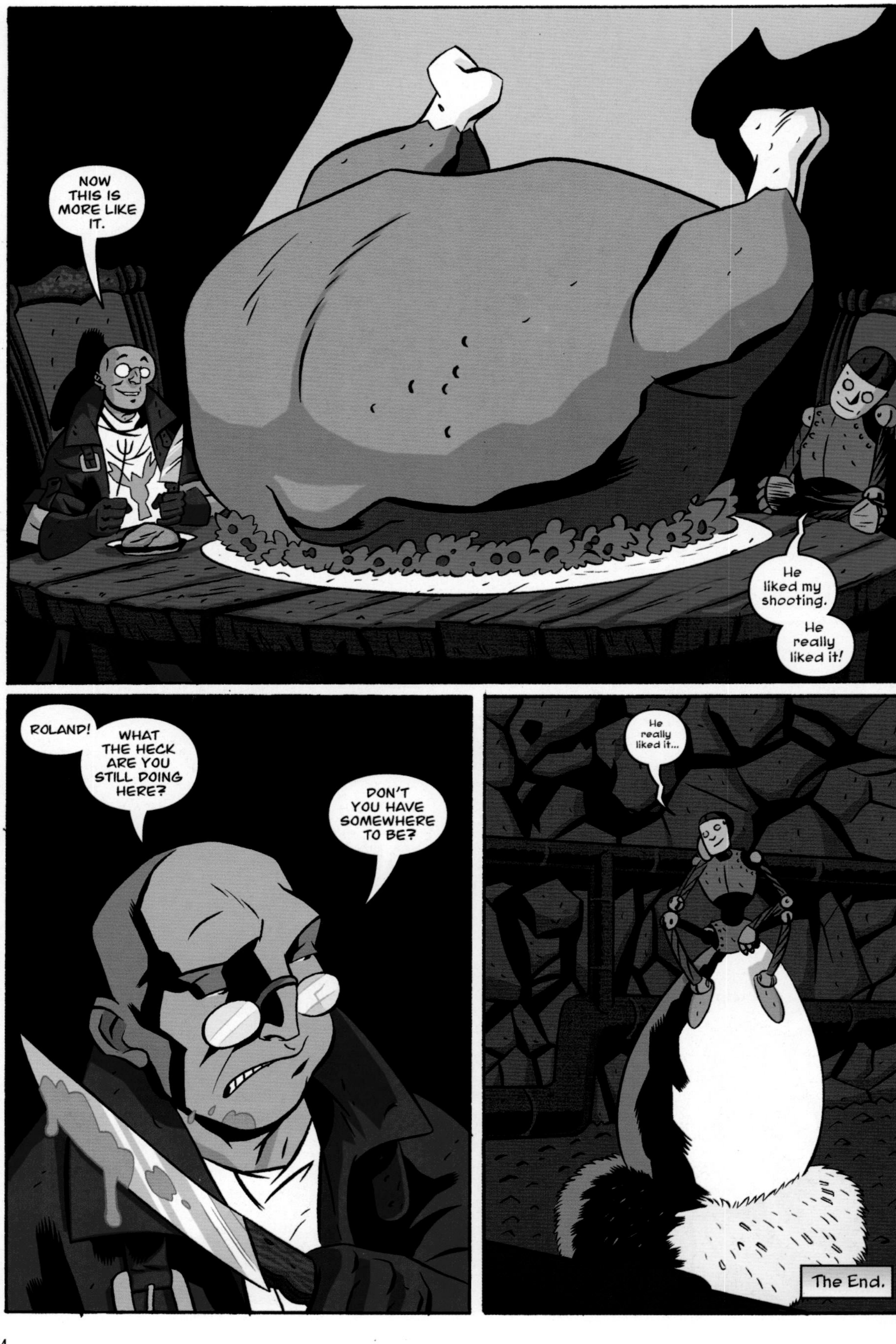
NOW THIS IS MORE LIKE IT.
He liked my shooting.
He really liked it!
ROLAND!
WHAT THE HECK ARE YOU STILL DOING HERE?
DON'T YOU HAVE SOMEWHERE TO BE?
He really liked it...
The End.

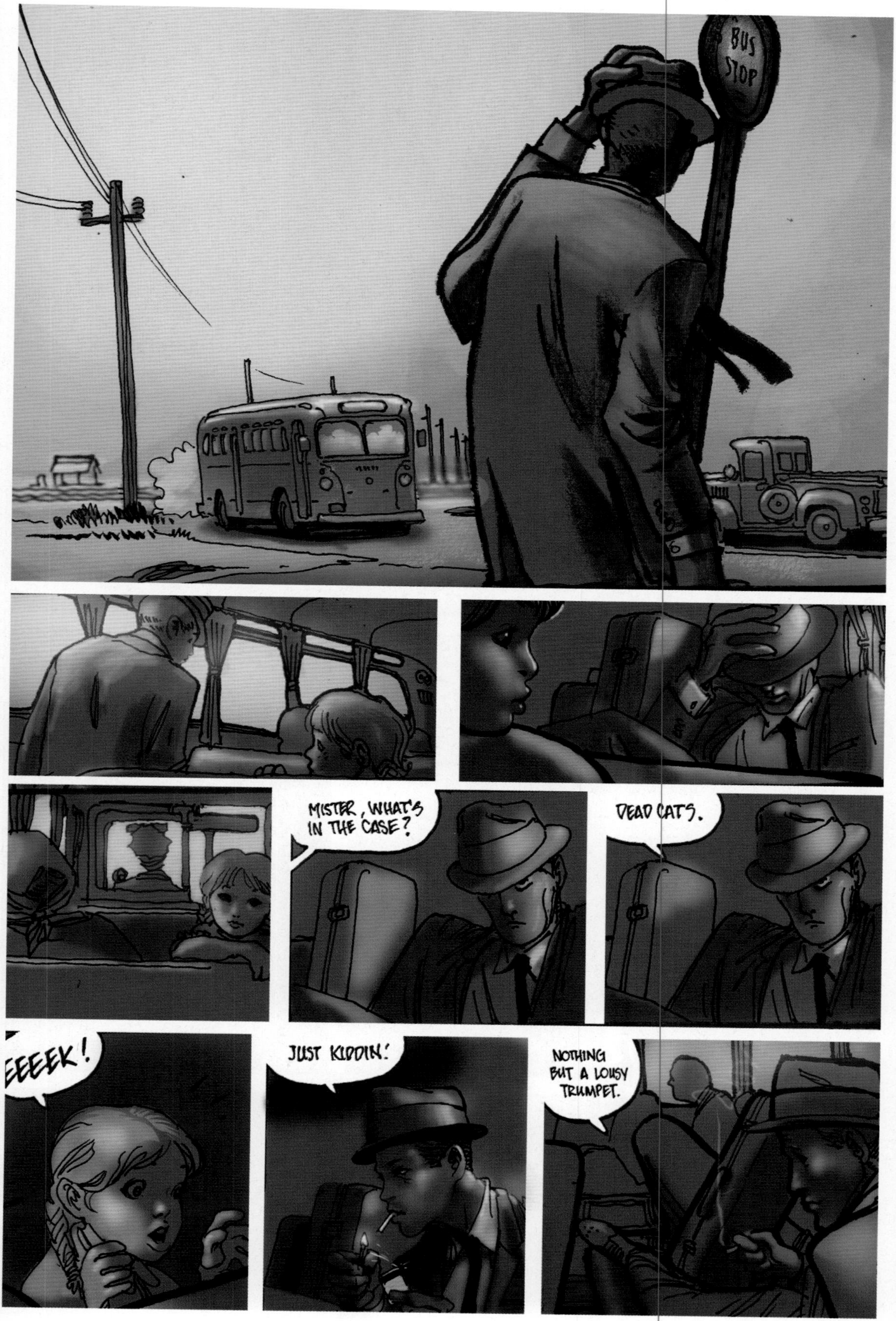
BUS STOP
MISTER, WHAT'S IN THE CASE?
DEAD CATS.
EEEEK!
JUST KIDDIN'!
NOTHING BUT A LOUSY TRUMPET.

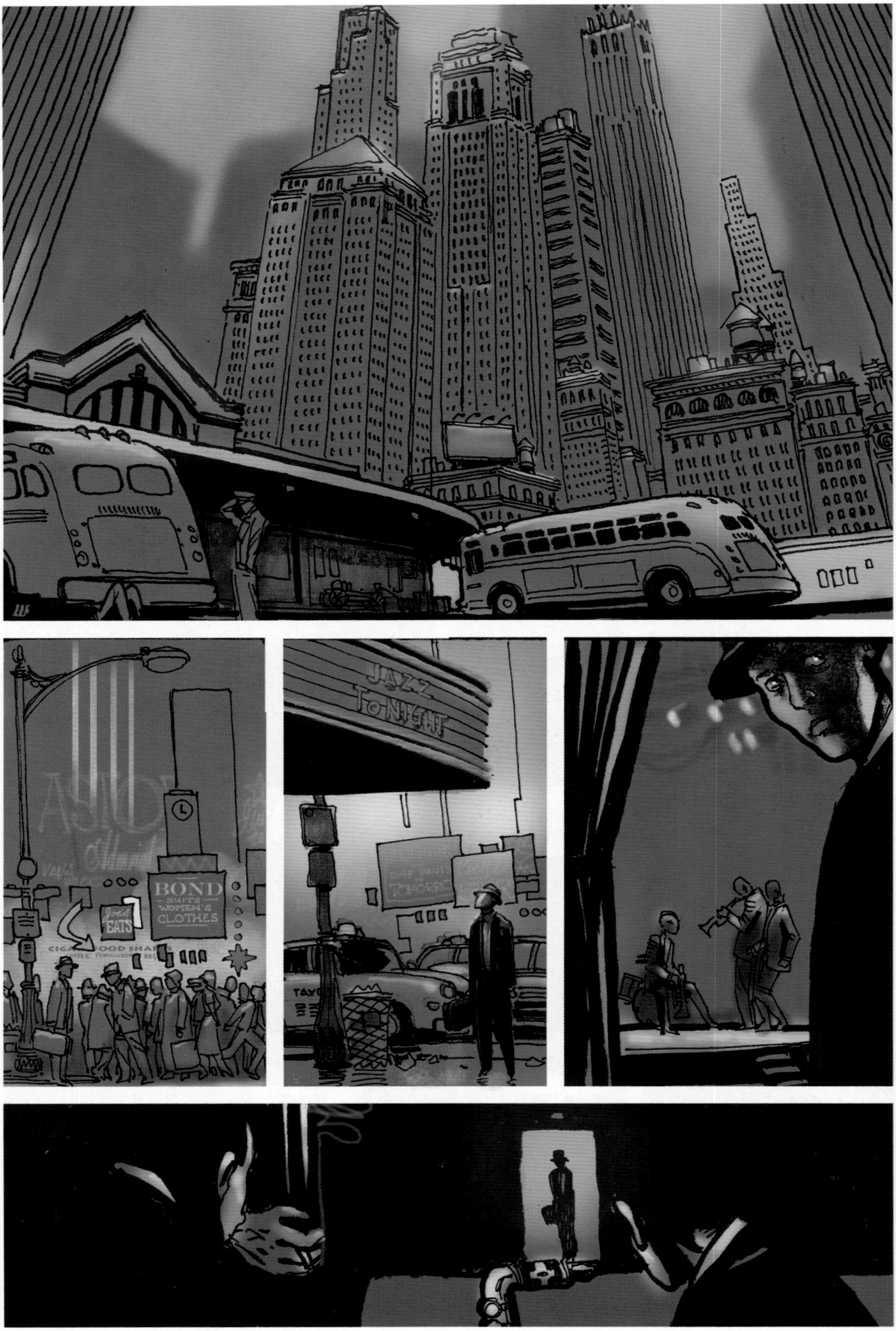
BOND
SUITS
WOMEN'S
CLOTHES
Joe's
EATS
JAZZ
TONIGHT

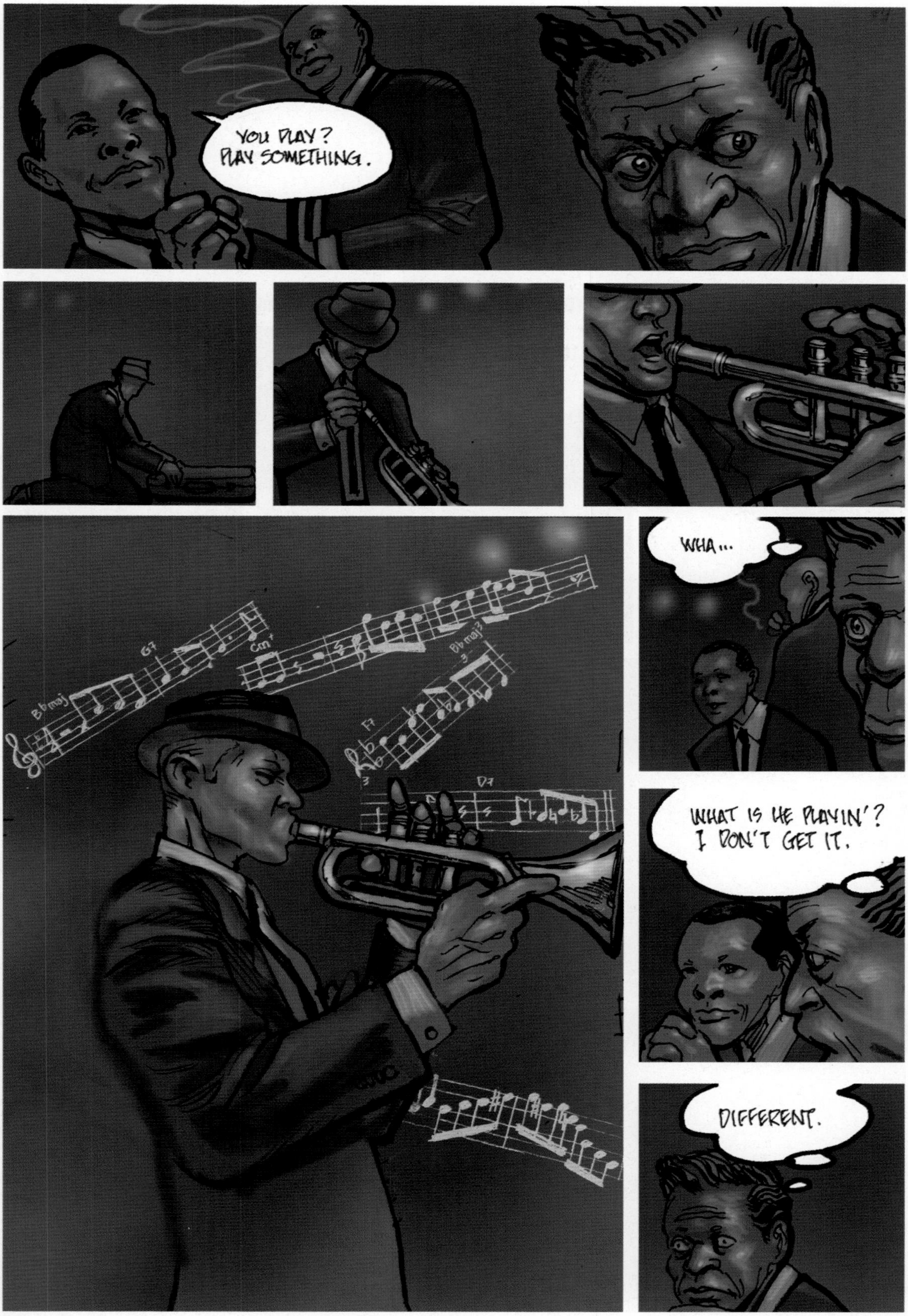
YOU PLAY? PLAY SOMETHING.
WHA...
WHAT IS HE PLAYIN'? I DON'T GET IT.
DIFFERENT.

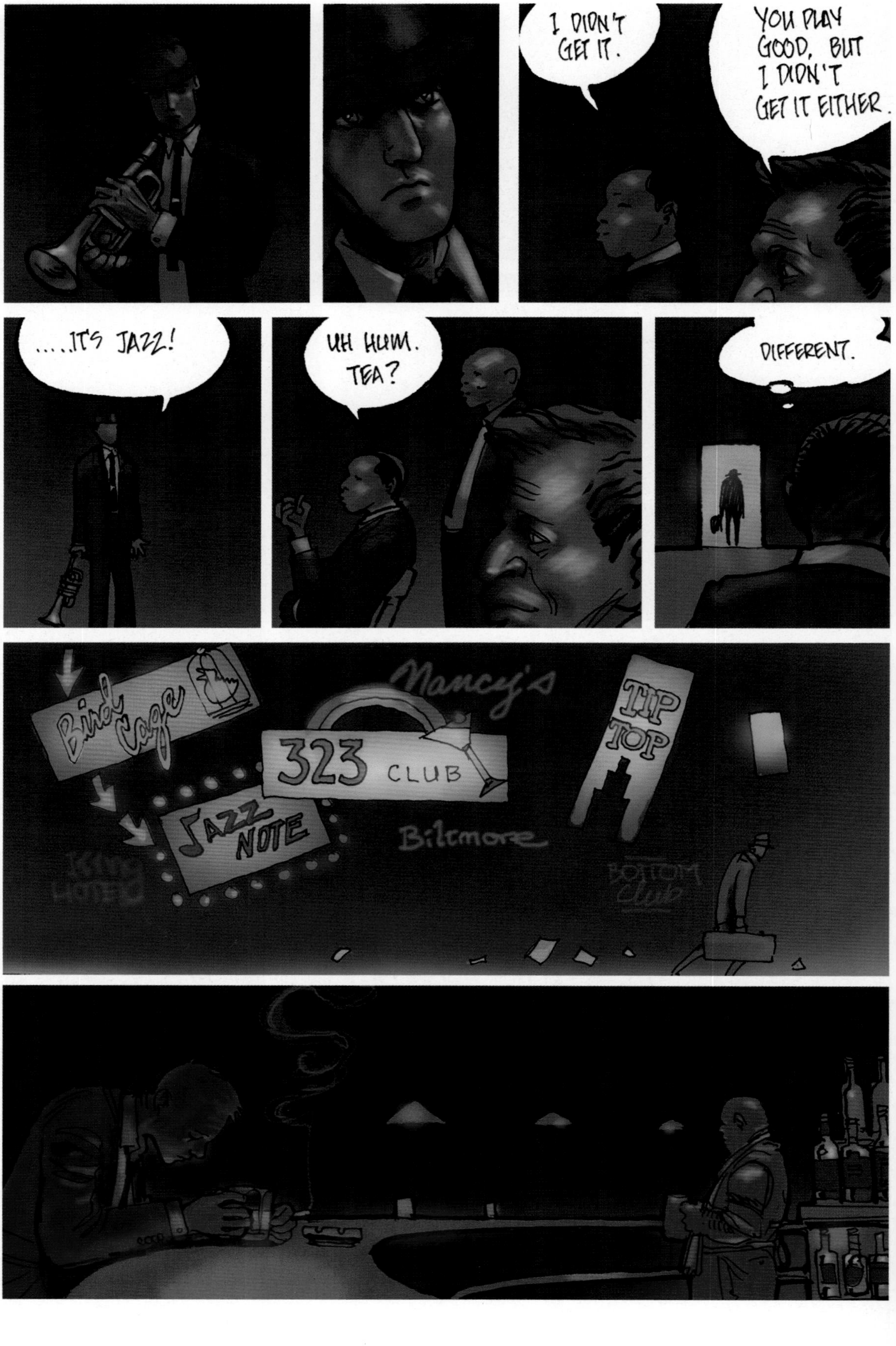
I DIDN'T GET IT.
YOU PLAY GOOD, BUT I DIDN'T GET IT EITHER.
.....IT'S JAZZ!
UH HUM. TEA?
DIFFERENT.
Bird Cage
Nancy's
323 CLUB
TIP TOP
JAZZ NOTE
Biltmore
BOTTOM Club

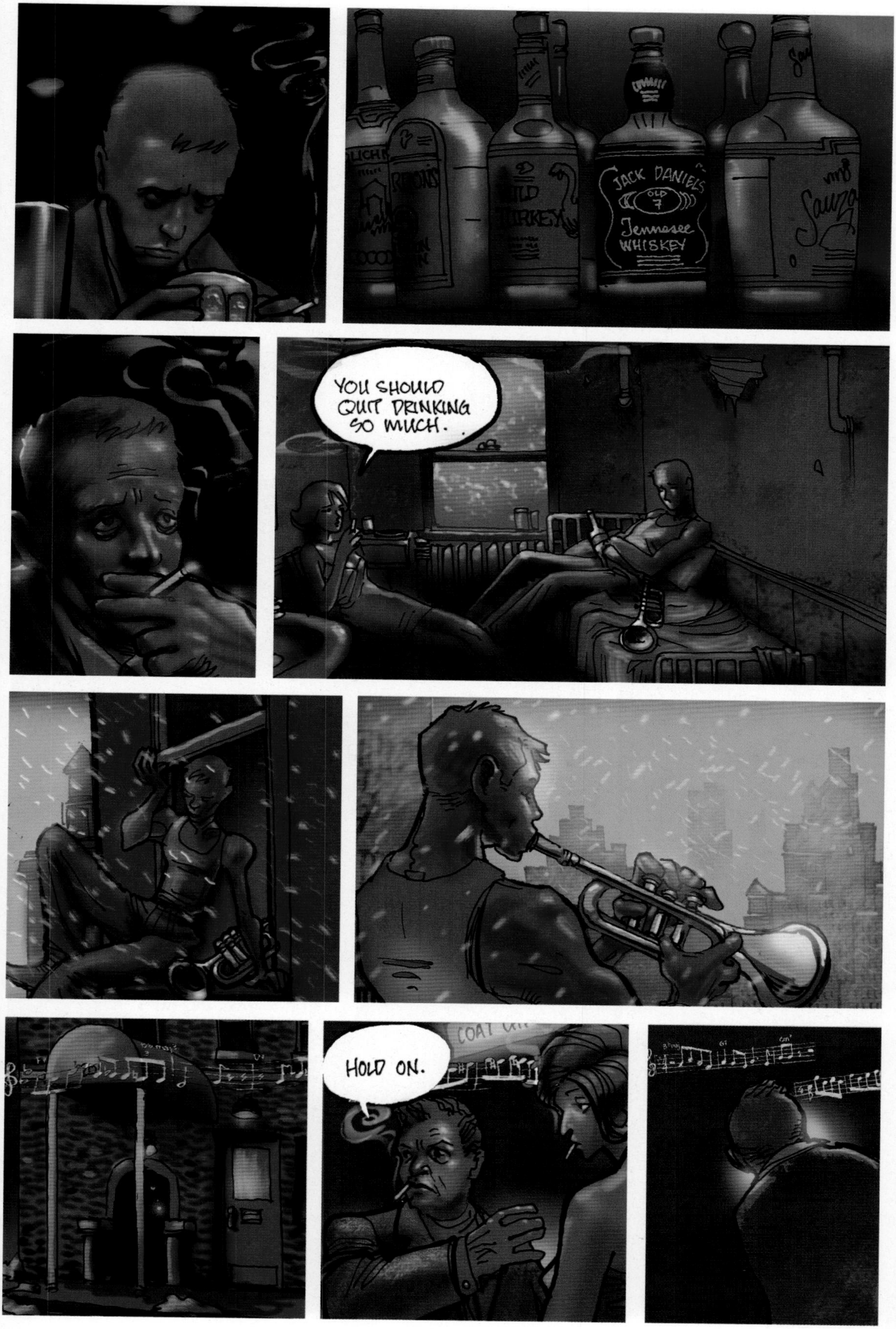
JACK DANIELS
OLD 7
Jennesee
WHISKEY
YOU SHOULD QUIT DRINKING SO MUCH.
HOLD ON.

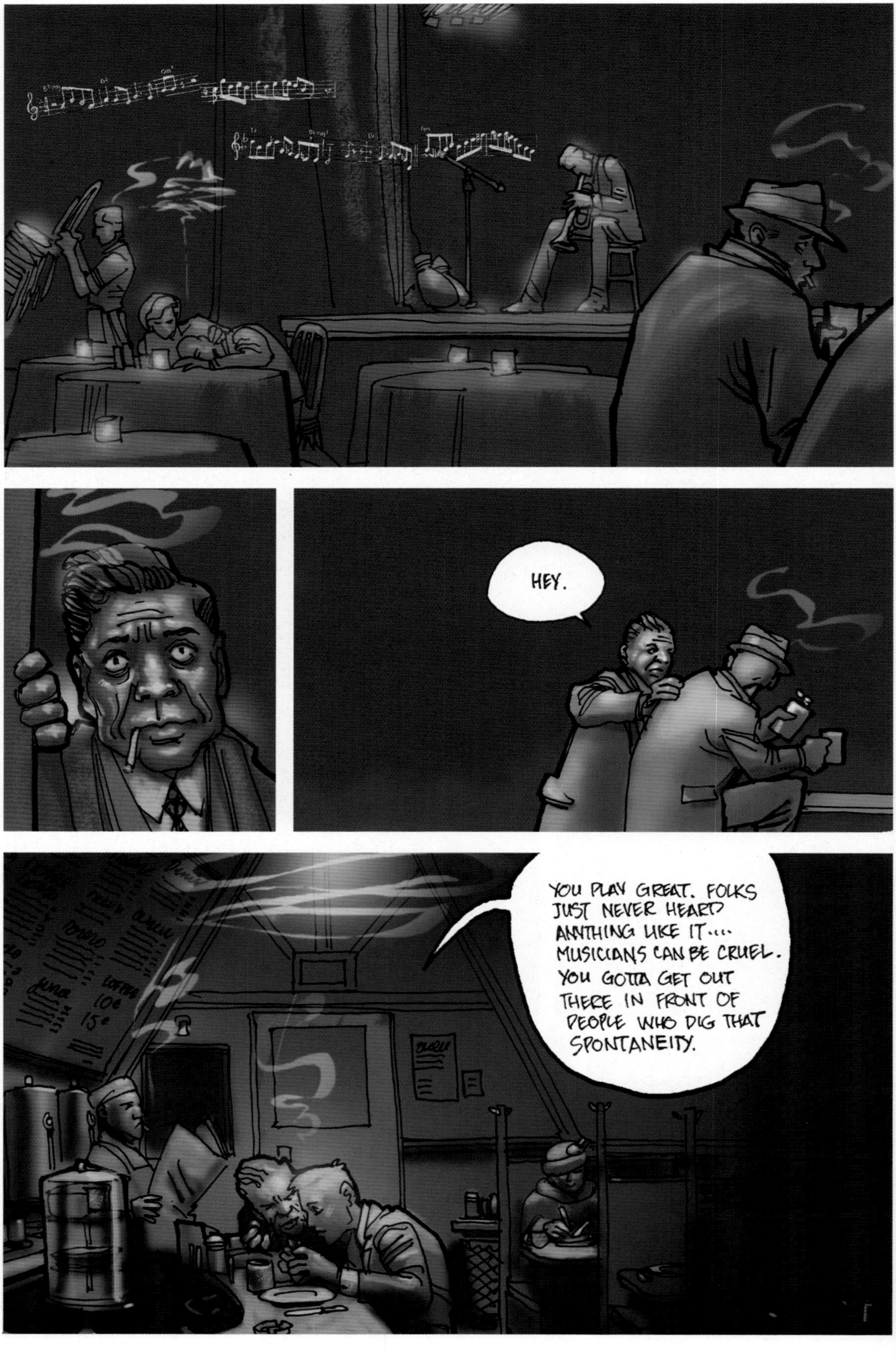
HEY.
YOU PLAY GREAT. FOLKS JUST NEVER HEARD ANYTHING LIKE IT.... MUSICIANS CAN BE CRUEL. YOU GOTTA GET OUT THERE IN FRONT OF PEOPLE WHO DIG THAT SPONTANEITY.

OKAY, OKAY, LET'S TAKE IT FROM THE TOP.

— LESS SPONTANEITY THIS TIME.

STAGE DOOR

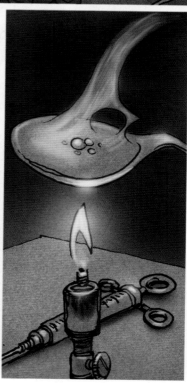

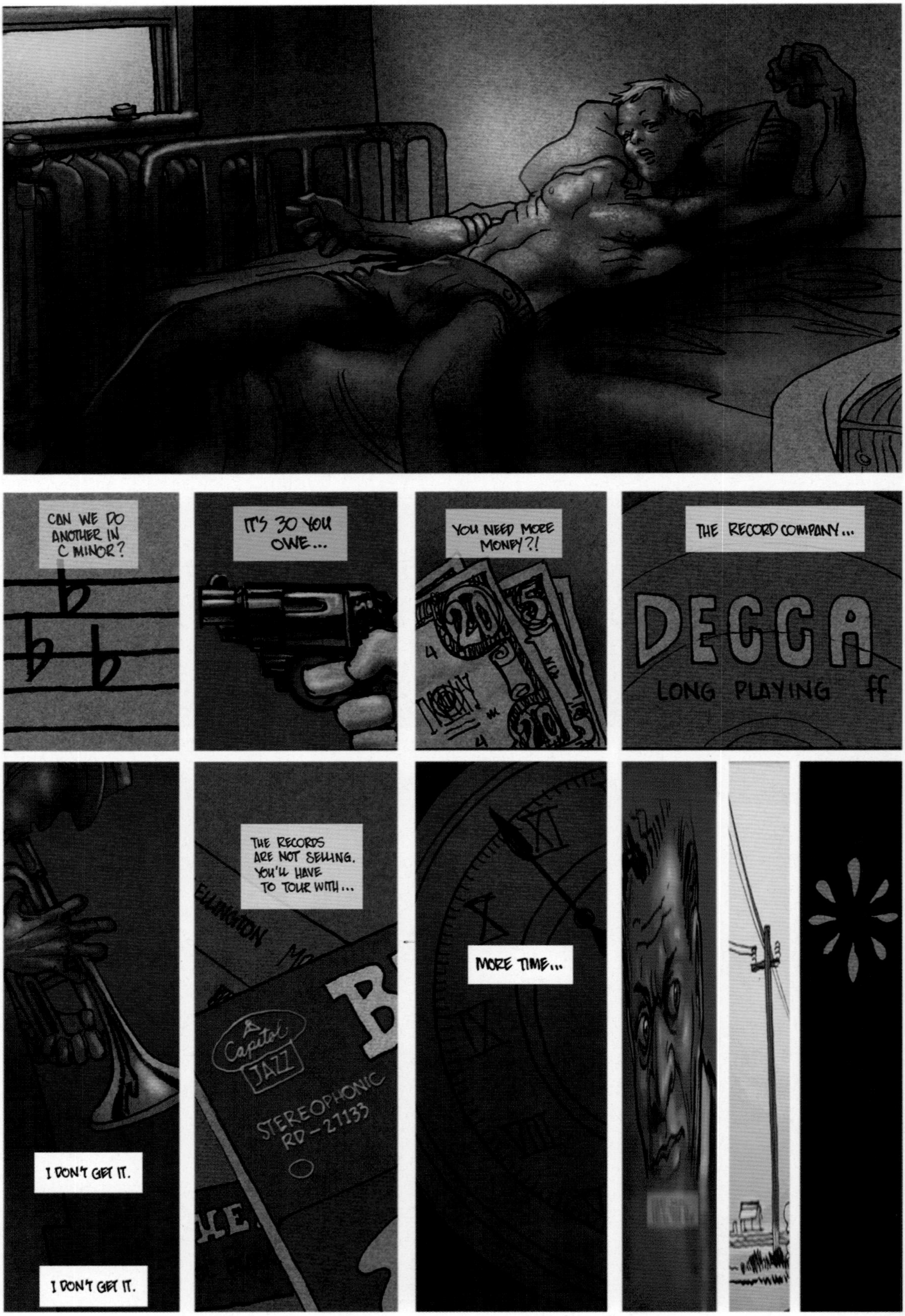
CAN WE DO ANOTHER IN C MINOR?
IT'S 30 YOU OWE...
YOU NEED MORE MONEY?!
THE RECORD COMPANY...
DECCA
LONG PLAYING ff
I DON'T GET IT.
I DON'T GET IT.
THE RECORDS ARE NOT SELLING. YOU'LL HAVE TO TOUR WITH...
ELLINGTON
Capitol JAZZ
STEREOPHONIC
RD-27133
MORE TIME...

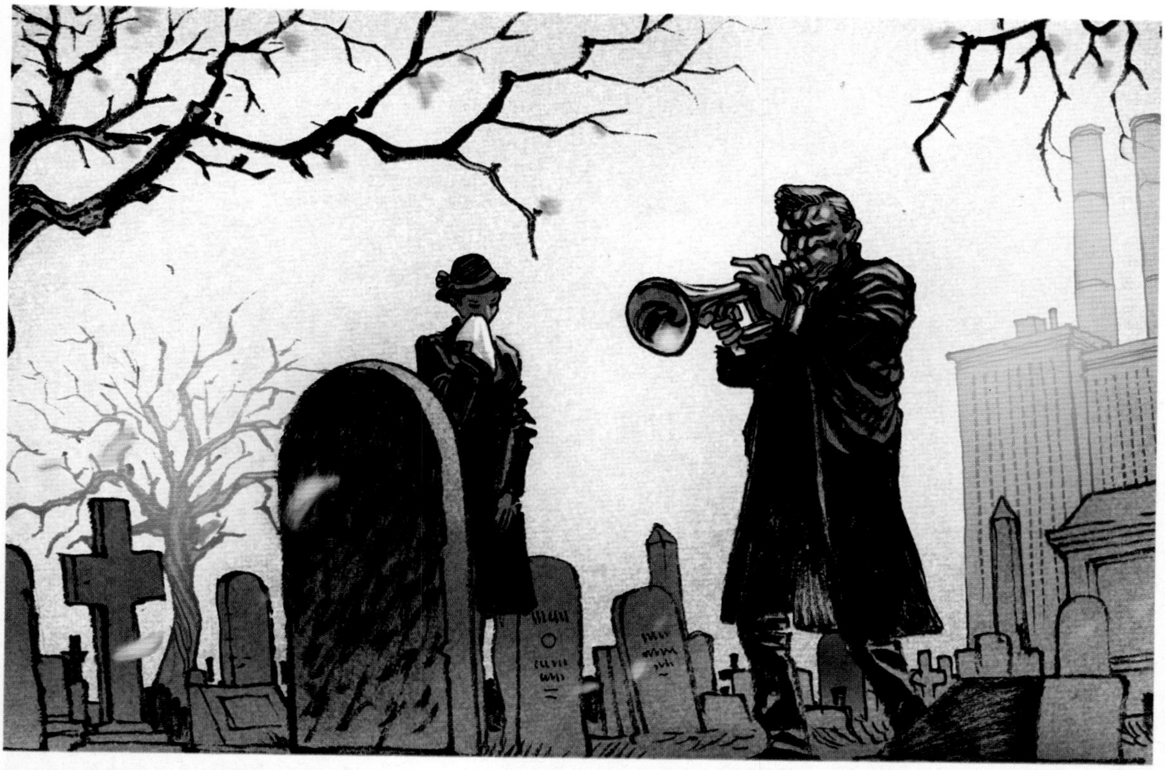

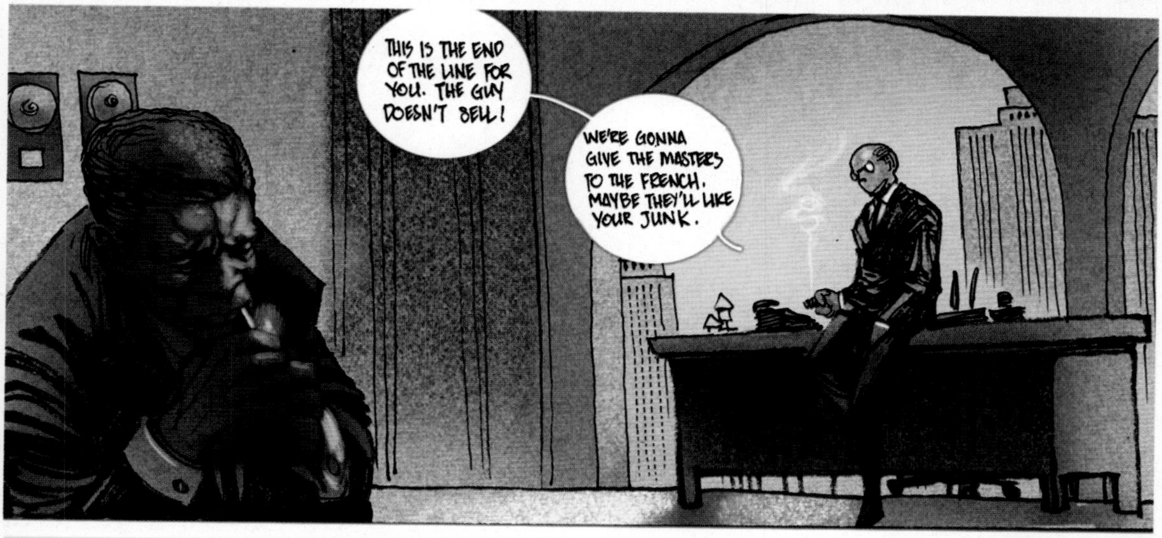

THIS IS THE END OF THE LINE FOR YOU. THE GUY DOESN'T SELL!
WE'RE GONNA GIVE THE MASTERS TO THE FRENCH. MAYBE THEY'LL LIKE YOUR JUNK.

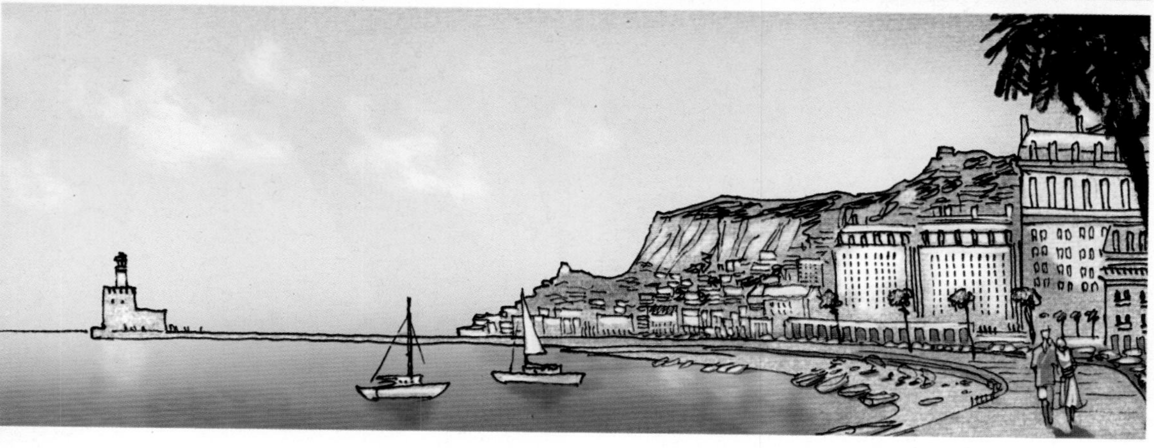

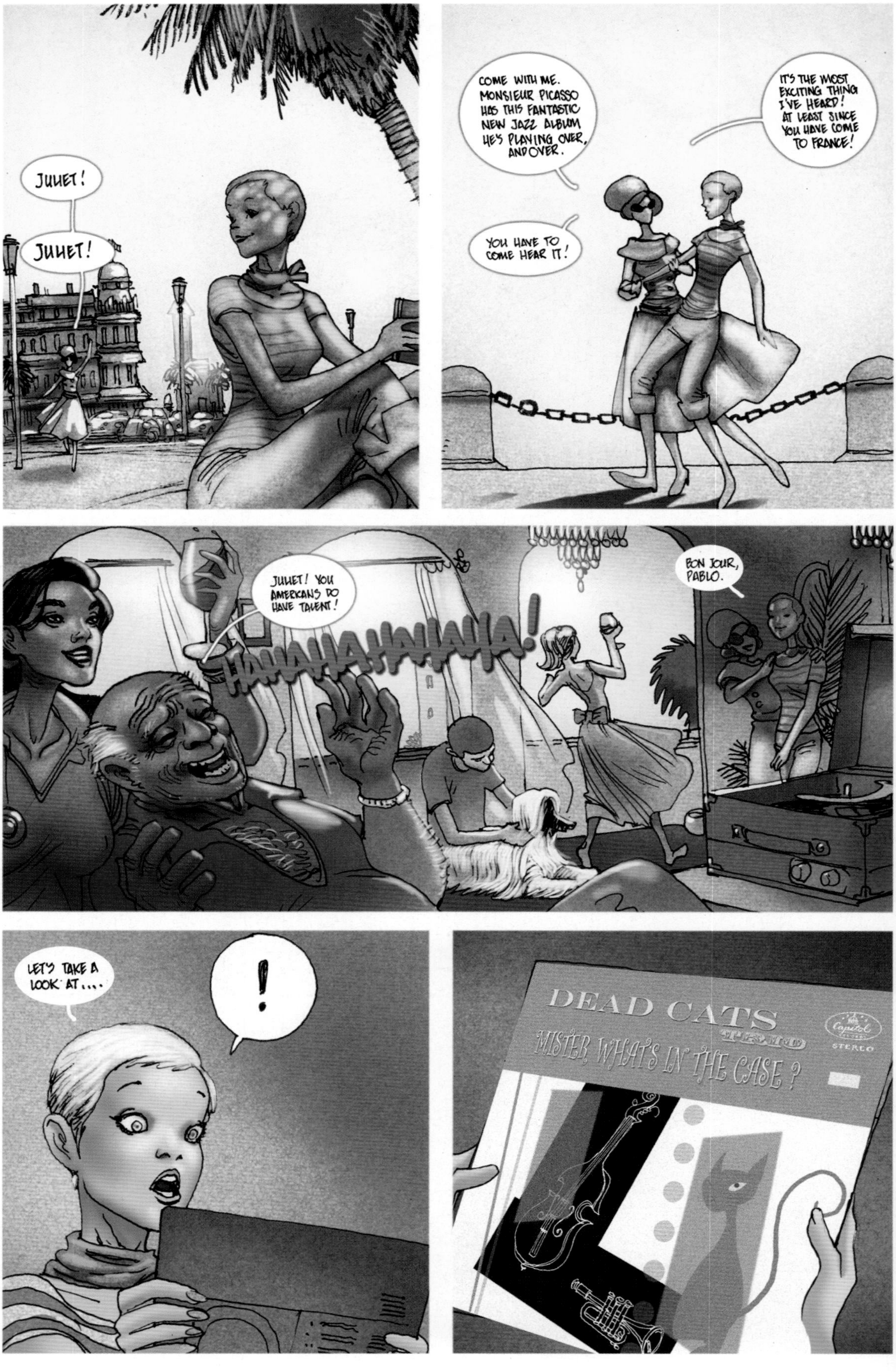
JULIET!
JULIET!
COME WITH ME. MONSIEUR PICASSO HAS THIS FANTASTIC NEW JAZZ ALBUM HE'S PLAYING OVER, AND OVER.
YOU HAVE TO COME HEAR IT!
IT'S THE MOST EXCITING THING I'VE HEARD! AT LEAST SINCE YOU HAVE COME TO FRANCE!
JULIET! YOU AMERICANS DO HAVE TALENT!
HAHAHAHAHAHA!
BON JOUR, PABLO.
LET'S TAKE A LOOK AT....
!
DEAD CATS
TRIO
Capitol
STEREO
MISTER WHAT'S IN THE CASE ?

La Llorona

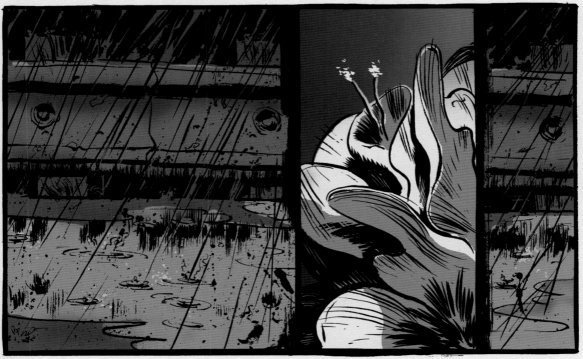

marcus White
& ed Tadem

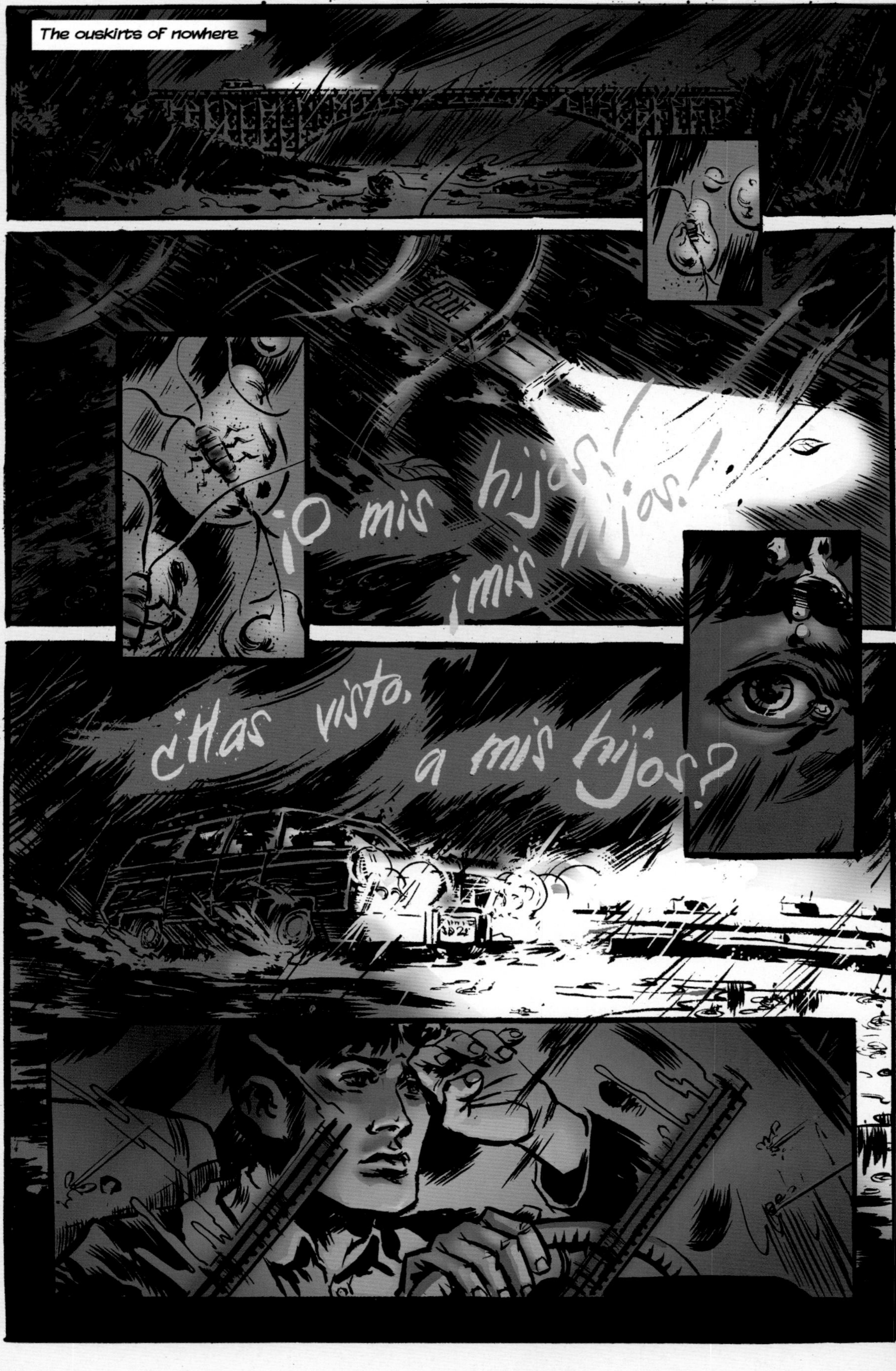
The ouskirts of nowhere
¡O mis hijos!
¡mis hijos!
¿Has visto, a mis hijos?

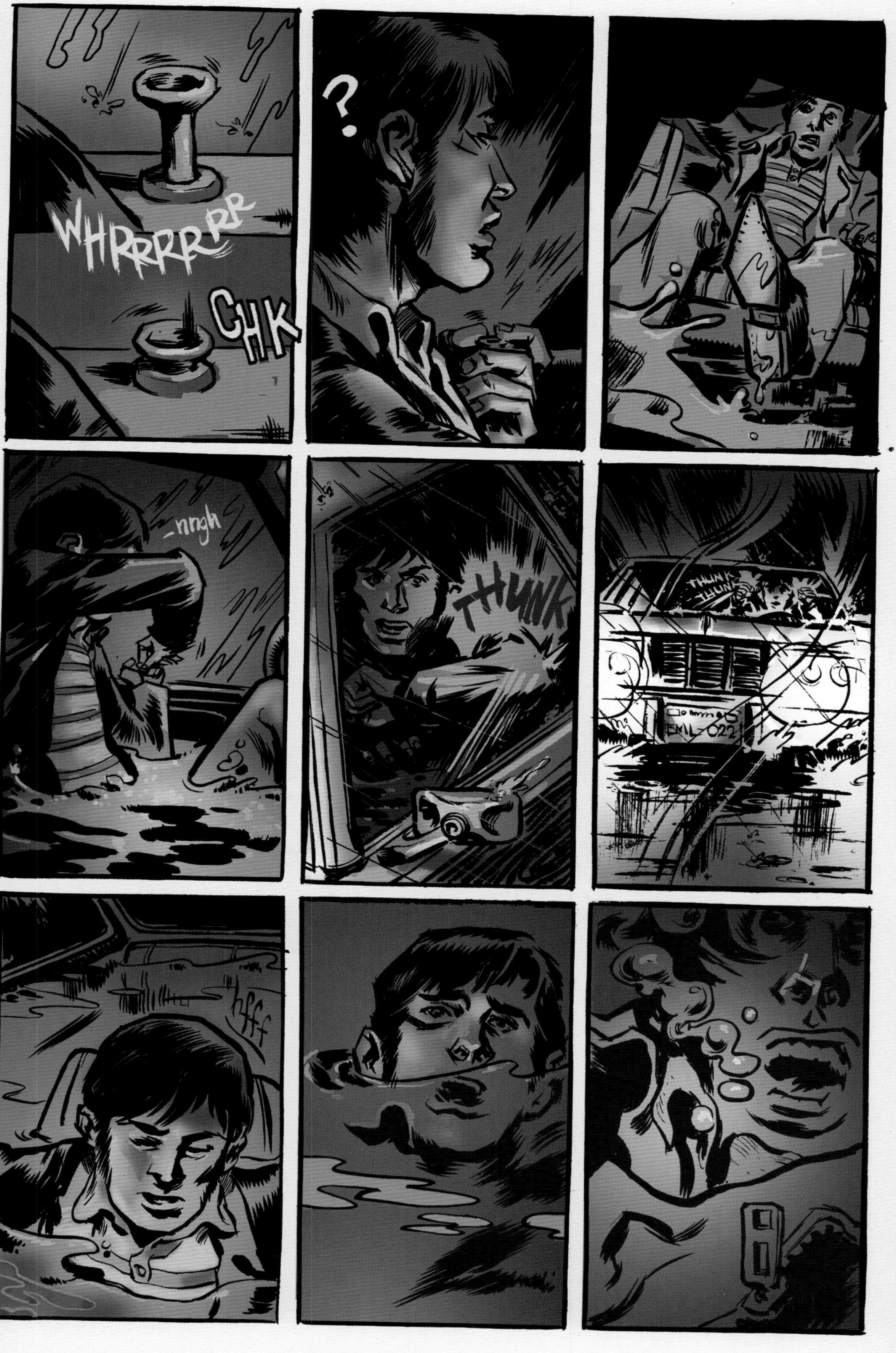
WHRRRRRRP
CHK
?
_nngh
THUNK
THUNK
THUNK
EML-022
hfff

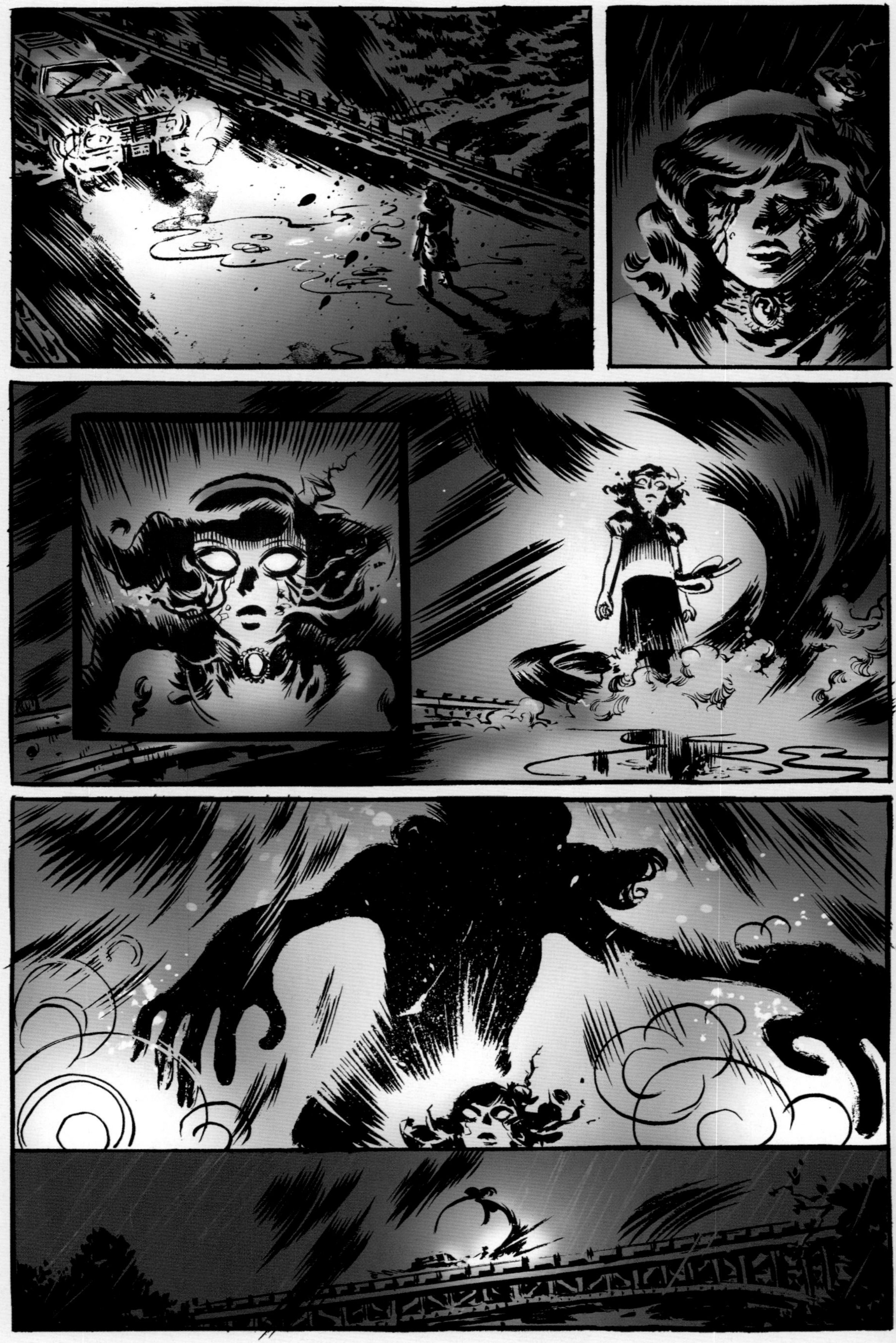

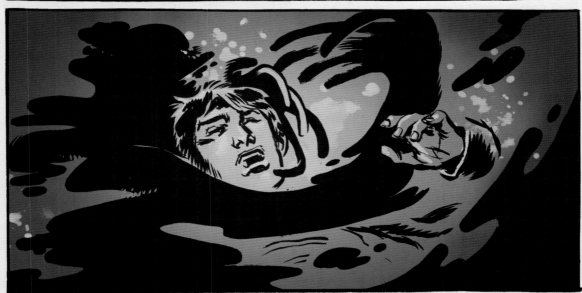

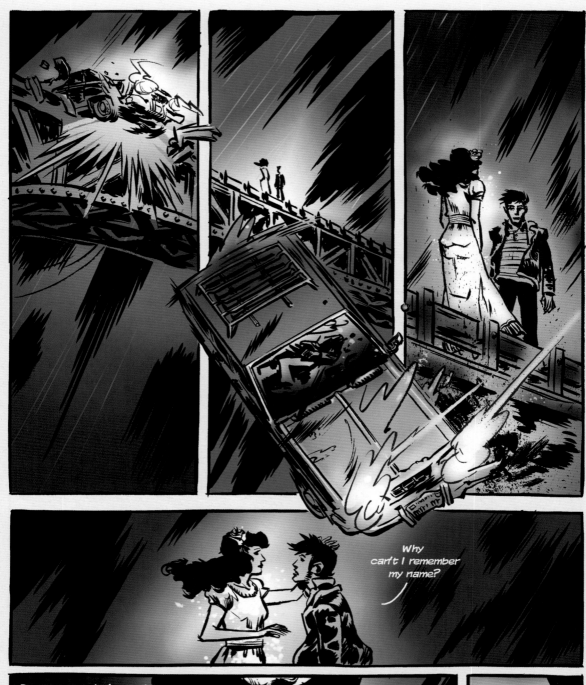

Why can't I remember my name?

Because you don't need it anymore.

You belong to me now.

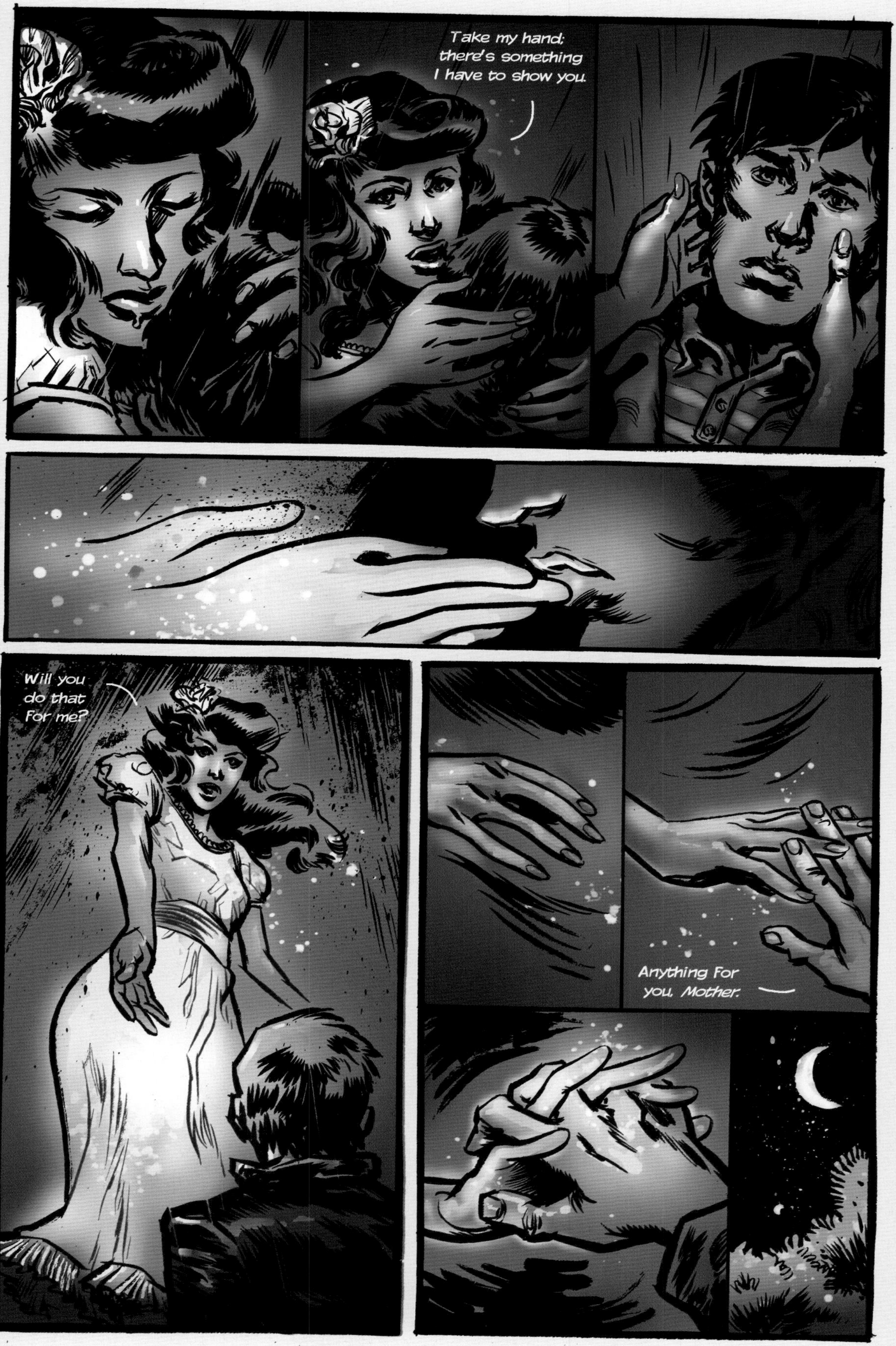
Take my hand;
there's something
I have to show you.
Will you
do that
for me?
Anything for
you, Mother.

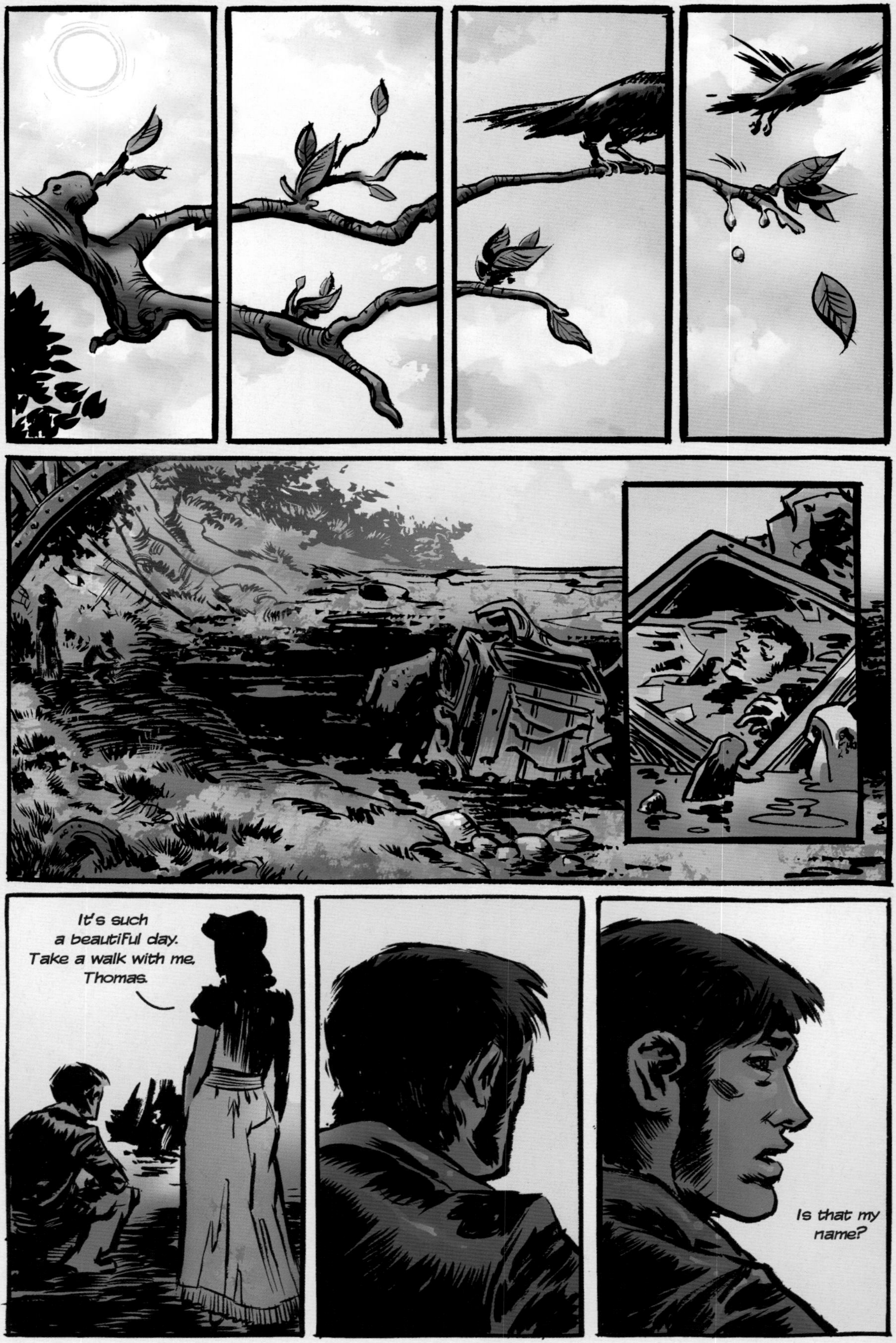
It's such a beautiful day. Take a walk with me, Thomas.
Is that my name?

fin.

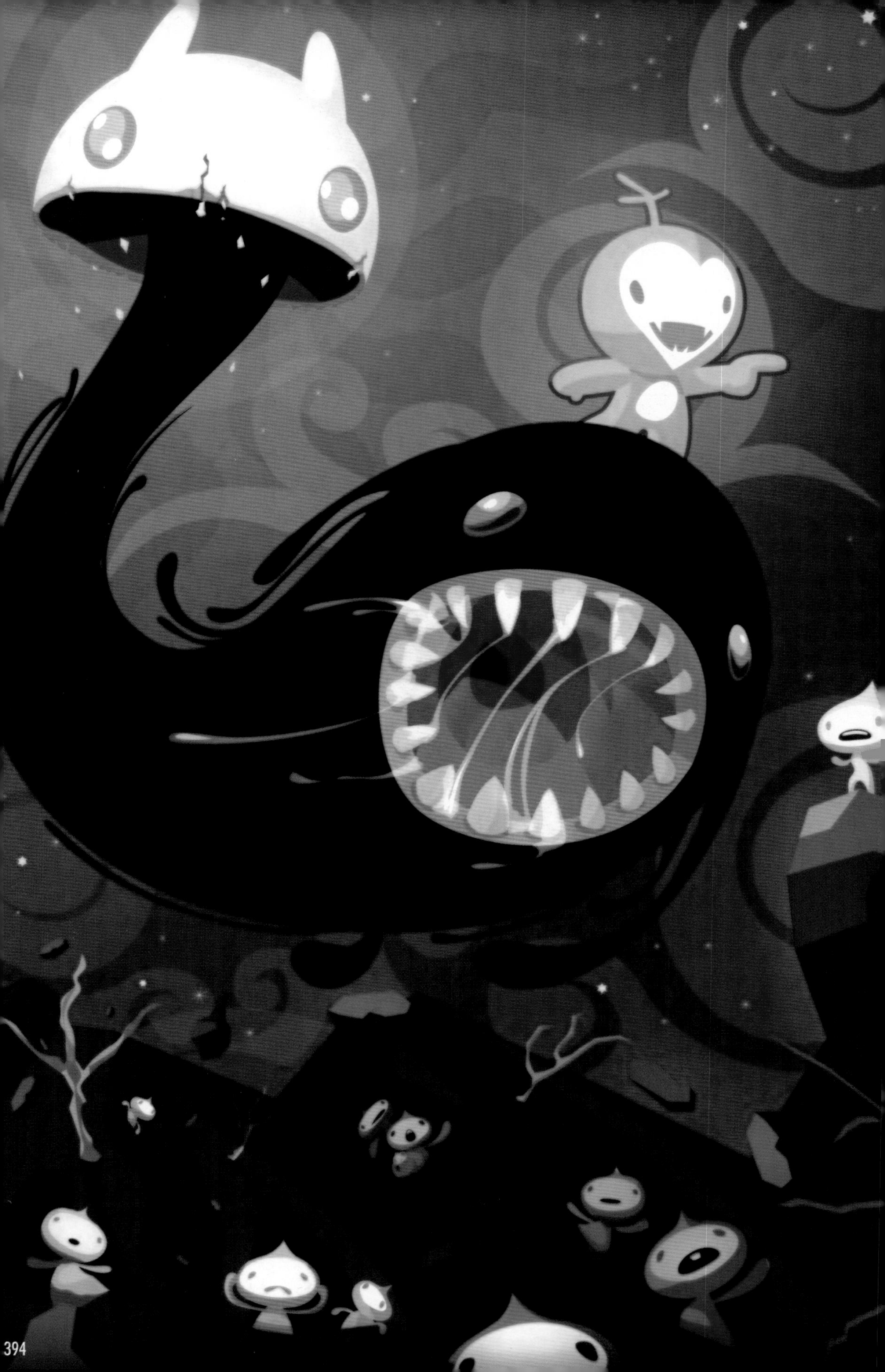

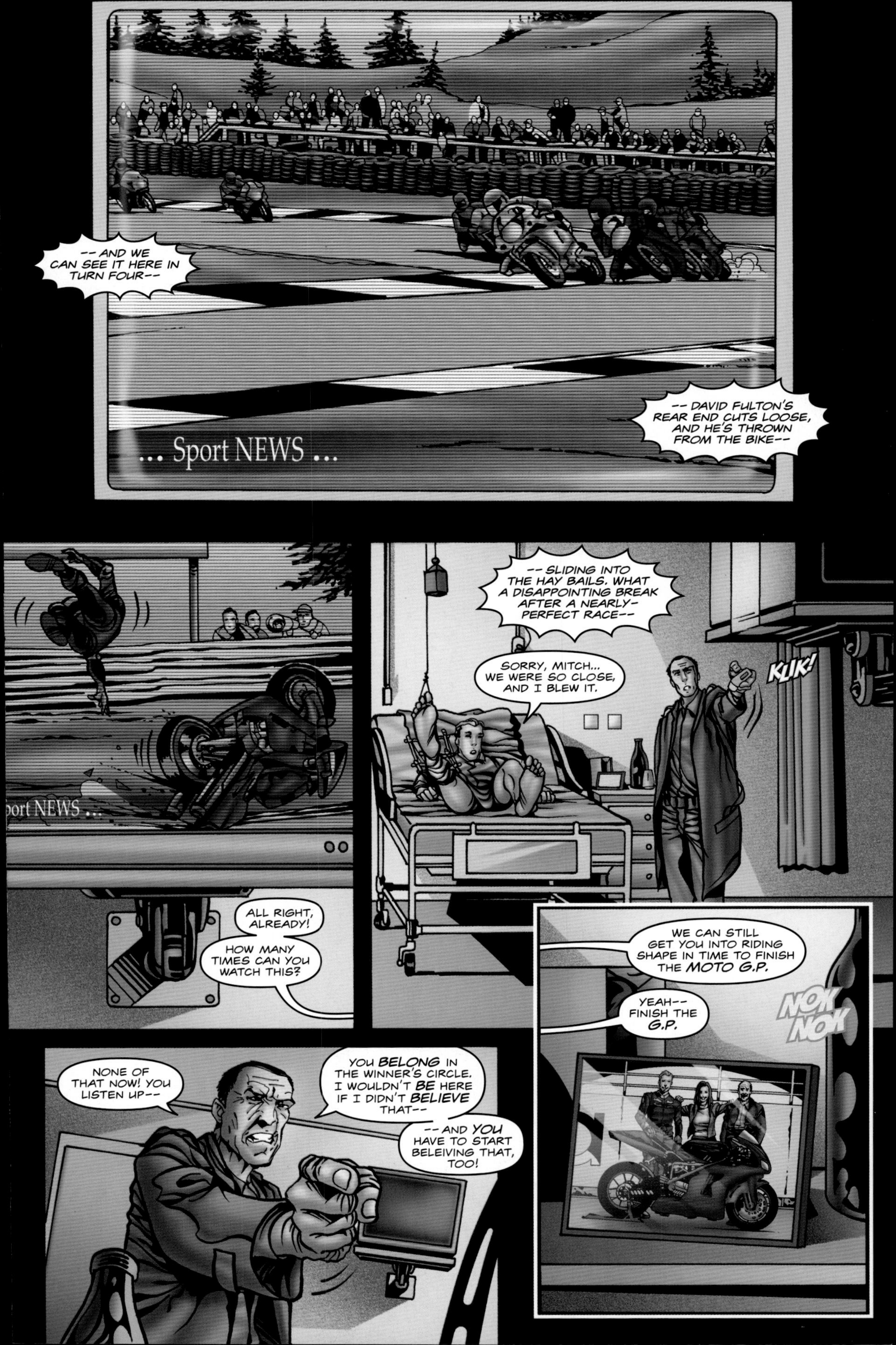
-- AND WE CAN SEE IT HERE IN TURN FOUR--
-- DAVID FULTON'S REAR END CUTS LOOSE, AND HE'S THROWN FROM THE BIKE--
... Sport NEWS ...
port NEWS ...
--SLIDING INTO THE HAY BAILS. WHAT A DISAPPOINTING BREAK AFTER A NEARLY-PERFECT RACE--
SORRY, MITCH... WE WERE SO CLOSE, AND I BLEW IT.
KLIK!
ALL RIGHT, ALREADY!
HOW MANY TIMES CAN YOU WATCH THIS?
NONE OF THAT NOW! YOU LISTEN UP--
YOU BELONG IN THE WINNER'S CIRCLE. I WOULDN'T BE HERE IF I DIDN'T BELIEVE THAT--
--AND YOU HAVE TO START BELEIVING THAT, TOO!
WE CAN STILL GET YOU INTO RIDING SHAPE IN TIME TO FINISH THE MOTO G.P.
YEAH-- FINISH THE G.P.
NOK NOK

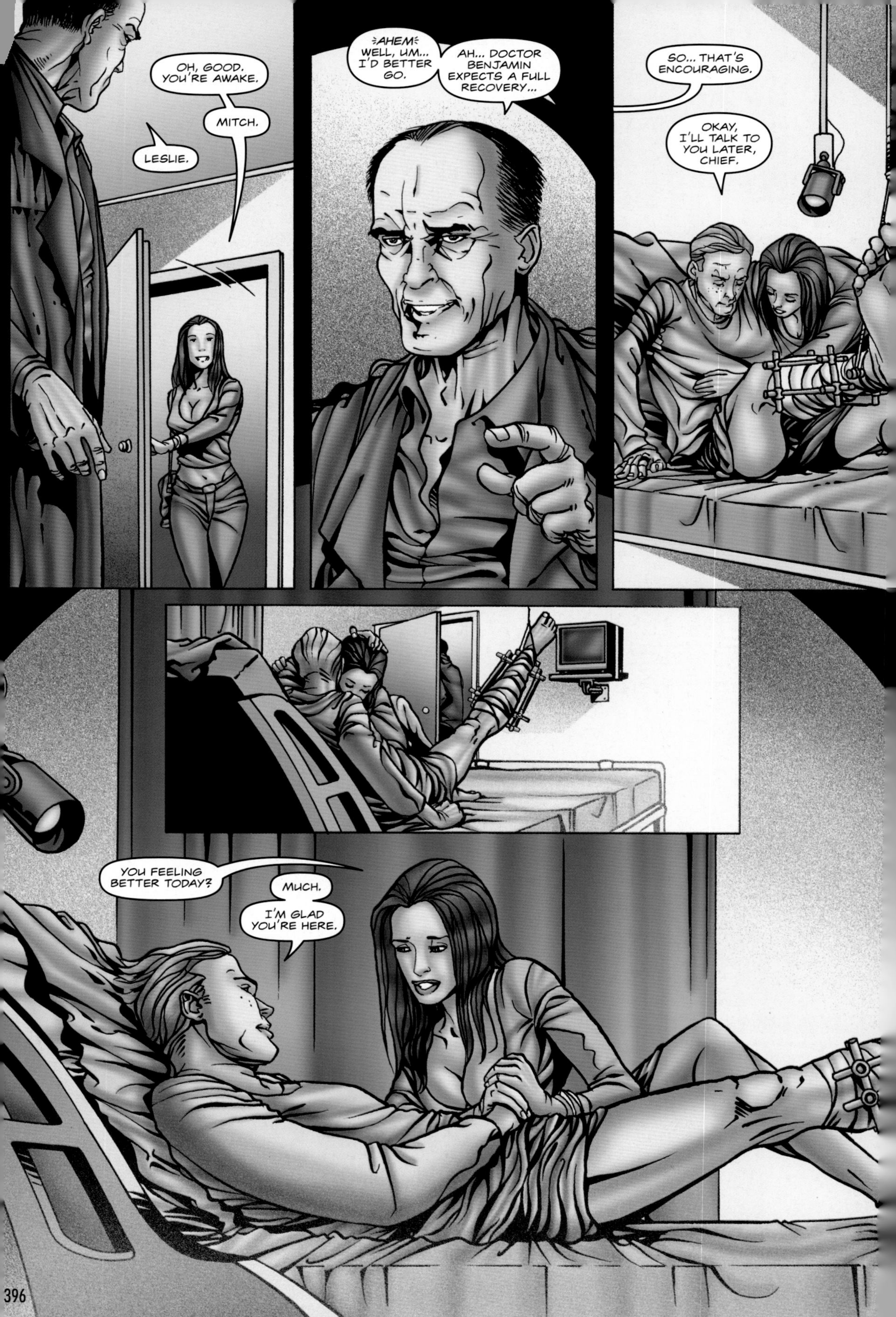
OH, GOOD. YOU'RE AWAKE.
MITCH.
LESLIE.
AHEM WELL, UM... I'D BETTER GO.
AH... DOCTOR BENJAMIN EXPECTS A FULL RECOVERY...
SO... THAT'S ENCOURAGING.
OKAY, I'LL TALK TO YOU LATER, CHIEF.
YOU FEELING BETTER TODAY?
MUCH.
I'M GLAD YOU'RE HERE.

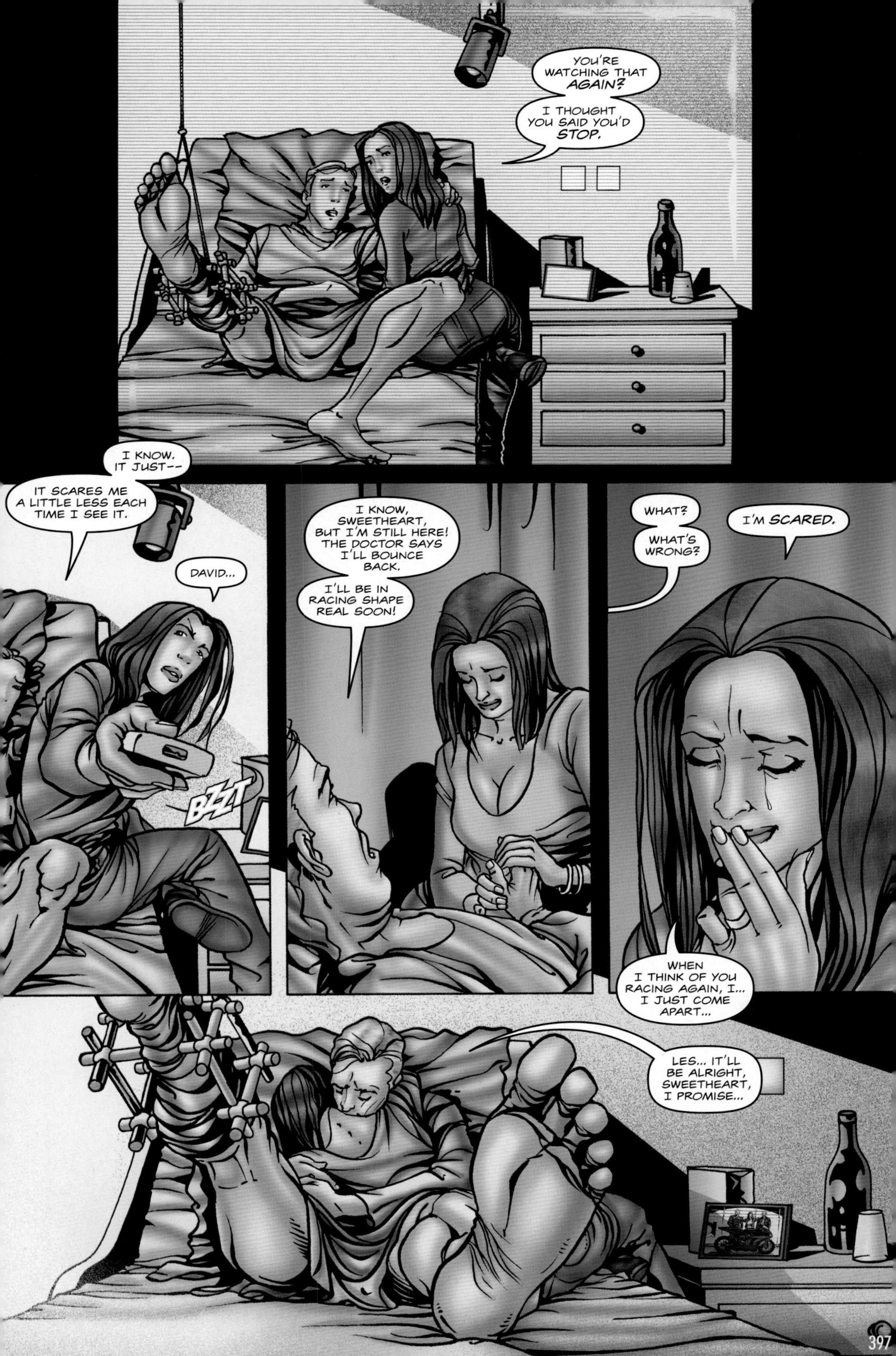
YOU'RE WATCHING THAT AGAIN?
I THOUGHT YOU SAID YOU'D STOP.
I KNOW. IT JUST--
IT SCARES ME A LITTLE LESS EACH TIME I SEE IT.
DAVID...
BZZT
I KNOW, SWEETHEART, BUT I'M STILL HERE! THE DOCTOR SAYS I'LL BOUNCE BACK.
I'LL BE IN RACING SHAPE REAL SOON!
WHAT?
WHAT'S WRONG?
I'M SCARED.
WHEN I THINK OF YOU RACING AGAIN, I... I JUST COME APART...
LES... IT'LL BE ALRIGHT, SWEETHEART, I PROMISE...

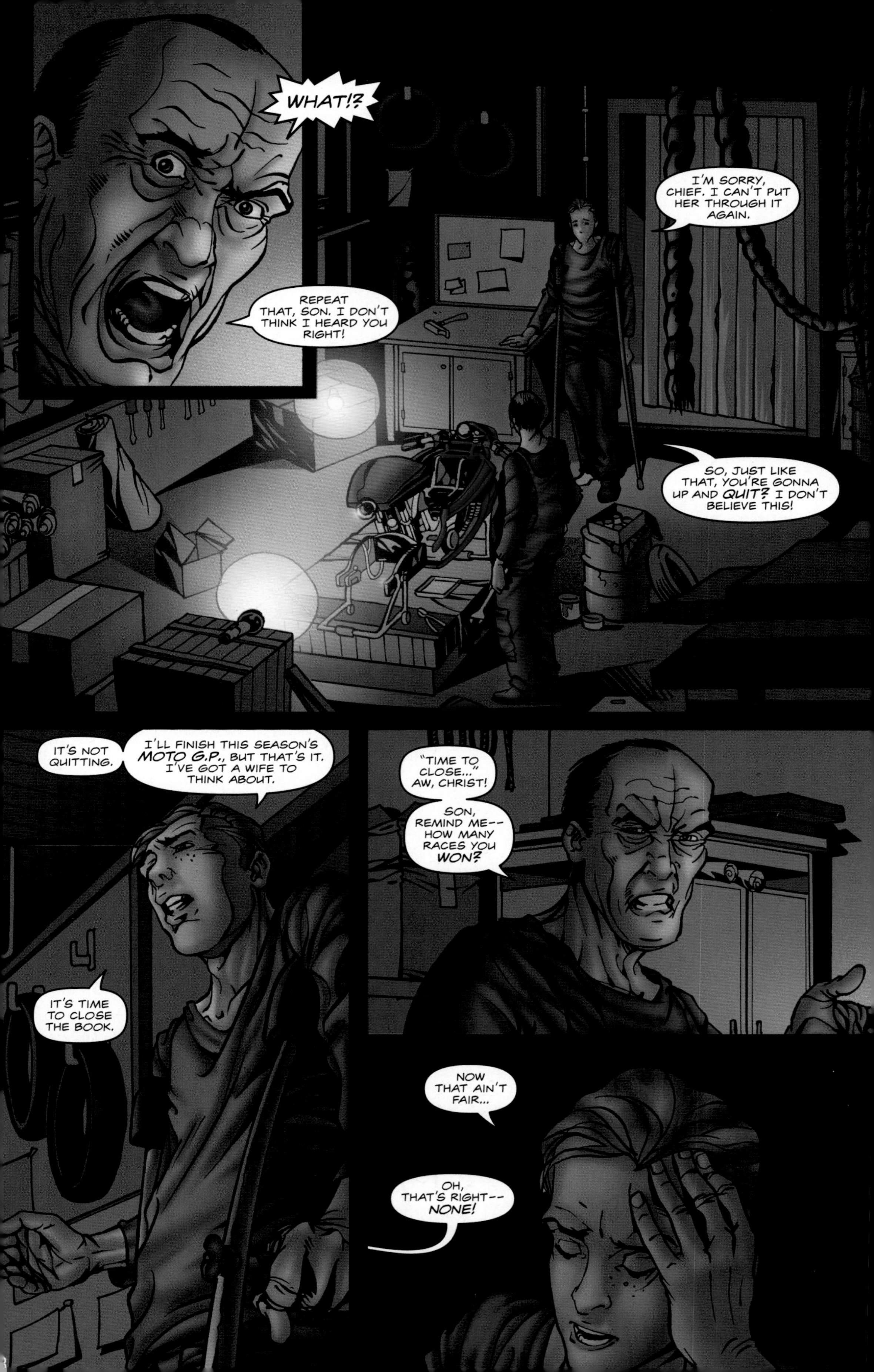
WHAT!?
REPEAT THAT, SON. I DON'T THINK I HEARD YOU RIGHT!
I'M SORRY, CHIEF. I CAN'T PUT HER THROUGH IT AGAIN.
SO, JUST LIKE THAT, YOU'RE GONNA UP AND QUIT? I DON'T BELIEVE THIS!
IT'S NOT QUITTING.
I'LL FINISH THIS SEASON'S MOTO G.P., BUT THAT'S IT. I'VE GOT A WIFE TO THINK ABOUT.
IT'S TIME TO CLOSE THE BOOK.
"TIME TO CLOSE..." AW, CHRIST!
SON, REMIND ME--HOW MANY RACES YOU WON?
NOW THAT AIN'T FAIR...
OH, THAT'S RIGHT--NONE!

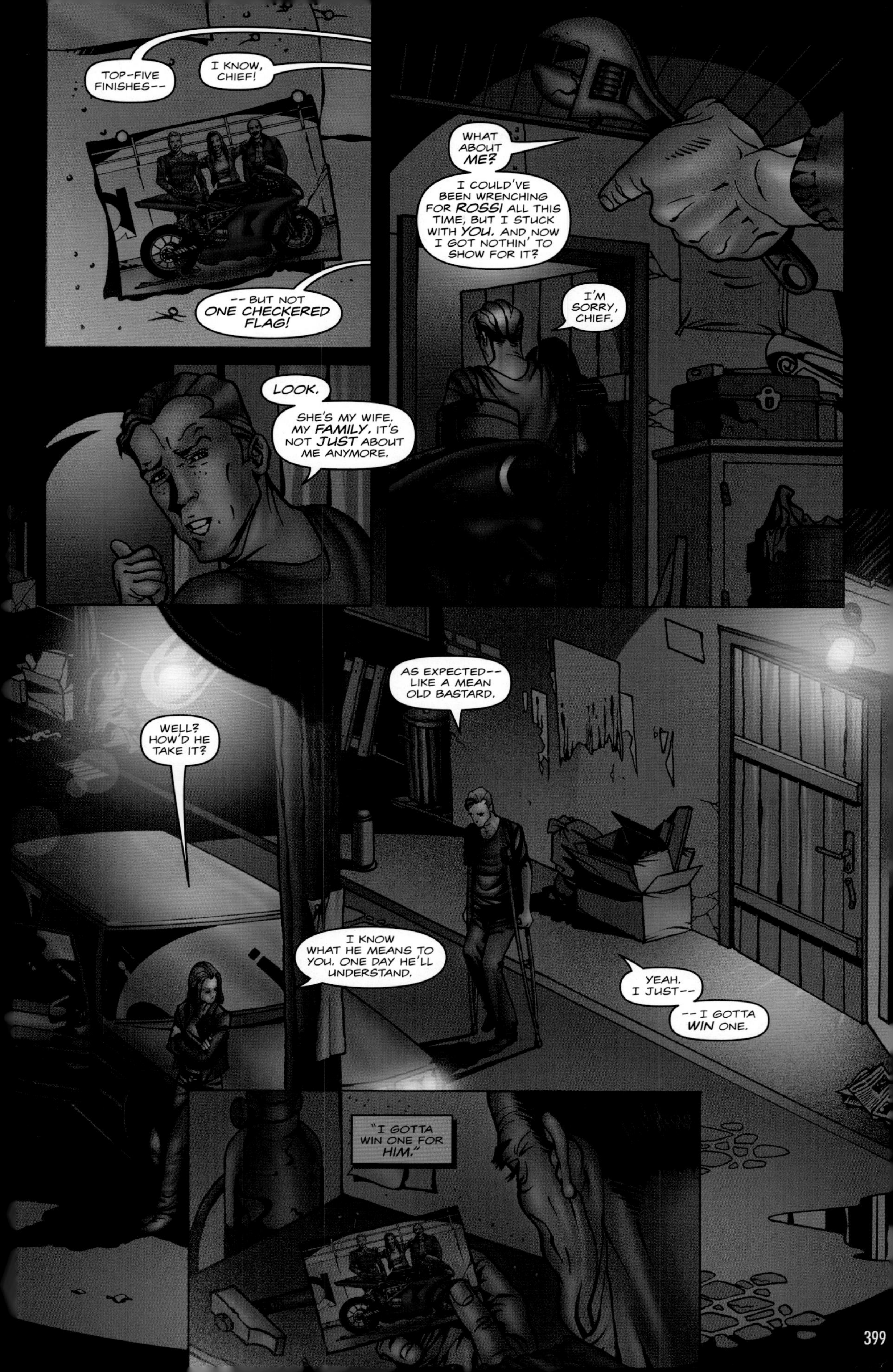
TOP-FIVE FINISHES--
I KNOW, CHIEF!
--BUT NOT ONE CHECKERED FLAG!
WHAT ABOUT ME?
I COULD'VE BEEN WRENCHING FOR ROSSI ALL THIS TIME, BUT I STUCK WITH YOU. AND NOW I GOT NOTHIN' TO SHOW FOR IT?
I'M SORRY, CHIEF.
LOOK.
SHE'S MY WIFE. MY FAMILY. IT'S NOT JUST ABOUT ME ANYMORE.
WELL? HOW'D HE TAKE IT?
AS EXPECTED-- LIKE A MEAN OLD BASTARD.
I KNOW WHAT HE MEANS TO YOU. ONE DAY HE'LL UNDERSTAND.
YEAH. I JUST--
--I GOTTA WIN ONE.
"I GOTTA WIN ONE FOR HIM."

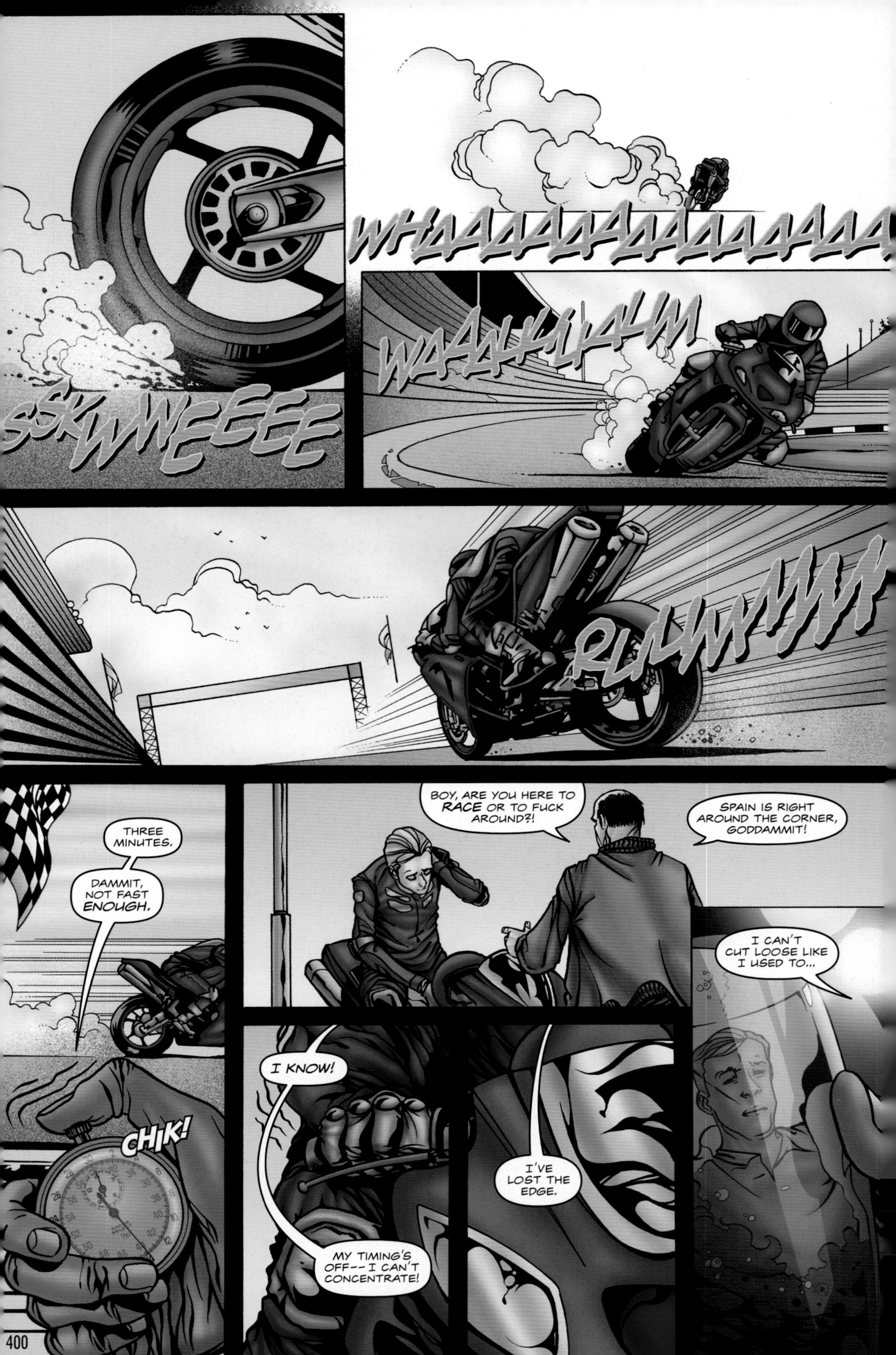
SSKWWEEEEE
WHAAAAAAAAAAAAAAA
WAAAHHHAHM
RUHWWWWW
THREE MINUTES.
DAMMIT, NOT FAST ENOUGH.
CHIK!
BOY, ARE YOU HERE TO RACE OR TO FUCK AROUND?!
SPAIN IS RIGHT AROUND THE CORNER, GODDAMMIT!
I KNOW!
MY TIMING'S OFF-- I CAN'T CONCENTRATE!
I'VE LOST THE EDGE.
I CAN'T CUT LOOSE LIKE I USED TO...

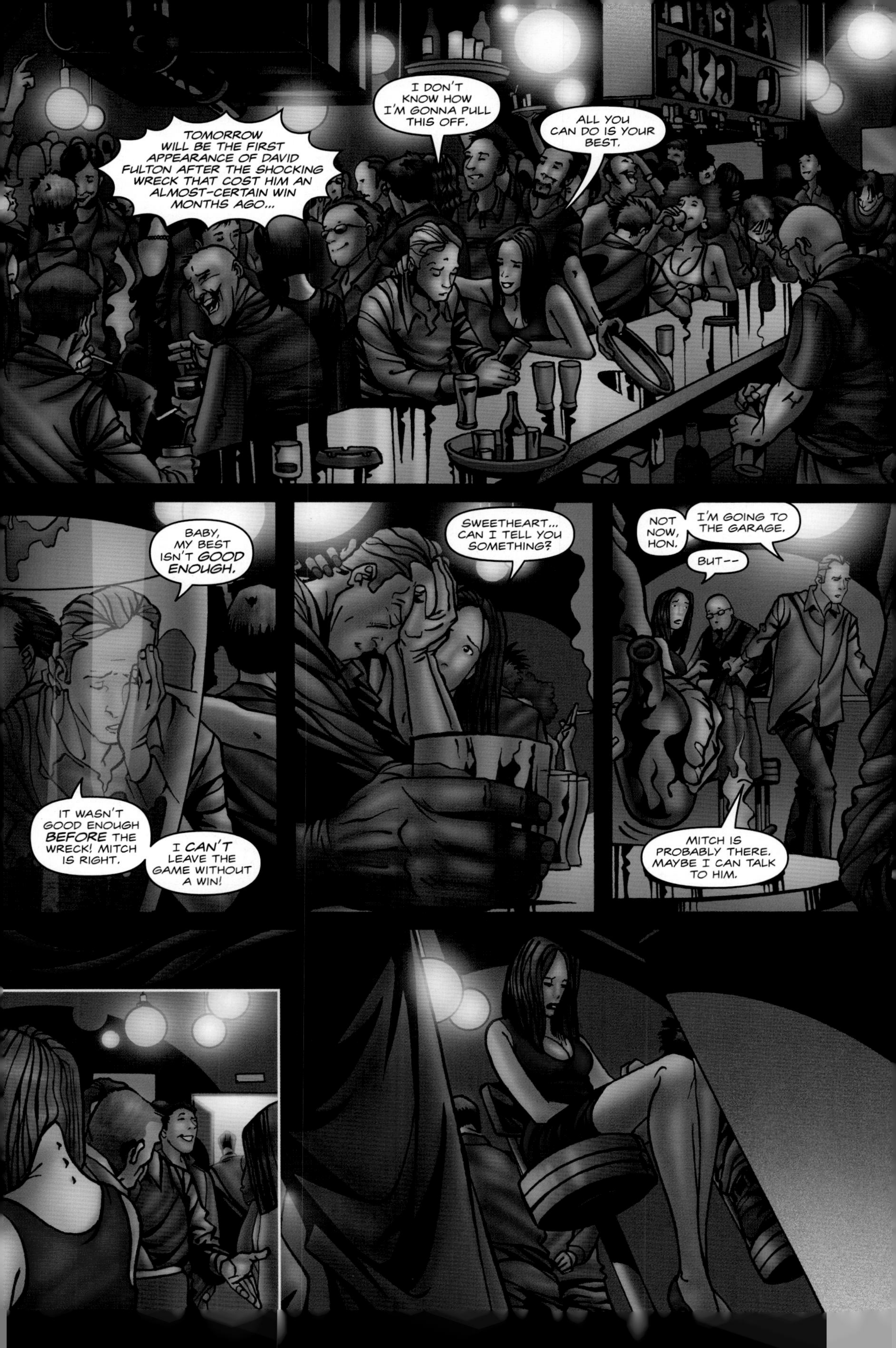
TOMORROW WILL BE THE FIRST APPEARANCE OF DAVID FULTON AFTER THE SHOCKING WRECK THAT COST HIM AN ALMOST-CERTAIN WIN MONTHS AGO...
I DON'T KNOW HOW I'M GONNA PULL THIS OFF.
ALL YOU CAN DO IS YOUR BEST.
BABY, MY BEST ISN'T GOOD ENOUGH.
IT WASN'T GOOD ENOUGH BEFORE THE WRECK! MITCH IS RIGHT.
I CAN'T LEAVE THE GAME WITHOUT A WIN!
SWEETHEART... CAN I TELL YOU SOMETHING?
NOT NOW, HON.
I'M GOING TO THE GARAGE.
BUT--
MITCH IS PROBABLY THERE. MAYBE I CAN TALK TO HIM.

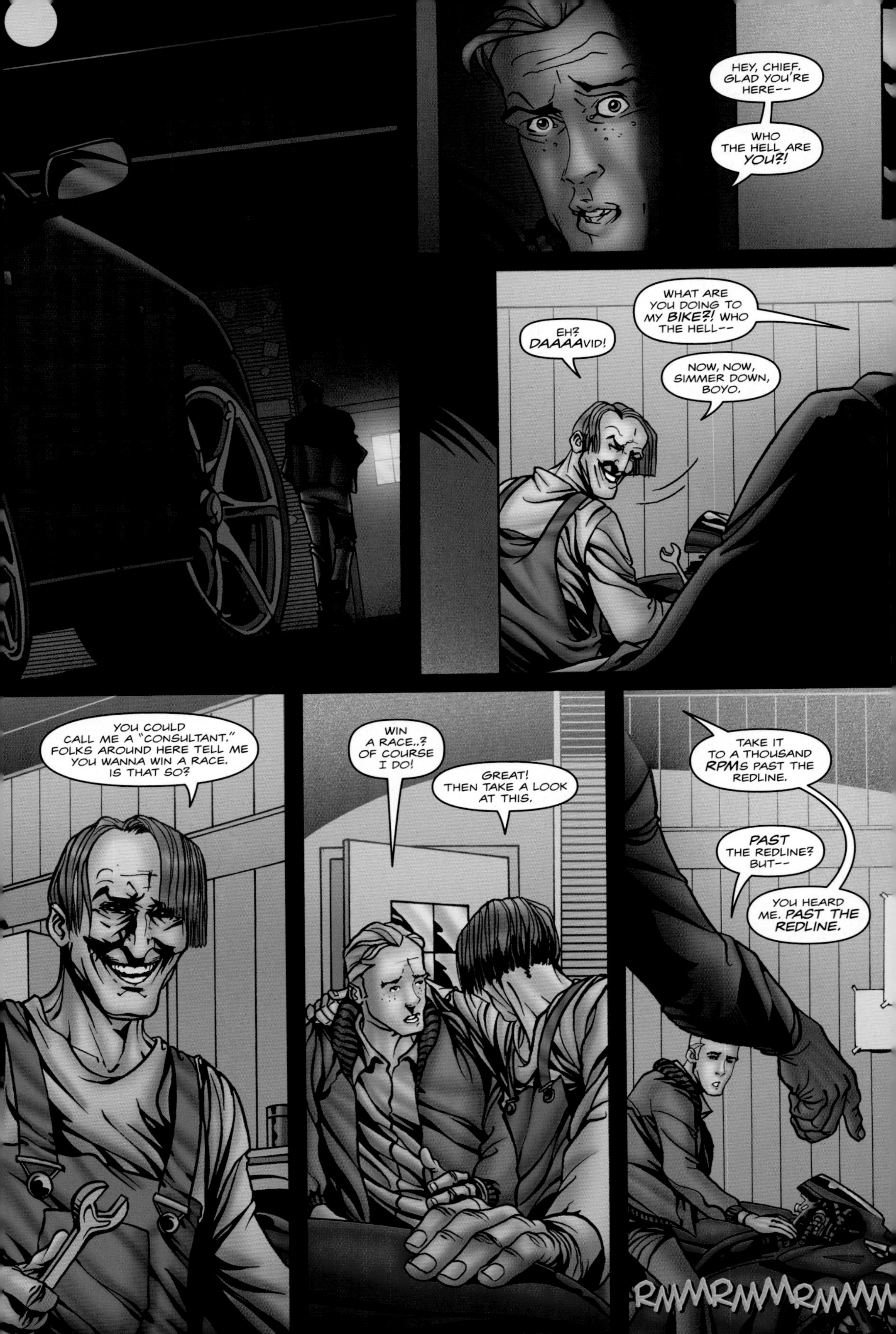
HEY, CHIEF. GLAD YOU'RE HERE--
WHO THE HELL ARE YOU?!
WHAT ARE YOU DOING TO MY BIKE?! WHO THE HELL--
EH? DAAAAVID!
NOW, NOW, SIMMER DOWN, BOYO.
YOU COULD CALL ME A "CONSULTANT." FOLKS AROUND HERE TELL ME YOU WANNA WIN A RACE. IS THAT SO?
WIN A RACE..? OF COURSE I DO!
GREAT! THEN TAKE A LOOK AT THIS.
TAKE IT TO A THOUSAND RPMS PAST THE REDLINE.
PAST THE REDLINE? BUT--
YOU HEARD ME. PAST THE REDLINE.
RMMRMMRMMM

X1000r/min

X1000r/min

THAT'S IT. HERE SHE *GOES...*

WHAAAAAAAAAAAEEEEEE

JESUS CHRIST!

WHAT DID YOU DO TO MY BIKE?!

THIS CAN'T BE WITHIN REGULATIONS.

OH, I KNOW HOW TO *TURN UP THE HEAT.*

KID, I PROMISE YOU-- -- THEY COULD TEAR THIS BIKE APART, AND THEY'D NEVER FIND A THING.

NOW, SHE'LL ONLY DELIVER THAT KICK FOR A FEW SECONDS, BUT IT'LL BE A *KILLER* WHEN YOU NEED IT. HEH, HEH...

AND YOU CAN HAVE THIS READY FOR ME TOMORROW?

YESSIR. BUT, AH... I'LL BE NEEDIN' SOMETHING FROM YOU.

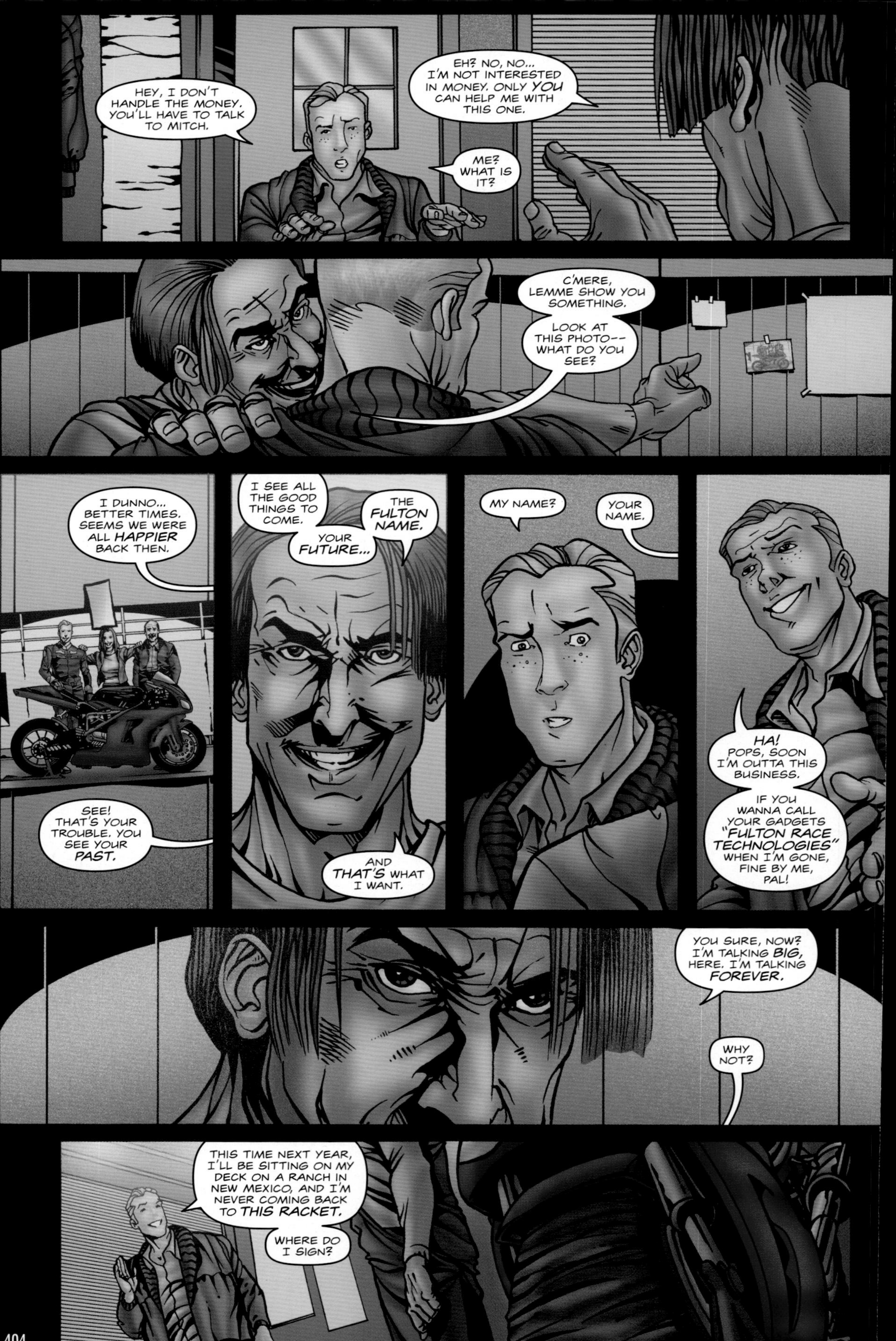

HEY, I DON'T HANDLE THE MONEY. YOU'LL HAVE TO TALK TO MITCH.
EH? NO, NO... I'M NOT INTERESTED IN MONEY. ONLY YOU CAN HELP ME WITH THIS ONE.
ME? WHAT IS IT?
C'MERE, LEMME SHOW YOU SOMETHING.
LOOK AT THIS PHOTO--WHAT DO YOU SEE?
I DUNNO... BETTER TIMES. SEEMS WE WERE ALL HAPPIER BACK THEN.
SEE! THAT'S YOUR TROUBLE. YOU SEE YOUR PAST.
I SEE ALL THE GOOD THINGS TO COME.
YOUR FUTURE...
THE FULTON NAME.
AND THAT'S WHAT I WANT.
MY NAME?
YOUR NAME.
HA! POPS, SOON I'M OUTTA THIS BUSINESS.
IF YOU WANNA CALL YOUR GADGETS "FULTON RACE TECHNOLOGIES" WHEN I'M GONE, FINE BY ME, PAL!
YOU SURE, NOW? I'M TALKING BIG, HERE. I'M TALKING FOREVER.
WHY NOT?
THIS TIME NEXT YEAR, I'LL BE SITTING ON MY DECK ON A RANCH IN NEW MEXICO, AND I'M NEVER COMING BACK TO THIS RACKET.
WHERE DO I SIGN?

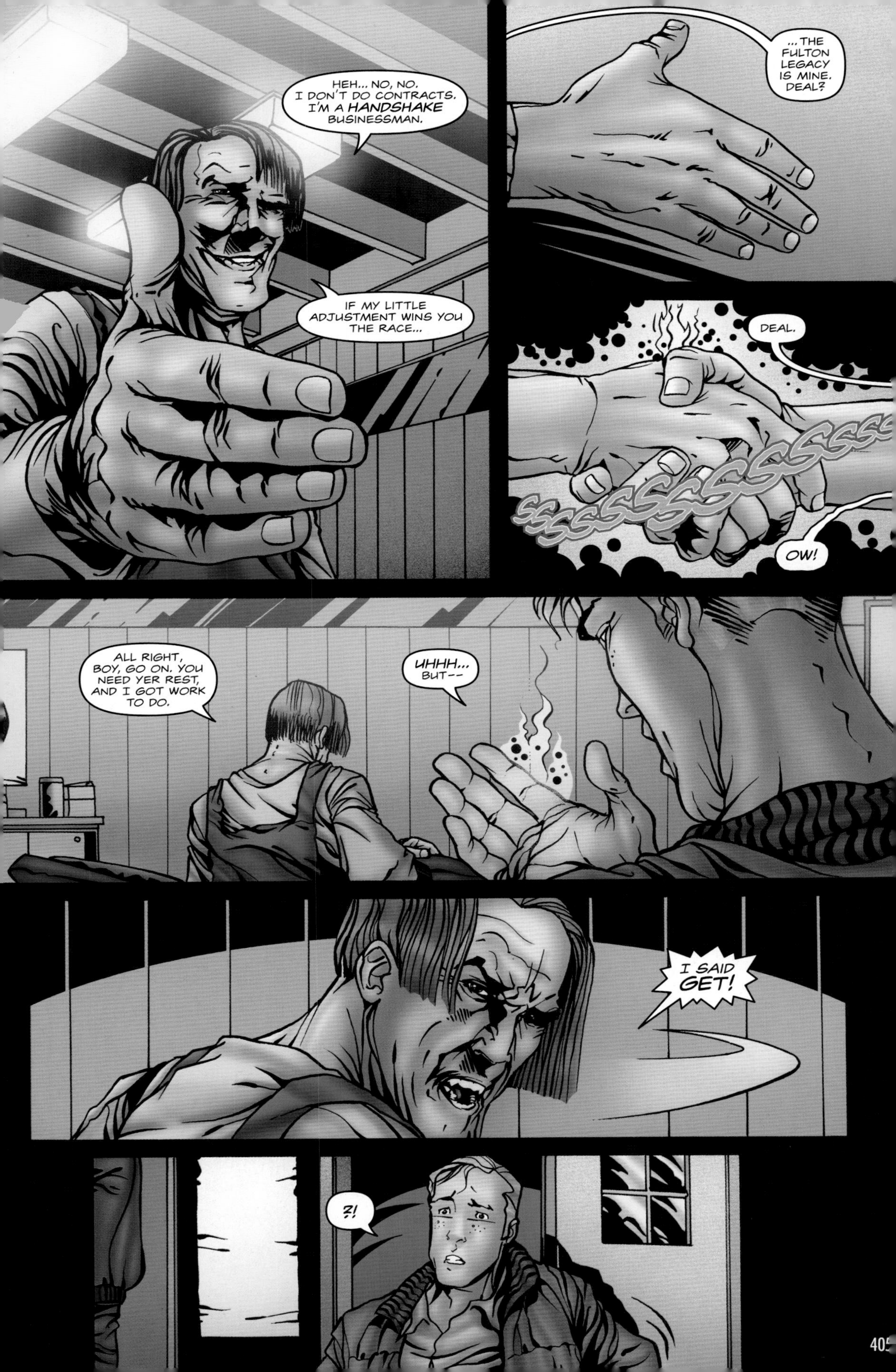
HEH... NO, NO. I DON'T DO CONTRACTS. I'M A HANDSHAKE BUSINESSMAN.
IF MY LITTLE ADJUSTMENT WINS YOU THE RACE...
...THE FULTON LEGACY IS MINE. DEAL?
DEAL.
SSSSSSSSSSSSSSSS
OW!
ALL RIGHT, BOY, GO ON. YOU NEED YER REST, AND I GOT WORK TO DO.
UHHH... BUT--
I SAID GET!
?!

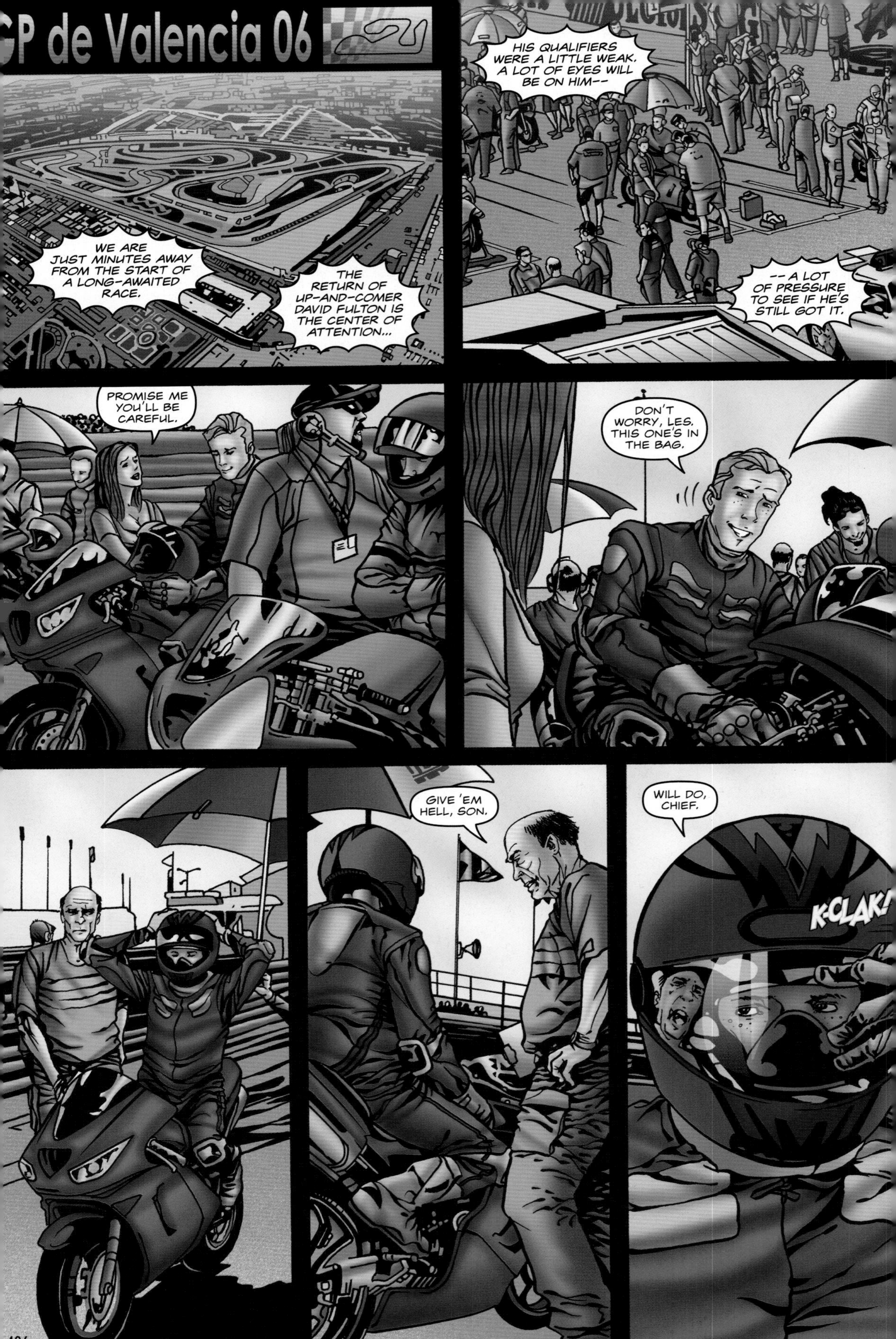
GP de Valencia 06
WE ARE JUST MINUTES AWAY FROM THE START OF A LONG-AWAITED RACE.
THE RETURN OF UP-AND-COMER DAVID FULTON IS THE CENTER OF ATTENTION...
HIS QUALIFIERS WERE A LITTLE WEAK. A LOT OF EYES WILL BE ON HIM--
-- A LOT OF PRESSURE TO SEE IF HE'S STILL GOT IT.
PROMISE ME YOU'LL BE CAREFUL.
DON'T WORRY, LES. THIS ONE'S IN THE BAG.
GIVE 'EM HELL, SON.
WILL DO, CHIEF.
K-CLAK!

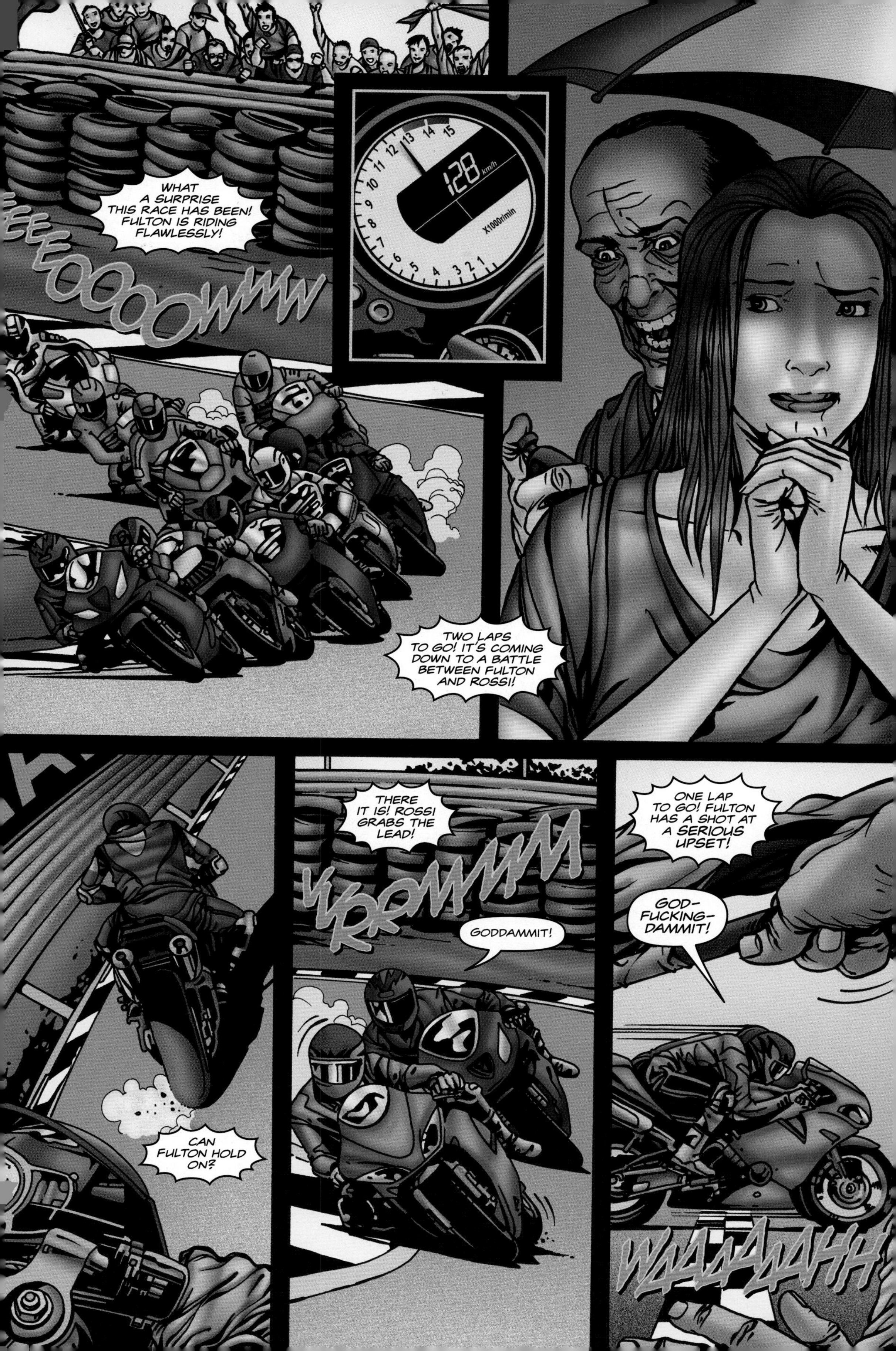
EEEEOOOOOWWWW
WHAT A SURPRISE THIS RACE HAS BEEN! FULTON IS RIDING FLAWLESSLY!
128 km/h
X1000r/min
TWO LAPS TO GO! IT'S COMING DOWN TO A BATTLE BETWEEN FULTON AND ROSSI!
CAN FULTON HOLD ON?
THERE IT IS! ROSSI GRABS THE LEAD!
VRRRMMMM
GODDAMMIT!
ONE LAP TO GO! FULTON HAS A SHOT AT A SERIOUS UPSET!
GOD-FUCKING-DAMMIT!
WAAAAAHH

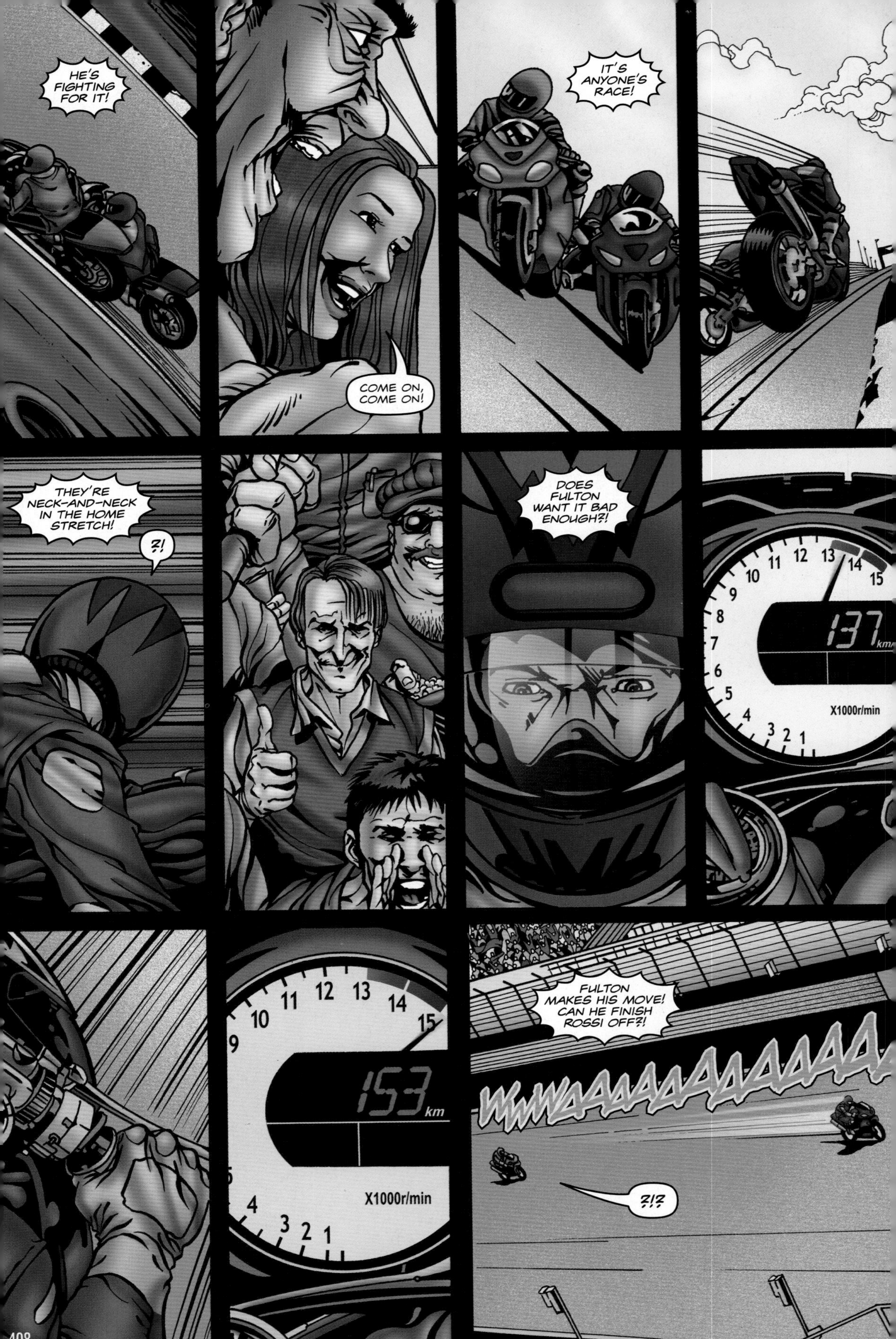

HE'S FIGHTING FOR IT!
COME ON, COME ON!
IT'S ANYONE'S RACE!
11 12 13 14 15
10
9
8
7
6
5
4
3 2 1
137 km
X1000r/min
THEY'RE NECK-AND-NECK IN THE HOME STRETCH!
?!
DOES FULTON WANT IT BAD ENOUGH?!
10 11 12 13 14 15
9
153 km
X1000r/min
4 3 2 1
FULTON MAKES HIS MOVE! CAN HE FINISH ROSSI OFF?!
WWWAAAAAAAAAAAAA
?!?

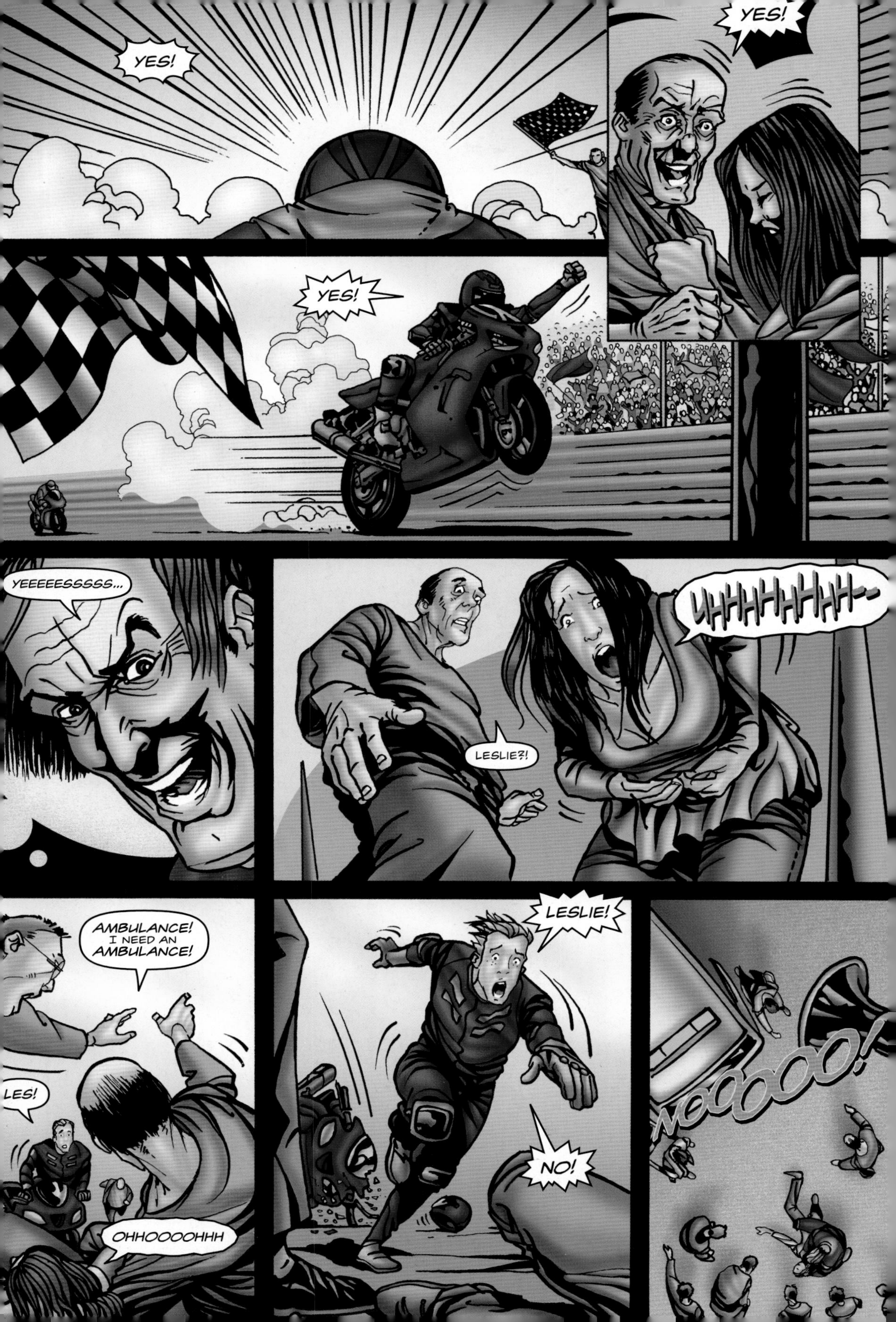
YES!
YES!
YES!
YEEEEESSSSS...
UHHHHHHHH--
LESLIE?!
AMBULANCE! I NEED AN AMBULANCE!
LES!
OHHOOOOHHH
LESLIE!
NO!
NOOOOOO!

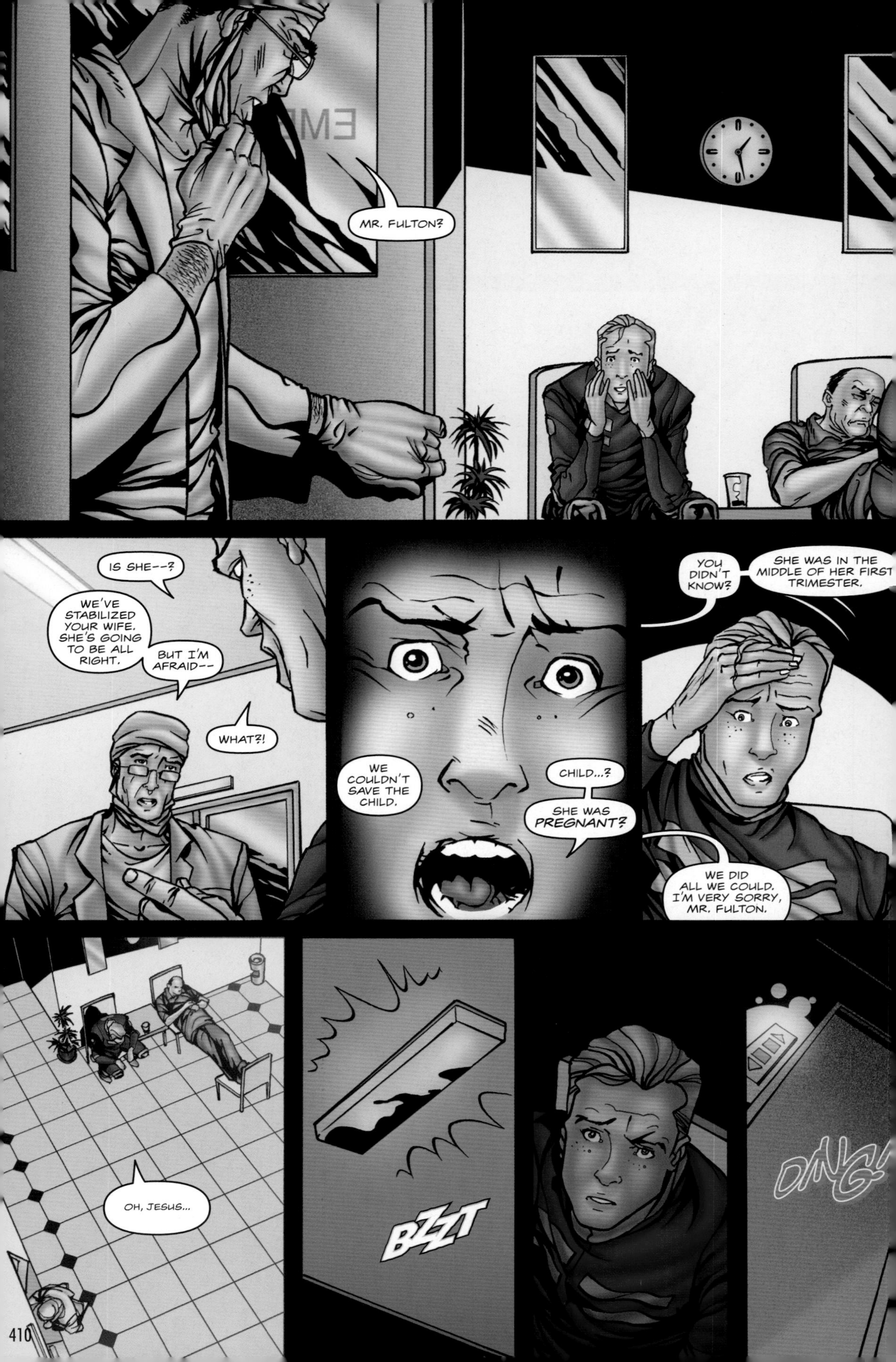
MR. FULTON?
IS SHE--?
WE'VE STABILIZED YOUR WIFE. SHE'S GOING TO BE ALL RIGHT.
BUT I'M AFRAID--
WHAT?!
WE COULDN'T SAVE THE CHILD.
CHILD...?
SHE WAS PREGNANT?
YOU DIDN'T KNOW?
SHE WAS IN THE MIDDLE OF HER FIRST TRIMESTER.
WE DID ALL WE COULD. I'M VERY SORRY, MR. FULTON.
OH, JESUS...
BZZT
DING

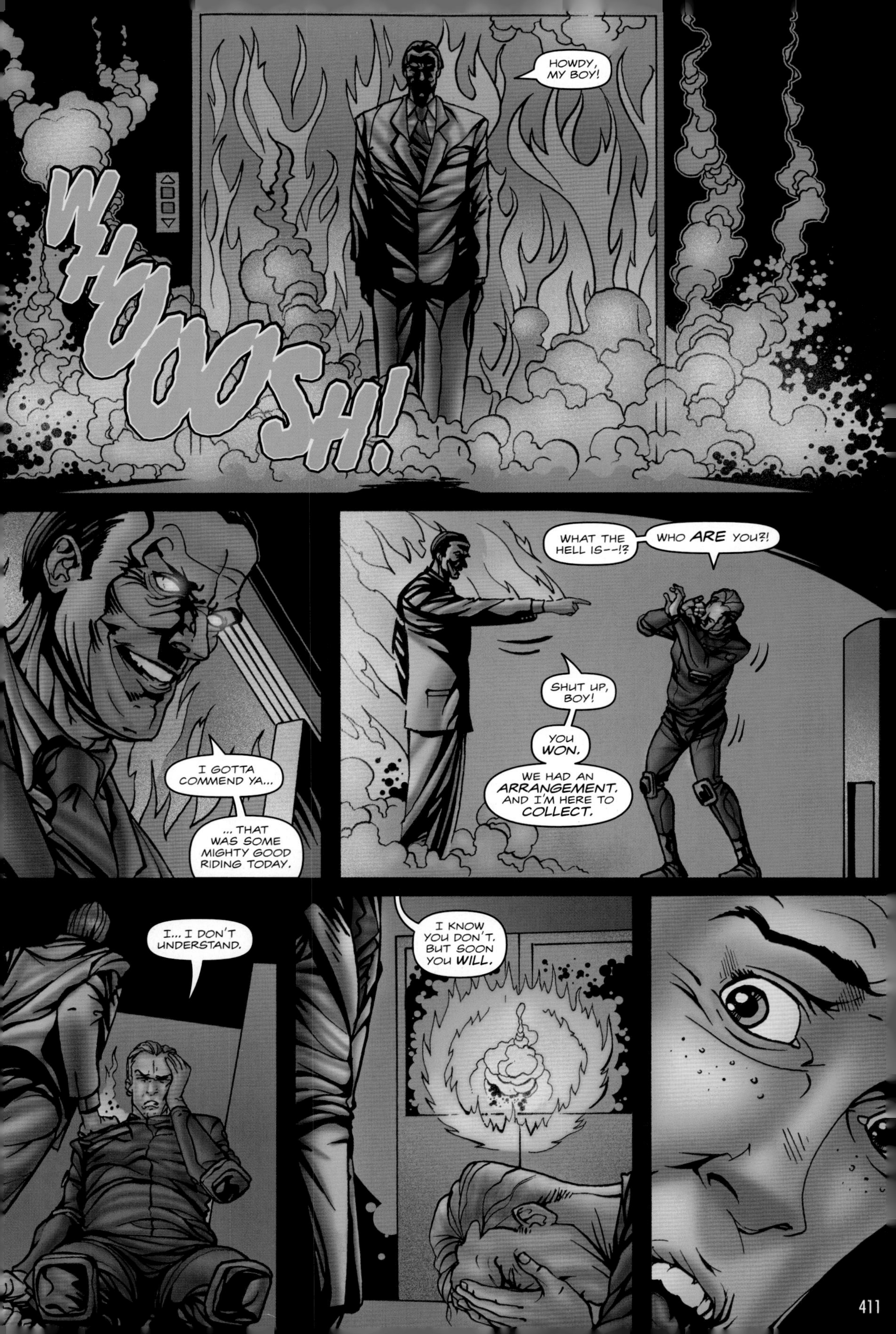
HOWDY, MY BOY!
WHOOOOSH!
I GOTTA COMMEND YA...
... THAT WAS SOME MIGHTY GOOD RIDING TODAY.
WHAT THE HELL IS--!?
WHO ARE YOU?!
SHUT UP, BOY!
YOU WON.
WE HAD AN ARRANGEMENT. AND I'M HERE TO COLLECT.
I... I DON'T UNDERSTAND.
I KNOW YOU DON'T. BUT SOON YOU WILL.

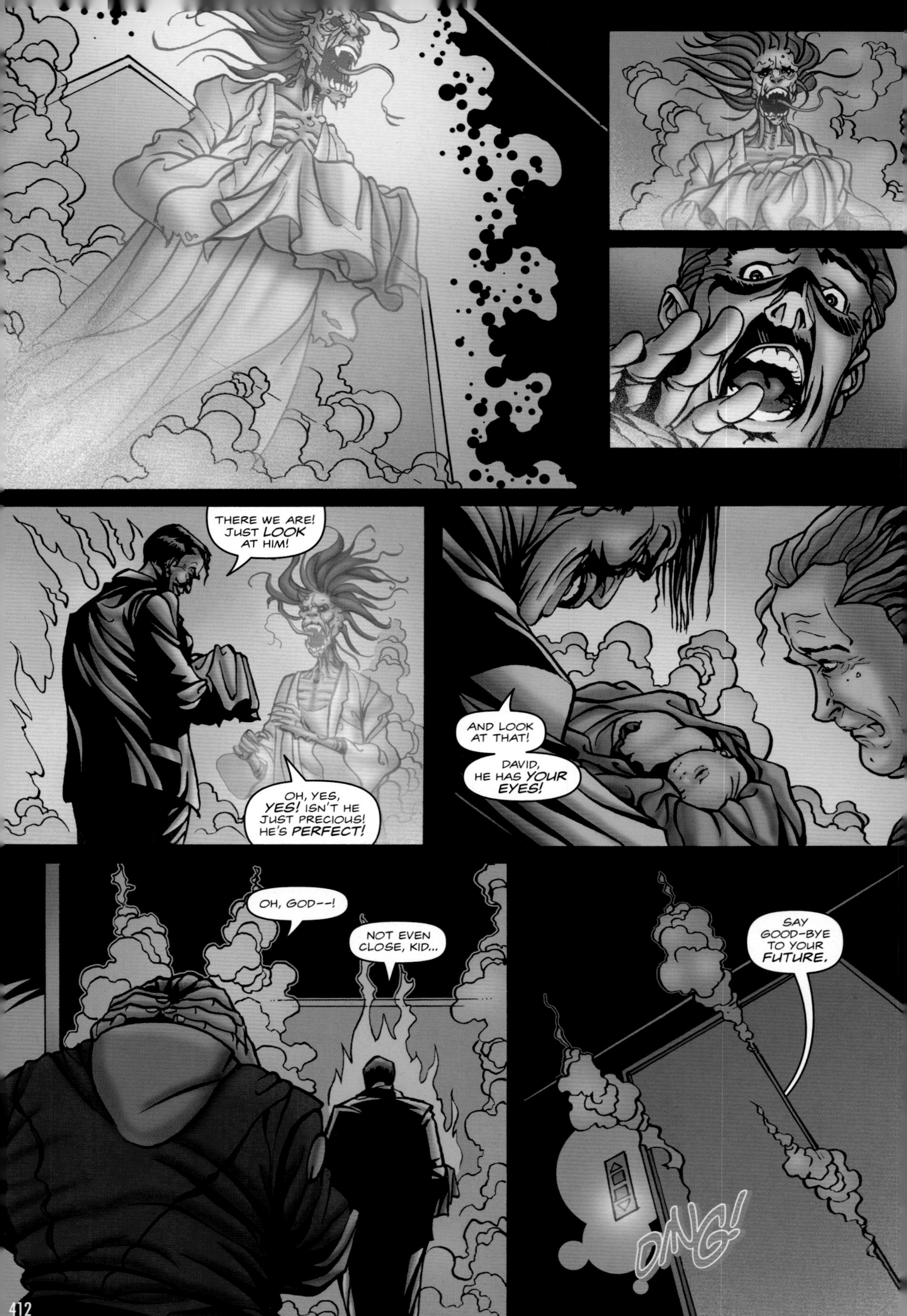
THERE WE ARE! JUST LOOK AT HIM!
OH, YES, YES! ISN'T HE JUST PRECIOUS! HE'S PERFECT!
AND LOOK AT THAT!
DAVID, HE HAS YOUR EYES!
OH, GOD--!
NOT EVEN CLOSE, KID...
SAY GOOD-BYE TO YOUR FUTURE.
DING!

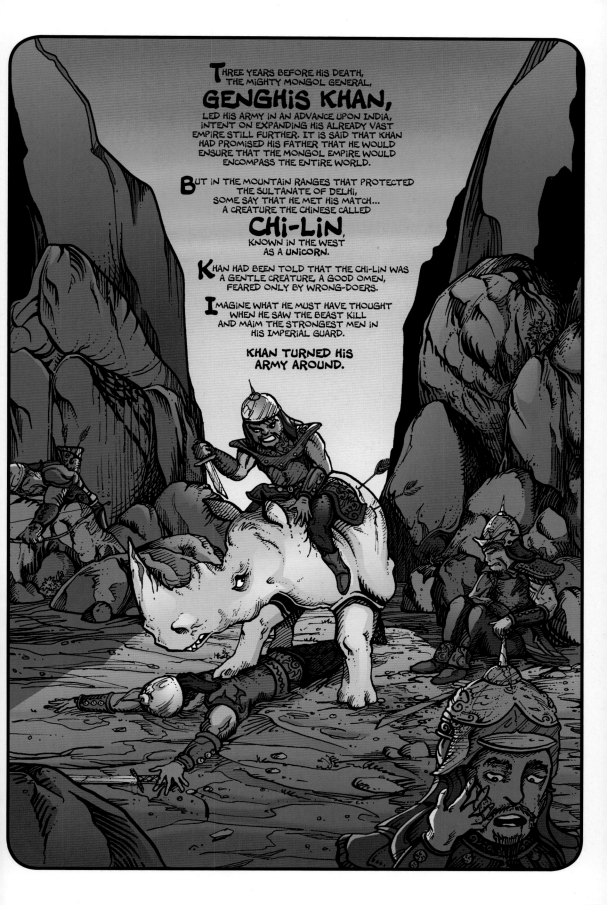

THREE YEARS BEFORE HIS DEATH, THE MIGHTY MONGOL GENERAL,

GENGHIS KHAN,

LED HIS ARMY IN AN ADVANCE UPON INDIA, INTENT ON EXPANDING HIS ALREADY VAST EMPIRE STILL FURTHER. IT IS SAID THAT KHAN HAD PROMISED HIS FATHER THAT HE WOULD ENSURE THAT THE MONGOL EMPIRE WOULD ENCOMPASS THE ENTIRE WORLD.

BUT IN THE MOUNTAIN RANGES THAT PROTECTED THE SULTANATE OF DELHI, SOME SAY THAT HE MET HIS MATCH... A CREATURE THE CHINESE CALLED

CHI-LIN,

KNOWN IN THE WEST AS A UNICORN.

KHAN HAD BEEN TOLD THAT THE CHI-LIN WAS A GENTLE CREATURE, A GOOD OMEN, FEARED ONLY BY WRONG-DOERS.

IMAGINE WHAT HE MUST HAVE THOUGHT WHEN HE SAW THE BEAST KILL AND MAIM THE STRONGEST MEN IN HIS IMPERIAL GUARD.

KHAN TURNED HIS ARMY AROUND.

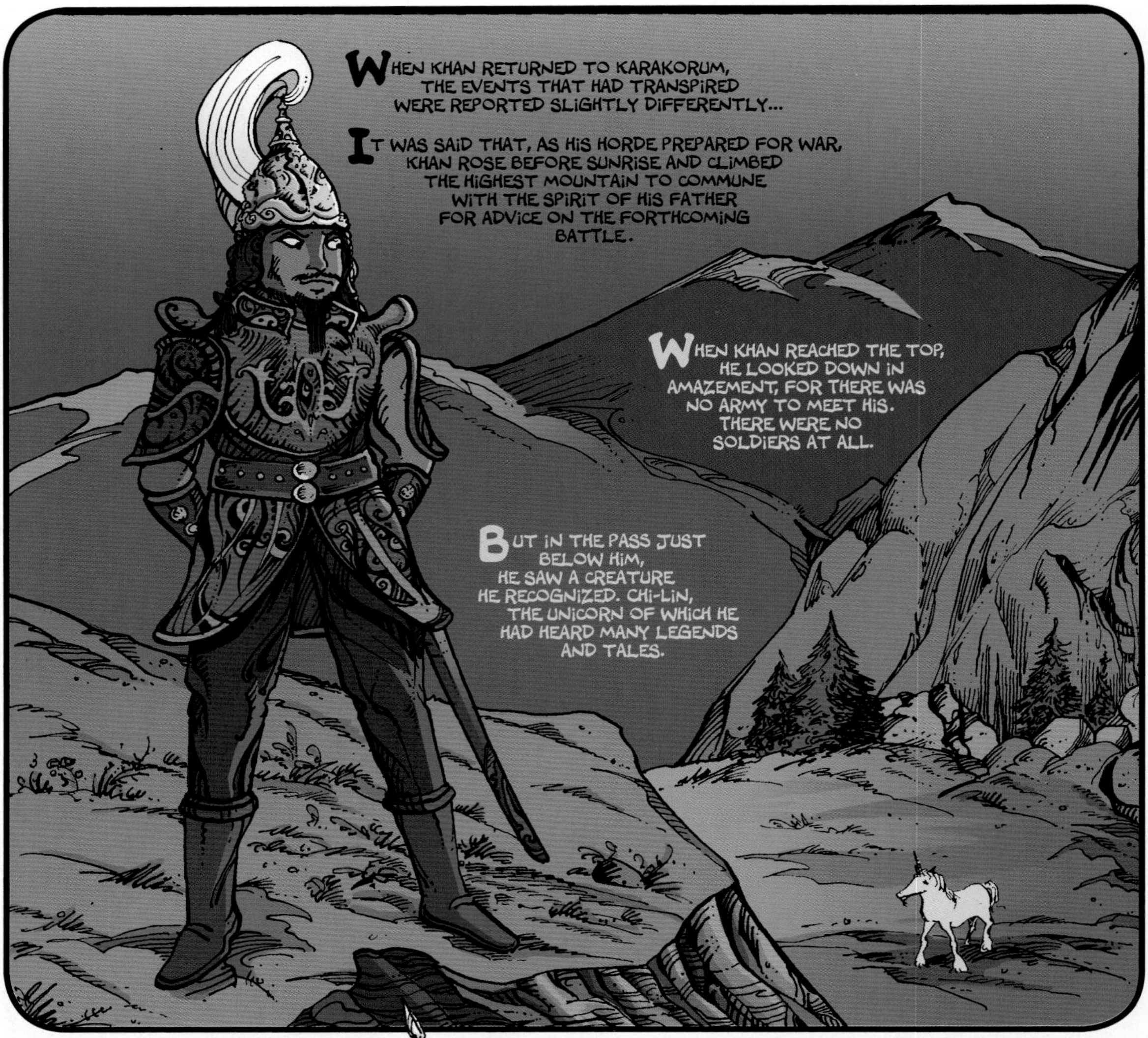
WHEN KHAN RETURNED TO KARAKORUM, THE EVENTS THAT HAD TRANSPIRED WERE REPORTED SLIGHTLY DIFFERENTLY...
IT WAS SAID THAT, AS HIS HORDE PREPARED FOR WAR, KHAN ROSE BEFORE SUNRISE AND CLIMBED THE HIGHEST MOUNTAIN TO COMMUNE WITH THE SPIRIT OF HIS FATHER FOR ADVICE ON THE FORTHCOMING BATTLE.
WHEN KHAN REACHED THE TOP, HE LOOKED DOWN IN AMAZEMENT, FOR THERE WAS NO ARMY TO MEET HIS. THERE WERE NO SOLDIERS AT ALL.
BUT IN THE PASS JUST BELOW HIM, HE SAW A CREATURE HE RECOGNIZED. CHI-LIN, THE UNICORN OF WHICH HE HAD HEARD MANY LEGENDS AND TALES.
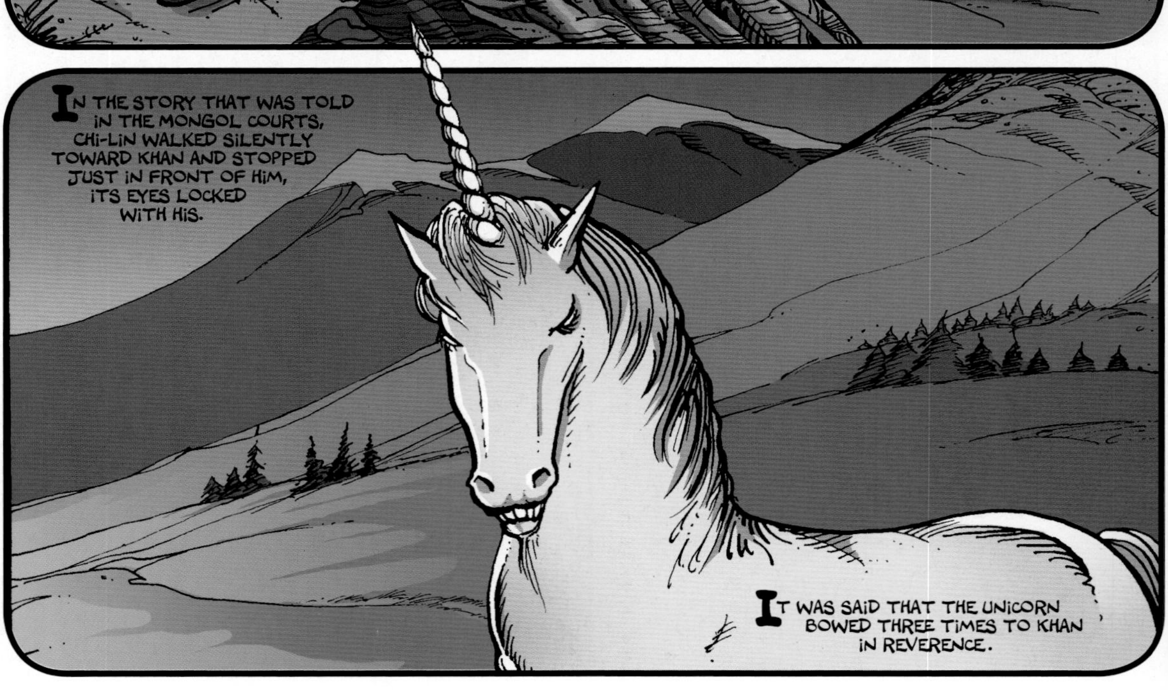
IN THE STORY THAT WAS TOLD IN THE MONGOL COURTS, CHI-LIN WALKED SILENTLY TOWARD KHAN AND STOPPED JUST IN FRONT OF HIM, ITS EYES LOCKED WITH HIS.
IT WAS SAID THAT THE UNICORN BOWED THREE TIMES TO KHAN IN REVERENCE.

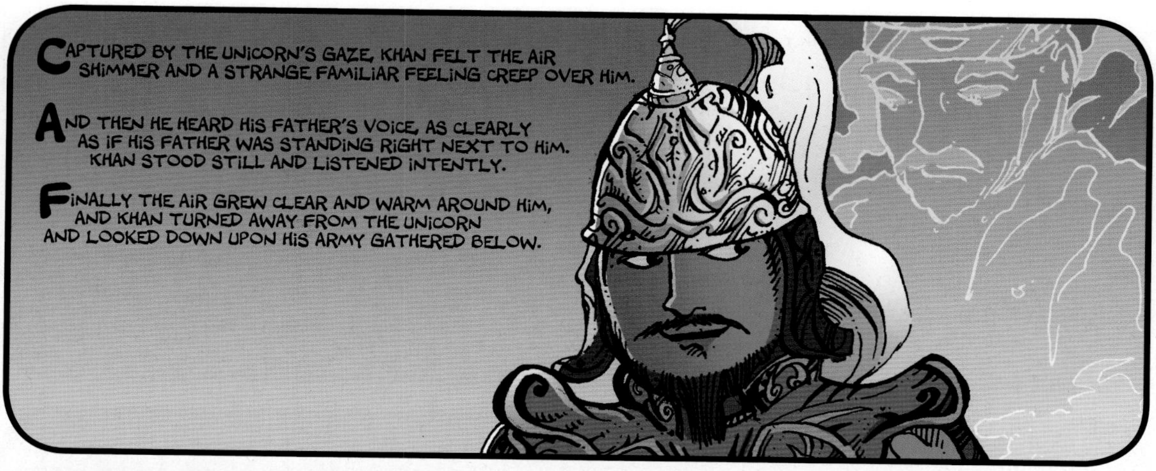
CAPTURED BY THE UNICORN'S GAZE, KHAN FELT THE AIR SHIMMER AND A STRANGE FAMILIAR FEELING CREEP OVER HIM.
AND THEN HE HEARD HIS FATHER'S VOICE, AS CLEARLY AS IF HIS FATHER WAS STANDING RIGHT NEXT TO HIM. KHAN STOOD STILL AND LISTENED INTENTLY.
FINALLY THE AIR GREW CLEAR AND WARM AROUND HIM, AND KHAN TURNED AWAY FROM THE UNICORN AND LOOKED DOWN UPON HIS ARMY GATHERED BELOW.

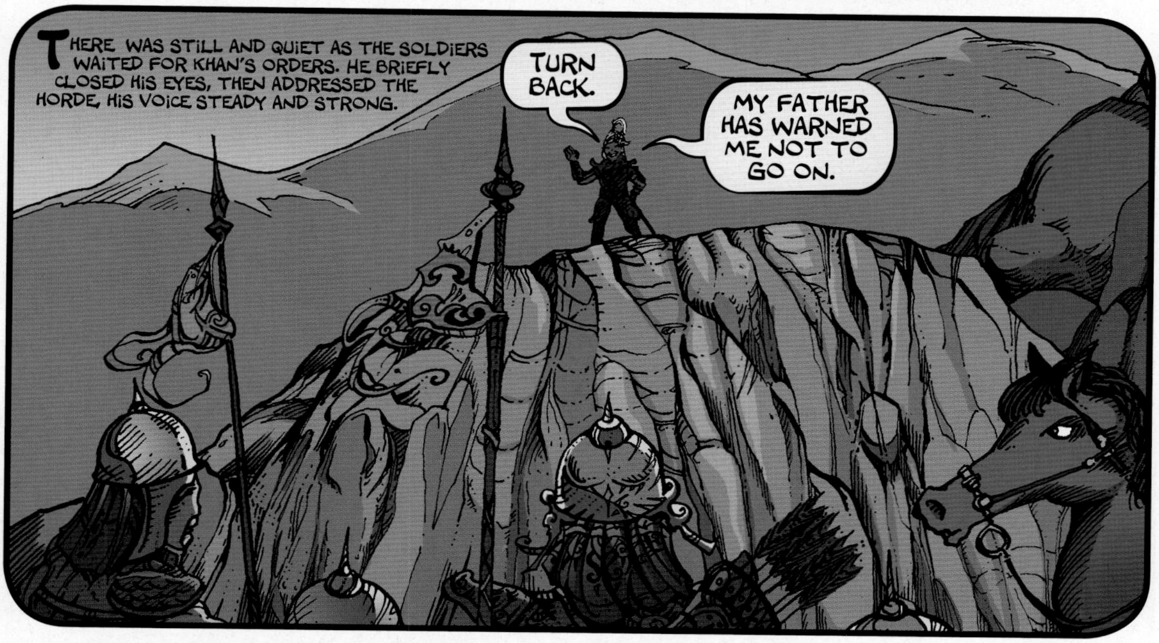
THERE WAS STILL AND QUIET AS THE SOLDIERS WAITED FOR KHAN'S ORDERS. HE BRIEFLY CLOSED HIS EYES, THEN ADDRESSED THE HORDE, HIS VOICE STEADY AND STRONG.
TURN BACK.
MY FATHER HAS WARNED ME NOT TO GO ON.

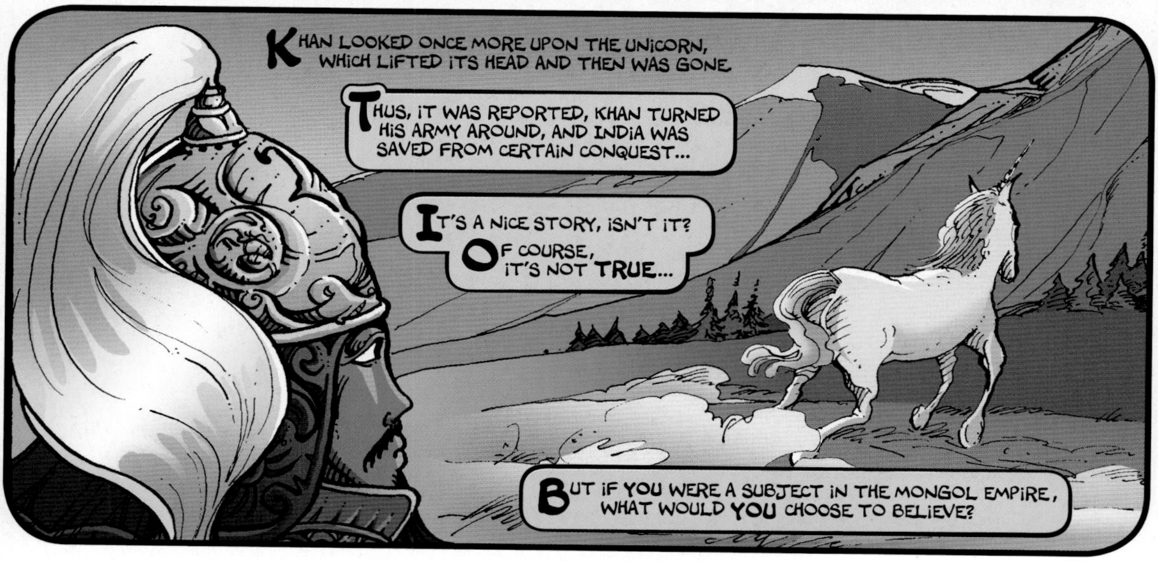
KHAN LOOKED ONCE MORE UPON THE UNICORN, WHICH LIFTED ITS HEAD AND THEN WAS GONE
THUS, IT WAS REPORTED, KHAN TURNED HIS ARMY AROUND, AND INDIA WAS SAVED FROM CERTAIN CONQUEST...
IT'S A NICE STORY, ISN'T IT? OF COURSE, IT'S NOT TRUE...
BUT IF YOU WERE A SUBJECT IN THE MONGOL EMPIRE, WHAT WOULD YOU CHOOSE TO BELIEVE?

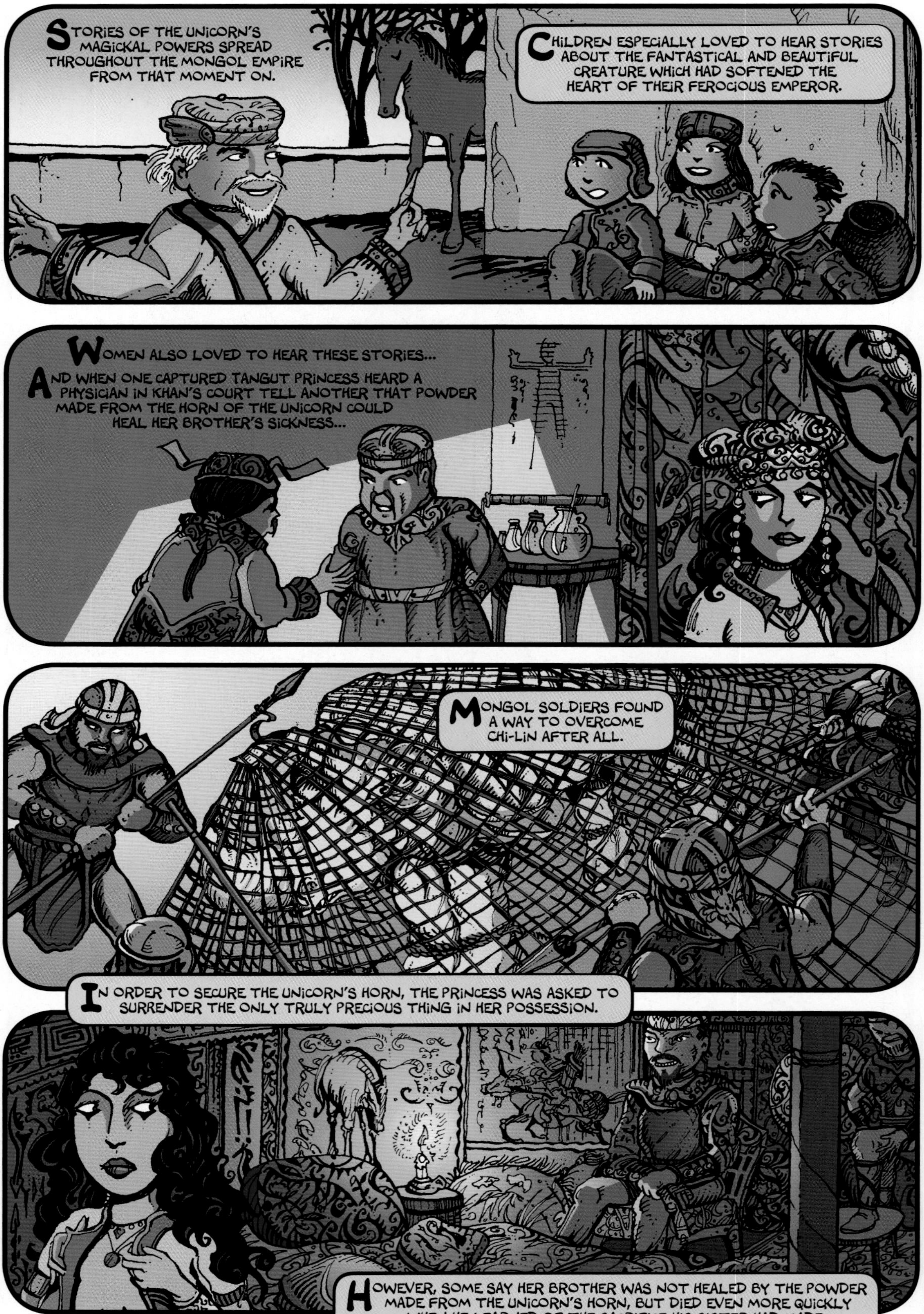
STORIES OF THE UNICORN'S MAGICKAL POWERS SPREAD THROUGHOUT THE MONGOL EMPIRE FROM THAT MOMENT ON.
CHILDREN ESPECIALLY LOVED TO HEAR STORIES ABOUT THE FANTASTICAL AND BEAUTIFUL CREATURE WHICH HAD SOFTENED THE HEART OF THEIR FEROCIOUS EMPEROR.
WOMEN ALSO LOVED TO HEAR THESE STORIES...
AND WHEN ONE CAPTURED TANGUT PRINCESS HEARD A PHYSICIAN IN KHAN'S COURT TELL ANOTHER THAT POWDER MADE FROM THE HORN OF THE UNICORN COULD HEAL HER BROTHER'S SICKNESS...
MONGOL SOLDIERS FOUND A WAY TO OVERCOME CHI-LIN AFTER ALL.
IN ORDER TO SECURE THE UNICORN'S HORN, THE PRINCESS WAS ASKED TO SURRENDER THE ONLY TRULY PRECIOUS THING IN HER POSSESSION.
HOWEVER, SOME SAY HER BROTHER WAS NOT HEALED BY THE POWDER MADE FROM THE UNICORN'S HORN, BUT DIED EVEN MORE QUICKLY WHEN HE LEARNED OF THE SACRIFICE HIS SISTER HAD MADE.

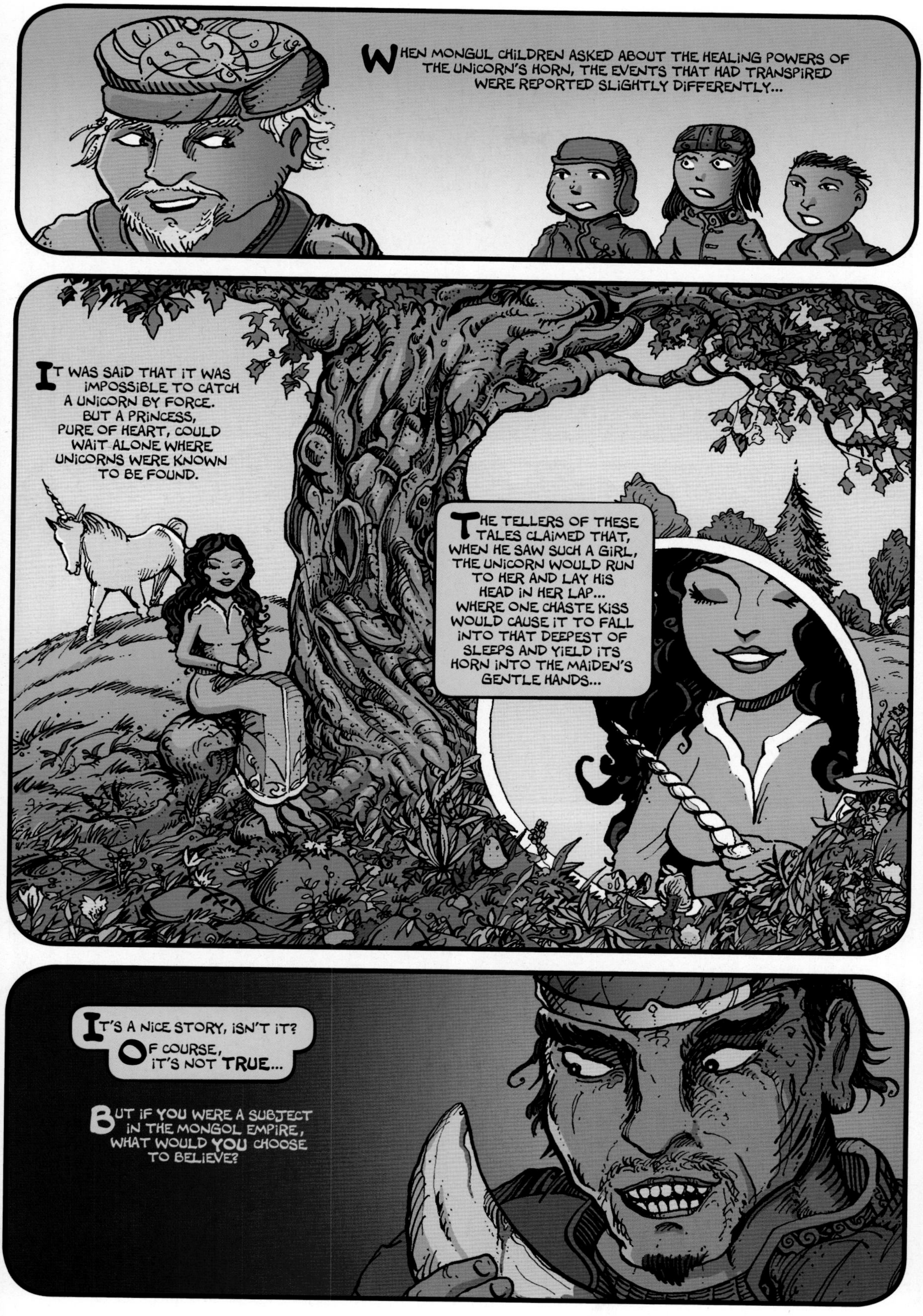
WHEN MONGUL CHILDREN ASKED ABOUT THE HEALING POWERS OF THE UNICORN'S HORN, THE EVENTS THAT HAD TRANSPIRED WERE REPORTED SLIGHTLY DIFFERENTLY...
IT WAS SAID THAT IT WAS IMPOSSIBLE TO CATCH A UNICORN BY FORCE. BUT A PRINCESS, PURE OF HEART, COULD WAIT ALONE WHERE UNICORNS WERE KNOWN TO BE FOUND.
THE TELLERS OF THESE TALES CLAIMED THAT, WHEN HE SAW SUCH A GIRL, THE UNICORN WOULD RUN TO HER AND LAY HIS HEAD IN HER LAP... WHERE ONE CHASTE KISS WOULD CAUSE IT TO FALL INTO THAT DEEPEST OF SLEEPS AND YIELD ITS HORN INTO THE MAIDEN'S GENTLE HANDS...
IT'S A NICE STORY, ISN'T IT? OF COURSE, IT'S NOT TRUE...
BUT IF YOU WERE A SUBJECT IN THE MONGOL EMPIRE, WHAT WOULD YOU CHOOSE TO BELIEVE?

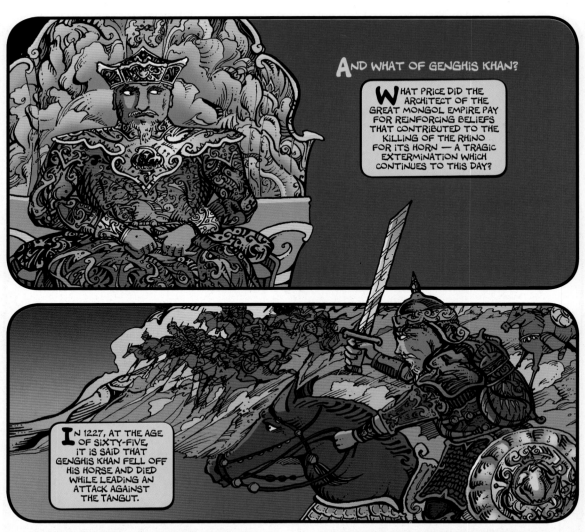

AND WHAT OF GENGHIS KHAN?

WHAT PRICE DID THE ARCHITECT OF THE GREAT MONGOL EMPIRE PAY FOR REINFORCING BELIEFS THAT CONTRIBUTED TO THE KILLING OF THE RHINO FOR ITS HORN — A TRAGIC EXTERMINATION WHICH CONTINUES TO THIS DAY?

IN 1227, AT THE AGE OF SIXTY-FIVE, IT IS SAID THAT GENGHIS KHAN FELL OFF HIS HORSE AND DIED WHILE LEADING AN ATTACK AGAINST THE TANGUT.

ON HIS DEATHBED, IT WAS SAID THAT HE SPOKE THESE LAST WORDS TO HIS SONS...

WITH HEAVEN'S AID, I HAVE CONQUERED FOR YOU A HUGE EMPIRE. BUT MY LIFE WAS TOO SHORT TO ACHIEVE THE CONQUEST OF THE ENTIRE WORLD.

THAT TASK... I LEAVE FOR YOU.

IT'S A NICE STORY, ISN'T IT? OF COURSE, IT'S NOT **TRUE**...

BUT IF YOU WERE A SUBJECT IN THE MONGOL EMPIRE, WHAT WOULD **YOU** CHOOSE TO BELIEVE?

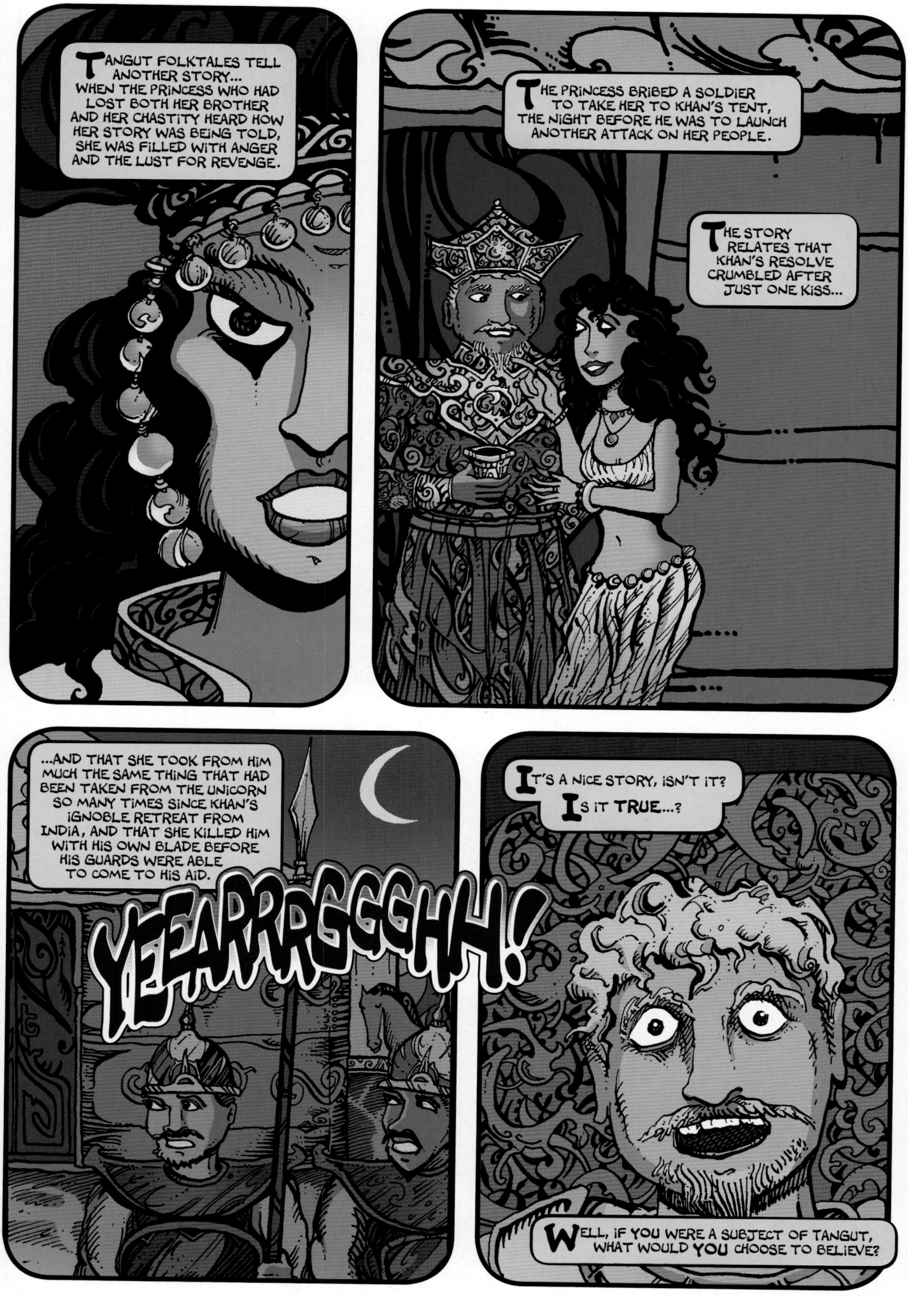

TANGUT FOLKTALES TELL ANOTHER STORY... WHEN THE PRINCESS WHO HAD LOST BOTH HER BROTHER AND HER CHASTITY HEARD HOW HER STORY WAS BEING TOLD, SHE WAS FILLED WITH ANGER AND THE LUST FOR REVENGE.
THE PRINCESS BRIBED A SOLDIER TO TAKE HER TO KHAN'S TENT, THE NIGHT BEFORE HE WAS TO LAUNCH ANOTHER ATTACK ON HER PEOPLE.
THE STORY RELATES THAT KHAN'S RESOLVE CRUMBLED AFTER JUST ONE KISS...
...AND THAT SHE TOOK FROM HIM MUCH THE SAME THING THAT HAD BEEN TAKEN FROM THE UNICORN SO MANY TIMES SINCE KHAN'S IGNOBLE RETREAT FROM INDIA, AND THAT SHE KILLED HIM WITH HIS OWN BLADE BEFORE HIS GUARDS WERE ABLE TO COME TO HIS AID.
YEEARRRGGGHH!
IT'S A NICE STORY, ISN'T IT?
IS IT TRUE...?
WELL, IF YOU WERE A SUBJECT OF TANGUT, WHAT WOULD YOU CHOOSE TO BELIEVE?

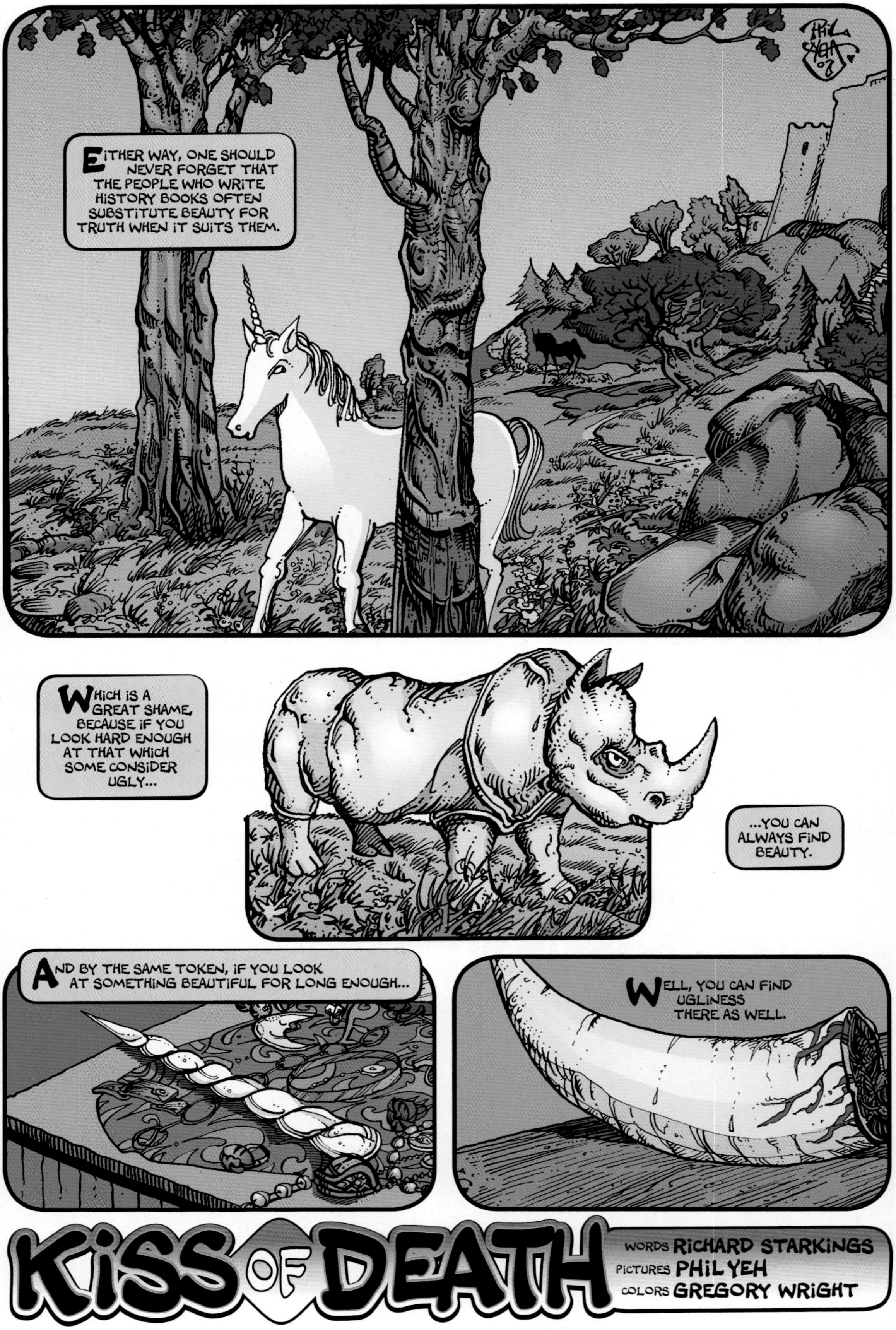
EITHER WAY, ONE SHOULD NEVER FORGET THAT THE PEOPLE WHO WRITE HISTORY BOOKS OFTEN SUBSTITUTE BEAUTY FOR TRUTH WHEN IT SUITS THEM.
WHICH IS A GREAT SHAME, BECAUSE IF YOU LOOK HARD ENOUGH AT THAT WHICH SOME CONSIDER UGLY...
...YOU CAN ALWAYS FIND BEAUTY.
AND BY THE SAME TOKEN, IF YOU LOOK AT SOMETHING BEAUTIFUL FOR LONG ENOUGH...
WELL, YOU CAN FIND UGLINESS THERE AS WELL.
KISS OF DEATH
WORDS RICHARD STARKINGS
PICTURES PHIL YEH
COLORS GREGORY WRIGHT

THE BLIND MONKEY STYLE

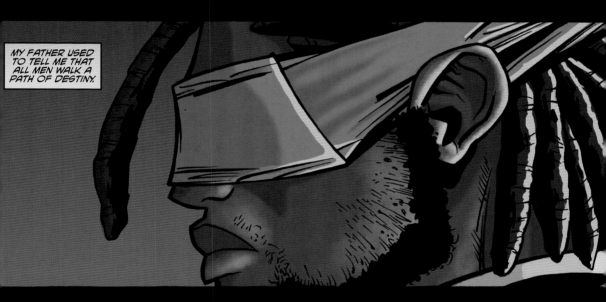

MY FATHER USED TO TELL ME THAT ALL MEN WALK A PATH OF DESTINY.

CHAPTER ONE
SMOKE and MIRRORS

WRITTEN BY
ROBERT LOVE & DAVID WALKER

ART BY
ROBERT LOVE

COLORED BY
PATRICK MORGAN

LETTERED BY
FONOGRAFIKS

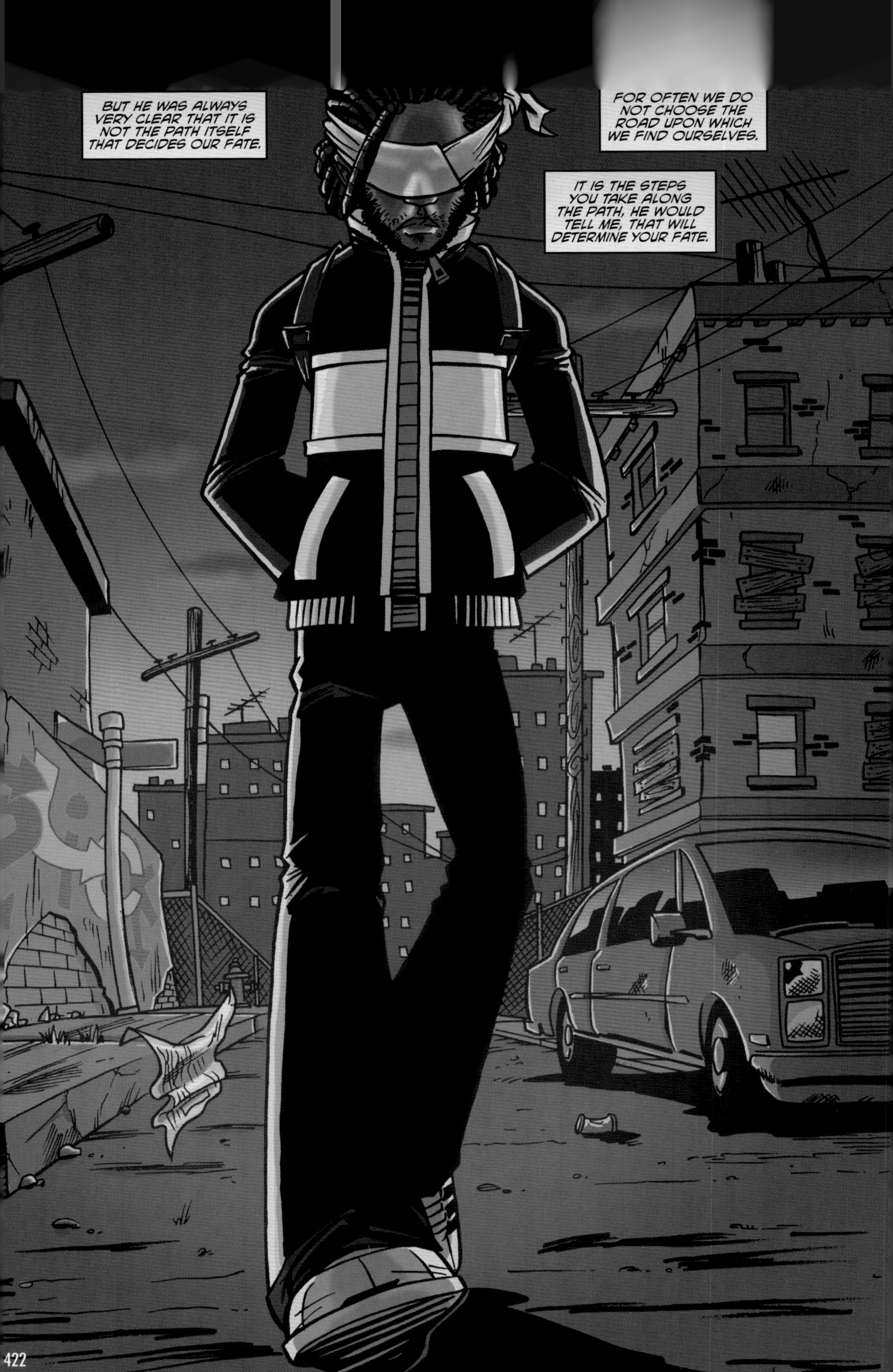
BUT HE WAS ALWAYS VERY CLEAR THAT IT IS NOT THE PATH ITSELF THAT DECIDES OUR FATE.
FOR OFTEN WE DO NOT CHOOSE THE ROAD UPON WHICH WE FIND OURSELVES.
IT IS THE STEPS YOU TAKE ALONG THE PATH, HE WOULD TELL ME, THAT WILL DETERMINE YOUR FATE.

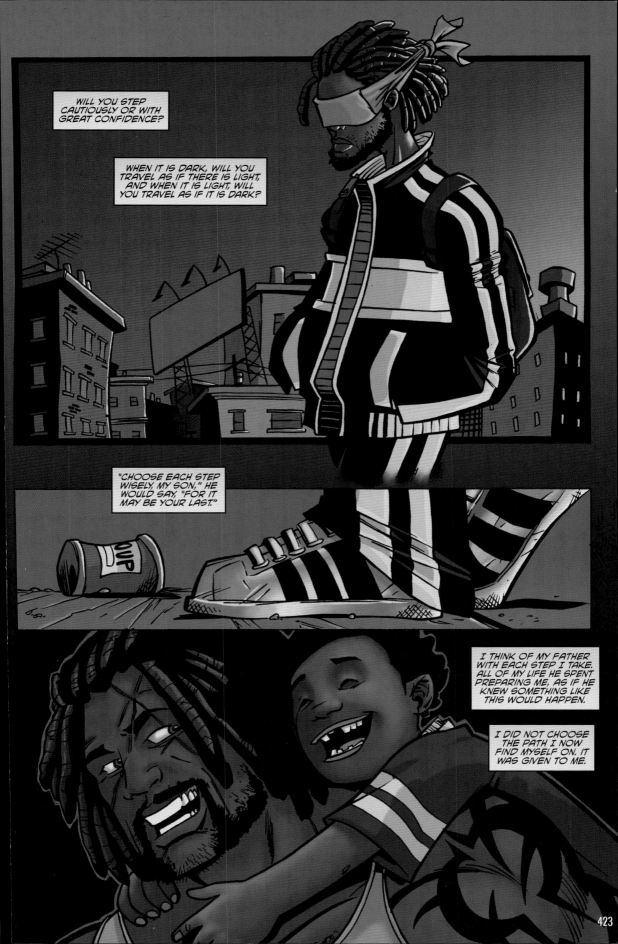

WILL YOU STEP CAUTIOUSLY OR WITH GREAT CONFIDENCE?

WHEN IT IS DARK, WILL YOU TRAVEL AS IF THERE IS LIGHT, AND WHEN IT IS LIGHT, WILL YOU TRAVEL AS IF IT IS DARK?

"CHOOSE EACH STEP WISELY, MY SON," HE WOULD SAY, "FOR IT MAY BE YOUR LAST."

I THINK OF MY FATHER WITH EACH STEP I TAKE. ALL OF MY LIFE HE SPENT PREPARING ME, AS IF HE KNEW SOMETHING LIKE THIS WOULD HAPPEN.

I DID NOT CHOOSE THE PATH I NOW FIND MYSELF ON. IT WAS GIVEN TO ME.

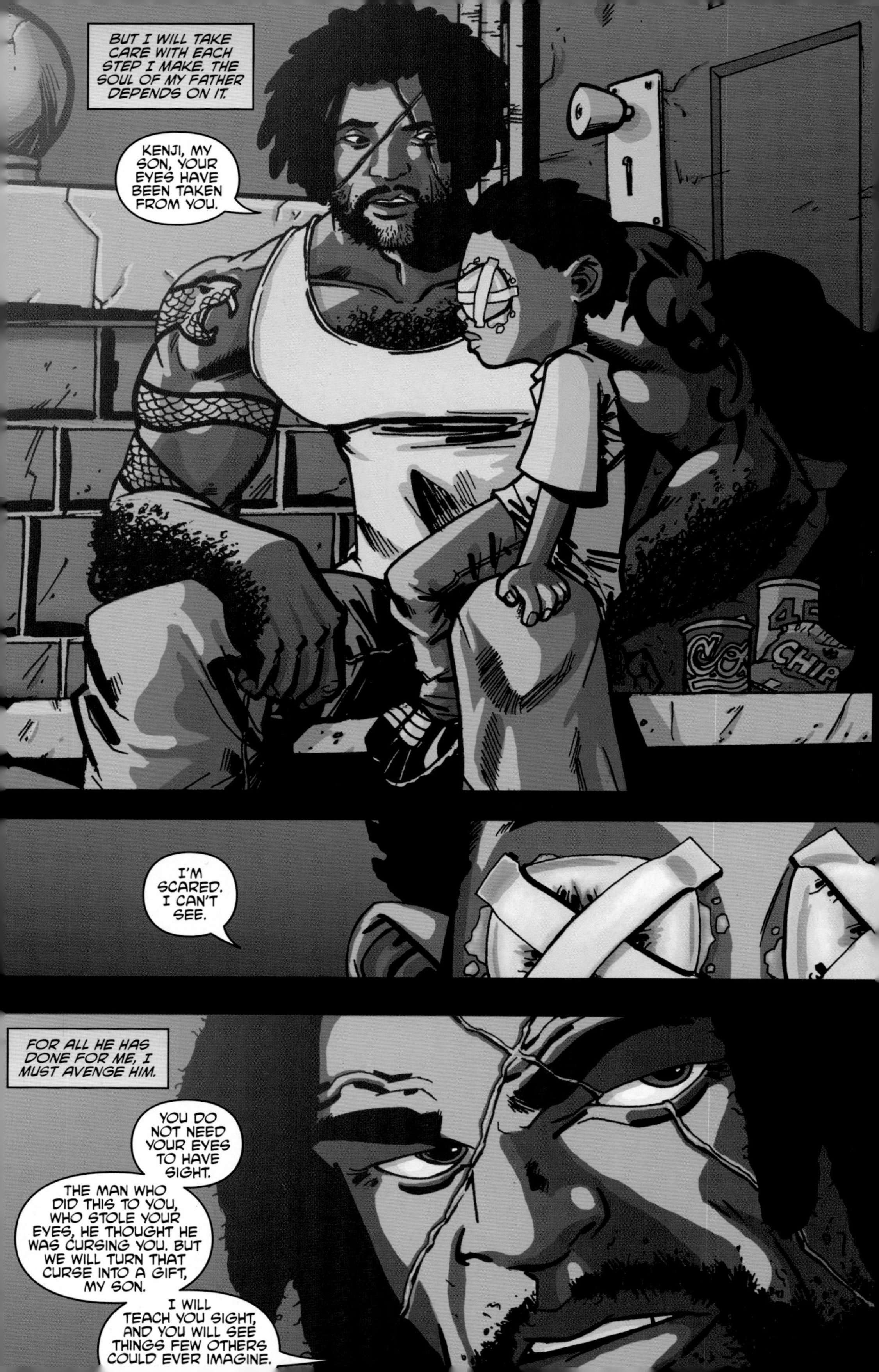
BUT I WILL TAKE CARE WITH EACH STEP I MAKE. THE SOUL OF MY FATHER DEPENDS ON IT.
KENJI, MY SON, YOUR EYES HAVE BEEN TAKEN FROM YOU.
I'M SCARED. I CAN'T SEE.
FOR ALL HE HAS DONE FOR ME, I MUST AVENGE HIM.
YOU DO NOT NEED YOUR EYES TO HAVE SIGHT.
THE MAN WHO DID THIS TO YOU, WHO STOLE YOUR EYES, HE THOUGHT HE WAS CURSING YOU. BUT WE WILL TURN THAT CURSE INTO A GIFT, MY SON.
I WILL TEACH YOU SIGHT, AND YOU WILL SEE THINGS FEW OTHERS COULD EVER IMAGINE.

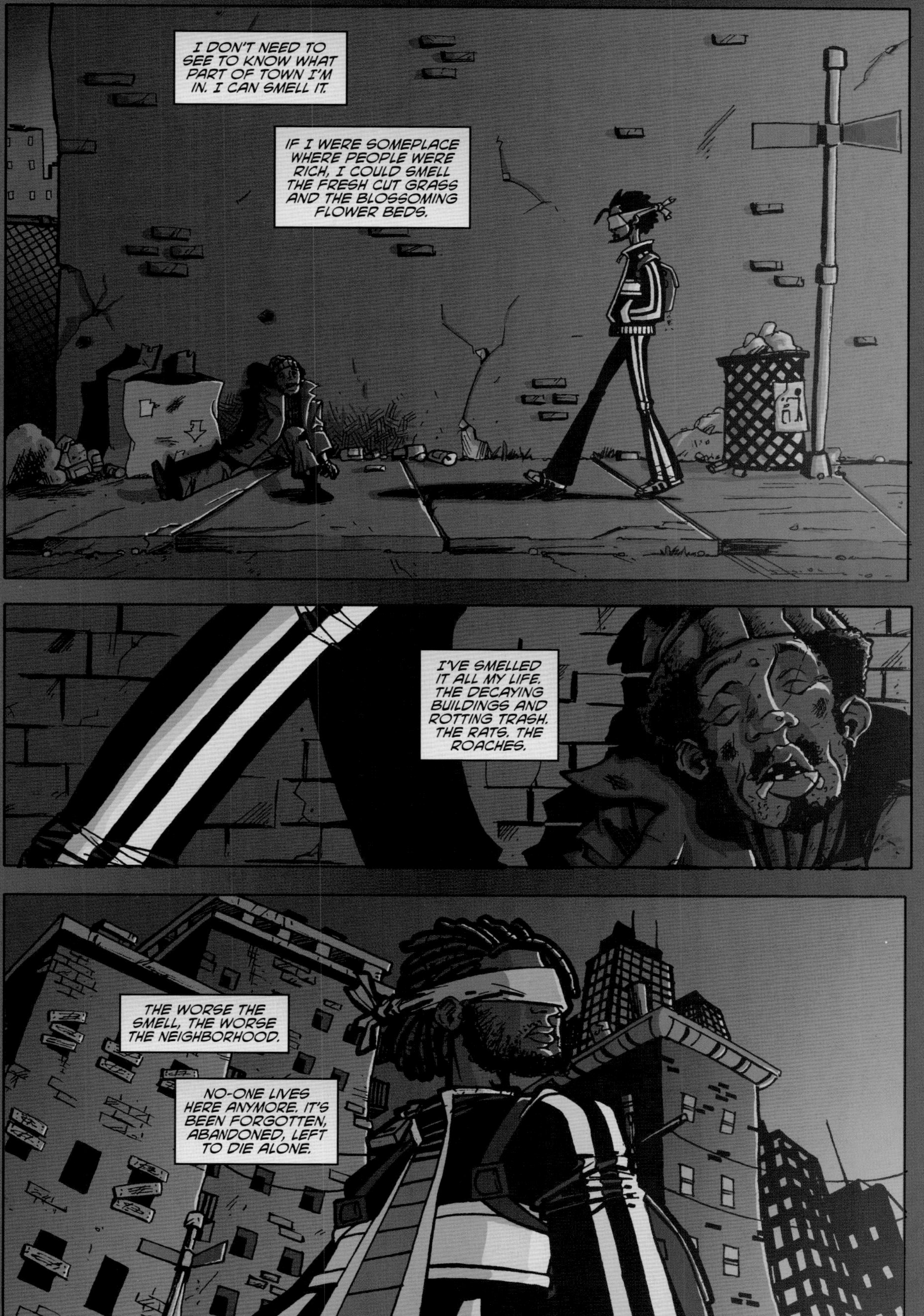
I DON'T NEED TO SEE TO KNOW WHAT PART OF TOWN I'M IN. I CAN SMELL IT.
IF I WERE SOMEPLACE WHERE PEOPLE WERE RICH, I COULD SMELL THE FRESH CUT GRASS AND THE BLOSSOMING FLOWER BEDS.
I'VE SMELLED IT ALL MY LIFE. THE DECAYING BUILDINGS AND ROTTING TRASH. THE RATS. THE ROACHES.
THE WORSE THE SMELL, THE WORSE THE NEIGHBORHOOD.
NO-ONE LIVES HERE ANYMORE. IT'S BEEN FORGOTTEN, ABANDONED, LEFT TO DIE ALONE.

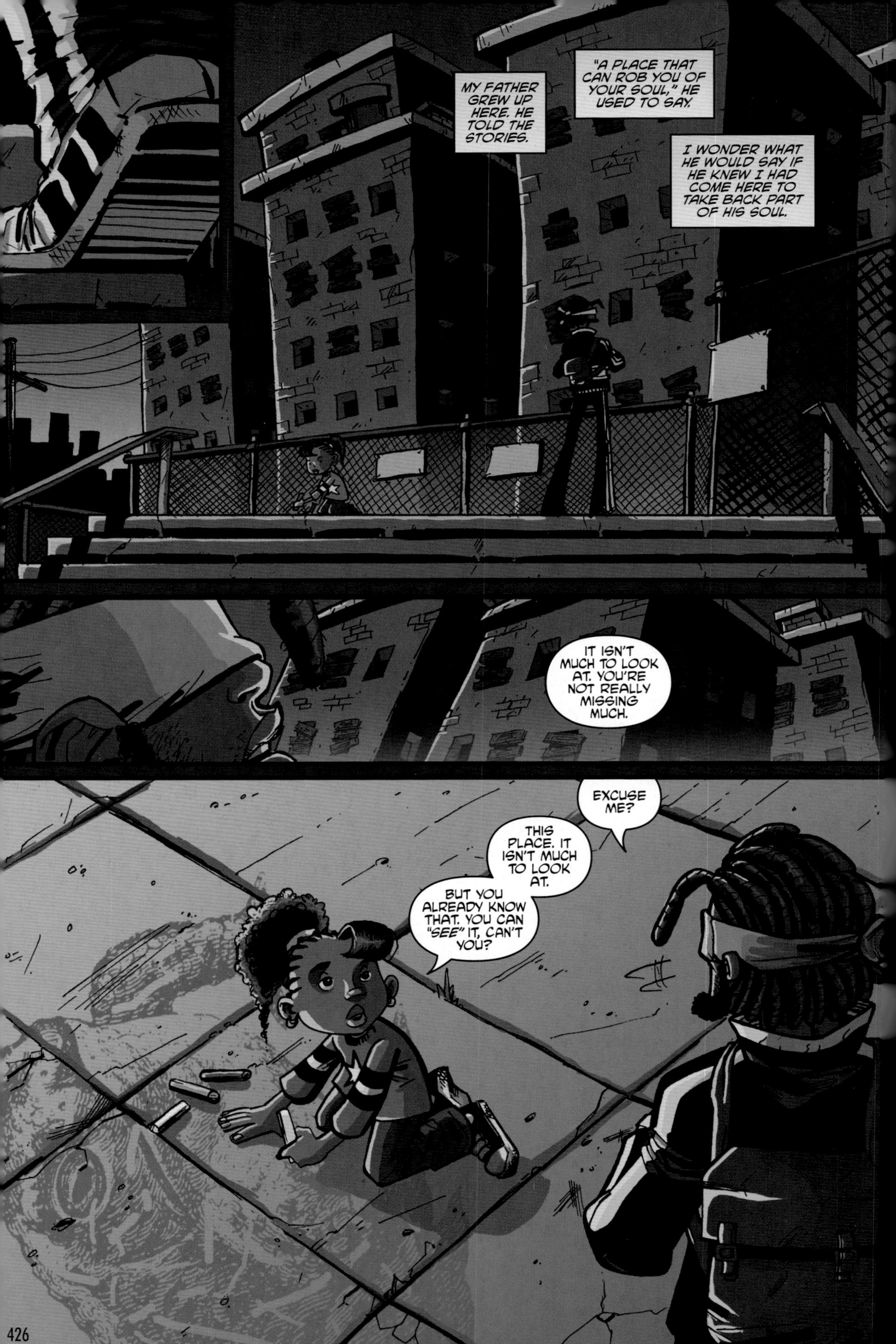
MY FATHER GREW UP HERE. HE TOLD THE STORIES.
"A PLACE THAT CAN ROB YOU OF YOUR SOUL," HE USED TO SAY.
I WONDER WHAT HE WOULD SAY IF HE KNEW I HAD COME HERE TO TAKE BACK PART OF HIS SOUL.
IT ISN'T MUCH TO LOOK AT. YOU'RE NOT REALLY MISSING MUCH.
EXCUSE ME?
THIS PLACE. IT ISN'T MUCH TO LOOK AT.
BUT YOU ALREADY KNOW THAT. YOU CAN "SEE" IT, CAN'T YOU?

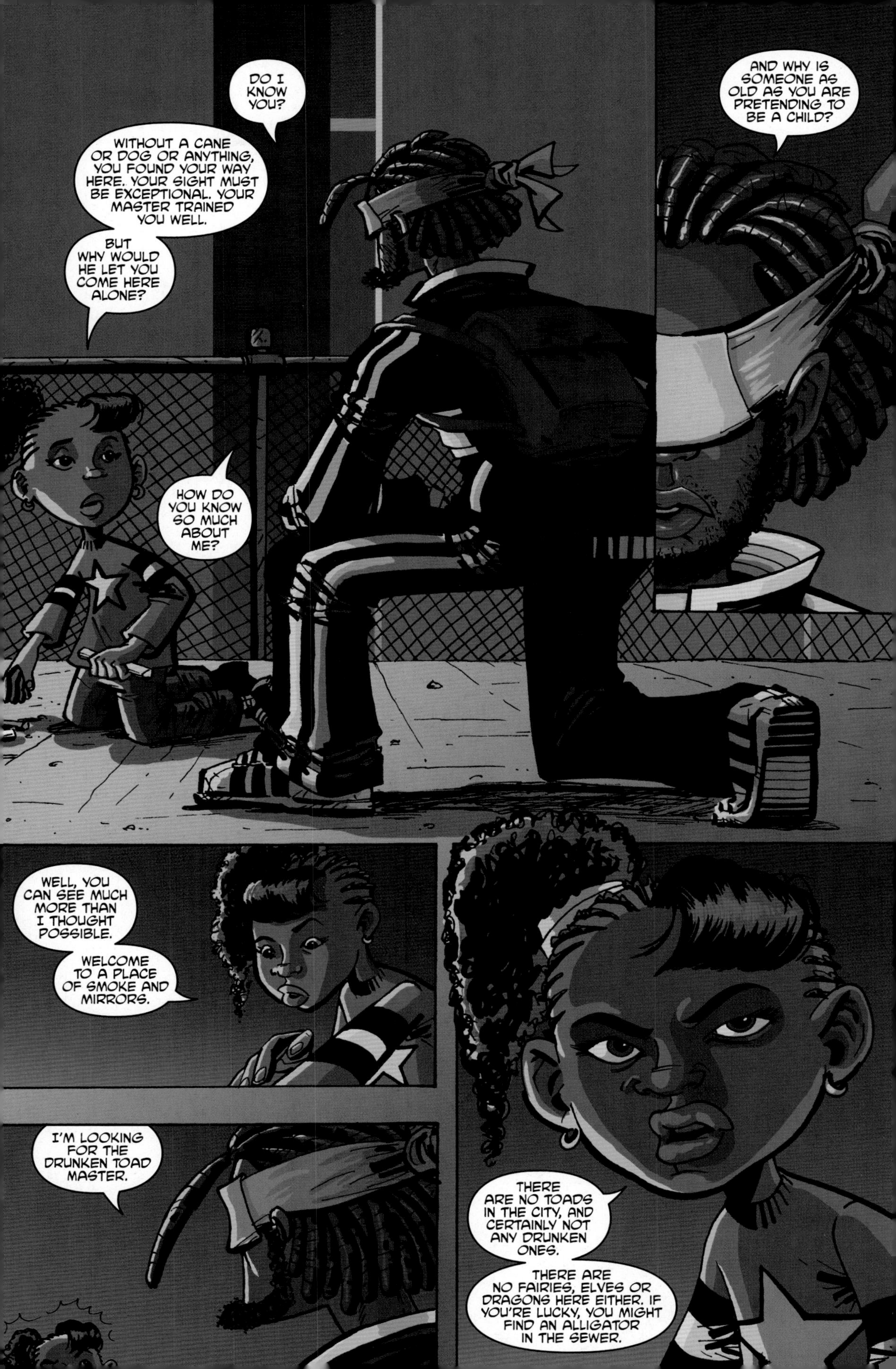
DO I KNOW YOU?
WITHOUT A CANE OR DOG OR ANYTHING, YOU FOUND YOUR WAY HERE. YOUR SIGHT MUST BE EXCEPTIONAL. YOUR MASTER TRAINED YOU WELL.
BUT WHY WOULD HE LET YOU COME HERE ALONE?
AND WHY IS SOMEONE AS OLD AS YOU ARE PRETENDING TO BE A CHILD?
HOW DO YOU KNOW SO MUCH ABOUT ME?
WELL, YOU CAN SEE MUCH MORE THAN I THOUGHT POSSIBLE.
WELCOME TO A PLACE OF SMOKE AND MIRRORS.
I'M LOOKING FOR THE DRUNKEN TOAD MASTER.
THERE ARE NO TOADS IN THE CITY, AND CERTAINLY NOT ANY DRUNKEN ONES.
THERE ARE NO FAIRIES, ELVES OR DRAGONS HERE EITHER. IF YOU'RE LUCKY, YOU MIGHT FIND AN ALLIGATOR IN THE SEWER.

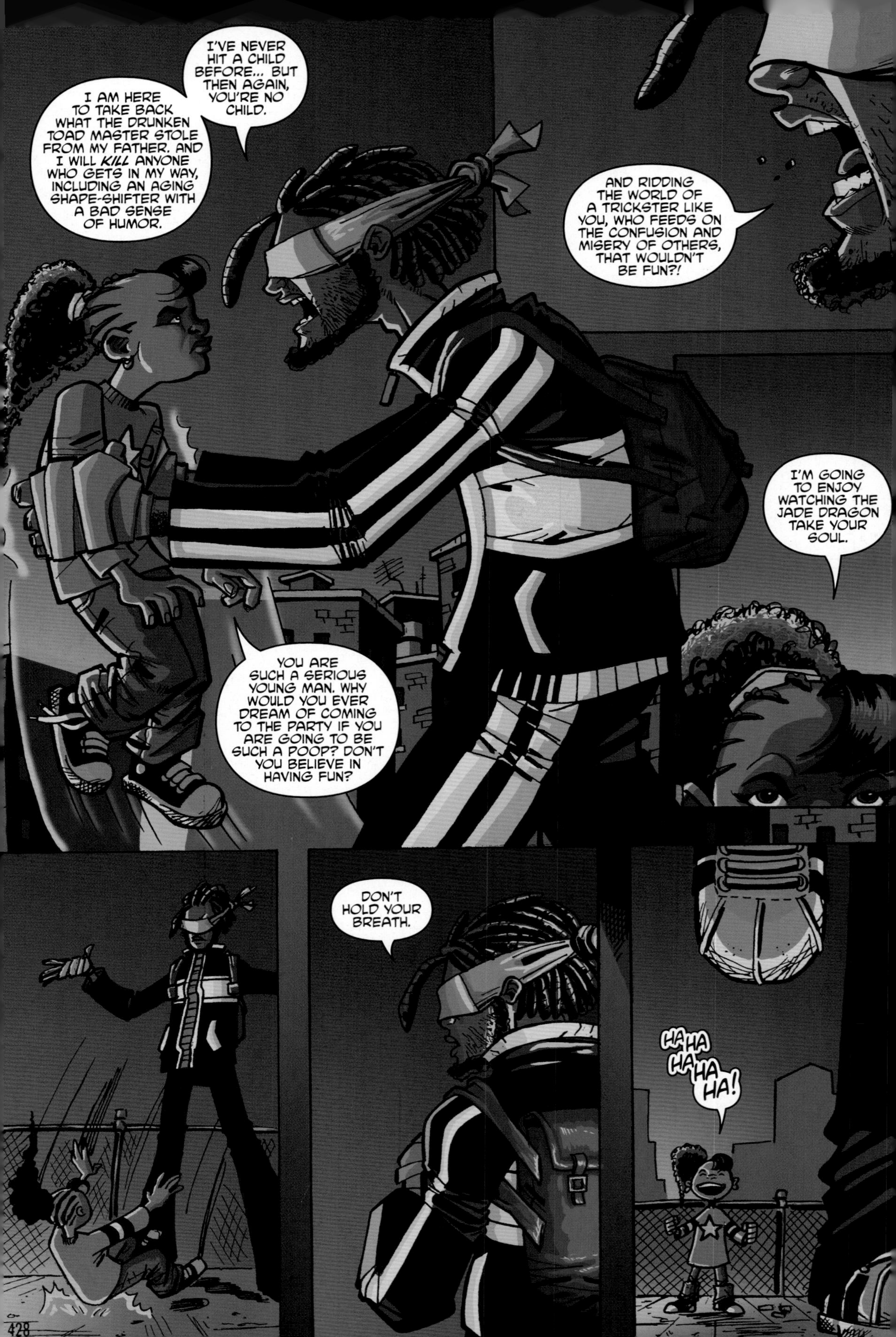
I AM HERE TO TAKE BACK WHAT THE DRUNKEN TOAD MASTER STOLE FROM MY FATHER. AND I WILL KILL ANYONE WHO GETS IN MY WAY, INCLUDING AN AGING SHAPE-SHIFTER WITH A BAD SENSE OF HUMOR.
I'VE NEVER HIT A CHILD BEFORE... BUT THEN AGAIN, YOU'RE NO CHILD.
AND RIDDING THE WORLD OF A TRICKSTER LIKE YOU, WHO FEEDS ON THE CONFUSION AND MISERY OF OTHERS, THAT WOULDN'T BE FUN?!
I'M GOING TO ENJOY WATCHING THE JADE DRAGON TAKE YOUR SOUL.
YOU ARE SUCH A SERIOUS YOUNG MAN. WHY WOULD YOU EVER DREAM OF COMING TO THE PARTY IF YOU ARE GOING TO BE SUCH A POOP? DON'T YOU BELIEVE IN HAVING FUN?
DON'T HOLD YOUR BREATH.
HA HA HA HA HA!

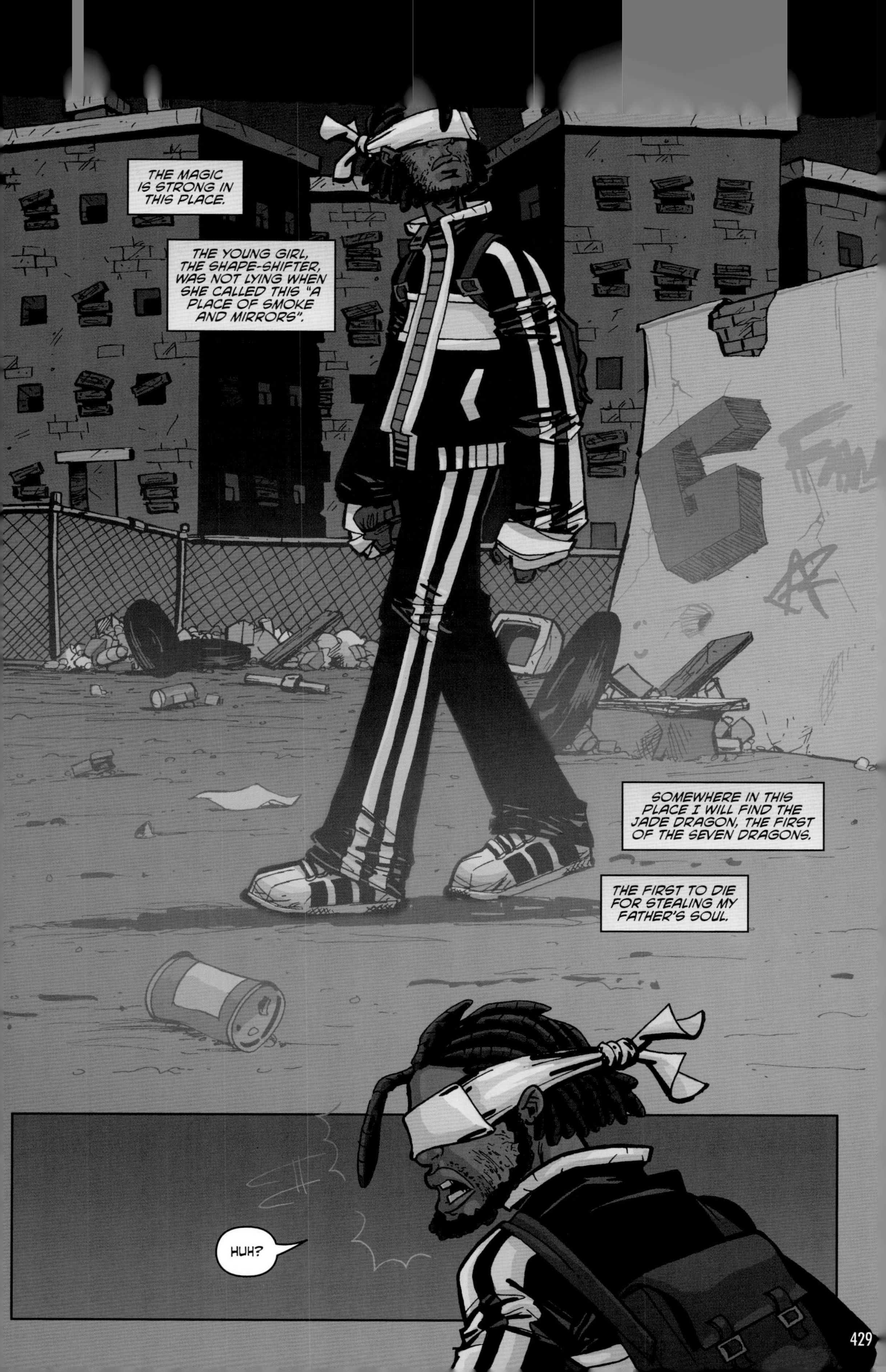
THE MAGIC IS STRONG IN THIS PLACE.
THE YOUNG GIRL, THE SHAPE-SHIFTER, WAS NOT LYING WHEN SHE CALLED THIS "A PLACE OF SMOKE AND MIRRORS".
SOMEWHERE IN THIS PLACE I WILL FIND THE JADE DRAGON, THE FIRST OF THE SEVEN DRAGONS.
THE FIRST TO DIE FOR STEALING MY FATHER'S SOUL.
HUH?

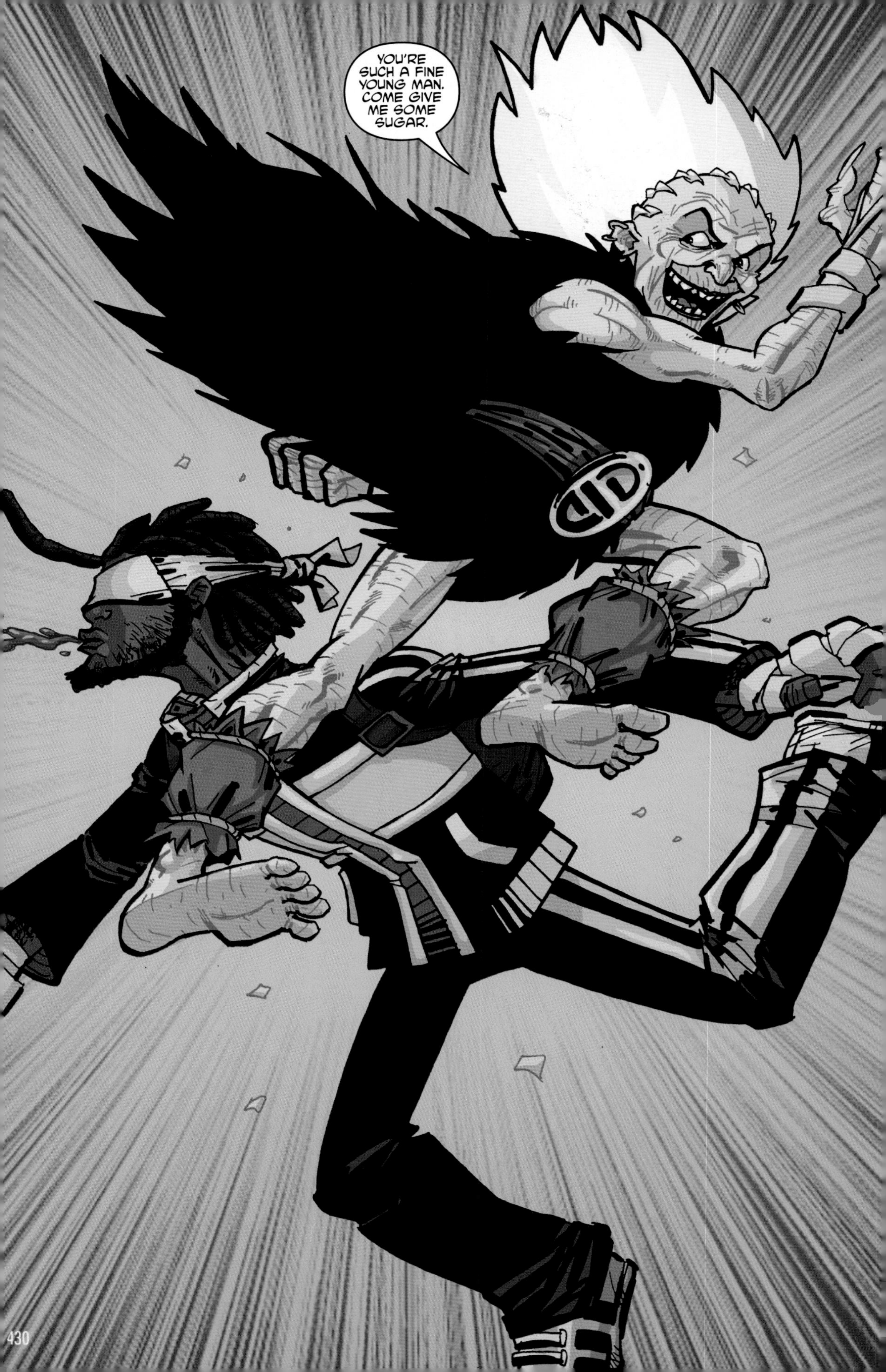
YOU'RE SUCH A FINE YOUNG MAN. COME GIVE ME SOME SUGAR.

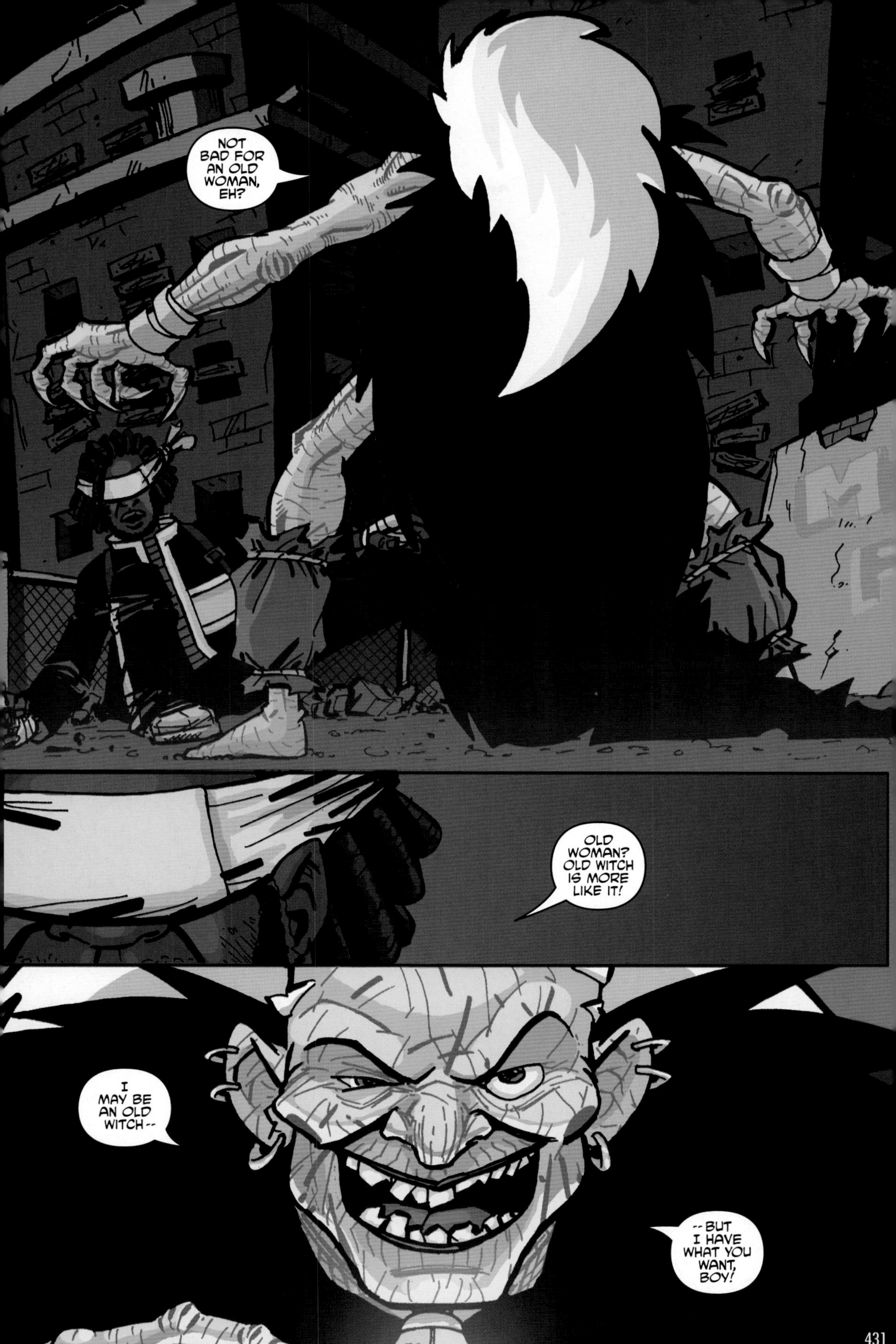
NOT BAD FOR AN OLD WOMAN, EH?
OLD WOMAN? OLD WITCH IS MORE LIKE IT!
I MAY BE AN OLD WITCH--
--BUT I HAVE WHAT YOU WANT, BOY!

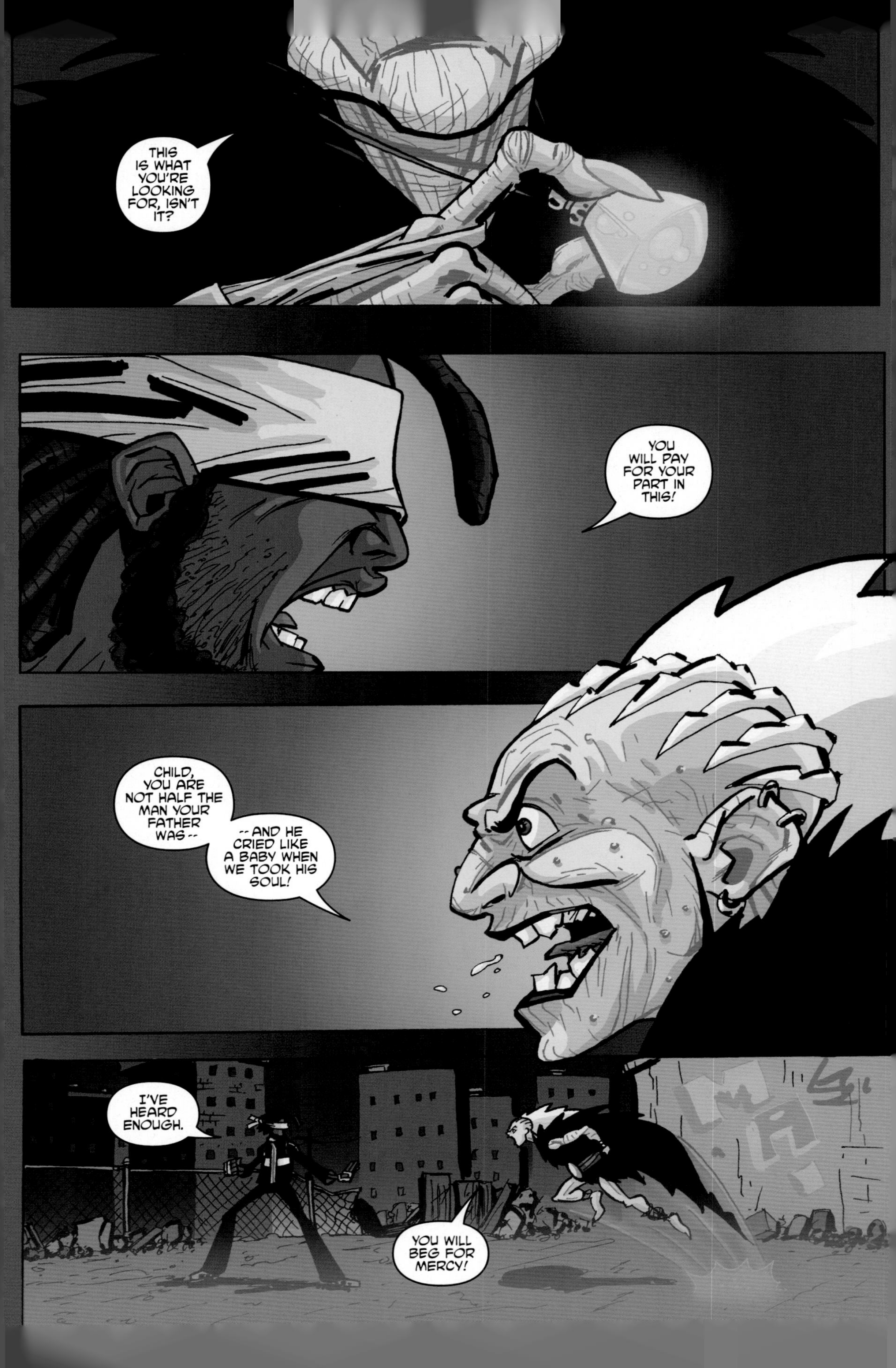

THIS IS WHAT YOU'RE LOOKING FOR, ISN'T IT?
YOU WILL PAY FOR YOUR PART IN THIS!
CHILD, YOU ARE NOT HALF THE MAN YOUR FATHER WAS--
--AND HE CRIED LIKE A BABY WHEN WE TOOK HIS SOUL!
I'VE HEARD ENOUGH.
YOU WILL BEG FOR MERCY!

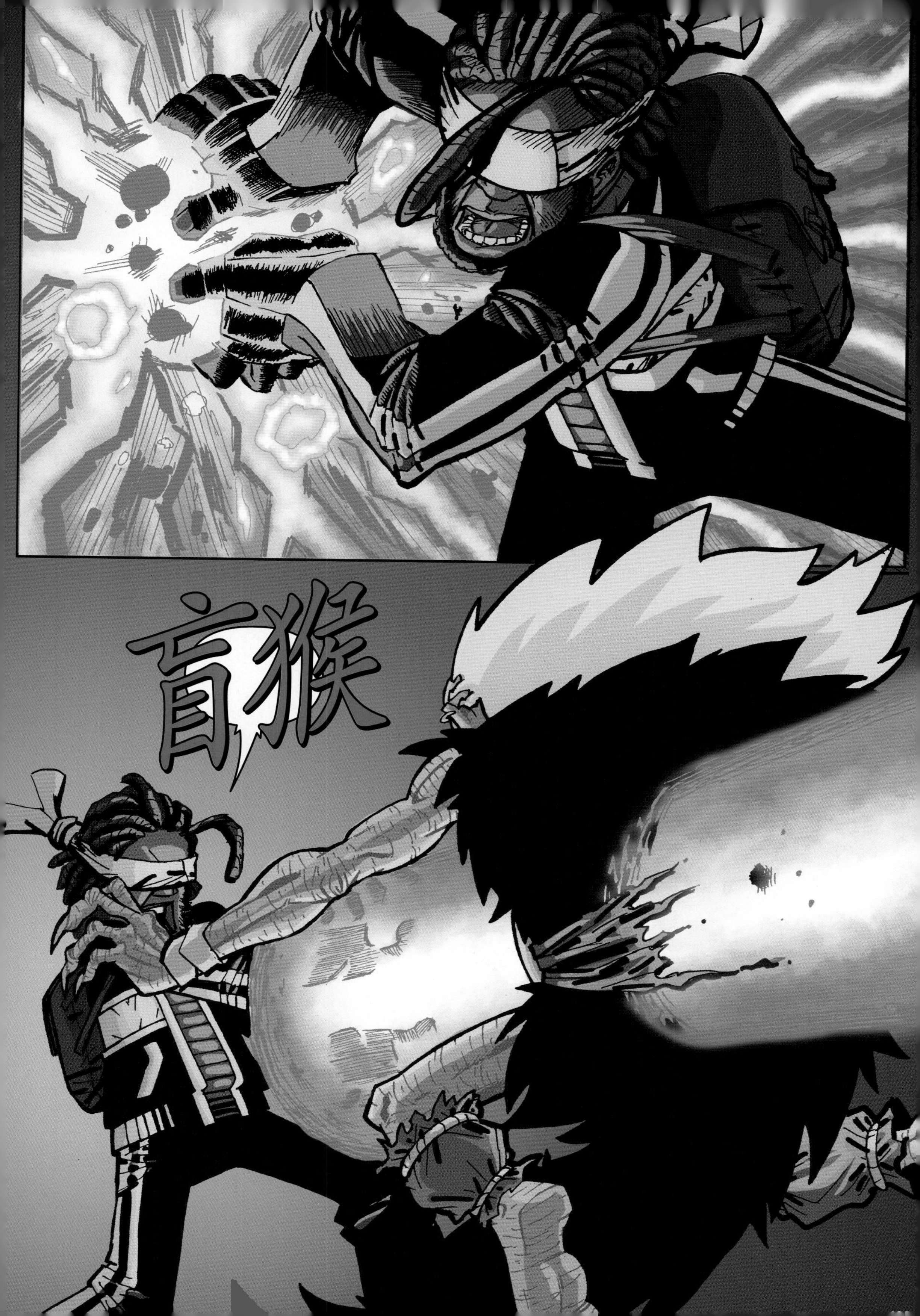
盲猴

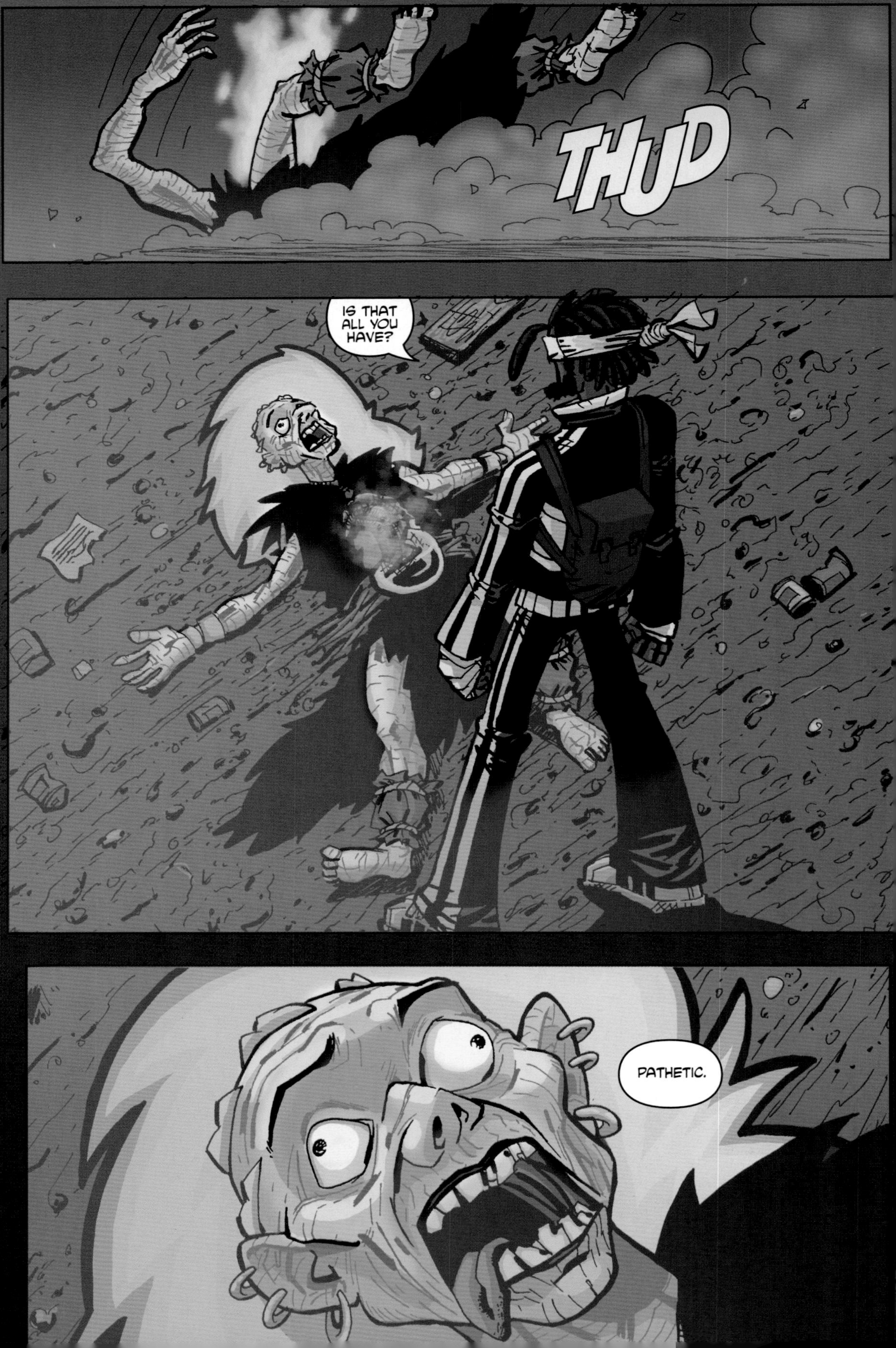
THUD
IS THAT ALL YOU HAVE?
PATHETIC.

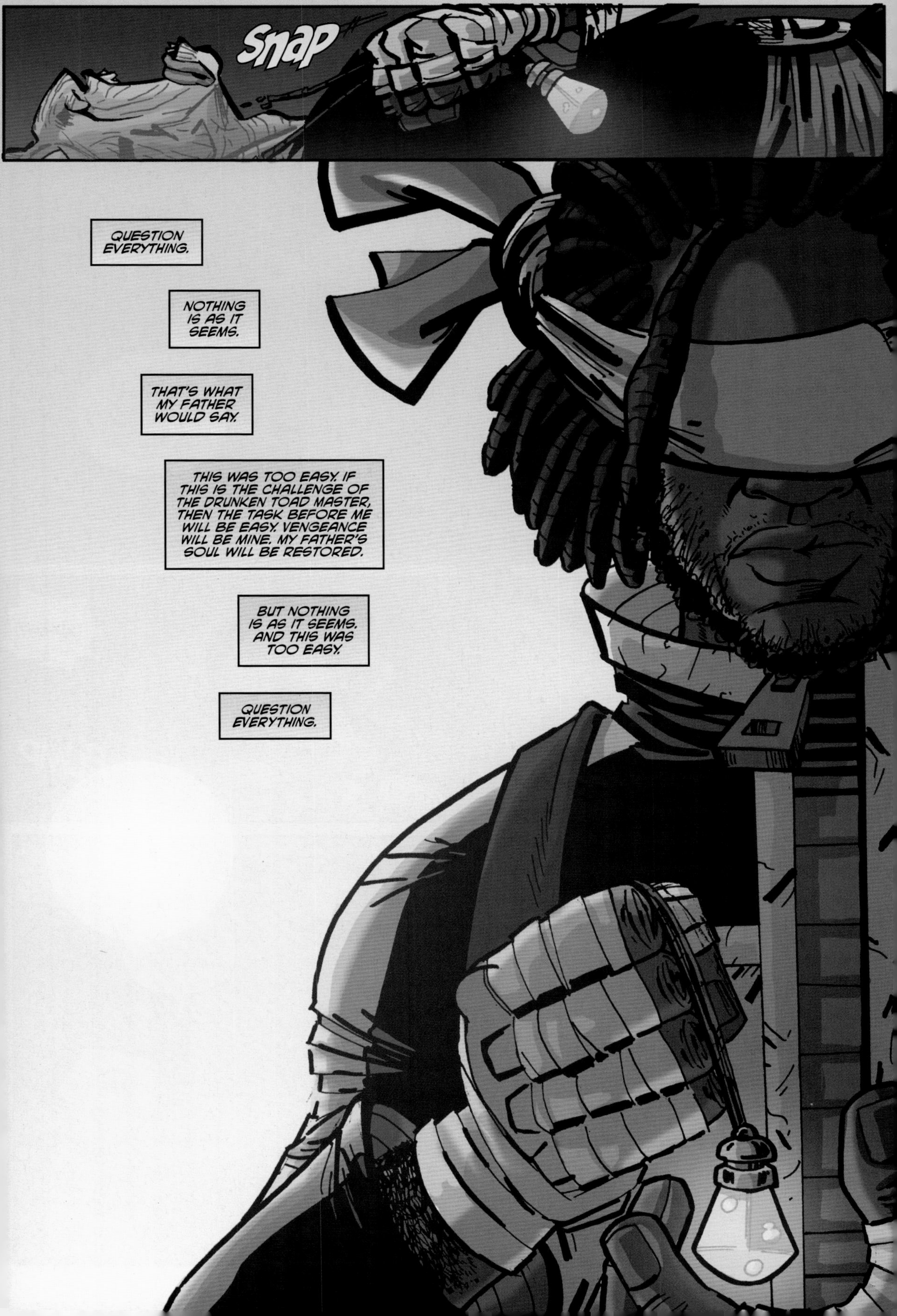
SNAP
QUESTION EVERYTHING.
NOTHING IS AS IT SEEMS.
THAT'S WHAT MY FATHER WOULD SAY.
THIS WAS TOO EASY. IF THIS IS THE CHALLENGE OF THE DRUNKEN TOAD MASTER, THEN THE TASK BEFORE ME WILL BE EASY. VENGEANCE WILL BE MINE. MY FATHER'S SOUL WILL BE RESTORED.
BUT NOTHING IS AS IT SEEMS. AND THIS WAS TOO EASY.
QUESTION EVERYTHING.

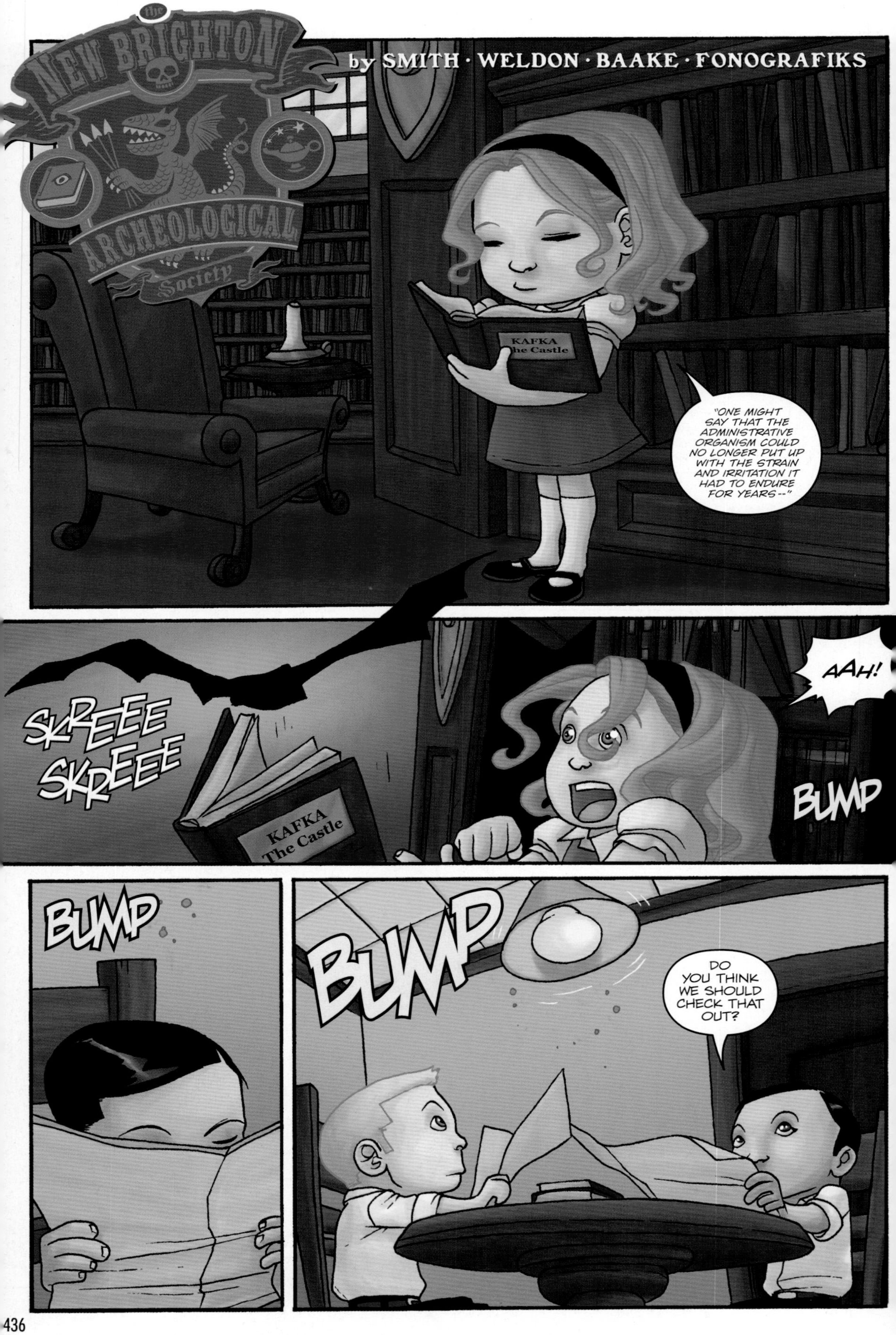
the NEW BRIGHTON ARCHEOLOGICAL Society
by SMITH · WELDON · BAAKE · FONOGRAFIKS
KAFKA The Castle
"ONE MIGHT SAY THAT THE ADMINISTRATIVE ORGANISM COULD NO LONGER PUT UP WITH THE STRAIN AND IRRITATION IT HAD TO ENDURE FOR YEARS--"
SKREEEE SKREEEE
KAFKA The Castle
AAH!
BUMP
BUMP
BUMP
DO YOU THINK WE SHOULD CHECK THAT OUT?

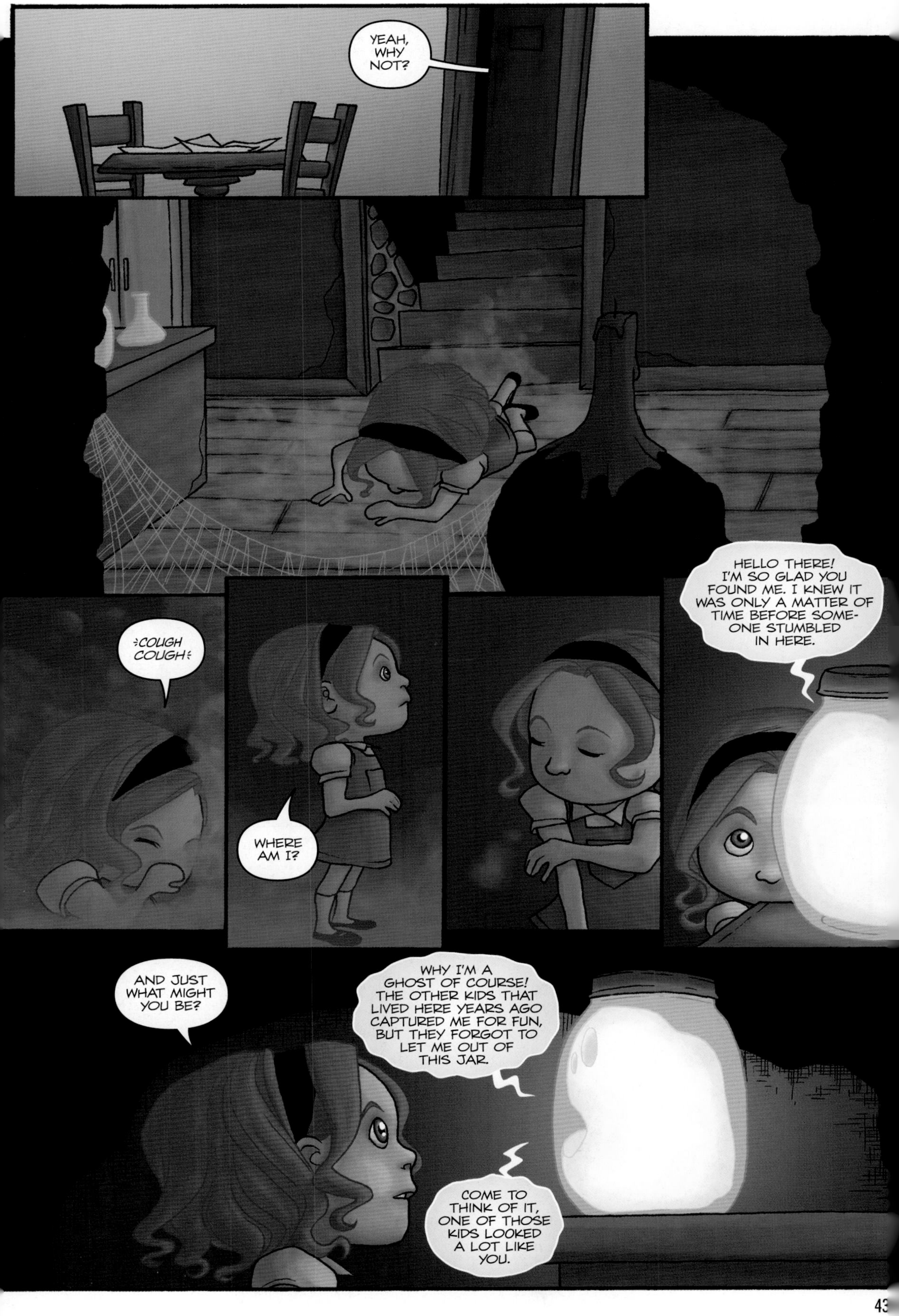
YEAH, WHY NOT?
≑COUGH COUGH≑
WHERE AM I?
HELLO THERE! I'M SO GLAD YOU FOUND ME. I KNEW IT WAS ONLY A MATTER OF TIME BEFORE SOME-ONE STUMBLED IN HERE.
AND JUST WHAT MIGHT YOU BE?
WHY I'M A GHOST OF COURSE! THE OTHER KIDS THAT LIVED HERE YEARS AGO CAPTURED ME FOR FUN, BUT THEY FORGOT TO LET ME OUT OF THIS JAR.
COME TO THINK OF IT, ONE OF THOSE KIDS LOOKED A LOT LIKE YOU.

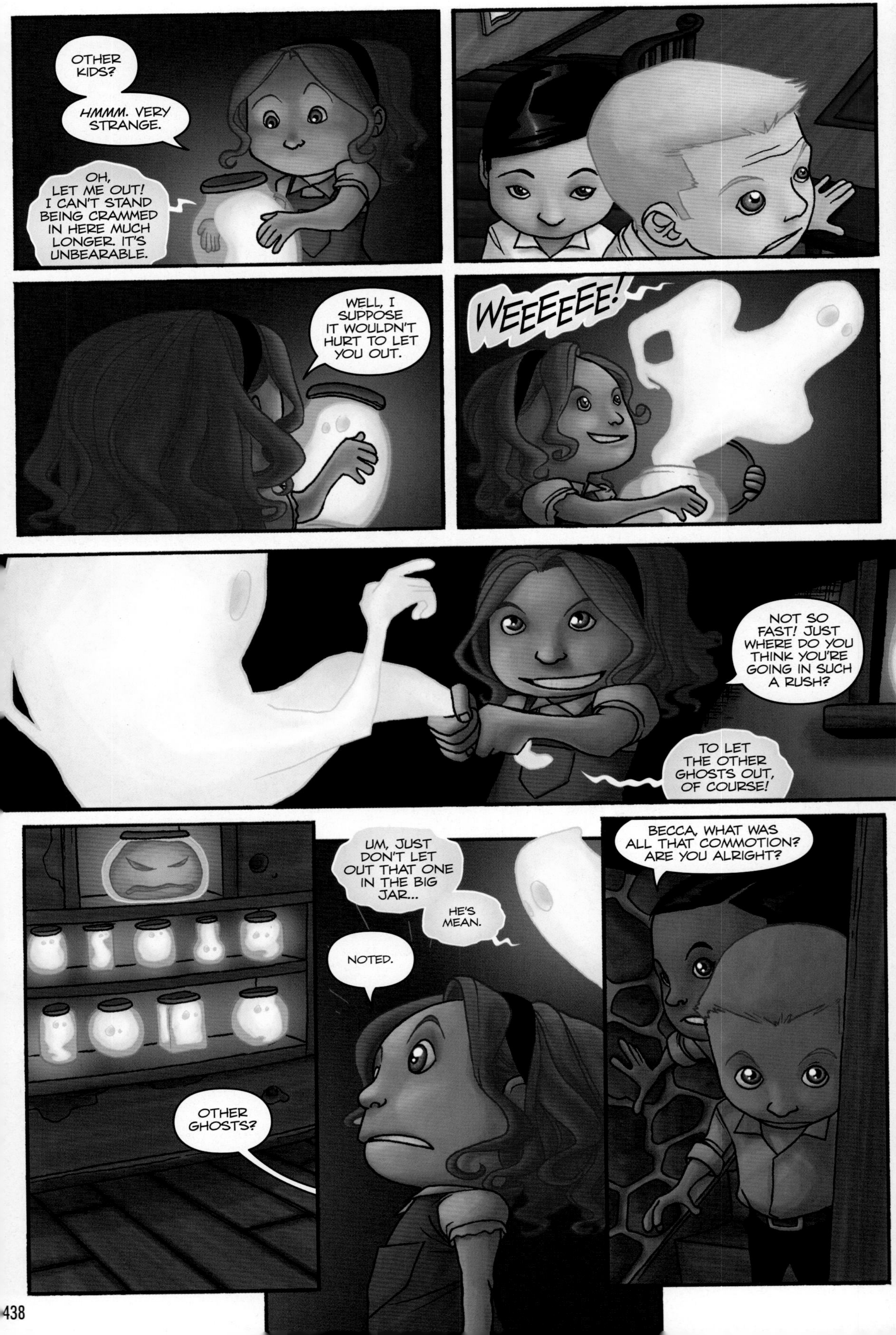
OTHER KIDS?
HMMM. VERY STRANGE.
OH, LET ME OUT! I CAN'T STAND BEING CRAMMED IN HERE MUCH LONGER. IT'S UNBEARABLE.
WELL, I SUPPOSE IT WOULDN'T HURT TO LET YOU OUT.
WEEEEEE!
NOT SO FAST! JUST WHERE DO YOU THINK YOU'RE GOING IN SUCH A RUSH?
TO LET THE OTHER GHOSTS OUT, OF COURSE!
OTHER GHOSTS?
UM, JUST DON'T LET OUT THAT ONE IN THE BIG JAR...
HE'S MEAN.
NOTED.
BECCA, WHAT WAS ALL THAT COMMOTION? ARE YOU ALRIGHT?

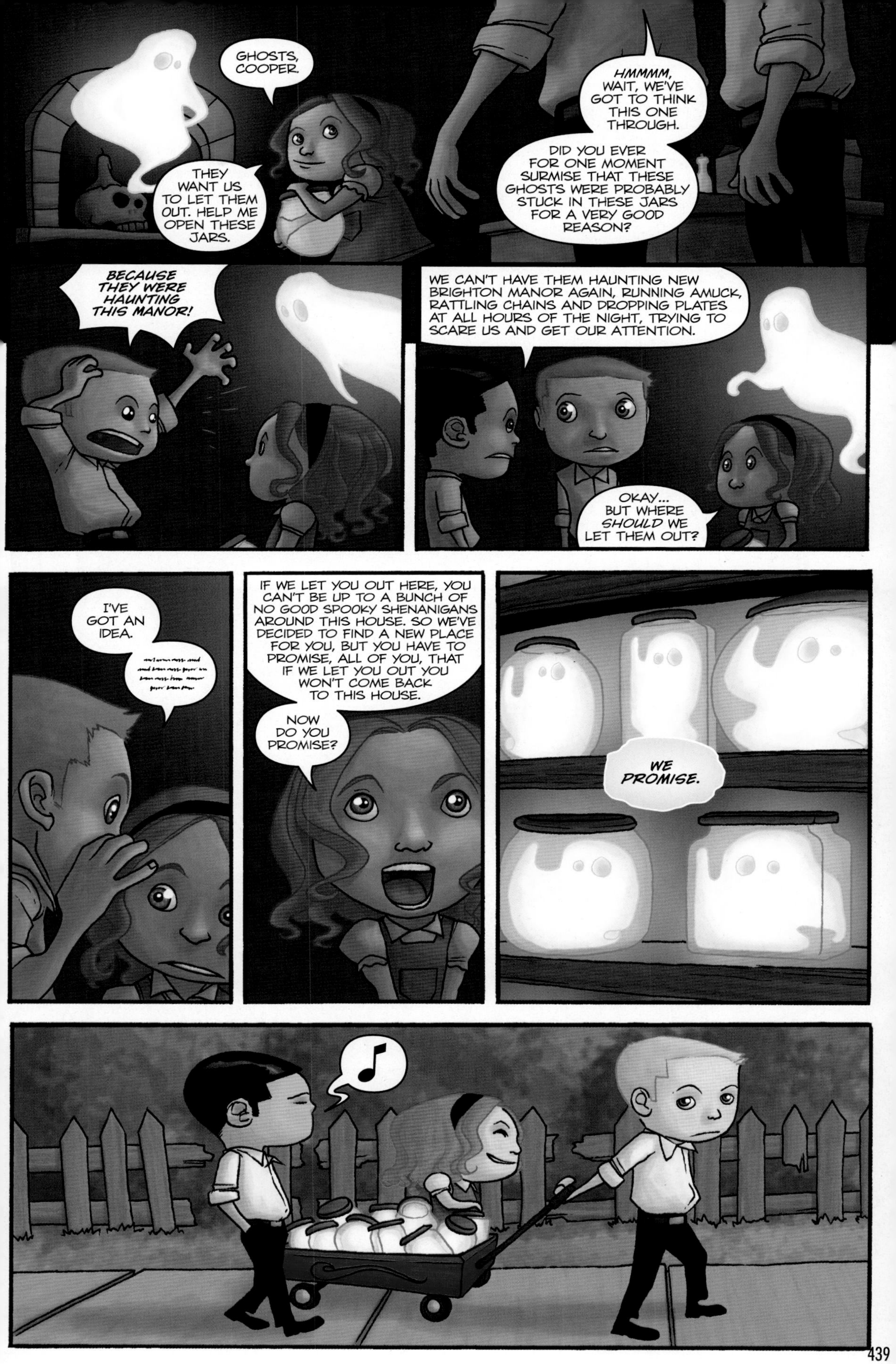

GHOSTS, COOPER.
THEY WANT US TO LET THEM OUT. HELP ME OPEN THESE JARS.
HMMMM, WAIT, WE'VE GOT TO THINK THIS ONE THROUGH.
DID YOU EVER FOR ONE MOMENT SURMISE THAT THESE GHOSTS WERE PROBABLY STUCK IN THESE JARS FOR A VERY GOOD REASON?
BECAUSE THEY WERE HAUNTING THIS MANOR!
WE CAN'T HAVE THEM HAUNTING NEW BRIGHTON MANOR AGAIN, RUNNING AMUCK, RATTLING CHAINS AND DROPPING PLATES AT ALL HOURS OF THE NIGHT, TRYING TO SCARE US AND GET OUR ATTENTION.
OKAY... BUT WHERE SHOULD WE LET THEM OUT?
I'VE GOT AN IDEA.
IF WE LET YOU OUT HERE, YOU CAN'T BE UP TO A BUNCH OF NO GOOD SPOOKY SHENANIGANS AROUND THIS HOUSE. SO WE'VE DECIDED TO FIND A NEW PLACE FOR YOU, BUT YOU HAVE TO PROMISE, ALL OF YOU, THAT IF WE LET YOU OUT YOU WON'T COME BACK TO THIS HOUSE.
NOW DO YOU PROMISE?
WE PROMISE.

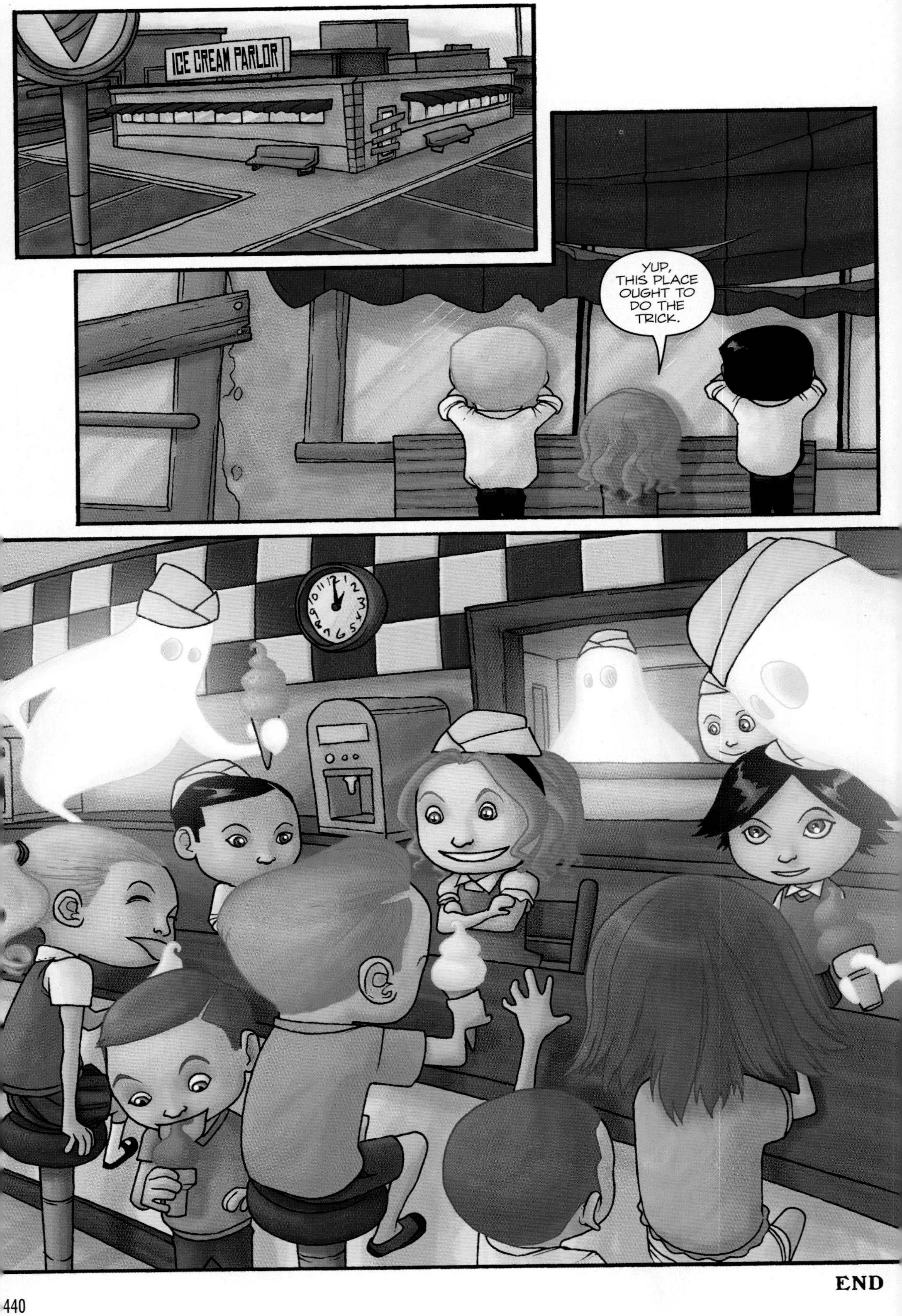
ICE CREAM PARLOR
YUP, THIS PLACE OUGHT TO DO THE TRICK.

END

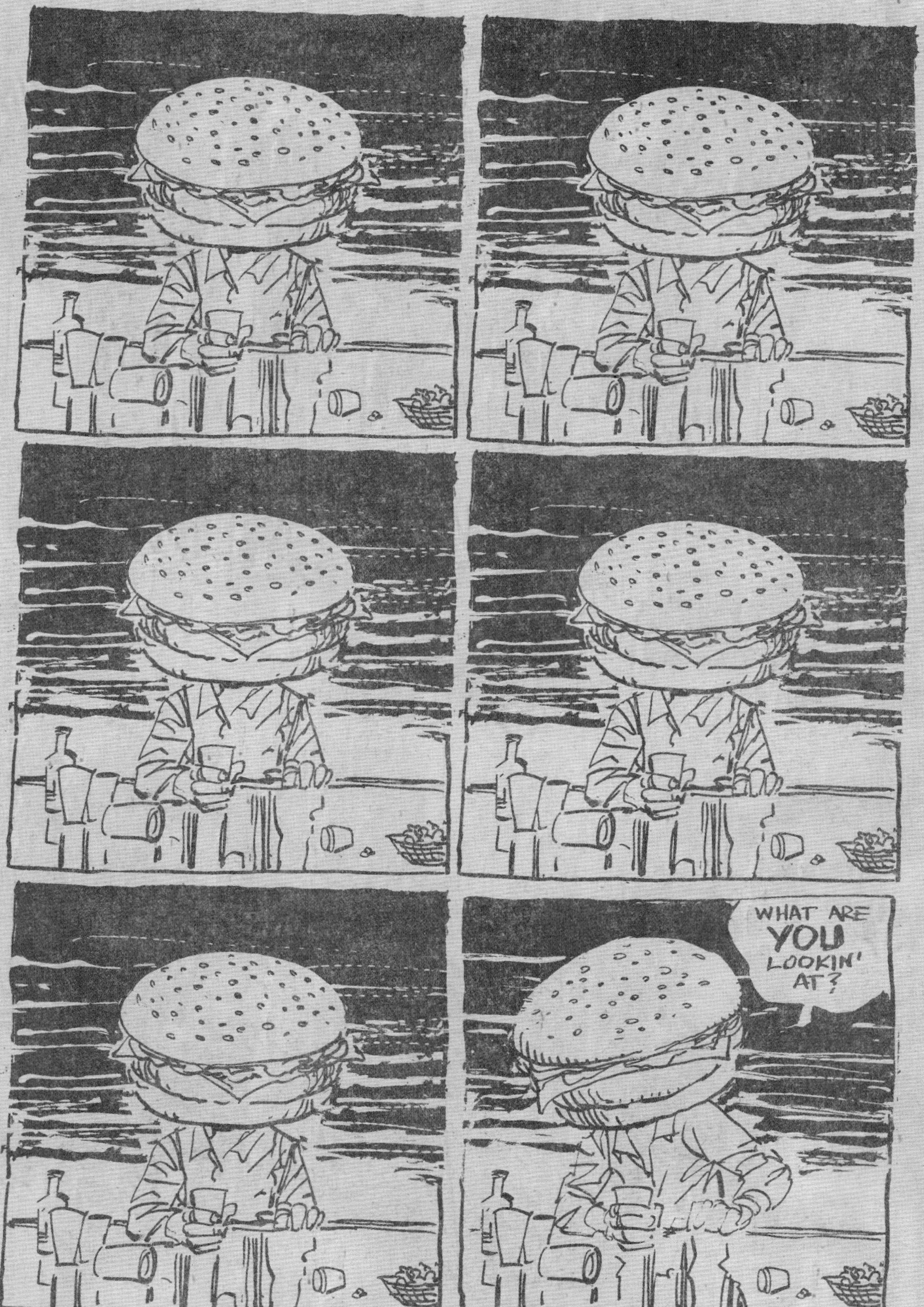
WHAT ARE YOU LOOKIN' AT?

AFTERWORD: GRAPHIC MUSIC

WRITTEN BY JOE KEATINGE

For years, my buddy Mark Andrew Smith and I only talked about two things:

Comics and music.

This came to a head about a year ago when Mark called with an idea that sent me flying through a wall.

He suggested combining our obsessions into an anthology.

The idea was to spread our love of comics by firing off artistic ammunition targeted at people we thought should enjoy them as much as we do.

A popgun, if you will.

And so, POPGUN, VOL 1 was born.

We were given the opportunity to include a variety of artists, writers and cartoonists. Each one with their own distinct style and voice, adding their own track to this mixtape of a graphic novel.

These folks are the reason this medium gets more and more fascinating every day. Each one is producing such fantastic work on their own that they no doubt will be able to accomplish something phenomenal by working together - being featured together.

There's never been a better time to be a fan.

If you're not an avid comic book reader, I really appreciate you trying something new and hope this book inspires you to read more.

For the longtime fans, we hope you enjoyed these looks into the previously secret parts of your favorite creators minds and a look into what the future holds from the current unknowns.

Huge thanks are due to each and every contributor. You gals and guys are the reason this book exists.

It may be hyperbolic to say you're the reason the state of the art will continue to grow leaps and bounds.

I hope to have all of you on board in future volumes. Huge special thanks are due to Eric Stephenson and Erik Larsen, who appreciated our vision enough to publish the book.

Thank you for reading.

Joe Keatinge
San Francisco, CA
10-07

DESIGNED BY VAL NUNEZ

Biographies

Mike & Laura Allred are the creative team behind MADMAN ATOMIC COMICS.

Anjin Anhut draws comics and concept art.

Kris Anka is interning for WB and attending CalArts.

Jacob Baake is a freelance artist and colorist.

Chuck BB is the co-creator and artist of BLACK METAL, published by Oni Press.

Ph'nglui mglw'nafh **Nate Bellegarde** Kentucky wgah'nagl fhtagn. Ia! Ia! Nate fhtagn!

Mike Bullock is the writer of LIONS, TIGERS & BEARS, and THE GIMOLES.

Benito J. Cereno III is the writer of TALES FROM THE BULLY PULPIT, HECTOR PLASM, and INVINCIBLE PRESENTS: ATOM EVE.

Brian Churilla is the artist of THE ENGINEER.

Paul Conrad works in animation and is an illustrator.

Graham Corcoran wrote "Triple Scoop," his first foray into the world of published comics.

Bill Crabtree is the colorist for such titles as INVINCIBLE and FIREBREATHER.

David Crosland is the artist behind SCARFACE: SCARRED FOR LIFE and EVERYBODY'S DEAD.

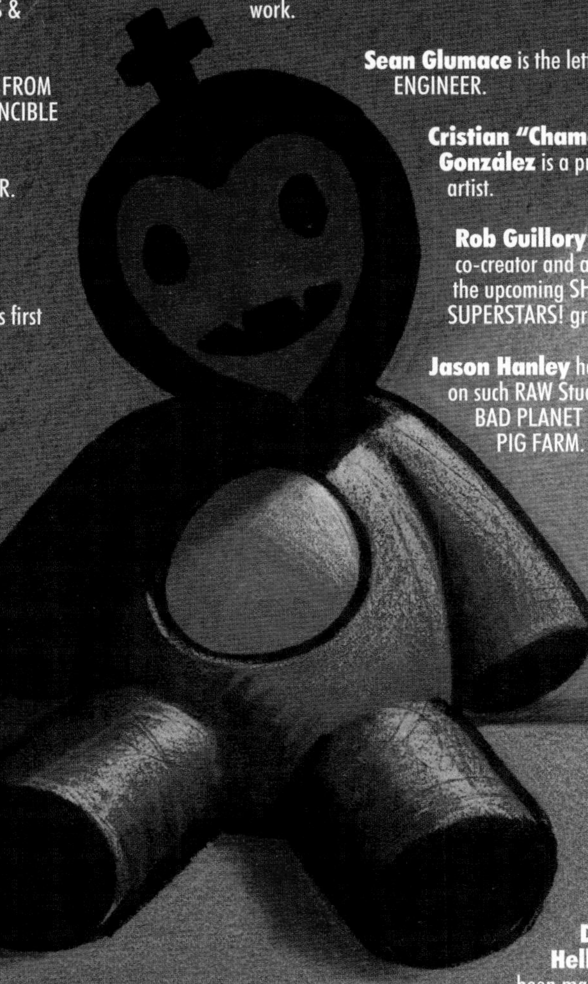

Toby Cypress is writing and illustrating his upcoming mini-series RODD RACER.

Jeremy Dale illustrates G.I. JOE for Hasbro, MISERABLE DASTARDS for 803 Studios/Dial C for Comics, and ABSOLUTE ZEROES for Heroforge.

Eric Derian is the colorist of two comic books featuring "Les enquetes des detectives Harley & Davidson."

Nick Derrington has illustrated X-STATIX, HAWAIIAN DICK, and MADMAN, among many others.

Marcelo Di Chiara is the artist for Marvel Comics' SPIDER-MAN FAMILY #1 and IRON-MAN/POWER PACK.

Adrian Dominguez is the creator of "Ellie Saves the World."

Coleman Engle attends the Savannah College of Art and Design.

Julio Figueroa is the writer of "Solomon Finch."

Joe Flood is now twenty-seven, draws comics, and lives in Brooklyn.

Fonografiks is a studio specializing in digital lettering, graphic design, and pre-press production for comic books.

Chris French wrote "Triple Scoop," his first published work.

Sean Glumace is the letterer of THE ENGINEER.

Cristian "Chamakoso" González is a professional artist.

Rob Guillory is the co-creator and artist of the upcoming SHORTBUS SUPERSTARS! graphic novel.

Jason Hanley has worked on such RAW Studios titles as BAD PLANET and ALIEN PIG FARM.

Danny Hellman has been making art for publication since 1988 and has worked for a wide variety of clients, including Time, Newsweek, Sports Illustrated, Fortune, Forbes, The Wall Street Journal, FHM, Guitar World, New York Press, and countless others.

Shepherd Hendrix is the artist behind the Eisner-nominated STAGGER LEE.

Jonathan Hickman is the creator of THE NIGHTLY NEWS and PAX ROMANA.

Dan Hipp is the co-creator/artist of THE AMAZING JOY BUZZARDS.

Josh Hoye is a professional illustrator graduating from Ringling College of Art and Design.

Derek Hunter is the writer and artist of PIRATE CLUB for Slave Labor Graphics and the upcoming MANNY GOLDEN IS: GROUNDED IN SPACE.

Joëlle Jones has worked for Viz, Image, DC/Vertigo, and Dark Horse.

Joe Keatinge is the PR & Marketing Coordinator of Image Comics.

D.J. Kirkbride is the writer of "Soulless, Man Without A Soul," his first published comic.

Sean Konot has lettered comics for all the major companies, including Image, Marvel and Dark Horse.

Andy Kuhn is the co-creator/artist of FIREBREATHER.

Erik Larsen is the creator of SAVAGE DRAGON and publisher of Image Comics.

Jason Latour has illustrated comics for Image and Oni.

Carlos Lerma is a graphic designer and visual artist.

Johann "Ullcer" Leroux has drawn two issues of "Les Enquêtes des Détectives Harley & Davidson."

Corey Lewis is the creator behind SHARKNIFE, PENG, and PINAPL.

Joseph Michael Linsner is the creator of DAWN and artist of DARK IVORY.

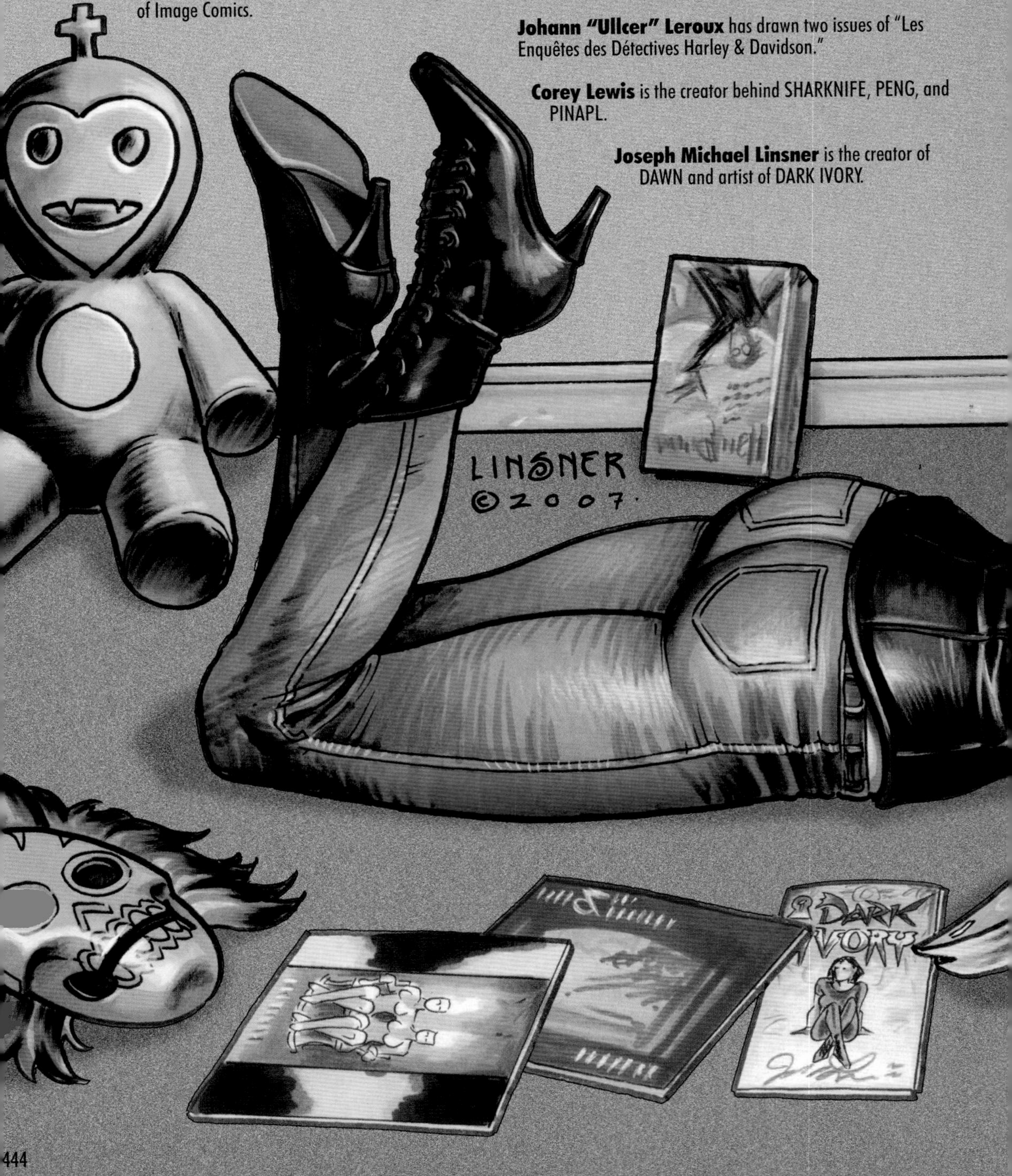
LINSNER
©2007
DARK IVORY

R.G. Llarena has appeared in HEAVY METAL.

Robert Love is an artist, a writer, and the co-creator of CHOCOLATE THUNDER and CREDENCE WALKER.

Nate Lovett is the artist on XOMBIE: REANIMATED from Devil's Due.

Russ Lowery is the colorist of AQUA LEUNG.

Jim Mahfood (a.k.a. Food One) is involved with comics, live art, flyer art, album covers, and t-shirt designs.

Thomas Mauer is a world-class letterer and the production manager at AAM/Markosia and Silent Devil.

Paul Maybury is the award-winning artist of the original graphic novel AQUA LEUNG. His work in this book is dedicated to the memory of his late friend Savvas.

Dylan McCrae is co-founder of the collective awesome known as SatelliteSoda and plays drums for his band IDDQD.

Derek McCulloch is the writer of STAGGER LEE and DISPLACED PERSONS.

Bernie E. Mireault is the creator of THE JAM.

Leah Moore & John Reppion have written ALBINON and WILD GIRL for Wildstorm among many others.

Chris Moreno is the artist on Paul Jenkins' SIDEKICK for 12 Gauge Comics/Image Comics and WORLD WAR HULK: FRONTLINE for Marvel Comics.

Patrick Morgan is studying animation at the Kansas City Art Institute.

Moritat is the artist of Image Comics' ELEPHANTMEN.

Kevin Myers is a freelance illustrator working in the advertising industry.

Val Nuñez is a professional video game concept artist and designer with forthcoming work in the comic HELL YEAH.

Elias Pate is a screenwriter.

Bob Pedroza is the colorist of SHADOWHAWK, INTIMIDATORS, and LIONS, TIGERS & BEARS.

Shin Pillan is a colorist.

Khary Randolph has worked on a number of properties in the animation and comic book industries, including BOONDOCKS, X-MEN, TEENAGE MUTANT NINJA TURTLES, SPIDER-MAN, and TEEN TITANS.

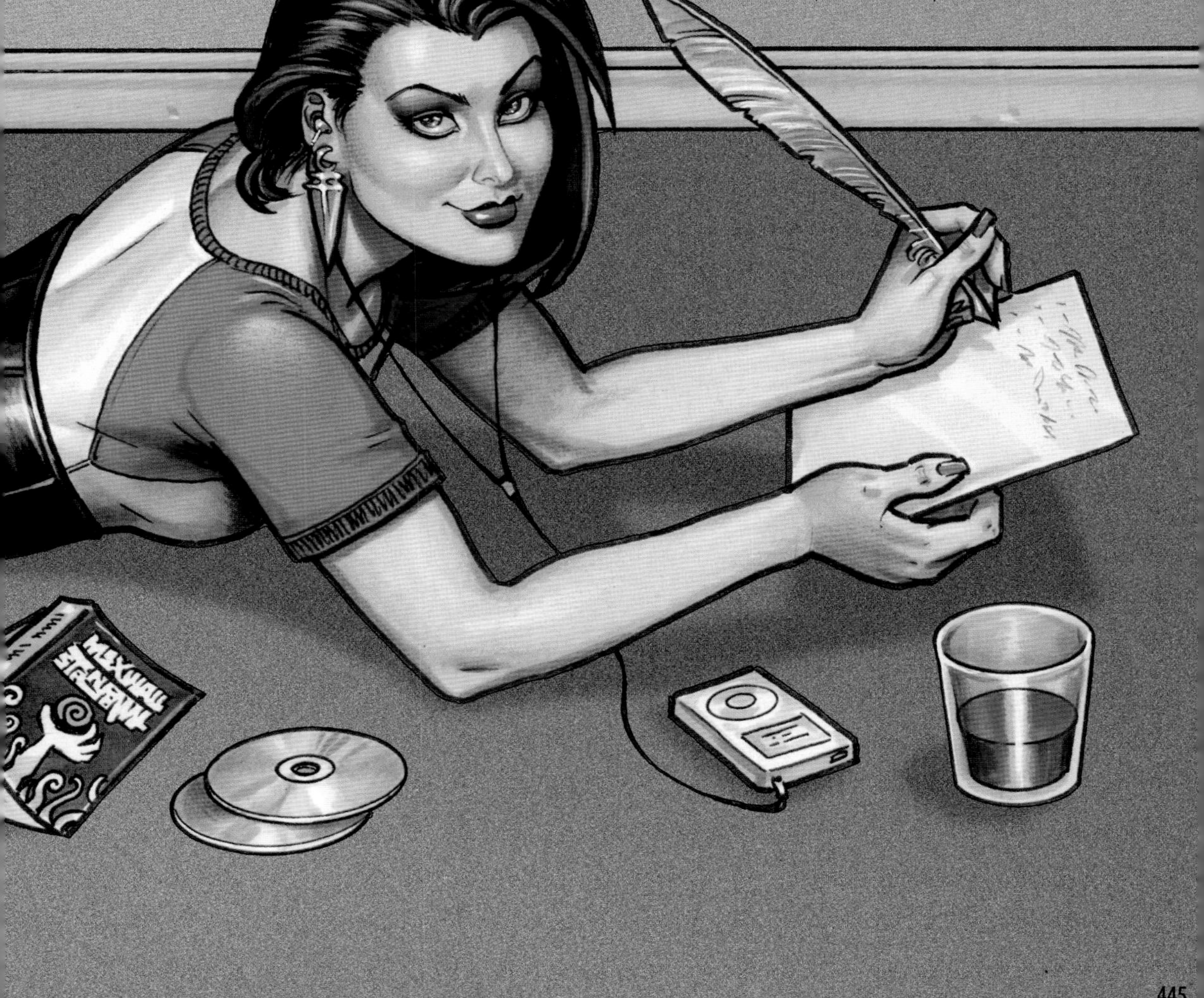

Rick Remender is the creator behind STRANGE GIRL, BLACK HEART BILLY, FEAR AGENT, SEA OF RED, NIGHT MARY, and DOLL AND CREATURE.

Jamie S. Rich is the author of the prose novels CUT MY HAIR and HAVE YOU SEEN THE HORIZON LATELY? as well as the ongoing comic book series LOVE THE WAY YOU LOVE.

Ben Roman is the artist of I LUV HALLOWEEN and CRYPTICS.

Mark Sable has written GROUNDED, FEARLESS SUPER GIRL, and TEEN TITANS for DC as well as the graphic novel for NBC's hit show HEROES.

Tim Seeley is the creator of HACK/SLASH.

Jeremy Shepherd is the co-creator/co-writer/colorist for "Egg-Centric," a mini story featuring THE ENGINEER.

M. Zachary Sherman is the writer of SEAL TEAM 7.

Mark Andrew Smith is the writer of THE AMAZING JOY BUZZARDS and AQUA LEUNG from Image Comics.

Jamie Snell is an inker.

Felipe & Milton Sobriero have appeared in HEAVY METAL magazine.

Aleksandar & Nikola Sotirovski are professional illustrators.

Nick Stakal has illustrated STRANGE GIRL and CRIMINAL MACABRE from Dark Horse.

Richard Starkings is the digital lettering pioneer behind COMICRAFT and the writer of ELEPHANTMEN.

Justin Stewart has had work in Viper Comics' SASQUATCH and Graphitti's TALES FROM THE CLERKS.

James Stokoe is the writer of WON TON SOUP and the upcoming MURDER BULLETS.

Joe Suitor is a professional designer.

Ed Tadem is the artist of. the "Jackie Karma" half of his first mini-series from Image Comics called '76 with writer B. Clay Moore.

Matt Timson is a British comic book artist who resides in Leicester.

Sheldon Vella is a professional artist and designer.

David Walker is a writer, filmmaker, and the creator of BadAzz MoFo.

Barnaby Ward is a professional illustrator.

Matthew Weldon has been laboring in the field of comic art since 2005.

Marcus White lives, writes, and sometimes sleeps in Houston, TX.

Keith Wood is a graphic designer at Dark Horse Comics and has previously done work for Oni Press and Marvel's Icon imprint.

Michael Woods is a writer and editor for comics.

Phil Yeh is the internationally renowned illustrator behind DINOSAURS ACROSS AMERICA.

Bryan Young scripts PIRATE CLUB with Derek Hunter for Slave Labor Graphics.